THE POST-IMPERIAL AGE: THE GREAT POWERS AND THE WIDER WORLD

The Postwar World
General Editors: A. J. Nicholls and Martin S. Alexander

As distance puts events into perspective, and as evidence accumulates, it begins to be possible to form an objective historical view of our recent past. *The Postwar World* is an ambitious new series providing a scholarly but readable account of the way our world has been shaped in the crowded years since the Second World War. Some volumes will deal with regions, or even single nations, others with important themes; all will be written by expert historians drawing on the latest scholarship as well as their own research and judgements. The series should be particularly welcome to students, but it is designed also for the general reader with an interest in contemporary history.

Decolonization in Africa *J. D. Hargreaves*

The Community of Europe: A History of European Integration since 1945 *Derek W. Urwin*

Northern Ireland since 1945 *Sabine Wichert*

A History of Social Democracy in Postwar Europe *Stephen Padgett and William E. Paterson*

'The Special Relationship': A Political History of Anglo-American Relations since 1945 *C. J. Bartlett*

Rebuilding Europe: Western Europe, America and Postwar Reconstruction *D. W. Ellwood*

The Pacific Basin since 1945: A History of the Foreign Relations of the Asian, Australasian and American Rim States and the Pacific Islands *Roger C. Thompson*

Central Europe Since 1945 *Paul G. Lewis*

International Relations since 1945. A History in Two Volumes *John Dunbabin*

The Cold War: The Great Powers and their Allies

The Post-Imperial Age: The Great Powers and the Wider World

International Relations Since 1945
A History in Two Volumes

The Post-Imperial Age: The Great Powers and the Wider World

J.P.D. Dunbabin

Longman
London and New York

Longman Group UK Limited,
Longman House, Burnt Mill,
Harlow, Essex CM20 2JE, England
and Associated Companies throughout the world.

Published in the United States of America by Longman Publishing, New York

First published 1994

ISBN 0 582 22719 4 CSD
ISBN 0 582 22720 8 PPR

British Library Cataloguing-in-Publication Data

A catalogue record for this book is available from the British Library

Library of Congress Cataloging-in-Publication Data
Dunbabin, J.P.D.
International relations since 1945 : a history in two volumes / J.P.D. Dunbabin
p. cm. – (The Postwar World)
Includes bibliographical references and indexes.
Contents: 1. The cold war : the great powers and their allies – 2. The post-imperial age : the great powers and the wider world.
ISBN 0-582-22866-2 (v. 1). – ISBN 0-582-22719-4 (v. 2). – ISBN 0-582-49365-X (pbk. : v. 1). – ISBN 0-582-22720-8 (pbk. : v. 2)
1. Cold War. 2. World politics–1945- 3. Great powers.
I. Title. 11. Series.
D843.D774 1994
909.82'5–dc20 93-28429
CIP

Set by 7.00 in 10/12 New Baskerville
Produced by Longman Singapore Publishers (pte) Ltd
Printed in Singapore

Contents

Abbreviations

AFPFL	Anti-Fascist People's Freedom League (Burma)
AHC	Arab Higher Command (Palestine)
AID	[US] Agency for International Development
AIOC	Anglo-Iranian Oil Company
ANC	African National Congress (South Africa)
APEC	Asia-Pacific Economic Cooperation
ARVN	Army of [South] Vietnam
ASEAN	Association of South-East Asian Nations
BP	British Petroleum
bpd	barrels per day
CAP	Common Agriculture Policy (European Community)
CARICOM	Caribbean Community and Common Market
CCP	Chinese Communist Party
CENTO	Central Treaty Organisation (Turkey, Iran, Pakistan, USA, UK, France; successor to the Baghdad Pact)
CGDK	Coalition Government of Democratic Kampuchea (coalition of exiled forces opposing the Vietnam-installed regime)
CIA	Central Intelligence Agency (USA)
CIS	Commonwealth of Independent States (comprising most of the former Soviet Union)
Comecon	Council for Mutual Economic Assistance (CMEA – communist countries)
COSVN	US term for the 'Vietcong' headquarters, situated just over the border in Cambodia
CPP	Convention People's Party (Ghana)
DDR	German Democratic Republic (East Germany)
DM	Deutschmark

DPP	Democratic Progress Party (Taiwan)
EC	European Community
EDC	European Defence Community (projected)
EEC	European Economic Community (later the EC)
EFTA	European Free Trade Area
EMS	European Monetary System
EOKA	National Organisation of [Greek] Cypriot Fighters
EPU	European Payments Union
ERM	Exchange Rate Mechanism (within the EMS)
FBI	Federal Bureau of Investigation (USA)
FLN	National Liberation Front (Algeria)
FLOSY	Front for the Liberation of South Yemen
FMLF	Farabundo Martí Liberation Front (El Salvador)
FRAP	Popular Action Front (Chile)
FRELIMO	Front for the Liberation of Mozambique
FRUS	*Foreign Relations of the United States*
G7	The group of the seven leading OECD members: USA, Japan, Germany, France, UK, Italy, Canada
G5	As above, less Italy and Canada
G10	USA, Japan, Germany, France, UK, Italy, Canada, Belgium, Netherlands, Sweden
Group of 77	The signatories of a Joint Declaration annexed to the 1964 Final Act of UNCTAD; (the 'Group of 77' has grown in numbers and functions as a caucus to press the interests of developing countries)
GATT	General Agreement on Tariffs and Trade
GDP	Gross domestic product
GNP	Gross national product
IAEA	International Atomic Energy Agency
IATA	International Air Transport Association
IBM	International Business Machines
ICJ	International Court of Justice
IDF	Israel Defence Forces
IISS	International Institute for Strategic Studies
ILO	International Labour Organisation
IMF	International Monetary Fund
INF	Intermediate range nuclear force
IPC	Iraq Petroleum Company
IRA	Irish Republican Army
ITO	International Trade Organisation (projected)
ITT	International Telephone and Telegraph (a US conglomerate, operating *inter alia* in Chile)

IZL	National Military Organisation (Palestine: ultra-Zionist)
JCS	Joint Chiefs of Staff
KANU	Kenya African National Union
KGB	State Security Committee; Soviet Secret Police
KMT	Kuomintang (nationalist radical party) (China)
KRDC	Korean Representative Democratic Council
LDP	Liberal Democratic Party (Japan)
MEC	Middle Eastern Command (projected)
MEDO	Middle Eastern Defence Organisation (projected)
MITI	Ministry of International Trade and Industry (Japan)
MPLA	Popular Movement of Liberation of Angola; in the 1970s and 1980s supported by Cuba and the USSR
NAFTA	North American Free Trade Agreement
NATO	North Atlantic Treaty Organisation
NICs	Newly industrialising countries
NIEO	New International Economic Order
NLF	National Liberation Front
NPA	New People's Army (Philippines)
NSC	National Security Council (USA)
OAPEC	Organisation of Arab Petroleum Exporting Countries
OAS	Secret army organisation; of settler resistance in Algeria
OAS	Organisation of American States
OAU	Organisation of African Unity
OECD	Organisation for Economic Co-operation and Development
ONUC	United Nations Force in the Congo
OPEC	Organisation of Petroleum Exporting Countries
OSS	Office of Strategic Studies (USA; the fore-runner of the CIA)
PFLOAG	Popular Front for the Liberation of the Occupied Arab Gulf
PKI	Communist Party of Indonesia
PLO	Palestine Liberation Organisation
PRC	People's Republic of China
PRI	Party of Institutionalised Revolution (Mexico)
RENAMO	Mozambique National Resistance; opposed to FRELIMO
RIIA	Royal Institute of International Affairs
ROC	Republic of China (the regime preceding the PRC; since 1950 it has controlled only Taiwan)

ROK	Republic of Korea (South Korea)
SACEUR	Supreme Allied Commander Europe (NATO)
SACLANT	Supreme Allied Commander Atlantic (NATO)
SALT	Strategic Arms Limitation Talks (or Treaty)
SAARC	South Asian Association for Regional Cooperation
SAVAK	Iranian secret police
SCAP	Supreme Commander Allied Powers and his staff; the occupation authority for Japan 1945–52
SCUA	Suez Canal Users Association (projected)
SDRs	Special Drawing Rights
SEATO	South-East Asia Treaty Organisation
SELA	Latin American Economic System
START	Strategic Arms Reduction Talks (or Treaty)
SWAPO	South West Africa People's Organisation (Namibia)
TVA	Tennessee Valley Authority
UAE	United Arab Emirates
UAR	United Arab Republic
UDI	Unilateral declaration of Independence (S. Rhodesia)
UMNO	United Malay National Organisation
UN	United Nations
UNCTAD	United Nations Conference on Trade and Development
UNEF	United Nations Expeditionary Force [Sinai]
UNESCO	United Nations Educational, Scientific and Cultural Organisation
UNFICYP	United Nations Peace-keeping Force in Cyprus
UNIFIL	United Nations Interim Force in Lebanon
UNITA	National Union for the Independence of Angola; supported in the 1970s and 1980s by South Africa and the USA
UNRRA	United Nations Relief and Rehabilitation Administration
UNRWA	United Nations Refugee Works Administration
UNSCOP	United Nations Special Committee on Palestine
WEU	Western European Union
WHO	World Health Organisation

Preface

> 'I know that it will be said by many, That I might have been more pleasing to the Reader if I had written the Story of mine own times . . .. To this I answer that whosoever in writing a modern History shall follow truth too near the heels, it may haply strike out his teeth.'

Fortunately the enterprise is no longer so dangerous as in Sir Walter Raleigh's time. My thanks are due in the first instance to the series editors for suggesting that I undertake it, and more particularly to Tony Nicholls for many helpful comments and suggestions; also to Longman both for accepting and producing the book and for important advice as to its structure and coverage. Responsibility for mistakes, of course, rests with me.

I am naturally greatly indebted to Oxford libraries and colleagues. Of the libraries, the Bodleian must have pride of place; but I should like to take this opportunity of thanking my former pupil, Andrew Peacock, for gifts that have made my college library far more useful, in this context, than one would a priori have expected. As for colleagues, it would be invidious to single out any of the living; but I owe much to both Alastair Buchan and Hedley Bull. The tragedy of Hedley's early death is of special relevance to this project. For it was originally hoped that he would accompany my narrative with a companion, and more analytical, volume; it is a great loss that he was not able to do so.

Beyond Oxford, I have (particularly in the mid-1980s, when British libraries were going though a bad phase) benefited from hospitality, talks, seminars, libraries and bookshops; especially in North America. My thanks are due to: the Canadian Institute of International Affairs; the libraries of the University of Toronto and of McMaster University; the Woodrow Wilson Center; the Library of

Congress; the Hoover Institution; the libraries of Stanford University and of the University of California, Berkeley; and to Princeton University (at which time my wife was at the Institute of Advanced Study). On two of these journeys I enjoyed support as a British Academy/Leverhulme Foundation Visiting Professor; otherwise, the current politics of academic funding compel me to add, work for this book was done on the basis of salaries and sabbatical leave from my college and university (in that order of magnitude).

My greatest debt, though, is to my wife Jean, for more than I can easily record, and to my daughters Bridget and Penny – at least the latter will not be able to say of this, as of my more domestic academic writing, that it is just 'the history of the garden wall'.

St. Edmund Hall, Oxford

Author's Note

All told, this book is quite long. For ease of reading and handling, it has been divided into two volumes, the first covering the Cold War, the second other major developments (like, for instance, decolonisation, the rise of the Rim of Asia, the Arab-Israeli dispute, or the evolution of the international monetary system) that, though they were certainly influenced by East-West rivalry, were essentially separate and autonomous. Save in its treatment of Western Europe (and of Yugoslavia), the first volume does not seek to go beyond the end of the USSR in 1991, and so excludes the wars of succession and the partial revival of the nineteenth century 'Great Game' in Central Asia and the Caucasus. The second volume has no such natural terminal point; many of its stories are still unfolding, and important developments (sometimes, indeed, dramatic transformations) are dealt with down to the summer of 1993. Naturally the author would prefer people to buy both volumes; but each is meant to be capable of standing on its own, covering one or more of the major themes of post-war international history. To make this possible a few (though very few) topics, like the Korean and Vietnam wars, figure in both, albeit in a somewhat different context.

Two other points should be noted. Most Chinese names are rendered according to the *pinyin* phonetic system commended by the People's Republic in 1979, but for Kuomintang and pre-communist names the old transliterated spelling is retained: thus Mao Zedong, but Chiang Kai-shek. Secondly, where the seasons of the year are used to give a general idea of date (as in 'the summer of 1993' above), they refer to the seasons of the northern hemisphere.

Editorial Foreword

The aim of this series is to describe and analyse the history of the World since 1945. History, like time, does not stand still. What seemed to many of us only recently to be 'current affairs', or the stuff of political speculation, has now become material for historians. The editors feel that it is time for a series of books which will offer the public judicious and scholarly, but at the same time readable, accounts of the way in which our present-day world was shaped by the years after the end of the Second World War. The period since 1945 has seen political events and socio-economic developments of enormous significance for the human race, as important as anything which happened before Hitler's death or the bombing of Hiroshima. Ideologies have waxed and waned, the industrialised economies have boomed and bust, empires have collapsed, new nations have emerged and sometimes themselves fallen into decline. While we can be thankful that no major armed conflict has occurred between the so-called superpowers, there have been many other wars, and terrorism has become an international plague. Although the position of ethnic minorities has dramatically improved in some countries, it has worsened in others. Nearly everywhere the status of women has become an issue which politicians have been unable to avoid. These are only some of the developments we hope will be illuminated by this series as it unfolds.

The books in the series will not follow any set pattern; they will vary in length according to the needs of the subject. Some will deal with regions, or even single nations, and others with themes. Not all of them will begin in 1945, and the terminal date may similarly vary; once again, the time-span chosen will be appropriate to the question under discussion. All the books, however, will be written by expert historians drawing on the latest fruits of scholarship, as well as their own expertise and judgement. The series should be particularly welcome to students, but it is designed also for the general reader with an interest in contemporary history. We hope that the books will stimulate scholarly discussion and encourage specialists to look beyond their own particular interests to engage in wider controversies. History, and particularly the history of the recent past, is neither 'bunk' nor a intellectual form of stamp-collecting, but an indispensable part of an educated person's approach to life. If it is not written by historians it will be written by others of a less discriminating and more polemical disposition. The editors are confident that this series will help to ensure the victory of the historical approach, with consequential benefits for its readers.

A.J. Nicholls
Martin S. Alexander

PART I
Decolonisation

CHAPTER ONE

General Considerations

INTERNAL AND OVERSEAS EMPIRES; INTERNATIONAL ATTITUDES TOWARDS 'SELF-DETERMINATION' AND COLONIES

Early in the twentieth century there had been two kinds of *formal* empire.[1] Those of, for instance, Britain and the Netherlands represented chiefly the rule by a mother-country of overseas dependent territories that were, in the British case often and in the Dutch always, colonies of a different ethnic background from that of the metropolis. It is to the ending of these empires that the term 'decolonisation' usually refers, and the present chapter is primarily directed to this process. However, one should not forget the existence of empires of a different type. The Tsar of all the Russias, the Habsburg Emperor, and the Ottoman Sultan had no 'colonies' but ruled over contiguous land masses inhabited by diverse ethnic groupings, of which many were clearly subordinate to the 'peoples of state' and some would have preferred to establish their own national states. The First World War did not result from rivalry for

1. More sweeping definitions, deriving indirectly from Lenin, see imperialism as the manipulation and exploitation by the 'centre' of the 'periphery', whether formally or in de facto partnership with local elites in nominally independent countries. The most influential exponents of this view have been Latin American 'dependency' theorists; but it also provides a context in which the formal decolonisation with which this chapter is concerned appears simply as the substitution of invisible (and less costly) for visible empire. The approach has some merits, but it is highly subjective: are South Korea and Taiwan being thus exploited, are they being helped by the international system to develop to the mutual benefit of themselves and their trading partners, or are they (as a growing climate of protectionism in the developed world would have it) enjoying a free ride on the back of the markets that these partners provide?

colonies, but it did to a considerable extent derive from the disintegration (or feared disintegration) of multinational empires. The subsequent peace settlement was quite largely an attempt to rearrange Europe on the principle of 'national self-determination' out of their ruins. In this way it was hoped to avoid the troubles that had led to the First World War and many of its predecessors.

The attempt was not a success, and Hitler was able to make the principle of national self-determination work for him to dismantle Czechoslovakia. It was accordingly much less to the fore in 1945. The new dominant power in Eastern Europe was the Soviet Union, which had succeeded in reconstituting in one state most of the former tsarist empire. Lip-service was admittedly paid to the equality of the Soviet peoples, buttressed by a federal system, autonomous regions, and an enlightened but paper constitution; but Stalin's practice had been quite otherwise. Although his successors were milder, when central power waned after 1988 the national problems evident after 1917 came back. In 1991 Lithuania, Latvia and Estonia – which Stalin had re-annexed in 1940 – again made good their independence. At the end of 1991 the remaining republics followed suit (though they sought to retain links in what at present seems an increasingly insubstantial confederal 'Commonwealth of Independent States'). Two years later this collapse of 'empire' had brought no more than friction to and between the major successor states, but extensive fighting (generally internal, but sometimes – as between Armenia and Azerbaijan – inter-state) in Central Asia, the Caucasus, and Moldova. In Yugoslavia, too, the collapse of communist power was followed in 1991 by the proclaimed secession of Slovenia and Croatia, leading in the latter case to heavy fighting with its Serb minority backed by the – now Serbian-controlled – federal army; in 1992 Bosnia opted for independence, and promptly dissolved into horrifying communal fighting and 'ethnic cleansing' that eventually drew in (so far rather ineffective) UN peace-keeping forces and mediation; fears were being voiced that similar disturbances might break out in Kossovo or Macedonia and draw external powers (like Albania, Greece and Bulgaria) into the conflict. 'Decolonisation' in its nineteenth- and early-twentieth-century form, the dissolution of multinational empires, has therefore again become a component of European and Central Asian politics.

Nor are secessionist tendencies, based on nationality, uncommon elsewhere. Indeed the ranks of multinational states were greatly swollen by the end of the old overseas empires. For the boundaries of their colonies had seldom been drawn along ethnic lines, and matters had sometimes been further complicated by the migrations of peoples permitted or positively encouraged by imperial rule. The Indian subcontinent provides an illustration. Loosely unified by the British, India was partitioned on independence into two countries, one secular and multinational (India), one Muslim (Pakistan). Pakistan was composed of two separate pieces over a thousand miles apart; in 1971 East Pakistan broke away (with Indian help) to form a new Bengali state, Bangladesh. West Pakistan remains intact, but there has been friction between its provinces, while Afghanistan has constantly promoted the idea of carving out an independent Pakhtunistan along the north-west frontier. India has not been subject to such intense strains, but it has seen substantial internal reconstruction of state boundaries along linguistic lines, and currently (1994) faces secessionist movements in Kashmir and the Punjab. Meanwhile the Tamil Tigers are fighting a long and bloody war to create an independent Tamil Eelam out of the north and east of Sri Lanka.

In short a high proportion of all countries have minority or multinational problems; discord or varying levels of insurgency are not uncommon. It is, however, and always has been, rare for countries voluntarily to allow part of their metropolitan territory to secede in the name of self-determination. *Much* more usual is a refusal, whether on the part of Abraham Lincoln of the United States or of General Gowon of Nigeria, to suffer the erring brethren to depart in peace.[2] Inevitably some countries are happy to back their enemies' autonomist or secessionist movements when it suits them. Thus Iran has frequently supported the Iraqi Kurds, but it sometimes has difficulties with its own, as does Turkey. None of the three existing states, Turkey, Iraq and Iran, shows any enthusiasm for an independent Kurdish nation-state carved out of their territory. Nor does the international community (though the USSR played with the idea during the Cold War as a means of destabilising its anti-communist southern neighbours); for the redrawing of state boundaries along national lines could open a Pandora's box and upset a high proportion of existing governments. Accordingly the 1963 Charter of the Organisation of

2. In this context the readiness of the Soviet Union (not usually thought of, even under Gorbachev, as the most liberal of countries) to abandon first its control over Eastern Europe in 1989 and then the Baltic states in 1991 (with only minor attempts at repression) is most remarkable. Also notable, at the end of 1992, was the 'velvet divorce' between the two halves of Czechoslovakia

African Unity (OAU) affirmed 'Respect for the . . . territorial integrity of each member-State';[3] Metternich would have approved.

Elsewhere, however, the Charter uses more 'Wilsonian' language: 'it is the inalienable right of all people to control their own destiny'. This clearly did not mean all *people*, for instance the African secessionists of the southern Sudan who have fought an endemic insurgency against the Arab north for most of the period since independence, but rather 'all territories under colonial rule or the rule of local European minorities'. To this latter end the OAU established a 'Liberation Bureau' and sought contributions 'for the purpose of liberating non-free Africa', though by now it was pushing on a largely open door. The UN General Assembly had in 1960 declared (without dissent but with nine abstentions) that 'All peoples have the right of self-determination. . . . Inadequacy of political, economic, social or educational preparedness should never serve as a pretext for delaying independence.' Admittedly Soviet attempts to add a time-limit – 'not later than 1961' – for such independence were rejected. But next year a Special Committee was established to secure the implementation of the Declaration, and the metropolitan countries were requested 'to take action without further delay' to comply.[4]

In most cases implementation was conceptually fairly straightforward, but some have thrown up potentially awkward conflicts of values. In September 1961 the Netherlands had invited the UN to take charge of Western New Guinea and organise a plebiscite to enable its inhabitants to say whether they wanted to join Indonesia or proceed to independence on their own. Indonesia insisted on a simple transfer. No Resolution could be found that would command a two-thirds majority in the UN General Assembly; but by fifty-three votes to thirty-six (with fourteen abstentions) the Assembly did vote down the proposition that 'any solution which affects the final destiny of a non-self-governing territory must be based on the principle of the self-determination of peoples'.[5] A similar problem was to be posed by Gibraltar, a miniscule, if long-standing, British colony that enjoyed elective internal self-government and did not wish 'decolonisation' in the form of transfer to Spain, of which geographically it forms part. In 1968 the General Assembly resolved (sixty-seven votes to eighteen,

3. *Keesing's Contemporary Archives* (Keynsham, Bristol – from 1974, London; from 1987, *Record of World Events*), 19466 (hereafter *Keesing's*)
4. *Keesing's*, 17993, 18724
5. *Keesing's*, 18725

with thirty-four abstentions) that 'the colonial situation in Gibraltar' was 'incompatible with the UN Charter', and Britain was called on (in vain)[6] to 'terminate the colonial situation' by October 1969 through negotiations with Spain. In short the existence of a 'colonial situation' should, at least in conjunction with the geographical and rather distant historical claims of another country, take precedence over the wishes of the local inhabitants.[7] The pendulum had indeed swung away from the overseas colonial empires that had still been so much to the fore during the UN's inaugural years.

PROBLEMS OF GENERALISATION; THE CONTRASTING EXPERIENCES OF: CANADA; THE PUNJAB; KUWAIT AND ZANZIBAR; SINGAPORE AND HONG KONG

'Imperialism' has tended to attract overarching explanatory theories that treat it as a single phenomenon and too often mask the diversity of individual colonies. As a corrective, it may be helpful to illustrate this diversity by giving examples of the very different ways in which individual territories entered, and later left, the British Empire.

Canada (with its French settlers) was conquered in 1759–63. It was not much valued, but was defended against the United States in the wars of 1775–83 and 1812–15. It became an area of population settlement, chiefly British and American. Minor rebellions in the 1830s were followed by the advent of self-government within the individual colonies of British North America, which all (bar Newfoundland) coalesced in 1867–73 into the internally autonomous confederation of Canada. This continued to look to Britain, both for sentimental reasons and because the connection provided security against the United States. Full control of external relations came, legally, in 1931 after discreet Canadian, and more

6. Instead Gibraltar's 1969 Constitution affirms that Britain 'will never enter into arrangements under which the people of Gibraltar would pass under the sovereignty of another State against their freely and democratically expressed wishes': *Keesing's*, 23453

7. *Keesing's*, 23194. Gibraltar had been taken by Christian Spain from the Islamic Emirate of Granada in 1462, by Britain from Spain in 1704. The 1713 Treaty of Utrecht that ratified Britain's acquisition also precluded the further passage of sovereignty to any country other than Spain, which is taken to rule out independence

direct South African and Irish, pressure. But the transformation of the psychological connection with the 'British Empire' took longer. Two symbolic steps at the latter end of the process – the 1965 replacement of the old British-derived flag by the new maple-leaf one and the 'repatriation' to Canada in 1982 of all aspects of the Constitution-making process[8] – were also attempts to address an upsurge of separatist feeling among the French-speaking Québecois.

After its founder's death, the imposing early nineteenth-century Sikh-ruled state of the Punjab collapsed into first an unsuccessful pre-emptive attack on British India, then national-cum-religious revolt that ended in 1849 with complete annexation – followed for the next half century by considerable Sikh enthusiasm for the Raj. In the final years of British rule the Punjab's Muslim majority came to support the Muslim League, undercutting the previously dominant coalition of moderate landlords of various faiths. In 1947 the Punjab chose partition between Pakistan and India, then dissolved into communal violence. This was accompanied by mass migrations of Muslims westward, non-Muslims (mainly Sikhs) eastward – in all of over 9 million people. The outcome was a homogeneous Muslim West Punjab within Pakistan, but within India pressure for the division of East Punjab into a Hindi-speaking state and a Punjabi-speaking one in which the Sikhs would constitute a majority. This was achieved in 1966, but was followed by extremist agitation – beginning in 1971 and becoming serious in the 1980s – for a fully independent Sikh Khalistan.

The sheikhdom of Kuwait was constituted under the Al Sabah family in 1756. In 1899–1904 the British acquired control of its external affairs and established a local political agent to advise the ruling family, whose interests in nullifying Ottoman suzerainty meshed with British wishes to hold Russian and German penetration away from the Gulf. These controls were ended in June 1961, by which time Kuwait's importance had been transformed through the development of oil. In July British troops had to be rushed in to prevent Iraq forcibly making good claims to Kuwait derived from the Ottoman Empire. Kuwait was then accepted by the Arab League, and two years later by the UN and Iraq. Iraq, however, unexpectedly invaded and annexed it in 1990, only to be ejected in 1991 by the military force of a US-led coalition acting on UN Resolutions.

8. In 1931 the formal enactment of constitutional changes had, to reassure the provinces, been left to the UK Parliament, albeit acting on Canadian advice

Somewhat similar in origin, though not outcome, were British relations with the Arab Sultan of Zanzibar. Here British informal influence, appreciable before 1873, deepened thereafter when the Sultan accepted the suppression of the slave trade in exchange for support against his local rivals and unruly subjects. The sudden advent of German colonialism in Tanganyika precipitated the demarcation of German and British spheres in East Africa, and in 1890 British influence hardened into a Protectorate. By the later 1950s the question of independence rose over the horizon in an island divided between an Arab upper class and an African majority. In December 1963 Zanzibar became independent under the Sultan, after an election in which the rival Afro-Shirazi party had won 54 per cent of the votes but (through over-concentration) only a minority of seats. In January 1964 the Sultan was toppled by a leftist coup whose leaders had supposedly trained in Cuba. Tanganyikan police then helped stabilise the situation; in April Zanzibar entered into a very loose federation with Tanganyika to form Tanzania.

In Singapore (1819) and Hong Kong (1841) Britain took possession of virtually uninhabited islands to prevent the Netherlands and China respectively from shutting out its trade, though without violence in the former case and through a small war in the latter. (Hong Kong was further expanded by war in 1860 and 1898.) Both became major cities inhabited by a predominantly Chinese population, and also (at times) important strategic centres. Singapore proceeded to substantial internal self-government in 1958. In 1963 its full decolonisation took the form of joining Malaysia, but in 1965 it seceded to become an independent republic. Singapore continued to welcome the basing of British troops, which provided some reassurance in respect both of its neighbours and of internal security, as well as a source of income; it was Britain's wish to save money that led to their withdrawal in 1974. Hong Kong's proximity to China appears to have precluded internal democratisation, and a booming economy has been governed by an essentially bureaucratic regime tempered by discreet consultation with the (increasingly Chinese) local economic elite and with the unofficial agents of the People's Republic. Through all its own internal twists and turns China has valued Hong Kong as a window to the outside world and a source of trade and convertible currency. From Hong Kong's perspective, the future was clouded by the approach of the end (in 1997) of the 1898 lease of the New Territories, without which Hong Kong would not be viable. Intensive negotiations began in 1982, and in 1984

Britain and China agreed that all Hong Kong should revert to the People's Republic in 1997, but as a 'Special Administrative Region' in which 'Hong Kong's previous capitalist system and lifestyle shall remain unchanged for 50 years'.

One could continue, finding examples to suit most interpretations of imperialism, but the chief conclusion must be the continuing importance of local conditions.

COMPETITION BETWEEN COLLABORATORS AND NATIONALISTS; MIX OF 'MODERN' AND 'TRADITIONALIST' ELEMENTS WITHIN THE NATIONALIST MOVEMENTS

Some scholars have concluded, from the extraordinarily small numbers involved – under 1,200 in the covenanted Indian Civil Service (by 1940 half Indians), about 900 in the French colonial corps for Sub-Saharan Africa[9] – that, outside colonies of settlement, imperialism depended on a mixture of non-interventionism and local cooperation. In the mid-twentieth century both were evaporating. Economic development and urbanisation (often stimulated by wartime or postwar developmental needs) had diluted the old self-sufficient rural societies. It thereby created groups that were more easily mobilised, and by making government more obtrusive rendered its control correspondingly more attractive. Local cooperators always continued to be forthcoming, but there were often built up alongside them rival elites. Some had been frustrated or snubbed by the colonial administration. Some were anxious to displace traditional rulers (who commonly survived in local government). Some had imbibed 'European' ideas of liberty/ nationalism/socialism, and wished to put them into practice at home. In the Gold Coast, Nkrumah was able to weld such groups into a pervasive and dominant Convention People's Party (CPP); from 1951 onwards Britain felt there was little option but to work with it. Elsewhere the mix was different. In Kenya, Jomo Kenyatta combined the support of such 'modern' African nationalists with

9. Raymond F. Betts, *Uncertain Dimensions: Western Overseas Empires in the Twentieth Century* (Oxford, 1985) p.193. Colonial administrators were, however, supplemented by people, frequently expatriates, running public utilities, education and the professions, churches and often the larger commercial undertakings

the traditional aspirations and grievances of the Kikuyu people to become the indispensable figure. In southern and more especially south-eastern Nigeria, leaders of the same stamp as Nkrumah emerged and pressed for independence. The Muslim and conservative North at first hesitated, then decided to compete in the hope that its numbers would offset the greater southern activism and development. The 1963 census showed that it would become steadily more dominant, so in 1966 murderous coups ensued that led eventually to civil war. Another variant can be seen in Morocco, where Sultan Mohammed encouraged the largely urban independence party, Istiqlal. In 1953, after anti-European attacks, France joined with his rival El Glaoui, the Berber Pasha of Marrakesh, in deposing him. This only increased his prestige; the substitute Sultan commanded little credibility and violence increased. So in 1955 first El Glaoui, then France, gave way; Mohammed was restored and was in a strong enough position to stand out for full independence, which he received in 1956. The rest of the 1950s saw struggles with Berber 'tribalism', then with some leftist Istiqlal politicians; in the 1960s there were several attempts to murder Mohammed's successor. He survived them all, and has remained in full control up to the present (1993).

EASE OF COLONIAL ACQUISITION; RISING COSTS OF POSTWAR COLONIAL GOVERNMENT

From the perspective of the colonial powers (if *not* always from that of the colonised peoples), most empires were acquired on the cheap. Imperial arms sometimes accepted defeat in minor wars. But, if one excepts wars between the Great Powers themselves,[10] arguably the only wars in the century before 1945 that demanded a major effort on the part of the would-be empire-builders were Japan's attempt from 1937 to 1945 to bring China into its system of informal empire, the 1919–22 Greek incursion into Anatolia, and the 1899–1902 British conquest of the Boer republics of the Transvaal and Orange Free State. That other colonial wars were much less demanding affairs was due to the then enormous margin of power between 'Europeans' and most 'non-Europeans', itself

10. The two twentieth-century world wars, plus the Crimean War, the 1877–8 Russo-Turkish War and the 1904–5 Russo-Japanese War

partly the product of political accident (like the decline of the Indian Moghul Empire in the eighteenth century and of the Chinese empire in the nineteenth century) but chiefly of differential technical, economic and organisational progress. Not only had empires been fairly easy to acquire, once pacified, they were also usually easy to rule. In 1885 British India had some 73,000 British and 154,000 Indian troops, in 1938 57,000 British and 139,000 Indian (with 37,000 Indian reserves); while in 1914 German Cameroun had 215 German officers and 2,750 African police and soldiers.[11]

After 1945 challenges became increasingly common, and the amount of force needed to handle them increased greatly. Colonial governments did sometimes resort to straightforward suppression, and they were seldom if ever *militarily* defeated.[12] But their staying power was limited; Ho Chi Minh is supposed to have told a French official that 'I will lose ten men to every one of yours, but I will win and you will lose', as indeed proved to be the case against first France, then the United States. Even where colonial governments were successful, as against the Mau Mau in Kenya, they were often reluctant to risk repeating the experience, and altered course accordingly. Or, as in Malaya, they might suppress an unwelcome insurrection, but do so partly by enlisting, and handing over to, a more congenial group. In most cases a trial of arms was avoided: nationalists accepted a degree of cooperation with the colonial government in the expectation of securing the reversion of power that (in the short to medium run) they were not strong enough to seize; their governors accommodated them both to avoid trouble and unpleasantness and to influence, while they were still able, the attitudes of their successors.[13]

11. D.K. Fieldhouse, *The Colonial Empires* (1966) pp.276–7, 396; N.H. Gibbs, *Grand Strategy: Volume 1 Rearmament Policy* (1976) p.831. Post-independence requirements appear to be *much* greater

12. The exceptions are Portuguese Guinea, where the resistance claimed control of over two-thirds of the country, and Vietnam, where after the defeat of Dien Bien Phu the French could have hoped only to hold enclaves, albeit considerable ones. Also India seized Portugal's Goa enclave in 1961

13. Many nationalists also accepted that they should proceed by constitutional and non-violent means, and turned to insurrection or violence only where this route was (as in Rhodesia or South Africa) persistently blocked

WANING METROPOLITAN ENTHUSIASM FOR IMPERIAL RULE (BRITAIN)

In this context one should note that in the metropolitan countries there had always been – alongside the small (if sometimes effective) imperial lobbies and a more general pride in empire – critics, whether of its cost or of its morality. Thus in 1882 its Parliament would not allow France to join Britain in suppressing the Egyptian Arabi Pasha, while Jules Ferry's career was damaged by the 1881 take-over of Tunis, then destroyed in 1885 as a result of the war that established French control over Vietnam. In Britain politics were convulsed by Gladstone's 1885 conversion to Irish 'Home Rule', an unpopular policy but one which most Liberals were prepared to accept and to which by 1920 the Conservatives had largely come over. By then events had admittedly moved on, and in 1921 it was necessary (but also quite popular) to concede 'dominion home rule' to southern Ireland. No sooner had the Irish question been thus apparently settled than an Indian one opened up – did the 1917–19 promises of eventual 'responsible government' commit Britain to the goal of 'dominion status'? In 1929 the Viceroy, under a Labour government, pronounced that they did. He was backed by the Conservative Opposition Leader, Stanley Baldwin, who was anxious to prevent British politics being torn apart over India as they had been for a generation over Ireland. He also saw concession as the only way to keep India in the Empire/ Commonwealth, given 'the wind of nationalism and freedom blowing round the world'. This precipitated the most bitter debate ever to occur within the Conservative Party over decolonisation – focused around the half-way house of the Government of India Act, 1935, but embracing much broader issues.[14] Somehow this debate served to inoculate the Conservative Party, with the result that when, after 1945, decolonisation came for real, resistance was a good deal weaker. Admittedly 1954–6 saw the formation within the party of the Suez Group, anxious to put an end to what it held to be a policy of scuttle. But its attitudes were soon discredited, not so much by the Suez expedition itself (which, if it bitterly divided the country, appears to have had at least majority support) as by its outcome. Decolonisation has caused far less division in postwar British politics than have relations with the European Community.

14. K. Middlemas and J. Barnes, *Baldwin* (1969) pp.698, 707, 713; Robert Rhodes James, *Churchill: A Study in Failure 1900–1939* (1970) p.201

On the left there had always been a body of opinion opposed to imperial expansion. After the apparent conciliation of the Transvaal by the 1908 restoration of (white) representative government, it was possible to see such decolonisation as the way to keep the connections and better features of empire without its unattractive side. When Attlee ended the Raj in 1947, such hopes seemed to have been justified by the subsequent decision of the successor states, India and Pakistan, to remain within the Commonwealth. So, particularly between 1957 (the independence of Ghana and Malaya) and 1963 (that of Kenya), there was a good deal of positive British enthusiasm for decolonisation. This is not to say that there was automatic concession to nationalists; but while (as we have seen) coercion needed more force than heretofore, readiness to deploy force was less. This was partly for financial reasons: an official 1957 analysis saw the empire as costing the British taxpayer £51 million per year,[15] while a decade later the decision to withdraw all troops from East of Suez (pressed strongly by the Labour Left on other grounds) was at least ostensibly taken for financial reasons. Considerations of public opinion were quite as important, however: the 1959 revelation that eleven Mau Mau prisoners had been beaten to death at the Hola Camp, and the likelihood that such incidents would recur, did much to stimulate a reassessment of policies towards Kenya. In the same year the Devlin Commission of Inquiry into the Nyasaland emergency and its fifty-two deaths set in motion a train of events that led to the break-up of the white-ruled Central African Federation. It was not that Nyasaland could not have been held down, but it seemed pointless, as well as wrong, to do so: 'We British have lost the will to govern'.[16]

BELGIUM AND THE CONGO

Most colonial powers reached this position sooner or later. The quickest shift was that of Belgium, which for most of the 1950s believed its (profitable) colonies immune to nationalism. December 1957 saw the first ever elections (municipal) in the Congo, and in 1958 successful African politicians started talking about home rule or independence. January 1959 saw both serious riots and a Belgian

15. D.J. Morgan, *The Official History of Colonial Development* v: *Guidance Towards Self-Government in British Colonies 1941–1971* (1980) p.102

16. Sir Roy Welensky, *Welensky's 4000 Days* (1964) p.319

promise of ultimate independence. By October this had become one of freedom to opt for independence in 1964, and in January 1960 independence was agreed on for 30 June.[17] Belgium was not prepared to govern in the face of nationalist resistance, nor was it deterred by the mounting violence that accompanied its precipitate departure.

FRANCE AND ALGERIA

After 1945 France *was* set on maintaining its empire, and was quite prepared to use force – reconquering southern Indo-China, seeking to strengthen its bargaining position in Syria, and suppressing nationalist disturbances in Algeria (1945) and Madagascar (1947). From December 1946 this landed it with war in Indo-China against the Vietminh. By 1953 French ministers were expressing doubts as to their country's willingness to continue. In 1954 the Dien Bien Phu débâcle led to a determination to get out, to which Mendès-France gave effect at the Geneva Conference. He also called off repression in Tunisia and began negotiations; his successor did the same in Morocco, and both became independent in 1956. Algeria, however, was different, legally part of metropolitan France and settled by nearly 1 million Europeans. It is worth dwelling a little on the Algerian independence struggle: it was one of the more traumatic episodes in postwar decolonisation; it accelerated French decolonisation elsewhere in Africa; and Algeria is one of the few European colonies to have gained its independence through prolonged fighting.[18] It has always claimed that, as a result, it is more truly independent than countries that have had sovereignty handed to them on a political plate, though the record of its subsequent relations with France does not necessarily bear this out.

When risings broke out in 1954 there was general agreement between mainland France, the settlers and the army that they should be put down. In military terms so they were, albeit by methods involving torture and the forced resettlement of one-tenth of the population that eventually came to worry metropolitan

17. *Keesing's*, 16755, 17089, 17315

18. Others are Vietnam, Zimbabwe, Guinea-Bissau and (possibly) Mozambique. The total of killings in the war and its aftermath will never be known; Alistair Horne reckons them at well over 300,000 though below the 1 million that now constitutes the official Algerian figure: *A Savage War of Peace: Algeria 1954–62* (1977) p.538

liberals. The main forces of the nationalist FLN were driven over the border into Tunisia and Morocco, and in 1958 the French army was able to deliver Muslim voters for *Algérie française* candidates. Both settlers and army were, however, on the alert against any possibility of backsliding on Paris's part (the settlers' interest is obvious, while the army regarded Algeria as a last stand after a run of defeats and saw its honour as pledged to its Muslim collaborators).[19] In 1958, fearing that a new French government would bow to American–British pressure to disengage, they took over Algeria and appeared ready to move on Paris. To avoid possible civil war, power was transferred to General de Gaulle (the only leader who commanded confidence in all quarters) with the clear intention that he should settle the Algerian problem one way or another.

First, however, he made sure that France should never again be so bogged down, by pre-emptively decolonising Sub-Saharan Africa. Here 1956 had already brought elective assemblies with some administrative powers. In 1958 the colonies were invited to vote for or against the new French Constitution. Only Guinea voted against, and was ejected into independence with the withdrawal of French aid and goodwill. The remainder accepted self-government within a French-dominated federal Community, but then resumed pressure for greater local control via the devolution of Community functions. De Gaulle proved accommodating, either because he had never believed in the Community as more than a political device or because he had his hands full elsewhere. In 1960 France recognised the 'international sovereignty' of most of its African dependencies, and concentrated instead on maintaining close relations with them through a mixture of aid and informal involvement.[20]

Ever since 1955, de Gaulle had been remarking privately that Algeria would some day be independent, but that 'There can be no question of my saying anything [in public] before I have the means to act'. In dealing with the army and the settlers in 1958 he was, therefore, deliberately vague: he implied support (and once, during his June 1958 tour of Algeria, shouted – in the heat of the moment? – for *Algérie française*), but he did not otherwise commit himself. On his return, he observed, 'They're dreaming' and 'We can't keep

19. In 1959 120,000 of the 550,000 security forces were local Muslims (*Keesing's*, 17128), far more than served in the nationalist forces. Come independence many (with their families, 80,000 in all) fled to France, fearing murder or internment: ibid, 19496, 25089

20. J.D. Hargreaves, *Decolonization in Africa* (1988) pp.152–6, 172–5

Algeria. . . . We have to find a form of cooperation in which the interests of France will be protected'.[21] His first public move came in September 1959, when he introduced the idea of a direct Algerian vote, to be held four years after the restoration of peace. He also offered an extra choice – complete secession – but seemed to aim at a self-governing Algeria composed of communal groupings, 'in close association with France in the fields of economy, education, defence and foreign relations'.[22] The prospect was to touch off a settler insurrection in January 1960; unlike his Fourth Republican predecessors, de Gaulle stood firm and it collapsed. There followed the curious episode of negotiations initiated by the commanders of one of the FLN's six military districts. Hard pressed, and disgusted by the absence of any tangible assistance from FLN headquarters abroad, they appeared to offer to stop fighting. De Gaulle met them personally in June 1960, but then (for reasons we can only guess at) immediately undercut them by openly inviting the FLN government-in-exile to talks in France. The talks led nowhere, but inevitably (and intentionally?) conferred a degree of recognition on the FLN.[23] In November de Gaulle further alarmed conservatives by slipping into a broadcast mention of 'an Algerian Republic, which will one day exist'. His tour of Algeria in December 1960 sparked settler riots against him, followed by anti-European counter-riots and pro-FLN demonstrations in Algiers. De Gaulle was impressed, and on the plane home said that he now doubted whether it would be possible to find a third Algerian force between the party of integration and that of independence: 'We must find an arrangement with the FLN'.[24]

In January 1961 a referendum (held in both metropolitan France and Algeria) accepted the principle of Algerian self-determination. But the doubling, since 1958, of the Algerian abstention rate (to 41 per cent) served to illustrate the degree of FLN influence, more especially in urban areas where French army control was less obtrusive. In April 1961 de Gaulle explained bluntly that Algeria cost France a good deal more than it brought in, asking:

21. Jean Lacouture, *De Gaulle: The Ruler 1945–1970* (1991) esp. pp.160, 185, 189–90

22. De Gaulle had apparently canvassed these options privately in Feb. 1958: Lacouture, *De Gaulle* p.161

23. Horne, *A Savage War of Peace* pp.387–95, 325; Lacouture, *De Gaulle* pp.264–6

24. Lacouture, *De Gaulle* pp.272–3

> Why should we remain tied to domination that is costly, bloody, and without future, when our country has to be renewed from top to bottom, and when all the underdeveloped countries ask our aid. . . . Why . . . should we give this aid and support if it is not worth our efforts, if there is no cooperation, and if what we offer brings no return?

Accordingly it would be necessary to submit to a vote 'a solution resulting from a preliminary agreement between the [French] Government and the different political elements, notably the rebellion'. This touched off another rebellion – one of French generals in Algeria. It soon collapsed in the face of firm broadcasts by de Gaulle and a consequent lack of enthusiasm on the part of the French conscripts serving there.[25] However, it was followed by the resort to terrorism (both in Algeria and France) on the part of the 'Secret Army' (OAS) of dissident officers and disgruntled settlers.

From May to July 1961 France attempted to negotiate a settlement at Evian with the FLN. Talks broke down over the post-independence rights of non-Muslim communities and the French determination to exclude from an independent Algeria the oil-rich Sahara; de Gaulle then raised the possibility, if no settlement was reached, of regrouping the pro-French population around Algiers and Oran, and of expelling Algerian workers and immigrants from metropolitan France. But in September 1961 he removed one obstacle by accepting future Algerian sovereignty over the Sahara and insisting only on 'an association which safeguards our interests'. Secret negotiations resumed, and led in March 1962 to a second Evian Conference. This produced a cease-fire and a general declaration on Independence and Cooperation, which was to be ratified that summer by referendum. Although the FLN ceased fire, the OAS did not. Communal rioting had been mounting since autumn 1961; the OAS did its best to provoke it by murders and explosions, in the hope of producing such a Muslim rising that the French army would have to intervene. It also embarked on 'scorched earth' destruction of schools and public buildings. By the time it recognised its mistake and came to terms with the FLN, it was too late. Conditions had triggered a general exodus of Europeans, their money, and many of their former Muslim collaborators. The result was massive unemployment (supposedly over 2 million). Nor were matters improved by revenge killings of 5,000–6,000 Europeans and a far larger number (perhaps between

25. ibid, chaps. 23–6; *Keesing's*, 17127, 17331 ff, 17574, 18060 ff, 18093, 18511 ff

30,000 and 150,000) of Muslim auxiliaries, or by sharp (if brief) fighting within the FLN, partly personal, partly Arab–Berber.[26]

From de Gaulle's perspective, however, he was at last free of colonial entanglements. Although OAS trouble within France took some time to die down (and nearly claimed his life), he was able to use his prestige and indispensability to complete the establishment of an executive-dominated French political system – and employ his resulting freedom of action to shape the future of the European Economic Community, withdraw from the supranational NATO command, and attempt to transform the US and Soviet 'hegemonies'.

France also managed to establish remarkably close relations with Algeria. The Evian agreement had provided for these. Its detailed provisions did not last. Thus its guarantees to French citizens in Algeria became irrelevant when most of them left. The military facilities retained by France for fifteen years proved of declining utility and were given up in 1968–70. Above all Algeria gradually eroded the advantageous position conceded at Evian to French oil interests, then in February 1971 took them over offering little compensation. France responded by threatening an end to economic aid and Algerian immigration, blocking World Bank loans, and discouraging purchases of the nationalised oil by threatening the buyers with law suits. In June 1971 a settlement was reached that improved the French position in detail but left Algerian control intact.

This episode was seen at the time as ending Algeria's 'privileged relationship' with France, but in fact ties proved more durable. Evian had stipulated that French economic aid (much boosted in 1958 as a counter to the FLN) should continue for three years at existing levels. It then declined somewhat but remained high (about £300 million for 1965–70 inclusive) and earned France much credit both with Algeria and (by extension) the Third World. Algeria continued to look to France for educational and technical assistance – from 1963 onwards French army conscripts could again serve in Algeria, as teachers: such arrangements were formalised by a twenty-year agreement in 1966. Evian also provided for free movement between France and Algeria. This proved embarrassing, and controls were instituted. Nevertheless the Algerian population in France continued to rise. It was not particularly welcome, which

26. *Keesing's*, esp. 18801 ff, 19145 ff, 19492 ff, 19807. The Algerian crisis is also discussed, from the perspective of its impact on French politics, in Dunbabin, volume 1, *The Cold War* chap. 13

sometimes involved the two governments in friction. But Algeria appreciated the remittances, estimated at £150 million in 1971, and (given its alarmingly high birth-rate) could not contemplate the closing of the safety valve that emigration afforded. This was only one aspect of the two countries' economic linkage: when in 1969 *Pravda* boasted of the growth in Algerian–Soviet trade, *Le Monde* observed that Algerian–French trade had been sixteen times higher. Ideologically, indeed, Algeria may have had more in common with the Soviet Union, but economically the USSR could replace France only in fairly limited fields (like wine).[27] The cautious Boumedienne, who ousted the more flamboyant Ben Bella in 1965, appreciated this.[28]

PORTUGAL AND AFRICA

Algeria illustrates the strains that a major war of repression might impose on the political system of the metropolitan country, and the Portuguese experience provides a further example. In the 1960s Portugal, though probably the weakest of the imperial powers, seemed able to buck the general trend. Of its African colonies, Guinea-Bissau was not particularly profitable, but Angola and Mozambique were.[29] When insurrection broke out in 1961–4, the Portuguese responded with force. The effort involved was not overwhelming: military expenditure rose from 4.6 per cent of GNP in 1960 to 8.3 per cent in 1971, over half the troops in the contested colonies were African, and total Portuguese dead (to 1974) numbered 7,700.[30] Nor were Portuguese arms unsuccessful: the Guinea-Bissau insurgents claimed (presumably with some exaggeration) to control two-thirds of the country, but their Angolan counterparts made little progress, while in Mozambique FRELIMO

27. In 1964 France agreed to import 8 million hectolitres at double the world price, but it progressively reduced imports, partly for market reasons, partly in response to Algerian nationalisations. In 1968 the USSR agreed to take 5 million hectolitres, but in a barter deal and at less than half the French price

28. *Keesing's*, 18801 ff, 22567, 23388, 24400, 25084 ff

29. Angola had oil and other minerals. Portugal was paid in gold for the earnings in South Africa of miners from Mozambique, while passing on to them the equivalent in local currency; Mozambique also had transport and tourism earnings

30. Hargreaves, *Decolonization in Africa* pp.214–16; *Keesing's*, 25755, 26116, 26088, 26196, 26489

was still largely confined to the north, and, even there, was unable to halt the construction of the great Cabora Bassa dam.[31] The Mozambique war had, however, reached the stage of extensive population displacement, and of massacres of non-combatants that Portugal was unable to keep hidden.[32] The army was clearly unhappy: in February 1974 the former commander in Guinea-Bissau and current Defence Minister, General Spinola, published a book proclaiming that there 'was no military solution to Portugal's overseas question' and calling (like de Gaulle) for self-determination.[33] There were rumours of plots by conservative soldiers against the long-standing authoritarian regime. This was suddenly displaced in April 1974 by more junior officers, radicalised by the war and (in some cases) by the socialist propaganda with which they had had to familiarise themselves in the course of counter-insurgency.

The new government promptly sought to decolonise. Guinea-Bissau, where there were no settlers and a strong liberation movement, was easy. Mozambique was harder: as we have seen, FRELIMO was largely northern, while the settlers were opposed and sometimes violent. The new leader, Samora Machel, brought chaos by his rapid introduction of 'socialism' and extrusion of the settlers: he was later to warn Mugabe against repeating these mistakes in Zimbabwe. Since he opened his territory to Mugabe's anti-Rhodesian guerrillas, Rhodesia returned the compliment by sponsoring his RENAMO resistance (which was later taken over by South Africa). In Angola no single liberation movement was pre-eminent, so Portugal simply left in 1975, with the three rival movements (plus their foreign backers) already scrambling for power. A Cuban expeditionary force secured initial victory for the (Marxist) MPLA, but there then ensued prolonged guerrilla warfare between this and its rival UNITA (with both receiving substantial external assistance until the end of the Cold War).[34] Meanwhile the

31. For a map of FRELIMO areas, see *Keesing's*, 25755. Nor did FRELIMO losses, a total of 2,057 killed over ten years (ibid, 27634), suggest very intensive activity

32. A subsequent UN report concluded that Portuguese and Rhodesian units had, during 1971–4, tortured/massacred over a thousand Mozambiqueans: *Keesing's*, 27246. No comparable investigation was made into Portuguese claims of similar FRELIMO atrocities

33. *Keesing's*, 26485

34. Events to 1975 are discussed in Hargreaves, *Decolonization in Africa* pp.212–18, and in *The Cold War* chap. 11; for the subsequent civil war and its (temporary) resolution, see also pp. 74–5 below

prospect of independence (and still more the subsequent civil war) produced a mass exodus of European and mixed-race settlers.[35]

DIFFERENT TYPES OF SETTLER COLONIES

The course of decolonisation was clearly much influenced by the presence or absence of settlers, and by their constitutional position. At one extreme were those colonies (all, in the twentieth-century, British)[36] where settlers constituted a clear majority of the population. This had not always been a guarantee against violence: the thirteen American colonies reached independence in 1783 through a long war and the extrusion of the many 'loyalists' who had been active on the losing side. But, profiting from earlier mistakes, Britain proved ready in the nineteenth century to devolve government in comparable circumstances. Although milestones can certainly be discerned in the development of such self-governing colonies into fully self-standing countries, the process was so gradual as to occasion few problems and comparatively little controversy.

Things were very different in colonies where there were appreciable numbers of settlers but they were not in a majority. Initially such settlers strengthened the hand of the colonial power, since they naturally identified with it and afforded it useful support on the ground. But their life-styles almost always ran to a colour bar, official or otherwise, and could well, in the later stages of imperial rule, exacerbate indigenous hostility. Politically, too, settlers have tended towards repression rather than concession – unlike charity, decolonisation starts away from home – and have generally preferred to insist on short-term safety rather than risk immediate concessions in an attempt to preserve longer-term interests. There were, of course, exceptions. Up to the 1950s the Europeans in Kenya fitted this pattern well: their presence did much both to provoke and to suppress the Mau Mau insurrection. But in 1960–3 they let themselves be jollied into permitting the expansion of the franchise, then accepting a government led by

35. *Keesing's*, 27498 puts departures (mostly for Portugal) in May–November 1975 at about 400,000

36. Canada, Australia, New Zealand and Newfoundland (responsible government 1854, return to direct British rule for financial reasons 1934, accession to Canada 1949)

their former bogeyman, Jomo Kenyatta. To ease the transition, British money was provided to buy white-owned farms (ultimately 4 million acres) for distribution mainly to Kikuyu smallholders. This enabled many settlers to leave, while others found Kenyatta's rule unexpectedly benign.[37] Where settlers were numerous, however, transitions were not generally so smooth. We have seen that in Algeria the *colons* tended to dig in: under the weak Fourth Republic, their intransigence served in 1956–8 to block the inclinations towards conciliation felt by a number of Paris governments; only the regime of General de Gaulle (exceptionally strong not only by reason of de Gaulle's own character, but also because the mainland felt that all other alternatives had been exhausted) could set them aside.

In much of southern Africa settlers were even stronger. Southern Rhodesia had been accorded full internal self-government in 1923 and South Africa dominion status (in effect independence) in 1910 – both under elective white rule. The position of their African majorities raised few political problems, and no international concern, until after the Second World War. The subsequent flood of decolonisation made it increasingly anomalous; opponents of white rule managed to bring about striking changes both in the values of international society and in public opinion within Western Europe and North America; 'natives' in southern Africa itself slowly became more ready to struggle against their inferior status. Such factors led Britain, in the early 1960s, to refuse full sovereignty to Rhodesia, whose Prime Minister Ian Smith accordingly took it in 1965 with a 'Unilateral Declaration of Independence'. This the international community did not accept; in 1966 Rhodesia's status (hitherto only a question between itself and the UK) became also a concern of Commonwealth conferences and of the United Nations – to which latter Britain turned in order to impose economic sanctions on the 'rebel' Rhodesian regime. Rhodesia was, however, supported by both South Africa and Portugal, whose colony of Mozambique flanked its longest and most vulnerable border, so its position remained strong until the 1974 Portuguese revolution. This disrupted the hitherto solid bloc of white-ruled states and colonies that covered most of southern Africa. It thus opened up Rhodesia's eastern border to guerrilla 'freedom fighters', and convinced South Africa that the existing Rhodesian regime could not last

37. Hargreaves, *Decolonization in Africa* pp.129–31, 193–5; *Keesing's*, 29481. Europeans numbered some 56,000, to 177,000 Asians and 8.4 million Africans: Hugh Tinker, *Race, Conflict and International Order* (1977) p.65

indefinitely. South Africa therefore started nudging Smith towards a negotiated settlement with at least some African nationalists. In 1977 negotiations collapsed; fighting grew into a nasty civil war, which threatened to involve the whole region as Rhodesia increasingly retaliated against guerrilla bases on its neighbours' territory. At the eleventh hour, the prospect of general disaster led, in 1979, to the negotiation of a settlement whereby Britain briefly resumed colonial control and in 1980 held elections on the basis of universal suffrage, then transferred sovereignty to the resulting African government. Although the destiny of Rhodesia/Zimbabwe was thus resolved, white-ruled South Africa continued to overshadow the region, intimidating (or interfering in) its neighbours (former colonies of Britain and Portugal), and until 1990 administering its own former League of Nations mandate, Namibia. Although South Africa was not a colony in the sense used in this chapter, its regime was widely perceived as having colonial overtones and has therefore attracted much condemnation and some pressure from the international community. (A fuller account of southern African developments will be found in Chapter 4 in this volume.)

CHAPTER TWO

Indonesia, Indo-China, and India

DECOLONISATION TO 1945; US WARTIME ATTITUDES TOWARDS COLONIALISM

Space will not permit a blow-by-blow account of decolonisation, but a brief overview may be helpful. The process had, of course, begun before 1945. The white self-governing British Dominions became fully independent juridically in 1931. Afghanistan had in 1919 repudiated British control over its foreign policy (at the cost of the accompanying subsidy). Egypt was propelled into 'independence' in 1922, albeit subject to the reservation of extensive British rights in the Canal Zone and the exercise of much neocolonial influence. The League of Nations Covenant did not contemplate self-government for the ex-German colonies in Africa or the Pacific, but did accept that the Arab parts of the former Turkish Empire 'have reached a stage of development where their existence as independent nations can be provisionally recognized subject to the rendering of administrative advice and assistance by a Mandatory [Power] until such time as they are able to stand alone' (Article 22). Iraq was the first such Mandate to reach formal independence (and League membership) in 1932; in 1936 the French popular front government agreed with Syria and the Lebanon on independence in 1939, though in 1938 the French Parliament reversed this policy. Lastly the Philippines: after defeating the colonial power (Spain) the USA had in 1899–1901 gone to some trouble to suppress nationalist insurgency instead of allowing the islands independence. Between the wars it changed course, partly for ideological reasons but chiefly because independence would allow it to shut out Filipino agricultural exports.[1] In 1933 the reluctance was on the Filipino side, but in 1934 all was settled: there should be complete internal self-government, with the USA for ten years retaining responsibility for defence and foreign affairs.

By the 1930s, then, the older empires had begun to pull back. But Germany, Japan and Italy were to make determined attempts to conquer new ones. Their efforts led to the Second World War, in the course of which France and the Netherlands were overrun, Britain severely weakened, and European racial prestige damaged by the ease with which Japan forced the surrender of British forces in Singapore and US forces in the Philippines. In the end, though, it was the Axis Powers that were defeated, and this naturally entailed the loss of most of the Italian colonies[2] and all the Japanese ones (Germany had already lost its colonies in the First World War). Of the Japanese colonies, China acquired Taiwan de facto, and the United States (for strategic reasons) took the Pacific islands (as UN trusteeships) plus the Ryukyus from Japan proper. Korea was temporarily occupied by the USA and USSR. In December 1945 they agreed in principle on the formation of a single provisional government, followed by a period of trusteeship. Nothing came of this, thanks chiefly to the mounting Cold War but also to Korean hostility to the idea of trusteeship. Further US–Soviet talks failed in mid-1947, and 1948 saw the formation of the rival Republic and Democratic People's Republic of Korea. Each claimed to speak for the whole country; the upshot was the outbreak in 1950 of the Korean War.

The major imperial powers emerged from the Second World War heavily dependent on the United States. The USA was, at one level, strongly anti-colonial – 'as a people, as a country,' wrote Roosevelt, 'we're opposed to imperialism – we can't stomach it'. Like President Wilson before him, Roosevelt talked of using US strength to impose his concept of the international system on his allies: 'We will have more trouble with Great Britain after the war than we are having with Germany now'. He urged India's claims to

1. Ideological reasons also led the USA to end its direct involvement in Latin America and embark on a 'Good Neighbor' policy towards the countries to its south

2. Various factors delayed a settlement until 1949. Britain then orchestrated a UN decision that Libya should by 1952 become an independent Kingdom (relying heavily on rent paid for British and US bases). The UN also granted Italy trusteeship over its former Somali colony until 1960. Eritrea, which the Italians had detached in 1889, was returned to the Ethiopian Empire in 1952 as an autonomous unit: in 1962 its autonomy was ended; a revolt broke out in 1966 that concluded with military success in 1991, followed by full independence in 1993

independence on Churchill; and he hoped that, after the war, Britain would not resume its Japanese-occupied colony of Hong Kong but allow it to revert to Chiang Kai-shek's China.[3] France, however, was Roosevelt's real *bête noire*; he frequently talked of its unfitness to recover Indo-China and of the desirability of transferring this to international trusteeship for about twenty years until it was ready for independence. (In expansive moods he added as suitable for such treatment a long list of other territories, like the Malay States, the Dutch East Indies, and even Thailand, of whose existing independence he was apparently unaware.) Roosevelt was also attracted by the idea of using the United Nations to ensure that this time the USA continued to provide international security after the war. To this end Dakar should be taken from France and become 'one of the prime United Nations strategic strongholds', a euphemism for passing to US military control.[4]

By 1945, however, Roosevelt was drawing back, perhaps because of a reluctance mortally to offend France and Britain, given his growing concern about the Soviet Union. When Churchill exploded at Yalta against what he took to be the US trusteeship proposals,[5] he was assured that only existing League Mandates, ex-enemy territory and colonies voluntarily placed under UN control were in question. Roosevelt still hoped for an Indo-China trusteeship, probably to be exercised jointly with China, but he told reporters that to press it 'would only make the British mad. Better to keep quiet just now'. In March 1945 he remained largely unresponsive to French pleas that arms be dropped so that the ex-Vichy forces in northern Indo-China could contest a complete Japanese takeover. But he came to accept that the trusteeship should be offered to France, provided it undertook to prepare the area for independence. Debate continued in Washington on US Indo-China policy, but shortly after Roosevelt's death (April 1945) France was finally assured that there was no disposition to question its sovereignty.[6]

3. R. Dallek, *Franklin D. Roosevelt and American Foreign Policy 1932–1945* (New York, 1979) pp.324, 428–9, 604n. The Americans tried, mildly, to impede the actual British return to Hong Kong, but took no action when Britain simply went ahead: *Foreign Relations of the United States* (Washington, DC) hereafter *FRUS*, 1945 vii pp.120, 500 ff

4. Dallek, *Roosevelt and American Foreign Policy* p.460; D. Cameron Watt, *Succeeding John Bull. America in Britain's Place 1900–1975* (Cambridge, 1984) p.223

5. He would never 'consent to forty or fifty nations thrusting interfering fingers into the life's existence of the British Empire'

6. Dallek, *Roosevelt and American Foreign Policy* pp.511–13; Watt, *Succeeding John Bull* esp. pp.213–19, 239

FRENCH INDO-CHINA AND THE DUTCH EAST INDIES 1945–6

In some ways the outcome of the war left colonial powers quite well positioned. From 1943 de Gaulle controlled the Maghreb. Britain dominated the Middle East, and had also, after much inter-Allied infighting, secured the South-East Asia command. As far as the conduct of the war was concerned this command proved marginal; but in political terms, it meant that British forces would take the surrender of Japanese troops in Malaya, Singapore, the Dutch East Indies and southern Indo-China. This may have proved more important than had been foreseen, by reason of local developments in the two latter areas at the close of the Japanese occupation.

Japan would have preferred simply to annex the Dutch East Indies; but, when driven on to the defensive, it began to cultivate Indonesian nationalism in the hope that this would help counter the anticipated Allied invasion. Planning was quite leisurely, and the Japanese surrender on 15 August 1945 forestalled the proclamation of an Indonesian Republic that would also have incorporated Malaya, North Borneo and Portuguese Timor. Japan had, however, established an Indonesian defence force. When popular fervour in Java pushed Sukarno into proclaiming an Indonesian Republic on 17 August, this force became the Indonesian army; it facilitated the rapid consolidation of the Republic, at least in Java, and prevented the Japanese from holding the ring, as they were instructed to do, until the arrival of Allied forces.

Vichy France had allowed Japan to station troops in Indo-China in 1940–1, and Japan in return had left French rule intact. But, fearing (correctly) that the French would turn on it in the event of an Allied invasion, Japan struck first in March 1945, interning the French army and administration. The obliteration of French rule left a vacuum. Japan would have preferred it to be filled, in northern Vietnam,[7] by the Emperor Bao Dai, who appointed a nationalist premier and Vietnamised the civil service. However, his prestige was limited; the vacuum was more effectively filled by Ho Chi Minh's 'League for Vietnam's Independence' (Vietminh). This was a communist-dominated coalition, formed in southern China in 1941, that had been establishing guerrilla bases in rural Tonkin since 1943 and a 'liberated zone' in early 1945. Its attraction

7. The former Protectorates of Tonkin and Annam; direct rule was to be retained over the former colony of Cochin China, the chief rice-producing area

extended to Bao Dai's viceroy in Hanoi. The Japanese turned power over to him on 16 August 1945; three days later, in the context of mounting popular demonstrations in Hanoi, he passed it on to the Vietminh. Later this also took over in Annam, and, as part of a broader coalition, in Saigon. Bao Dai abdicated in its favour on 25 August, and on 2 September 1945 in Hanoi Ho Chi Minh formally proclaimed the Democratic Republic of Vietnam.[8]

So by the time the Allies arrived to take the Japanese surrender a Vietnamese and an Indonesian Republic were already in existence. In retrospect it is a pity that they were not left undisturbed; it is possible, though unlikely, that they might have been, had the reactions of those taking the Japanese surrender been different. In the Middle East the British had themselves recently prevented France from forcibly reasserting its authority in Syria, though the damage that the episode caused to Anglo-French relations meant that it was unlikely to be repeated. The Chinese, who took the Japanese surrender in northern Indo-China, prevented French troops from returning – not through any love of the Vietminh but in order to push their own interests – until the February 1946 treaty of Chungking exchanged French concessions in China for Chinese recognition of French sovereignty over Indo-China. The delay enabled Ho Chi Minh's Republic to consolidate itself so that it could never be completely eradicated. The third Allied Power that might have taken over from the Japanese was the USA. This was in principle anti-colonialist; the Office of Strategic Studies (OSS the fore-runner of the CIA) was uncritically enthusiastic for the Vietminh. Also, though the USA was itself quite happy to use Japanese troops during the transitional period in Korea and northern China, General MacArthur was appalled when the British employed them against the Vietminh in Saigon: 'If there is anything that makes my blood boil, it is to see our allies in Indo-China . . . deploying Japanese troops to reconquer these little people we promised to liberate'.[9] So it is possible that he would have behaved differently had South-East Asia come under his command. On the other hand, he had earlier favoured a strong French military presence in Indo-China. He had also reached agreement for the restoration of Dutch civil administration in the East Indies; when the Dutch had cause to complain of British lukewarmness on their

8. Jan Pluvier, *South-East Asia from Colonialism to Independence* (Kuala Lumpur, 1974) p.249 and Part IV

9. Watt, *Succeeding John Bull* pp.240–1; Hugh Higgins, *Vietnam* (1975) p.19

behalf they came to wonder whether they would not have been better off with the Americans.[10]

Be that as it may, Britain wished to restore both Indo-China and Indonesia to its allies, but at the same time urged the latter to reach an accommodation with the local nationalists (as it was itself doing in Burma).[11] In both countries, however, the restoration of colonial rule was, to begin with, only partial.

In Indo-China the fears of the British commanding officer, General Gracey, that Saigon was slipping towards chaos and bloodshed, led him to disregard orders not to involve himself in matters of internal security[12] and to arm the former French prisoners, who then seized control of the town from the Vietminh-led 'National Executive Committee'; the Vietnamese responded with killings and kidknappings, strikes and guerrilla resistance. The British not only arranged a truce and negotiations in early October, but also accelerated the shipment of French troops (whose passage east Roosevelt had earler deliberately impeded). The negotiations broke down, with both sides far apart and the Vietminh also admitting their inability to control other Vietnamese factions. Gracey then, with the aid of Japanese troops, secured Saigon and a hinterland in which to concentrate the Japanese for evacuation home. From this base the French, in late October, mounted a military drive that had, by February 1946, recovered effective control of southern Indo-China, reducing the Vietminh to comparatively minor guerrilla resistance. Opinion differs as to the

10. Louis Allen, 'Studies in the Japanese Occupation of South-East Asia . . . II "French Indo-China" to "Vietnam" ', *Durham University Journal* lxiv (1971–2) p.123; H. Baudet in J.S. Bromley and E.H. Kossman (eds) *Britain and the Netherlands in Europe and Asia* (1968) pp.215–17

11. Most of the Burmese nationalists who had welcomed the Japanese occupation became disillusioned (despite the proclamation of 'independence' in 1943), and the Burma National Army changed sides in 1945. Returning British civilian authorities proved less sympathetic than had the military, concentrating on economic rehabilitation rather than immediate constitutional advance. Had this course been persisted with, the Anti-Fascist People's Freedom League (AFPFL) might have rebelled. But Attlee changed the governor in mid–1946, the AFPFL was brought into the Executive Council in September, and Burma progressed fairly smoothly to independence in January 1948

12. Mountbatten was cross, but reported to the Chiefs of Staff that it would be unsafe to revoke Gracey's 20–1 September proclamations once they had been issued. Since France did not yet have the capacity to enforce them, the Chiefs authorised Gracey on 1 October to use troops to support France; in passing this on, Mountbatten told Gracey to be preventive, not offensive. Gracey then met the Vietminh and arranged a truce and (abortive) negotiations with France: Allen, ' "French Indo-China" to "Vietnam" ', pp.124–7; Philip Ziegler, *Mountbatten. The Official Biography* (1985) pp.158, 161

importance of Gracey's actions: had he, as General Leclerc said in a moment of enthusiasm, 'saved French Indochina', or was Cochin China so divided internally, and the Vietminh so weak there, that French forces (which by early 1946 numbered 35,000) would have recovered control anyway? Either way, in early 1946 the French, though now securely based in the south, faced a Vietnamese Republic that controlled the north. Their initial response was to seek to negotiate on the basis that it should form an autonomous unit within a federal (but not sovereign) Indo-Chinese state.[13]

The Dutch reached the same position, though by a different route. By the time the British arrived, the Indonesian Republic was far more firmly entrenched in Java and Sumatra than was the 'National Executive Committee' in Saigon. Unlike Gracey, General Christison was ready to cooperate with it; any other course would have endangered the 100,000 Dutch internees scattered in camps throughout Java and Sumatra. As it was, the British had to fight (using Indian troops, and impeded by a US refusal to provide shipping) for a month to secure Surabaya as a base. Such episodes led them to limit the number of towns they themselves occupied in Java and, until March 1946, to ban the dispatch of Dutch forces to Java or Sumatra. Meanwhile the British had insisted on negotiations between the Dutch and the Indonesian Republic.

FRENCH–VIETMINH AND DUTCH–INDONESIAN NEGOTIATIONS 1946

Both the French-Vietminh and Dutch-Indonesian negotiations seemed at first to prosper. Ho Chi Minh welcomed a limited French presence in order to exclude the Chinese: 'It is better to sniff France's dung for a while than eat China's all our lives'.[14] March 1946 saw the Ho–Sainteny agreement, whereby 15,000 French troops were admitted to the north (where they replaced the Chinese) while France recognised the Vietnamese Republic as a 'free state' within an Indo-Chinese federation. Using this as a model, the Dutch Governor persuaded the Indonesian Republic to embark on discussions of a similar solution for the East Indies. In

13. Allen, ' "French Indo-China" to "Vietnam" '; Ziegler, *Mountbatten* pp.331–3; Philippe Devillers, *Histoire du Viêt-Nam de 1940 à 1952* (Paris, 1952) pp.153–69; Higgins, *Vietnam* pp.18–20

14. Higgins, *Vietnam*, p.20

both cases subsequent negotiations proved very difficult, but some sort of agreements were ultimately reached. In November 1946 the Dutch and Indonesians concluded a truce and the outlines of an agreement. This looked to the participation of the Indonesian Republic (with authority over Java and Sumatra) as one component of a 'United States of Indonesia', that would itself form with the Netherlands a Union for foreign affairs, defence, and some economic purposes. It was ill received by the Dutch Parliament, however, and it was only with considerable reservations on both sides that the Linggadjati Treaty was finally signed in March 1947. Meanwhile the Fontainebleau Conference on Indo-China had broken down. But this was partially offset by the last-minute signature in September of the Ho–Moutet *modus vivendi*, whereby Vietnam accepted in principle the Indo-Chinese monetary and customs union, and France undertook to grant democratic rights to the people of Cochin China (which Ho hoped would lead to its incorporation into his Vietnamese Republic).

THE FRENCH DECISION TO USE FORCE IN VIETNAM 1946

Both Linggadjati and the Ho–Moutet agreement soon collapsed. The French High Commissioner, d'Argenlieu, had never liked the negotiations, and was alarmed at the possible collapse of the 'free state' he had set up in Cochin China: the lifting of restrictions consequent on the Ho–Moutet agreement made it clear that the towns favoured unification with Ho's Republic, and, caught between such pressures and the French, the Chief Minister committed suicide. D'Argenlieu went to Paris to lobby, leaving his deputy Valluy instructions not to exclude 'the hypothesis of being compelled to resort to an act of direct force against the Hanoi government'. So after the moderate commander of the French troops in the north, General Morlière, had damped down an incident in Haiphong, Valluy bypassed him and told his subordinate to give the Vietnamese 'a severe lesson' and 'make yourself completely master of Haiphong' – which he did, in the process shelling the city with heavy casualties. If Valluy hoped this would precipitate a final breach with the Vietminh, he was disappointed. But in early December 1940 he effectively superseded Morlière, by sending Sainteny to Hanoi with instructions to make no major concessions and 'if it came to a breakdown carefully to leave the initiative to our partners [the Vietminh] while taking precautions not to be surprised by events'. On 19 December the Vietminh militia obliged by delivering a pre-emptive but muddled attack on French forces, which were soon able to go on to the offensive and take over the main buildings of Hanoi. Valluy's general line had in November had the approval of the principal ministers in Paris. But on 12 December the dove-ish Blum formed a caretaker government, and Ho Chi Minh started to cable him with proposals for a settlement. Equally Blum sent Ho a top priority pacific message on the 18th. However, messages had to pass through Saigon, which so delayed them that neither Ho nor Blum received their cables before the events of the 19th. Meanwhile Blum ordered Valluy to pursue a cease-fire if this were possible without compromising the position of French troops and civilians. Valluy held that it could not be done, and eventually Blum gave way. His position was further weakened when his colonial minister, Moutet, whom he had immediately sent out to try to arrange a truce, endorsed Valluy's actions and asked for reinforcements. So fighting became general: the resultant war can be seen as having lasted at least until Hanoi's conquest of Saigon in 1975. The events of 1946 provide plenty of scope for regrets: if only French officials had not taken matters into their own hands, if only Vietminh irregulars had not precipitated things on 19 December.[15] But pre-emption of Paris by colonial officials was commonplace under the Fourth Republic. Nor was France contemplating anything like real independence: Valluy had been instructed that, unlike the USA (whose economic strength would enable it to control a formally independent Philippines) and the USSR (which could dominate neighbouring Eastern Europe through the threat of invasion), France was both weak and far off; so if, as the Vietnamese wished, the French Union developed into a 'Commonwealth with purely symbolic allegiance', France would soon come to 'total abdication . . . and the sacrifice of all its interests'.[16]

15. They were not initially supported by Giap's main forces; together with Ho's appeals to Blum, this may suggest spontaneous action by Vietminh militants

16. Stein Tønnesson, 'The Longest Wars: Indochina, 1945–75', *Journal of Peace Research* xxii (1985) esp. pp.13–15

DUTCH 'POLICE ACTIONS' IN INDONESIA 1947–8

The Linggadjati Treaty of March 1947 had looked to the construction of a 'United States of Indonesia', but further negotiations soon deadlocked. July saw a Dutch ultimatum, followed by the occupation of parts of Sumatra and Java (the first 'police action'). The Indonesian Republic was clearly the weaker party, but it had been actively cultivating international support: India and (Labor-led) Australia brought the conflict before the UN Security Council, which called in August for a cease-fire and negotiations. The Dutch officially ended the 'police action'; but minor hostilities and extensions to Dutch-occupied areas continued, despite a degree of monitoring by Security Council members, until an Australian-Belgian-US Committee of Good Offices secured in January 1948 the Renville agreements (named after the US warship on which they were signed). Even then Indonesian irregulars (not necessarily under full government control) continued to irritate the Dutch, who often felt the firm restoration of order to be a prerequisite for any lasting settlement.

For the rest of 1948 unproductive negotiations continued. Meanwhile the Dutch accelerated the construction of the other federal units that they envisaged would participate, on a more or less equal basis with the much more populous Republic, in a federal Indonesia. Within the Republic the chief event was a communist rebellion in September (that was in many ways – including the murders committed by, and subsequent massacres of, the insurgents – an anticipation of events in 1965).[17] It is unclear how far the insurrection was the work of local activists, how far it represented a new policy from Moscow. But the Americans saw it as the latter, not unreasonably since it immediately followed the return from the Soviet Union of the exile Musso to take over the Indonesian Communist Party. Sukarno's readiness to denounce and suppress it further increased his stature in American eyes; it reduced the credibility of Dutch claims that their policies represented the only guarantee against the growth of communist influence in the area.

Dutch–Indonesian negotiations looked quite promising in November 1948, but both sides drew back under pressure from hard-liners. On 4 December the Dutch announced their failure, a step that was correctly seen as a prelude to military action before the monsoon season. Accordingly the USA sent a note to the effect

17. For which, see *The Cold War* chap. 8

that such action might 'jeopardise continuation of [Marshall] aid'. The note was rejected, and the USA instead tried pressing the Indonesians for further concessions (something its local agent had hitherto been distinctly reluctant to do). This came to nothing, partly as a result of foot-dragging by the Dutch Governor. On 19 December the 'second police action' went ahead, despite further US threats. Though a military success – the leaders and major towns of the Republic were seized – it was a disastrous political failure. It was condemned by the hitherto pro-Dutch politicians in the other units of their prospective federal Indonesia, and it worsened rather than cured Republican guerrilla resistance. It also created an international storm at the UN and elsewhere. Presumably it was the combination of these factors that decided the Dutch Cabinet to change its mind – after rejecting the idea of trying to blackmail the USA by threatening to pull out at once and leave the whole area in chaos. In late February 1949 it issued general invitations to a constitutional conference in the Hague and indicated a readiness to hand over power by mid-1950.

INDONESIAN INDEPENDENCE (1949) AND ITS AFTERMATH; WEST IRIAN

Negotiations were still difficult, as the Republican leaders declined to attend until their administration was reinstated on the ground. But, with UN mediation, the preliminary Roem–van Royen agreements were reached in May, Dutch troops started withdrawing in June, and an armistice was concluded in August 1949. By now the federal politicians had switched to seeking the best terms they could get from the Republic. The Hague Conference in the autumn agreed on a federal state, with seven constituent members and Sukarno as President. This would form a voluntary and equal Union with the Netherlands under the Dutch crown, but the Union's functions were to be far fewer than many Dutch partisans of empire had hoped. On this basis Indonesia became independent on 27 December 1949.

The aftermath was discouraging, with widespread insurgency (Muslim, communist, adventurist and separatist). Sukarno proceeded to tear up the Constitution, and in mid-1950 established a unitary state. Among the areas that resisted was the Melanesian and Calvinist island of Ambon, which had had strong connections with the Dutch army and which became from April to November the centre of the breakaway Republic of the South Moluccas. After its suppression many Ambonese had to be evacuated to the Netherlands, temporarily it was hoped, but in fact permanently. This was an unfortunate augury for Dutch–Indonesian relations, but the real stumbling block was to be Western New Guinea (West Irian), which was also racially distinct from Indonesia. The Hague conference had agreed only that this should be discussed within a year of Indonesian independence. Meanwhile the Dutch Parliament had attached to the Independence Act an amendment requiring the Dutch government to ensure that the Hague agreements on rights of self-determination, and so on, were honoured in practice. They were not, and this inevitably stiffened the Dutch position over West Irian. So no agreement was reached; and Sukarno's determination to acquire West Irian was to prove an important factor in radicalising his stance in international affairs. In 1956 Indonesia denounced the Union with the Netherlands; in 1958–9 it nationalised Dutch enterprises, which led to enormous economic dislocation and, in 1960, to the evacuation of the many Dutch nationals from Indonesia. There followed the threat of military confrontation, and in 1962 the transfer of West Irian to Indonesia through US pressure.[18]

THE FRENCH WAR IN INDO-CHINA 1947–53

Indonesian decolonisation was troubled, but far smoother than that of Indo-China. Although events in the two areas had initially run parallel, the French persisted with their resort to force whereas the Dutch did not. External pressures on the Netherlands perhaps contributed less to the decision to withdraw than did the changing Dutch reading of Indonesia's politics and of its economic value.[19] But it is interesting to note that France was not subjected to such pressures. In early 1947 the US Ambassador was instructed to hint

18. Pluvier, *South-East Asia* part VI; Dirk V. Stikker, *Men of Responsibility* (1966), Part I chap. 3, Part II chap. 1; *The Annual Register: A Review of Public Events at Home and Abroad*, 1949 and 1950; see also *The Cold War* chap. 8

19. The prewar Dutch East Indies had been immensely profitable, but by 1947 the Governor was already saying that the Dutch economy would recover quicker without them; they were constantly needing Dutch credits, and at independence 2 billion guilders (£188 million) of debt accumulated since 1945 had to be written off: *Britain and the Netherlands in Europe and Asia* pp.228–31

at UN involvement; but though France conceded no more than the dismissal of High Commissioner d'Argenlieu, the USA fixed with the UN Secretariat that a Vietnamese appeal should be filed, not circulated.[20] France probably owed its virtual immunity from pressure partly to its internal weakness – the USA had begun to bolster anti-communist forces and did not wish to risk upsetting the French political applecart – and partly to its status as a Great Power: the alienation of France would, in a Cold War context, be far more serious than that of the Netherlands; and France could have vetoed hostile resolutions in the UN Security Council. For the time being, therefore, the USA stood on the sidelines over Indo-China.

French arms were at first not unsuccessful, but they did not gain a complete victory. To supplement them France sought to enlist the prestige of Bao Dai – a tricky operation since, to be credible, he needed to exhibit nationalist credentials. Eventually in 1949 a bargain was struck: Bao Dai returned to Vietnam, acquired Cochin China (which France had been so determined to withhold from Ho Chi Minh in 1946), and proceeded to a distinctly circumscribed 'independence' within the French Union (as did the other Indo-Chinese kingdoms, Laos and Cambodia). The deal was not very credible; even the non-communist nationalist Ngo Dinh Diem declined to serve under Bao Dai.

The nationalist strategy paid only limited dividends, but France was soon able to reinforce it with an anti-communist one: Mao's triumph in China began to cast a shadow over South-East Asia. The British, already embroiled with communists in Malaya, began to feel it in 1948 and to seek a coalition to contain it. Initially the USA was not interested, but by late 1949 Acheson had been won over. The year 1950 saw an internationalisation of the Vietnam War. The United States and Britain formally recognised Bao Dai's Vietnam in February. The first US grant (of $10 million) for Indo-China was announced in May. Shortly thereafter the Korean War seemed to confirm the wisdom of thus containing China, so aid increased, ultimately covering 80 per cent of French financial costs. It was accompanied by some logistic and technical assistance, and by the proferring of military advice that the French seldom took. On the other side Chinese communist troops reached the border in December 1949; the People's Republic recognised Ho's regime in

20. Tønneson, 'The Longest Wars', p.17 and notes 10–14

January and brought the USSR to do likewise.[21] China went on to become Ho's main arms supplier (a position that was to give it considerable negotiating leverage at the Geneva Conference).

The year 1950 also constituted a military turning-point, in that the Vietminh passed from purely guerrilla actions to conventional offensives that, in October–November, forced French withdrawal from the towns on the Chinese border. In 1951 they tried to follow this up with an assault on the Red River delta, but were repulsed. However, France proved unable to capitalise on this success; in late 1952 renewed Vietminh offensives took over the territory along the Laotian border, while 1953 saw a major incursion into Laos to aid Pathet Lao resistance to the pro-French government. By now France was starting to tire of the war, and the Americans were demanding a more aggressive strategy for their money. The result was General Navarre's determination to bring the Vietminh to battle on his own terms, which led him to reoccupy Dien Bien Phu in November 1953. France was, however, no longer seeking a complete victory but only to establish a favourable position for negotiations (or, at worst, the gradual 'Vietnamisation' of the war). In the event Dien Bien Phu's fall served as backdrop for the Geneva Conference of 1954 that, in a formal sense, ended colonial rule in Indo-China.[22]

INDIA 1936–45

Far larger than Indo-China or Indonesia, indeed the largest 'colony' the world has ever known, was India. There is a vigorous and unresolved debate as to whether it could have been brought to independence as a single unit had the pace of decolonisation been faster between the wars and/or had different policies been followed in and after 1939. On the eve of the Second World War the position of the nationalist Congress Party appeared extremely strong: as a result of the 1936–7 elections it predominated in the governments of eight of the eleven provinces of British India; and its weakness in Muslim constituencies was obscured by the poor

21. The Eurocentric Stalin had supposedly 'wanted first a Communist takeover in France and a solution to . . . [Vietnamese] independence later'. Stalin was also suspicious of Ho's wartime liaison with OSS and his unwillingness to consult the USSR before taking action. Even after according him recognition, Stalin continued to doubt Ho's prospects: J. Radvanyi, *Delusion and Reality* (South Bend, Ind., 1978) pp.4–5, 269n; Jerrold L. Schecter with Vyacheslav Luchkov (eds) *Khrushev Remembers. The Glasnost Tapes* (Boston, 1990) – hereafter *Khrushchev Remembers iii* pp.154–6

22. See also *The Cold War* chap. 5

electoral showing of the Muslim League. However, in the aftermath of the elections the League's leader, Jinnah, was able to transform it into a mass party, playing none too scrupulously on fears of Hindu domination and drawing in many hitherto independent Muslim parties and organisations. His aim (which certainly ran ahead of the facts) was to secure its recognition as *the* Muslim party; this was much forwarded by events during the war.

When war broke out, the Viceroy, Linlithgow, announced India's automatic involvement. This was constitutionally correct, but Congress found it offensive. There was, admittedly, a good deal of sympathy for the anti-Nazi struggle, but also a feeling that the opportunity should be turned to advantage. Congress accordingly demanded, as the price of cooperation, a (satisfactory) declaration of British war aims, its own accession to the central government of India, and the promise of a constituent assembly and independence at the war's end. Had Linlithgow consulted earlier and more sympathetically, Congress might perhaps not thus have put him on the spot. But the Congress demand could not readily be met: given the unhappy precedent of Wilson's Fourteen Points, the British government was not in the business of defining war aims; and the Muslim League promptly made it clear that it would reject Congress's ideas of constitutional change. So Linlithgow went no further than generalities about postwar constitutional consultations and an offer to establish an Indian *advisory* war committee. Congress found this unacceptable, and (after some hesitation) decided to resign from provincial governments. It may have been hoping to be recalled on its own terms, but Linlithgow simply dispensed with it and instead looked increasingly to the Muslim League. In November the British government declared that it regarded Hindu-Muslim agreement as a precondition for constitutional change; and in March 1940 the League countered Congress demands for complete independence with a call for a separate Muslim state (soon to be known as Pakistan).[23]

After the European disasters of mid-1940 Congress made a new approach – an ambiguously worded offer of cooperation in the 'defence of the country', in exchange for an immediate 'National Government' plus a declaration of independence to take effect after the war. Linlithgow approached the British Cabinet for an overture

23. Gowher Rizvi, *Linlithgow and India* (1978) chaps 4–5; B.N. Pandey, *The Break-up of British India* (1969) chaps 5–6. Subsequent paragraphs also draw largely on R.J. Moore, *Escape from Empire. The Attlee Government and the India Problem* (Oxford 1983) and Ziegler, *Mountbatten* Part III

based on a promise of 'dominion status'[24] within a year of the war's conclusion, but the Cabinet would not thus tie itself down to dates and its offer fell flat. As a result Congress moved towards civil disobedience, though both this and its repression were comparatively restrained and had largely died down by late 1941. The Japanese victories of 1941–2, which brought them to the Indian border, reopened the constitutional question: the United States felt, wrongly, that India would not fight unless it was first freed. Labour members of the British Cabinet insisted that another effort be made. At one point even Churchill favoured the pre-emptive offer of a representative but *consultative* Defence Council that would at the end of the war become a constituent assembly. The outcome was Sir Stafford Cripps's mission to India. He brought with him a plan for postwar transition to independence that included the right of any province to opt out and become independent on its own. Most political parties found fault with this 'option clause', but the mission was shipwrecked on the more immediate issue of the Executive Council. By now this had a majority of Indians, albeit not of party representatives, and it worked perfectly smoothly. But Linlithgow, after initially allowing Cripps to discuss a Council that would 'approximate to a cabinet', then drew back and (with London's support) insisted on his power to overrule the Council if he thought fit; his chief responsibility was the war effort, and he doubted whether this would be a political Council's primary concern. Congress felt cheated, but the collapse of the negotiations was so presented that Congress was partially discredited in American (and even some Indian) eyes as having rejected a generous offer. There followed a 'Quit India' movement, but this was suppressed and the Congress leadership imprisoned. The government remained clearly in control for the rest of the war; again the Muslim League strengthened its position by cooperating.

In 1944 there was an attempt at reconciliation between Gandhi and Jinnah. Although this failed, it should be noted that Gandhi suggested a sovereign Muslim Pakistan,[25] albeit one whose viability

24. 'Dominion status' then entailed acceptance of the UK monarch as one's constitutional head of state; but it afforded full internal self-government and the ability (if one wished) to control one's own foreign policy, an ability dramatically illustrated by the Irish Free State's decision to remain neutral in the Second World War. For the most part, though, dominions did not choose to operate as states totally distinct from the UK. Indian leaders were surprisingly slow to appreciate that there was (after 1931) no substantive difference between 'dominion status' and 'independence'

25. Moore, *Escape from Empire* pp.55–7

Jinnah doubted because it excluded the non-Muslim areas of Bengal and the Punjab. It was to be on this solution that everybody ultimately fell back after three years of incessant further negotiation. Linlithgow's successor as Viceroy, Wavell, set the ball rolling when, in the closing months of the war, he finally secured permission to try to bring the parties on to his Executive Council on the basis of equal representation for Muslims and caste Hindus. But the Simla Conference broke down over Jinnah's insistence that all the Muslims be nominated by the League. Many eminent Muslims, including the then President of the Congress Party, were *not* League members. However the 1945 elections were to show that Jinnah's claim was no longer as far-fetched as it once had been: the League won all the Muslim seats for the central assembly, though in the more important provincial elections Congress retained the (wholly Muslim) North-West Frontier Province while the League just failed to topple the governing coalition in the Punjab.

The other important 1945 elections were those in the UK. Churchill had been a bitter opponent of the Government of India Act, 1935, and he remained unenthusiastic about the liquidation of the British Empire. He would almost certainly have been prepared to hand over power in India,[26] but he would probably have shown considerable sympathy to princes and provinces that did not wish to leave the Empire or that sought independence in close association with it. Labour's election made it certain that (with Attlee and Cripps continuing their long-time involvement in Indian affairs) early withdrawal would be a high British priority – though it took some time to convince the Congress leaders (who had, after all, recently been imprisoned by the Churchill–Attlee coalition). Britain had two further concerns. One was not to lose control of the situation during the withdrawal, a process that was itself corrosive of British authority. The other was to retain close links with the Indian successor government. As Cripps had put it to Churchill, 'My great anxiety is to keep India within the [British] Commonwealth of Nations because I believe that it is of very great importance to our future position in the world both economically and politically'.[27]

26. His purely Conservative caretaker government had approved Wavell's Simla initiative

27. Moore, *Escape from Empire* p.19

PARTITION AND THE TRANSFER OF POWER 1946–7

In 1946 things went badly. A Cabinet mission, dominated by Cripps, reached India in March. It nearly secured agreement on the basis of a coalition Interim Government and of a confederal Union, but agreement collapsed in the face of differing interpretations and mental reservations on the part of Congress and the League. Jinnah further suspected (with some justice) that, in the event of disagreement between the two, the Labour government would always choose to appease Congress. So in July he reverted to demanding an independent Pakistan, and called for direct action. Initially Wavell was ready to do without Jinnah and asked Nehru to form a government. Later, shocked by communal riots in which 5,000 were killed in Calcutta, Wavell induced Nehru to accept League nominees into his government; this took effect in October, but the resultant Cabinet did not work well. Constitutional agreement seemed no nearer, and the situation on the ground continued to deteriorate. Meanwhile Wavell's thoughts turned increasingly to breakdown plans, and in the autumn he pressed London hard to adopt a phased withdrawal (first from the south and by spring 1948 from the whole subcontinent). The Cabinet found this defeatist, and Attlee decided to see whether a new Viceroy, Mountbatten, could not break the deadlock.

The announcement in February 1947 of Mountbatten's appointment was coupled with a declaration that if agreement was not reached by June 1948, Britain would leave, handing over power to whatever bodies 'may seem most reasonable'. This sought to put pressure on the various parties to reach agreement. Another factor was the mounting violence and disorder: in March 1947 Muslim League paramilitaries sparked riots in the Punjab that killed 3,000, brought down the ruling coalition, and were never forgiven by the Sikhs. By now some Congress leaders (Patel and possibly Nehru) seem to have concluded that partition was preferable to a slide into civil war.[28] Mountbatten reached India in late March and plunged into a bewildering round of talks. At a personal level he made an excellent impression on Congress leaders – he had already charmed Nehru during an earlier encounter in Singapore – and they came to trust him. This was just as well, since, as regards the substance of the negotiations, several balls were in the air at once: immediate acquisition of 'dominion status' by the 'interim government', which

28. Pandey, *The Break-up of British India* p.195

would supervise the drafting of a full 'independence' constitution by mid-1948 and the departure of Muslim regions that would not accept it; immediate dominion status for both India and Pakistan; self-determination by province which raised the possibility of independence also for Bengal and the princely states. It is unclear how much of this represented manipulation (not only by Britain, but also by the various Indian politicians involved), and how much straightforward incomprehension by overworked people (notably Mountbatten and Nehru) not remarkable for their grasp of detail. The dénouement came in May, when Nehru was staying with Mountbatten at Simla. Shown the wording of the plan the British Cabinet thought had been agreed, he recoiled at its potentialities for Balkanisation, and fell back on an alternative scheme for the immediate transfer of power to two, and only two, 'dominions', India and Pakistan. These would remain temporarily within the Commonwealth and use its facilities for easing their transitional relations. By early June 1947 this had been sold to the British Cabinet, and, with more difficulty, to Jinnah (who still found it hard to accept the partition of Bengal and the Punjab it would inevitably entail).

There followed a period of impetuous preparation for the transfer of power by mid-August. Mostly things went well. But there were two exceptions – the Punjab and the disposition of certain princely states. Any partition of the Punjab along Muslim/non-Muslim lines would leave nearly half the Sikhs under Muslim rule, which they rejected; no other demarcation was really possible since the Sikhs were nowhere in a majority. The Sikhs had responded violently to the ousting of the coalition Punjab government, and conditions continued to worsen. But nobody seems to have anticipated the scale of the massacres that broke out on independence, swamping the 55,000-strong Punjab Boundary Force. In early September the Indian Cabinet recalled Mountbatten, now the supposedly non-political Governor-General, to take charge of its Emergency Committee. Order was not restored until October, after the loss of anything from 200,000 to 500,000 lives, and refugees continued to stream across the border (in both directions) till November.[29]

29. I.A. Talbot, 'Mountbatten and the Partition of India: A Rejoinder', *History* lxix (1984); Ziegler, *Mountbatten* chap. 34; Moore, *Escape from Empire* pp.326–32

KASHMIR, JUNAGADH AND HYDERABAD

The Punjab did not help Indo-Pakistani relations, but the real damage was done by what seemed at the time as the comparatively minor problem of Kashmir. This was one of the many princely states that had retained internal self-government (generally autocratic) but submitted to British paramountcy. Legally the end of the Raj would mean their recovery of full sovereignty. Congress found the prospect unacceptable; it was also unlikely that many rulers could have maintained themselves in the face of India's hostility and the possible unrest of their subjects. So, once the future of British India was agreed, the princes were pressed to accede (on terms of substantial internal autonomy, though this did not last long) to either India or Pakistan. Mountbatten's dynastic prestige as a cousin of the King-Emperor was a useful weapon in this connection: his advice was generally accepted. But three states stood out: Junagadh and the much larger Hyderabad (both land-locked Hindu states with Muslim rulers), and the Hindu-ruled, but predominantly Muslim, Kashmir, which bordered on both India and Pakistan. Mountbatten managed to secure for Hyderabad an offer of continued independence in exchange for internal constitutional reforms that would probably have led to its ultimate accession to India; but the Nizam turned it down, and in 1949 Indian troops moved in. Junagadh opted for Pakistan. India found this hard to accept and suggested a plebiscite. Pakistan should have closed with the offer, as it would have constituted a valuable precedent for Kashmir, but did not. A government-in-exile was then established in Bombay, and soon the state was in such confusion that the Nizam fled and India was invited to restore order.

Kashmir was not so easily settled. The Maharaja refused to opt for either India or Pakistan, probably hoping that he would be able to secure independence – and in retrospect there is much to be said for such a solution. In late October 1947 Pakistan sought to nudge him by unleashing an unofficial but violent invasion by local tribesmen. The Maharaja appealed for Indian military assistance. Inexplicably Mountbatten insisted that he first formally accede to India. Mountbatten saw this as a temporary and legalistic move, to be followed by a plebiscite and partition (along communal lines) between Pakistan and India. But Kashmir's accession to India was bound to be at the least a complication, since its subsequent disposition would then be looked to as a precedent by other areas. Actually it proved far worse: Nehru was himself of Kashmiri origin and was highly emotional on the subject; at one point in June 1947 he had declared 'that Kashmir meant more to him at the moment than anywhere else'.[30] So, though he could be brought to promise a plebiscite, he never honoured such promises; in 1953 he even imprisoned his former friend, Sheikh Abdullah, who (though a partisan of adhesion to India) sought for Kashmir what Nehru regarded as an unacceptable degree of autonomy.

Militarily Indian intervention was highly successful, holding the tribesmen away from the bulk of the settled country. But it nearly led to full-scale war, since Jinnah at one point ordered his army to reply; its commander was, however, still British, and he declined to strike without the approval of General Auchinleck, still (albeit tenuously) Supreme Commander of both armies.[31] Instead there were Indo-Pakistani discussions, but to little purpose. In 1948 India took the issue to the United Nations, which eventually secured a cease-fire (from January 1949). It also called for a plebiscite, and in subsequent years supplied a whole string of mediators – but to no effect. Muslim Pakistan might in any event have drifted away from India. But Kashmir made the two into enemies, and later blocked a number of moves for reconciliation.

INDO-PAKISTANI DIVERGENCE; THE WARS OF 1965 AND 1971

Pakistan, smaller and industrially less developed than India, sought protection by staying closer to Britain and the USA. In 1953 Nehru used the prospect of a US–Pakistan military alliance to scrap agreements for a Kashmir plebiscite. The alliance went ahead in 1954, and was reinforced by Pakistani participation in SEATO (the South-East Asia Treaty Organisation) and the Baghdad Pact; the resulting military aid assisted the build-up of a Pakistan army that was in reality directed chiefly against India.

Eisenhower nevertheless appreciated India's policy of international neutrality, which he saw as keeping one of China's borders quiet.[32] In the late 1950s he embarked on a long-term effort to mend the Indo-Pakistani rift. The 1958 advent of political stability in Pakistan – through military rule by General Ayub Khan –

30. Ziegler, *Mountbatten* pp.413, 445
31. ibid, p.447
32. Stephen E. Ambrose, *Eisenhower the President* (1984) p.380

provided a favourable context. By 1960 the preliminary problem of the sharing of irrigation water for the Indus basin had been resolved with the aid of World Bank mediation. But Nehru remained resistant to Pakistani attempts to proceed to a Kashmir plebiscite. Ayub was disappointed. When the Sino-Indian border dispute burst into war in 1962, he tended to blame India; he rejected Kennedy's plea that he earn Nehru's goodwill by signalling that India could safely transfer troops from the Pakistan border to the war zone. Kennedy, for his part, turned down Ambassador Galbraith's suggestion that India be bribed to make a generous offer on Kashmir;[33] instead (with Britain) he rushed equipment to the Indian army in the aftermath of its defeat by what he saw as an aggressive China. Ayub deplored this. Indian defeats (in reality the result of poor leadership and inadequate acclimatisation to high altitudes) may have led him to underestimate the quality of the Indian army. He may also have hoped that Nehru's successor as prime minister, Shastri, would prove weak. In 1965 he took the initiative (before the reconstruction of the Indian army was complete) first in the Rann of Kutch (where Britain mediated a cease-fire), then (in August–September) in Kashmir itself. Ayub was wrong; India gave as good as it got, and Pakistan eventually accepted UN calls for a ceasefire.

In January 1966 at Tashkent the Soviet Union mediated the restoration of diplomatic relations and military withdrawals to the 1949 cease-fire line. Shastri's sudden death in that city generated an ephemeral wave of goodwill. But no progress was made on Kashmir, and in its absence Pakistan rejected ideas of a 'no-war' agreement.[34] So matters continued, until Pakistan began to fall apart and the government embarked (in 1971) on massive repression in East Pakistan. Indira Gandhi then took her chance, liberated that country to become 'Bangladesh', and definitively established Indian supre- macy within the subcontinent.[35] This led in 1972 to a summit conference at Simla between Mrs Gandhi and the new Pakistani President, Bhutto, at which both committed themselves to peaceful

33. Mohammed Ayub Khan, *Friends Not Masters: A Political Autobiography* (1967) pp.107–13, 242–3, chap. 9; Theodore Sorenson, *Kennedy* (1965) p.664. Later President Johnson concentrated his attention not on the Kashmir issue but on pressing India (with some success) to pay more attention to developing its agriculture: Lyndon B. Johnson, *The Vantage Point: Perspectives of the Presidency, 1963–1969* (1972) pp.224–31

34. *Keesing's*, 21187 ff, 21325 ff; in 1959 it had been India that had rejected such ideas

35. See also *The Cold War* chap. 8

coexistence, the resolution of differences by peaceful means, and the respecting of the existing cease-fire line in Kashmir; Bhutto subsequently told Parliament, in effect, that Pakistan had no hope of bringing Kashmir self-determination.[36] Thereafter relationships within the subcontinent undoubtedly improved, a trend that led India, Pakistan, Bangladesh, Nepal, Bhutan, Sri Lanka and the Maldives to establish in 1983 a cooperation committee with regular meetings of ministers. It takes very little to upset India and Pakistan, however: in 1986 there were significant clashes on the Siachin glacier, followed in December 1986 to February 1987 by alarming troop concentrations on the border.[37] Late 1988 saw a promising attempt to restore cordial relations, but it has been more than counterbalanced by the continuing Sikh agitation in the Punjab (which India sees as fomented from Pakistan) and by the secessionist uprising that has convulsed Indian Kashmir since 1989, occasioning serious clashes on (and calls for hot pursuit across) the cease-fire line.

INDIA, BRITAIN AND THE COMMONWEALTH

Given this record of conflict, the transfer of power in India was not without its shadows. But – by contrast to events in, say, Indonesia – it had been performed with considerable panache and a remarkable degree of Indian–British goodwill. One symbol of this was India's readiness to remain in the Commonwealth on a long-term basis, instead of opting (like Burma) for independence *tout court.* When Attlee raised the question of long-term membership, Nehru replied in April 1948

> If anyone had asked . . . about a year ago, I have little doubt what the answer would have been, and this answer would have been almost unanimous. . . . Indeed it is remarkable what Lord Mountbatten, and may I add Lady Mountbatten also, have done to remove many of the old causes of mistrust and bitterness between India and England.[38]

Indian membership of the Commonwealth had been widely seen in London as a considerable prize: Churchill told Mountbatten in May 1947 that if he 'could achieve Dominion status for both Hindustan

36. *Keesing's*, 25432
37. *Keesing's*, 32975, 35513. From 1985 the regional group has been known as the 'South Asia Association for Regional Co-operation' (SAARC)
38. Moore, *Escape from Empire* p.348

and Pakistan, the whole country would be behind us, and the Conservative Party would help to rush the legislation through'.[39] What such membership would amount to in practice, it was impossible to say: it was of the nature of the Commonwealth that its links could never be precisely defined. Juridically Dominions were fully independent; practically the Second World War had shown that the Empire/Commonwealth (bar the Irish Free State) could still act as a unit.

London saw Commonwealth membership as contributing to two complementary goals: the mitigation of the effects of Indo-Pakistani partition, and common action with the rest of the Commonwealth. It had been hoped that, after independence, Mountbatten would be the first Governor-General (acting head of state) of both India and Pakistan, and, as such, help build organs of inter-state cooperation (like the Joint Defence Council). In the event Jinnah insisted on becoming Pakistan's first Governor-General; and though Mountbatten continued to hold Pakistan's interests in mind, inevitably he came to adopt – and, more important, be perceived as adopting – an Indian perspective. In any case two countries that were on the brink of war over Kashmir were unlikely to cooperate extensively; the idea was periodically revived in the 1950s, but the two countries' very different attitudes to international relations also constituted an impediment.[40] However, if London's highest hopes were not realised, nor were its worst fears; the subcontinent has at least proved militarily self-sufficient, and has not required British (or any other) forces to assist it with external defence or the maintenance of internal order and stability.

The other gains looked for from continued Commonwealth membership were thus summed up in 1949:[41]

> India is anti-communist and in the present dangerous state of world affairs, that means a great deal to us. Asia [especially China] . . . is becoming more and more overwhelmed by communism. If we lose . . . the co-operation of India, then not only the Commonwealth but the anti-communist Western Powers will lose . . . an extremely important foothold in Asia. . . . In recent years, certain parts of the Commonwealth have broken away. . . . The impression may easily be created . . . that the Commonwealth is disintegrating. . . . The decision . . . [to allow India to retain membership despite becoming a Republic] was undoubtedly a decision that will give the world a

39. Ziegler, *Mountbatten* p.385
40. Ayub Khan, *Friends Not Masters* pp.126–8, 131–2
41. By the South African Prime Minister (India's campaign against his racial policies notwithstanding)

> different impression that the Commonwealth is still a power in world affairs

'We shall', Attlee's Secretary of State for Commonwealth Affairs told him, 'be making an act of faith based on the belief that' India's 'contact with us will work a speedy and effective evolution', enabling Britain to 'seek to mould her views and influence her action'. Such hopes extended not only to foreign but also to military policy, in which context (one historian notes) 'the spate of draft military agreements' prepared in Whitehall 'until 1950 suggests a surprising degree of wishful thinking'.[42] For Nehru followed a policy (of anti-colonialism, criticism of white rule in Africa, and non-alignment in the East–West conflict) that contrasted strongly with that not only of the rest of the Commonwealth but also of most of the then independent non-European states, but which was over the next two decades to prove extremely influential in the Third World. Accordingly India remained detached during the Korean War (while playing a useful role in handling prisoners of war after the armistice). Unlike Australia and New Zealand, it provided no support for British operations in South-East Asia (though it did acquiesce in continuing British recruitment of Gurkha troops from the Himalayan kingdom of Nepal, and made major contributions to UN forces in Egypt and the Congo).

But if Nehru diverged sharply from British foreign policy, he remained in many respects anglophile: he once described himself as the last Englishman to rule India. He established good relationships with successive British premiers from Attlee to Macmillan; and while differences with British foreign policy were always clear, in the early 1950s Indian and British assessments of both China and Indo-China had enough in common to irritate the United States considerably. All this helped forward another British hope, that the Commonwealth connection would keep India from turning to the USSR. Indeed, though India accepted Soviet economic aid after Khrushchev's 1955 visit, Nehru promised Britain in 1956 not to buy Soviet military aircraft. The British attack on Egypt over Suez came as a great shock, and ended the practice whereby Commonwealth representatives would foregather before any international or UN meeting to exchange views on the way they would play things, a

42. Anita Inder Singh, 'Keeping India in the Commonwealth: British Political and Military Aims, 1947–49', *Journal of Contemporary History* xx (1985) pp.477–8, 480–1n

custom that offered the UK considerable scope for unofficial leadership. Admittedly relations were soon patched up, but there were to be other points of Anglo-Indian divergence, and in the 1960s the Commonwealth receded from the priorities of both countries.[43] Under the stress of defeat by China in the 1962 border war and of fighting with Pakistan in 1965, India both turned increasingly from the general world scene – which Nehru had hoped to transform through a highly personal diplomacy – and looked to the Soviet Union as a reliable opponent of Pakistan. (The result was a defence relationship culminating in the 1971 treaty[44] and an Indian tendency to avoid criticising Soviet foreign policy, but not much more.) Meanwhile Britain was focusing on Europe and abandoning its 'east of Suez' role. It found the Commonwealth a correspondingly less useful grouping; the tendency of its by now Third World majority to use the Commonwealth (from 1966) as a vehicle for attacking British policies over Rhodesia further diminished its attractions.

This 'Third World' majority owed something to India's example. For the prominence within the Commonwealth of so large and independent-minded a country did much to dissipate its neo-colonial image. Also India had insisted on becoming a republic. Since the only formal link was the Crown, this would normally have entailed leaving the Commonwealth – as Eire did in 1949. To retain India, the Commonwealth decided (after much debate) to confine the sovereign's role to the extremely nebulous one of 'Head of the Commonwealth'; this enabled states wishing to become republics (as most new states have in fact wished) to petition for continued membership – usually a formality, though not in the cases of South Africa (1961) or Fiji (1987). British colonies usually joined the Commonwealth on independence, and (given the unexpectedly rapid pace of decolonisation) this inevitably changed its nature. In the 1950s Commonwealth conferences still represented the gatherings of a primarily Anglo-Saxon family.[45] By the later 1960s they approximated rather to a cross-section of the United Nations,

43. S. Gopal, 'Nehru and the Commonwealth' in D. Dilks (ed.) *Retreat from Power. Studies in Britain's Foreign Policy of the Twentieth Century* ii (1981) chap. 5

44. See *The Cold War* chap. 8

45. 'It used', Macmillan told its 1962 conference, 'to be fashionable to refer to the Commonwealth as a family', but now 'we can best think of' it 'as a group of friends and relations': Harold Macmillan, *Memoirs* vi p.527. Privately Macmillan tended to think in terms of the 'old' Commonwealth members (still the majority when he became Prime Minister) and the 'new'

and the organisation's cohesion reduced accordingly;[46] the contrast in this respect between Macmillan's memoirs and Wilson's is striking.

One other unanticipated consequence, very possibly in the long run the most important, lay in the field of immigration. For Britain's anxiety to retain its position as the centre of the Commonwealth, together with the ease with which people had always moved between the UK and the white dominions, led it (unlike the rest of the Commonwealth) to retain until 1962 free access for citizens of any Commonwealth state. In the 1950s most immigrants were probably of British descent, but enough came from the West Indies and the Indian subcontinent to lay the basis of communities that will probably stabilise at about 10 per cent of the UK population, and that have already given rise to a society far more multiracial than was then envisaged. The acceleration of such immigration in the early 1960s led to the controversial imposition (and subsequent progressive tightening) of immigration controls. There are survivals of an older order: citizens of Commonwealth states, unlike those of EC members (other than of the Irish Republic), can vote in UK elections. But the very visible contrast between controls on Commonwealth immigration and (from 1973) free movement to and from the rest of the European Community underlines, at a day-to-day level, the marked shift that has occurred since the 1950s in the UK's outlook and identity.

46. Though not quite to vanishing point. Links of language and education make technical cooperation much easier on a Commonwealth than on a UN basis. Membership entails a certain sharing of diplomatic information. Some powers, notably Canada, find the Commonwealth an attractive forum for aid and diplomatic activity. Conferences occasionally reach agreements (e.g. on sporting contacts with South Africa – 1977) or launch initiatives (like the 1979 Rhodesia constitutional conference or the 1985–6 'Eminent Persons Group' on South Africa), and more often provide opportunities for quiet mutual lobbying by heads of government

CHAPTER THREE
The End of Empire

THE SURVIVAL IN THE 1940s OF IMPERIAL ATTITUDES, DESPITE EXTENSIVE DECOLONISATION

The most extensive round of decolonisation was that effected in the later 1940s; to the countries already described [Taiwan (to China de facto, 1945), Philippines (1946), Pakistan, India (1947), Burma (1948), Korea (two de facto sovereign states, 1948), Newfoundland (to Canada, 1949), Indonesia (1949)] should be added Ceylon (now Sri Lanka), whose independence came calmly in early 1948, and Syria, the Lebanon and Palestine, where in 1946–8 the French and British Mandates terminated with considerable incident that will be more conveniently discussed in Part III of this volume. But if, on a population basis, the greater part of the formal empires had thus been wound up, attachment to and expectations from empire had not. In 1947–8 the British Colonial Secretary was hoping 'to strengthen the position of Western Europe internationally by building up the economy of Africa and linking Africa more closely with this country and other countries of Western Europe', while Bevin sought thus

> to develop our own power and influence to equal that of the United States of America and the USSR. We have the material resources in the Colonial Empire, if we develop them, and by giving a spiritual lead now [to the formation of a Western Union] we should be able to carry out our task in a way which will show clearly that we are not subservient to [either superpower].[1]

1. Hargreaves, *Decolonization in Africa* pp.103–5

Admittedly further study soon showed that colonial resources could not be developed to such effect. But the time was one of high prices for primary products, of which metropolitan powers took full advantage. In the British case this involved a combination of state involvement in trading and a tight organisation from London of the 'sterling area' – 'More completely than ever before, economics and empire had come together'.[2] Empires, accordingly, were not regarded as obsolete, and colonial powers were ready to repress revolts. The process of independence never came to a complete standstill: Libya gained sovereignty in 1951, Sudan, Tunisia and Morocco in 1956; but the early 1950s represented something of a lull.

MALAYA AND THE GOLD COAST (GHANA) 1948–57

Nevertheless developments in 1948 in Malaya and the Gold Coast (now Ghana) had made further decolonisation certain. The two countries shared the position of being, through their raw material exports, major net dollar earners; indeed in a mercantilist sense they were the only really profitable parts of the formal British empire.[3] Although Malayan independence can be seen as somewhat belated by Asian standards, the Gold Coast inevitably set precedents for the rest of black Africa.

During the Japanese occupation of Malaya, the (almost entirely Chinese) Communist Party mounted minor guerrilla resistance from the jungle and so was sent some British arms. After the war these were mostly cached; the communists turned to trying to take over the local trade unions, which flourished under the influence of postwar inflation. The authorities at first viewed the process benignly; but in 1948, concerned by intimidation, strikes and estimates that nearly two-thirds of the unions were communist controlled, they cracked down. The other British U-turn came in the constitutional field. After the war the small traditional Malay kingdoms were reorganised to create in 1946 a 'Malay Union', in which the large Chinese community (of fairly recent immigrants)

2. John Darwin, 'British Decolonization since 1945: A Pattern or a Puzzle', in R.F. Holland and G. Rizvi (eds) *Perspectives on Imperialism and Decolonization* (1984) p.97

3. In 1954–6 the Malayan area's average annual trade surplus with the non-sterling area was over £51 million, that of the Gold Coast £19 million; East Africa and Aden contributed over £10 million (but were in overall trade deficit), while the rest of the empire (excluding Hong Kong) had a £17 million deficit: Morgan, *Official History of Colonial Development* v p.99

should enjoy equal rights with the indigenous Malays. The Malays feared that Chinese industry and commercial acuity would rapidly bring them to predominance. So the United Malay National Organisation (UMNO) sprang into existence and soon persuaded the British to revert to a Federation of Malaya, upgrading the Malay rulers and ending automatic citizenship for non-Malays. Counter-agitation proved ineffective, the Federation came into being in February 1948, and disillusion further inclined much of the Chinese community towards the communists. Debate continues as to whether the revolt that had broken out by June 1948 was the spontaneous outcome of these disappointments, or whether it was touched off by Soviet instructions.

The British expected to suppress it quickly, by drafting in troops and police formerly employed in Palestine. But defective strategy, stemming partly from administrative overlap and partly from lack of experience in confronting jungle-based guerrillas, made progress slow; nor was morale improved by the High Commissioner's 1951 death in an ambush. However, the British had many advantages: Malaya is a peninsula, and though the guerrillas could take refuge in less firmly administered southern Thailand, they had no access to external support and supplies. Their numbers were not great (4,000–5,000 hard-core fighters, though these were supported by a more numerous periphery of part-time activists). Also their appeal was confined to the Chinese; since these were mostly not citizens they could be influenced by the fear of deportation and the carrot of improved rights and conditions. Meanwhile the Malay majority was generally supportive of the government. Under Sir Gerald Templer, the British were able, from 1952, to turn these advantages to good account in what was to become the classic postwar demonstration of successful (if relatively small-scale)[4] counter-insurgency. Half a million Chinese squatters on the edge of the jungle were compulsorily concentrated into fortified villages, but at the same time supplied with services and land titles. The villages were then required to defend themselves and stop supplying the guerrillas with food, and were rewarded or punished according to their compliance. The now hungry guerrillas were pursued into, and bombed and ambushed within, the jungle. An extensive propaganda campaign was mounted to win the 'hearts and minds' of the people (the term was first used in Malaya).

4. Troops and police numbered about 110,000, the local home guard over 200,000; but total deaths (to 1960) were only 6,710 'terrorists', 1,865 soldiers/police, and 2,473 civilians: *Keesing's*, 17572

This campaign included, from 1951, the introduction of local government elections, and these provided a forum for growing political activity. Here the decisive development proved to be the 'Alliance' negotiated in 1953 between UMNO and the conservative and business-oriented Malay Chinese Association. The British had made it clear that some such intercommunal cooperation was a prerequisite for constitutional advance; and though the Alliance had initially to exert some pressure (withdrawing its representatives from governmental councils in 1954), in 1955 agreement was reached on an elective majority for the Legislative Council. UMNO swept the board at the elections, and its leader, the Tunku Abdul Rahman, became 'chief minister'. He initially insisted on holding talks with the communist insurgents; but these failed since the communists sought their party's legalisation, whereas the Tunku would offer only the sequence of surrender, screening and amnesty. After the talks' failure he bore down on the guerrillas with the combination of military pressure, offers of amnesty to deserters, and emphasis on Malaya's progress to independence; the insurrection continued to peter out, to the point where the state of emergency could be formally ended in 1960. Given the Tunku's attitude towards the communists, the British had every incentive to accommodate him, and no doubt felt (as they earlier had of Ceylon)[5] that 'if we treat them strictly as a Dominion, they will behave like a very loyal colony: whereas if we treat them as a Colony, we may end by driving them out of the Commonwealth'. So Malaya moved to independence in 1957, while retaining British (and Australian) military assistance and, with Singapore, providing Britain with bases that could be used for operations elsewhere. We have already noted the continued cooperation between Britain and the Tunku in the early to mid-1960s over the creation of Malaysia and its defence against Indonesia;[6] the subsequent winding down of the British military presence was the product not of local resentment but of UK financial needs.

Malaya had a communist emergency in 1948; the Gold Coast merely feared one. Constitutional reform had already begun; indeed the 1946 constitution had provided for an (indirectly elected) African majority on the Legislative Council. But there was no real feeling of urgency: 'Somewhere in West Africa within a century, within half a century', a 1943 Commission on Higher

5. Gordon-Walker to Attlee, March 1948, quoted in Holland and Rizvi, *Perspectives on Imperialism and Decolonization* p.195

6. See *The Cold War* chap. 8

Education had reported, 'a new African state will be born'.[7] The jolt came in early 1948: discontent was widespread, largely as a result of bureaucratic interference with economic activity, and rioting broke out after police fired on an ex-servicemen's protest. Initially there was a disposition to blame the Kremlin; even when this passed, it was succeeded by a determination 'to remove the causes of discontent which alone would make a Communist *putsch* conceivable'. There followed commissions of inquiry, then the extension of the franchise in the more developed south, though not the introduction of representative government. Meanwhile Kwame Nkrumah broke with the moderates who had brought him into politics, and in mid-1949 established his own Convention People's Party (CPP) with the aim of 'Positive Action' to secure 'Self-Government NOW'. 'Positive Action', a general strike, collapsed in early 1950, and Nkrumah was imprisoned. It was at first hoped that his absence would open the way for moderate politicians, but the CPP managed to effect substantial political mobilisation and to establish a widespread presence. Indeed British officials may have exaggerated its strength, viewing it as the counterpart of the Indian Congress Party. When in early 1951 it won thirty-four of the thirty-eight elective seats, Nkrumah was released from prison and invited to form a government. He accepted a transitional period of tutelage; but in 1952 he and the Governor between them convinced the (now Conservative) Colonial Secretary that to refuse constitutional advance 'would bring an end to settled government by consent, and forfeit the goodwill towards the United Kingdom and the desire to retain the British connection which are common to all parties in the Gold Coast'. So the chief factor delaying independence proved to be the reluctance of the tribally distinct northern Opposition to lose British protection. London was not prepared to embark on a confrontation on their behalf, and the Gold Coast became independent (as Ghana) in March 1957. Like Tunku Abdul Rahman, Nkrumah had promised to remain in the sterling area; but, under the combination of his gross economic mismanagement[8] and of the fall in the world cocoa price, Ghana ceased to be an economic asset.

7. Hargreaves, *Decolonization in Africa* p.64; subsequent pages draw extensively on this book

8. D.K. Fieldhouse, *Black Africa 1945–80: Economic Decolonization and Arrested Development* (1986) chap. 5

NIGERIA

A 1957 survey for the British Cabinet of Nigeria, easily the most populous state in Sub-Saharan Africa, doubted whether there remained time enough to complete 'our civilising and unifying mission. The pass had been sold' by the 1948 Commission on the Gold Coast, whose recommendations not only 'set the pace' there but, by 'so doing, . . . cost us some fifteen to twenty years in Nigeria. Successive Governments had since then considered that the risks of going too slowly were rather greater than' those 'of proceeding too fast'.[9] One problem had been Nigeria's size and heterogeneity.[10] Inertia, and the simple absence of national parties, led to an emphasis on the three existing Regions rather than on the federal level. Concern for the interests of the largest, least developed, and most pro-British Northern Region may also have been a factor. 1951 saw the advent of elected Regional governments, each Region being controlled by the party of its predominant tribe. The two southern Regions began to press for independence by 1956. When northern politicians demurred (fearing that a rapid British withdrawal would entail permanent southern dominance), they were insulted by the Lagos mob. So they went home making secessionist noises; southern politicians followed them to campaign in the north for the 1956 independence date. The upshot was four days of rioting in the northern city of Kano. The 1953–4 constitutional conferences, meeting in the riots' aftermath, saw a firm British refusal to name a date for independence, but an offer of full self-government in 1956 for those Regions that wanted it. In fact 1956 saw a reconciliation between northern and southern leaders, and a 1957 conference witnessed widespread support for full independence in 1960.[11] A commission was appointed 'to enquire into the fears of Minorities and the means of allaying them', but it produced a Pollyanna-ish report denying the existence of the problem. Nigeria became independent in 1960 under a coalition government of the north and east, whose displacement in 1966 by a murderous coup led to civil war. The federal forces won, but (to prevent any repetition)

9. Morgan, *Official History of Colonial Development* v p.97 – closely *paraphrasing* the original document

10. Nigeria would never have existed as a unit had the British not created it in 1906–14 by merging their disparate colonies in the area

11. James S. Coleman, *Nigeria: Background to Nationalism* (Berkeley, Calif., 1958) pp.398 ff

replaced the old 'regions' by smaller 'states' that would reflect Nigeria's ethnic diversity without threatening its unity.

THE ENSUING SCRAMBLE TO DECOLONISE

By the late 1950s, then, most of the former British and French colonies were either already independent or well on the way to becoming so. Hence the metropolitan countries had less and less reason to bother about the remainder. Decolonisation also now became contagious, partly because newly independent countries promoted the decolonisation of their neighbours. Thus Tunisia provided hospitality for the government and army of the Algerian FLN, and exerted itself to help negotiate a settlement with France. In 1958 Nkrumah staged an All-African People's Congress attended by leaders like Banda (Nyasaland/Malawi), Kaunda (Northern Rhodesia/Zambia), Lumumba (Belgian Congo/Zaïre) and Mboya (Kenya), whose nationalist activities, on their return home, soon became significant. But the sheer force of example was probably even more important. Togoland had been partitioned, in the First World War, between France and Britain, with the British share being linked to the Gold Coast. In the 1950s France felt that, to head off pressures in their share, they would have to go some way to match the Gold Coast's constitutional progress; so in 1956 Togo became an autonomous republic within the French union. This in turn had repercussions for other French African colonies, and contributed to their general acquisition, through the 1956 *loi cadre*, of appreciable internal self-government. From 1958 to 1960 it was France that forced the pace, not wishing to add, to its Algerian entanglement, trouble south of the Sahara. The acquisition of independence by a multitude of French colonies, many very small and poor, as well as by the Belgian Congo (see pp. 14–15), left the remaining British colonies in Africa looking rather conspicuous. The result was a sharp acceleration in their constitutional progress, and the dropping of previous ideas of maintaining 'our authority in each territory until a transfer of power could be shown to be generally desired by its people and they had shown that they could live at peace with one another and were capable of sustaining independent status with a reasonable standard of government'. Further contributory factors were the 1960 UN Resolution that 'Inadequacy of . . . preparedness should never serve as a pretext for delaying independence', and Macmillan's conviction that further dependency until they were 'ready' for freedom would not in fact train African leaders in the arts of government but merely embitter them.[12]

In so thinking, Macmillan had East Africa very much in mind. In 1959, the year 1970 had been suggested as a possible independence date for Tanganyika; Uganda would gain independence at much the same time, Kenya (a richer country, but one where the presence both of white settlers and of African tribal rivalries posed problems) not till 1975. In 1960 Nyerere's TANU (Tanganyika African National Union) swept the board at the Tanganyikan elections; next year there were fears that, unless Britain speedily reached agreement with him, the UN might seek to revoke the Trusteeship on which British rule was based; independence came that December. Uganda followed in 1962, after its tribal problems appeared to have been resolved by a coalition between the party of the major Buganda tribe (which had threatened to pursue independence on its own) and one of the nationalist leaders, Milton Obote – though the alliance collapsed in 1966, and for the next two decades the country was afflicted by repressive (often murderous) rule, tribal rivalries, and civil war. In Kenya the British would, arguably, have liked by electoral engineering to keep power from Kenyatta and the Kikuyus (who were seen as tainted by Mau Mau); but this was not something they were prepared to stick to in the face of opposition. Events moved fast: in 1960 a bare African majority of elected seats; in 1961 a coalition government of the Kenya African Democratic Union and the moderate European New Kenya Party. This government insisted on Kenyatta's release from prison even though his Kikuyu/Luo KANU (Kenya African National Union) was in opposition. In 1962 there was a coalition of the two African parties, secured by the introduction of a highly devolved Constitution (torn up after independence) to protect the weaker tribes; finally in 1963 KANU gained so great an electoral victory that Kenyatta (who three years earlier had been termed 'leader to darkness and death') became Prime Minister. The possibility was much canvassed that Tanganyika, Uganda and Kenya would then pursue the advantages of scale by converting their existing Common Services Organisation into an East African federation. Indeed Kenyatta secured early independence for Kenya in December 1963 by representing it as the necessary prelude to such

12. Whereas in 1954–9 Britain had had 'confidential agreements with the representatives of many Colonies not to accede to their public demands for' faster decolonisation, 'for which the representatives realised they were not sufficiently prepared': Morgan, *Official History of Colonial Development* pp.22, 102; Macmillan, *Memoirs* v pp.118–19

a federation. In the event nothing came of federation, and the three countries went their different (and in the 1970s distinctly hostile)[13] ways.

Further south, Macmillan abandoned the attempt to preserve the Central African Federation (see p.66); in 1964 its two northern components became independent as Zambia and Malawi. The settlers in Kenya and the Central African Federation had had many sympathisers within the British Conservative Party, so handling them had posed tricky political problems. There was no comparable interest in other countries, and London was by now ready to accommodate the aspirations for independence of any of its African colonies – except white-ruled Rhodesia. (Indeed in the 1970s it showed itself positively cool towards the Seychelles' Prime Minister's desire *not* to seek independence.)[14] This led to independence for a number of states that would not previously have been regarded as viable (like Lesotho, which is entirely surrounded by South African territory). But the British West Indies set more far-reaching precedents in this direction. It had been intended to bring them to independence as a federation. But in 1961, when the federation was on the eve of independence, Jamaica pulled out (fearing the other islands would prove a drag on its development). In 1962 Jamaica and Trinidad became independent on their own. The smaller islands formed associations with the UK whereby they secured full internal self-government but left Britain to conduct their foreign affairs. Either country could terminate the arrangement, and over the years most (though not all) islands have chosen to do so. This has given rise to a number of mini-states in the Caribbean. The example has been quite widely followed in the Pacific and Indian oceans, not only by ex-British/New Zealand colonies,[15] but also by some French ones, though France, unlike Britain, also operates a

13. The Common Services Organisation was dissolved in 1977, and Tanzania closed its border with Kenya until 1983 (with rail and steamer links not restored till 1985). Nyerere also resented Obote's 1971 ousting by Idi Amin, and seems in 1972 to have backed an unsuccessful coup to restore him. Subsequent relations were frigid. Then in 1978 Amin gave Nyerere another opportunity by repossessing the Kagera Salient by force. In response Nyerere managed in 1979 to liberate Uganda – but then used his dominant position in 1980 to reimpose Obote (whose rule, until 1985, proved quite as murderous as Amin's)

14. This coolness, and OAU financial support for his opponents because they did seek independence, led Prime Minister Mancham to change his mind in 1974. He became President of an independent Seychelles in 1976, which opened the way to his overthrow next year by a coup: *Keesing's*, 26500 ff, 28485

15. An important precedent was set here by Nauru (pop. 6,800), which opted for full independence in 1968 so as to secure for the islanders the benefits of their principal resource (a massive phosphate mine) before these were all dissipated

constitutional system whereby overseas territories can be treated as departments of the metropolitan territory.[16]

SYSTEMIC IMPLICATIONS OF DECOLONISATION

It is not, of course, my contention that formal empires had been completely liquidated by the mid-1960s, but by then all the Belgian and the greater part of the British, French and Dutch empires had become independent.[17] So colonies were now very much the exception in what had become 'a world of states' – of very different sizes, wealth and power, but all formally sovereign. The earlier decolonisation of the 1940s had affected more people, and, generally speaking, established more substantial countries, but the sheer number of new, if often small, states that became independent around 1960 was in itself important. For in most international forums states are theoretically equal; the UN General

16. This system offers small and well-affected communities a number of advantages, both financial and in terms of security; but Portugal gave it a bad name by claiming to possess no 'colonies', only 'overseas provinces'. The United States has successfully operated two variants. Hawaii was in 1959 incorporated into the Union as a state (despite some misgivings about the size of its Asian population). In 1952 Puerto Rico became a self-governing Commonwealth, with powers broadly similar to those of a state and enjoying both US citizenship and a favourable fiscal regime, but not participation in US federal politics; it may ultimately decide to seek statehood. The British were less imaginative. In 1955 Malta suggested integration into the UK, but the island was divided on the issue, the position of the Roman Catholic Church raised legal problems, and the idea fell through. Instead Malta became independent in 1964; integration has not been considered as an option for other small colonies. From 1954 the Dutch operated what was in effect a system of autonomous association with Surinam and the Netherlands Antilles – but with common citizenship. When Surinam moved towards full independence, one-third of its population is supposed to have exercised its right to settle in the Netherlands while there was still time: *Keesing's*, 27515. The Dutch found Surinam's 1975 independence rather a relief, both because it ended this right to immigrate and by reason of their concern over Surinam's internal politics

17. For Portuguese decolonisation, see pp.20–2. Spain began to decolonise in the late 1960s, but retained its Spanish Sahara where it opened an enormous phosphate mine in 1972. In the 1970s it intended conferring independence on the territory (settled population about 30,000 plus, sometimes, up to 45,000 nomads) after a referendum. But in late 1975 it was intimidated into turning the territory over to Morocco and Mauretania (which had rather tenuous historical claims). Mauretania subsequently dropped out, but Morocco has continued to occupy and defend the area against the Polisario liberation movement (backed by Algeria): *Keesing's*, 24125, 26714, 27413, 27575. A settlement was reached in 1988, though the UN-supervised referendum it envisaged has (1993) not yet been held

Assembly, in particular, operates on the basis of one-state one-vote. UN membership went from 76 in late 1955 to 122 in late 1966; expansion in membership did much to change its politics. Other bodies, admittedly, were far less affected, and the attempt in the 1970s to reorient world politics to reflect primarily the agenda and concerns of the new majority (for a 'New International Economic Order') did not succeed. But any comparison of, say, the inter-war and the post-1945 period will show that the provenance of major international problems and the identity of the actors has become far more diffuse. Sometimes this reflects the greater opportunities for international disagreement now that empires have departed: Kashmir could become such an issue only once there was an India and a Pakistan to compete for it, while France's predominance in Indo-China froze a pre-existing struggle between Vietnamese and Cambodians (Khmers) that revived after its departure. Equally decolonisation has encouraged the establishment of contact between neighbouring states formerly kept apart because they were in different imperial systems – ASEAN (Association of South-East Asian Nations) forms one notable example, the Arab League another.

THE SUPERPOWERS' LIMITED ROLE

If decolonisation has represented one of the most significant transformations of the postwar international scene, the superpowers' contribution to it was comparatively limited. In the case of the USSR this is unsurprising: it had few openings to exert direct influence within the colonies. The most obvious was the arming of liberation movements. This has occasionally been important – particularly, perhaps, in the case of the Jewish Agency/Israel.[18] But only a minority of colonies have gained independence by armed struggle; and there have generally been other backers and suppliers besides the USSR. More widespread has been the impact of the Cold War. 'Communism' was perceived as a major threat during the two postwar decades within which decolonisation was concentrated; the enlistment against it of local nationalism was regarded as an important counter not only by the United States but also by Britain. We have seen that this was done positively in the face of the

18. Arnold Krammer, *The Forgotten Friendship: Israel and the Soviet Bloc 1947–53* (Urbana, Ill., 1974)

(genuinely communist) Malay 'emergency', pre-emptively in the Gold Coast. Concern was also voiced during the transfer of power in India that nothing be done either to disrupt the country or to drive it into the Soviet Union's arms. Although such anti-communism is important, it is difficult to regard it as the dominant motive for decolonisation on the side of the metropolitan powers, still less on that of the nationalists.

The United States was far better placed to act directly, since most colonial powers looked to it for economic/military assistance, and since (for a decade after the war) it commanded the largest bloc of votes in the UN. Occasionally it did so act (though less often than might have been anticipated from its anti-colonial rhetoric). Thus, though less forward than Australia, the USA played the major role in prompting UN interposition between the Dutch authorities and the Indonesian Republic; its mediation contributed much to both the Renville and the Roem–van Royen agreements. But its effort to head off the second Dutch 'police action' by threatening to halt Marshall Aid was simply rebuffed, as were threats in connection with NATO. Subsequently US pressure may have been more efficacious in inducing the Netherlands to abandon West Irian; but it did not stop the British establishing Malaysia. Over Indo-China the USA initially questioned, but did not resist, French coercion of the Vietminh. Later, on anti-communist grounds, it funded the French war effort, though urging that it be combined with real independence for the Associated Indo-Chinese States.

In the Middle East the United States played a decisive role in the emergence of Israel (see pp.251–5). The Middle East was also the scene of the United States' most dramatic assertion of power over its allies, its halting by economic pressure of the 1956 Anglo-French 'Suez' attack on Egypt. But this is too readily taken as a paradigm case. In fact British policy successfully diverged from the USA's both over the Buraimi Oasis dispute between their respective clients (Saudi Arabia and the Trucial Gulf States) and over the repression of insurrection in Oman (see pp.301–2). More seriously US–British support for Tunisia in 1957–8, over incidents with French Algeria, backfired to precipitate the fall of the Fourth Republic and the advent of a de Gaulle government apparently dedicated to *Algérie Française*. In fact de Gaulle decolonised both Algeria and most of the French Empire with remarkable speed, but for his own reasons and *not* in deference to the Anglo-Saxons. Finally, if Kissinger is to be believed, the United States was successfully negotiating with Pakistan the independence of Bangladesh when India moved in and effected it by force. But this exhausts the list of overt US interventions.[19] Its brevity suggests that decolonisation was primarily a question between the colonies and their metropolitan countries. US attitudes and ideas were no doubt influential in moulding the general climate of opinion; colonial powers were often concerned to stand well in American eyes. But the real opening for US (or Soviet) penetration of an area did not come until after independence.

19. The USA involved itself from the mid-1970s in negotiations for a Rhodesian and a Namibian settlement, but these problems, while still technically 'colonial', had already become internationalised

CHAPTER FOUR

Southern Africa

The rule of much of southern Africa by a white settler minority had colonial origins and overtones, even in the case of the Union (later Republic) of South Africa, whose independence was always internationally recognised. By the 1960s it had come to be widely perceived as one of the world's major problems, and, in so far as it relates to South Africa, it had, in 1993, not yet ended. It may, therefore, be worth a rather more detailed account than was possible above.

THE CENTRAL AFRICAN FEDERATION 1953–63

In the 1950s the question was rather one of the expansion of settler rule northward from Southern Rhodesia (which already enjoyed full internal self-government) to Northern Rhodesia and Nyasaland (where London had devolved considerably fewer powers). The European population in Southern Rhodesia, and its much smaller counterpart in copper-rich Northern Rhodesia,[1] applied intense pressure for a federation. This was seen in London as economically desirable, and perhaps necessary to prevent Southern Rhodesia from gravitating into South Africa. It also provided an opportunity to unload the slightly more populous, but in resource terms less

1. Each country had about 1.9 million Africans in 1950. Southern Rhodesia had some 129,000 Europeans (to whom the 1930 Land Apportionment Act reserved half the land and ownership in urban areas), Northern Rhodesia 36,000 (well represented in mining and urban areas, but not farming on the scale of the south). For Rhodesian developments generally, see e.g. Hargreaves, *Decolonization in Africa* pp.134–8, 165–7, 189, 198–203, 218–26, and Peter Calvocoressi, *World Politics since 1945* (1977 edn) pp.366–77

well-endowed, Nyasaland – where European settlement was negligible. Admittedly African opinion in Northern Rhodesia and Nyasaland did not wish to exchange mildly protective rule from London for control by Southern Rhodesian settlers, but this did not seem too serious an obstacle: federation would be justified by its economic benefits, and by a policy of 'multiracialism' and 'partnership' (though the Southern Rhodesian Prime Minister, Godfrey Huggins, once likened this all too clearly to the partnership between a horse and its rider). The Central African Federation was accordingly brought into existence in 1953, subject to a number of safeguards, some illusory but others (notably the retention of British protectorates over Northern Rhodesia and Nyasaland) in the last resort real. A further constitutional review was set for 1960, and was widely expected to bring the federation to independence.

Federation's appeal to the Africans was further damaged by London's 1957 acceptance of some changes opposed by the African Affairs Board, and by the downfall of the Southern Rhodesian Premier in 1958 as a result of enacting too great an increase in African wages. African political organisations spread, especially in Nyasaland to which the charismatic Dr Hastings Banda returned after a long absence to lead a drive for secession. Fears of an impending rising and massacre (Mau Mau style) led in early 1959 to repression in Nyasaland and emergencies in all three countries, then to British Commissions of Inquiry. The Monckton Commission recommended that Northern Rhodesia and Nyasaland should have the right to secede from the federation, though it concentrated on suggesting changes that would stop them wanting to do so. But once London had, in 1960, made the Nyasaland government elective with Banda as Prime Minister, Northern Rhodesian Africans naturally sought parity. There followed years of intricate negotiations and complicated electoral changes, designed to save the federation. In 1962 Macmillan decided that this would be impossible. Eventually it was allowed to break up at the end of 1963, and Northern Rhodesia and Nyasaland became independent (as Zambia and Malawi) in 1964.

SOUTHERN RHODESIA (ZIMBABWE)

In retrospect the real question was what would happen in Southern Rhodesia. This had always provided the power behind the federation, and it naturally inherited the latter's substantial armed forces. Since 1958 its European politics had been moving to the right. The 1962 elections were won by the Rhodesia Front, which demanded independence on the break-up of the federation. It enjoyed a good deal of sympathy within the British Conservative Party, but this was counterbalanced by Commonwealth pressure for 'No independence before majority African rule'. In April 1963 Macmillan told the Queen that 'it would not need very much' in the way of Southern Rhodesian concessions to African opinion to enable him 'to carry an Independence Bill through the House of Commons with the assent of the great majority of the Conservative Party. But I cannot say, frankly, that it will be easy to carry independence unless some concession is made by [the Rhodesian Premier] Mr Field'.[2] Field made no such a concession. He also failed to link Rhodesian independence with either the break-up of the Central African Federation or independence for Zambia and Malawi. So his party replaced him in 1964 with Ian Smith. When further negotiations in 1965 still did not succeed, Smith reshuffled the army command and launched a Unilateral Declaration of Independence (UDI).

This divided European Rhodesians, and it is just possible that the Declaration would not have been made had Britain been prepared to threaten military action and perhaps make symbolic air strikes. Such a threat would, however, have been a bluff. The British government had some doubts as to its forces' readiness to fight. In any case it would be extremely difficult to assemble a large enough army and supply it from land-locked and underdeveloped Zambia, while the attempt to do so might simply bring South Africa in on the other side. Nor did the British Prime Minister, Wilson, believe it to be necessary: economic pressure would do the job instead, in (as he told a Nigerian-chaired Commonwealth Conference in January 1966) 'weeks not months'. Actually it was the Nigerian government that was dead within a week, whereas the Smith regime consolidated itself. Wilson had much trouble at the next Commonwealth Conference in September, but secured its acceptance of a final attempt to negotiate a settlement with Smith – failing which mandatory sanctions would be sought from the UN. In December 1966 Wilson met Smith on HMS *Tiger* and (with difficulty) secured his personal acceptance of a plan providing for the independence of a white-ruled Rhodesia, but subject to guarantees that there

2. Macmillan, *Memoirs* vi p.329

would be no interference with progress to (eventual) majority rule. The deal was rejected by Smith's Cabinet, which feared the degree of British power during the interim period of return to legality.[3] Britain accordingly approached the UN, which called for mandatory sanctions.

Sanctions had been imposed by many countries on a voluntary basis ever since UDI; from the spring of 1966 Britain had maintained, with UN support, a naval patrol to stop oil being landed in Beira for transit to Rhodesia. Sanctions were not a total failure; there were initially severe oil shortages. Later most of the visible ill effects were overcome, and the need for import substitution even provided a certain economic stimulus. But the cost of evading sanctions was appreciable; although the initial cessation of Rhodesian debt and dividend payments was helpful, the absence of external investment eventually inhibited the modernisation of manufacturing plant. By the later 1970s Rhodesia came to wish the ending of sanctions; but since only the UN could legally lift them, it was highly desirable that the final settlement be such as to earn UN commendation. This did not, in fact, prevent either Wilson or Heath from contemplating solutions that would have legitimised a considerable period of independent white minority rule; but it must at least have stiffened their insistence on this being acceptable to African opinion in Rhodesia and on guarantees that the African electorate would ultimately become predominant.

Yet if sanctions had some effect, they were very far from decisive, and in many respects ludicrous. South Africa had every interest in preventing the establishment of a successful precedent and stood firmly behind Rhodesia. Switzerland openly increased its Rhodesian trade. Many other countries either did so clandestinely or were deliberately inefficient in enforcing sanctions. In 1972 the USA restarted buying chrome for strategic reasons. Zambia gave up rail connections with Rhodesia in 1973, but was forced by the inadequacy of alternative routes and the general collapse of its economy to resume them in 1978; by next spring it was seeking secret credits to buy Rhodesian maize. Meanwhile Britain, sanctions' other principal sponsor, had concluded by 1968 that they would not bring Smith down 'unless we are prepared to apply them to South Africa'; so it acquiesced in continued oil supplies for Rhodesia,

3. Rhodesian politicians held that Britain had doublecrossed the leaders of the Central African Federation, and were correspondingly, though perhaps excessively, suspicious

using French and South African intermediaries.[4] For most of its duration the Beira patrol was therefore an expensive sham.

Wilson held further talks with Smith in late 1968, but to no effect. In 1971 the subsequent Conservative government reached a tentative settlement. This was, however, (like the *Tiger* proposals before it) conditional on a Commission of Inquiry's ascertaining that it was acceptable to the Rhodesian people as a whole; in May 1972 it was found unacceptable, and the deal collapsed. Guerrilla resistance to the regime began on an appreciable scale in 1973, but remained perfectly manageable. With the 1974 Portuguese revolution, however, it became possible to foresee a decolonised and hostile Mozambique, which would enormously increase the area of Rhodesia open to guerrilla penetration. That autumn the South African Prime Minister, Vorster, declared that the price of 'escalating conflict' 'would be high, too high for southern Africa', and started to work with President Kaunda of Zambia for a settlement to be agreed between Smith and the nationalists.[5] Although Smith could be brought to the water he could not be made to drink; he had repeated contacts with African nationalists, both direct and through South African–Zambian mediation, but to no purpose. Eventually Kaunda told the veteran nationalist Joshua Nkomo, 'Get majority rule and you are right. Fail and you become irrelevant'. In March 1976 Nkomo failed.[6]

That summer Kissinger took a hand. He supposedly offered various inducements for South African cooperation, and was thus enabled to present Smith in September 1976 with a package deal providing for a two-year transition to majority rule. If Rhodesia

4. James Barber, 'Economic Sanctions as a Policy Instrument', *International Affairs* lv (1979) esp. pp.373, 377–80; *Keesing's*, 29440, 30074; Foreign and Commonwealth Office, *Report on the supply of petroleum . . . to Rhodesia* (by T.H. Bingham and S.M. Gray) (1978) esp. pp.105–11, 118 and chap. 14. Apparently the top South African management of British oil multinationals did seek to restrict the supply of oil to Rhodesia, though their subordinates and customers did not. By late 1966 it was clear that to continue to do so would be commercially disastrous, and (with some encouragement from the British ambassador) they began to concentrate only on not breaking British law. In 1967 the British government also abandoned thoughts of preventing oil from getting through, and sought only to be able to say that no *British* oil was doing so. In 1968–9 it blessed an arrangement whereby (through an exchange agreement) Shell/BP South Africa indirectly supplied South African companies known to be forwarding oil to Rhodesia; in 1971 direct supply to these companies was resumed

5. *Keesing's*, 26909. In return Kaunda indicated that African countries would not fight South Africa, but leave its people 'the primary task of shaping their own destiny'

6. *Keesing's*, 27689–90

accepted, substantial economic assistance would be forthcoming; if not South Africa would cut off all aid, including oil. Smith accepted in principle.[7] But the resulting conference in Geneva was a failure, partly because of rivalry between different nationalists, partly because of nationalist attempts to alter Kissinger's proposed transitional arrangements. Vorster then declined in January 1977 to press Smith further (and the Carter administration was less fitted than its predecessor to persuade him). Anglo-American diplomatic initiatives continued, but the focus shifted on the one hand to Smith's attempt to secure an internal settlement with moderate nationalists, on the other to guerrilla attempts, principally by Mugabe's Mozambique-based fighters, to overthrow him.

In a sense both succeeded. A deal was eventually struck with Bishop Muzorewa and a biracial interim government formed in March 1978. In April 1979 elections were held, with some reserved European seats but otherwise on an adult suffrage basis. There was a 64 per cent turnout, which observers saw (according to their political preferences) as a substantial endorsement of the new regime or as the result of army pressure. Meanwhile fighting escalated: official figures suggest that almost twice as many people (13,000) were killed within Rhodesia in 1978–9 as in 1972–7.[8] The Rhodesian army was still dominant both within the country and in its ability to mount cross-border raids; many saw its commander, General Walls, as Rhodesia's real ruler. But the effort was beginning to tell: defence spending had risen to 37 per cent of the 1979–80 budget, guerrilla disruption of cattle dipping led to meat shortages, one-third of white-owned farms were reportedly abandoned, and Europeans were leaving. The 'internal settlement' with Muzorewa had brought neither peace nor international recognition.

The new British Conservative government was especially anxious to secure a settlement since it would otherwise face major domestic problems over the continuance of sanctions. However it was prevented by Foreign Office and Commonwealth pressure from simply recognising the Muzorewa regime on the basis of the April 1979 elections. Eventually a Commonwealth Conference in Lusaka determined on a new conference in London; Muzorewa attended in hopes of regularising his position, and the 'front-line' African states delivered his rivals with the threat that they would otherwise be left

7. *Keesing's*, esp. 28042

8. *Keesing's*, 29442, 30072; Hargreaves, *Decolonization in Africa* p.225 – but claims that casualties were really much higher were supported by the 1984 discovery of mass graves: *Keesing's*, 33137

out. Between September and December 1979 difficult negotiations produced a new Constitution, control by an interim British Governor pending elections, and a cease-fire followed by the return of guerrillas from neighbouring states. The election campaign was very tense, and could well have been followed by hostilities between Mugabe and a coalition of all his opponents. In the event Mugabe won convincingly. General Walls pressed Mrs Thatcher to annul the elections on grounds of intimidation,[9] but she refused. In March 1980 the results were announced amid general appeals for calm, Mugabe was invited to form a government, and everybody hastened to make terms with him.

Voting had, however, been tribal, with Smith still commanding the Europeans, Nkomo the Matabele, and Mugabe the Shona majority. Mugabe's government (of what became, on independence, Zimbabwe) initially drew on all three. Although, for economic reasons, he cultivated the Europeans (more especially farmers) despite his own advanced socialist principles, he fell out with the Matabele. In 1982 Nkomo was dismissed, amid allegations that he had been preparing (and seeking South African aid for) a coup. Disturbances followed in Matabeleland; in and after 1983 they were repressed with considerable violence, but sporadic resistance (and the need to protect white farmers) continued. In December 1987, however, Nkomo was brought to accept (at long last) the merger of his party with Mugabe's; an amnesty and surrender of guerrillas/bandits has followed.[10]

SOUTH AFRICA AND APARTHEID

There are obvious similarities between Rhodesia and South Africa, but in the latter the Europeans are far more deeply entrenched, both historically and numerically. In 1910 the previously self-governing colonies merged to form the Union of South Africa, as a British Dominion under elective white rule. Between the wars South Africa enjoyed a relatively high profile, contributing to the formation of the League of Nations and securing a League Mandate over the German colony of South-West Africa that it had conquered in 1915. Later it became a valued member of the United Nations; indeed its Prime Minister drafted the preamble to the Charter

9. *Keesing's*, 30904

10. *Keesing's*, esp. 30165 ff, 30365 ff, 31550 ff, 32240 ff, 34917 ff, 35626 ff; *The Independent*, 1 June 1988 p.11

(though, unlike other mandatory powers, he did not transfer supervision of his Mandate to the UN). From the beginning, however, India used the UN to express concern over South African treatment of its Indian population. In 1948 the (Afrikaner) Nationalist Party won the South African elections, and in the 1950s it set about perfecting legal arrangements for the separation of the races, with the whites clearly on top – apartheid. Many countries discriminate de facto, a few de iure; in several, repression has been considerably more bloody.[11] But nowhere else has a state been based on so open, sophisticated and pervasive a system of discrimination by colour. In the 1950s South Africa was clearly set on moving against the grain of international society. Both its domestic and its South-West Africa policy attracted UN attention, and from 1955 to 1958 it boycotted the General Assembly in protest.

The early 1960s showed the extent to which South Africa had become a pariah. March 1960 saw police shooting into anti-pass law[12] demonstrations at Sharpeville and Langa, killing eighty-three people; this was followed by riots, arrests and a state of emergency that lasted till May. It was not the best of backgrounds against which to raise the question of South Africa's continued membership of the Commonwealth; but the issue was inescapably posed by the 1960 decision to become a Republic.[13] A country making this change has to apply to retain Commonwealth membership; by 1961 this had become a formality. But, at a Commonwealth conference in March 1961, Ghana, Malaya and Canada were particularly critical, while the then much admired leader Nyerere had made it

11. A partial parallel is provided by Rwanda and Burundi (which together have one-third as many people as South Africa, if vastly less importance). In both, the pygmy Hutu majority was traditionally dominated by a small Tutsi ruling class. The Hutus came to power in Rwanda in 1960, which produced some 200,000 Tutsi refugees over the next two years. Tutsi guerrilla incursions led in 1964 to mass reprisal killings, perhaps of 8,000–15,000 Tutsi (though the totals were heavily disputed). Burundi saw an attempted Hutu coup and rising in 1965; another rising in 1972 may have killed 5,000 (the government said 50,000) Tutsi and prompted massive retaliation (put by missionaries at 100,000 though this could be an overestimate); there were further massacres in 1988; 1993 brought the unexpected election of a Hutu president, whose murder four months later in a Tutsi coup attempt set off tribal civil war, with some 200,000 casualties by the end of the year: *Keesing's*, 20085–6, 21113, 21324, 25324; *The Economist*, 27 Aug. 1988 p.47. The international community cannot be said to have been much concerned

12. Till their abolition in 1986, passes (which adult Africans had to carry at all times) were the chief instrument for controlling influx into white/urban areas; in 1960 arrests for pass law offences were running at about 500,000 per year

13. The decision, taken by (white) referendum, can be seen as the final settlement of the struggle between Afrikaner and Briton that had been the main theme in South African politics for ninety years

clear that, if South Africa was allowed to stay, Tanganyika would not join the Commonwealth on becoming independent. In the circumstances South Africa withdrew. There followed a campaign against South Africa in the UN and its agencies. By 1965 it had been forced out of the International Labour and World Health organisations, though not the International Atomic Energy Agency (IAEA), where its uranium production gave it some standing. After 1974 it was no longer allowed to speak in the UN General Assembly. In 1962 the General Assembly had urged a complete trade boycott; although this had no chance of acceptance by the Security Council (as would be necessary to make it mandatory), the latter did in 1963 call for an embargo (made mandatory in 1977) on arms sales to South Africa. The question of South-West Africa was also pursued, from 1960 to 1966 unsuccessfully through the International Court at the Hague, thereafter by UN resolutions to the effect that the South African Mandate was terminated and that the UN had taken over its administration; in 1971 the International Court upheld these.

Results of a kind seemed to flow from this pressure, and from the numerous public and private boycotts associated with it. Vorster discovered in the 1970s that the language of self-determination could mesh well with that of apartheid. Separate development had, in the 1960s, involved the erection of partially self-governing tribal units in the native reserves, one of which (the Transkei) started pressing for independence. In 1972 Vorster declared that it was 'our policy to lead our peoples to self-determination'; in 1976–81 four Bantustans became independent, while remaining within the South African currency and customs union.[14] This meant that people deriving from them, even if ordinarily resident in South Africa proper, became foreigners, present only on sufferance. It opened up a prospect of a congerie of (frequently discontinuous) mini-states, dependent on a Republic of South Africa whose only citizens were white and which retained most of the area's resources. Since the new states thus reinforced the apartheid design, the international community declined to recognise them (though some differed little in practice from land-locked Lesotho, whose 1966 decolonisation was acceptable since it came from the British).

14. Transkei (1976), Bophuthatswana (1977), Venda (1979), Ciskei (1981). (Other homelands, notably Kwa Ndebele and Chief Buthelezi's Kwazulu, went some way towards self-government but deliberately stopped short of 'independence'.) Coups brought to power in the Transkei (1987) and in Ciskei and Venda (1990) governments sympathetic to the ANC and desirous of reintegration into South Africa, but Ciskei (at least) had again broken with the ANC by 1992. ANC policy is that all should be reintegrated after the 1994 elections

SOUTH-WEST AFRICA (NAMIBIA) AND ANGOLA

In the 1950s South Africa was clearly contemplating the annexation of South-West Africa. UN pressure blocked this and in 1975 Vorster switched to the idea of an independence to be negotiated internally, but without the participation of SWAPO (the South-West Africa People's Organisation, the party of the numerically predominant Ovambo tribe, to which the UN was committed). He was headed off in 1977 by a 'contact group' of the USA and four other Western Powers; in 1978–9 this group almost succeeded in mediating a settlement between Vorster and the Presidents of 'front-line' African states, based on disengagement and free elections. Unfortunately South Africa was pressed a little too hard over interim arrangements and backed away. In the 1980s South Africa seemed to find its position in Namibia increasingly valuable as the basis on which to rest a forward defence by supporting UNITA's operations in southern Angola. The tendency was to suggest that the Cuban presence in Angola formed part of a much wider overall communist strategy directed at securing control of southern Africa's strategic minerals: if the Russians and Cubans were allowed to succeed in Angola, President P.W. Botha declared in 1985, their next target would be Namibia, followed by Botswana and then South Africa itself.[15] So, despite the 1984 Lusaka agreement (promising South African withdrawal in return for Angola's undertaking to stop SWAPO infiltration into Namibia – see p.77), periodic raids and clashes continued. The climax came in late 1987, when some 9,000 South African troops repulsed an MPLA attack on UNITA positions in the south, and then advanced to besiege Cuito Cuanavale from November 1987 to March 1988. They were in their turn threatened by the deployment of some 20,000 Cubans (well equipped by the USSR and enjoying air superiority). The prospect of incurring serious casualties seems to have softened the South African outlook, while Gorbachev's USSR (no doubt acutely conscious of the costs involved) was now ready to lean on its Cuban and Angolan clients. Previously token negotiations came to life, and in May secret talks between Angola, Cuba, South Africa and the USA cleared the way for the thrashing out of a settlement between August and December 1988.[16]

15. Barber and Barratt, *South Africa's Foreign Policy* pp.221–4, 314

16. Over $2 billion of Soviet arms had supposedly been sent to Angola in recent years: *Keesing's*, 36076–80, 36132, 36380; *The Independent*, 16 Nov. 1988 p.19; Barber and Barratt, *South Africa's Foreign Policy* pp.341–4

This provided for immediate South African and more gradual Cuban departure from Angola,[17] and for the holding of UN-sponsored elections in Namibia in 1989. Implementation was not straightforward: the agreement had been made over SWAPO's head, and in April 1989 SWAPO broke it by infiltrating guerrillas; a burst of fighting ensued, and the guerrillas were badly mauled by South African forces anxious to prevent their victorious return from dominating the elections (as Mugabe's men had allegedly done in Rhodesia in 1980). It is also said that major covert financial and propaganda efforts were made to stop SWAPO getting a two-thirds majority and imposing a 'winner-take-all' Marxist constitution. These efforts were helped by claims that SWAPO forces in Angola had tortured and killed people they suspected of spying. Whatever the reason, SWAPO's vote outside the Ovambo area was disappointing and the party achieved only a bare majority overall. It was therefore ready to compromise to secure the adoption of a constitution, and the count-down to independence in March 1990 went surprisingly smoothly.[18]

SOUTH AFRICA UNDER P.W. BOTHA 1978–89

Namibia, of course, was one thing, the Republic of South Africa quite another. By its own standards, it had for many years been moving towards reform: 1969 had already seen a breakaway from the ruling National Party in protest. The pace increased in 1978 with the replacement of Vorster, as Prime Minister and party leader, by P.W. Botha (amid a scandal over secret attempts to buy favourable publicity and influence abroad). In 1979–82 Botha lifted the ban on non-white trade unions; in 1982 his talk of cautious constitutional reforms prompted another, and more significant, breakaway from the National Party. The reforms, however, only flanked the white Parliament with subordinate Indian and Coloured chambers. The black majority remained excluded, and elections in

17. It did not end the Angolan civil war; indeed the USA merely took over from South Africa full financial and logistic support of UNITA. But the USA and USSR pressed UNITA and the MPLA to negotiate further; a settlement was reached in 1991 on the basis of a cease-fire, followed by UN-monitored elections in 1992. Unfortunately UNITA declared its defeat in these elections fraudulent and resumed hostilities: *Keesing's*, 1992 R3, 39082, 39128

18. *Keesing's*, 36576, 37031–2, 37116, 37296–7; *The Independent*, 11 June 1991 p.1

1984 served to swell rather than reduce violence and discontent. South Africa appears to have been subject to a cycle of shootings, riots, states of emergency, external pressures and blows to commercial confidence, followed by periods of recovery. Previous cycles had been inaugurated by the Sharpeville shootings of 1960 and the Soweto school riots of 1976. Another and more intense wave of township disturbances began in late 1984; by June 1985 they had accounted for 400 deaths, and in July Botha (now President under the new Constitution) proclaimed a state of emergency under which nearly 10,000 people were held for varying periods (plus a further 19,000 detained in the 'independent' homelands). The 'emergency' did not halt all domestic reform: 1985 saw the end of the legal bar on mixed marriages and 1986 the abolition of the hated pass laws (albeit not for citizens of the homelands). At a theoretical level this involved the abandonment of what Botha called 'the outdated concept of apartheid'. At a practical level, however, zoned residential separation by race continued, while political power remained firmly in white hands. In August 1985 Botha had made it clear that things would stay that way. South Africa did not consist 'of a white minority and a black majority', it was rather 'a country of minorities'; he rejected 'the principle of one-man one-vote in a unitary system', which would lead to 'domination of one over the others . . . and to chaos'.[19]

Township violence was domestic in origin; but the rioters often proclaimed their support for the African National Congress (ANC). This had originally been a legal, and non-violent, movement; but it had been harassed in the 1950s, with many of its leaders tried for treason or communism. In 1961, despairing of making progress through peaceful protest, it turned to what it hoped would be a major guerrilla onslaught to bring down the government. This proved little more than a damp squib. By 1965 its organisation within South Africa had been effectively broken up, but it had in 1960 set up an external wing abroad that soon assumed considerable dimensions. In 1969 the UN General Assembly recognised the 'legitimacy' of the struggle for majority rule in South Africa, and declared the ANC (and its smaller rival the Pan African Congress) the 'authentic representatives' of that majority.

The ANC thus enjoyed more success in campaigning abroad against the South African government than in trying to overthrow it

19. Barber and Barratt, *South Africa's Foreign Policy* pp.285, 310–11, 322, 383; *Keesing's*, 34723–4

through 'armed struggle' at home. It continued to train guerrillas in friendly African countries, and periodically sought to infiltrate them back. They achieved little beyond occasional incidents, such as the explosion of a bomb that killed nineteen people in a Pretoria street in 1983. P.W. Botha (who had a defence background) sought to use South Africa's military and special operations prowess to keep the ANC at a safe distance, partly by Israeli-style raids on its facilities abroad, but chiefly by pressuring the neighbouring African states into themselves barring guerrilla activity from their territory.

Botha enjoyed considerable success. Mugabe made it clear from the outset that Zimbabwe could not afford to host ANC guerrillas for fear of reprisals; nor could it participate in economic sanctions, since 90 per cent of its trade went through the Republic. South Africa provided various reminders of this vulnerability, ranging from the withdrawal of railway engines and a threat not to renew trade preferences in 1981 to the blowing up next year of much of the Zimbabwe air force.[20] But it is doubtful whether they were needed. Under FRELIMO, Mozambique had allowed guerrillas to operate against both Rhodesia and South Africa. Rhodesia had responded by supporting FRELIMO's rival, RENAMO. After the change of regime in Rhodesia, South Africa took over this support. The result was a bloody civil war (still – 1993 – not completely terminated) within Mozambique. In 1984 this led FRELIMO to conclude with South Africa the Nkomati 'co-existence' Accord whereby Mozambique was to expel the ANC and gravitate into the Republic's economic orbit while South Africa would end support for RENAMO. Mozambique would seem to have largely honoured Nkomati; but secret South African support for RENAMO continued, though it is not clear how far this represented official policy, how far the unauthorised actions of imperfectly controlled security and business forces. There was also the similar 1984 Lusaka agreement with Angola, whereby South Africa would withdraw and end its aid to UNITA in exchange for an Angolan undertaking to prevent SWAPO infiltration into Namibia. But it unravelled in 1985, when South African soldiers were captured while attempting to sabotage vital oil facilities in northern Angola. (Hostilities accordingly continued until 1988, with South African troops supporting UNITA as a cheap way of preventing SWAPO's establishment on the Angolan–Namibian border.) Another 1985 cross-border raid on

20. Barber and Barratt, *South Africa's Foreign Policy* p.268; *Keesing's*, 30906, 31054, 31553, 32244

ANC premises in Botswana, a country generally very careful not to provoke South Africa, led to the killing not only of ANC members but also of local citizens, and occasioned massive international criticism.[21]

THE IMPACT OF SANCTIONS ON SOUTH AFRICA

By now international sentiment was again running against South Africa. In the aftermath of Sharpeville the early 1960s had seen much pressure for sanctions, issuing in a 1962 UN General Assembly call for a complete diplomatic and trade break with the Republic and the more significant 1963 Security Council recommendation of an arms embargo. In 1977 this embargo was made mandatory in the aftermath of the Soweto rising and the death 'in custody' of the black activist Steve Biko. Similarly, following prolonged campaigns and the disruption of South African sporting tours abroad, South Africa was banned from the 1964 and subsequent Olympic Games and suspended from the International Football Federation in 1976, while in 1977 the Commonwealth agreed that its members should discourage all sporting contacts. Other individual countries introduced their own sanctions. South Africa was regularly assailed at the UN, and from 1974 prevented from speaking in the General Assembly, but not expelled from the organisation, since the West feared that this would create a precedent for the expulsion of Israel.[22]

The cold-shouldering of South Africa eased in the early 1980s. Arguably US official policy had begun to shift towards the end of the Carter administration, but the new approach became more visible under Reagan's Assistant Secretary of State for African Affairs, Chester Crocker. He favoured 'constructive engagement', a centrist approach neither exclusively condemnatory of South Africa because of its domestic policies nor wholly supportive for Cold War reasons. Under Carter, he felt, the USA had overplayed its hand and simply put South Africa's back up. Instead it should devote its 'limited influence' to pressing, in 'concrete issues', for 'sustained and orderly change' both within the Republic itself and more

21. Barber and Barratt, *South Africa's Foreign Policy* pp.270–4, 293–4, 313, 315–18. FRELIMO and RENAMO agreed a cease-fire in Oct. 1992. Implementation proved difficult; but a year later a time-table was arranged for disarmament, merger into a single national army, and elections in Oct. 1994 (all under UN supervision) – *Keesing's,* 39671, 39724–5, 1993 R17

22. Barber and Barratt, *South Africa's Foreign Policy*, pp.81, 167–70, 227–8

generally within Southern Africa.[23] The most obvious results were the diplomatic brokering that, with Zambian assistance, contributed significantly to the Nkomati Accord and the abortive Lusaka settlement of Angola/Namibia. In the wake of these agreements, P.W. Botha was able to make official visits to Portugal and many other West European states – that to Britain being the first by a South African Premier since the country had left the Commonwealth.

'Constructive engagement' was premised on the belief that there existed within South Africa the potential for 'meaningful evolutionary change', resting on sustained economic growth 'that could undergird change towards a more equitable order'. By late 1984 the economy was no longer growing fast enough to absorb the rising number of blacks of working age; the recent dramatic increase in black earnings was being eroded by inflation; and trouble broke out, first in the disadvantaged Eastern Cape and then more generally. The riots were internationally reported on television. Attention was further concentrated on South Africa by the award of the Nobel Peace Prize to Archbishop Desmond Tutu, who had used his position to fill the gap left by the banning of more conventional African nationalist politics. In the USA, there was a sudden upsurge of lobbying for sanctions (initiated by black Americans not only out of concern for South Africa but also because they had felt themselves marginalised in the recent US elections). President Botha, as we have seen, responded to the township riots by declaring a partial state of emergency in July 1985, a move that the European Community promptly condemned. But his Foreign Minister led the world to believe that he would accompany it by announcing major reforms in a speech in August. Instead Botha, while offering 'negotiations', made it clear that foreign pressure would not make him 'lead white South Africans and other minority groups on a road to abdication and suicide'. Archbishop Tutu declared himself 'devastated', and claimed that sanctions were now the only alternative to violence.[24]

The immediate consequences were economic. South African share prices and the foreign exchange value of the rand went into steep decline. Led by Chase Manhattan, major foreign banks took the unusual decision not to renew thair short-term loans to South Africa, ostensibly for commercial reasons but probably largely to escape domestic pressures in the United States. This drove South Africa into defaulting on foreign debt repayments, and it rattled South African business (always, admittedly, rather more 'liberal'

23. ibid, pp.274–9
24. ibid, pp.303, 306–8, 320–3

than the government), leading to declarations for further political reform and the unprecedented dispatch of a delegation to meet the ANC leader Oliver Tambo. For its part, the government initiated negotiations on debt rescheduling through the Swiss banker, Dr Leutwiler. An agreement was reached in early 1986, though only after Leutwiler had been assured that the 'process of reform' would continue (as indeed it did, with such measures as the abolition of the pass laws). Even so, in 1986–7 a growing number of large Anglo-American banks and corporations bowed to external pressure and sold off their South African operations.

The 1985 freezing of bank loans was probably the most dramatic, and unexpected, foreign pressure on South Africa; it was soon accompanied by further measures. Although Reagan vetoed a Bill to impose sanctions, he thought it politic to institute more limited embargoes by executive order. In 1986 Congress passed, over his veto, an 'Anti-Apartheid' Act that extended sanctions and looked to further measures in 1987 if South Africa had not moved to dismantle apartheid (though in the event these were not forthcoming). The European Community also imposed largely symbolic sanctions in 1985, despite British reservations. The question assumed its highest profile at the October 1985 Commonwealth Conference. Most of South Africa's neighbours were members; they generally pressed strongly for sanctions, while making it clear that they could not themselves afford to impose them. They enjoyed widespread backing, notably that of Canada and Australia (though this came easily inasmuch as both would profit from the elimination of South African trade competition). The chief cost would fall on the UK, which (while no longer South Africa's largest partner) still ran a comfortable surplus on their mutual trade and had the largest foreign investment there. Mrs Thatcher was passionately opposed to sanctions, not only because she disliked the ANC (in 1987 she called it a 'terrorist organisation') but also because she believed their chief effect would be the destruction of African jobs (especially agricultural ones). Unity was preserved by the decision to impose immediately only mild sanctions, but to appoint an 'Eminent Persons Group' to visit South Africa and inaugurate a 'process of dialogue . . . with a view to establishing a non-racial and representative government'. It is a measure of the nervousness of the South African government that it was prepared to permit such external interference; but the Eminent Persons Group was initially quite well received (and the state of emergency lifted). However in May 1986 South Africa undercut the process by raiding

ANC premises in Botswana, Zimbabwe and Zambia; in June Botha reimposed the state of emergency, roundly declaring that 'Neither the international community at large, nor any particular state, will dictate to us what the contents of our political programme should be'.[25]

In response the European Community returned to discussing sanctions; but as Germany, Britain and Portugal were opposed, further time was bought by dispatching the then President of the Council of Ministers (the British Foreign Secretary) on a fruitless last-ditch tour of Southern Africa. In August 1986 the Commonwealth reviewed the failure of negotiations and sought to tighten sanctions. Thatcher was now backed into a corner. The Indian Prime Minister declared that 'if Britain cannot gauge the pulse of the Commonwealth it cannot retain the leadership'; President Kaunda's language was stronger, though his credibility was not enhanced by his own taste for South African wine or by Zambian Airways subsequent institution of a service between the Republic and the USA to replace those cut off by the 1986 US sanctions. Eventually the Commonwealth agreed to disagree, provided that Britain undertook to implement the EC's upcoming decision on sanctions. The Community did indeed ban new investment in South Africa (which had dried up anyway) and the import of gold coins and of iron – but not that of coal (German purchases of which in fact increased). UN attempts in 1987 to generalise these measures by imposing mandatory sanctions were vetoed by the UK and USA. Nevertheless there continued pressures in the USA for further measures, though they did not issue in agreed legislation. The 1987 Commonwealth Conference, over British objections, appointed a committee of Foreign Ministers to monitor developments and make recommendations to the 1989 conference.[26]

By then, as we shall see, politics in the Republic had begun to change. It is not clear how much external pressures had contributed. Sanctions did not bring South Africa to its knees. They were perhaps most successful in severing sporting links. Given white South Africa's addiction to sport, this was certainly felt. It led both to attempts to induce 'rebel' foreign teams to breach the boycott by paying them over the odds, and to the integration (at least at national level) of many South African sports. More could hardly be expected. Economically the 1980s sanctions did reduce South

25. ibid, pp.324–34; *Keesing's*, 33892–3, 34594–5, 35624–5
26. *Keesing's*, 34597–8, 34627–8, 34647–51, 35624–5

African trade, perhaps by 7 per cent; but some countries' cuts were offset by increases on the part of others (in absolute terms notably Japan and Germany, in relative ones Switzerland, Argentina, Turkey, Taiwan and Brazil). Although South Africa was clearly anxious that the process should not be taken further, it had itself many cards to play. In August 1986 it had declared that 'The inevitable consequence of extending sanctions against South Africa must be that the economies of our neighbours will be harmed', and had taken steps to emphasise the heavy dependence of countries as far north as Zaïre on its transport facilities and goodwill; two years later it warned the US Congress against wrecking moves towards a Namibian settlement by tightening sanctions.[27] South Africa could clearly live with sanctions, but they reduced the ability of its economy to keep pace with its relentless population growth and will thus have encouraged those people who worried about such things towards a negotiated settlement. A cut off of oil might perhaps have worked more quickly, but South Africa devoted great efforts to securing it clandestinely, maintaining a strategic reserve, and substituting coal; the easier supply conditions of the 1980s seem to have cut the premium it had to pay above the world price.[28] Arms embargoes too could be worked around, both by theft and (at least until 1987, when US pressure seems to have curtailed it) by cooperation with that other pariah state, Israel. During the currency of the UN embargo, a local industry was built up that was itself capable of exporting.[29] South Africa enjoyed almost effortless military supremacy over its neighbours, but in 1975 its artillery, and in 1988 its aircraft, could not match the Soviet equipment with which Cuban forces in Angola had been supplied. As we have seen, in 1988 President Botha concluded that the Republic had become over-extended, and reversed his earlier tough forward policy by accepting measures that would lead to the decolonisation of Namibia.

27. *Keesing's*, 34600–1, 36335–6, 36862. Significant international aid (with Britain a highly visible contributor) was devoted to trying to lessen the dependence on the Republic of South Africa's neighbours, but to little immediate effect

28. In 1980 one tanker was scuttled at sea in an attempt to hide its earlier diversion to South Africa. In the later 1980s the premium that South Africa had to pay allegedly sank below $1 a barrel (as compared with $8 a decade earlier); most supplies came from countries claiming to impose an embargo: *Keesing's*, 33899–90; *The Independent*, 14 Sept. 1988 p.8

29. Barber and Barratt, *South Africa's Foreign Policy* pp.101–4, 158, 233–8

DE KLERK RELEASES MANDELA 1990

Whether Botha would also have contemplated domestic reversals is doubtful, but in early 1989 he suffered a stroke and resigned as leader of the ruling Nationalist Party. His successor was the hitherto cautious de Klerk, who defeated two more liberal opponents in the leadership elections. In mid-year he was talking of 'drastic changes' but not majority African rule, very much in Botha's language. But things seemed to be stirring. In July 1989 Botha himself met and talked with Nelson Mandela, the ANC leader jailed in the early 1960s, whose release had been one of the chief demands of the Eminent Persons Group and had now clearly become the pre-requisite for dialogue with any credible African politicians. In August Kaunda announced that de Klerk would be visiting Zambia and implied that he would establish at least indirect contact with the ANC. Botha resigned from the presidency in protest.

De Klerk's Zambian talks were, at least overtly, confined to Angola; he did not rock the boat until the South African parliamentary elections were out of the way and he had been safely confirmed as President. He then appealed to the world at large to give his new administration time; the Commonwealth Conference in October 1989 decided to wait for six months before taking any further decisions on sanctions. There followed further presidential meetings with Mandela, and releases of other important nationalist prisoners. Then in February 1990 de Klerk (apparently encouraged by the general diminution of the Soviet threat and by the collapse of communism in Eastern Europe) told the new session of Parliament that he would release Mandela, lift the ban on the ANC, and start negotiations for 'a totally new, just, constitutional settlement in which every inhabitant will enjoy equal rights'. Mandela was indeed freed that month; in August 1990 the ANC 'suspended' the armed struggle, while the government promised to release 'political prisoners' and to facilitate the safe return of ANC exiles (though it took a year to agree all the details of the necessary amnesties); and by July 1991 the remaining apartheid and land reservation laws had been repealed. External pressure on South Africa was correspondingly relaxed, with its sports teams returning to international competition in 1991, many countries dropping or diluting sanctions, and the Commonwealth agreeing in 1991 on their phased lifting in step with South Africa's progress to majority rule.[30]

30. *Keesing's*, 36387, 36647, 36803, 36837, 36880, 36963–4, 37232–4, 38047, 38178–9, 38270, 38376, 38553, 38705, 1992 R19–20

THE ROCKY ROAD TO A NEGOTIATED SETTLEMENT

On the ground, however, conditions in many ways worsened, Low-level fighting had started in rural Natal as early as 1986 between the more traditional Zulu Inkatha and the ANC, which (though professedly non-tribal and supported by some Zulus) was resisted by others as a Xhosa-led interloper. With the prospect of real political change, the struggle for local control intensified. So in 1990–1 violence spread to townships in the rest of the country, with affrays between Inkatha Zulu workers in migrant hostels and ANC militants, plus apparently aimless terrorist killings on (for instance) African commuter trains. Estimates of casualties vary, but are of the order of two to three thousand a year in 1990–1 and 3,500 in 1992 – well above the level of earlier disturbances. The security forces proved, at best, ineffective; this generated suspicion that they harboured a 'third force' that promoted violence in order to derail the government's declaratory policy of reconciliation. It has indeed transpired that, in its early years, Inkatha enjoyed covert official aid as an African movement opposed to sanctions. Despite official denials, such support is known to have continued until at least January 1991. Later that year the security forces launched an operation to infiltrate and compromise the ANC's military wing, Umkhonto we Sizwe. This may have been only one among many.[31]

The honeymoon following Mandela's release therefore waned; and real negotiations as to South Africa's political future were perhaps damagingly slow to start. However December 1991 saw the inauguration of a widely, though not universally, attended negotiating forum whose decisions would require both government and ANC consent. It got off to a good start in March 1992, when de Klerk secured 69 per cent support in a referendum asking the white electorate to endorse 'continuation of the reform process . . . aimed at a new constitution through negotiation'. But negotiation deadlocked over minority guarantees; and in June the ANC pulled out in the wake of a serious township shooting at Boipatong. In September 1992, a further shooting in the Ciskei led de Klerk and Mandela to step back from confrontation and resume negotiations. In February 1993 they agreed on: a new, elected, constituent assembly that would take decisions by a two-thirds, not (as de Klerk

31. *Keesing's*, 37951, 38087, 38271, 38318–9, 38376, 38663, 38705, 38948, 39177–8, 1992 R 19, 1993 R21–2

had initially sought) by a three-quarters, majority; a single non-rotating (and presumably ANC) President; and a 'government of national unity' to last for the five years after the elections, to include all parties that had secured a given proportion of votes (which de Klerk expected to preserve for the Nationalists at least some continued grip on the levers of power). This paved the way for the resumption of multi-party talks, the fixing of an April 1994 date for the constituent assembly elections, and for the establishment (authorised in September 1993 by the old white Parliament) of a shared Transitional Executive Council to supervise the government and the security services in the meantime. Thereafter, de Klerk and Mandela jointly appealed for the ending of all economic pressures on South Africa.

Most of these agreements had been reached bi-laterally between the government and the ANC, with the former giving the more ground. They also reversed the earlier nationalist strategy of seeking to build with Inkatha an alliance capable at least of blocking the ANC in any elected assembly, and so enforcing consociational power-sharing and the protection of minority rights. The reversal led to the growth of an opposition alignment of Inkatha, the Conservatives, and various home-land leaders. By mid-1993 this seemed to pose serious dangers: white conservative forces were grouped in May into the Afrikaner Volksvront, chaired by a former head of the armed forces and possibly enjoying the sympathy of many serving personnel; and in July Inkatha withdrew from the multi-party talks, announcing that it would boycott the April 1994 elections and warning of the danger of civil war. Behind the scenes there would appear to have been attempts to pacify them by concessions over the powers and geography of regional government that might provide both Afrikaners and Zulu Inkatha with a de facto homeland; but in early 1994 the future remained unclear.[32]

32. *Keesing's*, 1993 R21–2, 39302, 39446, 39497; *The Independent*, 15 Feb. 1993 p.12, 9 Sept. 1993 p.11; *The Economist*, 25 Sept.–1 Oct. 1993 pp.70–1

PART II
East Asia and the Pacific

CHAPTER FIVE

The Chinese Civil War

Early in the twentieth century US Secretary of State Hay declared grandiloquently that the Mediterranean was the sea of the past, the Atlantic that of the present, the Pacific the sea of the future. In the interwar period Europe still remained the centre of the world stage, but the crumbling of the liberal international order is usually dated from the Japanese take-over of Manchuria in 1931. It was the intermeshing of European and Far Eastern challenges that the principal status quo Power, Britain, found so hard to handle: witness the oft-repeated warning that it was

> a cardinal requirement of our national and imperial security that our foreign policy should be so conducted as to avoid the possible development of a situation in which we might be confronted simultaneously with the hostility, open or veiled, of Japan in the Far East, Germany in the West, and any power on the main line of communication between the two.[1]

Similarly, though the USA was far more European than Asian in character, it was, until 1941, usually more active in a western Pacific than in a European international context; and it was brought into the war by Japan's attack on Pearl Harbor. In the war priority was given to the European theatre; but at its end the United States was the dominant power in the West Pacific, and it remained generally more conscious than its European allies of the importance of East Asia: indeed its two major wars since 1945 have both been fought there. If one surveys our period as a whole, one is conscious of two great US set-backs – the 'loss' of China to the Communists and the

1. Third Report of the Defence Requirements Sub-committee, Nov. 1935

long and ultimately unsuccessful war in Indo-China. But it can be argued that these were more than counterbalanced by numerous, though generally less spectacular, successes, and that, while the western Pacific order now presents the United States with a number of economic problems, it nevertheless represents a considerable achievement.

CHINA TO 1945

In his rather hazy way Roosevelt had been unusually conscious of the coming importance of China. 'Our policy', he explained in 1945, 'was based on the belief that despite the temporary weakness of China and the possibility of revolutions and civil war, 450,000,000 Chinese would someday become united and modernised and would be the most important factor in the whole Far East.' Partly for this reason, partly because it was in the mean time under strong US influence,[2] Roosevelt cast China as one of the 'four policemen' around which he sought to structure the postwar international order; he succeeded in making it one of five Permanent Members with vetoes on the UN Security Council. Roosevelt also gave Eden the impression that he hoped to use the traditional American feeling for China 'to lead his people to accept international responsibilities' (which they had refused to do after the First World War).[3]

In 1945 China was in a bad way. The Japanese had occupied its major cities. With the puppet government of Wang Ching Wei, they dominated north-eastern China, though their hold over its more remote countryside was distinctly tenuous. Manchuria they had detached to constitute a separate state, from which both nationalist and communist influence was successfully excluded. The communists (CCP) were based on the poor district of Yenan, on China's northern periphery. There they had reconstituted their forces around the principles of austere living and the cultivation and mobilisation of the peasants. The Yenan model was to be much hyped; but it contrasted favourably with the corruption and indiscriminate brutality of the nationalist forces, and was to prove a

2. Roosevelt told Eden that 'in any serious conflict of policy with Russia' China 'would undoubtedly line up on our side'; Churchill saw the Chungking government, not 'as representing a great world Power', but as 'a faggot vote on the side of the United States in any attempt to liquidate the British overseas Empire': R. Dallek, *Franklin Delano Roosevelt and American Foreign Policy 1932–1945* (New York, 1981) pp.389–90

3. ibid, pp.391, 501

major asset in the Chinese Civil War. The CCP was also advantaged by the fact that, though Japanese troops were unbeatable in conventional warfare, they were thinly spread and so left openings for the penetration of guerrillas. Guerrilla warfare had always been Mao's forte; his supporters operated far more effectively in Japanese-held areas than did the more conventional nationalist armies (which, in any case, Japan regarded as its main opponents). By 1945 the CCP claimed to control 96 million people, mostly in islands of 'liberated' territory; the claim was exaggerated, but communists were strong in and around Shantung province. Lastly Chiang Kai-shek, the head of the internationally recognised Republic of China, ruled most of the south and west from the inland city of Chungking. His power had always been based chiefly on his army, but it had been exercised also through the Kuomintang (KMT), which sought to be a dominant and pervasive modernising nationalist movement. In 1937 the Japanese had driven Chiang into the interior, extruding KMT influence from the rising coastal and central trading and industrial centres. By so doing they also reduced his tax base, and in Chungking the KMT degenerated towards becoming just another regional war lord regime. In particular Chiang never managed to build an effective state apparatus. Thus in the peak years of 1942–3 only two-thirds of the land tax due – or a little over 8 per cent of total wheat and rice production – seems to have been collected officially. Later the system deteriorated further: in 1947 land tax from the whole of China produced only 57 per cent, in 1948 perhaps 33 per cent, of that raised from nationalist areas in 1942.[4] Much of what was collected was spoilt in transit or evaporated through corruption (itself a natural consequence of the failure of official salaries to keep pace with inflation). So government, and still more armies, resorted to ad hoc levies and to foraging (which were more inequitable and unpopular than regular taxation, and bore especially hard on areas already disrupted by fighting). Similarly, while the armies cannot be regarded as large in relation to China's population, they were (as a series of US advisers told Chiang) too large to be effective. Fewer units,[5] properly fed, trained and

4. Lloyd E. Eastman, *Seeds of Destruction: Nationalist China in War and Revolution 1937–1949* (Stanford, Calif., 1984) pp.59–60

5. General Stilwell urged a reduction from 300 to 30 divisions, though he seems never to have appreciated its possible consequences for the KMT power structure. Also, when demobilisation was tried after 1945, some, at least, of those thus rendered jobless simply transferred to the communists – F.F. Lin, *A Military History of Modern China* (Port Washington, New York, 1976 edn) pp.228–9

equipped, would have been militarily preferable. Moreover the need to raise troops was met by press-gangs that (at least by 1948) often seized villagers by night and marched them off roped together. The morale of those so recruited was not high: one calculation is that over half the 14 million men conscripted from 1937 to 1945 simply deserted.[6]

Another feature of Chinese politics was that, at least after the initial years of the war, the parties were keener on opposing each other than on fighting the unbeatable Japanese. This is usually seen in the context of KMT–communist rivalry, but is in fact more complex. General Yen Hsi-shan (ostensibly Vice-Chairman of the KMT Military Affairs Committee) ruled his section of Shansi as a private fief, where 'enemy' meant chiefly the communists, but secondarily the national government (whose troops he would not permit on his territory); lower on the list came Japan's Chinese clients, while with the Japanese themselves he maintained amicable official liaison.[7] By the same token Chiang Kai-shek used force, in 1945, to oust the ruler of Yunnan province, after having first dispatched most of his troops to take the Japanese surrender in northern Indo-China.[8] Against this background it is the less remarkable that the civil war between Chiang and the communists never really ended. In the 1930s Chiang had had Mao on the run; the communists may well have owed their survival to the feeling (which their propaganda exploited) that China should unite against Japanese expansionism rather than pursuing domestic quarrels. Such a front was indeed formed, ostensibly under Chiang's leadership, in 1936–7, but it was very flimsy. Chiang no longer assaulted Yenan, but he continued blockading it – using, the Americans believed, 400,000 good troops to do so in 1943. An attempted communist penetration of the Yangtze valley led to a severe clash with KMT forces in 1941. Mao, for his part, had declared as early as 1937 that 'Our fixed policy should be 70 per cent expansion, 20 per cent dealing with the Kuomintang, and 10 per cent resisting Japan'.[9]

6. Eastman, *Seeds of Destruction* p.260
7. ibid, p.12
8. Following their withdrawal from Hanoi in 1946 they were not returned home but sent north to fight the communists, whose propaganda sought with some success to demoralise them by playing on the way Chiang had treated Yunnan: ibid, pp.36–41
9. Immanuel C.Y. Hsü, *The Rise of Modern China* (New York, 1990 edn) pp.589, 603

THE FAILURE OF US MEDIATION 1943–6

After Pearl Harbor the USA became deeply involved in bolstering China's war effort, and, as a result, gained some leverage over politics in Chungking. In 1943, at Cairo, Roosevelt secured Chiang's promise to bring the communists into his government.[10] In 1944 the USA started pressing for action. In June Chiang accepted a US offer of 'assistance' in reaching agreement with the communists, and finally agreed to the dispatch to Yenan of a US mission (commonly known as the 'Dixie Mission'). This consisted mostly of young diplomats who had been appalled by the corruption of Chungking; they were bowled over by Yenan's contrasting environment and became zealous advocates of a tilt towards the communists. (Liberal Americans exposed to the realities of Nationalist China had a tendency to transfer their idealistic illusions to the communists.) The CCP naturally encouraged this: Mao stressed that he would welcome 'democratic American influence' and that Chinese industrialisation required free enterprise and 'the aid of foreign capital'; later he proposed visiting Washington to explain the Chinese situation to the President.[11] It is sometimes suggested that the USA missed a major opportunity by not responding to these initiatives: this can neither be proved nor disproved. It is, though, worth remembering that Mao's concern was not long-run future relations but the imminent struggle with the KMT. In similar circumstances in Yugoslavia the British did switch their aid from Mihailovic's Chetniks to Tito's communists, but this did *not* stop Tito subsequently aligning with Stalin against them.

Be that as it may, the USA stuck to its policy of supporting the existing Chinese government but attempting to negotiate it into a coalition with the CCP. Initially this task fell to Roosevelt's special representative, Hurley, who reported optimistically that there was little real difference between the two: both 'are striving for democratic principles'.[12] He hoped to reach a settlement through persistence and personal charm, though the exercise of the latter

10. Partly by promising Chiang support against the following: British return to Hong Kong; reconstitution of the pre-war extra-territorial arrangements in other ports; Soviet encroachment on Manchuria: Richard C. Thornton, *China: The Struggle for Power 1917–72* (Bloomington, Ind., 1973) pp.353–4

11. W.P. Head, *America's China Sojourn . . . 1942–1948* (Lanham, Md, 1983) p.102; Barbara Tuchman, 'If Mao Had Come to Washington: An Essay in Alternatives', *Foreign Affairs* li (1972–3) p.44

12. Tuchman, 'If Mao Had Come to Washington' p.54

took eccentric forms (on first arriving in Yenan he let out a Red Indian war whoop, and such behaviour led Mao to dub him 'the clown'). The CCP (as the weaker party) was prepared for an arrangement – some kind of central coalition and nominal military unification that would leave its local power intact. In November 1944 Hurley secured its assent to his outline coalition proposals. The KMT promptly altered them to provide for the integration of communist troops into a centrally controlled National Army. Unsurprisingly this was declined. Hurley attributed the rejection, after an initially encouraging reply, to an unauthorised approach (through the Dixie Mission) to the communists for combined action in Shantung, which (he felt) suggested that the USA was on the point of shifting support from the central government. The episode increased Hurley's suspicion of the Dixie Mission, as did its later attempt to arrange behind his back for Mao to visit Washington. A final collision occurred in March 1945. Most of the US diplomats in China telegraphed a criticism of his policy as encouraging Chiang's obstinacy and leading to civil war; one official added that future US–Chinese relations should not be left 'in the hands of a bungler like Hurley'.[13] Hurley was not pleased. Holding out the hope of success by the end of April 1945,[14] he persuaded Roosevelt to endorse his approach and reassign his critics. In fact he managed to keep talks going (flying Mao to Chungking and guaranteeing his safety), but little more. In November he resigned, then exploded with public charges that his policies had been deliberately undercut by the professional diplomats. To calm matters down Truman appointed the extremely prestigious former Chief of Staff, General Marshall, to succeed him.

Meanwhile Japan's decision in August 1945 to surrender had created a sudden power vacuum in China that both the KMT and the CCP rushed to fill. The USA backed the KMT, instructing Japanese commanders to surrender only to Chiang Kai-shek; Nationalist troops were airlifted to Nangking and Shanghai, where they beat off a communist assault. But the real competition came in the north;[15] indeed after lengthy negotiations the CCP agreed in October to stand down most of its southern forces and transfer

13. *United States Relations with China* (State Dept, Washington, DC, August 1949) pp.87 ff; Michael Schaller, *The United States and China in the Twentieth Century* (New York, 1979) pp.105–6

14. Hurley hoped that the Yalta agreement on China with the USSR (see *The Cold War* chap. 15) would make the Chinese communists more cooperative

15. Thornton, *China: The Struggle for Power* p.179

them north. After some deliberation the Americans decided not only to extend airlifts to cities like Peiping (Beijing) but also (in October) to land their own marines to hold key positions and supervise the evacuation of Japanese troops. Chiang decided, however, not to make a major effort in Hopei and Shantung, where the communists were strong, but to concentrate instead on Manchuria: a centre of industry, and an area where both communists and KMT were starting from scratch. General Wedemeyer, the US military representative, believed this to be foolish: Chiang should concentrate on securing northern China (which would itself be a slow process); logistic problems, which Wedemeyer thought Chiang did not appreciate, meant that he would not for 'many years' be in a position to occupy Manchuria. But Washington decided that, if Chiang did not occupy Manchuria, the Soviet Union was bound to take it over. So Chiang's forces should be transported there, though General Marshall should have considerable latitude in arranging this, to help him bring pressure to bear on both the KMT and the communists for a compromise.[16]

At first things went well. The KMT had begun clearing the railway into Manchuria, but in January 1946 Marshall secured a cease-fire, to be supervised by tripartite US–KMT–CCP teams: troop movements in northern China were to stop, and the CCP would allow the railways to run. There followed agreements on an interim administration, and on the freezing of existing patterns of control over local government. A scheme was even worked out for the reduction of both KMT and CCP forces and their ultimate integration into a non-party army. On the ground conditions were less satisfactory, with low-key infiltration and expansion by both sides. It was in Manchuria that things really unravelled: communists (largely unarmed) had been streaming thither overland in the wake of its conquest by the USSR. Although Soviet troops were chiefly interested in looting the region's industrial plant, they gave the CCP a head start by impeding KMT access until October and thereafter restricting it to small forces in the main southern cities. The communists supposedly picked up 300,000 ex-Japanese rifles, 138,000 machine guns and 2,700 artillery pieces; and their tolerant policy towards soldiers who had previously taken a different side enabled them to enrol 75,000 troops from the former (Japanese puppet) Manchukuo army. In a remarkable effort they also took

16. State Department, *Foreign Relations of the United States* (*FRUS*), 1945 vii pp.650–60, 762–73

over local government and began mobilising the locals.[17] In March the USSR suddenly began a withdrawal, timed to suit its own convenience and without advance notification (at least to the Nationalist government) of its local moves. Both CCP and KMT scrambled to replace them. In April the communists overwhelmed the small Nationalist garrison in Changchun. Heavy nationalist counterattacks occupied the main industrial areas, and the CCP sought a truce. Marshall managed to arrange one in June, but Chiang warned that 'this would be his final effort at doing business with the communists, that the present indeterminate situation with communications blocked, coal barely obtainable . . ., cities starving could not be endured economically or otherwise, that all-out war would be preferable'.[18] In subsequent negotiations he therefore insisted on communist withdrawal from key railway lines in northern China.

Agreement was not reached, and there ensued a process of fighting while talking. Both sides mounted offensives, but the KMT enjoyed the general initiative. In July Chiang told Marshall that 'it was first necessary to deal harshly with the communists, and later, after two or three months, to adopt a generous attitude' – by which time they were likely to make the 'compromises' 'necessary for a settlement'.[19] Chiang slightly improved his position in Manchuria, but most of the fighting was in northern China, where the KMT took a number of cities and drove the communists from the strategic railways (though it could not always prevent their filtering back). Marshall sought to dissuade it by imposing an embargo on arms and ammunition deliveries that took effect in August. There has since been controversy as to how far this damaged the KMT position.[20] At the time Chiang remained confident of an early victory: in December he told a sceptical Marshall that the communist forces outside Manchuria 'could be exterminated in 8 to 10 months'.[21] He had in fact called a further cease-fire in November to permit the convocation of a National Assembly, but as this met without the provisions designed in January to give the CCP

17. For events in Manchuria see Steven I. Levine, *Anvil of Victory: The Communist Revolution in Manchuria, 1945–1948* (New York, 1987). Figures for arms and ex-Manchukno recruits come from KMT and US sources: Lin, *A Military History of Modern China* pp.228–9

18. *FRUS*, 1946 ix p.978

19. Hsü, *Rise of Modern China* p.628

20. See Thornton, *China: The Struggle for Power* pp.202–4, 209–11, 367, and (for the opposite view) *United States Relations with China* pp.354–9

21. *FRUS*, 1946 x p.577

and its allies a veto, it only made matters worse, and communist negotiators and truce supervisors withdrew to Yenan. General Marshall had for some time been threatening to end his mediation, as no longer serving any useful purpose; in January 1947 he was recalled to become US Secretary of State. Talks still continued sporadically; in March the USSR proposed discussing the Chinese situation in the Four Power Conference of Foreign Ministers (though neither the USA nor the KMT were agreeable). Meanwhile fighting expanded; in July the communists were proclaimed to be in open rebellion. But by then the tide had turned; indeed Washington was already discussing whether the weakening of the KMT's military position required US counteraction.

NON-MILITARY FACTORS IN THE KMT DEFEAT

The KMT débâcle was mostly military, but its mishandling of the economy made an important contribution. Before 1945 industry and commerce (which were concentrated in the areas controlled by Japan) had been integrated into its Co-prosperity Sphere, whose collapse was bound to lead to disruption. Matters were not improved by seizures of the property of 'collaborators' and (often) its acquisition by KMT bigwigs. Also holders of the old currency were forced to exchange it at exorbitant rates for Republic of China notes. This sort of behaviour made 'liberation' seem rather like conquest. More generally China suffered one of the world's great inflations. It had shifted from a silver-based to a paper currency in 1935. From 1937 onwards the government (driven into the interior and cut off from much of its usual revenue) met its expenses chiefly by printing. The habit continued after 1945, Chiang maintaining in December 1946 that 'while the situation was serious in the cities', the basically agrarian nature of the Chinese economy meant 'that there was not the danger for about two years of a collapse' of the kind Marshall was prophesying. The result was a vast increase in the quantity of notes in circulation (and hence of inflation) from 1.9 billion Chinese dollars in early 1937 to 1,032 billion in 1945 and 24,600,000 billion in late 1948; August 1948 saw a currency reform, but it failed (the note issue expanding 4,524 times by April 1949).[22] The collapse of the currency did not directly destroy the

22. *FRUS*, 1946 x p.577; Hsü, *Rise of Modern China* pp.612, 640–1

government, but it made for problems in supplying the armies. It further encouraged speculation and corruption (long-standing KMT problems), and contributed to the general collapse in morale that helps explain why the communists met with so little resistance after they had crossed the Yangtze river.

Another factor is more problematic. It is often contended that the CCP earned the reward for its Yenan policy of austere living and cultivating the peasantry, who, of course, constituted the vast majority of the population. Some scepticism is in order: by 1948 communists in 'liberated areas' were already being accused of appropriating the best houses, riding in cars, and growing fat in restaurants.[23] However, they had the advantage of the KMT in two interconnected respects. Where they were strong they forcibly displaced local elites, and were thus able to establish a far more effective control than could the nationalists. Admittedly we know less about its operation, but it enabled the CCP to levy supplies, conscript manpower, and above all feed their forces more reliably than did their opponents. It also avoided much of the diversion of official demands on to exclusively peasant shoulders that alienated nationalist areas (though the effect could be tarnished by the stirring up of class war that provoked sporadic resistance and had therefore to be curtailed during the agricultural growing season). Again the KMT generally fought a conventional war without trying to win 'hearts and minds', whereas the CCP made much more of a propaganda effort to mobilise and motivate, and to reassure people that, if conscripted, they would in due course be brought home again. It also returned something in exchange for its inevitable military exactions, by limiting rents and distributing some of the property seized from the wealthy. Anyway, whether through force or sympathy, the CCP mobilised enormous bodies of men (through labour service quotas) to support its soldiers.[24] Mostly this was a matter of transporting guns and heavy equipment and so enabling communist armies (unlike their opponents) to operate without fixed (and vulnerable) lines of supply; but at the great battle of

23. Philip Short, *The Dragon and the Bear* (1982) p.135

24. Levine, *Anvil of Victory*, discusses these themes with special reference to Manchuria. (He sees the CCP as successfully *mobilising* peasants, but as unprepared to accept their autonomous actions and preferences – which was, after victory, to have disastrous consequences, borne chiefly by the peasants.) Eastman concludes that, though peasants did not rise against the KMT, 'In important, indirect ways . . . they withheld their support', whereas in communist areas most peasants apolitically accepted the new regime and some, 'particularly the youth', actively supported it: *Seeds of Destruction* p.88

Huai-Hai, KMT tanks were boxed in and immobilised by ditches dug by a huge collection of peasants. In some regions the CCP may indeed have tapped long-standing traditions of self-conscious rural resistance to authority. However, the KMT was not swept away by a peasant rising: it lost its armies in large-scale conventional warfare – to which we must now turn.

MILITARY OPERATIONS 1946–9

The KMT would probably have done better had it either attempted less or staged an all-out offensive instead of falling in with Marshall's mediation in early 1946. The latter course would have been risky, especially given Chiang's dependence on the Americans. But his best troops were southern, and they deteriorated when employed on garrison duty in the very different north. By contrast the delay worked in favour of the previously ill-equipped communist forces. The safer option, however, would have been to accept US advice and purchase agreement with the communists by conceding them much of the north China plain and Manchuria. Had the KMT done this, it would still have enjoyed international recognition, and have occupied what was to become the more valuable half of the country. As it would not have over-extended its forces, it would have proved very difficult to dislodge. Given the long-standing KMT commitment to Chinese unity, this approach was unthinkable. Nor could Chiang even bring himself to withdraw troops on a large enough scale in early 1948, though this might still have enabled him to salvage the centre and south.

There were two main theatres – Manchuria and northern China. In Manchuria fighting was limited during the second half of 1946, since Chiang was broadly content with his occupation of the smaller but more valuable part of the region and did not wish to risk provoking the USSR by taking Harbin.[25] Such restraint was probably wise, but the communists used the respite to restructure their hitherto rather unimpressive armies, acquiring from the USSR 1,200–1,800 artillery pieces and 370–700 tanks. They were also joined in 1947 by North Korean units, and by some of their own forces whom the Soviets had regrouped after they had been driven

25. *FRUS*, 1946 x p.577. He did, however, occupy the south-eastern province of Antung

over the Korean border.[26] After periodic probing attacks from November 1946, in May 1947 they launched a major offensive to cut the railway links between the main nationalist centres. The KMT had repulsed it by July, but only at the cost of abandoning half its Manchurian territory with considerable losses of equipment. Further offensives in September and December again drove the KMT to concentrate on the defence of major cities. That of December led the KMT to airlift in two further divisions, after which it claimed to have stabilised the situation. In fact further communist attacks from January to March 1948 succeeded in isolating the garrisons of Changchun and Shenyung both from each other and from northern China. Their resupply by air was expensive and inadequate; but Chiang still refused US advice to evacuate them, and could not even persuade his local commander to move his men to the least exposed area, Chinchow. Between September and November 1948 the communists took all three cities, with a total KMT loss of 400,000 of what had once been its best troops. They then came south to besiege Peiping.[27]

Fighting in northern China was more confused, and at first resembled guerrilla warfare. Initially the communists tended to evade sweeps by superior nationalist forces and either attack elsewhere or filter back later. In March 1947 the KMT secured a psychological success in capturing Yenan; but the men involved could have been better used elsewhere, and were in fact to be withdrawn a year later. The KMT's other main goal was to clear Shantung. It never quite succeeded, as ejected communist forces moved down towards central China and the KMT had to abandon some of its gains to counter them. By the second half of 1947 the disparity in strength between KMT and CCP forces was beginning to lessen; the communists started to embark on sieges, and in the spring of 1948 also on conventional battles. Meanwhile the KMT showed, as in Manchuria, a tendency to adopt defensive positions in towns rather than actively seeking out the enemy. Outcomes fluctuated, but by mid-1948 the communists had at least recovered their losses of 1946. In particular they had by May driven the KMT from most of Shantung and penned up 60,000 troops in its capital

26. Thornton, *China: The Struggle for Power* p.207; the high estimates are Soviet, the low Chinese. V. Petrov puts the Korean numbers at 100,000: in O.B. Borissov and B.T. Kaloskov (eds) *Soviet–Chinese Relations, 1945–1970* (Bloomington, Ind., 1975) p.26; see also R.R. Simmons, *The Strained Alliance: Peking, Pyongyang, Moscow and the Politics of the Korean War* (New York, 1975) p.32

27. For this and subsequent paragraphs see Levine, *Anvil of Victory* chap. iv, and L.M. Chassin, *The Communist Conquest of China* (Cambridge, Mass., 1965)

Tsinan. Again Chiang decided to defend it and airlifted soldiers in rather than out. It fell in September 1948, more (the US Consul felt) out of defeatism on the part of its disillusioned and primarily southern garrison than from any military necessity. At this point Chiang did pull back troops to cover the crucial cities of Nanking and Shanghai. But, instead of defending the line of the Yangtze, he sought a major battle a little further north. The CCP accepted the challenge. Both sides had about 600,000 men; the KMT also enjoyed air support, and had a distinct edge in tanks (though this was blunted by mud and by communist energy in digging ditches). In the event KMT armies allowed themselves to be cut off and encircled individually; between November 1948 and January 1949 most were annihilated, taken prisoner, or induced to change sides.

COMMUNIST VICTORY 1949

After the battle of Huai-Hai the KMT position crumbled rapidly. On 21 January 1949 Chiang went through the motions of resigning and going into retirement on Taiwan, whither he was to transfer art treasures, the Republic of China gold reserve, and military, air and naval units. In 1949 there was a general atmosphere of *sauve qui peut*. This might mean joining Chiang on Taiwan, or escaping to Hong Kong. It could as easily involve going over to the communists, who welcomed deserters provided they brought their rifles with them. On 23 January the large garrison of Peiping surrendered, accepting incorporation into the People's Liberation Army. (Several units had preceded them, and many more were to follow.)[28] Against this background Chiang's temporary successor as President sought to negotiate, in the hope of retaining China south of the Yangtze. Mao insisted on crossing the river 'come peace or come war', even though he felt that the USA might 'send troops to occupy some of the coastal cities and fight us directly'. His military plans were framed with this worst case scenario in mind,[29] but in

28. Too much should not be read into what was mostly a pragmatic response to war weariness and defeat. For the process could operate the other way: while there were no significant desertions in Korea, 14,000 out of the 20,000 Chinese prisoners-of-war refused repatriation and opted to go to Taiwan: David Rees, *A Short History of Modern Korea* (Post Erin, Isle of Man, 1988) pp.126, 135

29. J. Chen, *The Sino-Soviet Alliance and China's Entry into the Korean War* (Woodrow Wilson Center, Washington, DC, 1992, *Cold War International History Project*, Working Paper no. 1) p.2

April he was able to cross the Yangtze virtually unopposed. A month later the communists had occupied the capital Nanking, Hangchow and Shanghai. In October the new capital Canton followed, at the end of November its replacement Chungking.[30] In December 1949 the Republic of China's capital was transferred to Taiwan. Mao had already proclaimed the People's Republic in Beijing on 1 October; in 1950, after a little further mopping up, he controlled all mainland China bar the British colony of Hong Kong.

US DETACHMENT IN THE CIVIL WAR

Given the value that the USA had once placed on Chiang, it is surprising how little was done to help him in the civil war. In December 1945 Washington had agreed that, even if Chiang's obstinacy were to cause the failure of the Marshall mission, he would still have to be helped to move troops north; otherwise 'there would follow the tragic consequences of a divided China and of a probable Russian reassumption of power in Manchuria, the combined effect of this resulting in the defeat or loss of the major purpose of our war in the Pacific'.[31] In 1946 Chiang seemed strong enough to make this unlikely; indeed Marshall invoked an arms embargo to restrain him. The March 1947 Truman Doctrine of support for 'free peoples . . . resisting attempted subjugation by armed minorities or by outside pressures' might have suggested a change. Acheson was at pains to reassure Congress that it did not – unlike Greece, China's government 'is not approaching collapse. It is not threatened by defeat by the Communists'.[32] As Chiang had just occupied Yenan this was not an unreasonable position. Lin Biao's Manchurian offensive of May–June 1947 put it in doubt, and forced Washington to consider action to prevent a possible communist victory. The Chiefs of Staff argued that US 'security interests require that China be kept free from Soviet domination'

30. The only serious resistance to this advance came from local particularists and regional warlords, which suggests that the KMT should (in 1945) have bid for Manchurian sentiment by restoring its former ruler Chang Hsueh-liang, who had been driven out by the Japanese in 1931. Instead they continued to hold him under house arrest for having kidnapped Chiang in 1936 to force him into an anti-Japanese front with the communists

31. *FRUS*, 1945 vii p.768

32. Thornton, *China: The Struggle for Power* p.208; Dean Acheson, *Present at the Creation: My Years in the State Department* (1969) p.225

since otherwise all Asia was likely to follow; they hoped minor military assistance would (as in Greece) enable the KMT to recover. The State Department was sceptical, doubting Soviet ability 'to make China a going concern' even if the CCP won, and fearing the consequences of entering the war on the side of the Kuomintang; it also cited a military study in May that had placed China 'very low on the list of countries which should be given . . . assistance'.[33] The upshot was a relaxation of the arms embargo and the dispatch of General Wedemeyer on a fact-finding mission. He reported in September 1947 that the most important thing was for the KMT to put its own house in order. But he did advocate some economic assistance (tightly controlled by US advisers), the supply of military munitions and spare parts, and US retraining and rehabilitation of KMT units (though only outside combat areas).[34] His recommendations were scaled down, a mere $27 million of economic aid and a small Army Advisory Group being accorded in October. Some saw this as deplorably little and talked of blocking 'Marshall Aid' in Congress unless more was done: '[We] have got to win in Asia, too, or we will ultimately lose in Europe. I cannot . . . vote to put some $20,000,000,000 into holding the line on one front and then ignore another front vital to our future'. Even people who felt like this did not advocate commitment of US troops, however, and Congress as a whole was unenthusiastic: in late 1947 the KMT bid for $1.5 billion over four years. In February 1948 Truman proposed $570 million over fifteen months; Congress actually voted $400 million.[35]

In 1948 the administration became resigned to a KMT collapse. Truman privately regarded the KMT leaders as a bunch of incompetent crooks. Marshall was very clear that the USA should not become entangled in the war; as he subsequently put it, 'we would literally have [had] to take over the country in order to insure that the [KMT] armies functioned with efficiency . . .. At that time . . . we had one and a third divisions in the entire United States'.[36] Getting no sympathy, Chiang turned to the Republicans, whose presidential candidate, Dewey, promised massive financial and military aid. Against most expectations,

33. *FRUS*, 1947 vii pp.843–4, 849

34. He also revived his proposal of an international trusteeship over Manchuria, an obvious non-starter: *United States Relations with China*, esp. pp.767, 810–14

35. Hsü, *The Rise of China* (1990 edn) p.634; (1975 edn) p.762

36. John L. Gaddis, *The Long Peace: Inquiries into the History of the Cold War* (New York, 1987) p.78. For Marshall's expression of similar sentiments in October 1948, see *United States Relations with China* p.281

Truman was re-elected; his administration's subsequent policy towards China was to prove ambiguous and perhaps inconsistent.

One reason for the relaxed official attitude towards communist victory there had been a belief that China did not greatly matter. The Joint Chiefs of Staff had worried more about it than had the State Department, but in 1947 they had placed it thirteenth in a list of countries whose defence was important to the USA. In 1948 a State-War-Navy-Air Force committee dropped it to seventeenth; in 1949 it was held that, for logistic reasons, China would be of little immediate military use to the USSR, while 'our position is not directly jeopardized by the loss of China so long as the security of the islands [of the West Pacific, notably Okinawa and the Philippines] continues to be maintained'.

US COMMITMENT TO TAIWAN 1949–51

Even as this last was being written in November 1949, the USA was moving to support the French war effort in Indo-China to prevent 'another Communist triumph in Asia, following on the heels of China', which would itself have knock-on effects. The CCP's victory had, therefore, helped spread 'containment' to South-East Asia. Moreover common sense suggested that the USA's ability to project power from the West Pacific island chain would be much reduced if the CCP took over Taiwan and let the Soviets establish bases there. To forestall such a contingency Truman approved, in February 1949, the idea of detaching Taiwan from China by secretly promoting a movement for autonomy. This might well have been popular locally: Taiwan had been a not unhappy Japanese colony, and the harshness of KMT rule had generated a minor rebellion in 1947. By May 1949 it was clear that the island was 'packed with troops' loyal to Chiang Kai-shek; so the US administration determined that it had no option but to let events take their course, except in the event of war with the USSR (in which case the military had plans to intervene). The USA stood aside when the CCP overran China's other large offshore island, Hainan, in April 1950; in June Truman's publicly stated policy of not intervening, directly or indirectly, to protect Taiwan still stood. However, it was being increasingly questioned, both by the military and within the State Department. Once the Korean War had broken out, Truman was read a powerful memorandum from General MacArthur arguing that 'unless the United States' political-military strategic position in the Far East is to be abandoned, . . . the time must come . . . when a line must be drawn beyond which Communist government will be stopped'. Perhaps as a temporary measure, Truman authorised the 'interposition' of the Seventh Fleet between Taiwan and the mainland. He still said he would not give the nationalists a nickel, but in August 1950 he approved the establishment of military contacts with, and $14 million defence aid for, Taiwan. As the Korean War dragged on, Taiwan came to look increasingly attractive and to receive both economic aid ($98 million in the year from June 1950) and in 1951 a permanent military mission. The USA had become committed to the survival, on Taiwan, of the KMT's Republic of China. From Beijing's perspective, it had now intervened to prolong the civil war.[37]

US POLICY TOWARDS THE PEOPLE'S REPUBLIC FROM 1949

In 1949, however, the USA's Chinese policy had been, as Acheson put it, one of 'waiting till the dust settled'. It is sometimes claimed that in mid-1949 a chance was missed of rapprochement with the victorious communists. In fact the latter feared 'military intervention in China's affairs, just as . . . imperialist countries did to the Soviets after the Russian Bolshevik revolution'. Since September 1948 Mao had been looking to visit Stalin; from May 1949 the ground was being prepared, with increasing cordiality, for such a visit.[38] The US ambassador in Nangking did hold a number of informal conversations with a protégé of Zhou Enlai's, but (despite some tantalising rumours) they led nowhere.[39] In September 1949

37. Gaddis, *The Long Peace* chap. 4; Hsü, *The Rise of China* pp.746–7

38. Chen, *The Sino-Soviet Alliance and China's Entry into the Korean War* pp.2–3, 6ff

39. On 31 May Ambassador Stuart received a message, supposedly from Zhou, to the effect that the CCP was divided between a pro-Moscow faction under Liu Shao-chi and a moderate one under Zhou, with Mao still to make up his mind. The message also recalled past friendly contacts and hinted at China's need for economic aid. Truman authorised a friendly, though non-committal, reply. Zhou's office refused to receive it. Hints were then dropped that Mao and Zhou would meet Stuart were he to visit Beijing; but the effect was spoilt by Mao's near-simultaneous declaration that China belonged firmly 'to the side of the anti-imperialist front headed by the Soviet Union'. The State Department felt that a Beijing visit would come uncomfortably close to recognition; in July the tone of conversations with Stuart hardened

Acheson explained to Bevin that the USA should eschew not only 'outright hostility' to China, but also 'conciliatory gestures' – partly as they would be unpopular, but also because they would confirm the Marxist image of a 'desperate' US 'need for markets'. The CCP should be left to learn 'the hard way' that China 'will lose much more than it will gain' by its association with the USSR. The British did not find this altogether convincing, and formally recognised the People's Republic in January 1950 – almost inevitably, given their position in Hong Kong. This did them so little good in terms of day-to-day frictions with the new regime as to furnish Acheson with further arguments for caution, for 'the nations that have recognized to date appear to be in little if any better position than those who have not'.[40]

The reality of KMT collapse did not fully come home to US public opinion until 1949; after all Chiang still governed the majority of the country as late as that January. The 'loss' of China then prompted a search for scapegoats. In a Cold War atmosphere treachery seemed a plausible explanation, despite the publication in August 1949 of a lengthy account of *United States Relations with China* since 1944 that, Acheson claimed, showed that 'nothing this country did or could have done within the reasonable limits of its capabilities could have changed that result'.[41] The State Department, Acheson and Truman became the target of McCarthyite paranoia. A 'China lobby' sprang up (through conviction, opportunism and KMT money); it enjoyed easy access to the press, and Chinese harassment of US consular officials and extrusion of missionaries and businessmen provided it with plentiful ammunition.[42] All this was an obstacle to recognition of the CCP as the government of China. But it was, initially, probably not the chief determinant of policy.

Although Acheson expected that the CCP would begin by going out of its way to cooperate with the USSR, the hope was that this would not last. Truman foretold 'that the Russians will turn out to be the "foreign devils" in China and that the situation will establish

40. Edwin W. Martin, *Divided Counsel: The Anglo-American Response to Communist Victory in China* (Lexington, Ky, 1986) esp. chaps 7, 9 and pp.67–8, 138. Canada too was reportedly put off by the treatment accorded to Britain and India

41. *United States Relations with China* p.xvi

42. An apparently well-informed Chinese dissident later claimed that 'the People's Republic had been blinded by pro-Soviet ideology. We should have normalized relations with the United States right away. It could have been done despite the American Government's resistance had we only thought things out properly and made certain concessions': Martin, *Divided Counsel* p.249

a Chinese government that we can recognize and support'. Acheson explained privately in April 1950 that one of his chief objectives was 'to drive a wedge between Peiping and Moscow'. This became harder to work for after the start of fighting in Korea. For the war, as the British ambassador noted, generated a wave of feeling that led Americans 'to want to bash anything that can be labelled Red' and made it 'easier to talk of "No more Munichs with China" . . . than it is to see the varying shades of Red in the [communist] areas of the world'. In December 1950, after the Chinese intervention, Attlee warned against forcing Beijing into Moscow's arms as there was still 'a chance of Titoism';[43] Acheson agreed in principle, but added that 'The question was not whether this was a correct analysis but whether it was possible to act upon it'. 'Perhaps in ten or fifteen years we might see a change in the Chinese attitude but we do not have that time available . . . If in taking a chance on the long future of China we affect the security of the United States at once, this is a bad bargain'. Truman agreed; the Chinese would remain a Soviet satellite 'as long as the present Peiping regime is in power . . . The Chinese people do, of course, have national feelings. The Russians cannot dominate them for ever, but that is a long-range view and does not help us just now'.[44]

This appeared to close the door. During the December 1950–January 1951 crisis of the Korean War, the USA adopted a hard line in public. Admittedly it so far yielded in January to British and Commonwealth pressure as to accept proposals offering China, in exchange for a cease-fire, an international conference on such questions as Taiwan and Beijing's claims to the Chinese seat on the Security Council – but only because Acheson guessed correctly that China would reject them, and that this would pave the way for the UN to condemn it as an aggressor.[45] At the very same time, however, he was secretly negotiating (through an intermediary) with someone connected with the Beijing regime who claimed that Zhou Enlai and other 'patriotic communists' knew of his undertaking. The USA warned that China's current dedication to Soviet interests risked dragging it into a war in which it would be devastated; but if, instead, it broke with Moscow and ended the war

43. Tito, while remaining a communist, had broken with Stalin in 1948

44. This and the two next paragraphs draw extensively on Gaddis, *The Long Peace* pp.161–73; see also Nancy B. Tucker, *Patterns in the Dust: Chinese–American Relations and the Recognition Controversy, 1949–50* (New York, 1983) chap. ix and p.175

45. Callum A. MacDonald, *Korea: The War before Vietnam* (Basingstoke, 1986) pp.82–6

in Korea, US recognition of, and UN membership for, Beijing would follow and Taiwan would prove 'a solvable problem'. The USA was led to hope that this might come about either through a change of stance on Mao's part or, more probably, through a coup. Had all this become known, there would no doubt have been a political explosion in the United States, but the occasion did not arise: the chief US negotiator returned disillusioned from a visit to Hong Kong in May 1951 and reported that the Beijing 'regime is thoroughly locked into collaboration with Moscow'.[46]

So, Acheson told Churchill in 1952, while there had been 'a real possibility' of a Sino-Soviet split before the Korean War, Chinese intervention 'had made this hope seem very distant and impossible of attainment at the present'. It did not, admittedly, evaporate: the succeeding Eisenhower administration shared the same goal. But it looked to achieve it by increasing the pressure on the People's Republic, and thus appeared to fan the unconditional hostility of the China lobby that portrayed Beijing as more alarming even than Moscow.[47] The Chinese, for their part, had the uncomfortable experience of living under the shadow of US nuclear weapons, which were credibly brandished against them on a number of occasions in the 1950s. Only when the USA had come to seem less dangerous, and the USSR more so, did relations change. In the 1970s they switched suddenly from deep enmity to not-so-tacit partnership.[48] Roosevelt's dream of China as a manipulable Great Power was never realised, but equally the USA turned out not to have 'lost' China for good. In the mean time, however, fear of China was to play a major role in shaping US policies elsewhere in Asia.

46. *FRUS*, 1951 vii pp.1,476–503, 1,519–20, 1,530–5, 1,542–8, 1,550–2, 1,557–62, 1,652–64, 1,667–71, 1,697–8, 1,711–12, 1,716

47. Gaddis, *The Long Peace* pp.164–87

48. For which see *The Cold War* chap. 10

CHAPTER SIX

The Indo-Chinese Wars

Many people came to see the Chinese civil war as a great American failure; but, if so, it was at least one in which the USA had refused to become directly involved. The United States' other East Asian failure – perhaps the most painful foreign policy failure in its entire history – came in Indo-China, after prolonged and extremely controversial military intervention. It will be convenient first to trace and explain this intervention, and then briefly to assess some of the reasons for, and implications of, its failure.

Although the USA had not, historically, had strong connections with the area, its participation in the Second World War had stemmed directly from the sanctions that it imposed after Japan's 1941 occupation of southern Indo-China; unable to lift them by negotiation, Japan attacked the US Fleet in Pearl Harbor and overran the Philippines and South-East Asia. After the war (as we have seen) the USA sought to mediate between the Dutch and Indonesian nationalists, eventually exerting considerable pressure for Indonesian independence. It would not so tangle with France, even though Ho Chi Minh had in 1945 received aid from (and engaged the admiration of) the OSS. But neither was Washington initially responsive to British attempts to interest it in containing communism in the area. This changed in 1949 for two reasons. One was the collapse of the KMT: 'the extension of communist authority in China', declared NSC 48/1, 'represents a grievous political defeat for us: if Southeast Asia also is swept by communism we shall have suffered a major political rout the repercussions of which will be felt throughout the world'.[1] The

1. June 1949, *Pentagon Papers* (Boston, Mass., Senator Gravel edn, 1971) i p.37; cf. also pp.361–2 for prophesies that if Indo-China went communist so would Thailand and Burma

second reason related to Japan, whose future economic health was seen as depending heavily on trade with Asia. Some people thought Japan should look primarily to South-East and South Asia; although the administration as a whole was – till late 1950 – prepared to see a revival of traditional economic links with China, everybody accepted that Japan should not become exclusively dependent on a now communist China. This brought Acheson to appreciate, and subsidise, the French role in combatting the communist Vietminh – even though he also stressed the need to foster local nationalism as the surest preventative of communism. Nor did the subsequent Republican administration differ: Dulles had worked with the Democrats over the Japanese peace treaty, had played a major role in barring Japanese contacts with China, and was convinced that South-East Asia was the only area to which Japanese trade could safely be directed.

NORTH AND SOUTH VIETNAM (1954–60)

In 1954 French will to continue fighting in Indo-China collapsed. It might conceivably have been steadied had the USA intervened massively to save Dien Bien Phu, but Eisenhower would not do so. France therefore settled (at the Geneva Conference) with China, which 'delivered' a reluctant Ho Chi Minh. The USA was unhappy, but could do little beyond itself refusing to sign the Geneva agreements. In this refusal it was joined by the French-created but theoretically independent Vietnamese government, which continued to control the country south of the 17th Parallel. This was headed by Ngo Dinh Diem, a non-communist nationalist of the kind that the USA had been looking for; despite some initial hesitations, the USA proceeded from late 1954 to back him in the hope of building a viable state that would keep communism north of the parallel. In so doing the USA and what we can now call South Vietnam were disregarding the Geneva Agreements, which prescribed the holding of elections in 1956 to reunite Vietnam. This perhaps sat ill with US advocacy of elections to reunite Germany and Korea, but it was not otherwise remarkable. Neither the USA nor South Vietnam was a party to the agreements. China (which had negotiated them) apparently favoured Vietnam's continued partition, provided that South Vietnam did not become a vehicle for US influence.[2] North

2. See *The Cold War* chap. 5

Vietnam itself broke the provision that any civilians who wished to leave for the other part of the country 'shall be permitted and helped to do so'; for the resulting exodus might, as Ho and Giap admitted, have tilted the numerical balance from North to South Vietnam.[3] Diem's refusal to contemplate elections cannot be said to have harmed his legitimacy in the short run. North Vietnam secured only token support even from the USSR and China; although in 1957 the USSR vetoed UN membership for South Vietnam alone, it proposed the simultaneous admission of both North and South (a suggestion that, in retrospect, the USA would clearly have done well to accept).[4] But the general assumption had been that the communists would have won elections in 1954.[5] Diem's refusal to hold them did much, in the 1960s and 1970s, to undercut his state's appeal in the West.

Initially both North and South Vietnam concentrated on internal consolidation. In the North, General Giap later said, 'We attacked on too large a front and, seeing enemies everywhere, resorted to terror, which became far too widespread'. Land reform was instituted to redistribute holdings and root out 'landlords' and 'rich peasants'. The number of executions involved was later magnified by southern propaganda, but more recent guesstimates are of the order of 5,000 (plus an unknown number of imprisonments). In 1956 the process, together with the regime's anti-Catholic policies, sparked a revolt, which was firmly put down. During 1956–7 there was a change of Party Secretary, some backtracking, and a pause before the country proceeded to collectivisation.[6]

Consolidation in the South was a good deal harder. Diem was at first unexpectedly successful, purchasing, coopting, and outmanoeuvring the religio-political sects in 1955, and staging a referendum that converted the state into a republic under his

3. D.A. Ross, *In the Interests of Peace: Canada and Vietnam 1954–73* (Toronto, 1984) p.111 and chaps 4, 5. In all about 150,000 Vietminh troops and dependants but only 4,300 'civilians' went north. Some 890,000 people (including 250,000 troops, officials and dependants) went south (ibid, p.104), and many more Catholics and 'rich peasants' wished to. The Church and the Americans certainly prompted flight for propaganda reasons. This has led observers to discount it as an authentic choice, but given the widespread eagerness to leave Vietnam after the final communist victory, it should probably be taken at face value

4. *Pentagon Papers*, i p.247

5. *FRUS*, 1952–4 xiii Part 2 pp.1,794, 2,191, 2,407–8

6. William S. Turley, *The Second Indo-China War* (paperback edn, 1987) p.19; E.A. Moise, 'Land Reform and Land Reform Errors in North Vietnam', *Pacific Affairs* xlix (1976) esp. p.78; *Pentagon Papers*, i p.246; Philip B. Davidson, *Vietnam at War* (Novato, Calif., 1988) pp.286–7

presidency. His initial success not only led the USA to decide definitely that he was worth supporting but also convinced the British that, contrary to their earlier expectations, South Vietnam could be salvaged.[7] Diem did attempt a land reform, but a very limited one.[8] Basically, though, he relied on the building up of his military power with US assistance, and on the rooting out of subversives. Some say that this led to more political executions in the South than in the North. Its effect was not only to reduce Communist Party membership from about 55,000 in 1954 to 5,000 in 1959, but also to alienate a wide spectrum of unattached opinion. Hanoi had originally expected the Southern regime to collapse in a welter of faction fighting. By 1959 it feared the complete elimination of communist cadres if nothing were done, but it also judged conditions propitious for armed struggle. Southerners had been pressing for this for some time; their position in Hanoi was strengthened by the rapid political rise of Le Duan, who had commanded in the South against the French.[9] In May 1959 the Politburo authorised the resumption of armed struggle; that summer saw the start of the reinfiltration south of cadres evacuated in 1954 and the creation of rudimentary facilities to supply them. Late in 1960 local colouring was provided by the creation of an ostensibly non-communist National Liberation Front for South Vietnam (NLF).[10]

LAOS 1956–75

The first major crisis, however, came not in South Vietnam but in Laos. In 1956 and 1957 Prince Souvanna Phouma, to US irritation, negotiated agreements for some (communist) Pathet Lao ministers to join his government and for the incorporation of some Pathet Lao troops into the Royal Army; the remainder were supposed to disband, but did not. By mid-1958 Souvanna Phouma was

7. Ross, *In the Interests of Peace* pp.170, 199, 213

8. Landlords were allowed to keep as much as 100 hectares; although rents were reduced, the state made possible their collection in many areas where they had lapsed during the anti-French insurgency. Implementation was also distinctly patchy

9. He came north to Politburo membership in 1957 and was by 1960 First Secretary

10. Turley, *Second Indo-China War* pp.19–20, 24, 33; *The Pentagon Papers as published by the New York Times* (paperback edn, 1971) subsequently *Pentagon Papers* (NYT), pp.76–7

disillusioned and talked of ousting the Pathet Lao ministers. But he himself encountered opposition from right-wing parties, lost his parliamentary majority, and was replaced (probably with CIA encouragement) by a strongly anti-communist premier – who in turn was ousted in December 1959 by a coup led by Phoumi Nosovan. When, from mid-1959, these rightist governments faced a Pathet Lao rebellion, the USA supported them and established a military training mission. In August 1960 a further coup by a young neutralist captain, Kong Le, reinstated Souvanna Phouma. Phoumi Nosovan took up arms, with Thai and CIA assistance. So Souvanna Phouma turned to the Pathet Lao, and by December was also receiving airlifted Soviet supplies.

This open external support for rival sides in the civil war was extremely ominous; the USA was under strong Thai and some Filipino pressure to intervene militarily to keep the communists at a safe distance. Eisenhower sought Macmillan's consent to a SEATO intervention, if necessary, but he did not himself wish one. Eisenhower told President-elect Kennedy that he should avoid *both* a Laotian coalition government containing communists *and* intervention: 'it is like playing poker with tough stakes and there is no easy solution'.[11] Kennedy was deeply suspicious of the communists; Congressmen were briefed that, 'if [it] goes Communist', Laos would probably infiltrate guerrillas into Thailand. In March 1961 Kennedy secured SEATO agreement to the defence of western Laos, and in April (after rumours of a neutralist–Pathet Lao offensive) he seriously considered intervention. Unlike Eisenhower, however, Kennedy was ready to accept Laotian neutrality: 'If in the past there has been any possible ground for misunderstanding of our support for a truly neutral Laos', he announced in March, 'there should be none now'.[12] He accordingly backed British efforts to gain Soviet cooperation in reconvening a Geneva conference on Laos; in April 1961 the UK and USSR, as co-chairmen of the 1954 conference, jointly called for a cease-fire and conference. Sporadic fighting continued, but the three Laotian factions (rightist, neutralist, and Pathet Lao) met periodically to discuss the formation of a unified government. The difficulty came over who should get which portfolios; in 1962 the USA began exerting financial pressure on the rightists to induce them to cooperate. Such support of Laotian neutralism alarmed Thailand, which had to be reassured

11. Macmillan, *Memoirs* v pp.331–3; Ambrose, *Eisenhower* pp.614–15
12. Martin E. Goldstein, *American Policy toward Laos* (Cranbury, NJ, 1973) p.236

(in early 1962) by guarantees of its security and promises that the USA would prevent a communist take-over of Laos.[13] The occasion to redeem these undertakings appeared to have come in May 1962, when the Pathet Lao routed the rightist army. The United States duly sent further troops to Thailand,[14] and token Australian, New Zealand and British forces were offered. But it was made plain that they would not support Phoumi. Thus weakened, he finally agreed to a coalition. The Pathet Lao, too, were restrained from further exploiting their – or more probably North Vietnam's – military victory. So in June 1962 a united neutralist government under Souvanna Phouma came into being, and the Geneva Conference was able to conclude with a Declaration on the Neutrality of Laos.

Inasmuch as the civil war had been prevented from escalating into major conflict between outside communist and anti-communist powers (as in Korea), this was a great success. But in Laos itself not much had changed. By late 1962 cooperation between Pathet Lao troops and Kong Le's 'neutralist' forces had broken down, and the USA began supplying the latter. In April 1963 the Pathet Lao left the government after mutual political murders, and sporadic fighting resumed. The USA now supported Souvanna Phouma's 'neutralist' government, and successfully blocked attempted 'rightist' coups in 1964 and 1965. Outside involvement steadily deepened in response to the intensification of the war in Vietnam. In June 1962 Hanoi had told Souvanna Phouma that, though happy to see him lead a united Laotian government, it insisted on continued freedom to use the trails through Laos to South Vietnam: so the 1962 Geneva provision prohibiting such use was bound to be a dead letter. By the end of the decade Hanoi had 67,000 troops in Laos to operate the trails and hold anti-communist forces away from them. This enabled the Pathet Lao to control the eastern half of the country and gradually to extend its position. From 1965 the USA, with Souvanna Phouma's permission, embarked on massive bombing in an attempt to cut the trails. It had already been drawn into air strikes to bolster the government in the north, to which end it later came to finance small numbers (6,000 in 1972) of Thai 'volunteers'. Finally the CIA came during the 1960s to recruit a private army (15,000 full time, 40,000 in all) from the minority Hmong (or Meos). This was, all too probably, partly financed by drug trading;

13. B.M. Blechman and S.S. Kaplan (eds) *Force without War: U.S. Armed Forces as a Political Instrument* (Washington, DC, 1978) p.141

14. Taking the total to 7,000, some deployed near the border opposite Vientiane; 5,000 more were on stand-by

although it at first brought great prosperity, in the end Pathet Lao counter-offensives killed or drove into exile an alarmingly high proportion of the Hmong.[15] The Laos civil war accordingly remained very much alive. It was conducted largely clandestinely, however, and attracted little international attention, partly because for both the Americans and the North Vietnamese (who provided most of the fighting power of the rival parties) it was essentially subsidiary to the struggle for South Vietnam. Once that was over, the remainder of Laos fell (as Khrushchev had forecast in 1961)[16] to the Pathet Lao 'like a ripe apple' in 1975.

SOUTH VIETNAM: KENNEDY AND DIEM

When Kennedy became President he was prepared for trouble over Laos, but he was shocked by the condition of South Vietnam: 'This is the worst yet. You know, Ike never briefed me . . . '.[17] Kennedy approached Vietnam from two angles. He took very seriously Moscow's proclaimed support for 'wars of national liberation' and strategy of overcoming capitalism by first detaching the Third World. Politically, too, as he told his adviser Walt Rostow, he could not 'take a 1954 [French-style] defeat today'. As we have seen, he was prepared to pull back from earlier US policies and accept the neutralisation of Laos. But this made firm action elsewhere all the more important, both to impress Khrushchev (who had reactivated the question of Berlin) and to reassure pro-American Asians. Vice-President Johnson, after a rapid Asian tour in May 1961, argued strongly that

> Laos has created doubt and concern about the intentions of the United States throughout Southeast Asia. No amount of success at Geneva can, of itself, erase this. The independent Asians do not wish to have their own status resolved in like manner in Geneva.

15. Goldstein, *American Policy toward Laos* p.330; John Prados, *Presidents' Secret Wars: CIA and Pentagon Covert Operations since World War II* (New York, 1986) pp.292, 296; Thomas Powers, *The Man Who Kept the Secrets: Richard Helms and the CIA* (paperback edn, 1981) pp.226, 451

16. Goldstein, *American Policy toward Laos* pp.245–6. The previous paragraphs are drawn chiefly from Goldstein, from David Hall, 'The Laotian War of 1962 and the Indo-Pakistani War of 1971' in Blechman and Kaplan, *Force without War*, and from Prados, *Presidents' Secret Wars* chap. 14

17. Arthur M. Schlesinger, *A Thousand Days: John F. Kennedy in the White House* (1965) p.291

. . . the leaders visited want – as long as they can – to remain as friends or allies of the United States . . .

Our mission arrested the decline of confidence in the United States. It did not . . . restore any confidence already lost. The leaders . . . [made] it clear that deeds must follow words – soon.

. . . If these men . . . were bankers, I would know – without bothering to ask – that there would be no further extensions on my note.

. . . Asian Communism is compromised and contained by the maintenance of free nations on the subcontinent. Without this inhibitory influence, the island outposts – Philippines, Japan, Taiwan – have no security and the vast Pacific becomes a Red Sea.

. . . Vietnam and Thailand are the immediate – and most important – trouble spots . . .

The basic decision in Southeast Asia is here. We must decide whether to help these countries . . . or throw in the towel in the area and pull back our defenses to San Francisco and 'Fortress America' concept. More important, we would say to the world in this case that we don't live up to treaties and don't stand by our friends.[18]

Johnson was perhaps particularly vehement, but Kennedy received little or no advice not to increase US involvement: even pessimistic reports suggested that, if the worst came to the worst, the USA could probably succeed by increasing its commitment, or inducing North Vietnam to back off through bombing and other pressures.[19] Perhaps the strongest advice to keep out came from de Gaulle, who urged Kennedy to take a tough line on Berlin at the Vienna summit, but to keep clear of Indo-China: 'You will find that intervention in this area will be an endless entanglement. Once a nation has been aroused, no foreign power, however strong, can impose its will upon it'; 'you will sink step by step into a bottomless military and political quagmire, however much you spend in men and money'.[20] De Gaulle was no doubt thinking of French experience in Indo-China and Algeria; but Americans were apt to regard this as irrelevant, since they were both stronger than France and free from the taint of old-fashioned imperialism. William Bundy saw the danger 'that we would wind up like the French in 1954; white men can't win this kind of fight', but nevertheless believed that early and forceful action had a 70:30 chance of success.[21] The military, who had opposed involvement in Laos, favoured sending troops to South Vietnam since they did not

18. *Pentagon Papers* (Senator Gravel edn) ii pp.57–9
19. See e.g. ibid, pp.95–7
20. De Gaulle, *Memoirs of Hope* (1971) p.256
21. *Pentagon Papers* (NYT) p.98

believe this would provoke major external intervention of the kind that had occurred in Korea.

Kennedy felt otherwise: open US troop commitments could upset the Laos cease-fire; he feared, too, that they might convert Vietnam 'into a white man's war, [which] we would lose as the French had lost a decade earlier'. Kennedy is said to have compared them to an alcoholic taking a drink: 'The effect wears off, and you have to take another'. There were also presentational problems; in contrast to Korea there had been no overt aggression: 'These Diem's own people; difficult operating area. If go beyond advisers need other nations with us. . . . Pres receiving static from Congress; they against using US troops'.[22] So in November 1961 Kennedy took a middle course, rejecting (for the time being) direct military participation, but increasing aid and providing South Vietnam with training, helicopter transport and 'combat advisers'. This was less than President Diem had asked for; perhaps for this reason, the USA did not insist on anything like the degree of control over his government that it had originally requested, and greatly watered down its demand for 'real administrative political and social reform' and a sharing 'in the decision-making process in the political, economic and military fields'.[23]

Providing Diem with enhanced resources but still leaving him essentially in control was not a success. Indeed it is remarkable how rapidly his government's position declined. In 1959, as we have seen, he seemed to have the communists on the run and to have gone far in recovering control over the countryside: in the province of Long An only 6 per cent of assessed land taxes had been collected in 1955 but 82 per cent in 1959.[24] However, when the communists resumed the offensive, things rapidly went into reverse. In Long An the Tet festival of January 1960 was marked by 26 murders and 2 kidnappings; government agents in outlying areas accordingly made themselves scarce: in one such area 90 of 117 hamlet chiefs resigned, and by the end of 1960 only 6 hamlet chiefs remained.[25] Government forces increasingly withdrew into the safer areas; the percentage of land tax collected (which may be taken as

22. ibid, pp.106, 108 (unsigned notes of 15 Nov. 1961 NSC meeting); *Pentagon Papers*, ii p.117

23. *Pentagon Papers* (Senator Gravel edn) ii pp.120, 126

24. Jeffrey Race, *War Comes to Long An* (Berkeley, Calif., 1972) p.284

25. This is not to say that the revolutionaries' losses were not higher (797 as against 175 on the government side in 1960); but a feature of the Vietnam War was that the insurgents were consistently ready to accept far higher casualties than were government forces

a proxy for other aspects of control) fell steadily to 21 per cent in 1964.[26]

Diem's 1962 recipe for stopping the rot was a 'strategic hamlets' programme modelled on British actions in Malaya. In Malaya, however, the British had had to deal only with the Chinese minority, not with the entire population; although the compulsory relocation of the rural Chinese had its harsh side, it did provide an immigrant community with the right to remain in Malaya, with land, and with amenities. Most of these inducements were not applicable to indigenous Vietnamese peasants; these were, if anything, more likely to feel indebted to the insurgents (whom it will be convenient to call Vietcong). Diem's land reforms had been very limited, while his restoration of order had enabled landlords to return to areas from which they had been driven by the Vietminh. By contrast the Vietcong reduced rent and redistributed landlords' lands, while carefully avoiding antagonising middle (and generally even rich) peasants. In any case the strategic hamlets programme was, despite warnings, pushed through far too fast – 7,200 had purportedly been built by mid-1963 – with the result not only that amenities were lacking but also that their fortifications left much to be desired. Nor, probably, were all its mistakes accidental, since the man in charge in Saigon was a secret Vietcong supporter. Even so the hamlets posed problems for the Vietcong, but they would work only if they could be defended; given the political turmoil that set in in mid-1963 this ceased to be the case.[27]

This turmoil stemmed from a collision between the Roman Catholic-dominated government and the Buddhists, who constituted the overwhelming majority of the population. In April 1963 official support was given to Roman Catholic celebrations in Hué. Then, just before Buddha's birthday in May, the government chose to enforce a generally ignored ban on the display of religious flags. Buddha's birthday was nevertheless defiantly celebrated in Hué. The army dispersed the festival crowds, killing nine people, which sparked first mass demonstrations, then a Buddhist campaign for the punishment of those responsible, freedom to celebrate and an end of arrests. In June 1963 a monk, Thich Quang Duc, alerted the press and burnt himself to death by way of protest, an action that had enormous impact on both national and American public opinion. As time went on Buddhist protest was aimed increasingly

26. Race, *War Comes to Long An* esp. pp.113–16

27. ibid, pp.132–4 and pictures; Turley, *Second Indo-China War* pp.49–50; Truong Nhu Tang, *A Vietcong Memoir* (New York, 1985) pp.46–7

at the Diem regime and sought a neutralist and nationalist state. These aspirations were quite genuine, and a similar movement was to manifest itself in the mid-1970s after the communist take-over of South Vietnam (when it was again to be given short shrift by the new authorities).[28] But Diem and his entourage saw the movement only as subversive; Diem's sister-in-law announced (plausibly enough) that it had been infiltrated by communists and ridiculed Thich's suicide as a 'barbecue'. So the gestures made, under US pressure, by the regime were neither convincing nor effective. The last straw came in August when, shortly after Diem had promised the USA to be conciliatory, his brother Nhu sent troops into the pavilions and arrested 1,400 monks. Washington's response was to cable its ambassador that

> Diem must be given the chance to rid himself of Nhu and his coterie and replace them with best military and political personalities available.
>
> If . . . Diem remains obdurate and refuses, then we must face the possibility that Diem himself cannot be preserved.[29]

Diem's position had never been completely secure – a 1960 coup had nearly unseated him – and the Kennedy administration had always had at the back of its mind the possibility of switching support elsewhere if Diem proved a failure. In August 1963, after the pagoda raids, conspirators approached the US embassy in Saigon. Ambassador Lodge responded to the Washington cable quoted above by advising his superiors that there was no chance of Diem's discarding his brother and sister-in-law and that to make the demand would only warn them of an impending coup. So he sought, and obtained, approval to let the conspiring generals go ahead.[30] In fact, on prudential grounds, they decided not to.

This led to prolonged US reappraisal, both in Saigon and in Washington, in the course of which, for the first time, the idea of disengaging from Vietnam was raised. A National Security Council meeting heard it argued that the Diem regime would get little support either from the military or the country at large and that, over the next six to twelve months, 'as the people see we are losing the war, they will gradually go to the other side and we will be obliged to leave'. So 'it would be better for us to make the decision to get out honorably'. Such thinking was firmly ruled out by

28. *Keesing's*, 27896, 28279, 28911
29. *Pentagon Papers* (Senator Gravel edn) ii pp.226–8, 235
30. *Pentagon Papers* (NYT) pp.167–73

Secretary Rusk and Vice-President Johnson. But Robert Kennedy later took up the question:

> As he understood it we were there to help the people resisting a Communist take-over. The first question was whether a Communist take-over could be successfully resisted with any government. If it could not, now was the time to get out of Vietnam entirely. . . . If . . . it could, but not with a Diem–Nhu government as it was now constituted, we owed it to the people resisting Communism to give Lodge enough sanctions to bring changes that would permit successful resistance. But the basic question of whether a Communist take-over could be successfully resisted with any government had not been answered, and he was not sure that anyone had enough information to answer it.

Attempts were made to get this information: a rapid two-man inquiry produced reports so diametrically opposed that the President asked whether their authors had visited the same country.[31] The fundamental issue was not pursued, and the USA drifted into support for further coup planning. Diem and Nhu, who had preserved some contacts with Hanoi, responded to US pressure by opening discussions on ditching the Americans and taking the National Liberation Front into a coalition government. It is unclear whether this was a serious initiative or simply an attempt to blackmail the USA (Nhu leaked the story to an American journalist).[32] In any case nothing had come of it by the time the presidential palace was attacked in early November 1963. Diem unwisely rejected Ambassador Lodge's offer of personal protection; he and Nhu were shot.

In countenancing a coup, the USA had deepened its commitment to the continued prosecution of the war. Indeed in August 1963 Lodge had been authorised to 'tell appropriate military commanders we will give them direct support in any interim period of breakdown [in] central government mechanism'.[33] In December 1963 the North Vietnamese Central Committee concluded, though from different premises, that the USA faced a choice between accepting defeat and introducing its own troops. The second course might well enable the Saigon government to develop into a neo-colonial dependency able to withstand a purely Southern revolution. So the North would have to increase its involvement and build up 'main force' units capable of annihilating their regular

31. ibid, pp.204–5; *Pentagon Papers* (Senator Gravel edn), *ii pp.243–4*

32. Stanley Karnow, *Vietnam: A History* (New York, 1983) pp.291–2; Ross, *In the Interests of Peace* pp.276, 441

33. *Pentagon Papers* (Senator Gravel edn) ii p.734

Southern army (ARVN) counterparts. Accordingly 1964 saw preparations for escalation on both sides; in April North Vietnamese units started training to move south, and their infiltration began in October.[34] Even before then Washington was convinced that Hanoi controlled the southern insurgency and could call a halt if it wished. So in 1964 a number of low-key sabotage operations were launched against the North and plans made for major bombing, which, it was felt, would require a congressional resolution of support. Against this background a warning was sent to Hanoi in June that, unless the insurgency in the South was halted, the USA 'would carry the war to the north'. The North Vietnamese Premier rejected it,[35] and President Johnson took no immediate action, perhaps for domestic political reasons.

THE 'GULF OF TONKIN' INCIDENT AND CONGRESSIONAL RESOLUTION, 1964; JOHNSON'S 1965 DECISION TO COMMIT US FORCES

The situation was transformed by a naval incident in early August 1964. A US electronic intelligence destroyer, patrolling close to North Vietnam in the aftermath of a South Vietnamese commando raid, was attacked by Northern torpedo boats but emerged unscathed. Johnson took no action beyond warning against a repetition. Two days later radar and sonar indicated another attack, and avoiding action was taken. Neither the US destroyers involved nor the aeroplanes they summoned actually saw the attackers; radio intercepts appeared to indicate North Vietnamese orders to attack the destroyers, but were problematic and could indeed have referred to the earlier incident.[36] Whether or not the episode was a false alarm, Johnson responded by bombing North Vietnamese naval bases – and by securing a near-unanimous congressional resolution that authorised the President not only to repel any further attacks on US forces but also 'to take all necessary steps, including the use of armed force, to assist any member or protocol state of the South-East Asia Collective Defense Treaty requesting assistance in defense of its freedom'.[37] This was later to be known

34. Hitherto the infiltration (about 44,000 since 1959) had been chiefly of Communist cadres of Southern origin: Turley, *Second Indochina War* pp.44, 57–61

35. Ross, *In the Interests of Peace* pp.275–6; *Pentagon Papers* (NYT) p.256

36. Karnow, *Vietnam* pp.366–76

37. *Pentagon Papers* (NYT) pp.257, 264–5

as the 'Gulf of Tonkin Resolution'. It resembled that passed during the 1954–5 Chinese Offshore Islands Crisis (which could have led to even more serious consequences) and that launching the Eisenhower Doctrine for the Middle East in 1957. Johnson subsequently treated it as *carte blanche* for US military participation in the Vietnam War; but he had obtained it in a fit of patriotic revulsion against an apparent unprovoked attack, without addressing the 'disagreeable questions' (as to the type of force that might be involved and the need to take such action anyway) that had been identified during earlier contingency planning for such a resolution.

Johnson wanted to contest the November 1964 presidential elections as the peace candidate (in contrast with the hawkish Republican, Goldwater), so he made little immediate use of the Gulf of Tonkin Resolution except to reinforce a second (and equally unavailing) warning to Hanoi. But the expectation was that sustained air attacks on North Vietnam would probably have to be launched 'early in the new year'.[38] In November–December Johnson's advisers prepared options: a limited enhancement only of measures against Hanoi, which would probably fail; immediate and severe bombing; or something between the two. Unsurprisingly Johnson favoured the third, and in January 1965 approved retaliatory bombing of North Vietnam 'immediately following the recurrence of a spectacular enemy action'. The opportunity came in February with a Vietcong attack on a US special forces camp at Pleiku; by March retaliatory raids had escalated into the continuous but controlled bombing of the North. Johnson had, however, already expressed doubts: 'I have never felt that this war will be won from the air, and it seems to me that what is much more needed . . . is a larger and stronger use of . . . military strength on the ground. . . . I myself am ready to substantially increase the number of Americans in Vietnam if it is necessary to provide this kind of fighting force against the Vietcong' (December 1964). From February to July 1965 the presidential circle debated the wisdom and nature of such a commitment. Given Johnson's inclinations, commitment was always likely. The combination of major Vietcong victories and of the sixth governmental coup since the fall of Diem probably made it inevitable. The US commander, General Westmoreland, a strong partisan of intervention, reported in June that 'The South Vietnamese armed forces cannot stand up to this

38. ibid, p.307

pressure without substantial U.S. combat support on the ground', and asked for 180,000 men; on 28 July 1965 Johnson announced his decision to meet Westmoreland's requests.[39]

JOHNSON'S STRATEGIC MISTAKES

On paper Johnson's decision had been reached after an impressive weighing of the options. From late 1964 onwards George Ball had emerged as a critic, worried about unending escalation by both sides, and doubtful whether 'an army of westerners can successfully fight orientals in an Asian jungle'. Under Ball's influence, too, a working group found that the most likely result of a US refusal to escalate 'would be a Vietnamese negotiated deal under which an eventually unified Communist Vietnam would reassert its traditional hostility to Communist China and limit its own ambitions to Laos and Cambodia'.[40] But Ball was not taken very seriously. The more usual view was Rusk's: the 'nature and integrity of the US commitment was fundamental'; 'If the Communist world finds out we will not pursue our commitments to the end, I don't know where they will stay their hand'. It was generally accepted that Vietnam was a test case for the strategy of wars of national liberation. Even Ball conceded that, if South Vietnam was allowed to collapse, there would be trouble in Thailand and South Korea. McNamara doubted the possibility of holding Thailand, and added 'Laos, Cambodia, Thailand, Burma, surely affect Malaysia. In 2–3 years communist domination would stop there, but ripple effect would be great [in] Japan, India. We would have to give up some bases. Ayub [Khan of Pakistan] would move closer to China. Greece, Turkey would move to neutralist positions'. And so on. Some concern was expressed about American staying power. As against this, Johnson privately feared that failure in Vietnam would unleash a right-wing backlash, comparable to that occasioned by the 'loss' of China in 1949, which would prove fatal to all he stood for in domestic politics.[41] The real debates, therefore, were over the extent of US intervention. The military would have liked a more rapid and intensive bombing of

39. Karnow, *Vietnam* chap. 9; *Pentagon Papers* (NYT) chaps 6, 7

40. *Pentagon Papers* (NYT) p.326; G.McT. Kahin, *Intervention: How America Became Involved in Vietnam* (New York, 1986) p.374

41. Kahin, *Intervention* pp.360–1, 374 ff; Charles De Benedetti in R.A. Divine (ed.) *Exploring the Johnson Years* (Austin, Tex., 1981) p.31

the North; Johnson preferred gradual escalation as less likely to upset US domestic opinion or to push China into intervention.[42] Westmoreland wanted US troops to play a major role in fighting the Vietcong; Maxwell Taylor (formerly Chairman of the Joint Chiefs of Staff, but now Ambassador in Saigon) wanted to use them only to hold enclaves, releasing ARVN forces to fight the Vietcong but not relieving them of the principal responsibility for the conduct of the war. After some wavering, Johnson decided for Westmoreland.

It can be argued not only that the decision to escalate was mistaken,[43] but also that the wrong strategy was adopted. More bombs were supposedly dropped on North Vietnam than on Germany in the Second World War, and the spectacle placed the USA in a very bad light. Damage was naturally considerable: 85 per cent of fixed electricity generating plant was destroyed, most industries flattened; cities were partially evacuated, troops tied up in restoring communications and manning air defences, and civilian casualties considerable.[44] However, no attempt was made to bomb the North 'back into the stone age'. Johnson chose targets (personally at first) with considerable restraint so as not to provoke Chinese intervention – to avoid which he quietly promised in 1965 not to destroy the vital Red River dams or attack the Chinese border. Even so there might have been scope for mining the North Vietnamese ports, as Nixon did in 1972.[45] In the absence of such actions, and given that it was safeguarded by China from direct invasion,[46] Hanoi was under no overwhelming pressure to discontinue its southern interventions. Nor did the USA do all it could to prevent supplies and troops coming down from the North. The Ho Chi Minh Trail in Laos was bombed repeatedly, but no major attempt was made to cut it on the ground until 1971, perhaps for fear of repercussions within Laos (which was in 1965 again in

42. On the other hand gradual escalation increased US losses by allowing time for the installation of anti-aircraft missiles

43. As Rusk conceded, 'the harder we tried and then failed, the worse our situation would be' (Nov. 1964)

44. How great nobody knows; the USA put them in 1969 at 52,000 (Turley, *Second Indo-China War* p. 202), Karnow at 100,000 (*Vietnam* p. 458). That Vietnam has not claimed higher totals is confirmation that (unlike the Second World War Allies) the USA was not practising obliteration bombing

45. A 1965 study noted that 65 per cent of North Vietnam's imports came through Haiphong, but felt they could be trucked in from China: Kahin, *Intervention* pp. 337–8. This might not have been easy; also China was later to bar the transit of Soviet supplies, so they had to come by sea

46. T.M. Gottlieb, *Chinese Foreign Policy Factionalism and the Origins of the Strategic Triangle* (Rand, Santa Monica, Calif., 1977) pp.5–6, 8n

the international limelight). The USA also acquiesced in the dispatch of supplies via Cambodia, and allowed the Vietcong to use Cambodian territory as a sanctuary. Finally, within Vietnam itself the Americans tended to put too much emphasis on conventional search and destroy operations directed against major enemy units. There were, of course, reasons; the Americans had a clear conventional superiority and, if they could drive major Vietcong forces to the periphery of the country, the South Vietnamese (who should have had more local knowledge) could then take care of the remainder. But the side-effects, especially in 'free fire zones', were massive destruction and (despite efforts to avoid them) substantial civilian casualties. Also the hunted Vietcong often made themselves scarce (or hid in the tunnels they excavated with remarkable industry), only to return when their assailants withdrew. Moreover since attention was fixed on large-scale operations, local protection, reconstruction and the winning of 'hearts and minds' generally received too low a priority.[47] It was, indeed, not until May 1967 that US civil and military pacification programmes were brought together under a single director.

US intervention nevertheless staved off collapse in 1965; by 1966 US operations were apparently inflicting heavy casualties. Stable government followed, though more slowly. In 1965 General Thieu became President and Air Vice Marshal Ky Premier. In March 1966 Ky blundered into a confrontation with Buddhists in the North that developed (probably unnecessarily) into a rebellion that was not suppressed till June. But the central government was not again challenged, which left its forces more leisure to fight the communists. In 1967 Thieu secured confirmation as President in imperfect, though not completely fraudulent, elections,[48] and thereafter progressively consolidated his power.

THE TET OFFENSIVE (JANUARY 1968)

None of this discouraged Hanoi. It had decided in 1963–4 to increase its involvement in the South and was unmoved by Soviet counsels of caution. Nor did it have any use for Chinese advice to

47. For a critique of this policy, see Race, *War Comes to Long An* chap. 5

48. In the elections 84% of the electorate voted. Thieu won 35% of the votes, doing best in outlying areas where military influence was greatest, but losing the big cities. A proponent of peace negotiations came second with 17%

fight a prolonged guerrilla war. It looked to an ultimate 'general offensive and general uprising', and apparently hoped for one in 1965. US intervention supervened, but Hanoi still decided late that year 'to win a decisive victory on the southern battlefield in a relatively short period'.[49] The military strategy was that of General Thanh, the commander in the south. After his death in mid-1967 it was somewhat scaled down in response to General Giap's caution. Attacks on isolated US outposts began in September, and proved costly. They climaxed in January 1968 with an assault on Khe Sanh that Washington took to be an attempt to repeat Dien Bien Phu; this diverted US attention and troops, but was inexplicably prolonged until April despite some 10,000 communist losses. Meanwhile in late January, during the agreed truce for the Tet festival, the communists flung 70,000–80,000 troops against 100 towns all over the country, with audacious attacks on the US embassy, the Presidential Palace, and the Saigon radio station. Surprise was complete: half the ARVN was on leave. But the attacks failed to spark any sympathetic rising; and, now that they had come out of hiding, communist forces were cut down in large numbers by superior firepower. The largest city captured was Hué; the insurgents then murdered some 3,000 people,[50] and held it for a month before being destroyed in bitter fighting. By March the USA reported 2,000 American, 4,000 ARVN and perhaps 50,000 insurgent deaths in the Tet fighting.[51] But the effort was continued with renewed attacks on cities in May and August 1968, both (lacking surprise) repulsed fairly easily.

In military terms the Tet offensive was a disaster; as one of its planners later wrote, 'we suffered heavy losses of manpower and material, especially of cadres . . ., which caused a distinct decline in our strength. Subsequently, we not only were unable to preserve all the gains we had made but also had to endure myriad difficulties in 1969–70'.[52] Major communist attacks accordingly declined sharply until 1972. As a disproportionate number of the Tet

49. W.R. Smyser, *The Independent Vietnamese: Vietnamese Communism between Russia and China, 1956–1969* (Athens, Ohio, 1980) pp.73–94; Turley, *Second Indo-China War* p.101; D. Pike in P. Braestrup (ed.) *Vietnam as History* (Washington, DC, 1984) p.71; Karnow, *Vietnam* p. 453

50. 2,800 bodies were later found and 200 civilians went missing. The communists had certainly eliminated 'reactionary elements' (as they had done in the countryside at the start of the war); but government counter-terror and crossfire during fighting accounted for other victims: Karnow, *Vietnam* pp.532, 530–1; Turley, *Second Indo-China War* pp.109, 118

51. Karnow, *Vietnam* p.534

52. Turley, *Second Indo-China War* p.116

casualties had been Southerners (since Giap sought to husband his Northern regulars), growing numbers of Northerners had to be sent to take their places. These were less familiar with the territory. Countermeasures, too, were now more effective in that, since 1967, Vietcong cadres were being deliberately sought out for arrest or elimination by counter-intelligence. This CIA-sponsored Operation Phoenix was morally dubious; like much else in the South it was also corrupt, with 70 per cent of those arrested supposedly able to buy back their freedom. But subsequent Vietcong testimony suggests that it was still distinctly damaging, though the claim that it accounted for 60,000 authentic agents cannot be tested.[53] After Tet, too, more emphasis was placed on 'rural construction', while in 1970 Thieu recognised the land redistribution effected by the Vietcong and embarked on a further programme that halved tenancy in the populous Mekong delta.[54] All this helped the extension of government power: US statistics, indeed, suggest that, while less than half the population lived in 'secure' areas in 1965, over three-quarters did in 1971[55] (though such figures, necessarily imprecise, were also inflated by the tendency of people to flee from war zones to the safety of cities).

There would, then, have been a case for *increasing* the US war effort after the Tet offensive. Instead Tet broke the American will to fight. This had been eroding for some time: even in 1965 Johnson had worried about the question, 'Are we starting something that in two or three years we simply can't finish?'[56] By 1967 there were signs of weakening within the administration: McNamara, in particular, was disillusioned with the bombing of the North, and so was eased out of office in February 1968. Tet contradicted the official optimism about the course of the war, and public confidence in Johnson fell sharply. It also raised the question of dispatching more troops. Johnson had already shown reluctance in early 1967: Westmoreland had requested an additional 200,000 men but received only 45,000. In February 1968 the military sought another 200,000 (half for Vietnam, half to fill the gaps that Vietnam had created in US strength elsewhere), but told Johnson it would mean mobilising the reserves. This was something that Johnson had

53. Karnow, *Vietnam* pp.601–2

54. Turley, *Second Indo-China War* pp.135–6. It is not clear how far these reforms benefited Thieu's government, but they left a landowning peasantry that resisted later communist exactions and attempts at collectivisation: Nguyen Van Cahn, *Vietnam under Communism 1975–82* (Stanford, Calif., 1983) pp.30–3, 38, 139

55. Braestrup, *Vietnam as History* pp. 42–3 and Appendices

56. Kahin, *Intervention* p.383

always been reluctant to contemplate, so he asked the new Defense Secretary Clark Clifford to conduct a study: 'Give me the lesser of the evils'. Clifford recommended cautious de-escalation. It became clear, too, that even congressional hawks opposed significant troop increases. Then on 12 March 1968 Johnson almost lost the New Hampshire primary to the previously insignificant peace campaigner, Senator Eugene McCarthy. This really proved little,[57] but it encouraged Bobby Kennedy to enter the presidential lists as an opponent of the war, and it convinced Johnson that he needed 'a peace proposal'. The last straw came in late March, when the group of elder statesmen whom Johnson periodically consulted on foreign affairs reversed their previous stance and advised disengagement.[58] On 31 March Johnson finally decided to send only 13,500 more troops to Vietnam. He also announced his intention not to seek re-election, discontinued the bombing of most (later all) of North Vietnam,[59] and proffered unconditional peace negotiations, which, to his surprise, Hanoi promptly accepted.[60] Talks began in Paris in May 1968. Although they made absolutely no progress, the US administration was to come under increasing pressure from an anti-war movement convinced that just one more concession would get them off the ground.

NIXON'S PLANS TO END THE WAR 1968–9

The three main US presidential candidates in 1968 all held out hopes of ending involvement in Vietnam. Humphrey had to be careful not to upset Johnson, but he eventually declared for 'de-Americanisation', and promised a complete halt to the bombing of the North 'as an acceptable risk for peace' that 'could lead to success in negotiations'. Wallace would end the war by really

57. Only 50,000 votes were cast; many of McCarthy's supporters seem to have wanted to end the war by intensifying, not abandoning, the bombing

58. The State Department's Philip Habib briefed them, and later Johnson himself, that South Vietnam was in such a state that real progress might take five to ten years

59. Bombing of the southern areas directly supporting infiltration was halted in October, largely to help Humphrey's presidential candidature

60. Karnow, *Vietnam* pp.545–66; *Pentagon Papers* (NYT) pp.607–23. There had been, Johnson says, seventy earlier attempts (by all kinds of intermediaries) to arrange negotiations. But Hanoi always insisted on a prior bombing halt, which Washington had conditioned on an ending of supply and infiltration from the North that Hanoi would not accept

bombing North Vietnam till it gave up. Nixon claimed that 'New leadership will end the war and win the peace', as it had in Korea. Off-the-record he said:

> I'll tell you how Korea was ended. . . . Eisenhower let the word go out . . . To the Chinese and the North Koreans that we would not tolerate this continual ground war of attrition. And within a matter of months, they negotiated. Well, . . . that should be our position.

To aid the process Nixon also sought, once elected, to enlist the good offices of the Soviet Union. In March 1969 he told his Cabinet he expected the war to be over in a year.[61] But neither of his approaches worked.

Khrushchev had discouraged Hanoi from escalation in 1964, arguing that its forces were unprepared for modern war. On taking over, Brezhnev switched to endorsing the 'heroic liberation struggle', while Kosygin went to Hanoi in early 1965 promising the resumption of the aid Khrushchev had cut. While he was there, US bombing of the North started. The Kremlin responded by denouncing it, by instructing West European Communist parties to protest, and by increasing its aid to North Vietnam. The USSR also rushed in missiles, which were (in due course) to shoot down appreciable numbers of US bombers. But it worried about growing US involvement, which (Brezhnev told the Hungarians) might change the current favourable military situation in the South. So Kosygin seems also to have talked in Hanoi and Beijing of de-escalation and of helping the USA 'find a way out' of Vietnam. Neither capital proved responsive. Despite the 1965 US commitment of combat troops, Shelepin may again have proposed negotiations in 1966. The Russians continued to worry about the possibility of major US escalation.[62] So Kosygin jumped at the chance (which appeared to present itself when he was in London in February 1967) of arranging the discontinuance of US bombing against a secret promise by Hanoi not to send any more troops South, in return for which the USA would undertake not to introduce any further troops. The ending of the bombing of North

61. Seymour M. Hersh, *The Price of Power: Kissinger in the Nixon White House* (New York, 1983) p.52; R.M. Nixon, *The Memoirs of Richard Nixon* (paperback edn, 1979) p.390

62. A former Hungarian diplomat claims that there were fears that the USA would respond to the open crossing of the Demilitarised Zone by Northern units with amphibious landings in North Vietnam – and that Chinese military intervention might lead to the use of tactical nuclear weapons: J. Radvanyi, *Delusion and Reality* (South Bend, Ind., 1978) pp.189–90

Vietnam in 1968, and the obvious US eagerness to disengage, probably stilled many of these fears. Soviet military aid certainly continued, but switched increasingly to the kind of equipment that would enable North Vietnam to launch a major conventional offensive (as it did in 1972).[63] By contrast Egypt was to be deliberately starved in the early 1970s of the weapons it needed to attack Israel (see pp.320–1).

The Nixon administration, however, initially hoped that the USSR could be brought to coerce Hanoi. Thus in April 1969 Kissinger broached with Dobrynin the idea that (while in Moscow for strategic arms talks) Cyrus Vance might meet a North Vietnamese negotiator and reach a settlement based on mutual withdrawal of US and North Vietnamese troops. He added, on Nixon's authority, that the request was a test of US–Soviet relations, since, though they might talk about progress in other areas, a Vietnam settlement was the key to everything. Dobrynin promised that the proposals would be forwarded to Hanoi, but said that the USSR would never threaten to cut off supply to North Vietnam. No answer was ever received to this feeler. In September 1969 Dobrynin was told that continued Soviet reluctance to help end the war would soon prove very serious, a point that Nixon further underlined next month: 'If the Soviet Union found it possible to do something in Vietnam, and the Vietnam war ended, then we might do something dramatic to improve our relations. . . . But until then . . . real progress will be very difficult'.[64] Given Hanoi's dependence on the USSR (inter alia for all its petroleum), the USSR could, in theory, have brought considerable pressure to bear (at the risk of driving Hanoi into Beijing's arms).[65] The USSR sometimes dealt very abruptly with its clients,[66] but on this occasion

63. ibid, esp. pp.38–40, 151, 167, 189–90, 204; Smyser, *The Independent Vietnamese* esp. pp. 73–4,76–7, 88, 94; Douglas Pike, *Vietnam and the Soviet Union* (Boulder, Colo., 1987) esp. chap. 5 and pp.120–2, 139; Wilson, *The Labour Government 1964–70* chap. 19; Karnow, *Vietnam* pp.495–6

64. Nixon, *Memoirs* pp.391, 399–400, 405–7; Henry Kissinger, *White House Years* (subsequently, *Memoirs* i) (Boston, Mass., 1979) pp.267–8

65. China could, presumably, have provided (lower-quality) substitutes for all Soviet military aid except, perhaps, missiles. Whether it would have greatly increased its aid to Hanoi at a time when it was seeking US support against Moscow is less certain

66. In 1967–9 the USSR successfully pressed Cuba to revert to the Soviet line by holding oil deliveries constant despite the 8% per year growth in Cuban demand and by imposing other economic sanctions: Tad Szulc, *Fidel: A Critical Portrait* (paperback edn, 1987) pp.678, 681, 684, 689. There was at least talk of its having forced Castro to accept the resolution of the 1962 missile crisis by threatening to cut off his oil: J. Radvanyi, *Hungary and the Superpowers* (Stanford, Calif., 1972) pp.135–6

it did not choose to do so; and unless subjected to intense pressure, Hanoi (like Israel) would go its own way. Nor, as things transpired, did the USSR have any reason to intervene. Nixon's threats notwithstanding, US–Soviet relations later improved dramatically, with a summit conference being arranged for May 1972. In April 1972 North Vietnam staged a long-awaited offensive even larger than that of 1968, despite US warnings of its possible impact on the summit. The Soviet Union had provided the wherewithal; but equally it reacted very mildly when the USA resumed bombing and also mined North Vietnamese harbours, a step that Johnson had never dared take. Despite a certain amount of bluster neither Nixon nor Brezhnev was prepared to let the episode prevent or spoil the summit. In short US–Soviet relations could not be 'linked' to events in Indo-China.

The other arm of Nixon's strategy was to threaten North Vietnam with terrible destruction unless it negotiated a compromise. But if there was ever a time for this approach, it had passed. There had been divisions within the North Vietnamese Politburo in the early 1960s as to how far it was right to put the country at risk by open intervention in the South. Probably hardliners like Le Duan were firmly in control by 1965; but Johnson might just possibly have been able to bargain for Northern restraint by making sufficiently convincing threats of all-out air attack. In fact his bombing lost much of its impact through gradual escalation, and was so far limited that Hanoi may by 1969 have come to believe it could live with the worst that the USA could do. Be this as it may, Nixon issued threats, telling Ho Chi Minh in July that, in default of a breakthrough by November, he would have recourse 'to measures of great consequence and force'. Many similar warnings were given, and 1 November 1969 was built up as a deadline. But to no purpose; in August Ho's reply simply reiterated demands for a US withdrawal, and in mid-October (after Ho's death) Pham Van Dong broadcast encouragement for the US anti-war movement's demand that Nixon 'immediately bring all American troops home'. Nixon's threats were not entirely empty since he had commissioned plans for intensive bombing ('Duck Hook'). Rather than further stir the cauldron of internal US unrest, however, Nixon allowed his bluff to be called and confined himself to a firm speech for domestic consumption.[67]

67. Nixon, *Memoirs* pp.393–411; Hersh, *The Price of Power* pp.120–34

VIETNAMISATION

If US forces were to be cut, the South Vietnamese would have increasingly to take over the fighting (whereas since 1965 they had been regarded largely as auxiliaries to the better equipped and more effective Americans). This policy of 'Vietnamisation' began early in 1969 while Nixon still hoped to bring North Vietnam to accept mutual troop withdrawal. When these hopes evaporated, only Vietnamisation remained. At one level it was quite effective. Troop cuts enabled the USA to reduce the draft, and the call-up machinery was also reformed. This did much to quieten US campuses, but the progressive reduction of US troops (from a peak of 543,000 in April 1969 to 157,000 by the end of 1971) opened up the possibility of their soon becoming militarily insignificant. An acute dilemma presented itself in early 1972 when a communist offensive seemed on the cards; but the compulsion to continue withdrawals was so strong that Nixon decided to halve US forces by May 1972. However, if troops departed, US air power could still be used: it cost relatively few US casualties and was much less sensitive politically than a conscript army. Still, as Nixon noted in 1972, 'all the air power in the world' would not save Saigon 'if the South Vietnamese aren't able to hold on the ground': Vietnamisation also demanded the further strengthening of the ARVN. Quantitatively this was easy; equipment was poured in, and numbers rose from the 820,000 of late 1968 to 1,048,000 (half full-time) four years later. Qualitatively the picture was more mixed; Kissinger once complained that 'The South Vietnamese seem to go in cycles. They're very good for about a month and then they seem to fold up'. Some ARVN units were indeed good, and South Vietnamese forces sometimes did well; in other circumstances (especially when deployed away from their home bases) they simply collapsed. 'The real problem', Nixon noted, 'is that the enemy is willing to sacrifice in order to win, while the South Vietnamese simply aren't willing to pay that much of a price in order to avoid losing.'[68] This must be qualified: ARVN deaths in battle (admittedly defending what was supposed to be their own country) were by late 1972 more than four times as high as the 46,000 that the USA found unacceptable. But they pale before 'Vietcong' and North Vietnamese losses (see Table 1).

68. Karnow, *Vietnam* pp.642–3; Nixon, *Memoirs* p.595; Braestrup, *Vietnam as History* (chronological table)

Table 1 Deaths in the Vietnam War[69]

	US	*South Korea, Australia New Zealand, Thailand*	*ARVN (to late 1974)*	*South Vietnamese civilians*	*Communist troops*	*North Vietnamese civilians*
Killed in action	45,900					
Missing (presumed dead)	2,500					
Non-combat deaths	10,300					
	58,700	5,200	220,400	250–430,000	951,000	perhaps 55,000

69. *Sources*: Turley, *Second Indo-China War* pp.201–3; Karnow, *Vietnam* p.653.
The figures for 'communist troops' (Vietcong and North Vietnamese) are US estimates (perhaps high) for the period 1965–74; those for 'North Vietnamese civilians' derive from US estimates of the cost of the 1965–8 bombing (52,000), North Vietnamese figures for those killed in Hanoi and Haiphong by the 1972 'Christmas bombing' (1,623), and some allowance for other bombing casualties. Braestrup gives slightly higher ARVN figures (223,748 to the end of 1973)

THE LON NOL COUP IN CAMBODIA 1970

A disastrous side-effect of Vietnamisation was the impact that it gave to the extension of the war in Cambodia. This had after 1954 been successfully governed by its former King, Prince Sihanouk, whose chief ambition had been to keep the country out of trouble. In the 1960s this involved leaning verbally towards China, which he judged the predominant power in the region, condemning US intervention, not contesting Vietcong use of thinly populated eastern border areas, and, from 1966, allowing shipment of Vietcong supplies through Cambodian ports. By December 1967 Sihanouk was having his doubts (the China of the 'Cultural Revolution' looked less impressive); so he suggested US 'hot pursuit' raids 'in uninhabited areas', which 'would be liberating us from the Vietcong'.[70] Johnson would not undertake them, but in early 1969 Nixon started bombing in border areas, seeking both to destroy or dislodge the Vietcong headquarters (COSVN) and to 'signal' his determination to Hanoi (which had launched a minor offensive in South Vietnam). Although Nixon told some leading Congressmen, he otherwise kept the operation secret from the US public; both Cambodia and North Vietnam also preferred to keep quiet about the bombing. North Vietnam did, however, begin to support the small communist resistance to Sihanouk, the Khmer Rouge.

As 1969 proceeded Sihanouk looked increasingly to the Americans, but others were more impatient. While Sihanouk was on holiday in France, anti-North Vietnamese demonstrations broke out; the Cambodian government seems to have encouraged a mob to sack the North Vietnamese and South Vietnamese NLF embassies on 11 March 1970; there followed indiscriminate attacks on ordinary Vietnamese. On the 13th all 'Vietcong' troops were ordered out of the country. On 18 March Sihanouk was formally deposed and a new regime constituted under General Lon Nol. Sihanouk might have prevented this had he risked dashing home when trouble first broke. Instead he followed his original plan of visiting Moscow, then Beijing – whence he immediately broadcast his intention of fighting Lon Nol. This undermined a French attempt to mount an international conference (along the lines of the Geneva Conference on Laos) to re-establish both Sihanouk and Cambodian neutrality.[71] In late April China instead arranged a

70. Karnow, *Vietnam* p.590

71. The French proposal would not have been easy to implement since both Hanoi and Saigon rejected it: ibid, p.605

meeting, under Sihanouk's chairmanship, of North Vietnam, the Southern NLF, Pathet Lao and the Khmer Rouge, which provided legitimation for the continued 'Vietcong' use of Cambodia and for both North Vietnamese and Chinese support for the Sihanouk–Khmer Rouge coalition. There has been controversy as to how far the United States was responsible for Lon Nol's coup. He had discussed ousting Sihanouk with US intelligence in 1968–9, and there seems to have been some infiltration of the Cambodian army by Khmer working for the CIA. But Lon Nol was probably acting independently in 1970, albeit in the belief that he was bound to get US support; both Nixon and Kissinger seem to have been taken by surprise.[72] Be that as it may, the effect was disastrous since it removed the constraints that had hitherto shielded Cambodia from full involvement in the Indo-Chinese struggle.

The North Vietnamese and Khmer Rouge were first off the mark, capturing or attacking several towns in April 1970 and cutting communications to the capital Phnom Penh. Official Washington was deeply divided as to whether to help Lon Nol militarily, but Nixon clearly felt that something should be done: 'They are romping in there, and the only government in Cambodia in the last twenty-five years that had the guts to take a pro-Western and pro-American stand is ready to fall'. US action, however, was geared chiefly to the needs of its existing war in South Vietnam: Cambodian developments provided a tempting opportunity to take out the Vietcong bases on the border, and in particular COSVN. So on 30 April Nixon announced joint South Vietnamese and US attacks on the 'sanctuaries', justifying them chiefly in terms of protecting US forces in Vietnam and guaranteeing 'the continued success of our withdrawal and Vietnamization programmes'. Then, to placate fears of getting bogged down in yet another Indo-Chinese war, he gave assurances that US troops would go no more than twenty-one miles into Cambodia and that they would leave by the end of June – which obviously limited the help they could give Lon Nol. South Vietnamese forces penetrated further and stayed longer; but after the acceleration of the schedule for US troop withdrawals from Vietnam, Thieu had to pull back the units that had been trying to keep open some important roads in

72. Karnow, *Vietnam* pp.603–7; Kissinger, *Memoirs* i pp. 457–70; Hersh, *The Price of Power* chap. 15; Chang, Pao-Min, *Kampuchea between China and Vietnam* (Singapore, 1985) pp.27–33

Cambodia.[73] Thereafter the only combat assistance provided to Lon Nol was from the air – at grave cost to Cambodian civilians.[74]

Although the 1970 incursion did little to save Lon Nol, it did relieve pressure on South Vietnam by capturing quite sizeable stocks of Vietcong weapons and equipment. It also inflicted appreciable casualties (Nixon was to claim 13,700 killed and captured). But it narrowly failed to intercept the bulk of COSVN personnel, who had begun to withdraw into the interior immediately after Sihanouk's deposition. So perhaps the USA's chief gain from the 1970 Cambodian developments was that they diverted enemy forces into fighting Lon Nol – 'If those [40,000] North Vietnamese weren't in Cambodia', Nixon declared, 'they'd be over killing Americans' – and prevented Vietcong supplies using Cambodian ports.[75]

THE 1971 SOUTH VIETNAMESE ATTEMPT TO CUT THE HO CHI MINH TRAIL; THE 1972 NORTH VIETNAMESE OFFENSIVE

With these supplies cut off, the Ho Chi Minh Trail down through Laos became correspondingly more important. The trail had originally been a collection of jungle paths that took six months to travel and carried a considerable risk of malaria. From mid-1964 it was constantly upgraded to take trucks (eventually finishing as paved roads, supply depots, and even an oil pipe-line).[76] The USA sought to block (or at least damage) the route by bombing, but it had not tried to cut it on the ground, since permanent blocking would have required large numbers of troops. Johnson, in any case, did not want cross-border forays. Now Nixon decided to seize the staging-point of Tchepone in February 1971 and destroy as many trail facilities as possible before withdrawing – but to do so using

73. They had, admittedly, behaved so badly as to be a very mixed blessing to Lon Nol

74. Precisely how grave has become a matter of controversy; in the Appendix to *Years of Upheaval* (1982: subsequently, *Memoirs* ii), Kissinger defends himself against charges of indiscriminate bombing. The Cambodian civil war cost about half a million lives, but we cannot reliably apportion these as between bombing, fighting and Khmer Rouge atrocities

75. *Keesing's*, 24145; Truong, *Vietcong Memoir* pp.176 ff; Hersh, *The Price of Power* p.303

76. Karnow, *Vietnam* pp.331–4, 659–60, 663

only the ARVN, since (in the aftermath of Cambodia) Congress had forbidden the use of US troops in either Cambodia or Laos. The operation was badly planned and executed, and showed the ARVN to be ill-fitted to fight offensive set-piece battles (especially in the absence of US advisers and communications experts). Tchepone was ultimately captured, but by 24 March the ARVN had pulled out in headlong and disorderly retreat. The incursion did delay the communist build-up, but its chief effect was to confirm North Vietnam's belief that it could beat the ARVN in conventional warfare.[77] The attempt was first made in June 1972, with the commitment of ten of North Vietnam's thirteen combat divisions. It almost succeeded: some cities were taken (provoking panic-stricken civilian flights), and guerrillas were able to return to 'pacified' regions when government troops withdrew to resist attacks elsewhere. The communists, too, made mistakes and encountered logistic difficulties; and they were battered by US air power, losing perhaps some 50,000 dead. Hanoi now decided that the time had come to bargain seriously.[78]

SECRET NEGOTIATIONS AND THE 1973 CEASE-FIRE AGREEMENT

The Paris peace talks that started in 1968 achieved nothing but propaganda. They were supplemented in 1969 by secret North Vietnamese meetings with Kissinger (also in Paris). Initially these fared no better. As a precondition for a cease-fire and the return of US prisoners-of-war, the North Vietnamese demanded that the USA remove President Thieu and his regime. This Washington would not accept. The United States no longer pursued its pre-1968 goal of a unilateral suspension of Northern infiltration, but it still sought mutual US–North Vietnamese withdrawal. Hanoi objected on principle, since it regarded Vietnam as a single country and rejected the equation of US and North Vietnamese troops as being both aliens in the South. It also knew that, whatever the situation had been in the mid-1960s, Saigon could now defeat the Southern insurgents if Northern forces withdrew. During 1970–1 both sides may occasionally have hinted at a softening of their positions, but, if

77. Kissinger, *Memoirs* i pp.987–1010; Turley, *Second Indo-China War* pp.141–3

78. US interdiction of its railways and mining of its ports may also have been a factor: Turley, *Second Indo-China War* pp.143–9; Karnow, *Vietnam* pp.639–47

so, this was never followed up. In late 1972, however, both wanted to settle before the November US elections, the communists probably fearing that a re-elected Nixon would be stronger and more obdurate, the Americans that the new Congress might legislate to bar even the use of air power in Indo-China. In October 1972, therefore, a deal was nearly reached on the basis of a cease-fire, the return of prisoners, an American – but *not* a North Vietnamese – troop withdrawal, and an interim arrangement in South Vietnam that (should it not lead to mutually agreed elections) would leave the government and the NLF to control whatever territory they occupied. At this point Thieu, who had not expected earlier negotiations to succeed and so had raised no objections, became seriously worried and demanded changes. This led to a stiffening of the North Vietnamese position. To break the deadlock, and demonstrate his resolution, Nixon launched the 'Christmas bombing', which was suspended when Hanoi accepted his timetable for negotiations in early January 1973. These soon proved successful; Thieu's acquiescence was secured by the promise (which the 'Christmas bombing' made appear more credible) that the USA would again punish Hanoi if it broke the agreement, plus the carrot of further aid and the threat that if Saigon proved obdurate the US would settle without it.

CONGRESS PRECLUDES US ACTION TO ENFORCE THE AGREEMENT (1973)

The cease-fire was concluded in January 1973. The chief lever that the USA had to enforce it was the possibility that it might resume bombing in the event of violations. 'We shall', Nixon declared in March, 'insist that North Vietnam comply with the agreement. And the leaders of North Vietnam should have no doubt as to the consequences if they fail to comply'. Kissinger may not always have been confident of Saigon's prospects,[79] but in March–April 1973 he certainly urged air strikes in response to what he saw as continued Northern infiltration. Nixon was hesitant; the outcome was raids in Laos (which may have promoted the implementation of the cease-fire there), but not the week's bombing of the Ho Chi Minh

79. John Erlichman claims that Kissinger said, on 23 January, 'if they're lucky they can hold out for a year and a half': *Witness to Power. The Nixon Years* (paperback edn, 1982) p.288

Trail that would have addressed the problem of infiltration. Both then and later Kissinger blamed Watergate: 'If we didn't have this damn domestic situation, a week of bombing would put this Agreement into force'. But Nixon had already been reluctant to continue in early January 1973, when he had insisted on an early settlement and noted 'that as far as our situation here is concerned, the war-weariness has reached the point that Option Two [involving continued bombing] is just too much for us to carry on'.[80] So even without Watergate he would have found bombing very difficult to renew.

Nixon's threats might still have had value as a bluff, but Congress largely undercut them. Once it had recovered US prisoners of war, it felt free to bolt the door against further military involvement. The immediate occasion was Cambodia, where no cease-fire had been arranged since Hanoi claimed that it could not control the Khmer Rouge. US air support for Lon Nol therefore continued. Amendments to delete all funds for this were attached in June to appropriations and other financial bills for the coming fiscal year. Nixon sought at first to resist. He was, however, being badly damaged by Watergate, and he eventually compromised on a measure that permitted continued bombing until 15 August, then cut off funds for all US military activity throughout Indo-China. The extension of bombing helped break a Khmer Rouge assault on Phnom Penh, but its real purpose was to buy time for discussions with China on Lon Nol's departure and the reconstitution of a neutralist coalition government under Sihanouk. Kissinger claims that Zhou Enlai's support for such an outcome evaporated when Congress halted the bombing.[81]

COMMUNIST VICTORIES 1975

In South Vietnam Thieu ignored the fig-leaf provisions of the January 1973 agreement for a tripartite National Reconciliation Council, and sought, in fairly low-key fashion, to expand the territory under his control. Saigon claimed the take-over of 1,000 hamlets by mid-1974.[82] But it suffered economically from the

80. Kissinger, *Memoirs* ii esp. pp.318–26, 1,237; Nixon, *Memoirs* p.743

81. Kissinger, *Memoirs* ii pp.343, 349–55, 358–9, 362–9; T.M. Franck and R. Weisband, *Foreign Policy by Congress* (New York, 1979) chap. 1

82. Turley, *Second Indo-China War* p.164

withdrawal of US troops and (in 1974) from the oil price rise. Nor did Congress's cut-backs of US financial assistance help. By 1974 the country was in the grip of an inflation that did much to undermine the morale of the army (and others on fixed salaries), and also led people to view the endemic official corruption with growing hostility. Meanwhile in March 1973, the Hanoi Politburo reaffirmed 'the path of revolutionary violence' in the South, but decided initially to concentrate on rebuilding its forces and only to fight where they had local superiority; so there was a relative lull in 1973–4. In October 1974, after some hesitation, Hanoi decided to try an offensive next year, though still in the belief that final success would probably not come until 1976. Communist troop strength in the South was supposedly increased (from 190,000) to 275,000 by March 1975.[83]

On paper the ARVN was the stronger force, but it was spread too thinly in an attempt to hold as much territory as possible; though still probably the better equipped, it had been trained to fight American-style with prodigal use of ammunition (in 1974 it used sixteen times as many shells as its opponents) and had difficulty in adjusting to reductions in its supply. Nor could its air force, though large, really replicate the US air strikes that had done so much to stem the 1968 and 1972 offensives. But the primary mistakes were those of command. After the relatively minor town of Banmethuot fell on 11 March 1975, Thieu ordered the evacuation of the central highlands. Commanders and some units left by air; other troops, their dependants, and panic-stricken civilians fled to the sea down an unmade road under shell-fire, and disintegrated as a fighting force. A second communist offensive in the North first broke the ARVN around Hué, then isolated and shelled Danang, which was swamped by up to 1 million refugees and in no condition to face a siege. An attempt was made to withdraw the garrison by sea, but most troops deserted or were left behind. After taking Danang on 29 March, Hanoi decided to drive on Saigon before Southern morale recovered. Only once did it meet prolonged resistance; and much of the ARVN command (like other high Southern officials) fled abroad. Saigon was taken on 29 April.[84] Phnom Penh, besieged since January, had already fallen to the Khmer Rouge. In Laos, after a symbolic Pathet Lao victory in May, rightist politicians fled and a

83. Karnow, *Vietnam* pp.659, 663–4; Chang, *Kampuchea* p.39

84. A puppet Southern government was established; then in 1976 North and South Vietnam were formally united

gradual communist political take-over was complete by December 1975.

REASONS FOR THE US FAILURE

There are many reasons for American failure. 'South Vietnam' was a bad country to back, internally so divided that Diem thought it could be ruled only by a ruthless centralisation of authority. With US aid he managed to create a state out of sectarian turmoil. But he took few pains to cultivate the peasants, the great majority of the population; it was left to the communist insurgents to effect the kind of land reform that so transformed Taiwan. Diem was not strong enough to withstand the renewal of communist rebellion, controlled and partially supplied from the North but initially undertaken mostly by Southerners; he also drifted into collision with the Buddhists. In the aftermath of his removal, the Americans came close to taking over the state. They eventually secured a fairly stable regime under President Thieu that, by the end of the decade, could probably have handled its own insurgents, but which was never a match for North Vietnam. Thieu's regime was both authoritarian and corrupt; but that is not unusual, and the communist government of a united Vietnam (after his fall) certainly shared both these characteristics and was, by its own admission, to prove economically highly incompetent.[85] Nor (whatever may have been the case in the 1950s) is it clear that the South Vietnamese would have chosen the Vietcong on a free vote. Thieu, admittedly, was careful not to put this to the test, but the NLF was never able to precipitate the 'general uprising' it called for. Most people, probably, simply wished to keep alive and out of trouble: hence the flight from the much fought-over country to the towns. But the great communist offensives precipitated not so much public enthusiasm as floods of refugees (which in 1975 helped reduce the initial planned ARVN strategic withdrawals to a shambles); this is not surprising, since there had been many in 1954 who fled (or sought to fly) communist rule in the North, and since an exodus from the country resumed by boat in 1978. It is, however, clear that South Vietnam was far less effective than either the NLF or North Vietnam in mobilising people and motivating them to risk their lives.

85. *Keesing's*, 35067 ff, 35900

Had Vietnam been a peninsula, its two halves might have been sealed off, and infiltration largely prevented, as in Korea – especially if the terrain had been open rather than jungle. But geography gave North Vietnam a considerable advantage. So did the memory of Chinese intervention in the Korean War, which China threatened to repeat were North Vietnam invaded. This threat ensured that, though North Vietnam suffered from its participation in the war, its regime was never in any danger. The USA was clearly right not to provoke Chinese intervention, but it is, with hindsight, arguable that, if the USA was going to intervene at all, other policies would have been more effective. Thus there may have been merit in Maxwell Taylor's 1965 advocacy of a lower key approach, whereby US ground forces held enclaves securely (and with relatively low casualties) but did not assume the main burden of the fighting. Alternatively it can be argued that more forceful actions might have worked better than those actually taken. Had Kennedy sent troops rather than 'combat advisers', he might have given Hanoi pause. It is *just* possible that more severe bombing of North Vietnam in 1965 could have led to negotiations. It was a mistake to leave until 1971 the attempt to cut the Ho Chi Minh Trail in Laos; and there would have been a case for earlier ground raids against Vietcong forces in the Cambodian border 'sanctuaries'. Another criticism concerns the nature of US strategy within South Vietnam: at least until 1968, too much effort was devoted to 'search-and-destroy' sweeps, not enough to the targeting of local 'Vietcong' cadres. Many of these were killed when they broke cover during the Tet offensive; subsequently resources were switched towards pacification with tangible results. Indeed the war might have gone differently had the USA *increased* its military effort after 1968.

That it did not was largely a function of its domestic politics. Although no one can be sure that the USA could have won, it clearly was not defeated in the military sense of the word, but rather outlasted. This, however, had always been a possible danger. General Marshall once doubted whether the USA could ever fight 'a seven years' war'. The Korean War (with which the US involvement in Vietnam is most directly comparable) lasted less than three years; and by November 1952 the US electorate was clearly looking to see it ended. Johnson was later to regard as a serious error his decision (taken for fear of reviving McCarthyism and of diverting attention from domestic reform) not to whip up warlike sentiment. The administration's general expectation in 1965 seems to have been that the war would take a couple of years, and it was conscious of dangers if things dragged on; McGeorge Bundy's summary of the objections to intervention included the query, 'Can we take casualties over five years?'[86] Arguably support for the USA's Vietnam involvement lasted nearly as long as that for the Korean War: it was not until mid-1967 that a majority came to see the Vietnam War as 'a mistake'. Responding to this perception, Johnson launched 'a public relations campaign to demonstrate' progress, and 'even hinted that the end was in sight'.[87] This backfired when the Tet offensive showed the Vietcong to be far stronger than it had been depicted: Dean Rusk recalls his relatives suggesting that 'if you can't tell us when this war is going to end, well then maybe we just ought to chuck it . . . The fact was that we could not, in any good faith, tell them'.[88] Later in 1968 all three presidential candidates were promising to end the war. The process took much longer than Nixon had expected; he was ready to incur severe political costs rather than simply pull out in a way he thought likely to damage the United States' international standing. But he was certainly seeking to reduce US involvement, not to maintain or increase it.

THE DOMESTIC US ANTI-WAR MOVEMENT AND ITS IMPACT

From 1967 US administrations were operating against the background of a strident anti-war movement, whose effectiveness was (from 1968–9) enhanced by much press sympathy. It was joined by many former supporters of the war – a notable example being the Defense Department official Daniel Ellsberg, who in 1971 leaked to the *New York Times* a mountainous internal study of official decision-making, the *Pentagon Papers.* The movement exposed official explanations – the phrase 'credibility gap' dates from the Johnson era – and brought out the indiscriminate destruction occasioned by US use of bombing, defoliation and fire power. It broadcast the unsavoury nature of the Saigon regime, and tended

86. Johnson had also worried about US staying power (see p.127); see also Kahin, *Intervention* esp. pp.368–9, 377, 383, 386

87. John Mueller, 'A Summary of Public Opinion and the Vietnam War' and tables in Braestrup, *Vietnam as History*; George Herring in Divine, *Exploring the Johnson Years* p.51

88. Karnow, *Vietnam* p.548

to romanticise the NLF and deny (or excuse) Hanoi's actions beyond its borders. Its arguments clearly came to sway many people inside as well as outside government.

Opposition to the war was, though, a matter not only of argument, but also of demonstrations – 'Hey, Hey, LBJ, How many kids did you kill today?' – and indeed, especially for substantial sections of educated youth, of a new mood and life-style. This had other sources besides Vietnam, notably the civil rights and black activist turmoil that had by 1967 degenerated into a 'long hot summer' of ghetto riots. The fact that it had close parallels in other countries, notably in 1968 in France and West Germany, suggests the presence of a general sociological phenomenon. As the Scranton Commission on Campus Unrest saw things in 1970:

> A great majority of our students and a majority of their elders oppose the Indo-China war. Many believe it entirely immoral. And if the war is wrong, students insist, then so are all policies and practices that support it. . . .
>
> Behind the student protest. . . . A 'new' culture is emerging. . . . Membership is often manifested by differences in dress and life style. Most . . . fear that nuclear war will make them the last generation in history. They see their elders as entrapped by materialism and competition and prisoners of outdated social forms. . . . They see the Indo-China war as an onslaught by a technological giant upon the peasant people of a small, harmless and backward nation. . . .
>
> But among the members of this new student culture there is a growing lack of tolerance, a growing insistence that their own views must govern, an impatience with the slow processes of liberal democracy. . . . A small number . . . have turned to violence; an increasing number, not terrorists themselves, would not turn even arsonists and bombers over to law enforcement officials.
>
> At the same time many Americans have reacted to this emerging culture with an intolerance of their own. . . . Distinctive dress is enough to draw insult and abuse. Increasing numbers of citizens believe that students who dissent and protest, even . . . peacefully, deserve to be treated harshly. Less and less do students and the larger community seek to understand the view-point and motivations of the other. If this trend continues . . . the very survival of the nation will be threatened.[89]

In the long run such fears proved excessive. But in 1968–9 the United States seemed in a bad way: Nixon's inaugural noted that 'We are torn by division', and in March he said of the by now endemic campus disorders 'this is the way civilizations begin to die.

89. *Keesing's*, 24311

. . . None of us has the right to suppose it cannot happen here'.[90] Accordingly one constraint on US decision-makers was their reading of the likely domestic effects of their actions. The anti-war movement was clearly not strong enough to induce them simply to pull out of Vietnam. George Herring doubts, indeed, whether it was a major factor in Johnson's crucial decision not to meet General Westmoreland's request for more troops in the wake of the 1968 Tet offensive; but he does feel that it had an important influence on Johnson's decision that March to stop bombing most of North Vietnam, offer negotiations, and not seek re-election as President.[91] Nixon devoted a great deal of attention to campus unrest. At one level this involved attempts to mobilise the so-called 'silent majority' of Americans against the protesters and to harass anti-war groups. He was also quick to amend the system of military conscription so that liability for service no longer hung over university students or men aged over nineteen. In due course this did much to calm things,[92] but before then protest reached a peak with the massive 'Moratorium' rallies – Nixon says that over a quarter of a million people came to Washington for that of 15 October 1969, and notes North Vietnam's encouraging message to them:

> with the approval and support of peace-loving people in the world, the struggle of the Vietnamese people and U.S. progressive people against U.S. aggression will certainly be crowned with total victory.
>
> May your fall offensive succeed splendidly.

And so, in a sense, it did; for Nixon had issued Hanoi with an ultimatum threatening terrible things if no negotiating progress was made by 1 November, and was thinking of acting on it by unleashing a 'savage bombardment' ('Duck Hook'). There may, perhaps, always have been an element of bluff in this. But his decision to let the deadline pass with no more than verbal abuse was influenced, he says, by the knowledge that 'after all the protests and the Moratorium, US public opinion would be seriously divided by any military escalation of the war'.[93] In May 1970 there was one more great eruption when the Ohio National Guard shot dead four

90. *Keesing's*, 23135; S.E. Ambrose, *Nixon*, ii *The Triumph of a Politician 1962–1972* (New York, 1979) p.263

91. 'The War in Vietnam' in Divine, *Exploring the Johnson Years* p.52

92. Ambrose, *Nixon* pp.264–5

93. Later he was to declare this the worst decision of his Presidency: Nixon, *Memoirs* pp.396, 398–9, 400–2, 404–5; Hersh, *The Price of Power* pp.124–30; Ambrose, *Nixon* p.306

Kent State students protesting against Nixon's incursion into Cambodia: 450 colleges went on strike, the National Guard was called to 21 campuses, and Governor Reagan closed down the whole California state university system. On the other hand New York construction workers stormed City Hall where the US flag was flying at half-mast after the Kent State shootings, beat up students and hippies, and later staged a massive demonstration in support of the President. Nixon responded to the turmoil by defending the Cambodian incursions as necessary to protect the American troops still in Vietnam but also by promising that all US forces would leave Cambodia by the end of June – which certainly reduced the military utility of their sweep.[94]

It was at this point that Congress began to take a hand. Previously it had given many indications of unhappiness, but had studiously avoided rocking the boat by impeding the financing or conduct of the war. Now it symbolically repealed the Gulf of Tonkin Resolution and voted to bar further ground operations in Cambodia; the possibility arose that it might go further. Defense Secretary Laird, in particular, had, as a former Congressman, always feared such a move, and sought to pre-empt it by phased troop withdrawals and 'Vietnamisation'. By 1972 the margin was becoming very close: that year's withdrawals were militarily risky, given the imminence of North Vietnamese offensives, but politically essential. In July the Senate narrowly passed an amendment setting a deadline for US troop withdrawals. This had no legal effect; but it was a sign of what the new Congress might do in January 1973, and it provided Nixon with a considerable incentive to conclude his peace negotiations by then.[95] This he managed to do. However the resultant withdrawal of US ground forces and return of US prisoners of war also removed the chief restraint on congressional activism – the fear of being seen to put them at risk. When US bombing continued in Cambodia (where no cease-fire took effect), Congress cut off funds. Initially Nixon managed to veto this, but only to see similar provisions attached to a string of other financial measures. He therefore accepted a compromise whereby Congress let the bombing continue until mid-August, but then cut off funds for all US military activities in Indo-China. So when Kissinger tried to pressure Dobrynin over Cambodia by reminding him that 'we will [not] forget who put us in this uncomfortable position', he

94. Ambrose, *Nixon* pp.348–59
95. Kissinger, *Memoirs* i pp.1,101, 1,166; Nixon, *Memoirs* pp.702, 718, 742–3

drew the retort, 'In that case you should go after Senator Fulbright, not us'.[96]

US PURPOSES IN FIGHTING THE VIETNAM WAR

Part of Johnson's, and still more Nixon's, problem lay in establishing what exactly the war was for. Unlike North Korea, North Vietnam had committed no clear-cut initial act of aggression, so its intentions were a matter of judgement. At first it was seen as part of 'international communism', which, having taken one country, would use that as a springboard for subverting the next (the 'domino' theory). Kennedy, though prepared to risk a neutralist coalition government in Laos, was still basically of this school, and believed it necessary to respond to Krushchev's backing of wars of national liberation. After the Cuban missile crisis, he worried less about the USSR, but more about China. Johnson continued in this frame of mind, and the 1964–5 Beijing–Jakarta axis confirmed the apparent threat to South-East Asia just when he was pondering whether to commit troops to stop South Vietnam collapsing. Nixon, however, did not believe China to be either so dangerous or so hostile; indeed he was to construct an alignment with it on the basis of mutual interest in checking Soviet power. But if North Vietnam was no longer viewed as the surrogate for an expansionist Great Power, its actions and ambitions were presumably only of fairly local scope.

Yet by the mere fact of backing South Vietnam and, until 1968, increasing its stake whenever challenged, the USA had engaged its own prestige in its client's survival. Preserving the credibility of such commitments had always been important, and it became Nixon's and Kissinger's chief concern to disengage in such a way as not to call it in question. As we shall see (see pp.217–18), the rest of South-East Asia *was* shaken by the 1975 communist take-over of Indo-China. But that did not prevent it responding to the shock by drawing more closely together within ASEAN, and continuing its general 'Western' economic and political orientation. Outside Eastern Asia it was not clear that people did link US credibility with its ability to sustain South Vietnam. In the Middle East the tests were rather its constancy in sustaining its local friends, notably Israel and the Shah of Iran; and even the Shah's fall (in January

96. Kissinger, *Memoirs* ii pp.356–9, 369–70; Nixon, *Memoirs* pp.888–9

1979) did not prove as great a blow to confidence in the USA as might have been expected. In Europe Gaullist doubts stemmed chiefly from the shift in the nuclear balance; given Soviet acquisition of an intercontinental capability, would the USA really risk its own cities to save those of its allies? These doubts stiffened Johnson's determination to act in Vietnam; however, as Ball told him, 'What they [the Europeans] are concerned about is their own security, that is, troops in Berlin have real meaning, troops in Vietnam have none'; indeed 'Western Europeans look upon us as if we got ourselves into an imprudent situation' there.[97]

CONSEQUENCES OF THE US INTERVENTION

The consequences of the US intervention in Vietnam are not easy to pin down.[98] Without it Hanoi would have taken over Saigon much earlier and with far fewer casualties. In 1954 Britain anticipated such a take-over, but hoped for the continued independence of a non-communist Laos and Cambodia (as, we now believe, did China). Hanoi's retention of troops in Laos and support for the Pathet Lao, despite the Geneva agreements, was ominous, but it is just possible that Sihanouk could have preserved the independence of Cambodia (where communists were very few) but for the Vietnam War. This Hanoi and the NLF could prosecute only by using Cambodian territory; by 1969–70 their presence had created an anti-Vietnamese backlash. Hanoi responded by encouraging the Khmer Rouge, then (after the Lon Nol coup) openly fighting for them. Without this help the Khmer Rouge might have made little progress, but after 1972 they developed a power of their own. The upshot, when they took over in 1975, was a uniquely horrible regime, dedicated to the creation of a cashless, family-less agrarian society, which had (by the time of its overthrow in late 1978) killed vast numbers of people and brought the country to the verge of starvation.[99]

97. Kahin, *Intervention* pp.375–6

98. One important intangible is drugs. Drug-taking spread among servicemen in Vietnam (something that China told the Egyptians it was deliberately trying to facilitate). Anti-war protest at home overlapped with the growing drugs culture

99. Mounds of skulls from the killing fields survive, but the scale of disaster can be calculated only demographically; one estimate is that 'over one million people – or one person in seven – died as a direct result of D[emocratic] K[ampuchea] policies and actions . . . Perhaps as many as one hundred thousand people were killed outright as enemies of the revolution' (David P. Chandler, *A History of Cambodia* (Boulder, Co., 1992 edn) p.212)

Kissinger's North Vietnamese negotiating partners told him that they were destined 'not merely to take over South Vietnam, but also to dominate the whole of Indo-China'.[100] By 1979 they had done so. To succeed thus to French ascendancy may well have been the limit of Hanoi's ambitions, but there were some grounds for fearing a further spillover: Thailand contains both minorities ethnically akin to Laos and low-key communist insurgencies that it might be tempting to support. Both the Khmer Rouge and Vietnam did help Thai (and in Vietnam's case also Malaysian) guerrillas, at least on occasion.[101] The fear of further communist expansion was by no means simply American: Thailand expressed extreme concern during the 1960–2 Laotian crisis, and (since it favoured forward defence) contributed in a number of ways to the Indo-China war. Singapore, and later Indonesia, also praised US military intervention and stressed that it was buying time for South-East Asian consolidation.[102] China was to claim, after Vietnam's 1978–9 conquest of Cambodia, that 'the spectre of "dominoes" is again present in Asia. People have anxiously asked: The Soviet–Vietnamese hegemonists have brazenly captured Kampuchea by force today; where will they strike tomorrow?' Accordingly it attacked Vietnam to teach it a 'lesson'.[103]

In the 1960s Australia and New Zealand (and also South Korea) sent token forces to South Vietnam. But Britain refused, to Johnson's intense displeasure, while France criticised him sharply and promoted schemes for the neutralisation of as much of Indo-China as possible. In general, the more time went on, and the further one was from Vietnam, the less plausible the 'domino' argument appeared and the more uncalled for US intervention. This was not new: Europe had had little use for US policy during the 1950s Chinese offshore islands crises. These had passed quickly, however; Vietnam did not. So it did much to dim the very favourable image that the USA had enjoyed in Europe in the 1940s and 1950s. 'Nowhere', Brandt writes,

100. Chang, *Kampuchea* p.34n

101. *Keesing's*, 27844, 28101, 28511, 29819, 30278; M. Leifer, *Conflict and Regional Order in South-east Asia* (International Institute for Strategic Studies (IISS) Adelphi Paper no. 162, 1980) p.5

102. W.W. Rostow, *The United States and the Regional Organization of Asia and the Pacific, 1965–1985* (Austin, Tex., 1986) p.14

103. Charles McGregor, *The Sino-Vietnamese Relationship and the Soviet Union* (IISS Adelphi Paper no. 232, 1988) p.33

> did the 'system' put itself more terribly in the wrong, in the eyes of young people, than Vietnam. Intervention in South-East Asia seemed to imply that the United States, once a refuge for the poor, oppressed and hopeless, was setting out on a road that would lead, via its own idea of a democratic world mission and concrete great power interests, to a repetition of all the original sins of imperialism.[104]

It is, too, often claimed that the war not only weakened the United States' ability to lead Europe through prestige and affection, but also so damaged its balance of payments as to leave it unable any longer to maintain and dominate the Bretton Woods international monetary system that it had been at such pains to foster. Certainly the system collapsed in 1971 when the USA ran out of gold (as is discussed on pp.492–4); but here Vietnam probably did no more than mildly accelerate a trend that had been apparent for over a decade.

In the United States itself, opposition to the war greatly encouraged the growth of a 'revisionist' historiography that depicted the USA as being at least as blameworthy as the USSR for the onset of the Cold War and subsequent confrontations. Nor was disillusion confined to historians. Leakage of information by opponents of the Vietnam War led the Nixon administration to unpleasant and illegal countermeasures. These spilt over into the Watergate scandal, which in turn led on to revelations of past CIA behaviour. All this served temporarily to depress US self-esteem and self-confidence, restoring which was to be a major goal of the Reagan presidency. As late as 1989 Bush chose to refer to Vietnam in his inaugural: 'That war cleaves us still. But' surely the 'statute of limitations has been reached . . . the final lesson of Vietnam is that no great nation can long afford to be sundered by a memory'.[105]

Like the Korean War before it, Vietnam sparked a concern never to get involved again. One expression was the 1973 War Powers Act (passed over Nixon's veto), which sought to prevent commitment of troops to a combat situation for more than 60–90 days without explicit congressional sanction. The Act is constitutionally dubious and has never been tested in practice, but Vietnam has certainly

104. Brandt himself had initially known little about Vietnam; 'I may even have preferred ignorance because enlightenment would have brought me into conflict with US policy, on which I was heavily dependent'. But he was hotly attacked by his teenage sons in 1965 for not dissociating himself from US bombing etc: Willy Brandt, *People and Politics: The Years 1960–1975* (1978) pp.200, 318, 320

105. *The Times*, 21 Jan. 1989 p.5

given rise to inhibitions. In 1977 Carter excluded intervention to stabilise Zaïre, and doubted US willingness ever again to undertake such missions.[106] However great Reagan's fear of communist penetration in Central America, he never committed 'combat advisers' to El Salvador as Kennedy had to Vietnam. On the other hand, Carter did establish a 'Rapid Deployment Force', and (after the Soviet invasion of Afghanistan in December 1979) he promised to resist any external attempt to gain control of the Persian Gulf. Reagan sent warships to the Gulf in 1987, even though Iranian attacks on them could be foreseen. In 1990 Bush committed troops to Saudi Arabia, at first to protect it from possible Iraqi invasion but soon with a view to driving Iraq out of Kuwait (though in the end he secured congressional authorisation before using them). What he would not do was risk a prolonged and possibly costly entanglement by allowing them, after their quick victory in the desert, to advance into the inhabited areas of Iraq.[107] Possible parallels with Indo-China were here very much in mind; the USA would seem to be in no mood to undertake anything beyond quick (though possibly large) in-and-out combat missions.

106. *Europa* (8 May 1977) p.iv – issued with *The Times* 3 May 1977

107. Troops did eventually go to Kurdistan to assure refugees that they could safely return; but the exercise was undertaken only as a result of British/European pressure, and was rapidly wound down

CHAPTER SEVEN

Japan

FIRST PHASE OF THE OCCUPATION 1945–7

Until its defeat in 1945 the leading power in the East Asian region had been Japan. Some of the most important decisions about its future were taken very early. It had generally been agreed that Japan should lose its colonies; at Yalta the Soviet Union was authorised (as a bribe to enter the War) to annex South Sakhalin and the Kurils; after Japan's surrender the USA formally detached from it, but did not annex, the Ryukyu and Bonin islands. The essential Japanese homeland was left intact, however, unlike that of Germany; nor was Japan split into semi-sovereign occupation zones.

Japan's defeat had been overwhelmingly the work of the United States, and the USA was determined to enjoy primacy in the subsequent reconstruction. It would not allow the USSR to occupy the northern island, Hokkaido, or China a zone in the south-west. In 1946 a British Commonwealth Occupation Force did take over nine prefectures including Hiroshima; but its operations (progressively curtailed by UK, Indian and New Zealand withdrawal in 1947–8) were of only minor importance.[1] What really mattered was SCAP (the office of the forceful Supreme Commander Allied Powers), even if MacArthur was sometimes rather more responsive to Allied suggestions than he liked to pretend. SCAP operated by issuing 'instructions' to a continuing Japanese government and bureaucracy. This had been decided on before the Japanese surrender

1. Samuel Chu, 'General S.M. Chu on the Allied Council . . .', in T.W. Burkman (ed.), *The Occupation of Japan: The International Context* (Norfolk, Va, 1984) p.33; Roger Buckley, *Occupation Diplomacy: Britain, the United States and Japan 1945–1952* (Cambridge, 1982) pp.xi, 91 ff

became effective; it was much easier than the establishment of a full-blown military government, but it afforded the Japanese some possibility of influence, at least through foot-dragging on unpopular policies like trust-busting. The other crucial decision, without which Japan would not have surrendered, was not to insist on ending the imperial system. Australia (and much US public opinion) would nevertheless have liked to try Hirohito as a war criminal, but SCAP's report that this would necessitate the increase of the occupation force to 1 million men ultimately proved decisive.[2] It was thus possible for conservative Japanese politicians (and most Japanese politicians were fairly conservative) to argue that, despite all the changes, the essential continuity of the Japanese polity (*Kokutai*) had been preserved.

SCAP was, however, like its counterpart in Germany, determined to root out the tendency to aggression that it saw as inherent in past Japanese history; some of its reforms were to be important, either per se or in terms of subsequent politics.

First, since Japanese politicians would suggest only minor changes, SCAP drafted a new Constitution and required the Diet to adopt it (under the threat of taking the issue directly to the electorate). The Constitution emphasised the Emperor's purely symbolic role as head of state, and provided that the government should be responsible to Parliament. Article 9 also declared that 'the Japanese people forever renounce war as a sovereign right of the nation and the threat or use of force as a means of settling international disputes'. To accomplish this aim, 'land, sea, and air forces, as well as other war potential, will never be maintained'.

Second, while Japanese politicians recognised the need for some land reform, SCAP considerably expanded it. Except in Hokkaido, no one might own more than about 7.5 acres of cultivated land. The government bought the rest for resale (on a thirty-year payment basis) to former tenants, who had previously rented nearly half of all arable land. Given the then rate of inflation, landlords suffered badly but tenants got their new holdings very cheap. Rural incomes therefore increased, and the countryside – driven by poverty to right radicalism in the early 1930s – became strongly conservative. Productivity per acre increased sharply – though this might have occurred anyway – but Japan was locked into small-scale farming that has, over time, come to need extensive price support and protection from more efficient producers (notably the USA).

2. Buckley, *Occupation Diplomacy* pp.62, 219

Third, American Labor had been brought into planning for the occupation of Germany and Japan, and MacArthur was directed to encourage unions. By 1947 three laws had been enacted, drawing on New Deal experience, to encourage collective bargaining and fair labour standards. Unions, previously suppressed, shot up to 6.8 million members by the end of 1948. Poverty, inflation, and the rise of unionism combined to generate industrial disputes (sometimes involving the seizure of control from management) that conservatives found alarming – especially as communists came to predominate (particularly in public sector unions) and to call a general strike for February 1947. After trying privately to dissuade them, MacArthur successfully banned the strike at the eleventh hour.

Fourth, in this initial phase, SCAP favoured decentralisation, most importantly of the police. It moved more slowly over industrial deconcentration, but in September 1946 the dissolution of the five largest *zaibatsu* (combines) was ordered; April 1947 saw a general Anti-Monopoly Law, and December a Deconcentration Law under which 325 companies were soon designated as candidates for break-up.

Finally, in a somewhat capricious selection made on the basis of past positions and political conduct, SCAP 'purged' (forced into retirement) 202,000 people and banned a further 204,000 (plus their relations) from holding future positions in the public service.[3]

CHANGING OCCUPATION POLICY 1947–9

The first phase of the Occupation was soon completed; in 1947 MacArthur suggested that it was time to sign a peace treaty to consolidate his achievements and withdraw. Such a treaty would have incorporated a twenty-five-year pact to enforce Japanese demilitarisation along the lines that the USA had suggested for Germany in 1945–6,[4] and a reparations regime: MacArthur had earmarked 505 plants for reparations in August 1946, and in November the Pauley Commission recommended very extensive dismantlement of heavy industry.[5] Japan was saved from what would have been a harsh peace partly by inter-Allied disputes as to the proper sharing out of reparations, but chiefly by Soviet and

3. *Keesing's*, 9354
4. See *The Cold War* chap. 3
5. *Keesing's*, 8560 ff

(Nationalist) Chinese insistence on preserving a veto over the peace terms.[6] Meanwhile Washington came to wonder whether an early settlement really was desirable: the military was reluctant to relinquish its bases in Japan, and Kennan worried that the country might be vulnerable to a communist take-over given the weakness of the central government (after the SCAP reforms), the degree of state ownership (pending the completion of land reform and of trust-busting), and the deplorable state of the economy.[7]

Since the Occupation continued, it was bound in some respects to change direction; trust-busting apart, MacArthur had largely completed the tasks originally set him. It is the nature of the change that has been hotly debated. MacArthur himself in 1949 declared it to be 'from the stern rigidity of a military operation to the friendly guidance of a protective force'.[8] Others have labelled it the 'reverse course' in which SCAP's New Deal elements were submerged, important reforms abandoned, and Japan wrenched from neutrality and locked into the role of an American offshore arsenal in the Cold War. Others again see Cold War motivation and reaction to the imminent 'loss' of China as less important than a simple desire to get Japan to stand, economically, on its own feet and not cost the US taxpayer quite so much. Nor is there agreement as to whether the economic cure prescribed in 1949 was successful or whether Japan was only rescued by the Korean War, that 'gift of the gods' as Prime Minister Yoshida called it.

There can be no doubt that both Japanese politics and internal occupation policy moved to the right. Of politics we need here only note that, whereas the 1947 elections had made the Socialist party the largest in the Diet and led to a period of Socialist–Democratic coalition government, those of 1949 gave Yoshida's Liberals an absolute majority – at a time when SCAP was returning increasing responsibilities to the Japanese. One of the clearest shifts of occupation policy related to trade unions. July–December 1948 saw drastic limitations on union activity in the civil service and nationalised industries. There was, too, a trimming of public sector employment under the 1949 economic austerity measures, the opportunity was taken (with SCAP's informal encouragement) to

6. In July 1947 the State Department suggested a preliminary conference of the eleven nations that supervised the Occupation – to reach decisions by a two-thirds majority. The USSR insisted that the issues be worked out instead in the Conference of Foreign Ministers; China accepted the proposed conference but demanded a veto: *Keesing's*, 8875–6

7. George F. Kennan, *Memoirs 1925–1950* (Boston, Mass., 1967) chap. 16

8. *Keesing's*, 10027

dismiss activists, a course imitated by private industry after the outbreak of the Korean War. These moves had been, in part, a response to communist militancy. They were complemented by internal attempts within the union movement from late 1947 onwards to roll back communist influence. These were, as in Europe, supported by American Labor; they reached a temporary high point in 1950, when some of the communist-leaning Japanese Congress of Labor Unions broke away to join the rival Japanese Confederation of Labor.

In economic terms the early stages of the Occupation had been extremely tough. US post-surrender policy had made it clear that

> Disarmament and demilitarization are the primary tasks of the military occupation. . . .
>
> The existing economic basis of Japanese military strength must be destroyed and not permitted to revive. . . .
>
> The policies of Japan have brought down upon the people great economic destruction and confronted them with the prospect of economic difficulty and suffering. The plight of Japan is the direct outcome of its own behavior, and the Allies will not undertake the burden of repairing the damage.[9]

The Japanese people seem to have taken things fairly stoically and blamed their former military rulers. But economic conditions were deplorable, with real per capita income in 1946 and 1947 only half the prewar level.[10] Declaratory US policy had softened only slightly by 1947, but in the second half of the year it encountered a good deal of questioning in Washington. By January 1948 the USA was telling its partners that, though many of the Allied objectives had been realised, these did not include 'the establishment of a self-supporting economy . . . without which the achievement of the occupation cannot be consolidated'. Indeed 'Economic chaos . . . has been prevented only at the expense of the American people who have financed the . . . vital [food and other imports] required to prevent widespread disease and unrest'. Accordingly 1948 was to see a steady shuttle across the Pacific of officials recommending economic rehabilitation: thus in April the Johnson Committee declared that the USA should 'now assist the recovery of Japan', urged the curtailment of reparations,[11] and endorsed a

9. 29 August 1945 – World Peace Foundation, *Documents on American Foreign Relations*, viii (July 1945–Dec. 1946) (Princeton, NJ) pp.267 ff

10. G.C. Allen, *Japan's Economic Expansion* (1965) p.280

11. As in Europe dismantled plant often proved hard to reassemble and was just left to rust. The number of plants held available for dismantlement was twice reduced in 1948, and deliveries were halted in May 1949: *Keesing's*, 10025

'recovery program' for Japan and Korea of $220 million in the ensuing year as 'essential in order to reduce and eventually eliminate spending in these areas for relief'.[12] This perspective made Americans look with more sympathy on people who had been purged: as Army Secretary Royall put it, 'the men who were the most active in building up . . . Japan's war machine . . . were often the ablest and most successful business leaders of that country, and their services would in many instances contribute to the economic recovery of Japan'. From 1949 onwards, therefore, the process went into reverse; by 1952 most of those purged had already been permitted to return to public activity, and the remainder followed shortly after independence.[13] (The subsequent return to high office of a number of people, like Shigemitsu Marmoru and Kishi Nobusuke, who had been prominent in the 1930s and 1940s suggests that the purges had less effect in Japan – outside the armed forces[14] – than did their counterparts in Germany, though they amounted to a good deal more than Soviet 'de-Stalinisation'.) Similarly trust-busting came to be perceived as harmful to industrial confidence and propensity to invest; so in 1949 it was restricted to only 19 of the 325 companies that had been targeted in 1947.

Thus far politicians like Yoshida could wholeheartedly approve. They were less happy with the US determination to squeeze out inflation (prices had gone from 16 times the prewar level in 1946 to 209 times in 1949)[15] through public sector austerity and control of the money supply. The policy (associated particularly with the 1949 Dodge Mission) did no more than slow the rate of growth, but it entailed a number of business bankruptcies and was represented as risking a full-blooded slump. Without it Japanese industry could probably not have responded to the surge in external demand generated by the Korean War. Another aspect of the policy was the restoration of international trade. This had started in 1948, but had been handicapped by a maze of different exchange rates. In 1949 these were reduced to a single all-purpose rate, set by Washington at 360 yen to the dollar, a level that proved remarkably durable; 1949 also saw the transfer to the Japanese government of most of

12. *Documents on American Foreign Relations, 1948* pp.160–2

13. J.W. Dower, *Empire and Aftermath: Yoshida Shigeru and the Japanese Experience, 1878–1954* (Cambridge, Mass., 1979) pp.332–3

14. Nobody above the rank of colonel was allowed back into the reconstituted Japanese forces

15. Allen, *Japan's Economic Expansion* p.276

the responsibility for controlling trade and the creation of the Ministry of International Trade and Industry (MITI). This was to weld a close business-government partnership (to close Japan's trade deficit) that was in due course to appear to some observers a model of intelligent anticipation of (and adaptation to) changing world trends in demand and manufacturing, to others the cornerstone of an aggressively mercantilist 'Japan Inc'.

THE 1951 PEACE AND SECURITY TREATIES

Washington was, as we have seen, deeply divided over the wisdom of an early peace treaty. In September 1949 Acheson agreed with Bevin to try for a treaty. By December he had won Truman's support for seeking one that would preserve US bases in Japan even if that meant that the USSR would not sign.[16] In the spring of 1950 the Republican John Foster Dulles was recruited to negotiate a treaty that would have enough bipartisan appeal to secure ratification by the US Senate. On the Japanese side successive governments had been preparing for a peace treaty almost since the moment of surrender. But in 1949 the general hope was for a treaty with all belligerents (including the USSR and China) that would remove US bases from Japan (though their continuance on neighbouring islands like Okinawa would be distinctly reassuring). Yoshida, however, decided that this was unrealistic: only if offered bases would the USA conclude peace, and (on these terms) the Soviet Union was unlikely to sign. So the choice lay between a separate treaty and indefinite postponement of the recovery of sovereignty. Sovereignty was Yoshida's overriding concern: in May 1950 he approached Washington with warnings of mounting Japanese impatience for the end of the occupation and with the offer of bases after independence; these could, if necessary, be provided for in an agreement separate from the main treaty.[17] Washington soon decided to proceed along these lines; the idea of a bilateral security treaty to accompany the multilateral peace treaty was finally settled with Japan in February 1951.

The other major problem was that of which China, if any, Japan should seek to make peace with: for Britain recognised the

16. T.W. Burkman (ed.) *The Occupation of Japan: The International Context* (Norfolk, Va, 1984) pp.230, 280

17. ibid, pp.199–205; Dower, *Empire and Aftermath* pp.373–6

(communist) People's Republic of China (PRC), the United States recognised the (Kuomintang) Republic of China (ROC) on Taiwan. The British position drove Dulles to some very plain speaking, but his final solution was a finesse. In May 1951 he secured private Japanese assurances that the government would prefer to deal with Taiwan,[18] then in June agreed with Britain that neither of the two Chinas should sign the peace treaty but that Japan should then conclude a parallel treaty with whichever it chose. This, as we shall see, did not dispose of the issue, but it made possible the summoning of a peace conference on the basis of a joint US–British text.

Britain was not the only country that had to be squared; this cost Dulles much peripatetic diplomacy. Even so India would not attend the peace conference since it disapproved of the exclusion of the PRC and of the likely alienation of the Soviet Union. Burma and Indonesia would not sign as their reparations claims had not been met. The United States induced the Philippines, Australia and New Zealand to go along only by concluding defence treaties that (in effect) guaranteed them against a revival of Japanese military power. It was, thus, a considerable feat to secure the assembly of forty-nine countries in September 1951 for the San Francisco Conference. Unexpectedly the USSR, Poland and Czechoslovakia were among them – but only for the purpose of reopening discussion. 'For one who had spent as long an apprenticeship as I had,' wrote Acheson, 'under Speaker Sam Rayburn of the House of Representatives and its Rules Committee, this did not present a perplexing problem.' He persuaded the conference to adopt highly restrictive rules of procedure modelled on that body, whose significance the Russians did not appreciate until too late.[19] Acheson thus foreclosed any possible filibuster and got his treaty intact – though the Russians did not sign.

The same day Japan signed a bilateral Security Treaty, desiring, 'as a provisional arrangement for its defence, that the United States of America should maintain armed forces of its own in and about Japan so as to deter armed attack on Japan'. This treaty, providing for the continuance of US bases, was (as we have seen) the prerequisite for the restoration of Japanese sovereignty. It was a distinctly unequal one: it contained no clear provisions as to either duration or renegotiation (thus giving the USA, Dulles believed,[20]

18. Burkman, *Occupation of Japan: The International Context* p.237
19. Acheson, *Present at the Creation* pp.54 ff
20. Burkman, *Occupation of Japan: The International Context* p.218

the right to station troops as long as it wished, without any obligation to do so when it did not). These troops were for 'the maintenance of international peace and security in the Far East' as well as for the specific defence of Japan. In contrast to the near-simultaneous treaties with Australia–New Zealand and with the Philippines, there was no provision for joint consultations as to their use. Finally, it was stipulated that they could render 'assistance given at the express request of the Japanese Government to put down large-scale internal riots and disturbances', which implied some continuing involvement in internal Japanese security.

REARMAMENT LIMITED BY JAPANESE RELUCTANCE

One reason for such involvement was the weakness of Japan's own security forces. The occupation had, in its early stages, not only dismantled the military but also decentralised the police – to the point where Kennan regarded the country as vulnerable (but for the US presence) to a communist take-over.[21] It had also erected significant psychological and constitutional barriers to the reconstitution of Japanese armed power. In 1949 industrial disputes (arising partly from the Dodge austerity) produced violent demonstrations and the occupation of a number of local police stations. During 1950–1 the communists adopted, at least formally, a policy of armed struggle.[22] By then the USA was coming to look for a Japanese capability to handle its own internal security and also to make some contribution to wider Western defence. In June 1950 Dulles and MacArthur discussed remilitarisation with Yoshida. Both then seemed ready to accept Yoshida's rejection of Japanese forces and to limit themselves to the reactivation of former munitions factories 'to assist in the reconstruction of American armaments'. In July, however, after the outbreak of the Korean War, SCAP inaugurated a 'National Police Reserve', ostensibly for use against domestic riots but with the clear (though unstated) intention that it should develop into a Japanese army.

There were, in this, a number of parallels with US designs for West Germany.[23] Whereas Adenauer had welcomed, if not a

21. Kennan, *Memoirs 1925–1950* pp.376, 390–2
22. M. Kosaka, *A History of Postwar Japan* (Tokyo, 1982 edn) p.99
23. For which see *The Cold War* chap. 4

national army, at least the idea of a German military contribution to Western security as the vehicle for recovering sovereignty, Yoshida always sought to delay and minimise Japanese rearmament. He wondered whether Japan could afford it economically. He feared that it would prove so unpopular as to be politically destabilising. Above all he worried that it could lead to a rerun of the 1930s.[24] The US ambassador was quite unable to persuade him that 'with civilian control the military could be the servant, not the master of Japan'. Yoshida had to yield somewhat to US pressure, and in February 1951 secretly proposed 'Initial Steps for Rearmament Planning'; but this was to involve only a navy (a fairly safe force, politically speaking) and a 50,000-man army (too small to be effective). He had to concede 75,000, still ostensibly policemen, though from later 1951 they trained with heavy weapons on US bases. At the San Francisco conference, Yoshida beat off pressure for at least 300,000 men, and would go no further than 110,000 in October 1952. One consideration was a fear that, with any more, Japan would come under pressure to join in the Korean War:

> Mr Yoshida shuddered every time he recalls how the Japanese army was bogged down in China. In that the people share his fears. Should Japan have 300,000 ground troops, a strong argument would be made that we don't need that many to defend Japan from attack and the United Nations, under your influence, would ask us to . . . [send] at least a hundred thousand to Korea.[25] Once these troops are despatched, there is no telling when they will be withdrawn.[26]

The Korean War ended in 1953. By 1954 Yoshida was prepared to contemplate a limited further expansion, including a small air force. The military nature of the undertaking was at last admitted by its redesignation as the Self-Defence Force. This has continued to expand, but very slowly – as may be seen from a comparison of

24. It may be important that the Army had then played the chief role in leading Japan into the 'dark valley'. In Germany that dishonour had fallen not to the army but to the Nazi Party. A further difference was that, whereas in the 1950s one could hope to contain West German rearmament within a collective framework like the European Defence Community, there was no such possibility in the Japanese case. Lastly, Dower maintains, Yoshida may have suspected that the military could prove a vehicle for communisation from above, the danger of which had been a major theme of the 'Konoe Memorial' he had drafted in early 1945

25. Yoshida need not have worried; Syngman Rhee refused point blank to contemplate such a return of Japanese troops

26. Dower, *Empire and Aftermath* esp. pp.377–400; Burkman, *Occupation of Japan: The International Context* esp. pp.214–15

Japanese and British defence personnel and expenditure in Table 2.[27]

Table 2 Comparison of Japanese and British defence expenditure

		Personnel (000s)	*Defence expenditure ($ million)*	*As % of GNP*
1951	Japan	74	86	0.6
	UK	841	3,217	7.8
1955	Japan	178	241	1.0
	UK	800	4,388	8.1
1960	Japan	206	421	1.1
	UK	502	4,640	6.4
1965	Japan	225	848	1.0
	UK	424	5,855	5.9
1970	Japan	259	1,640	0.8
	UK	373	5,950	4.9
1975	Japan	236	4,620	0.9
	UK	345	11,118	4.9
1980	Japan	241	8,960	0.9
	UK	329	24,448	5.1
1986	Japan	243	20,927	1.0
	UK	324	27,344	4.9

Not everybody shared Yoshida's attitudes to the army, but they do seem to have had very wide support; so in the 1970s and 1980s much political significance was attached to keeping defence expenditure below 1 per cent of GNP, despite persistent US

27. Derived from the International Institute for Strategic Studies (IISS), *The Military Balance, 1971–2* pp.62–3, *1981–2* pp.112–13, *1988–9* p.224. Britain, as an island that has (since 1960) relied like Japan on volunteer forces, provides perhaps the best comparison, but since 1965 French and West German expenditure has been broadly similar to Britain's. Japan's population is much larger (117 million in 1980, as compared to Britain's 56 million, France's 54 million and West Germany's 61 million). The yen's recent hardening has increased Japan's apparent expenditure as measured in dollars

pressure to the contrary. Notwithstanding the military build-up on the Soviet Pacific Coast, Japan, under the US nuclear umbrella, seemed to face few threats. Nor was it clear what an enlarged Japanese defence establishment would do. In 1957 the 'Basic Policy for National Defence' had been to rely on 'the Japanese–US Alliance [as] the major (if not the sole) shield against external attack'. In 1977 the goal was 'the maintenance of a full surveillance posture in peace-time and the ability to cope effectively with situations up to the point of a limited and small-scale aggression'. In 1980 Prime Minister Suzuki told the Diet that Japan could, consistently with the Constitution, protect shipping for a thousand miles out from its ports. Plans gave priority, not to the politically more alarming army, but to helping the navy and air force do this. The USA felt that it would require 'substantially greater' spending, but if both the Carter and Reagan administrations pressed for more, in 1977, 1981 and 1983 Japanese Premiers had to tour ASEAN giving assurances that Japan's intentions were purely defensive: 'it would', said Suzuki, 'be completely mistaken either to hope that Japan will play a military role in the international community, or to feel anxiety that Japan might again emerge as a military giant'. How near the surface memories still remained abroad of Japan's conquering past was to be dramatically illustrated in 1982 and 1986, when the authorisation of new Japanese school textbooks whitewashing it provoked protests from both Chinas, both Koreas, Singapore, Thailand, the Philippines, Hong Kong and the island of Okinawa.[28] Nor have things been helped by Japan's reluctance (in marked contrast to Germany) to apologise unequivocally for its past aggression. In such an environment, Japanese acquisition of a major strategic capability (for instance one sufficient to protect the Malacca Straits choke-point) would be distinctly counter-productive; there seems little disposition to undertake it. Indeed, during the 1990–1 Kuwait crisis, an anodyne proposal to send 2,000 Japanese troops to the Gulf in a non-combatant role collapsed in the face of Socialist opposition; instead Japan contributed some $9 billion to the US war effort, and even this passed only after it had been earmarked for non-combat activities.[29]

28. Y. Satoh, *The Evolution of Japanese Security Policy* (IISS Adelphi Paper no. 178, 1982) esp. pp.15–20; *Keesing's*, 30793–4, 30969–72, 32135, 32317, 34676

29. *Keesing's*, 37859–60, 38010–11, 38098, 38192

JAPAN FORCED TO RECOGNISE THE REPUBLIC OF CHINA 1952

To its Japanese critics, the San Francisco Conference had (in the light of the non-signature of India, Burma, and Indonesia) represented 'an Asian peace without Asians', while the Security Treaty bound Japan so tightly to the USA that its new status was best viewed as 'dependent independence'. This impression was reinforced by the manner in which Japan was constrained to recognise the Republic of China. Yoshida had (as we have seen) intimated to Dulles that this was his intention, but he might have behaved differently, had he really been free to choose. After his retirement he was strongly critical of US policy, arguing that China would never accept subordination to the USSR in the long run and that the United States should have exploited this inherent tension by adopting a positive policy towards the People's Republic. Even at the time he seems to have argued 'that China should be left alone. China may turn Red or Black – all the same. . . . What is an affair of China should be left to the Chinese. It will all settle down in the long run'. In August 1951 he mentioned to Dulles the possibility of a bilateral treaty with 'Communist China'. In September the US Senate (where the 'China lobby' was strong) made it clear that it would have none of this: fifty-six senators told Truman that were Japan so to recognise the PRC, they would never ratify the San Francisco peace treaty.[30] In October Yoshida was equivocating, telling one house of the Japanese Diet that Japan sought relations with Taiwan, the other that it would consider establishing an Overseas Agency in Shanghai.

The US Senate did not like this: so in December 1951 Dulles descended on Tokyo, flanked by the ranking Republican and Democrat members of its Far Eastern subcommittee, and read Yoshida (and the head of the British mission) a memorandum to the effect that the Senate 'will insistently want to know whether Jap. Govt. intends pursue foreign policies in Asia which are generally compatible with those of United States'; having made this point Dulles suggested that Japan negotiate a treaty with the Republic of China, but only 'on basis of its de facto actual control', thus leaving 'for future development the relations between Japan and any area of Chi. not under actual control of Natl. Govt.' In response Yoshida expressed concern about the British attitude – for Japan was 'in

30. Dower, *Empire and Aftermath* pp. 394–5, 403–5

almost impossible position when confronted by major difference between the two leading nations of free world' – and went on to beg for more latitude:

> The China problem cannot be solved by military force. The free nations should enlarge their contacts with China and give opportunities for the people under Communist control to expose themselves to the liberal atmosphere of the free nations. Because of its racial and cultural affinity with China, Japan may serve this purpose better than the United States and Britain. Please place your trust in Japan and let it lead the free nations in enlarging contacts with China.

Japan might thus 'be able to play important role in weaning China from domination by Sov. politburo'.[31] Dulles would have none of this. After a little further stalling, Yoshida accepted (with only minor amendments) a letter that Dulles drafted for him to the effect that Japan would not sign a treaty with the PRC, but would seek one with the ROC 'applicable to all territories which are now, or may hereafter be' under its control. Dulles released this letter, to considerable effect, just before the 1952 Senate hearings on the San Francisco treaties. Although Taiwan was unhappy that Japan would negotiate with it only in respect of territories under its control, a Japan–ROC treaty came into force that summer. Yoshida spoke of it as only a 'first step' towards 'an overall treaty' 'to establish a total good neighbour relationship with China in the future'.[32] For the time being, however, it closed the door on official relations with the PRC.

That Japan's China decisions were thus made for it was important psychologically. Some scholars believe that it was also crucial economically. Before 1941 Manchuria, China, Taiwan, Korea and Sakhalin had supplied 35 per cent of Japan's raw materials and absorbed 40 per cent of its exports.[33] Once the USA had begun to feel concerned about the state of the Japanese economy, Americans started worrying about the implications of this trade pattern: if it were resumed, would it enable 'international communism' to exert political leverage on Japan; if not, could anything else be put in its

31. Burkman, *Occupation of Japan: The International Context* pp.242–4; *FRUS*, 1951 vi pp.1,437–8; Chihiro Hosoya, 'Japan, China, the United States and the United Kingdom, 1951–2: The Case of the "Yoshida Letter" ', *International Affairs* ix (1984) p.249

32. Dower, *Empire and Aftermath* pp.407–10. The British were furious (though perhaps as a result of a misunderstanding) at Dulles's publication of the Yoshida letter, and the episode left bad blood between Eden and Dulles

33. Burkman, *Occupation of Japan: The International Context* p.168

place, or would permanent US subventions be required to prevent Japanese economic and political collapse? From 1947 onwards many geopolitical solutions were propounded. These often suggested the diversion of Japanese trade to South-East Asia, and go far towards explaining the new American focus on that area in and after 1949. Until the Korean War, however, their implications for Japan remained limited. Japan still wanted to trade with China: late in 1949 its Trade Minister anticipated that China would eventually account for one-third of all Japanese trade, and the USA was prepared to allow this. Truman had authorised SCAP to encourage Sino-Japanese trade, provided 'preponderant dependence' on China was avoided and efforts made to develop alternative raw material sources in southern Asia. Similarly in 1950 Dulles felt that to break the 'natural and historic' Sino-Japanese interdependence would antagonise Japan, whereas under conditions of 'normal' trade the USA's subsidy to Japan could fall from $270 million to $25 million. The Korean War changed this, as so much else. Following China's intervention, the USA cut off its own trade in December 1950 and took steps to reduce Japan's. During the 1952 treaty hearings in the Senate, Dulles stressed that constraints on Japanese exports to China went beyond those mandated by the so-called Battle Act of 1951. To prevent their softening after independence, Japan was induced, in a special agreement with the USA, to restrict China trade more tightly than did the USA's major European allies.[34]

JAPANESE DOMESTIC POLITICS

The United States had made Japan's bed; it remained to be seen whether Japan was happy to lie in it. Much of Japanese politics in the 1950s was devoted to resolving this question. Many of the issues, like the confrontation between the government and the teachers' unions, do not directly concern us; but we should note the consolidation of the Japanese political structure, the failure to conclude a peace treaty with the USSR, and the revision of the Security Treaty with the United States.

First, the political structure. In 1918–32 Japan had had something resembling two-party parliamentary-based government.

34. ibid, esp. pp.174, 235, 247, 268

Later the parliamentary elite had been largely pushed aside; but by 1945 military leaders, at least, had been completely discredited, and it was natural, as well as necessary, to return to earlier practices. The new 1946 Constitution further stipulated that governments be appointed by, and command the confidence of, the House of Representatives. Political parties reformed in November 1945, but not simply along 1920s lines; indeed by 1946 there were 13 'parties' operating nationally and 363 locally. In short there was much confusion and fluidity, one illustration of which was the frequency with which parties changed their names. The important parties were the Liberals and the Democrats (originally 'Progressives'), both comprising many pre-Surrender politicians, the Socialists and the Communists, both previously suppressed. Communists became strong in the trade unions and in extra-parliamentary agitation, but in electoral terms they have served chiefly to sterilise votes that might have gone to the Socialists.[35] After the 1946 elections the Liberal leader, Hatoyama, was about to head a coalition government when SCAP suddenly purged him. He was replaced by a former diplomat, Yoshida Shigeru, apparently on the understanding that Yoshida would return the party leadership to Hatoyama should the latter become able to resume political activity. SCAP saw Yoshida's government as too conservative; when it ran into criticism for its inability to improve economic conditions, MacArthur told him to seek a new mandate.[36] The April 1947 elections brought in a Socialist-led coalition government with the Democrats – the only Japanese government before 1993 to have contained Socialists. But the left Socialists chafed at the restraints of coalition, and this led to the coalition's reconstruction in February 1948 under a Democrat Premier. It then collapsed in October under the impact of a bribery scandal.[37] Yoshida returned to office and in January 1949 secured an absolute majority of parliamentary seats, largely on the rebound from the Socialists. This electoral triumph enabled him to preside over the recovery of Japanese sovereignty, and to retain the premiership until December 1954.

In a way Yoshida's achievements were his undoing. For when the ban on their political activities was lifted, people who had been purged returned to the Diet in remarkable numbers – among them

35. Their best performance was thirty-nine seats and 10.4% of the 1979 vote

36. *Keesing's*, 8560

37. Kosaka attributes the publicity accorded this scandal to faction fighting within SCAP, where conservatives resented past partiality for the Socialists: *History of Postwar Japan*, pp. 84–5

Hatoyama, who became Yoshida's enemy when the latter would not hand over to him. Another important development was the Liberals' sharp decline in the 1953 and still more the 1955 elections (when they gained only 112 seats), and the Socialists' recovery. This recovery was masked by the party's 1951 split into rightist and leftist factions; but in 1955 the Socialists (and their fringe allies) collectively obtained 160 seats, mostly leftist. Admittedly the real victors were the Democrats (whom Hatoyama had now joined) with 185; but the Socialist advance was coming to worry business, whose peak organisations had returned to politics in the early 1950s, partly as paymasters and partly to secure the further relaxation of the Occupation's anti-monopoly policy. Pressure seems to have been exerted for a merger between the Liberals and the Democrats; despite intense personal rivalries this was eventually achieved in November 1955 – one month after a similar process had reunited the Socialists. The two parties then competed to attach to themselves trade and professional associations, women's groups and other interests, with the Liberal Democrats (LDP), under the guidance of Secretary-General Kishi Nobusuke, proving markedly the more successful.[38] By 1958 the new face of Japanese politics had become clear: the LDP gained 287 seats (actually rather less than its constituent parties had held in 1955) to the Socialists' 166.

For many years thereafter there was little change. The LDP declined slightly, after 1976[39] sometimes failing to secure an absolute majority of seats. Even in such cases it would fall back on a cushion of like-minded Independents and others, and it encountered no difficulty in maintaining a Diet majority. Of course it had advantages: money matters in Japanese politics, and a business-oriented party of government was best placed to raise it, and also to perform constituency favours that were in turn electorally appreciated; the LDP gained, too, from rural over-representation. It was also by far the most popular single party: although no longer polling the 58 per cent of 1958 and 1960, even at its 1976 nadir it secured 41.8 per cent to the Socialists' 20.1 per cent. So dominant did the LDP prove that the real political competition was that between its highly organised internal 'factions'. This competition has policy components, but is very largely personal. LDP factions proved broadly content with Japan's international alignment. Their opponents in other parties did not –

38. ibid. pp.170–3

39. When it was badly hurt by the arrest of the influential ex-premier Tanaka in connection with the Lockheed bribery scandal

though in the later 1970s the Democratic Socialists and, in 1981, Komeito, came to accept the Self Defence Force and (with qualifications) the Security Treaty. Meanwhile the Socialists began to tone down their criticism. This softening of attitudes notwithstanding, Japan's postwar stance was clearly underpinned by continued LDP ascendancy – as Japanese leaders occasionally reminded the USA when pressed to take politically unpopular action.[40]

The 1990s brought an upset, the product of further scandal, economic slowdown, and (just possibly) of a world-wide impetus to change generated by the end of the Cold War. In October 1992 Kanemaru Shin, the head of the largest LDP faction, resigned as a result of an influence-peddling scandal – the next year he was found to have $60 million of hidden assets. In the ensuing contest, the faction leadership eluded both Kanemaru's preferred successor, Ozawa, and his nominee, Hata. Hata then formed a 'policy study group' that soon developed into an independent faction, and in April 1993 refused an offer to join what was by now an ailing government. In June, that government was defeated on a motion censuring it for not reforming the electoral system (so as to reduce rural over-representation and the scope for corruption). 39 LDP Diet members, mostly from Hata's faction, voted against it, and Hata then seceded to found a new centrist party (one of three to be established in 1992–3 by former LDP politicians). In the July 1993 elections, the real losers were the Social Democrats, whose representation in the Lower House of the Diet was cut almost in half; but this rejection of an archaic socialism served to make them more malleable and acceptable as coalition partners. The LDP lost only four seats, over and above those held by defectors to the new centre parties. However it no longer had an absolute majority; and after lengthy negotiations, a very broad non-LDP coalition (under Hosakawa Morihiro, but supposedly strongly influenced by Ozawa) took over in August. In foreign policy it sought to raise Japan's international profile, but promised to continue broadly along the lines of its LDP predecessors: it is too soon to say what will ensue in practice.[41]

40. J.A.A. Stockwin, *Japan: Divided Politics in a Growth Economy* (1975) esp. chap. 5; H. Fukui, *Party in Power* (Berkeley, Calif., 1970) esp. chap. 2; *Keesing's*, 30970

41. *Keesing's*, 39140–1, 39367–8, 39508; *The Economist*, July–Aug.1993

THE KURIL ISLANDS DISPUTE BETWEEN JAPAN AND THE USSR

The Yoshida–Hatoyama rivalry had contained, besides personal antipathy, a political element, for Hatoyama was anxious to restore full Japanese independence. This meant upgrading the armed forces and seeking (albeit unsuccessfully)[42] to amend the constitutional barriers to rearmament – policies with which the Eisenhower administration was very comfortable. It also entailed an attempt to mend relations with the USSR. Hatoyama succeeded Yoshida as Premier in December 1954, and talks with the Soviet Union began in June 1955. They promptly ran into trouble over the Kuril island chain that runs from Hokkaido to Kamchatka. At Yalta 'The Kuril Islands' were included among the territories promised to the Soviet Union to induce it to enter the war; in August–September 1945 it occupied them all – including the most southerly (Etorufu, Kunashiri, Shikotan and the Habomais) which Russia/the USSR had never previously ruled – and in due course expelled their inhabitants. SCAP initially acquiesced, but in 1949 Washington came to hold (with some justification in terms of past administrative patterns)[43] that 'there is sound basis for the legal contention that the Habomai and the Shikotan are not properly part of the Kuril islands', though Etorufu and Kunashiri definitely were. So, in his 1950–1 discussions with the USSR of a possible Japanese settlement, Dulles condemned only the Soviet occupation of Habomais and Shikotan; the San Francisco treaty included a Japanese renunciation of 'the Kuril Islands', partly as a bait to the Soviet Union to sign.[44]

When talks opened with the USSR in 1955, the Japanese envoy, Matsumoto, was instructed to claim all the Kurils, but if necessary to settle for Shikotan and the Habomais. In August the USSR offered them, though according to Khrushchev its offer was to be conditional on the closure of US bases in Japan (which would not have been easy to achieve). Whether as a result of US pressure or of factional infighting within Japan, Matsumoto then raised Japanese demands, so the USSR broke off talks. They resumed in 1956, but ran into the same obstacle – which Dulles did his best to magnify by warning that 'if Japan recognises Kunashiri and Etorufu as Soviet

42. The LDP has never in fact had the necessary two-thirds majority in the Lower House

43. J.J. Stephan, *The Kuril Islands* (Oxford, 1974) p.97; I use the islands' Japanese, not Russian, names

44. Burkman, *Occupation of Japan: The International Context* p.207

territory, the United States will ask her to confirm Okinawa[45] to be American territory'.[46] In the end no peace treaty was achieved. The USSR did, however, agree a declaration resuming diplomatic relations and promising further negotiations for a treaty that would include Japanese recovery of Shikotan and the Habomais. The USSR also lifted its ban on Japanese membership of the UN.[47]

Negotiations over the islands have continued sporadically ever since; in 1972 Gromyko complained that the issue was giving him a headache. The Soviet line did not change, partly, no doubt, because in 1964 Mao Zedong endorsed the Japanese position and linked it with China's claims on the USSR. In 1969 Kosygin insisted to the Japanese Foreign Minister that the outcome of the Second World War was irreversible; this was, of course, a familiar Soviet claim in the European context, and the USSR would not have wished to set up contrary examples in Asia. Also, with the growth of the Soviet Pacific fleet, the islands gained in strategic importance as controlling an exit to the high seas, and were correspondingly fortified. Of course the territorial dispute is not all that important; although it has led to many incidents with Japanese fishermen, it did not prevent the agreed delimitation of fishing zones in 1977.[48] Nor, probably, would it have prevented a more general accommodation had this been clearly in the two countries' mutual interest. But the USSR had a lot to overcome in Japan. Before 1941 anti-Russian and anti-communist feelings were far commoner there than anti-Anglo-American. After 1945 Japan reverted to former habits of enthusiastic, if selective, adoption of Western culture and practices, and came increasingly, if a little precariously, to see itself as a developed 'Western' state. Nor did it help that, by the time Japan had (in the 1970s) come to pursue closer relations with China, the latter was strongly anti-Soviet. What one can say is that the USSR passed up opportunities of capitalising on periods of US–Japanese friction and Japanese self-assertion.

One such episode, that of 1955–6, we have noted. Another

45. There was a parallel in that the USA had separated Okinawa from Japan after the war and developed it into a major military base, though from 1951 recognising 'residual' Japanese sovereignty

46. The State Department added a statement supporting Japanese claims to Kunashiri and Etorufu, but hinting that, if they *were* to be regarded as part of the 'Kuril Islands' renounced at San Francisco, then Japan had no right to pronounce on their present sovereignty

47. Stephan, *Kuril Islands* esp. pp.219, 246; *Keesing's*, 15195–7; *Khrushchev Remembers* iii pp.85–90

48. Stephan, *Kuril Islands* p.189; *Keesing's*, 28564

possible opportunity came in the early 1970s, when Japan suffered both the 'Nixon shocks' (see pp.178–9) and alarm about its oil supply and economy stemming from the 1973 Arab production cuts and price rises. In 1972, after a considerable interlude, Gromyko visited Tokyo to inaugurate a period of regular consultation and resume talks on a peace treaty; but the issue of the islands soon obtruded. Discussions were taken up again in 1973 and broadened to include the possibility of large-scale Japanese development of Siberian natural resources. Prime Minister Tanaka and Brezhnev had a set-to on the subject of the islands, however, and though the subsequent communiqué talked of a $2 billion Japanese loan, the subject was left rather vague. Further progress appeared to have been made in 1974, but in the end it all came to nothing. In 1975 the USSR warned Japan against drawing too close to China, and suggested an interim treaty of 'friendship and goodwill'. In 1976 Gromyko returned to Tokyo, 'obsessed' (as the Japanese Foreign Minister put it) with the possibility of a Sino-Japanese friendship treaty. The visit was a failure, and Japan indicated its intention to proceed with the treaty. Here too negotiations moved slowly; but in mid-1978 Japan brushed aside Soviet warnings and signed a peace treaty with China, including a statement of opposition to 'efforts by' any third country 'to establish . . . hegemony' in the Asia–Pacific region. The USSR took this, as China had intended, as a hostile act, and Soviet–Japanese relations froze until the Gorbachev era. Then in 1986 *Pravda* commented, in what looked like implicit criticism of past policy, that relations between the two countries 'do not correspond either to their political weight in world affairs or [to] their economic potential'. Shevardnadze twice visited Tokyo, but to little effect.[49] Instead Gorbachev gave clear priority to mending relations with China. Accordingly the Cold War thawed far more slowly in East Asia than in Europe; at the 1990 Western G7 summit Japan proved cool towards economic assistance for the USSR. In 1991 it did hint at a $26 billion aid package in exchange for the return of the islands, but Gorbachev was now too weak domestically to give them up; although he visited Tokyo nothing came of it.[50] After the August 1991 Soviet coup, negotiations began with Yeltsin, but, despite periodic bouts of official optimism, no settlement has yet (1993) been reached.

49. *Keesing's,* 25104, 25625, 26253, 27599, 29279–80, 34237–8; *Facts on File,* 1973 p.874; Stephan, *Kuril Islands* pp.233–4; *The Economist,* 24 Dec. 1988 p.62

50. *Keesing's,* 37629, 38148; *Daily Telegraph,* 20 Aug. 1991 p.4

DISTURBANCES OVER THE RENEWAL OF THE SECURITY TREATY 1960

Hatoyama had retired after Japan's admission to the UN in late 1956; in February 1957 the forceful Kishi Nobusuke became Premier. His term of office was confrontational: a major collision with the Teachers Union was followed by a controversial proposal to expand police powers. Kishi extended the Diet's 1958 session to force the latter through, thus creating a storm of protest, but subsequently backed off in face of an Opposition boycott. He also persuaded the USA to discuss revision of the Security Treaty (which it had refused in 1955), and in January 1960 to conclude a revised treaty eliminating the inequalities of that signed in 1951. But the continuation of *any* such treaty was opposed by the Socialists and Communists, who seriously embarrassed the government by their success in spinning out parliamentary discussion. On 19 May 1960 Socialist Members of the Diet forcibly prevented the Speaker from calling a vote to extend the session of the Lower House; Kishi had them removed by police, and the House then ratified the treaty in a late-night vote with only the LDP present. This was widely seen as the subversion of parliamentary democracy. Nor was the situation improved by the U2 incident and the collapse on 17 May of the Paris summit conference, which highlighted the possible dangers of military association with the USA.[51] Accordingly there were massive strikes and demonstrations against the Kishi government, the treaty, and the proposed visit of President Eisenhower to complete the ratification process; Kishi was trapped in the Diet building for twelve hours and Eisenhower's Press Secretary was penned in his car for eighty minutes until rescued by helicopter. Eisenhower duly called off his visit. The moment that ratification had been completed, Kishi (prompted by warnings from business) announced his intention to resign.[52]

The episode unleashed some political murders, alarming in view of Japan's past history. But it also constituted something of a catharsis. Socialist attempts to continue the agitation against Kishi's successor, Ikeda, fell flat. Ikeda lowered the temperature by promising 'to cooperate with my friends, the members of the opposition parties' and to protect 'the principles of parliamentary democracy'. In September 1960 he announced his ambitious plan

51. See *The Cold War* chap. 7. Three U2s had been based in Japan; they were withdrawn in July

52. Stockwin, *Japan* pp.72–3; Fukui, *Party in Power* p.163; *Keesing's*, 17263–4, 17525 ff

to double living standards within a decade. Then, well funded by business, he called elections, increased his majority, and declared the Security Treaty controversy 'settled'. For the next decade the government sought to avoid excitement, promote general good feelings (for which the 1964 holding in Tokyo of the Olympic Games, originally scheduled for 1940, proved an excellent vehicle), and, above all, to concentrate on economic growth.[53]

TRADE, GROWTH, AND THE JAPANESE ECONOMY

Growth represents both postwar Japan's most striking achievement and, probably, a major stabilising factor. It could, initially, by no means be taken for granted: with a large population and very limited natural resources, Japan depended on imports of raw materials and, in the long run, sufficient exports to pay for them. It had not satisfactorily resolved this problem before the Second World War – hence both its Asian conquests and its vulnerability to the 1941 US oil embargo. The war and subsequent upheaval had completely disrupted its trade with the Asian mainland. Part of the necessary adjustment came through a collapse in a standard of living already depressed by massive bombing, part through US supply of relief and commodities. The problem, in the 1950s, was how long US charity could be depended on, and what could be put in its place. One possible solution, trade with China, had been largely ruled out, not only by the Cold War, but probably also by the general evolution of the People's Republic.[54] Washington had been sure, in the late 1940s and early 1950s, that Japan's natural trading alignment was with Asia, and, as we have seen, South-East Asia was canvassed as either a supplement or an alternative to China; in May 1950 the US administration testified that it would be the 'principal market for Japanese products, and, of course, its principal source of raw materials'.[55] Trade with Asia was important, and the USA tried hard to promote it both by diplomacy and by

53. Kosaka, *History of Postwar Japan* chaps 11, 12; *The Times*, 29 Sept. and 22 Nov. 1960, p.11

54. Neither national pride, nor the 'Yenan' tradition of self-sufficiency, nor the Stalinist economic system adopted in the 1950s would have been conducive to Chinese resumption of the prewar pattern of trade with Japan

55. Burkman, *Occupation of Japan: The International Context* p.178

trying to aid purchases in Japan.[56] Nevertheless the relative importance of Asian trade declined in the 1950s.[57] The United States remained easily Japan's most important single economic partner. What changed was Japanese ability to compete in that market. Dulles had felt that the United States did not 'need or want many of their items since they are really cheap imitations of our own goods'; and between 1945 and 1964 Japan did run a trade deficit with the USA. There followed, though, first a rough balance, then an embarrassing surplus ($3.2 billion in 1971, $4.2 billion in 1972).[58] However, if Japan eventually became more than capable of supporting itself, it initially owed much to US assistance: 65 per cent of its imports were covered by aid during 1945–9. Aid was supplemented, then after 1951 replaced, by military-related 'special procurements'; at their 1952–3 Korean War peak of over $800 million per year, these covered 37 per cent of imports, and as late as 1959–63 8 per cent. Nor did the economic benefits of US foreign policy end there, since Japan was well placed to supply US logistic requirements for the Vietnam War; one estimate is that in 1967–8 such orders brought Japan nearly $1 billion per year, with almost as much coming in from the local spending of US bases.[59]

I have stressed trade since the balance of payments was the major constraint on the Japanese economy: in 1957, 1961 and 1963–4 'severely restrictive policies and subsequent recessions were made inevitable by the appearance of large current-account deficits'.[60] Some Japanese industries were always geared to the export market, notably shipbuilding (where, after much international debate, SCAP left intact the vast wartime capacity, and efficiency plus technological innovation brought the industry, at its peak in the 1970s, half of all world production). But, though essential, from

56. At its peak in 1960 such tied aid accounted for 10% of Japanese exports to South-East Asia: L.H. Redford (ed.) *The Occupation of Japan: Economic Policy and Reform* (Norfolk, Va, 1980) p.290

57. In 1954 Asia (including the Persian Gulf) provided 30.6% of Japanese imports and took 48.9% of its exports, while North America accounted for 46% of imports and 21.7% of exports; in 1960 the figures were Asia 30.4% and 36.0%, North America 42.8% and 33.2%; in 1967 30.7% and 34.1% as compared with 35.8% and 34.7%: Hugh Corbet (ed.), *Trade Strategy and the Asian-Pacific Region* (1970) pp.50, 54

58. Redford, *Occupation of Japan: Economic Policy and Reform* p.290; J. Halliday, *A Political History of Japanese Capitalism* (New York, 1975) p.287

59. Allen, *Japan's Economic Expansion* p.278; J.W. Dower, 'The Superdomino in Asia: Japan in and out of the Pentagon Papers', *The Pentagon Papers* (Senator Gravel edn, 1972) v p.120

60. A. Boltho, *Japan: An Economic Survey* (Oxford, 1975) p.55; 'recessions' involved the slowing, not the ending, of growth

1953 to 1972 trade accounted for little over half as much of the Japanese GNP as of the European.[61] What emerged in the 1950s – partly through the combination of rising incomes and little possibility of spending them on housing – was a high demand for manufactured goods like the 'three electric treasures'.[62] This was met primarily by domestic manufacture; after quality problems had been sorted out (SCAP had stressed the importance of quality control and the avoidance of the poor reputation of interwar Japanese exports), and when production had built to a level where marginal costs were low, these industries turned also to exports.[63]

The basic explanations of growth, then, are domestic, although it is easier to assert this than to pinpoint them precisely. There has, indeed, been much debate as to whether they are specifically Japanese, or whether Japan merely contained in abundance features that would produce growth anywhere. But the ability of other East and South-East Asian countries to tread the Japanese road suggests that it is not unique.[64] Conventional explanations include the setting of a very high value on economic growth by a society that saw it as essential to national security and consequence. In 1973 MITI recounted Japan's history since its forcible nineteenth-century 'opening' to foreign trade, and explained that 'feelings of isolation and alienation, anxiety and impatience, have become a burning desire to catch up [economically] and a source of national vitality';[65] not until the 1960s did any qualms come to be voiced at the great environmental costs. Japanese government has been exceptionally stable, capitalist and pro-business (though not *laissez faire*); its scope, and hence its claims on economic resources, are, by international standards, small. The level of saving is very high, and

61. ibid, p.140

62. Sales of washing machines went from 100,000 in 1953 to 800,000 in 1956; televisions and refrigerators followed a couple of years later. By the 1960s the popular goal was the acquisition of the three Cs (air conditioner, car, colour TV): Kosaka, *History of Postwar Japan* pp.136–7; Armin H. Meyer, *Assignment Tokyo: An Ambassador's Journal* (Indianapolis, 1974) p. 191

63. Boltho, *Japan* pp.154–60

64. A major (if inevitably controversial) 1993 World Bank study of the economic upsurge of Japan and the Asian rim concluded that, though some state interventions in domestic financial markets and efforts to promote exports had proved successful, direct industrial restructuring and government attempts to promote high technology usually had not. More important was the area's general orientation towards exports and the competitive discipline this imposed on local manufacturers. The study also noted that departures from *laissez faire* and the market had been far fewer than in most other developing countries (and had varied significantly in scale as between the East Asian countries themselves): *Financial Times*, 27 Sept. 1993 pp.3, 18, 34

65. Meyer, *Assignment Tokyo* p.188

has tended to be funnelled into economically productive investment. The labour force is well-educated and trained, and highly adaptable – partly because Japan (like many other countries) was able to draw down an initially sizeable agricultural workforce; partly because a secondary subcontracting sector serves as a buffer that enables the major concerns to pass on many of the costs of changing course; and lastly because the policy, in these concerns, of jobs for life discourages the growth of job-protective restrictive practices, while trade unions (though demanding large and regular wage increases) are happy to see production maximised so as to earn them. Naturally not everything works well: the main railways, though technically advanced, became financially bankrupt; the retail sector is far less efficient than the manufacturing; and agriculture is, by world standards, no longer competitive. However, most things were held together by an economic 'virtuous circle' that averaged 9.7 per cent per year growth over the period 1953–72, a performance clearly better than that of any other country. (At that rate over 20 years, 100 becomes 637.)

Admittedly the two oil price rises of 1973 and 1979 came as severe blows, putting Japan's balance of payments back into the red during 1973–5 and again in 1979–80, and slowing its growth rate between 1973 and 1983 to 4.3 per cent per year (still high by the standards of developed countries, but well below that of capitalist East Asia). The economy, however, remained flexible, moving out of energy-intensive (and polluting) industries, establishing subsidiary manufacture abroad, and seeking high-technology products less exposed to competition from Japan's imitators, the Asian 'newly industrialising countries' (NICs). In this process, Japan showed (as it had in its earlier development of shipbuilding) a remarkable gift for picking products that would prove in worldwide demand – an extreme instance being the new video cassette recorders, for which there were virtually no other sources of supply and that sold well even at the depth of the early 1980s world recession. The drawback is that, in conjunction with extensive US and European industrial obsolescence, this led to a balance of payments surplus (1983 $20.8 billion, 1984 $35 billion, 1985 $49.3 billion) so large as to become a serious international political liability.[66]

66. Boltho, *Japan* pp.8–9, 56; *The Asian Economic Handbook* p.8 and *The Pacific Basin: An Economic Handbook* (Euromonitor, London, 1987) pp.27, 184; G.C. Allen, *How Japan Competes* (1978) p.54; The Oriental Economist, *Japan Economic Yearbook, 1980–1* pp.36–7

THE NIXON SHOCKS 1971

Ikeda, and his successor as Prime Minister, Sato, had, then, delivered on the 'income doubling' promise of 1960. Sato secured a further welcome success by inducing the USA in 1969 to promise to return Okinawa to Japanese sovereignty[67] – in exchange for the continuance of the 1960 Security Treaty, and of a US base on Okinawa, with the tacit understanding that Japan would not look too closely to see whether nuclear weapons were brought there.[68] This happy calm was shattered in 1971 by what came to be known as the 'Nixon shocks'; the scene was further ruffled in 1976 by congressional revelations that the aircraft firm Lockheed had been bribing important Japanese politicians. The resulting uproar led Prime Minister Miki to tell President Ford that, if the scandal was not resolved, Japanese democracy might 'suffer a fatal blow'; for a time the LDP seemed electorally endangered, though the eventual outcome was no more than a rearrangement of its factional patterns.[69]

The first Nixon shock was the announcement in July 1971, with no real prior warning to Japan, that the President had accepted an invitation to visit Beijing. The idea that Washington might thus suddenly recognise the People's Republic of China was familiar in Tokyo as a 'nightmare'; now the USA had 'jumped over Japan's head' and done so.[70] The Japanese objection was not to the policy itself, only to the lack of consultation and to the possibility that Japan would now be left friendless and out on a limb. The episode caused problems for the Sato government; these were exacerbated by its quixotic decision that autumn to help the USA round up votes at the UN in what proved to be a vain attempt to enable Taiwan to keep a seat there. Sato survived a Diet censure motion, but decided in 1972 to retire (albeit on a high note after the return of Okinawa – and an unusually long premiership). His successor, Tanaka, who may have been chosen in the hope of a more robust foreign policy, moved quickly to liquidate the problem, promptly

67. This took effect in 1972; Sato vigorously drew the contrast with the USSR's behaviour in the Kuril islands

68. Ex-Ambassador Reischauer caused a furore in 1981 by revealing that this policy of casting a blind eye on US nuclear visits had been established at the time of the 1960 Treaty: *Keesing's*, 30972

69. Ex-Premier Tanaka, leader of the largest faction, was charged with receiving \$1.7 million; he continued to control his faction, but could never return to office: *Keesing's*, 27840–1, 28157

70. Meyer, *Assignment Tokyo* pp.113–14

securing an invitation to visit China, and in September 1972 opening formal diplomatic relations with Beijing and ending them with Taiwan. Although some feared that Nixon's action had 'cast a long shadow over the future of the two countries', in the event everything worked out smoothly. Indeed the Nixon–Kissinger visits to China foreclosed any possibility that pro-China factions in the LDP, and a mounting 'China fever' in the Japanese press, would force on Japan an embarrassing choice between US wishes and China. Furthermore, the new Chinese enthusiasm for bolstering the United States' position in the West Pacific (to contain the USSR) led it to favour the continuance of the US–Japanese Security Treaty that it had so often denounced before.[71] Japan's only problem was just how far it wished to go in pleasing China, given that the Soviet Union had responded to the new developments by reopening negotiations for a friendship treaty. As we have seen, Soviet stubbornness over the Kurile islands ultimately decided Japan to align verbally with China and to conclude, in 1978, a treaty with an 'anti-hegemony' (i.e. anti-Soviet) declaration.

Harder to handle was Nixon's second shock, the imposition in August 1971 – again without warning – of a temporary 10 per cent import surcharge. Nixon sought to halt the run on US gold reserves, and to force other countries to agree new exchange rates and trading practices that would eliminate the USA's deficit (see pp.492–4). Japan was only one of these countries, but it was particularly vulnerable since its surplus with the USA accounted for all the latter's 1971 trade deficit, while Nixon's advisers predicted worse to come. The problem had of course been recognised before, and Japan had made moves to correct it (including the liberalisation of foreign currency allowances for tourists[72] and the 'voluntary' restraint of many classes of export). But it was upset by Nixon's actions (following so closely after the earlier 'shock'); Japan initially regarded Treasury Secretary Connally's call for a $13 billion turn-around in the US balance of payments as 'Texas talk'. In one sense things sorted themselves out. The rest of 1971 saw much diplomatic fence-mending. In December the Smithsonian Agreement produced a 16.9 per cent revaluation of the yen *vis-à-vis* the dollar, and the removal of the import surcharge. In 1972 Japan reduced its own tariffs, and added over $1 billion 'emergency purchases' to help Nixon electorally. In 1973 it let the yen 'float' upwards.[73] With

71. ibid, chap. 4
72. In 1971 more Japanese than Britons visited the USA
73. Meyer, *Assignment Tokyo* chap. 5

the oil price rise, this did for a time control the problem, but not for long: Japan's surplus with the USA returned to $3.8 billion in 1976, $7.3 billion in 1977.[74] So this question, unlike that of the recognition of China, had no definite solution.

Although the mutual benefits of US–Japanese trade were enormous – Japan was the United States' second largest market, the USA Japan's largest – the imbalance has proved a perpetual and increasing irritant. There is in fact no agreement as to where the problem really lies. Japan is certainly agriculturally protectionist[75] (and will probably remain so, given the strength of the agricultural interest in the LDP); but this is not uncommon. It used to be overtly mercantilist: some surplus in manufactured trade is needed to cover the costs of importing raw materials and intermediate foods; and in 1971 the MITI minister confessed that Japanese leaders were still conditioned by an era of deficits when every yen spent abroad was like 'giving up a drop of blood'. Liberalisation had begun – under International Monetary Fund (IMF) pressure – with the phasing out of currency controls by 1964. In 1972 Japanese tariffs on manufactured goods fell to, and in 1982 below, the average for developed countries. Between 1969 and 1972 the number of items subject to import quotas was reduced from 120 to 33. From 1967 controls on inward investment were relaxed, with in 1980 an opening of the stock market and permission (in theory) for take-over bids. On paper, therefore, Japan can claim one of the world's more open markets, and ascribe foreign failures to penetrate it to: inferior products and an instinctive Japanese preference for domestic manufactures; inadequate marketing;[76] and ignorance of the Japanese language. Others, however, say that Japan maintains, not always consciously, a whole network of non-tariff barriers that are given up only very slowly and under extreme pressure: European skis were not licensed because Japanese snow was 'different', canned fruit could not be imported when labels failed to specify the exact number of pieces, and so on.[77]

74. Jon Woronoff, *World Trade War* (New York, 1984) p.139

75. Still it imports much farm produce, with the USA supposedly securing a disproportionate share of the orders since it has more political clout than competitors like Australia

76. In Jan. 1992 complaining US car manufacturers were reminded that they had never adapted their products to the fact that the Japanese drive on the left

77. Woronoff, *World Trade War* esp. chap. 3; Meyer, *Assignment Tokyo* pp.200–1, 224–5; for a different view, Jagdish Bhagwati, *The World Trading System at Risk* (Princeton, NJ, 1991) pp.24 ff. A 1983 French response to such supposed Japanese techniques was to admit Japanese video recorders only through a deliberately small and inconvenient customs post at Poitiers

THE PLAZA ACCORD 1985

Such disputes came to assume ever-growing importance. Japan's current account surplus was $7 billion in 1982, $24 billion in 1983 and $37 billion in 1984, mostly arising out of trade with the United States. This generated much criticism; in (at least) April 1984, March–April, July and October 1985 Japan introduced packages of measures to encourage imports by opening its market. Another line of thought saw the surplus as the natural result of an undervalued yen and an overvalued dollar. In September 1985 G5 Finance Ministers and Central Bankers representing the five leading currencies[78] met in New York and agreed, in the so-called Plaza Accord, to correct this by intervening in the market. In a sense they were successful: the dollar had by May 1986 dropped from 240 to 160 yen, and continued to fall more slowly until 1989. The change in relative prices certainly encouraged Japanese investment abroad; it also led Japanese imports in 1986–9 to grow rather faster than did those of other large Western industrialised countries.[79] US exports were disappointing, however, and by 1989 the trade deficit with Japan had grown to $49 billion. So US protectionist sentiment strengthened and, in some quarters, took on a distinctly 'Japan-bashing' tinge: in 1988 the Trade Bill, as at one stage proposed in the Senate, included the phrase 'When trading with adversaries, like Japan . . .'.[80] This was dropped from the final version, but the 1988 Trade Act authorised the USA to demand that other countries (in May 1989 Japan, India and Brazil) discontinue trade practices that it found unacceptable or face 100 per cent tariff barriers. 'Structural Impediments Initiative' talks began against this background: in contrast to the usual international practice, it was the *creditor* country (Japan) that was forced in 1990 to promise changes in the way it ran its internal affairs (notably by facilitating the spread of supermarkets – which are more open to imports than ordinary shops – and by spending more on housing and public

78. US dollar, yen, deutschmark, pound and French franc

79. *Keesing's*, 33668, 34557, 36619, 37278, 37394; Bhagwati, *World Trading System at Risk* pp.41–3; B.K. Gordon, *Politics and Protectionism in the Pacific* (IISS Adelphi Paper no. 228, 1988) p.26

80. C. Michael Aho, 'America and the Pacific Century: Trade Conflict or Cooperation?', *International Affairs* lxix (1993) p.22. Not that such sentiments were confined to Americans; in 1991 the French Prime Minister was credited with describing the Japanese as 'little yellow men' who 'stay up all night thinking about ways to screw the Americans and the Europeans. They are our common enemy': *Sunday Times*, 23 June 1991 p.17

works.)[81] Such promises went some way towards improving the US–Japanese atmosphere (though some of the good was undone by Japan's stance during the Gulf War); many trade issues were subsumed into the less antagonistic forum of the multilateral negotiations of the GATT 'Uruguay' round. But the bursting of Japan's domestic 'bubble' boom led to a sharp fall in consumer imports and a corresponding rise in the trade surplus with the USA ($107 billion in 1992); 1993 therefore opened with fears of a confrontation with the new Clinton administration,[82] while a year later (after the failure of summit talks) one seemed imminent. So far from the trade surplus directly enhancing Japanese negotiating power (as surpluses usually do), the constant need to explain or defend it has been a political liability.

JAPAN'S GROWING INTERNATIONAL STATUS

Nevertheless there are ways in which the surplus has increased Japan's international standing. Under US pressure Japan has, more especially since the later 1970s, increased international aid to become, by 1989, the world's largest donor.[83] Some of this is 'strategic' – to countries like Pakistan, Egypt and Turkey with which Japan has few historical links but whose stability is important for Western (and more especially US) foreign policy.[84] Much more aid has been oriented towards Eastern Asia, where it has complemented Japan's far more extensive direct investment. In particular, after an initially prickly relationship, Japan has since 1977 emerged as the major external patron of ASEAN (see pp.222–3). Aid, however, accounted for only a small part of the Japanese surplus. Capital outflow ($400 billion in 1985–8)[85] mostly went on overseas lending and investment. Partly a prophylactic against protectionism, such investment has by now given Japan an appreciable manufacturing presence not only in eastern Asia but also in North America and

81. In return the USA expressed the intent to cut its budget deficit, and received Japanese lectures on the need to save more, go metric and improve its educational system: *Keesing's*, 37319–20, 37279, 37376–7

82. 'Very Politely, Japan warns Clinton not to pick a fight', *International Herald Tribune* 10 Feb. 1993 p.1; *The Independent*, 23 Jan. 1993 p.17

83. $10 billion scheduled for 1989–90, as against the USA's $9 billion: *New York Times*, 23 Feb. 1989 p.A 10

84. Pakistan received 32 billion yen in the wake of the Soviet invasion of Afghanistan: Satoh, *Evolution of Japanese Security Policy* p.30

85. *The Economist*, 24 Dec. 1988 p.42, 6 April 1991 p.14

Europe (more especially the UK). It was complemented by the spread of Japanese banks and financial institutions, whose domestic base had swelled with growth, a booming stock market, and progressive rises in the international value (and usage) of the yen. By 1988 seven (or on different criteria ten) of the world's ten largest banks were Japanese, and Tokyo had become the world's second financial centre. In 1990 this was eventually reflected in a revision of the International Monetary Fund's quotas and votes (see p.481) that took Japan from fifth place to equal second (with Germany), displacing Britain.[86] All this clearly adds to significant *potential* Japanese power. To precisely how much is a matter partly of circumstance and partly of perspective, but those who in the 1960s attributed enormous importance to US multinationals must now be gazing at their Japanese successors.

Japan has hitherto been more concerned with status than with exercising political power, since the existing international situation suited it fairly well. Japan's international profile has accordingly been lower than that of West Germany, France or Britain, but its importance has become self-evident. In the 1950s and 1960s the Western foreign policy establishment was 'Atlanticist'. In the early 1970s the buzzword became 'trilateralism' (Europe, North America, Japan), and in 1973 took shape in the 'Trilateral Commission' (a study group for influential people from all three areas). In 1975 France invited the heads of government of the six leading OECD (Organisation for Economic Co-operation and Development) countries (in order of economic size, the USA, Japan, West Germany, France, Britain, Italy) to talks on the current problems of the world economy. These summits (termed, with the inclusion of Canada from 1976, G7) became annual,[87] and have extended their competence well beyond economic affairs. Japan is, therefore, very much part of the Western inner circle; in 1990–1 it used its position to cool European enthusiasm for economic aid to the USSR and to forward its claims to the occupied islands. But, as we have seen, the 1990–1 Kuwait crisis highlighted Japan's inability, for both constitutional and domestic political reasons, to commit troops to combat situations abroad. In 1992 the government sought to

86. *Facts on File*, 1988 p.586; *Keesing's*, 37474. By mid-1992, however, Japanese banks were under considerable pressure as a result of the interconnected collapse of property prices and of the share index (the latter to little over one-third of its 1989 peak)

87. Since the 1985 Plaza Accord they have been paralleled by meetings of Finance Ministers and Central Bank Governors of the Group of Five (or, since 1986–7, sometimes of those of G7)

address this deficiency (and bolster its claim to Permanent Membership of the UN Security Council) by forcing through – with great difficulty – legislation authorising up to 2,000 Japanese military personnel to participate in non-combatant UN operations; that autumn the first Japanese troops to serve on the Asian mainland since 1945 were dispatched to assist the UN in Cambodia.[88]

Japan's international consequence has thus grown by a steady succession of small steps. But it has probably been by example that Japan has most influenced the shape of the modern world. In 1954 Yoshida had warned that, 'If China's economic progress is such that she outstrips her neighbors substantially in the years ahead, the gravitational pull will be too much to resist, and Southeast Asia will fall to the Communists without a struggle', in which case Japan would also succumb.[89] He need not have worried. By the 1960s Taiwan and South Korea were imitating Japan. Later non-communist South-East Asia came to look that way; by 1980 the Malaysian Prime Minister (Mahathir, Mohamed) was telling his people to 'learn from Japan'.[90] After Mao's death, but more especially in the 1980s, China itself came to recognise that it had been economically eclipsed by its neighbours; it embarked on economic reforms, and opened 'special enterprise zones' to foreign capital (mostly from Hong Kong and Japan) in ways that were painful, and quite unprecedented, for a communist country. How far China should take these reforms remains controversial; but it has clearly joined the emerging economy of the Pacific Basin (now centred on Japan and the USA), and may in due course become one of its poles.

88. *Keesing's*, 38963, 39097
89. Dower, *Empire and Aftermath* pp.477–8
90. *The Economist*, 10 April 1982 p.58

CHAPTER EIGHT

The Pacific Rim

Japan had been a Great Power before the Second World War, and Kennan saw it as one of the four vital power centres that needed to be kept out of communist control. Before 1945 Taiwan and Korea had been no more than Japanese colonies. Thereafter they were not initially seen as being of particular strategic importance: both were excluded from the United States' 'strategic perimeter' in the West Pacific that Acheson defined publicly in January 1950.

US DECISION TO PROTECT TAIWAN 1950

There were, admittedly, critics, even within official Washington, of the idea of standing aside and accepting what Acheson then described as Taiwan's inevitable conquest by the communists. But it was not until after the outbreak of the Korean War that Truman reversed that policy by 'interposing' his Seventh Fleet between Taiwan and the mainland. Initially this was meant only to 'neutralise' the island, and to preserve the peace as much by preventing Chiang Kai-shek raiding the mainland as by barring off a communist conquest of Taiwan. Such even-handedness did not last: military shipments to the KMT were soon resumed, and in April 1951 a military assistance mission was established.[1]

All this constituted a belated recognition of the importance of denying the communists 'the equivalent of an unsinkable aircraft carrier and submarine tender'. Its positive advantages were less

1. Gaddis, *The Long Peace* pp.72–5, 80–9; Peter Lowe, *The Origins of the Korean War* (1986) pp.152–3

immediately apparent. The new relationship with Chiang meant that the USA could, in its dealings with China, now use Kuomintang assets. This may have been useful in the field of intelligence; later in the decade, Taiwan flew U2 reconnaissance planes on behalf of the United States. Even before the Korean War, the CIA had begun to train KMT guerrillas for raids on the mainland and in 1951–2 it built up nationalist troops stranded in Burma by the civil war so as to reinfiltrate Yunnan and thus distract communist forces.[2] Had China's reaction been less restrained, this might have had very serious consequences. More generally, US support for Taiwan could only appear to Beijing as intervention in the Chinese civil war. This probably did not cause communist Chinese hostility to the USA, but presumably deepened it. On two occasions, in 1954–5 and 1958, there was a real possibility that the USA's commitment to Taiwan would drag it into war with China.

THE CHINESE OFFSHORE ISLANDS CRISIS 1954–5

At the Geneva Conference on Indo-China in 1954 China had shown itself surprisingly accommodating, almost certainly in the hope that the area would be neutralised and so freed of US influence. Instead the United States proceeded to create the South-East Asia Treaty Organisation (SEATO) and to enhance its presence in South Vietnam. Chinese disappointment may have been reflected in the outbreak of a crisis over the 'offshore islands' that was to prove one of the most alarming in the entire postwar period.[3] These islands, Quemoy, Matsu and the Tachens, were very close to the mainland but still held by the nationalists on Taiwan. The communists started shelling them in September 1954, and were apparently building up towards an invasion. The islands themselves were of little military value, and European statesmen (in Eisenhower's words) considered

2. Similar efforts were made to keep China occupied in Central Asia by backing Tibetan resistance for over a decade after 1956; this produced useful hauls of intelligence material, but probably worsened conditions in Tibet: Prados, *Presidents' Secret Wars* pp.73–7, chap. 9; Thomas Powers, *The Man who kept the Secrets: Richard Helms and the CIA* (paperback edn, 1981) pp.102, 421; John Ranelagh, *The Agency: The Rise and Decline of the CIA* (1986) p.216

3. It is correspondingly controversial. My account derives from Gordon Chang, 'To the Nuclear Brink. Eisenhower, Dulles, and the Quemoy-Matsu Crisis' (which has a map) and H.W.Brands, 'Testing Massive Retaliation: Credibility and Crisis Management in the Taiwan Strait' – both in *International Security* xii (1988); cf. also Ambrose, *Eisenhower the President*, chaps 9, 10

'America reckless, impulsive and immature' in not letting them go. Chiang Kai-shek had, however, stationed 70,000 troops there, and Eisenhower worried that, if Chiang lost them, his regime might again unravel. Eisenhower recognised the dangers if the USA got deeply involved in defending them: 'When we talk of general war with Communist China, what we mean is general war with the USSR also'. But he felt fairly confident that he could prevent matters coming to such a pass. Eisenhower meant initially to ask the UN Security Council to secure the islands' demilitarisation. But Chiang's 'Republic of China' had a veto there. To prevent Chiang using it, he was offered a defence treaty that committed the USA to defending Taiwan and the Pescadores and left deliberately vague whether it would also protect the offshore islands. But Beijing then jailed thirteen US airmen shot down over its territory during the Korean War; this created such a domestic storm in the USA that it was thought best to put off making the UN initiative.

In January 1955 China overran one of the Tachen islands. The others (which were too distant for air cover from Taiwan) were thought to be indefensible; the Americans bribed Chiang into permitting their evacuation by promising to protect Quemoy and Matsu. The administration had originally decided to make this promise public for its deterrent effect, but it eventually decided not to – perhaps to ease the passage through Congress of a resolution giving Eisenhower the authority, if he judged it necessary, to commit US forces to action in defence of Taiwan and 'closely related localities'. Chiang felt betrayed.

By March things were worse, and Dulles returned from a Far Eastern visit convinced there was 'at least an even chance' that China would attack Quemoy and Matsu and that the USA would have to fight. He and Eisenhower started to prepare American – and Chinese – opinion for the use of nuclear weapons.[4] Privately, though, Eisenhower sought to bolster Chiang's own forces to avoid the need for direct intervention, and said that if the USA had to join in, it would do so first with conventional weapons; atomic ones 'should only come at the end'. Tension was further raised when the Chief of Naval Operations told the press that the USA had plans for all-out nuclear attack on China and that he personally expected hostilities by 15 April.

On 5 April 1955 Eisenhower wrote that they could no longer

4. 'Yes, of course they would be used. In any combat where these things can be used on strictly military targets and for strictly military purposes, I see no reason why they shouldn't be used just exactly as you would use a bullet or anything else'

inertly await the moment of decision 'between two unacceptable choices', war or a retreat in the face of Chinese attack that could lead to the disintegration of 'all Asian opposition' to communism, and asked for ideas. This led to a mission being sent to Chiang, offering, if he agreed to evacuate the remaining islands, to institute a naval blockade of the Chinese coast opposite Taiwan – which would have proved both provocative and dangerous – and threatening, if he did not, to drop the US promise to protect Quemoy and Matsu. Chiang still refused, citing his betrayal over the Tachen islands.

In the meantime China had changed course. The USA later heard, and credited, a rumour that Zhou Enlai had secretly flown to Moscow and been told that the Soviet Union would not support China in a war over the islands. Another view is that China had never meant to expel the nationalists from *all* the offshore islands. These were indubitably Chinese, whereas links between the island of Taiwan and China had been surprisingly tenuous before its cession to Japan in 1895; and in the 1950s the majority of Taiwan's inhabitants were probably quite prepared to embrace a specifically Taiwanese, as opposed to Chinese, political identity. From this perspective Chiang's retention of Quemoy and Matsu, and claim to be the ruler of all China, may also have been a *communist* Chinese interest: it would anchor Taiwan/nationalist China to China proper in a situation of 'one country/two systems' that still afforded some hope of future reunion.[5] Anyway at the Bandung Conference, Zhou made friendly noises towards the USA and offered negotiations. Eisenhower responded; Zhou went halfway towards giving the assurance that the USA had been seeking, declaring that China was 'willing to strive for the liberation of Formosa by friendly means as far as this is possible'. Tension was gradually wound down, the imprisoned US airmen were released, and quiet US–Chinese talks started in August 1955.

5. In late 1955 China was charging that the USA wanted to 'hoodwink world public opinion by arranging for the traitorous Chiang Kai-shek group to "quit" the coastal islands'; after the 1958 crisis Mao praised the Taiwanese public for its loyalty to the concept of a single China and claimed the Americans were trying 'to force on us [both] a Two China policy': Nancy Bernkopf Tucker in Immerman, *Dulles and the Diplomacy of the Cold War* pp.259–60

THE CHINESE OFFSHORE ISLANDS CRISIS 1958

Though these talks achieved little, the offshore islands remained quiet until mid-1958, when Beijing had occasion to mark its displeasure with what it saw as Khrushchev's readiness to make deals with the USA over China's head. Soviet visitors to China at the time were alarmed by its bellicose talk.[6] In August 1958 heavy artillery bombardment of Quemoy began, soon accompanied by broadcasts about its imminent invasion and Chinese determination to liberate Taiwan. Chiang Kai-shek had again concentrated on the offshore islands far more men than were optimal for defence, and their resupply was not easy. As in 1955 Eisenhower supported Chiang, convoying nationalist supplies in international waters but reserving to himself the decision as to further military action. This time he was rather more confident that he would not be pushed to extremes, but the apparent prospect of a major war for the offshore islands was even more unpopular: at one point Eisenhower told the more belligerent Dulles that 'two-thirds of the world, and 50 per cent of US opinion, opposes the course which we have been following'. Nevertheless he was succesful. One explanation is simply that the nationalists established air supremacy (with the aid of US Sidewinder missiles) and (using US-supplied landing craft) succeeded in fighting supplies through to Quemoy. Another view is that Beijing was worried by the flexibility that the USA showed in secret negotiations in Warsaw: this might have led to the abandonment of the islands and the establishment of a UN trusteeship over Taiwan, hence to Taiwan's definitive separation from China. In any case the bombardment was relaxed in October. In a flying visit to Taiwan, Dulles read the riot act, emphasising Chiang's political isolation and the suspicion that he positively 'wants to endanger the peace and involve the US, as the only means of returning to the mainland'. The Korean and Indo-Chinese 'civil wars' had been 'ended by armistice', and Chiang should in future behave as if an armistice were in effect. On 23 October Chiang renounced the use of force to return to the mainland; two days later Beijing declared that it would bombard Quemoy only on odd days of the month.[7] Hostilities thus gradually tapered off. But

6. *Khrushchev Remembers* ii p.260; Royal Institute of International Affairs (RIIA), *Survey 1956–8* p.538; Andrei Gromyko, *Memories* (paperback edn, 1989) pp.321–3

7. P.P.P.C. Cheng, *Truce Negotiations over Korea and Quemoy* (Washington, DC, 1977) chap. 3; Ambrose, *Eisenhower: The President* pp.482–5; Hoopes, *The Devil and John Foster Dulles* chap. 17; R.L. Garthoff (ed.), *Sino-Soviet Military Relations* pp.109–11, chap. 7

Taiwan still felt obliged to maintain large armed forces.[8] In 1962 Chiang readied them to support any rebellion that might result from the terrible privations on the mainland, and provoked counter-concentrations by the PRC. The USA calmed things down, and since then there have been no serious signs of conflict.[9]

TAIWAN'S ECONOMIC DEVELOPMENT

In the 1950s, Taiwan must have seemed a very doubtful asset, given both its potential for dragging the USA into Armageddon and the incompetence that its government had displayed during its recent defeat on the Chinese mainland. But its development was to prove impressive. Taiwan had inherited from its Japanese colonial rulers a relatively well-educated population, an agriculture geared to export, and some (admittedly war-damaged) industry. Its initial experience of Chinese rule had been unfortunate, leading in 1947 to anti-mainland rioting in whose suppression some 18,000–28,000 people were killed.[10] The effect, however, was to give the government a remarkably free hand. One set of local elites had been discredited through collaboration with the Japanese, while those who had hoped to succeed it suffered badly in and after the 1947 events. Finally when the 1.2 million mainlanders fled to Taiwan in 1949–50, they monopolised political power and made extensive precautionary arrests of suspected enemies, both communist and autonomist.[11] So, unlike the earlier position on the mainland, there were neither local nor political hindrances to land reform. Both Chiang Kai-shek and his US advisers saw inactivity in this respect as a major reason for the KMT's defeat, and were determined not to repeat it. Even before Chiang's arrival implementation had begun of the Chinese law, passed in 1930 but never really put into effect on the mainland, restricting rents to 37.5 per cent of the main harvest. There followed, from 1951, the sale (cheaply) to peasants of land originally set aside for Japanese colonists. Then from 1953 the government compulsorily purchased all holdings of more than 3

8. In 1958 650,000, falling to 500,000 in the later 1970s

9. Some pinprick and intelligence-gathering KMT raids did, however, continue until 1969: Ralph N. Clough, *Island China* (Cambridge, Mass., 1978) pp.15, 21, 106

10. *Keesing's*, 38765

11. René Dumont with Charlotte Paquet, *Taiwan, le prix de la réussite* (Paris, 1987) pp.22, 99

hectares of irrigated (or 6 hectares of dry) land, reselling it to smallholders and landless workers for payments below the level of rents. Owner-occupation, albeit of very small holdings, accordingly became the norm. This process was assisted by a Joint Sino-American Commission on Rural Reconstruction, to which, in 1951–3, half of all US aid was devoted. The government also provided credit and advisory services, though it used its control over fertiliser supplies to hold down the price of rice. Agricultural production comfortably outpaced population growth, and moved readily into exports of cash crops.

Landlords were paid for their expropriated property partly with shares in the industrial facilities that Japan had left behind, which were thus privatised. As they had no prospect of political advancement (given the mainlanders' domination of government), industry and commerce represented the chief routes to success. They benefited, too, from a friendly administration, a high national propensity to save, and the conquest in the early 1950s of inflation. The most interesting feature of the Taiwanese model was that production was initially small-scale, and increasingly located in the countryside to use labour that could not profitably be expended on the small farm holdings; from the 1960s agriculture became more and more a part-time occupation. In 1953 the country had been overwhelmingly agricultural; by 1962 manufacturing lay only very slightly behind agriculture, whether in terms of employment, contribution to GNP, or exports.[12] Heavy industry was added in the 1970s; but, for the most past, manufacturing remained relatively small-scale, entrepreneurial and flexible. When the (necessarily limited) home market was saturated, it diversified readily into exports. Like Japan, Taiwan initially ran a trade deficit covered by US economic aid totalling about $1.5 billion from 1950 to 1964/5,[13] when it was ended as no longer necessary. Its place was taken by loans, and by overseas investment, which Taiwan (unlike Japan) welcomed and which accounted for $1.9 billion between 1952 and 1978 and a further $2.6 billion by 1982. In 1970 the trade balance became positive, and remained so save for the oil shock years of 1973–4 and 1980; in the 1980s it became embarrassing, reaching $10 billion in 1985 and $19 billion at its peak in 1987.[14]

12. Dumont, *Taiwan* p.32

13. ibid, p.29. To this should be added military aid, much admittedly in kind, that had by 1969 amounted to some $3 billion (Clough, *Island China* p.23) and that continued till 1974

14. I.C.Y. Hsü, *China without Mao* (New York, 1983) p.176; Dumont, *Taiwan* pp.34,44; *Facts on File*, 1988 p.12

National income – remarkably evenly distributed – increased correspondingly, by an annual average of 7 per cent in the 1950s, 9 per cent in the 1960s, nearly 10 per cent in the 1970s and over 8 per cent in the 1980s; growth faltered in 1990, but the government hoped to return to a 7 per cent rate and to bring Taiwan by 2000 into the world's twenty richest per capita countries.[15]

TAIWAN'S POLITICAL EVOLUTION

Taiwan's economy, then, is a great success. Its problems have been political. One was the cleavage between the KMT mainlanders and the indigenous Taiwanese majority. This, admittedly, is now on its way to resolution: in 1988 a man of Taiwanese origin, Lee Teng-hui, succeeded to the presidency and appointed a Cabinet with a Taiwanese majority, and the 'senior parliamentarians' elected in the 1940s by mainland constituencies were eventually retired from the National Assembly to permit Taiwan-based elections in late 1991.[16]

TAIWAN'S INTERNATIONAL STATUS

More serious is the question of Taiwan's international status. In the 1950s conflict with the People's Republic of China was probably prevented only by the interposition of the US fleet. From the 1960s Beijing concentrated on securing the ROC's diplomatic isolation. Its greatest success came in the 1970s, with its recognition by the UN in 1971 and with the Sino-American détente. In 1972 Nixon visited the PRC and, in the Shanghai communiqué, acknowledged 'that all Chinese on either side of the Taiwan strait maintain there is but one China and that Taiwan is part of China. The United States Government does not challenge that position'; indeed it promised 'progressively [to] reduce its forces and military installations on Taiwan as tension in the area diminishes'. US aircraft were withdrawn by 1975; in 1979 the USA established full diplomatic

15. Hsü, *Rise of Modern China* pp.904–5; *The Economist*, 16 Nov. 1991 (A. Cowley, 'Asia's Emerging Economies' pp.6, 23); *Keesing's*, 38009

16. Hsü, *Rise of Modern China* pp.913–14; *Facts on File*, 1988 pp.525, 578–9; *Keesing's*, 35716, 38146–7, 38290. To prevent a formal breach with the mainland, Lee retained a few presidentially appointed 'overseas Chinese' representatives

relations with the PRC, terminating those with the ROC and allowing its Security Treaty to expire. However, Congress simultaneously imposed on the President a legal obligation to supply Taiwan with defensive weapons; Reagan's compliance with this caused occasional friction with China. Moreover the ROC remained, in many ways, more significant commercially than the PRC, and it has used its economic strength to reduce its political isolation. In 1989 it established a $1.2 billion development fund for 'friendly countries' that brought a number of small countries to reconsider their Chinese policy; in 1990 Nicaragua switched to become the twenty-eighth state to recognise the ROC. Trade with Eastern Europe shot up in 1991, and a delegation visited five states (including the USSR) in hopes of promoting 'substantive relations with them' through the offer of aid. Other countries (especially in South-East Asia) may be attracted by the prospect of Taiwanese investment. A number of states (including Australia and Canada) have upgraded their informal offices in Taipei.[17]

TAIWAN'S RELATIONS WITH THE PEOPLE'S REPUBLIC OF CHINA

Meanwhile the PRC has made repeated attempts to draw the Taiwan government into negotiations. Neither Chiang Kai-shek nor, after 1975, his son and heir Chiang Ching-Kuo, were tempted by promises of continued autonomy within a reunited country. But both continued to proclaim the unity of China and to persecute those who called for a legally distinct and independent Taiwan. Beijing found this encouraging, and its condolences on Chiang Ching-Kuo's death in 1988 stressed that he had 'opposed the independence of Taiwan and had stood for the reunification of the country'. By then Taiwanese politics had begun to unfreeze. In 1986 a new Democratic Progress Party (DPP) was, for the first time, unofficially permitted to contest elections. In 1989 it won twenty-two seats, of which seven went to a faction calling for Taiwan's independence as a separate state. Though such calls remained illegal (and were sometimes punished as sedition) until 1992, the

17. In 1992 Russia established an unofficial representative office (on the US and Japanese model), while Niger recognised the ROC in return for $50 million in aid, an offer that the PRC could not quite match: *New York Times*, 22 Feb. 1989 p.A3; *Keesing's*, 37670–2, 37859, 38190, 38993, 39095

DPP repeated them quite widely in the December 1991 National Assembly elections – and did badly as a result. A formal declaration of independence from China is in fact improbable, since it is the course most likely to prompt the PRC to military action. Still less likely is any early submission to Beijing, for Taiwan remains sceptical of the PRC's promises, citing the experience of Tibet. It has, however, followed a policy of progressive relaxation of restrictions on dealings with the PRC. Thus ordinary Taiwanese were, for the first time, permitted (from 1987–8) to visit the mainland.[18] Unofficial trade via Hong Kong increased, and by late 1990 Taiwanese investment on the mainland may have totalled $4 billion with more to come, much of it located inland of the offshore islands. The formal ending of the 'Period of Mobilisation for the Suppression of the Communist Rebellion' came in 1991, with President Lee acknowledging communist control of the mainland. The PRC has responded with numerous gestures, like the ending of the deafening propaganda broadcasts to the offshore islands; in April 1991, it hosted a visit by the new semi-official Taiwanese Straits Exchange Foundation. However, it has not been attracted by Taiwan's proposals for reunion on the basis of democracy and a free enterprise economy, to be negotiated by the two governments as independent and equal entities. 'Unofficial' talks have continued, with a second conference on relations and on peaceful reunification being held in Hong Kong in July 1992. But the PRC will not formally renounce the use of force; in late 1992 Taiwan sought to counter its military build-up through significant arms purchases of its own.[19]

KOREA 1945–50

Active US involvement had begun earlier in Korean than in Taiwanese affairs. Roosevelt had envisaged Korea as proceeding to independence only after a prolonged – he often said forty year – 'tutelage'. Stalin made no difficulties, but suggested a shorter time-span; in May 1945 he and Harry Hopkins agreed on a UN Trusteeship to be exercised by the USSR, USA, Britain and China.

18. Reportedly they returned unimpressed, and struck by their own vastly higher standard of living

19. *Facts on File*, 1988 p.12; *Keesing's*, 37122–3, 37670–2, 37917, 38098, 38146–7, 38190, 38814, 38912, 39005, 39095, 39236, 1992 R84

In August, with Japan on the verge of surrender and the Soviet Union moving into Manchuria and northern Korea, US Secretary of State Byrnes ordered planning for a joint US–Soviet occupation of the peninsula 'with the [dividing] line as far north as possible'. Accordingly the 38th Parallel was fixed on, without any very deep thought; Stalin accepted it without demur. It left two-thirds of the population in the south, but the more industrialised areas in the north.[20]

It now seems that the USSR had potentially conflicting interests in the peninsula. In strategic terms it was, in September 1945, chiefly concerned with acquiring sufficient control of parts of southern Korea (Inchon, Pusan, Cheju Island – and Tsushima island, which it wished transferred from Japan) that it regarded as 'of essential importance for securing dependable sea communications to the [recently reacquired] Soviet military–naval base at Port Arthur'; it looked to do this in the context of a joint four power trusteeship over the whole country. Equally 'the Japanese military and heavy industry in North Korea must be transferred to the Soviet Union as partial payment of reparations, and also as compensation for the huge damage inflicted by Japan on the Soviet Union throughout the time of its existence, including the damages from the Japanese intervention . . . from 1918 to 1923'. This too could be achieved within the context of a single Korean government, if an acceptable one could be arrived at. But it could equally be effected by partition; and, on the ground, the USSR moved in that direction far more rapidly than in Germany. By October 1945 it had sealed off its zone.[21] Within this the USSR initially worked through the leftist committees that sprang up at provincial level throughout the peninsula after Japan's decision to surrender, but in October it grouped them into an embryo state government. October also saw the foundation (under Soviet supervision and

20. This and subsequent paragraphs draw on David Rees, *A Short History of Modern Korea* (Port Erin, Isle of Man, 1988) chaps 8–9, Peter Lowe, *The Origins of the Korean War* (1986) chaps 1–2, Callum A. MacDonald, *Korea: The War before Vietnam* (Basingstoke, 1986) chap. 1, and Andrew C. Nahm, *Korea: Tradition and Transformation* (Elizabeth, NJ, 1988) chap. 9, and Kathryn Weathersby, *Soviet Aims in Korea and the Origins of the Korean War, 1945–1950: New Evidence from Russian Archives* (Cold War International History Project [CWIHP] Working Paper no.8, Washington, DC, 1993)

21. Any economic incentive to reopen it evaporated in early 1946. For the disappearance of southern rice surpluses (as a result of market reforms) prevented the US from acceding to a Soviet request for the reinstitution of the traditional barter of southern rice for northern coal (Lowe, *The Origins of the Korean War* p.26). In Germany it had been the Soviets who had occupied the agricultural areas but could not, or would not, supply the industrial west with grain

guidance) of a Communist Party whose First Secretary, Kim Il Sung, appears to have returned to Korea in the entourage of the Red Army. Reports to the CPSU Central Committee show that, that autumn, the 'occupation authorities were very active in creating Soviet-style social and political structures in northern Korea'. The winter saw the repression of a number of anti-communist riots and risings. On the other hand no effort seems to have been made to help the 'Korean Communist Party' in the south. Its members were told that 'the correct strategic line can take place only through a correct understanding of the international position of Korea . . . The ideals of the United States, the leader of capitalism, and the Soviet Union, the fatherland of the proletariat, are to be expressed in Korea without contradiction'.[22]

Korea was among the subjects considered at the December 1945 Moscow meeting of the Council of Foreign Ministers. Soviet briefing papers continued to assume the 'Necessity for the Restoration of the Unity of Korea'; one declared that 'it would be politically inexpedient for the Soviet Union to oppose the creation of a single Korean government', while noting that this would not be easy given the divergent Soviet and American policies. In the event, the Council called for the establishment of 'a four-power trusteeship for Korea for a period of up to five years'. 'Trusteeship' was an unfortunate term, given that Japan's post-1905 takeover had initially assumed that form; and the idea was repudiated by all Korean politicians except the communists. This seems to have brought the USSR to decide definitely in favour of partition. At the Joint Soviet–American Commission meetings in Seoul early in 1946, it insisted that, in preparing for a provisional government, only groups accepting the Moscow agreement – ie communists – were to be consulted. The USA refused, and talks were adjourned in May. Meanwhile the Soviet authorities moved in February to create (and closely supervise) a government (under Kim Il Sung), constitution and laws for North Korea.[23] Thereafter there was little doubt that the north had passed under communist control, though with tension and competition (as in Eastern Europe) between rival communist leaders who may have been marked by the different ways in which they had spent the years before 1945.

The interlude between the Japanese decision to surrender and the US arrival in the south had seen the proclamation of a 'Korean

22. Weathersby, *Soviet Aims in Korea and the Origins of the Korean War* pp.9–12, 15
23. ibid, pp.13–18

People's Republic', which sought to unite all politicians who had been opposed to the Japanese, but whose aims were broadly leftist though not necessarily communist. General Hodge, the US Commander, refused to recognise it, and instead operated first through the Japanese authorities and then through his own military government. Fear of communism led him, in conditions of sporadic risings and considerable social disturbance, to a tough maintenance of order which some historians see as a counter-revolution. And though Washington favoured trusteeship, its men on the ground seem to have been looking, by the winter of 1945–6, to devolve power progressively to conservative nationalists who, from exile in China, had opposed the Japanese. Accordingly February 1946 saw the constitution of an advisory body, chaired by Syngman Rhee, the 'Korean Representative Democratic Council' (KRDC). This process of the parallel evolution of potential Northern and Southern governments might have been halted by the Joint US–Soviet Commission talks, debating possible members of a provisional government (set in motion by the Moscow Council of Foreign Ministers), but, as we have seen, these failed: despite occasional signs of flexibility, the USSR would contemplate only 'democratic parties and organizations' who accepted the idea of a trusteeship, while the US pushed the KRDC, which vehemently opposed it.

Ironically General Hodge spent the next year or so quarrelling with Syngman Rhee, who was campaigning for the early establishment of an independent anti-communist South Korean government. Hodge's attempts in mid-1946 to draw together all non-communist southern politicans through a Coalition Committee failed. When the Right dominated the indirect (and rather questionable) October elections to an Interim Legislature, Hodge balanced it through his choice of nominated members; but the result was again deadlock. Meanwhile the government apparatus was gradually gaining power. A constabulary had been established in January 1946 which put down communist and harvest risings in October. The administration was 'Koreanised' in early 1947, then designated the South Korean Interim government in May; it was bolstered by a grant of $600 million over three years, decided on in parallel to the 'Truman Doctrine' aid to Greece and Turkey.

All this provided a potential alternative to the official policy of agreeing a provisional government for the entire peninsula, but it did not close the door. Indeed the Joint Comission was reconvened in May 1947 to search for such a government, and initially seemed to be making progress. But it then bogged down, possibly (though not necessarily) as a by-product of the Soviet decision to turn against Marshall Aid. Meanwhile the Americans were coming to doubt whether their administration of southern Korea could be sustained in the face of Rhee's campaign for independence. One option 'would be to arrange with the Soviet Union for mutual withdrawal of troops and let nature take its course which will eventually mean another Soviet satellite in Korea'. This prompted debate in Washington as to how much Korea mattered. Some held that 'If we allow Korea to go by default and to fall within the Communist orbit, the world will feel that we have lost another round in our match with the Soviet Union, and our prestige and the hopes of those who put their faith in us will suffer accordingly'. But the Joint Chiefs of Staff judged that 'from the standpoint of military security, the United States has little strategic interest in maintaining the present troops and bases in Korea'. The eventual decision was that, since 'the US position in Korea is untenable' but since, equally, the USA could not ' "scuttle" and run from Korea without considerable loss of prestige and political standing', it should seek a settlement 'which would enable the US to withdraw from Korea as soon as possible with the minimum of bad effects'.[24]

This meant installing an indigenous government, withdrawing, and hoping that South Korea did not collapse too quickly. The USA's chosen medium was the United Nations General Assembly. In late 1947 this appointed a Commission (on which the Ukraine declined to serve) to observe elections and advise on the installation of a government for the whole peninsula. The Commission was firmly excluded from the north, and recommended against holding elections only in the south since this could well perpetuate the peninsula's partition. But the UN decided (against the votes of Australia and, on a technicality, Canada) to go ahead. Elections were held in May 1948 under very disturbed conditions – the police did their best to make people vote, while the Far Left sought to disrupt proceedings by attacking polling booths and killing candidates. UN supervisors were very thin on the ground, but the results were recognised as a 'valid expression of the free will of the electorate in those parts of Korea which were accessible to the Commission and in which the inhabitants constituted approximately two-thirds of the people of all Korea'. The Right had won; the new National Assembly quickly adopted a Constitution and elected Syngman Rhee as President of the 'Republic of Korea' (ROK); in

24. Lowe, *The Origins of the Korean War* pp.34–6; Gaddis, *The Long Peace* pp.94–5

August 1948 this took over, with US blessing, from the military government. In December the UN recognised it as 'a lawful government' and 'the only such Government in Korea'. By implication the 'Democratic People's Republic of Korea' that had been proclaimed in the North in September was not lawful. But there were now, de facto, two Korean regimes both claiming authority throughout the peninsula.

The USSR withdrew its troops from the North in December 1948, and the USA followed suit in June 1949, being determined not to be sucked into hostilities by a Northern invasion (which it thought quite possible). However, the USA did not want to see South Korea collapse, and so continued to provide both economic and military aid. The new Republic got off to a bad start, with a major rebellion on the island of Cheju and (perhaps more ominously) a mutiny on the part of the police sent to suppress it in October 1948. In the autumn of 1949, the number of active guerrillas is supposed to have peaked at over 3,000; but by the spring of 1950 they had been worn down, despite substantial infiltration from the North. This success, however, had been won at the cost of a security effort that was pushing public expenditure out of control; by 1950 the USA was worried that South Korea would follow Kuomintang China into hyperinflation. In the May 1950 elections (held at US insistence) Rhee's party suffered an appreciable if limited set-back, while in June the price of rice rose by one-third (which could have had serious political repercussions).

Officially the US view was that South Korea could now handle anything short of an invasion actively supported by the USSR or China, and that this was unlikely. But there were doubts. The British (always rather sceptical observers of US Korean policy) produced a War Office report in December 1949 to the effect that 'there can be no doubt whatever that [the North's] ultimate object is to overrun the South; and I think in the long term there is no doubt that they will do so'. A little later the commander of the US Military Advisory Group also doubted Southern military capabilities, though admittedly by way of lobbying Washington to improve them. In May 1950 the chairman of the Senate Foreign Relations Committee told the press that he expected the communists to overrun Korea (and probably also Taiwan).[25]

25. Gaddis, *The Long Peace* p.96; Lowe, *The Origins of the Korean War* pp.57–67; R.R. Simmons, *The Strained Alliance. Peking, Pyongyang, Moscow and the Politics of the Korean War* (New York, 1975) p.115

KIM IL SUNG'S PLAN TO INVADE SOUTH KOREA 1949–50

These views appear to have been held also by Kim Il Sung. He had constantly been pressing on Stalin the urgency of reunion, and from 1949 he was advocating invasion and buying Soviet arms. According to a classified history of the war written in 1966 by the Soviet Foreign Ministry, Kim and other Korean leaders

> were firmly determined to unify the country by military means . . .
>
> Calculating that the USA would not enter a war over South Korea, Kim Il Sung persistently pressed for agreement from Stalin and Mao Zedong . . .
>
> Stalin at first treated the[se] persistent appeals . . . with reserve, . . . but he did not object in principle. The final agreement to support the plans of the Koreans was given by Stalin at the time of Kim Il Sung's visit to Moscow in March–April 1950.[26] Following this, in May, Kim . . . visited Beijing and secured the support of Mao . . .
>
> By the end of May 1950 the General Staff of the K[orean] P[eople's] A[rmy] together with Soviet military advisers[27] announced the readiness of the Korean army to begin concentration at the 38th parallel. At the insistence of Kim Il Sung, the beginning of military activity was scheduled for June 25, 1950.
>
> By the time of the attack, the North Korean armed forces had significant superiority over the South Koreans . . . The operational plan . . . envisioned that Korean troops would . . . in the main complete military activity within 22–27 days.[28]

Cautiously, though, after massively equipping the North Korean Army, Stalin pulled back all military advisers so that there should be no provable link with the USSR (for which Krushchev blamed him, feeling that the commitment of one or two Soviet tank corps would have settled the issue).[29]

26. According to his interpreter Kim urged that, with a surprise attack, the war would be won in three days; there would be a rising of 200,000 Party members in the south, plus support from the southern guerrillas; and the US would not have time to intervene (Weathersby, *Soviet Aims in Korea and the Origins of the Korean War*, p.26). Khrushchev says Kim had argued 'that South Korea was blanketed with Party organisations and that the people would rise up in revolt when the Party gave the signal', while Mao had held 'that the USA would not intervene since the war would be an internal [Korean] matter' (*Khrushchev Remembers* i pp.333–4 – cf. also ibid, iii pp.144–6, and Chen, *The Sino-Soviet Alliance and China's Entry into the Korean War* pp.18–21). Of course Rhee was just as keen to liberate the North (Simmons, *The Strained Alliance* pp.115–16); but the US did not give him the go-ahead

27. Weathersby claims that 'The evidence is persuasive that the [actual] battle plan used for the invasion . . . was drafted by Soviet advisers' (*Soviet Aims in Korea and the Origins of the Korean War* p.25n)

28. ibid, pp.24–5

29. *Khrushchev Remembers* i p.335

THE WESTERN RESPONSE

The invasion on 25 June 1950 caught Truman on holiday. He later wrote that, as he flew back to Washington, he recalled Manchuria (1931), Ethiopia (1935–6) and Austria (1938), where the democracies' inaction had simply encouraged further aggression:

> If this was allowed to go unchallenged it would mean a third World War, just as similar incidents had brought on the Second. . . . It was also clear to me that the foundations and the principles of the United Nations were at stake unless this unprovoked attack on Korea could be stopped.

Such perceptions were not confined to the USA; a leading French official thought that the loss of Korea would 'irretrievably impair' Western prestige and drew parallels with 1938. According to Acheson, 'the governments of many Western European nations appeared to be in a state of near panic, as they watched to see whether the United States would act or not'; there were US fears that, if it did not, Europe would go neutralist. The US decision to respond, therefore, was taken in the light not of feelings about Korea itself, or even about its strategic significance (which, in Japan at least, is regarded as considerable), but of a general view of the international system: 'We can't let the UN down!', Truman repeated to himself on 25 June, 'We can't let the UN down!'.[30]

The initial US (and British) contribution was of naval and air support, in line with the offshore nature of its then defence posture. Originally it was hoped (despite US Army scepticism) that this would suffice. By the end of June it was clear that it would not; Truman authorised the commitment of combat troops. Assessments of the forces needed steadily escalated, but by mid-July General MacArthur was confident: 'I intend to destroy and not to drive back the North Korean forces. . . . I may need to occupy all of North Korea. In the aftermath of operations, the problem is to compose and unite Korea'.[31] MacArthur's strategy, an amphibious landing at Inchon hundreds of miles behind the current front, had technical flaws. But when executed on 15 September 1950, it succeeded

30. Harry S. Truman, *Years of Trial and Hope, 1946–1953* (1956) p.351; Deborah Larson in Robert Jervis and J.L. Snyder (eds) *Dominoes and Bandwagons: Strategic Beliefs and Great Power Competition in the Eurasian Rimland* (New York, 1991) pp.96–8; Gaddis, *The Long Peace* p.97

31. *History of the Joint Chiefs of Staff [JCS]* (typescript, National Archives, Washington, DC) iii p.222. For a fuller account of the war, see *The Cold War* chap. 4

brilliantly: a fortnight later North Korean forces south of the 38th Parallel had been destroyed.

THE UN INVASION OF NORTH KOREA, CHINA'S INTERVENTION, AND US RESPONSES (1950–1)

Victory raised the question of what to do next. Initially the US administration had proclaimed that its intervention was intended only to restore the prewar position. But opinion had been hardening during the summer in favour of overrunning the North; on 27 September MacArthur was directed to do so provided there was no likelihood of major Soviet or Chinese intervention. In retrospect this was a disastrous mistake. At the time it was seen as a natural punishment for aggression, as the simplest way of preventing the regrouping of North Korean forces and another round of fighting, and, above all, as the implementation of the 1947 UN policy of reuniting Korea through free elections. On 7 October 1950 a British Resolution was carried overwhelmingly in the General Assembly calling on UN forces to cross the 38th Parallel, restore 'stability throughout Korea' and hold elections.[32] They then followed the South Koreans over. No restrictions were placed on MacArthur's deployments; although he had initially envisaged halting foreign troops on a defensible line at the narrowest point of the peninsula and using only Koreans beyond it, on 17 October he ordered a further bound and thereafter headed hard for the international frontier with China along the Yalu river. A final offensive to achieve this was launched in late November, but coincided with a Chinese counter-offensive and was swept away.

Khrushchev tells us that Stalin would have let Kim Il Sung go under, but that he accepted a Chinese offer to intervene. Their initial attack went very well, and their military was consistently over-confident: 'The American troops were crushed and the war ended many times in these battle reports'.[33] Like the UN forces they pushed their luck too far. In December 1950 Washington was in a flat spin, without a policy but revolving ideas of evacuating

32. With this in mind, the UN Command itself administered, until the 1953 armistice, occupied territory north of the Parallel, rather than simply turning it over to South Korea

33. *Khrushchev Remembers* i pp.336–7, iii p.147; Chen, *The Sino-Soviet Alliance and China's Entry into the Korean War* pp.22–30; see also *The Cold War* chap. 4

Korea and/or expanding the war beyond the peninsula. It would have jumped at a cease-fire, and endorsed Arab–Asian attempts to secure one through the UN. Zhou Enlai refused, declaring that the 38th Parallel had been 'obliterated forever' by the invasion of North Korea, and demanding the evacuation of all foreign troops plus American departure from Taiwan and the seating of Communist China in the UN. A further offensive (31 December–10 January) took the Chinese south of the South Korean capital of Seoul. On 11 January 1951 another cease-fire plan was put to the General Assembly, in many ways rather nebulous but involving withdrawal of foreign troops and a conference to settle the status of Taiwan and Chinese representation at the UN. The US administration accepted, preferring domestic political trouble to the risk of alienating its allies, and hoping that the Chinese would decline – as indeed they did. By then the USA had become more confident as to the military situation; at the end of the month it proceeded to have China declared an 'aggressor' under the new UN 'uniting for peace' procedure (see p.456),[34] despite Chinese warnings that this would 'close the door' on any possibility of peace.

Counter-offensives from late January to April took UN forces just past the Parallel; the USA now determined to seek a cease-fire. Late April saw a well prepared Chinese offensive, which at one point came within five miles of Seoul; at the end of May this was driven back with such heavy losses that the new UN Commander[35] could report that for the next two months the 'military situation [would offer] optimum advantages in support of . . . diplomatic negotiations'. Various soundings of the Soviet Union and China had already been made in mid-May, but to no purpose. So Kennan was asked to speak ominously but unofficially to the Soviet UN ambassador – to the effect that current Chinese policy risked precipitating a 'most dangerous [US–Soviet] collision'. 'If the drift to serious trouble was to be stopped, the method would seem to be an armistice and cease-fire in Korea at about where the forces stood.'[36] Whether through fear, or through a concern not to lose further territory in Korea, the Russians proposed talks; these began in early July 1951.

34. *History of the JCS*, iii pp.385, 428–30; Acheson, *Present at the Creation* p.513; Simmons, *The Strained Alliance* pp.188–90

35. MacArthur had been dismissed in April 1951 for issuing unauthorised statements and criticising administration policy

36. *History of the JCS* iii pp.502, 527, 564; Acheson, *Present at the Creation* p.532

CEASE-FIRE TALKS 1951–3; THE 1953 ARMISTICE

Fighting eased off but did not end, owing to an American concern that, if it did, public opinion would insist on bringing the boys home as in 1945, leaving the UN Command helpless if the communists chose to break off talks. In fact these talks dragged on for two years – which greatly soured the US domestic response to 'Truman's War'. Negotiations were always difficult, but in November 1951 agreement was reached on a potential armistice line along the current front (a position slightly more favourable to South Korea than the 38th Parallel). Thereafter the chief, and from May 1952 the only, issue was that of the repatriation of prisoners against their will.[37]

By October 1952 the UN Command had made a final offer, and, as it was not accepted, recessed the armistice talks indefinitely. Thoughts then turned to the possibilities of coercive action. Most US generals doubted the chances of any significant victory on the ground without major reinforcements; given the calls on US troops elsewhere, the Chiefs of Staff were unenthusiastic. During his visit to Korea in December 1952, President-elect Eisenhower made it clear that he favoured a cease-fire in place. Once in office he hinted discreetly in a number of quarters that, in the absence of satisfactory negotiating progress, he might use nuclear weapons and expand hostilities beyond the Korean peninsula. Whether for this reason, or as a result of Stalin's death on 5 March 1953,[38] on the 28th the communist commanders signalled a wish to resume negotiations. Once more these were slow; they were further complicated by Syngman Rhee's determined resistance to any armistice that left Korea divided; and they were marred by the escalation of US bombing and by heavy final communist offensives. Ultimately the communists dropped their demand for the forcible repatriation of prisoners, and a cease-fire took effect that has lasted (uneasily) to this day. The possibility of another Northern invasion

37. To China's anger two-thirds of all Chinese prisoners refused to return; the UN Command would not compel them to do so, not only for propaganda reasons but also because it did not want to expose them to the fate of the Russians returned after Yalta

38. Dwight D. Eisenhower, *Mandate for Change* (1963) p.181. In May he told the NSC that, if talks failed, he favoured decisive atomic strikes against China: 'the quicker the operation was mounted, the less the danger of Soviet intervention' (*The [London] Times*, 9 June 1984 p.3). The 1966 classified Soviet history claims that, 'after Stalin's death,' the USSR, with Chinese encouragement, 'in many ways facilitated the conclusion of the [armistice] agreement' (Kathryn Weathersby, CWIHP *Bulletin* 3 (1993) pp.15, 17, 18)

remained; partly for this reason, partly to induce Rhee to accept the armistice, the USA concluded a defence agreement with South Korea and retained troops there.

POSTWAR TENSIONS BETWEEN NORTH AND SOUTH KOREA 1953–87

Neither North nor South Korea has ever accepted the partition of the country as permanent. North Korea did not again seek reunification by force, but it has tried various forms of destabilisation. In 1968 there was an attempt to murder the South Korean President and the landing of guerrillas seeking to generate insurgency.[39] In 1974 a shot missed the President but killed his wife; infiltration tunnels running under the border demilitarised zone were then discovered, followed by others in 1978 and 1980. In 1983 an ROK delegation to Burma was blown up, killing seventeen but missing the President. In 1987 somebody confessed to blowing up an ROK airliner, acting on orders from the son of North Korea's leader.[40] Such episodes, and North Korea's declared readiness forcibly to support a southern rising, have kept tension along the demilitarised zone far higher than along, say, the border between East and West Germany. This has been felt to necessitate a large ROK army, which in turn has been the predominant factor in Southern politics and has used the Northern danger to justify authoritarian rule.

North Korea, although smaller than the ROK (in population and, from the 1960s, in wealth), seems to have spent more heavily on defence (supposedly 24 per cent of its GNP in 1985 to the South's 6 per cent), and to have achieved superior armed forces. Accordingly a US presence (until 1991 with nuclear weapons) on the ground was seen as necessary to deter invasion.[41] As part of his general reduction of US forces Nixon removed 20,000 men in 1970; but he also gained Prime Minister Sato's assent to a clause asserting that South Korean security was 'essential to Japan's own security'. In the early 1970s this proved controversial, and Japanese attitudes

39. Also the seizure on the high seas of the US intelligence ship *Pueblo*, followed in 1969 by the shooting down of a US surveillance aircraft: Rees, *Short History of Korea* p.162

40. ibid, pp.152, 166–7; *Keesing's*, 36590

41. Rees, *Short History of Korea* pp.177–9; *East Asia, the West and International Security, Part 3* (IISS Adelphi Paper no. 218) p.17; *Keesing's*, 1992 R71

towards South Korea cooled (in the light both of the 'Nixon shocks' and of the 1973 kidnapping from Japan of the Korean opposition leader, Kim Dae Jung). But in 1975 Hanoi's conquest of South Vietnam, and its enthusiastic welcome by North Korea, worried Tokyo as well as Seoul. When the Carter administration declared its intention of withdrawing ground forces over five years, Japan lobbied actively against this and presumably contributed to the 1979 decision to postpone the cuts – as it proved indefinitely.[42]

SOUTH KOREAN ECONOMIC AND POLITICAL DEVELOPMENTS

The cost of the Korean War had been horrific: perhaps 0.9 million Chinese, 1.5 million North Korean, and 1.3 million South Korean (mostly civilian) casualties, plus 34,000 US dead (and over 100,000 wounded).[43] Both Koreas were devastated. The North (exposed to US air power) must have suffered worse, but it recovered faster, partly because it contained most of the country's industry and mineral resources, partly as a result of successful communist mobilisation. In the South, Syngman Rhee managed, by 1957, to end runaway inflation, but despite $1.7 billion aid, little economic progress was made. The liberal parliamentary government that took over in 1960 inherited, but did not master, a financial crisis.[44] General Park Chung Hee, who staged a coup in 1961 and had by later 1963 finally consolidated his rule as President, was vastly more successful. A former officer in the Japanese army, he avowedly modelled himself on Japan's Meiji era modernisation and post-1945 recovery.[45] A Five-Year Plan, oriented towards producer rather than consumer goods, was announced in 1961. Park followed it up by seeking to normalise relations with Japan, previously poisoned by colonial memories and fishery disputes. This did not prove at all easy: 1964 saw demonstrations against Park's 'humiliating diplomacy' that led to the resignation of the Cabinet and proclamation of martial law; meanwhile Japan, though theoretically appreciating the need for economic aid 'to bring about political stability' in

42. South Korea needed this assistance, since its own persuasive power had been reduced by Koreagate (see p.448): Chong-sik Lee, *Japan and Korea: The Political Dimension* (Stanford, Calif., 1985) pp.72, 75 ff, 93–9

43. Simmons, *The Strained Alliance* pp.213, 242. War and refugee movements left the North Korean population 1 million lower in 1953 than it had been in 1949

44. Rees, *Short History of Korea* pp.141–3

45. Lee, *Japan and Korea* pp.62–3

Korea, proved in practice decidedly stingy. The USA sought to mediate. A treaty was finally signed in 1965, establishing full diplomatic relations, delimiting fishery zones, settling the status of Korean residents in Japan, and providing for Japanese payment of some $500 million in grants and soft loans, $300 million in commercial ones.[46]

These figures were well below Korea's original hopes, and below the $1 billion US aid during 1965–70 that Park earned, in part, by contributing troops to the Vietnam War.[47] But they unlocked further Japanese commercial loans, which served as catalysts in that the Korean government used them as guides in according domestic assistance to entrepreneurs.[48] The process brought corruption, but it worked. Korean growth would appear to have taken off in 1963; on one computation it averaged over 8 per cent per year both in the 1960s and (despite a severe slump in 1980) in 1971–80, nearly 10 per cent in 1981–90. It was led by industrial production in which huge firms modelled on the Japanese played an important role, though the 1970s were to see a major programme of agricultural development as well. Despite some foreign investment (half from Japan), it was high risk in that, into the 1980s, Korea consistently ran a trade deficit, financed by borrowing. By late 1982 its $37 billion foreign debt equalled that of the Argentine. However Korea did not default, but moved into surplus and started to repay its debt. (Its success was such that GATT ruled that from 1990 it should no longer restrict imports on balance of payments grounds, though in 1991 Korea again returned to deficit.) The South Korean economy, therefore, may now be nine or ten times as large as the North Korean.[49]

North Korea apparently achieved complete political stability by 1958, when Kim Il Sung purged his last rivals. He went on to establish a personality cult of more than Stalinist proportions (including a 500-foot statue in Pyongyang). Recently there have been some hints at political unease, but Kim clearly means to be succeeded by his son, Kim Chong Il. South Korea, by contrast, has so far oscillated between periods of firm rule and disturbed interregnums marked by major riots, generally student-led but

46. ibid, esp. pp.49–55

47. Rees, *Short History of Korea* p.148

48. Overall Japanese loans to Korea (1965–73) were $674 million commercial and $416 million governmental: Lee, *Japan and Korea* pp.63–6, 86

49. ibid, esp. pp.86, 91, 121, Table 6; *Asian Economic Handbook* p.8; Rees, *Short History of Korea* chap. 13; Cowley, 'Asia's Emerging Economies' p.6; *Keesing's*, 37281–3, 1992 R72

including demands for higher wages. In 1960 such protests against Syngman Rhee's electoral manipulations brought about his fall (see p.447). There followed a brief period of parliamentary rule, a coup, and General Park's consolidation of power, culminating in his successful re-election as President in 1963 against a divided Opposition.[50] Later Park found it necessary to change the Constitution, first to allow himself more than two presidential terms, later to enable him to nominate one-third of the National Assembly, which proved useful when his party was outpolled in the 1978 elections. In 1979 there were serious riots and calls for Park's resignation; that October he was murdered, probably as a prelude to a coup by the security services. This led both to the gradual assumption of power by General Chun Doo Hwan and to strikes, demonstrations and a popular uprising in Kwangju. The number killed in its suppression remains controversial to this day.[51] Chun wanted to hand over, after one seven-year term as President, to a hand-picked successor, Roh Tae Woo; but from 1986 onwards agitation mounted for, at the least, constitutional revision and a genuine election. By mid-1987 it had spilt over into violent demonstrations and widespread arrests, and seemed likely to endanger the holding of the 1988 Olympics. Roh then partially defused the situation by endorsing most opposition demands. He won the presidential elections in December 1987, though only because his opponents could not agree a single candidate, and took office in February; but his party failed in April 1988 to gain an absolute majority in the National Assembly. Disturbances continued, with a break for the Olympics. Roh moved to isolate his more extreme opponents (generally students) by liberal talk, by allowing the re-opening of scandals from Chun's regime, and by making overtures to the North. In late 1989 he struck a deal with the three main Opposition leaders by sacrificing politicians linked too closely with ex-President Chun and forcing Chun himself to testify on the Kwangju rising; he followed this up in 1990 with a merger with two Opposition parties. This gave Roh a large Assembly majority; it also brought into the ruling party one of his 1987 presidential rivals, Kim Young Sam, who (after various alarms) won what appear to have been open and competitive elections in 1992 to succeed Roh as President.[52]

50. Rees, *Short History of Korea* pp.140–6; see also pp.447–8 in this volume

51. At the time the government claimed 144 civilians, but 2,000 is now thought more likely: *Keesing's*, 30607, 36020

52. *Keesing's*, 35505 ff, 35769, 30621, 37123, 37282–3, 39234

LIMITED THAW BETWEEN NORTH AND SOUTH KOREA 1988–93; SOUTH KOREA'S SUCCESSES ON THE WIDER DIPLOMATIC SCENE

In mid-1988 Roh declared that 'dismantling the barrier separating the South and the North and building a road to a unified and prosperous homeland is a duty that history has imposed on every Korean alive today'. North–South Korean relations have been abysmal, far worse than those between East and West Germany; but the consciousness of belonging to one country is strong enough to prompt frequent propaganda proposals and periodic talks on reunion. Talks were held in 1971–3, in 1985–6 (resulting in permission for a limited number of family visits and reunions), and in 1985–7 (in a vain attempt to agree arrangements for the shared management of the Seoul Olympic Games).[53] By 1988 the South Korean regime's US orientation (and its refusal to concede Northern demands over the Olympics) were being attacked as blocks to reunion. President Roh was therefore more adventurous than his predecessors; Kim Il Sung also proved more forthcoming than in the past; the period since 1988 has seen a higher level of North–South contacts than ever before. At first little was achieved; late 1991 saw a renewal of tension, stemming from fears that North Korea was on the verge of becoming a nuclear power. Talks in December 1991, however, went unexpectedly well, and the two Prime Ministers signed a non-aggression pact, promising telephone links and freedom of travel across the cease-fire line, and undertaking to work for a nuclear-free peninsula.[54] However, little concrete followed in 1992. The chief obstacle remained suspicions of North Korea's nuclear programme and of its refusal to allow more than limited inspections by the International Atomic Energy Agency; 1992 ended with renewed tension and North Korean threats to break off negotiations altogether if the South resumed joint military exercises with the USA.[55]

More demonstrable progress was achieved by the other prong of South Korea's policy, the enhancement of its status relative to that

53. Rees, *Short History of Korea* pp.156, 163; *Keesing's*, 35904 ff

54. *Keesing's*, 36289–90, 37280, 38010, 38396, 1992 R71. The softening of North Korea's stance may have reflected grave economic difficulties and a wish to unlock Japanese economic aid. Equally South Koreans, looking to the German example, have recently come to be concerned at the likely cost of rehabilitating the north in the event of reunion, and so perhaps to favour a rather more gradual process than they did in the heady aftermath of German reunion in 1990

55. *Keesing's*, 38912, 38962, 39141, 39190

of North Korea and the improvement of its standing with the latter's communist allies. One milestone was its ability to stage the Olympics in 1988 without encountering communist boycotts. 1988 also saw the doubling of trade with China and the establishment of what were termed 'working trade agreements' with the USSR. In 1990 there was a meeting between Presidents Roh and Gorbachev, which the latter said had been inspired by the scale of commercial links; it was, as Roh had forecast, soon followed by the establishment of full diplomatic relations. Economic collaboration prospered, and Korea offered the USSR $3 billion in tied aid. In April 1991 Gorbachev paid a flying visit to South Korea. That summer diplomatic relations were established with China, which withdrew its opposition to UN membership for the ROK. North Korea had previously insisted that only a single Korea should be represented, but, fearing isolation, it too applied for membership. Both states joined in September 1991, amid further talk from Roh about reunion. Fifteen months later South Korea was chosen to chair the Group of 77 (see pp.473–4) developing countries for 1993.[56]

THE PHILIPPINES 1945–60

Indo-China apart, nowhere in the Western Pacific has international tension approached the level of the Korean peninsula or the Chinese offshore islands. Instead the story is mostly one of attempts, generally but not always successful, at national and regional consolidation and economic growth. Ironically this process proved unusually arduous in the Philippines, a US colony that proceeded to independence in 1946 with much goodwill, and a strong US orientation evidenced in mutual tariff and investment preferences and (from 1947) huge US military bases. Superficially Philippine politics consisted of largely non-ideological US-style two-party contests; under the surface, they represented competition between great families (and their clienteles) more reminiscent of Hispanic *caciquismo*, which, in many localities, descended to a liberal use of 'guns, gold and goons'. The chief threat to the system, the more alarming because of its proximity to the capital, was the rural Hukbalahap insurgency. The Huks derived from peasant protest of

56. *Keesing's*, 37089, 37533, 37715, 38147, 38396, 39050, 39251; Cowley, 'Asia's Emerging Economies' p.22

the 1930s. During the Second World War they had fought the Japanese, helping US forces but holding aloof from the official US-sponsored guerrillas. It is not clear how far they were under communist influence, but after 1945 many Americans saw this as considerable; both they and the landlords who controlled the Filipino government sought to disarm the Huks. The resulting collisions, violent disputes over rent and the blocking of political protest through electoral manipulation led to the renewal in 1946 of a rebellion that the Communist Party came to endorse (and seek to dominate). Even at their 1949–51 peak, the Huks were largely confined to central Luzon, could draw on no foreign support, and never secured a sanctuary or 'liberated area'. From late 1951 the tide turned, and by 1954 the rising had been substantially put down, by a combination of more competent military action, amnesties, and the wooing of peasant sympathies through (limited) land reform and the curbing of state and landlord brutality. This seemed an object lesson in how to handle a communist insurrection, credit for which went chiefly to Defense Secretary Ramon Magsaysay, helped by US advisers (some later famous in Vietnam) and comparatively small sums of aid.[57]

In 1953 Magsaysay duly won the presidency but he died in a plane crash in 1957 and proved hard to replace.

THE MARCOS ERA 1965–86

In the 1960s the most successful politician was Ferdinand Marcos, who secured an unprecedented re-election as President in 1969. He then ran into problems, both economic and of public disorder, though it is unclear how far he fomented violence himself in order to justify a constitutional coup. This came in 1972 with amendments to enable Marcos to continue indefinitely as President, followed by the declaration of martial law. Marcos then tried to replicate the Korean and Taiwanese economic miracles. By no means everything he did failed, but he made some instructive mistakes. He embarked on a Taiwanese-style land reform, but did not really carry it through in the face of opposition from plantation-owners. He followed Korea in favouring large privileged companies for strategic economic areas; but these 'crony capitalists' both damaged ordinary

57. From 1951 to 1956 $500 million (including $117 million military assistance), down from the $700 million of 1946–50: Benedict J. Kerkvliet, *The Huk Rebellion* (Berkeley, Calif., 1977) pp.240, 244

small-scale business and lacked the talent of their Korean counterparts (often needing to be financially rescued). In particular they did not really build out from the domestic market into exports; this not only harmed the balance of payments but also reduced pressure on their firms to become internationally competitive. Capital was, indeed, increasingly wasted, both on prestige building and property speculation, and on inappropriately capital-intensive industry. As in Korea, development was financed by international borrowing. Much was unavoidable, but the burden could have been reduced (as in Singapore, Malaysia and to a lesser extent Korea) had foreign commercial investment been more welcome, since this is less likely to go into uneconomic projects and (unlike bank loans) does not require servicing unless it is profitable.

The last straw was political weakness. Both the communist and the Muslim insurgencies spread in an atmosphere of general alienation. Living standards were under pressure, especially after the 1979 oil price rise. In August 1983 the opposition leader Senator Aquino decided to risk coming back, and was instantly murdered. This was perceived as an act of desperation on Marcos's part and prompted a massive flight of capital. In October the Philippines sought a debt moratorium, and the subsequent long-drawn negotiations with the IMF were not conducive to business confidence. Aquino's murder served also to galvanise the political oppositions, leading to repeated demonstrations, a high turn-out in the 1984 parliamentary elections, and the expectation that Marcos's fall would be only a matter of time. With such pervasive uncertainty, the Philippines failed to take advantage of the Reagan boom in the US economy and the surge in imports that had so striking an effect on Korea and Taiwan; indeed in 1984 and 1985 GNP dropped.[58]

Reagan had been reluctant to intervene lest Marcos's fall resulted (as in Nicaragua) in a communist takeover. But he was reluctantly convinced that the regime's continuance was in fact helping the communists, and in October 1965 began to put pressure on Marcos. Marcos responded by calling a snap presidential election for February 1986, hoping the opposition would be divided, but at the eleventh hour the Church arranged a coalition headed by Aquino's widow. Marcos's National Assembly declared him the victor, but this was so much at variance with unofficial counts as to provoke a crisis. Things were brought to a head by a small mutiny led by the Defense Secretary and the Chief of Staff

58. John Bresnan (ed.) *Crisis in the Philippines: The Marcos Era and Beyond* (Princeton, NJ, 1986) esp. chaps 5, 6; *Keesing's*, 34874

(Fidel Ramos). Marcos was restrained from crushing it by the interposition of enormous crowds, called out by the Church. President Reagan both appealed to him to retire and offered asylum; after some hesitation, Marcos went, with his vast ill-gotten wealth, into exile.[59]

THE PHILIPPINES 1986–93

Cory Aquino took over as President in February 1986. She managed, with considerable difficulty, to remain in power despite attempts at military coups and a quarrel with her Vice-President. In 1992 she was succeeded by Ramos, who had narrowly won elections in which no candidate achieved as much as one-quarter of the votes cast.

The economy has started to revive, but it remained (as one commentator put it) 'on the bottom tier of free Asia',[60] afflicted by inflation and foreign debt, and (since 1989) subject to IMF surveillance. There was, however, a diminution of insurgency, both regional and on the part of the Communists. These had in 1969 founded a New People's Army (NPA), looking to the Maoist guerrilla model. Its leaders were drawn more from the intelligentsia than had been those of the Huks, and their horizons were wider. Appealing not only to tenant farmers but also to a wide range of alienated and marginalised people, they expanded particularly in Marcos's last years. By 1984 they had appreciable influence in perhaps one-fifth of the country's *barrios*; in 1985 they are supposed to have had some 20,000 active guerrillas, and their advance occasioned both domestic and international concern.[61] Aquino's first instinct was to draw them back into the political process through the release of prisoners, amnesties and cease-fires. This annoyed the army, and did not induce the NPA to abandon armed struggle. Indeed the NPA continued to grow, and its activities expanded to include urban assassinations and the sporadic targeting of US officials. So the government resumed the offensive,

59. George P. Shultz, *Turmoil and Triumph. My Years as Sectretary of State* (New York, 1993) chap.31; *Keesing's*, 34928 ff. Nobody knows how much money was salted away abroad. In 1988 Marcos reportedly offered $5 billion for permission to return home. In 1987 it was claimed he had personally stolen $10 billion, his friends perhaps as much again, which accounts for much of the nation's international debt (of $26 billion in 1984): *Keesing's*, 35714; *Facts on File*, 1987 pp.560–1, 1988 p.722

60. That is, closer to Thailand, Malaysia and Indonesia than to Taiwan, Korea, Hong Kong, and Singapore (*New York Times*, 24 Feb. 1989 pp.D1, 4); cf. *Keesing's*, 37580, 38012

61. Bresnan, *Crisis in the Philippines* pp.130–4, 244–5; *Keesing's*, 39100

securing considerable successes through an intense and controversial offensive in 1989. Forced on to the defensive, NPA propaganda came to focus increasingly on opposing the US presence and bases; when in 1991 the Philippines' Senate rejected the treaty providing for their continuance, the NPA formally proclaimed a cease-fire. This did not in fact hold; but, shortly after taking office in June 1992, President Ramos began releasing communist prisoners as part of a general attempt at pacification. In September 1992 the ban on the Communist Party was lifted and peace talks were arranged, while overtures were made to the Muslim rebels (albeit initially in vain). Progress proved slow, and clashes continued. But in mid-1993 NPA forces had fallen to half their 1988 strength, and by the end of the year there were signs that both the communist and the Muslim insurgencies were winding down.[62]

Late 1992 also saw the United States' evacuation of their giant bases in the Philippines. These had once appeared to be of international importance: for the USA certainly valued their convenience, and implied that, without them, it would be hard to maintain US military supremacy in the Western Pacific and capacity to intervene further afield. At first the Philippines was only too pleased to have them: we have noted its 1951 insistence on a Security Treaty. Marcos reopened discussions, securing in 1979 a reduction in their size and a US payment of $500 million over 1980–4, then in 1983 another payment of $900 million for 1985–9. During the 1988 negotiations for 1989–91 the Filipino Foreign Secretary chose to play to a nascent, but by no means universal, anti-Americanism. But the real question was that of a new treaty that would permit the bases to continue after 1991. Cliff-hanging talks eventually produced such a treaty in 1991; when this was rejected by the Filipino Senate, Aquino seemed ready to take the question to the people through a referendum. But by then the world had changed: physically in that a volcano had buried the Clark air base in ash; politically in that, with the collapse of Soviet power, the USA no longer saw the Subic naval base as necessary and decided to draw it down or leave rather than become dependent on the course of Filipino politics.[63]

62. *Keesing's*, 35712–14, 37579–80, 38442, 39603, 39741, 39781, 1992 R80, 1993 R80

63. *Keesing's*, 36428, 38344–5, 38441–2, 38677, 39100, 39196, 1992 R80

THE ESTABLISHMENT OF ASEAN 1967

In 1965 the USA seemed to have had little luck with South-East Asia. It was militarily involved in South Vietnam. Laos had occasioned a major international crisis in 1960–2, followed by a low-level civil war. US actions there were, at least in part, designed to reassure an extremely nervous Thailand, which preferred to be defended beyond its borders. Indonesia had, despite recent US cultivation, aligned itself with China, and plunged into 'confrontation' with Malaysia and Britain. Britain's creation of Malaysia (against US wishes) had also annoyed the Philippines, which laid claim to Sabah. Malaysia's emergence appeared not even to have resolved the tricky problem of Singapore: this withdrew in 1965 with hard feelings on both sides, and its viability as an independent state was in considerable doubt. In retrospect the crucial change came with the attempted 1965 Indonesian coup and the subsequent manoeuvring aside of Sukarno.[64] The new ruler, Suharto, was both firmly anti-communist and anxious to mend fences with Malaysia. There had earlier been vague regionalist aspirations towards a grouping of Malaya, the Philippines, and Indonesia (Maphilindo) or Thailand (Association of South-East Asia). With the increasingly erratic and expansionist Sukarno gone, these schemes could now safely be resumed, for cooperation offered the non-communist states of the area their best chance of survival. Such sentiments were particularly strongly voiced by the Singapore Prime Minister Lee Kuan Yew: the United States was 'buying time' for the nations of Asia, but 'if we just sit down and believe people are going to buy time for ever after for us, then we deserve to perish'. Thailand, too, strongly supported US action in Indo-China, but looked to regionalism as reinsurance against the possible waning of the US presence.[65] The result was the establishment in 1967 of the Association of South-East Asian Nations (ASEAN), initially a rather nebulous organisation, but one that damped down conflict between its members and left them free to concentrate on their own development.[66]

Singapore was the most active, especially as it was faced with the

64. See *The Cold War* chap. 8

65. W.W. Rostow, *The United States and the Regional Organization of Asia and the Pacific, 1965–1985* (Austin, Tex., 1986) pp.14–15, 24–6; Girling, *Thailand* pp.114–15

66. Thus in 1969 Malaysia and the Philippines were induced to resume diplomatic relations, suspended as a result of the Philippine claim (not finally abandoned until 1992) to Sabah: *Keesing's*, 25941, 39100

rundown of its great British military base. It sought both to reduce population growth and to boost manufacturing by attracting multinationals (by 1983 it had received $4.7 billion of foreign investment).[67] Later it was able to go up-market (perhaps a little too fast in the 1980s), though still relying substantially on petrochemicals and ship repair, and to become a major commercial and tourist centre. Singapore is usually classed with Taiwan, Korea and Hong Kong as one of the 'Four [economic] Tigers'. The other ASEAN members also enjoyed economic growth, albeit slightly less rapid and from a lower starting-point.[68] Growth did not always prove so stabilising, however: Malaysia was briefly shaken by racial riots in 1969, while the Philippines and Thailand both experienced appreciable domestic insurgencies in the 1970s (that of Thailand partly the result of groups and areas which felt they were missing out on development).

THAILAND IN THE 1970s

Thailand also faced political instability. In 1968–9 the military-based government inaugurated elections under a new constitution, only to suspend this in 1971. In 1973 student demonstrations and demands for the constitution's reinstatement escalated into massive disturbances; the King and the army withdrew support from the government, and its leaders went into exile. This inaugurated a period of highly visible leftist agitation, demonstrations and strikes, which caused much alarm even though the 1975 and 1976 elections produced centrist (if unstable) governments. The response was massive right-wing organisation in the name of 'nation, religion and king', which culminated in the 1976 sacking of Thammasat University after students had hung the Crown Prince in effigy. There ensued a period of right-wing repression that drove many moderate leaders to take refuge with the insurgents, then from 1977 milder military rule. This has since settled down, with royal

67. Jan Woronoff, *Asia's 'Miracle' Economies* (Armonk, NY, 1986) p.133

68. Indonesia 3.5% per year GDP growth 1960–70, 8% 1971–80, nearly 6% 1981–90; Malaysia 6.5%, 8% and nearly 6%; Thailand 8.2%, nearly 10% and nearly 8%; Singapore 8.8%, over 8% and over 6%; Philippines 5.1% in 1960–70, 5.4% in 1973–83, but a distinctly slower pace thereafter: *Asian Economic Handbook* p.8; Cowley, 'Asia's Emerging Economies' p.6

backing and from 1979 also an electoral element.[69] In the mid-1970s, however, Thailand's domestic situation looked far from secure, and various books depicted the country as a potential 'domino'.

Thailand had also to contend with the aftermath of its long-standing connection with the USA in a region where communism now seemed triumphant. Already by 1973 the previously supportive Prime Minister was expressing qualms. After the fall of Saigon in 1975 there were calls for 'equidistance' and an attempt to place more controls on US troops stationed in Thailand. The USA found these controls unacceptable and so simply pulled its troops out; nor would it return them after the 1976 coup, despite the new government's play on the communist danger.[70] Thailand therefore returned to the pre-coup policy of mending fences with its eastern neighbours. But it also sought to reinsure elsewhere, notably through a 1978–9 exchange of diplomatic visits with China. In 1979 China both invaded Vietnam as 'punishment' for its conquest of Kampuchea and issued repeated warnings against any attack on Thailand. If the Vietnamese ever contemplated such an attack it was presumably China that deterred them; certainly Thailand's ASEAN partners were in no military position to do so.[71]

ASEAN, CAMBODIA, AND VIETNAM

At a lower level ASEAN proved useful; the shock of the communist triumph in Indo-China led it to draw together. 'As never before', Lee Kuan Yew declared, 'the future of non-communist Southeast Asia rests in the hands of' its own 'leaders and peoples'. At the 1976 Bali summit meeting he expressed the hope that an effective

69. In 1991 there was a military coup. This was not immediately contested; but May 1992 brought riots in Bangkok, with forty-four deaths before the situation was resolved by royal intervention. Later the 'angel' parties narrowly defeated the 'devil' (or pro-military) ones in elections, and military powers to act against internal unrest were trimmed: David K. Wyatt, *Thailand: A Short History* (New Haven, Conn., 1984 edn) chap. 10; *Keesing's*, 1992 R85, 38894–5, 39093, 39195

70. Girling, *Thailand* pp.239–45

71. Lee Kuan Yew saw an acute dilemma: had there been no Chinese intervention, 'we would face Vietnamese supremacy, which in this case means Soviet supremacy. If the intervention is over-successful, . . . there will [eventually] be an assertion of influence . . . by a Communist power that has influence over all guerrilla movements in . . . Thailand, Malaysia, Singapore and Indonesia': M. Leifer, *Conflict and Regional Order in South-East Asia* (IISS Adelphi Paper no. 162, 1980) p.16

ASEAN could prevent 'incipient emergencies' from developing into 'full-scale revolutions'. Although the measures agreed were very general, the climate of mutual goodwill facilitated some bilateral agreements on anti-insurgency cooperation, notably that between Thailand and Malaysia. ASEAN was also concerned to stress that it was not simply the old Western-dominated SEATO under another name, and renewed its call for South-East Asia to become a 'Zone of Peace, Freedom and Neutrality'. Vietnam was unconvinced. Instead it called for 'peace, genuine independence and neutrality' and made a number of derogatory remarks to the effect that 'The policy of setting up such military blocs as ASEAN . . . has failed and passed for ever'. Instead it urged the individual ASEAN countries to conclude with it bilateral treaties of friendship.[72] There were some signs of softening in 1978, but they ended abruptly with Vietnam's alignment with the USSR and the invasion of Kampuchea that brought its forces to the borders of Thailand.

ASEAN states could not but align with Thailand, and the prospect of bilateral deals with Vietnam receded. China embarked on a long-run policy of squeezing Vietnam by forcing it to maintain high military readiness on its northern border, while encouraging continued guerrilla resistance in Kampuchea whereby 'Vietnam will be tied down and its plan to realise an "Indochina Federation" – a direct menace to Southeast Asia – will be delayed. The longer the delay, the greater will be the consumption of the national strength of Vietnam'. Apparently China did consider resupplying Khmer Rouge guerrillas through its contacts with Burmese and Thai communist insurgents, but concluded that there was no alternative to working with the Thai authorities. This gave Thailand, and through it the rest of ASEAN, a degree of diplomatic leverage. Extensive negotiations led to the formation in 1980 of a coalition of all the Cambodian resistance groups, and in 1982 of a Coalition Government of Democratic Kampuchea (CGDK) – headed by the non-communist Prince Sihanouk, who (though militarily weaker than the Khmer Rouge) was internationally far more acceptable. This was then duly accepted by the UN.[73]

Vietnam's invasion of Kampuchea and the 1979 famine had led to a massive flight into Thailand. Many refugees returned when conditions improved in 1980, but over 100,000 did not. Rather than

72. Rostow, *The United States and the Regional Organization of Asia and the Pacific* pp.83–4; *Keesing's*, 27676; Leifer, *Conflict and Regional Order in South-East Asia* pp.34–5

73. Charles McGregor, *The Sino-Vietnamese Relationship and the Soviet Union* (IISS Adelphi Paper no. 232, 1988) pp.47–8, 52; *Keesing's*, 31885, 31889

let them settle in the interior and become yet another potentially subversive minority, Thailand restricted them to the border area, and allowed them to receive foreign (mostly Chinese) military aid and continue operations against the Vietnamese-installed Kampuchean government. This risked retaliation, and fighting did occasionally spill over the border, notably in 1980 and 1984–5. On the whole Kampuchea and Vietnam showed considerable forbearance.[74] The success of their 1984–5 operations suggested that they had mastered the problem posed by CGDK resistance. In 1985 Vietnam began partial troop withdrawals with the declared aim of leaving entirely by 1990. Its intention, no doubt, was to legitimise the Kampuchean regime it had installed, and it reserved the right to return if necessary.[75]

A new complexion was given to events by Soviet determination to woo China and by the latter's highlighting of the Vietnamese presence in Kampuchea as one of the three main obstacles to reconciliation. Shevardnadze declares, indeed, that it was the principal obstacle. He does not explain how it was overcome; but Vietnam depended very heavily on Soviet aid – without Soviet oil and spare parts its military effectiveness would have plummeted – and was presumably subjected to pressure.[76] Vietnam's initial claims of troop withdrawals had met considerable foreign scepticism, but that of November 1987 carried more conviction. Indonesia had already brought Kampuchea to talk with the CGDK; this inaugurated a process of interminable cliff-hanging negotiations. At first the Kampuchean government was probably seeking only to detach Prince Sihanouk from the Khmer Rouge, but he insisted on the creation of a new coalition administration formed from all parties to the conflict. Four years later this was finally agreed, though only after the UN had become involved (pursuant to an Australian peace plan), the United States had been persuaded by the USSR to talk directly to Vietnam, and Vietnam had itself become reconciled to China. A cease-fire of kinds was agreed in May 1991; in November the exiles returned to Phnom Penh to inaugurate a UN-assisted period of joint rule prior to elections in 1993. A rapturous

74. This may have been due to fear of China and/or to restraint by the USSR (which had apparently promised Thailand in 1979 that Vietnam would pose no threat): Girling, *Thailand* pp. 248, 282. It can indeed be argued that Vietnam's invasion of Kampuchea actually helped stabilise Thailand by ending Khmer Rouge support for its insurgents

75. *Keesing's*, 30669–77; McGregor, *The Sino-Vietnamese Relationship and the Soviet Union* pp.34, 44–5

76. McGregor, *The Sino-Vietnamese Relationship and the Soviet Union*, pp.68–9; E. Shevardnadze, *The Future Belongs to Freedom* p.159

reception was accorded to Sihanouk, but *not* to his Khmer Rouge counterpart. This proved an ill augury. By the end of 1992 the Khmer Rouge stood alone in refusing to comply with the 1991 peace plan. Despite UN sanctions, it was apparently supported by China and by the Thai army (with which it traded wood and gems). There were fears that it would sabotage the 1993 elections, which it termed a 'theatrical farce to hand over Cambodia to Vietnam'. Actually polling was quiet, though the narrow victory of Sihanouk's son's party nearly prompted a coup to restore the pre-1991 pro-Vietnamese regime. A coalition government was put together with some difficulty; but under pressure from prospective Western donors, Sihanouk reluctantly excluded Khmer Rouge participation. Low level clashes followed, but not (at least in 1993) the feared resumption of civil war.[77]

VIETNAM'S 'BOAT PEOPLE' REFUGEES; ECONOMIC DIFFICULTIES AND THE TRANSFORMATION OF ITS STANCE IN INTERNATIONAL RELATIONS

In 1979 there had seemed a possibility that Vietnam would achieve an ascendancy in South-East Asia through its military prowess and (possibly) its revolutionary appeal. In fact it has made more impact on its neighbours by landing them with unwanted refugees. These had been leaving ever since the fall of Saigon, but their numbers increased sharply in 1978–9. Although perhaps one-third were lost at sea, over 100,000 managed to reach land in May and June of that year. Malaysia saw them as likely to upset its politically delicate population balance (especially as most were, at this stage, ethnically Chinese); it threatened to repel newcomers and expel those already there unless other countries accepted more for resettlement. The upshot was a widely attended conference under UN auspices, at which Vietnam agreed to try to stop departures while non-regional countries pledged both money and resettlement places. This eased things; but, though slowed, the exodus continued, becoming increasingly Vietnamese, indeed northern Vietnamese and so directed more towards Hong Kong. This had a long tradition of repatriating would-be *Chinese* immigrants lest it be swamped, and pressure mounted against Vietnamese ones. In the 1980s some 1.5

77. *Keesing's*, 35967–9, 36588–9, 36615–17, 36881–2, 37186–7, 37598, 38150, 38194–5, 38440–1, 39276, 39324, 39415–16, 39513–14, 39560, 39601, 39687, 39780, 1992 R62, 1993 R63–4. During the process of change Kampuchea gradually reassumed its former name of Cambodia

million refugees were resettled (mostly in the USA and Australia), but external sympathy waned, and the number left where they had first landed rose accordingly. In 1988 Hong Kong, and in 1989 all the ASEAN countries, started screening arrivals to distinguish 'political refugees' from the great majority of 'economic migrants' who could (in theory) be sent back. This, however, assumed that Vietnam would take them, but it proved reluctant. Vietnam did not wish to upset the United States, reconciliation with which it had now come to see as a condition of economic revival; and the USA (though itself practising forcible repatriation in other contexts) thought it wrong to return anybody to a state like Vietnam. It was not until 1992, at which time there were 55,000 'boat people' detained in deplorable holding camps, that Britain and Vietnam were able to reach agreement on the forcible repatriation of 'economic refugees'.[78]

Vietnam's December 1986 Party Congress was dominated by depressing economic reports, and led to a major clear-out of the top leadership. Subsequently some moves were made to open up the economy; and by March 1991 Vietnam had attracted promises of $1.4 billion in foreign industrial investment to take advantage of its cheap labour. But this was only a fraction of similar investment in ASEAN countries: the nature of Vietnam's regime was clearly an obstacle, as was the USA's continued blocking of assistance from the World Bank. Meanwhile the USSR, which had hitherto subsidised Vietnam to the tune of at least 1 billion roubles a year, decided in 1991 to shift its dealings on to a commercial basis. The Vietnamese government was therefore in difficulties. It had shown itself very reluctant to turn to China, apparently refusing in late 1990 an offer of aid with foreign policy strings. A year later it was ready to bite the bullet – especially in view of the collapse of communism in the USSR; so November 1991 saw a top-level visit to Beijing, the world's new communist centre.[79] The relations thus so painfully re-established were in fact to be ruffled in 1992 by disputes over the Spratly islands (see pp.224). But Vietnam made considerable progress in mending relations in other directions. In July 1992 it acceded (with Laos) to ASEAN's 1976 Treaty of Amity and Cooperation and was rewarded with 'observer status' in the Association it had spurned a decade and a half before; this was intended to lead eventually to full membership. Another indication of the fraying of the cold-

78. *Keesing's*, 30075–83, 31692, 36526, 37121–2, 38123, 38395, 38912

79. *Keesing's*, 30085, 38149, 38440–1, 1992 R86; Cowley, 'Asia's Emerging Economies' pp.11–12; *The Independent*, 12 Dec. 1990 p.10, 23 Feb. 1991 p.11, 6 Nov. 1991 p.12

shouldering of Vietnam was the inauguration of (limited) Japanese and Australian economic aid. Unofficial US–Vietnamese relations continued to mend: Vietnam met US conditions by releasing the last former South Vietnamese officials from 're-education' camps,[80] and cooperated with the USA's attempts to satisfy itself that none of its military personnel captured during the war were still being detained.[81] It was rewarded in July 1993 by the lifting of US opposition to IMF and other international lending, and by an aid conference that November which pledged $1.96 million. The ban on US companies trading with Vietnam was not lifted until early 1994. But by then it was no more than an irritant, since investment has started to flow in from the rest of the Pacific Rim and international oil companies had become distinctly interested in Vietnamese waters.[82]

THE DEVELOPMENT OF ASEAN

With Vietnam thus in no mood to make difficulties, pressure on ASEAN relaxed. The Philippines apart, its individual members have prospered; the grouping seems in good heart. For the most part this is a matter of coordinated diplomacy; from 1982 its foreign ministers have had annual collective talks with those of the major Pacific powers and of the European Community (see p.227). There have also been attempts to build ASEAN up as an economic bloc. This has been uphill work, given member states' very different economic philosophies – Singapore, as an entrepôt, favoured openness, while Indonesia was strongly dirigiste. The 1976 Bali summit could agree only on 'progress towards the establishment of preferential trade arrangements as a long-term objective'.[83] Meanwhile there has been some attempt at the planned distribution of major investment and manufacturing projects. In 1977 the Japanese Prime Minister Fukuda (anxious to allay the anti-Japanese feeling that had burst into riots during his predecessor's 1974

80. Overall 100,000 are supposed to have passed through them, though by 1992 only 25 were thought to remain: *Keesing's*, 38963

81. North Vietnam seems, in 1973, to have lied about the number of US prisoners it had taken. Recent tantalising reports of surviving Americans have generated feelings in the USA that will have to be satisfied before the full establishment of relations. But further investigations, with what appears to be full Vietnamese cooperation, have not (1993) located any 'Missing in Action' survivors

82. *Keesing's*, 39005–6, 39416, 39559, 39602, 1993 R85–6; *Financial Times*, 4 Feb. 1994 p.8

83. *Keesing's*, 27676

South-East Asian tour) promised $1 billion for schemes of ASEAN's own choice; his successors pledged further assistance during their 1981 and 1983 tours. The process of agreeing and implementing these projects has been slow: the economies of individual ASEAN members are aligned to trade with Japan and the USA rather than with each other. Accordingly we find the Malaysian Prime Minister contrasting ASEAN's growing political influence with its 'mediocre or worse' achievements in the field of trade cooperation.[84] Internal trade had nevertheless risen (from 14.7 per cent of all ASEAN trade in 1975 to 22.5 per cent in 1983), and mutual trade barriers were reduced. But there were still divergent views on the direction in which ASEAN should seek to move, with Singapore suggesting in 1989 a free trade agreement with the USA, Malaysia pushing in 1991 for an East Asian Economic Caucus that would include Japan but not the USA, and Thailand advocating an ASEAN free trade bloc. Eventually Thailand won out, and the January 1992 summit agreed to move (over fifteen years) to an ASEAN Free Trade Area in manufactured products.[85] These markedly divergent goals only reflect a greater uncertainty as to the way in which the whole Pacific region should develop; it is to this that we should now turn.

TRENDS IN THE DEVELOPMENT OF THE PACIFIC BASIN

The US ambassador to Japan, Mike Mansfield, declaimed in 1984: 'The next century will be the century of the Pacific. When you look at the whole picture you have to admit that that's where it all is, that's what it's all about, and that's where our future lies'. The concept of a Pacific Basin attracts boosterism. But there can be no doubt that the importance of the Western Pacific has been transformed since 1945. The two most obvious changes are those of greater internal stability and of explosive economic growth. They are clearly interconnected, though economic growth does not require complete confidence in political stability: Hong Kong continues in the early 1990s to prosper, though nobody can be sure how it will fare after the return to China in 1997 and those who can afford to do so are trying to insure themselves by acquiring

84. *Keesing's*, 26454, 28616, 30793–4, 32317, 33782

85. Sinclair, *The Pacific Basin: An Economic Handbook* p.149; *Keesing's*, 37569, 38101, 38345–6, 38729, 39560, 39691, 1992 R87, 1993 R86. In 1993 ASEAN also agreed to establish an Economic Caucus partially, but not entirely, within the APEC forum

footholds in more dependable countries like Canada. Nor can either political stability or continued economic prosperity be taken for granted. One possible political danger zone is Korea. North Korea's apparent determination to develop nuclear weapons has dampened moves towards a détente on the peninsula, and threatens to bring it into collision with the UN; trouble could also arise in the event of an internal collapse as a result either of Kim Il Sung's death or of economic disaster.

Other Pacific problems include those of the delimitation of offshore boundaries. China's claims, backed by the seizure of strategic islets,[86] are very large. Feathers were ruffled in early 1992 when China and Vietnam both took it on themselves to license companies to drill for oil in the Spratly Islands; although the Chinese Foreign Minister spoke of the possibility of joint development, talks to resolve their dispute have so far (1993) failed. China's growing defence spending (and rumours that it would purchase an ex-Soviet aircraft carrier) prompted fears that it 'would like to convert the entire South China Sea into an inland lake' and led South-East Asian countries both to rearm and to call on the USA to maintain a continued protective presence in the area. Finally, though conflict between the People's Republic and the Republic of China now seems remote, it could revive (were, for instance, the Taiwan independence movement to make too much headway), and Taiwan has been buying arms accordingly.[87]

At present, such scenarios appear less likely than that of economic friction leading to political alienation. To a considerable extent the area's postwar success has come from the subordination of politics to economics; economic growth has eased many potential strains. It has, however, been uneven growth, as most countries run a deficit with Japan and a surplus with the USA. The US economic expansion of the 1980s greatly helped other countries recover from the multiple shocks of 1979–81; and though eyebrows were sometimes raised, in the early 1980s, at the degree of Korean borrowing, no West Pacific state now looks in danger of Latin

86. In 1974 China took the Paracel Islands in the South China Sea from South Vietnam. Since 1975 both China and Vietnam have maintained forces in the Spratly Islands to the south (where Taiwan, Malaysia and the Philippines also have positions), and there have been a number of clashes: *Keesing's*, 27872, 35902, 39005–6 (map). A less serious dispute is that between Japan (the possessor), China and Taiwan over the Senkaku Islands: ibid, 28564, 29280

87. Admittedly the Ukraine denied selling the aircraft carrier: *Keesing's*, 38862, 39005–6, 39094–5, 39143, 39217; *The Independent*, 13 Feb. 1992 p.14, 12 July 1992 p.21 ('Asian states shape up for war over oil atolls')

American-style debt problems. The United States itself has passed within a decade from the world's largest creditor to (on paper) the world's largest debtor; the process obviously cannot continue indefinitely. Nor are the Americans prepared to let it. Protectionist sentiment grew in the later 1980s, and the USA showed a new determination to open up foreign markets and/or to shut out imports. The potential for friction, or even 'trade war', is obviously considerable, especially as the United States inclines towards unilateral action in determining the 'fairness' or 'unfairness' of other countries' competition. Export-oriented states (like the Four [West Pacific] Tigers) are probably extremely vulnerable. Lee Kuan Yew told Congress in 1985 that

> Putting up barriers to American markets would . . . send a signal that the model provided by the countries of East and Southeast Asia is no longer an available option. . . . Does America wish to abandon the contest between democracy and the free market on the one hand versus communism and the controlled market on the other, at a time when she has nearly won this contest for the hearts and minds of the Third World?[88]

Moreover once relations sour in one connection there is likely to be a spillover into others. Anti-American feeling is potentially serious in the Philippines and Korea. In the former a certain reaction has developed to the long 'neocolonial' presence and to US involvement (until late in the day) with the Marcos regime; it was reflected in the Senate's 1991 vote against the treaty renewing US military bases. In Korea students and the Far Left blame US support for past authoritarian regimes; some see the US military presence as a bar to national reunion. Lastly, and most importantly, a real trade war between the USA and Japan might drive the latter to rethink its whole 'Western-oriented' international alignment.

Although if it is easy to paint gloomy scenarios, they are less probable than those of continued adjustment with only minor frictions. The contrast between the present and the past is striking. East Asia has been one of the more disturbed areas of the world, with civil war in China, the Korean War, crises over the Chinese offshore islands, the long civil wars in Indo-China, and Sino-Soviet and Sino-Vietnamese border clashes. With the possible exception of Cambodia, none of these troubles seems likely to recur. Although

88. *Washington Post*, 10 Oct. 1985 p.E2. Lee did, however, support US action to open the Japanese market: 'It is right that she should be made to abide by the rules that have brought her to her present unprecedented prosperity'

the USA 'lost' both China and Indo-China, this did not have the wider repercussions that it feared. Most neighbouring states proved able to stand on their own feet. In South-East Asia they created in ASEAN a regional organisation apparently capable of managing local problems; their economic growth was such that, so far from falling inevitably into China's orbit, they constituted a far more attractive model – one which China itself was moved in the 1980s to imitate. This growth has its insecurities, which may be highlighted if the early 1990s (like the early 1980s) prove to be years of widespread recession, but it has proved broadly stabilising and vastly preferable to African or Latin American experiences. In some respects it constitutes a major challenge to the old developed world: a 1992 OECD guesstimate was that China and the Pacific Rim's present one-quarter of world output might grow to a one-third in 2010 and to a half by 2040.[89] But it also brings the latter's consumers many benefits: the author cannot be unusual in possessing a Japanese microwave, a Korean computer, a Taiwanese telephone . . .

What has been slower to emerge is a distinct focus of Pacific power. The idea of a Pacific Community was floated in 1980–1 by the Australian ex-Premier Gough Whitlam with some Japanese encouragement. It has led on to the constitution in 1989 of an 'Asia–Pacific Economic Cooperation' (APEC), with a membership that includes North America (and, since 1991, China, Hong Kong and Taiwan). There has also been advocacy of (and some jockeying over) a more purely ASEAN and Pacific rim 'East Asia Economic Grouping'. But Pacific states are probably too disparate in both their internal politics and their economic strategies to find a 'supranational' body à l'Européenne attractive;[90] many still have reservations about Japan and/or a reviving uneasiness about a newly powerful China. So for the foreseeable future official institutional links may well not go beyond the annual 'Post-Ministerial conference' talks on trade and regional security issues between the six ASEAN foreign ministers[91] and their 'dialogue partners' (the

89. *The Independent*, 1 July 1992 p.21

90. Proposals drawn up by senior officials in 1993 said that ASEAN must 'strive to be, not a supranational community as envisaged by proponents of the European Community's Maastricht treaty, but a community of different nations and different peoples with their own identities' and policies (*International Herald Tribune*, 23 Feb. 1993 p.5); and this must apply *a fortiori* to the wider Pacific area

91. Brunei joined ASEAN on becoming fully independent in 1984; as we have seen, the idea has been canvassed of Vietnam, Laos, and (if order is restored) Cambodia joining in due course; Burma (Myanma) might be a conceivable member were its politics to change

USA, Japan, Australia, New Zealand, EC, Canada (and – from 1991 – South Korea), plus China, Russia, Vietnam, Laos and Papua New Guinea in their capacities as 'observers' and/or members of the new (1993) 'Regional Forum' on security.[92] Informally, however, there is far more inter-governmental cooperation, buttressed by annual meetings (since the early 1980s) of the Pacific Economic Cooperation conference of government officials (ostensibly in their private capacities), businesspeople and academics, and by the Pacific Basin Economic Council of influential businesspeople (dating from 1967). Such bodies are, in turn, reinforced by a network of academic and professional societies meeting on a 'Pacific Basin' basis. Enthusiasts hope that they will ultimately generate a real 'Pacific' consciousness. The idea is no more utopian than 'European union' must have seemed when first broached in the 1920s. But there has been close cooperation across the Atlantic throughout the postwar period, initially accompanied by considerable 'mid-Atlantic' enthusiasm, without it developing into anything more concrete. Much, obviously, will depend on whether the current broadly multilateral pattern of world trade survives, or whether it fragments into separate European, American (or North American), and East Asian systems. Much too will be determined by whether the Pacific Rim countries react to the rising power, both economic and military, of China by accommodation (or even gravitation into its orbit), or by fearfully keeping their distance and looking to the United States (and Japan) for support that might or might not be forthcoming.

92. *Keesing's*, 36817, 37044, 38101, 38345–6, 39560. In imitation of ASEAN, the South Pacific Forum (Australia, New Zealand, and thirteen smaller island states) conducts talks with seven 'dialogue partners' with South Pacific trade and/or territorial interests

PART III

The Middle East

CHAPTER NINE
The Middle East Setting

The importance of the 'Middle East' in the postwar period is more easily recognised than defined. The Suez Canal, 'the route to India', and the exit from the Black Sea have historically all been focuses of strategic and imperial concern; more recently they have been joined by the Hormuz Straits out of the Persian Gulf. In the early twentieth century the chief significance of the Middle East was as a crossroads; it has since become progressively more important in its own right. Already by 1919 Clemenceau could say of Lloyd George's Middle Eastern interests that 'he smells of oil'. Oil was then still of only secondary importance; but after 1945 Middle Eastern production developed rapidly, and the area came to be recognised as containing the world's largest, and most cheaply worked, reserves. Awareness of this did not necessarily dictate the policy of outside countries, but it was, at least, always a consideration. The way in which Middle Eastern oil was managed and developed was to prove of great economic importance, particularly to Europe and Japan.

Before 1914 most of the Middle East, apart from a weak Iran, still belonged to the Ottoman Empire. Even at the peak of its power, this had generally operated on the basis of expecting the leaders of its various religious and national communities to organise their day-to-day affairs, and of holding them accountable for the loyalty and behaviour of their peoples. This engendered in would-be local leaders the habit of looking for outside support to confirm and strengthen their authority over their own communities; as the Ottomans declined, the range of such external supporters broadened to include European Great Powers. The habit continued even after the passing of Ottoman rule; some contend that it has produced a political culture of seeking foreign intervention to promote one's own interest, and, correspondingly, of enlisting clientelistically in the connections of one's external patrons. Such patrons, equally, became accustomed to working through, and trying to strengthen, their own partisans: 'our friends in the Middle East', as the British termed them.

The First World War completed the expulsion of Ottoman rule from the Arab world. The chief external agent, and beneficiary, was the British Empire. The Middle East represented its last major extension; between the two world wars Britain dominated, less by direct administration (which was exercised only over Cyprus, Palestine and Aden) than through the combination of military bases (notably along the Suez Canal) and influence over the local Arab rulers. Defence of this position constituted one of Britain's highest priorities during the Second World War, at the end of which British control had been, geographically, yet further extended. This apparent strength was, however, misleading; the post-war period saw a steady shrinkage of British influence. By the later 1950s the question arose of how what Eisenhower termed the 'vacuum' was to be filled: by one or other of the superpowers; by the local states as a body; or perhaps by one of them reconstituting the long past, but still remembered, glories of the early Arab Caliphates or of the Persian Empire. The Middle East's geopolitical position ensured that the outcome would be of much international concern.

The Middle East is also the geographical centre of three of the world's major religions. Good Muslims should, if they can, make the pilgrimage (hadj) to Mecca at least once in their lives, which produces a certain sensitivity to Middle Eastern concerns throughout the Muslim world. Christian veneration for the Holy Land is less strong (for many Christians Rome is a major competitor); but there has historically been a record of concern over the disposition of the Holy Places around Jerusalem. Jews, during their long Diaspora, retained their identity through a religion that looked to eventual supernatural return and to the rebuilding of the Temple – 'Next year in Jerusalem . . .'. In the twentieth century some determined to reconstitute, by secular means, a Jewish state in Palestine as a sanctuary from persecution, a necessary condition for the rebuilding of their nation, and as a centre even for those Jews who choose not (or are not permitted) to migrate to it. Few Jews are indifferent to the security of the state thus created in 1948. Most Arabs regard it as planted by force and deception on Arab land at the expense of the local inhabitants. The actual numbers involved are small – currently just over 4 million Israelis and rather fewer 'Palestinians' – but external support has ensured that both Israel and its neighbours are very heavily armed. The Arab–Israeli dispute has attracted far more interest, and consumed far more of statesmen's time, than the affairs of other and by many criteria more important parts of the world (for instance the Persian Gulf).

THE NORTHERN TIER OF TURKEY AND IRAN

One of the major themes of nineteenth-century international relations was Russia's attempt to expand southwards. This was resumed in 1945–6; at the onset of the Cold War the United States supported Turkey and Iran in blocking it. The result was to leave Turkey a firmly anti-communist and pro-Western state, an alignment further confirmed by its participation in the Korean War and its entry into NATO in 1952. Thereafter relations with the USSR mellowed; Turkey prudently refrained from impeding the Soviet naval build-up in the Mediterranean. There were also tensions with the USA in the 1970s, when Congress insisted on withholding aid as a reprisal for Turkey's 1974 invasion of Cyprus. On a number of occasions, too, rival claims to sovereignty in the strategic and potentially oil-bearing Aegean Sea have brought Turkey quite close to clashing with Greece. But Turkey's international posture remained essentially unaltered until the Soviet Union's collapse.[1] It reflected not only the commitment bequeathed by the founder of the modern state, Kemal Atatürk, to become part of Europe, but also the considerable degree of domestic political stability and the guidance of its strong armed forces.[2]

1. Since when Turkey has assumed a high profile as a patron of, and potential role model for, the new states of Central Asia, many of which are Turki-speaking. Its position, Western alignment, religion, and Kurdish minority make it a key player in the handling of northern Iraq

2. The new postwar international climate led in 1946 to the creation of a two-party system. The Democratic Party, the more conservative and less secularist of the two, gained power through the 1950 elections. Ten years later it was toppled by a military coup, concerned to prevent the erosion of the Kemalist legacy, but by 1965 the Justice Party (often seen as its successor) had recovered office. It was ousted in 1971 by the threat of a coup; this inaugurated a decade of political instability, the emergence of extremist political parties, and mounting left and right-wing violence (that supposedly cost 1,800 lives in the first nine months of 1980). The period was

The international alignment of Turkey's eastern neighbour, Iran, was also long determined by the 1946 episodes in which the USSR was eventually induced to withdraw its troops and the Shah's government later expelled its communist members and subdued the Soviet-sponsored Kurdish and Azerbaijani autonomous states.[3] In 1951–3 Iran's pro-Western outlook and regime was, as we shall see (pp.342–7), endangered by the dispute with Britain over oil revenues. But the nationalist Premier Mossadegh was toppled, and the Shah restored to full powers, by a USA–UK orchestrated royalist counter-coup. He ruled, apparently with growing success, for the next quarter-century, but was ousted in 1979 by a revolution. The resultant Islamic Republic turned abruptly away from the United States, which it portrayed as 'the Great Satan', but this did not impel it to embrace the atheistical Soviet Union. Instead it sought a wholly distinct policy based on militant Shi'ite Islam.

For most of the period covered by this book, then, the USSR was separated from the Arab world by a 'Northern Tier' of pro-Western states. In 1954–5 Turkey, Pakistan, Iraq and Iran came together to form the Baghdad Pact. The Pact marked the high point of Turkey's readiness to involve itself in the affairs of the Arab world: it was eager to use force in 1957 to topple the Left-leaning Syrian government and in 1958 to reverse the Iraqi revolution.[4] Such policies probably reflected not only the climate of the times but also the preferences of Prime Minister Menderes; they did not outlast his fall in 1960. The linkage with Iran and Pakistan, however, proved more durable; when in 1959 Iraq withdrew from the Baghdad Pact, its remaining members reconstituted it as the Central Treaty Organisation (CENTO).[5] This played a useful, though scarcely a major, role, improving communications (notably through the 1971 strategic railway between eastern Turkey and Iran bypassing the USSR), and serving as a vehicle for transferring weapons to Pakistan in connection with its Indian wars. It collapsed in 1979 when Iran pulled out after the fall of the Shah, followed quickly by Pakistan.

---

ended in September 1980 by an army take-over. After political and economic restructuring, elections were again held – and won by the economically liberal and politically centrist Motherland Party (not the army's preferred choice). In late 1991 elections forced President Ozal (of the Motherland Party) to share power with Suleyman Demirel (formerly leader of the Justice, now of the True Path, Party)

3. See *The Cold War* chap. 3
4. Below, pp.298–9, 300
5. Turkey, Iran, Pakistan, USA, UK and France

BRITAIN'S DEPENDENCE ON DEFENCE TREATIES AND BASES

Further south the British position had, during the Second World War, rested on two defence treaties, that accompanying Iraqi independence in 1932, and that of 1936 with Egypt. Both enjoined mutual support in time of war, both permitted British use of strategic bases, and both were stretched to their limits in 1941–2. The Iraqi treaty was invoked in 1941 to counter the intended juncture of German paratroops and the pro-Axis insurrectionary government of Rashid Ali. A subsequent attempt to drive the British out of the Habbaniya air base led to Rashid Ali's defeat and Iraq's reversion to its more usual pro-British stance. Meanwhile the British Middle Eastern Command was located in Cairo. Britain used Egyptian facilities freely throughout the war, and in February 1942 moved tanks to the palace in Cairo to force King Farouk to appoint a more sympathetic government. Such high-handed behaviour was deeply resented by younger nationalists (notably junior army officers and intellectuals) and (in Egypt) by the Muslim Brotherhood. Opposition politicians were always ready to play up to such sentiments, more especially in Egypt (where the British presence was of much longer standing and more obtrusive than in the rest of the Arab world).[6] It would have been prudent, at the end of the war, to retire rapidly to the Canal Zone and reduce the British profile; in fact the last troops did not leave the Cairo citadel until 1947.

Such delays reflected lack of imagination and military foot-dragging, but there was also a more fundamental debate about the nature of the future British presence. It is difficult to be sure of Attlee's real views, as he may sometimes simply have acted as devil's advocate: but until 1947 he repeatedly criticised the idea of maintaining a strong military presence in the Middle East as both expensive and unnecessarily provocative of the USSR; instead he favoured the conversion of the area into a neutral zone, preferably under the aegis of the UN.[7] Such thinking contributed to the passing up in 1947 of responsibility for financial aid to Greece and Turkey, and to the eventual decision to withdraw from Palestine. It

6. De facto British control had been established in 1882. Britain formally decolonised Egypt in 1922, but reserved many rights; a settlement was reached only in 1936 when Egyptian fear of Italy eclipsed dislike of Britain and so permitted the conclusion of the Anglo-Egyptian Defence Treaty

7. Raymond Smith and John Zametica, 'The Cold Warrior: Clement Attlee Reconsidered, 1945–7', *International Affairs* lxi (1985)

was, though, usually outweighed by the perception of Bevin (and the Chiefs of Staff) that the Middle East was of 'vital consequence' for Britain and the Empire. This consequence, indeed, would be yet further enhanced as relations with the Soviet Union worsened; for in the event of war, it would provide bases both for the bombing of the USSR and for eventual return to the European mainland, which (it was assumed) would be again overrun in the early stages of the fighting.

The Chiefs of Staff did consider defending British interests in the Middle East from a distance, but found no substitute for local bases. Considerable thought was given, however, to possible alternatives to the Suez Canal Zone, the most valuable position but also that most exposed to local politics. One such alternative might be the British Mandate of Palestine, but only if its political problems could be overcome. Transjordan could offer only limited facilities, but was ready (indeed anxious) to do so; its progression in 1946 to formal independence was accompanied by a defence treaty.

Another possibility was Libya. Britain had taken this from Italy during the Second World War, but, instead of at once settling things to its own liking, had reserved the country's disposition to postwar international consideration. This proved acrimonious. Britain wanted trusteeship over, and a base in, Cyrenaica (which it had promised the Senussi would not be returned to Italian rule).[8] The USSR put in a bid for Tripolitania, but the idea of its thus gaining access to the Arab world appalled first Eden and then Bevin; alternatively the USSR favoured, as did France, Libya's return to Italy under a UN trusteeship. Anglo-Italian negotiations produced a tentative solution in 1949, but it failed to secure UN approval. Britain then gave Cyrenaica self-government; in November 1949 the UN opted for the independence of a united Libyan state, duly constituted in 1951 under the Senussi leader King Idris. Libya relied heavily on Britain, and in 1953–4 offered bases to both the UK and the USA; but the process had taken too long to make much of a contribution to Britain's postwar problems with Middle Eastern bases.

Finally, there was Cyprus, a British possession, but one whose predominantly Greek population was likely at some stage to demand union with Greece. The British posture in the 1940s was that of hoping such a contingency would not arise, in case Cyprus

8. In theory Italy had gained Libya from Turkey in 1912. In practice Senussi resistance was not conquered until the later 1920s, and then harshly

were to become militarily crucial, but also of not developing the expensive port facilities that would be needed to convert Cyprus into an effective base.

RENEGOTIATIONS OF THE BRITISH DEFENCE TREATIES

Meanwhile nationalist pressure made it advisable to renegotiate the existing British defence treaties with Egypt and Iraq. Renegotiation proved possible in London, but in neither case could it be carried into effect locally. The new 1948 Treaty of Portsmouth provoked violent street demonstrations in Iraq and was never ratified. In practice, however, the existing treaty was allowed to remain in operation; and the pro-British Nuri al-Said continued to dominate the political scene. In 1954 he launched a new initiative, first proposing in London the replacement of the Anglo-Iraqi Treaty (due to expire in 1957) by a multilateral pact,[9] then sounding Turkey out on a defence agreement. In January 1955 (with a speed that rather took Britain and the USA aback) Turkey and Iraq concluded such an agreement. Britain took advantage of this to negotiate the 'sale' to Iraq of its air bases, which would, however, still be available for training and exercises, and in April 1955 signed what became the Baghdad Pact.[10]

Dealings with Egypt went less smoothly. A treaty was negotiated in 1946 with Sidki Pasha providing for complete British withdrawal by late 1949 against a promise that the bases could be reactivated in the event of aggression against 'countries adjacent to Egypt'. The deal promptly became embroiled with the question of the Sudan. Since its reconquest in 1899 this had been governed ostensibly by an Anglo-Egyptian condominium, but in fact chiefly by Britain. Egypt aspired to incorporate the Sudan, and, on Britain's refusal to budge, its Parliament rejected the Bevin–Sidki agreement.[11] In 1947 Egypt took the issue of treaty revision to the United Nations, which merely shelved it. Further attempts at negotiation continued, but to little effect. A visit to Cairo in early 1950 eventually convinced Bevin

9. Sir Evelyn Shuckburgh, *Descent to Suez* (1986) pp.237–8, 252

10. This was soon joined by Pakistan (which already had defence pacts with Turkey and the USA) and Iran

11. In retrospect it might have been better to allow Egypt the Arab north, but to detach Sudan's African south

that a purely bilateral settlement was unlikely, and by May Britain had started to sound Egypt out on the possibility of subsuming existing defence arrangements into a multilateral pact. It received no encouragement; but the idea remained very much in evidence for the next three years, the US Joint Chiefs of Staff warming to it after the outbreak of the Korean War (as a way of helping Britain handle the Middle East, for which they did not think they would be able to spare any troops for the first two years of a global war).

Late in 1950 Egypt threatened to denounce the 1936 treaty. This softened Bevin's position; but his successor as Foreign Secretary, Morrison, set his face against further concessions. Instead he pushed preparations for Middle Eastern Command (MEC), to be managed chiefly by the UK, Turkey, USA and France; Egypt would be invited to participate, and offered the Canal Zone base on condition that MEC troops could use it at all times. For, Morrison told Acheson in August 1951, 'Egypt is not, and never will be, able to defend herself against aggression by a major power'; moreover 'we cannot hope to defend the Middle East . . . without the existence of a main base in Egypt. . . . We cannot move it out of Egypt, because not only would the expense be prohibitive, but also there is nowhere else where it can conveniently go'; so 'We cannot afford to leave Egypt entirely', nor could any British Government 'offer to do so and hope to remain in office'.[12] By September the details were tied up, and Turkey (which had just secured its coveted invitation to join NATO) agreed to join in pressing the concept on Egypt. In October 1951 Egypt set about abrogating both the 1936 defence and the 1899 Sudan Condominium treaties; although Britain insisted on presenting Cairo with the MEC proposals, they were unsurprisingly rejected.

Thereafter matters deteriorated fast. Egypt sought to force British withdrawal by sabotage and guerrilla attacks on the base. The new British Conservative government sent in further troops, taking the total there above 80,000. In January 1952 they responded to attacks by forcibly disarming the police in Ismailia, killing forty in the process, which in turn set off major anti-European riots in Cairo. All this further weakened the prestige of the Egyptian regime, already badly damaged by defeat in the 1948–9 Israeli war, corruption and brazen royal extravagance. The climate proved favourable for a long-prepared coup by middle-ranking officers, who took over in July 1952 and soon dispatched the King into exile.

12. *FRUS*, 1951 v pp.373, 375

Initially it seemed that the new regime might be more forthcoming. Indeed the Sudan dispute was settled in February 1953, on the basis of self-determination within eight years. Cairo expected the Sudan to opt for accession to Egypt, and the 1953 elections were duly won by the party of union. Eden pushed ahead, believing correctly that, given a choice, Sudan would prefer independence; this came in January 1956, although not before the outbreak of what has proved endemic southern secessionist insurgency. But if Egypt was ready to settle over the Sudan, it remained unattracted by MEC (now renamed Middle Eastern Defence Organisation – MEDO): it was still determined to secure the withdrawal of all British troops and – despite the new regime's CIA contacts – it did not feel threatened by the Soviet Union, which it saw as a distant country with no record of colonialism in Arab lands. This was borne in on the new US Secretary of State, Dulles, during a Middle Eastern tour of May 1953. He was unimpressed with Egypt, which he expected to remain unstable for years to come, and concluded that Middle Eastern defence could more profitably be anchored on Turkey and other Northern Tier countries. He realised, too, that negotiations over MEDO had little future, and feared a degeneration into open Anglo–Egyptian hostilities. On his return home he publicly expressed concern that too close an association with French or British colonial interests might lead to the USA's becoming tarred with the same brush. During Lord Salisbury's July visit to the United States, Dulles induced him, after some plain speaking, finally to drop MEDO and resume direct negotiations with Egypt.[13]

Negotiations were not easy, but various factors softened the British position: the 1936 treaty would in any case expire in 1956; the Canal Zone was now vulnerable to nuclear attack; a Northern Tier defence seemed to be emerging instead. In any case, as Eden put it:

> We are not now expecting war with the Soviet Union in the immediate future . . . the problem . . . is largely that of meeting our peacetime commitments. . . . In the present cold war situation, it is through a settlement with Egypt that we could best secure our interests in the area, including our oil interests and the use of the Suez Canal . . .[14]

13. *FRUS*, 1952–4 ix pp.25–6, 379 ff, 394 ff, 2,108–24
14. Cabinet Memorandum, 7 Jan. 1954 (Public Record Office, CAB 129)

This settlement, finally concluded in October 1954, provided for complete British evacuation by June 1956. Egypt would then maintain the base with the aid of British technicians, and it could be reoccupied in the event of an attack (other than by Israel) on any Arab League state or Turkey (but not Iran).

CYPRUS 1954–93

The agreement went down badly with the Right of the British Conservative Party, where a back-bench 'Suez Group' was formed to lobby against further scuttle. Nor had Britain really solved the problem of finding alternative East Mediterranean facilities. Middle East Command was transferred to Cyprus, which had adequate airfields but not harbours. Cyprus was, moreover, itself becoming politically untenable. Agitation for union with Greece (*enosis*) had been mounting since 1950, led by Archbishop Makarios. Greece would, at the time, have been happy to offer Britain whatever facilities it wished after *enosis*, and there are those who say that Turkey would not then have intervened. Greek public opinion, and (more reluctantly) the Greek government, supported the *enosis* agitation; and in 1954 Greece took the issue to the UN (to no immediate effect). In 1955 'EOKA' (the 'National Organisation of [Greek] Cypriot Fighters'), under Colonel Grivas, launched a 'terrorist' offensive against the British, who proved unable to put it down despite their 1956–7 deportation of Makarios.[15] September 1955 saw a British-Greek-Turkish conference in London at which Britain advocated internal self-government, Greece called for self-determination in the reasonably near future, and Turkey categorically ruled out *enosis*. Towards the end of the conference an explosion in Thessaloniki damaged the birthplace of Atatürk (the founder of modern Turkey) and sparked major (and, as Greece believed, officially orchestrated) riots against the Greek minorities in Istanbul and Izmir. Graeco-Turkish animosity, arising from the Greek wars of liberation and from Greek incursions into Turkey after the First World War, was only thinly buried; and the situation of Cyprus – four-fifths Greek and one fifth Turkish – was calculated to reawaken it. Also Turkey, whose western seaboard was already

15. During the 1955–9 emergency 506 people were killed, with 97 inter-communal murders in July 1958: *Keesing's*, 16481, 16833

dominated by Greek islands, was not prepared to see the same happen to its southern ports; it therefore advocated either a continuation of British rule over Cyprus or the island's return to Turkey. Initially Britain may not have found this bar to *enosis* unwelcome, but in 1956 it began to contemplate eventual Cypriot self-determination if British and Turkish interests could be protected.

In 1957 the new Macmillan administration altered course, releasing Makarios (following Eisenhower's intercession) and replacing the military governor by a diplomat, while Turkey switched to advocating partition. Mid-1958 brought communal rioting in Nicosia and growing activity on the part of the Turkish imitation of EOKA (the 'Turkish Defence Organisation'). In June Macmillan personally proposed the association of representatives of the Greek and Turkish governments with the Governor of Cyprus in supervising a communally based administration of the island; if this worked well, Britain would, after seven years, be prepared to share sovereignty. This alarmed the Greeks, who saw the enhancement of Turkey's position as unacceptable, but who feared that, if Turkey cooperated and Greece did not, the result would be a Turkish presence on the island sufficient to force partition. Makarios reacted by calling for Cypriot independence; Greece by once more taking the issue to the UN. At the UN, however, in contrast to its earlier limited successes, Greece found itself placed on the defensive, partly by Turkish lobbying of the Muslim states, and partly because it seemed the least conciliatory of the three countries involved. While the Greek Foreign Minister, Averoff, was digesting the consequences, he was unexpectedly approached by his Turkish counterpart, who (Averoff suspects) had been alarmed by the recent Iraqi revolution (see pp.300–1) and who did not wish to add the fatal antagonisation of Turkey's western neighbour. The two Foreign Ministers held a succession of private talks (with British blessing). Their Prime Ministers then reached agreement at Zurich and London. Cyprus was to become independent, with the Turkish minority's position protected by an elaborate structure of power sharing and divided local government. Its constitution was guaranteed by Britain, Greece and Turkey, each with the right of intervention. Britain retained two bases under full sovereignty, while Greece and Turkey would maintain token forces on the island. Ominously Makarios, who had endorsed not only the talks but even the Turkish proposal of separate communal municipalities, jibbed at the last moment and had to be pressured into accepting the agreements in London in February 1959.[16] Still he did accept, and in 1960 Cyprus became independent, with Makarios as President, amid considerable initial enthusiasm.

Britain had solved its basing problem; though progressive withdrawal from the Middle East made this of diminishing value. But the power-sharing provisions of the Cyprus Constitution were never really implemented. Greek Cypriot criticism of the Zurich and London agreements mounted. By 1962 Makarios seems to have been cogitating constitutional amendments, though he failed to enlist President Kennedy's sympathy and was, in April 1963, strongly warned off by the Greek government.[17] After the fall of that government had led to elections in November 1963, Makarios, without further consultation, proposed constitutional amendments very much to the Turks' detriment. Communal fighting broke out, and in December 1963 Britain restored order with Greek and Turkish consent. The sequel, however, was an unsuccessful conference, further fighting, and the drift of Turkish Cypriots into blockaded enclaves. Turkey assembled an invasion fleet and this led Makarios to appeal to Moscow. NATO canvassed plans for a peace-keeping force, but Makarios rejected it and Moscow warned heavily against NATO intervention. The question was accordingly taken to the UN, which, in April 1964, itself deployed a peace-keeping force (UNFICYP). This did not immediately bring calm. In June, Washington warned Turkey that, if it intervened and triggered a Soviet response, it should not count on NATO aid; the USA also suggested a new settlement based on *enosis* plus substantial Turkish sovereign bases on the island, but Makarios rejected the idea. August saw further alarming fighting, followed by a UN-mediated cease-fire. In its aftermath 10,000 Greek troops were clandestinely introduced onto the island and the numbers of the National Guard unconstitutionally built up. In 1966 and 1967 Greece twice sounded Turkey out about a settlement over Makarios's head, but to no effect. Then in November 1967, fighting in mixed areas led the National Guard to push aside UNFICYP and attack the Turks. Turkey then threatened intervention, and was prevented only by heavy US pressure. One consequence was the proclamation of a 'Provisional Cyprus Turkish Administration', supposedly to operate

16. Evangelos Averoff-Tossizza [Greek Foreign Minister, 1956–63], *Lost Opportunities. The Cyprus Question, 1950–1963* (English translation, New Rochelle, NY, 1986) chaps 13–18; Nigel West, *The Friends* (paperback edn, 1990) pp.103–4.

17. Averoff, *Lost Opportunities* pp.424–30

until the full restoration of the 1960 Constitution.[18] Another was endless, but unavailing, inter-communal talks. By the early 1970s the situation was unravelling fast. Grivas returned to Cyprus to press for *enosis*, and in 1973 his EOKA-2 resumed terrorism. In July 1974, Makarios publicly accused Greece of controlling the organisation, and of using Greek officers serving with the National Guard to seize power. The National Guard mounted a coup on 17 July and appointed a former EOKA gunman, Nikos Sampson, as President (though British forces managed to whisk Makarios off the island away from probable murder).

The coup gave Turkey its chance. Consultations were held with Britain under the Treaty of Guarantee; but Britain, though ready to censure the Greek government, would not permit the introduction of Turkish forces via its sovereign bases. They therefore landed in northern Cyprus on 20 July. The USA managed to secure a cease-fire on the 22nd, after which both the Sampson government in Cyprus and the military junta in Greece collapsed. Anglo-Greek-Turkish talks were then held in Geneva: Turkey insisted on a settlement that would afford definitive protection to the Turkish minority, and, though briefly prepared to consider Greek and Turkish cantons within a unitary state, eventually held out for an autonomous region in northern Cyprus. Britain anticipated further Turkish military action; it offered, given UN consent (which would probably have been forthcoming) to deploy heavily armed troops in blue berets across the line of the Turkish advance and so put on Turkey the onus of attacking them and thus challenging the UN. However it would do so only with US approval; this was not forthcoming, partly because Washington was preoccupied with the fall of the Nixon administration, but chiefly because Kissinger doubted whether anything could stop Turkey and thought it best to avoid a first class crisis and let matters take their course with no more than diplomatic intervention. With British interposition thus ruled out, the Greek and Greek Cypriot sides began to contemplate a Turkish autonomous region. But Turkey demanded immediate control of an area covering a third of the island. On 14 August its troops simply took the territory they wanted amid widespread inter-communal fighting and massacre; about one third of the island's total population are said to have fled as refugees, south,

18. In 1967 Turkey secured the departure of the clandestine Greek troops, but not the reduction of the National Guard's numbers: Robert McDonald, *The Problem of Cyprus* (IISS Adelphi Paper 234, 1988–9) pp.11–17, 83; *Keesing's*, 22435–6

north or into the British bases.[19] 1975 saw the creation de facto of a Turkish Cypriot Federated State, which was to be consolidated by the move of Turks northwards and (with some prompting) of Greeks southwards, plus some Turkish settlement from the mainland. This state said that it would form part of a new Cyprus confederation.[20] But interminable (if occasionally promising) UN-monitored negotiations between the federated state and the Cyprus government have so far (1993) produced no settlement. Meanwhile the Greek two-thirds of the island has made a remarkable economic recovery, although the Turkish area in the north has not.

19. When fighting resumed in August, Greece sounded Britain on joint military intervention; Britain stalled until after a cease-fire had been arranged: James Callaghan, *Time and Chance* (1987) chap. 11; McDonald, *The Problem of Cyprus* pp.17–20, 85; Kissinger, *Memoirs* ii pp.1,188–92

20. To strengthen its hand, it proclaimed its formal independence in 1983, but has secured minimal international recognition

CHAPTER TEN

Palestine to the Establishment of the State of Israel

By 1918 Britain had driven Turkey from the 'Fertile Crescent' with the aid of the 'Arab Revolt'. In the process Britain had given promises – to France (the Sykes–Picot agreement), to Hussein Sherif of the Hejaz (the McMahon–Hussein correspondence), and to the Zionists (the Balfour Declaration) – that, though their exact historical content remains arguable,[1] were at least potentially conflicting. France got Syria and the Lebanon (ultimately as League of Nations Mandates); given its weakness on the ground and need for support in Europe, France proved accommodating about the subsequent demarcation of Anglo-French spheres of influence. But French ascendancy in Syria clashed both with the great Arab Kingdom based on Damascus that Hussein's son Feisal aspired to, and with local nationalism. Feisal *might* have been brought to accept a measure of French tutelage. However in March 1920 a Damascus assembly proclaimed him king of a sovereign greater Syria; there followed attacks on French coastal positions, and in July France responded by occupying Damascus and driving Feisal out. In 1921 he was installed as king of Iraq, with the expectation of early independence under British guidance. Also in 1921 Britain accepted Feisal's brother, Abdullah, as Emir of an Arab state in Transjordan, provided he abandoned his proclaimed design of driving the French from Damascus. Transjordan was extremely poor and depended on British subsidies. In the 1920s it needed British defence against incursions from King Saud's new Wahhabi state which had ousted Hussein from the Hejaz; as a result Britain

1. For the contention that deception was *not* practised on Hussein, see Elie Kedourie, *In the Anglo-Arab Labyrinth: The McMahon–Husayn Correspondence and its Interpretations, 1914–1939* (Cambridge, 1976)

officered and trained a small Arab Legion that was, in the later 1940s, generally agreed to be the best of the Arab armies.

PALESTINE 1917–45

The third British pledge, the Balfour Declaration of 1917, undertook to aid 'the establishment in Palestine of a national home for the Jewish people, . . . it being clearly understood that nothing shall be done which may prejudice the civil and religious rights of existing non-Jewish communities in Palestine'; in 1920 Britain converted its occupation of Palestine into a League of Nations Mandate, charged with implementing the Declaration. Here the separation of Palestine from Syria may have been crucial. The Ottoman *vilayet* had included much of Syria, Palestine and Transjordan; had it remained united, Jewish immigration could never have endangered the continuance of an Arab majority. In January 1919, on this basis but *only* on this basis, Feisal promised the Zionist leader Weizmann free immigration into Palestine.[2] However, when Britain would not support Feisal against France over Syria, he backed away from the Weizmann agreement and denounced both the separation of Palestine from Syria and Zionist aspirations for a state.

The Balfour Declaration did not necessarily entail statehood, but a Jewish state was the ultimate goal of the Zionist movement, and the nightmare of the Palestinian Arab population (hereinafter the 'Palestinians'). In the British Cabinet there had been two schools of thought. Some felt that Palestine could support only a small population and that the – almost exclusively Arab – existing inhabitants would not be content 'either to be expropriated for Jewish immigrants, or to act merely as hewers of wood and drawers of water'. Others claimed that, with active and scientific development (at Jewish expense), Palestine could easily accommodate more people. In a sense both were right; the population of Palestine increased from under 700,000 in 1917 to just under 2 million in 1947, since when it has tripled. Development did not reconcile most Palestinians to the Jewish presence, however: 1920, 1921 and 1929 saw riots, each leading to some controls on Jewish immigration.

2. Feisal was attracted by the prospect of securing Jewish money and support against France

Nevertheless things were still manageable, since, once calm and prosperity was restored in Europe, not many Jews wanted to come to Palestine. In the 1930s East European depression and Hitler's advent to power produced a flood of refugees; this was one of the factors that set off the 'Arab Revolt' of 1936.

The resultant Peel Commission of Inquiry concluded in 1937 that the gulf between Jew and Arab was widening dangerously. It therefore recommended partition: a small independent Jewish coastal state, a corridor from Jerusalem to Jaffa under permanent British Mandate, with the rest of the county to be merged with Transjordan under Abdullah's rule. Abdullah was naturally delighted. The main Zionist leaders favoured acceptance of any Jewish state, however small, but the Zionist Congress rejected it in the hope of securing improvements by further negotiation. Such tepid support cooled British enthusiasm and afforded time for Arab mobilisation against the proposals. A second round of the 'Arab Revolt' was launched and the agitation extended outside Palestine. The British Foreign Office concluded that partition would upset the Middle East and that, in the then state of international affairs, Britain could not risk driving the Arab states into the arms of Italy. So the government backtracked.[3] The eventual upshot was a White Paper in May 1939: Palestine should move (over ten years) to independence as a single state with an Arab majority; Jewish immigration should be limited to 75,000 over the next five years, after which further immigration would depend on Arab consent. This was to prove the best offer ever made to the Palestinians. Under the influence of Amin al-Husayni, the uncompromising Mufti of Jerusalem, they rejected it.

The Second World War greatly weakened the Palestinians' position. The Mufti did not improve his standing by first helping with Rashid Ali's Iraqi coup, then fleeing to, and endorsing, Germany. More importantly Hitler shook loose, and did his best to murder, the Jewish population of Europe. This powerfully reinforced the view that Jews would never be safe except in a state of their own; they had, after all, been quite well integrated into pre-Nazi Germany. It may also have made Jews less ready to dismiss threats to drive them into the sea (to which many Arab leaders were prone) as mere rhetoric, since Hitler's *Mein Kampf* had once been written off as such. It enabled the Zionists' excellent propaganda

3. T.G. Fraser, 'A Crisis of Leadership: Weizmann and the Zionist Reactions to the Peel Commission's Proposals, 1937–8', *Journal of Contemporary History* xxiii (1988)

machine to pin on their opponents the now damaging charge of anti-Semitism. Lastly the war transferred the leadership of the West from Britain to the United States. Despite Poale Zion's affiliation to the Labour Party, Zionist influence in Britain had been chiefly through the lobbying of sympathisers in government circles. This could be done in the USA as well; but in addition the Jewish vote was thought to be decisive in the electorally crucial state of New York (and of some importance elsewhere). The US State Department and the military (as in Britain, and for the same reasons) plus the oil companies put up powerful countervailing pressure, and US policy was often not pro-Zionist. It was, though, subject to sudden lurches, some at least attributable to electoral considerations;[4] the unpredictability of American behaviour (hence the unreliability of US support), together with the fear that friction over Palestine would endanger the whole spectrum of Anglo-American relations, contributed substantially to the eventual British decision to quit.

During the war a number of ambitious schemes for the reordering of the Middle East were floated. Perhaps King Saud might assume the overlordship of the Fertile Crescent and, in exchange for this plus £20 million from the Zionists, accept a Jewish state in western Palestine as an independent federal unit in his Arab Caliphate.[5] This can never have been a starter; if Saud did nibble, he killed it in 1943. More promising was the idea of combining the partition of Palestine with the reconstitution of a Greater Syria. British, and at one stage apparently Egyptian politicians, felt that this might make Jewish (and Christian Lebanese) independence acceptable to the Arabs, though Nuri al-Said was prepared to contemplate only their 'semi-autonomy'.[6] But on examination in 1944 a Cabinet Committee dropped the scheme, partly for fear of expanding French influence should this continue dominant in Syria, partly because Abdullah of Transjordan was only likely to join if he could rule the resulting state, something the Syrians would probably not accept.[7] The committee thus returned to recommending the partition of Palestine much along the lines of the Peel Commission; but Eden was opposed and the military urged

4. For a moderate discussion of the impact of such considerations, chiefly in connection with the New York mayoral election (Nov. 1945), the 1946 mid-term and the 1948 presidential elections: see Michael J. Cohen, *Palestine and the Great Powers, 1945–48* (Princeton, NJ, 1982) pp.47–8, 51, 58, 64–5, 163–70, 381–9

5. Michael J. Cohen, (ed.) *The Rise of Israel: A Documentary Record*, vol. 32 (New York, 1987) *passim*

6. ibid, esp. pp.206–7, 214

7. *The Rise of Israel: A Documentary Record*, vol. 33 p.223

that nothing be done before the end of the war. Presumably for these reasons, and also because he was angered by the Jewish murder in November 1944 of the British Minister in Cairo, Churchill shelved the committee's recommendations. By July 1945 he was suggesting countering US criticisms by inviting them to take over the mandate: 'I am not aware of the slightest advantage which has ever accrued to Great Britain from this painful and thankless task. Somebody else should have their turn now'.[8]

JEWISH AND US PRESSURE ON BRITAIN 1945–7

The task was indeed getting increasingly painful: Jewish extremists, notably Menachem Begin's Irgun (IZL) and the 'Stern gang', had already begun a campaign to drive the British out by explosions and murders. Until the defeat of Germany, mainstream Jewish organisations cooperated with the authorities against IZL, but in October 1945 and June 1946 the mainstream paramilitary force, Haganah, joined in the sabotage of Palestinian railways and bridges, first to show that Jewish wishes could no longer be safely overridden, then that, without Jewish consent, military bases in Palestine would no longer be very valuable. Also in July 1946 the British administrative headquarters in the King David Hotel were blown up, killing 92 people. Security operations were, despite the existence on paper of ferocious legal powers, not impressive. Mid-1946 saw the arrest of 2,700 Jewish leaders in an attempt to break up the Haganah and to open the way for more moderate politicians. Neither purpose was achieved, but the episode did lead to the ending of Haganah attacks on the British and to limited attempts to restrain the IZL. Unwillingness to upset this détente, and impair prospects for political agreement, made the High Commissioner reluctant to authorise further drastic action. By late 1946 the army was restive; in January 1947 Montgomery gained Cabinet authority for a more forceful response to terrorism. This came in March with the replacement of civil by military government over much of Tel Aviv and Jewish Jerusalem. But little effective use was made of it, and it was lifted after a fortnight. The Chiefs of Staff then backed off, claiming that the continuation of such action would place a major strain on their troops and risk the alienation of

8. ibid, p.269

the mainstream of the Yishuv (the Jewish community). Nor were other innovations more successful. The now standard tactic of special patrols to ambush terrorist squads was proposed in 1947; the first attempt in May led to the murder of a young suspect, and the effort was abandoned when this became known. So the security forces adopted a fairly passive posture. Their discipline was poor: on a number of occasions terrorist acts sparked reprisal rampages.[9] Also their quality may not have been high. (They were not, as we saw on p.54; very effective when first transferred to Malaya; success there came only after much reorganisation, and with the ability to take far more drastic action in regard to the local Chinese community than was ever permitted *vis-à-vis* the Yishuv.)[10]

The main believers in the value to Britain of remaining in Palestine were the Chiefs of Staff. In answer to Churchill's suggestion of passing it to the USA, they had claimed that 'Handing over the mandate' would lead to a loss of 'our predominant position in the Middle East. The psychological effects of this on world opinion are incalculable.' Moreover, apart from Cyprus and Sudan (neither very satisfactory), 'Palestine is the only territory between Malta and Aden in which we can confidently expect to have facilities for the stationing of troops'.[11] Their enthusiasm later waned. But Palestine would be useful for at least some of the facilities to be removed from Egypt under the 1946 Bevin–Sidki agreement; in January 1947 they were still pressing for a solution that would permit the continued stationing of forces there. Later they accepted that this might prove impossible, and concentrated on urging that, whatever the outcome in Palestine, it should not alienate the Arab world and so jeopardise the possibility of negotiating other military arrangements.[12]

The immediate issue confronting the incoming Labour

9. Cohen, *Palestine and the Great Powers* esp. pp.85–90

10. A comparison of Palestine and Malaya is instructive. In both, immigrants were potentially numerous enough to swamp the native population, and in both, immigration controls were introduced (in response to local pressure) in the 1930s. In both, the immigrants were more dynamic than the locals, and in both, they sought, after the Second World War, to drive the British out. But in Malaya – strategically and economically more valuable than Palestine – the British put down the 'emergency', which (though on a larger scale than the 1945–7 Jewish operations against Britain) was communist and had little international appeal (especially to the USA). So a Jewish state emerged to dominate Palestine, whereas Malaya proceeded to independence, after a Malay–Chinese agreement, but with the Malays politically preponderant and using this power to counteract Chinese economic competition. Malaya has had the quieter history

11. On 10 July 1945: Cohen, *Palestine and the Great Powers* pp.16, 37–8

12. *The Rise of Israel*, vol. 36 esp. pp.53–63, 195–8, 215 ff

government in 1945 was immigration. This had been controlled broadly in line with the 1939 White Paper; the quota of 75,000 would soon be exhausted, after which further immigration should depend on Arab consent. Zionists had never accepted such a cut-off; their chief efforts were devoted to getting it lifted, on the one hand, and circumventing it on the other by organising illegal immigration from a war-torn Europe full of Jewish displaced persons in former prison camps. Truman had sent an emissary, Harrison, to inquire into their condition and wishes, and in July 1945 asked Churchill at Potsdam to lift restrictions on immigration to Palestine. In August he passed London Harrison's report, which claimed that almost all the Jews in German camps wanted to go to Palestine and recommended acceptance of a Jewish Agency petition for 100,000 entry permits to clear the problem. London initially restrained Truman from going public, Bevin threatening to counter by demanding four US divisions to help maintain order. But in late September, probably with an eye on the New York mayoral election, the White House issued a statement that suggested Britain had simply ignored Truman's earlier letter. London was not only angry, but also worried about the possible repercussions on Anglo-American relations. Bevin's solution was a joint Anglo-American inquiry into the immigration and other Palestinian issues, and this was eventually agreed. British concern at Truman's diplomatic style and apparent carelessness as to Arab reactions is comprehensible, but it has been argued that an opportunity was missed. Britain eventually more or less endorsed the 100,000 figure. Had it been conceded at the outset, it would have cleared (and perhaps permitted the closure of) the camps under Western control,[13] and removed a major lever from Zionist propaganda. Also Truman might, if given his political and moral triumph, have retired to the sidelines, leaving more scope for the natural disposition of the State Department and US military to support the British lead in this area.[14]

Be that as it may, politics in 1946 revolved around immigration. The Arab states' tacit acquiescence was secured for its continuance at the existing rate of 1,500 a month. In April 1946 the Anglo-American inquiry recommended the immediate admission of the 100,000 and, much more vaguely, the continuation of the mandate

13. At the time they contained some 50,000 Jews, but a year later more than 250,000 (as a result of a massive flight, aided by the Zionist underground, from Eastern Europe)

14. This is the view of Cohen, *Palestine and the Great Powers* esp. pp.56–7, 393–4, and also of Alan Bullock, *Ernest Bevin: Foreign Secretary, 1945–1951* (1983) pp.174–5. Much of the following paragraphs derives from Cohen

over a state based on Arab–Jewish power-sharing. Under considerable Zionist pressure Truman again jumped the gun, releasing the immigration recommendation and glossing over the remainder. Equally undiplomatically Bevin told the Labour Party Conference that American pressure stemmed from the wish not to have to admit too many Jews into the USA. A further joint working party was set up, and in July 1946 produced the Morrison–Grady recommendations for separate Jewish and Arab provinces, albeit for the time being within a single state under British control; arrangements were worked out to transport 100,000 Jews to Palestine, but only after general acceptance of the plan. Truman was attracted, but backed off (in response to Zionist and electoral pressure) just before the issue of a joint Anglo-American announcement. Britain continued to try to sell something along Morrison–Grady lines to Jews, Palestinians and representatives of the Arab states (not helped by a further Truman electoral statement on the eve of Yom Kippur that was taken as endorsing Jewish demands for partition).

By 1947 British expectations of securing general agreement were slim; ministers were divided and had begun to discuss the option of returning the question to the United Nations. A resumed conference in London soon reached deadlock, with Zionists demanding partition, Arabs immediate independence for a unitary state. In February the Cabinet agreed to advance a final plan: the admission of 96,000 Jews over two years, with subsequent immigration to be determined (if necessary) by the UN; a single state, but with a measure of local devolution and of central power sharing; and independence after five years. Zionist rejection was unsurprising, that of the Palestinians foolish, since they lost the chance of proceeding, with British military assistance, to independence on a majority basis. Having thus reached a dead end, Britain carried out its threats of referring the question to the UN.

This reference was originally regarded as something of a ploy to secure last-minute concessions; it was noted that, if it did, the reference could then always be withdrawn, that the General Assembly could not finally decide till the autumn, and that in any case a two-thirds majority was unlikely. But in September 1947 the Cabinet decided to pull out of Palestine come what might.

One reason was the human costs of staying. By the standards of some subsequent colonial wars British casualties were not high.[15]

15. From July 1945 to August 1947, 135 killed and 259 wounded: Parl. Deb. 5th series 441 (12 Aug. 1947) 2307

But there was a steady, and much resented, stream of well-reported murders (almost entirely by Jews). The last staw was IZL's July 1947 hanging (in reprisal for the execution of two of its members) of two kidnapped sergeants whose bodies were then booby-trapped. The Chancellor of the Exchequer told Attlee

> that the time has almost come when we must bring our troops out of Palestine altogether. The present state of affairs is not only costly for us in manpower and money, but is, as you and I agree, of no real value from the strategic point of view – you cannot in any case have a secure base on top of a wasps' nest – and it is exposing our young men, for no good purpose, to most abominable experiences, and is breeding anti-Semites at a most shocking speed.[16]

Parliament reassembled for emergency debates:

> The feeling there expressed [reported the Colonial Office] that Great Britain should withdraw from Palestine was, of course, largely engendered by the strong public reaction . . . so long as we remained in Palestine we could be exposing our troops to a succession of outrages which we apparently could do very little to prevent. Our feeling here is that this reaction is not transitory and . . . the debates have made a great impression on Ministers.[17]

The other major consideration was the course of events in the United Nations. In May 1947 Palestine was referred to a special committee (UNSCOP). To everybody's surprise, the USSR indicated support for partition; this upset previous calculations that the UN would favour independence for a united Palestine with an Arab majority. UNSCOP reported in August 1947, a majority favouring partition, a minority a federal state with Arab preponderance. Bevin believed that neither would work, and that Britain could only lose by association with the attempt. A definite British determination to withdraw 'might conceivably' induce Jews and Arabs 'to cooperate in order to avoid the otherwise inevitable civil war', but it should not be contingent on such cooperation. The Cabinet agreed, Attlee

16. *The Rise of Israel*, vol. 36 p.171. Palestine was tying up 100,000 British troops at a cost, since mid-1945, of £100 million, a significant sum given Britain's 1947 financial crisis

17. ibid, p.191. A further consideration was the collapse of the attempt to deter illegal immigrants by transferring them, not to the now choked transit camps in Cyprus, but back to their ports of departure. This was done in July to the 4,500 passengers on the *Exodus*. But amid a blaze of publicity they refused to disembark in France, and the French government would not make them; so in late August they were sailed to Hamburg. This forcible return to the land of their persecution raised such an outcry that the experiment was never repeated

declaring that 'there was a close parallel between the position in Palestine and the recent situation in India',[18] where the announcement of a British determination to leave by a given date *had* brought an agreement between the parties (see pp.42–3).

UN DECISION FOR PARTITION NOVEMBER 1947

The UNSCOP reports were referred to three UN subcommittees, one to work on partition, one on a unitary state, and one to investigate possibilities of conciliation. In November 1947 the third subcommittee reported failure and the recommendations of the second were voted down. Those of the first were passed to the General Assembly, by one vote short of a two-thirds majority and with many abstentions. There followed ferocious lobbying. Hitherto the United States (though itself endorsing partition) had not lobbied, since the State Department disliked the policy. But, according to Michael Comay (then running the Jewish Agency's New York office),

> an avalanche descended upon the White House while some newspapers openly accused officials in the State Department of sabotage. The President, we learned, became very upset and through [*sic*] his personal weight behind the effort to get a decision. . . . It was only in the last 48 hours . . . that we really got the full backing of the United States.[19]

This was quite something. Bernard Baruch threatened France with the cut-off of US aid, though the decisive approach may have been an appeal by Weizmann to Léon Blum: the Liberian President Tubman was told that the Firestone Rubber Company might cut its investment plans; Liberia's UN delegate later complained of a warning that, unless Liberia voted for partition, it 'could expect no further favors from Congress'; similar threats had, he said, also been made to Haiti. His Cuban counterpart claimed that one Latin American vote had been bought for $75,000. Such pressure had its limitations; Greece resisted it and voted against partition, supposedly in exchange for Arab support over the Greek civil war. Lobbying for the Arabs was led by Pakistan, but hampered by the Palestinians' refusal to make any conciliatory noises. Comay said it

18. *The Rise of Israel* pp.199–212
19. On 3 Dec. 1947: ibid, vol. 37 pp.187 ff

drew on 'color sympathies' among non-white countries.[20] In the event partition (into Jewish and Arab states, plus a permanent UN trustee-ship over Jerusalem) was endorsed on 29 November 1947 by thirty-three votes to thirteen, with ten abstentions. Palestine then slipped into Jewish–Arab hostilities.

SUBSEQUENT US FLUCTUATIONS

The USA soon became concerned both at the bloodshed and at the likely long-run consequences of British withdrawal, and so sought to repair the situation. It was, however, very late to turn back; US diplomacy was fatally undercut both by unreadiness to commit troops and by the long record of alternation between State Department and presidential policies. Britain was correspondingly unforthcoming. February 1948 saw Security Council consultations, March a proposal that a trusteeship be established and partition temporarily shelved. In April the USA backed away, reluctant 'to buy into a war between the Jews and Arabs of Palestine'.[21] In May it was again suggesting a truce and a brief prolongation of the Mandate to allow for last-minute negotiations. Britain would not budge without the promise of a US military commitment. The Jewish leaders ultimately decided not to comply, despite State Department threats that they could lose all future US support. The last resort, worked out with the British and Canadian UN delegations, was a call for a truce and the appointment of a UN mediator. Just as this was going through the General Assembly on the last day of the Mandate, 14 May, the US delegation discovered to its mortification that Truman had already recognised the state of Israel (which had been proclaimed some hours earlier). The Assembly nevertheless voted to appoint a mediator, and on 29 May 1948 the Security Council called for a cease-fire.

20. He also claimed that Egypt induced Ethiopia to abstain, while Chile did so 'as a result of joint British–Arab pressure. Britain was officially neutral; but while most of its delegation was 'coldly correct', Comay saw some hardline Foreign Office men as active opponents: ibid, pp.187–8, 197; Cohen, *Palestine and the Great Powers* pp.297–8

21. Briefing of the American UN delegation: Cohen, *Palestine and the Great Powers* p.367

JEWISH–ARAB HOSTILITIES NOVEMBER 1947 TO MAY 1948

But this is to get ahead of events. The UN had made no serious provision for the implementation of its 29 November 1947 Resolution.[22] Britain, whose primary concern was its standing in the Arab world, had always made it clear that it would not impose a solution that it disagreed with. If Britain would not, nobody else could, since Britain also insisted on undivided authority as long as it still retained the Mandate. In any case probably only the USA and USSR had the resources to do so. Soviet intervention was not offered and would never have been accepted; and at no stage between 1945 and 1948 would the USA commit troops, nor indeed could it (the Joint Chiefs held in 1948) without a partial mobilisation that would bust the budget.[23] Although Britain was no longer seeking to control the situation,[24] the manner of its departure was to prove extremely important. It would not go in a hurry, since it wished (in an increasingly crisis-prone world situation) to evacuate the large quantities of military stores stockpiled in Palestine. Withdrawals from specific areas were staged to suit British needs; but they affected local Jewish–Arab fighting, benefiting sometimes one side, sometimes the other (with the disadvantaged attributing the outcome to political partiality). More importantly, Britain ensured that, as long as the Mandate lasted, the regular armies of the Arab states stayed out of Palestine – with the exception of the Arab Legion, which (being under joint British–Jordanian control) was allowed to occupy some Arab areas after local British withdrawals, and which became involved in fighting around Jerusalem.

The initial struggle, then, was between Jews and Palestinian Arabs (rather ineffectively reinforced by irregulars of the 'Arab Liberation Army' under Arab League sponsorship). Until March 1948 it was mainly a matter of mutual terrorism and of (fairly successful) Arab

22. The UN did appoint a five-man Commission progressively to take over the direction of central administration and supervise partition. But the British would not admit it until almost the end of the Mandate, chiefly because they would then have had to protect it and provide the force to execute its decisions

23. Cohen, *Palestine and the Great Powers* pp.348–9, 367

24. Up to February 1948 British forces could still limit major attacks on Jewish settlements, shepherding the Arab Liberation Army away from Tirat Zvi; in April they sought (ultimately unsuccessfully) to prevent the Jewish reduction of Jaffa. There were also ad hoc peace-keeping interventions – and controversial failures to intervene

attempts to ambush traffic and cut roads. Without artillery the Arabs could not capture Jewish settlements, but a number were in danger of being starved out; also the road to Jerusalem was cut in late March and Jewish morale there plummeted. In April 1948, however, the pendulum swung sharply towards the Jews, who had by then converted the Haganah from a primarily defensive militia into a body capable of mounting strategic offensives. The Yishuv had, in fact, a number of advantages. Although smaller than the Palestinian Arabs, as a largely immigrant community it contained more men of military age,[25] 20,000 of whom had served with Allied armies during the Second World War. Also, despite rifts between the Haganah and IZL, military planning was far more centralised than on the Palestinian (or later the Arab) side;[26] in March the first sizeable shipments of clandestine arms started arriving from Europe. April 1948 saw a series of offensives intended 'to gain control of the area allotted [by the UN] to the Jewish State'; by the end of the month Tiberias, Haifa and Jaffa had been either completely or virtually captured.[27] Also, though the siege of Jerusalem was not lifted, convoys were forced through and an Arab suburb captured. Among the Arab villages along the Jerusalem road was Deir Yassin; this had observed a local non-aggression pact with the Haganah, but was attacked by the IZL; when it resisted, its entire population was massacred, some deliberately after being first paraded through Jerusalem. The atrocity was denounced by the Haganah, and a telegram of apology sent to King Abdullah; but it was to prove a turning-point, both in precipitating Palestinians into refugee flight (as the IZL had intended) and in inflaming Arab feelings further afield.

Among its effects was that of putting great strain on the private deal between Abdullah and the Jews. Abdullah had always hoped to expand his role westwards, and had long maintained friendly contacts with the Yishuv. He secretly received Golda Meir in November 1947; on the assumption that the UN would vote for a Jewish and an Arab state in Palestine, they agreed that Abdullah should annex the latter with Jewish acquiescence, and that there would be no occasion for conflict between them. In February 1948

25. Cohen claims 50% more: *Palestine and the Great Powers* p.307

26. In early April the Arab Liberation Army leader, Quawukji, agreed to stand aside and give the Jews a free hand in attacking pro-Mufti forces: Avi Shlaim, *Collusion across the Jordan: King Abdullah, the Zionist Movement, and the Partition of Palestine* (Oxford, 1988) pp.158–9

27. Cohen, *Palestine and the Great Powers* pp.335–6; Ritchie Ovendale, *The Origins of the Arab–Israeli Wars* (1948) pp.119–20

Abul Huda, Transjordan's Prime Minister, cleared this with Bevin. He explained that Palestinian Arabs had made no preparations for either governing themselves or establishing an army. So, if things were left to drift, either the Jews would take all Palestine or the Mufti would return and try to take over Arab Palestine. Neither outcome would suit Transjordan or Britain. So Transjordan proposed, at the end of the British Mandate, to send the Arab Legion to occupy those neighbouring parts of Palestine that the UN had awarded to the Arab state.[28] Bevin's response was, 'It seems the obvious thing to do', though he also secured Abul Huda's assurance that Transjordan would not go on and invade areas allotted to the Jews. Bevin seems to have remained confident, right up to the end of the Mandate, that this Transjordan–Jewish understanding was still in place. It had, he told US Secretary of State Marshall on 11 May 1948, always been his hope that the Jews would keep to their own zones, that Jerusalem would be put under a truce, and that King Abdullah might use his forces temporarily to keep order in the Arab areas.[29] In short, things would work out without a major explosion, much as they were deemed to have done in India.

For this to happen very delicate handling would have been necessary. One problem was that the Mandate's formal continuation until May 1948 left plenty of time for things to go wrong. If the Jews were to take over the Arab areas within the boundaries allotted them by the UN,[30] the process was bound to involve Arab defeats and humiliations that would inflame feelings elsewhere in the Arab world. Within limits this could help Abdullah (provided, of course, that he did not himself get carried away) by enabling him to pose as the protector of the Arabs on the West Bank. But the other Arab states had a shrewd idea of his intentions and one of their chief concerns was to make things difficult for him. Initially this led to an Arab League[31] policy of supplying the Palestinians with weapons and volunteers, but *not* committing regular armies (so as to give Transjordan no occasion to intervene). In April 1948 it

28. That is, roughly, Judea and Samaria (or the 'West Bank'), but not Gaza or western Galilee (which had also been awarded to the Arab state but which the Legion could not easily have reached)

29. Shlaim, *Collusion* esp. pp.112–16, 133–8, 175, 190

30. These had been so drawn as to include almost all the Jewish areas outside Jerusalem, but at the price of producing a state that would be half Arab in population, much more than half in landownership

31. The idea of an Arab League had initially been urged as part of an Iraqi scheme for dominating the Fertile Crescent. But, as actually constituted in 1945, it included also Egypt, Saudi Arabia and the Yemen; this made it much less amenable to Iraqi and Jordanian influence

became clear that this would lead to a Jewish victory; so the League switched to intervention, but to a *joint* intervention designed to limit Transjordan's freedom of action as far as possible. (This was, however, not to prove all that far, since the League never managed to agree on a meaningfully united command.)

Abdullah never denied to the Jews that there had been an agreement, but Deir Yassin changed the atmosphere. On 17 April 1948 he told an Egyptian newspaper that he regarded it as tantamount to a declaration of war. Four days later he informed the Arab News Agency that, because of this and other incidents, he had given up hope for a peaceful solution and would, if invited, defend Palestine; the Jews could settle the dispute only by agreeing to enter an Arab state, albeit with autonomy for areas in which they formed a majority. Privately he told his British adviser, Sir Alec Kirkbride, that, in view of the publicity that some of his exchanges with the Jewish Agency had attracted, he could go no further than this offer of autonomy; he did not expect it to be accepted, but hoped thus to keep the door open for subsequent negotiations when tempers had cooled.[32] Meanwhile he both shared the general feeling of anti-Jewish outrage and used it to secure an appeal from the Arab League to send in the Legion to protect the Palestinians. On 29 April he agreed with the League on a joint intervention.

Early in May 1948 Abdullah made a final approach to see whether the Yishuv would cede some of the territory the UN had allotted it, which he could then use as an argument to induce the Arab world to accept partition. In reply the Jews warned that, if the partition scheme was not implemented peacefully, they would no longer feel bound by its borders. Meir also secured another meeting (on 10 May), but it was not a success. She simply warned that the Jews were now far stronger than in time past; they would respect the UN borders if there was peace, but not otherwise. Abdullah sought a one-year cooling-off period and offered only Jewish autonomy. Since his earlier understanding with her, events like Deir Yassin had occurred; he no longer had freedom of decision, but was one of five Arab states acting together. He gave the impression of being reluctantly caught up, but emphasised that he was always ready for talks even 'after the battles start'.[33]

32. Shlaim, *Collusion* pp.165n, 170–1

33. ibid, pp.205–10. It is sometimes said that, given Abdullah's prejudices, it was a mistake to send a *woman* to deliver what amounted to an ultimatum; also that Meir (who had apparently been given some latitude on borders) showed neither flexibility in this respect nor readiness to build on earlier Legion–Haganah contacts to try to restrict hostilities to token confrontations

Abdullah's freedom of manoeuvre was further reduced, two days later, when Egypt finally decided on intervention. But in any case Amman appears (like other Arab capitals) to have been swept by a mood of unreasonable optimism. On 15 May 1948 Abul Huda forecast victory within a fortnight, and told Kirkbride that, though he and Abdullah basically adhered to their original intentions, Transjordan would not be able 'to stop at the frontiers of the Jewish state if the line of the Arab armies was sweeping all before them'.[34]

WAR AND ARMISTICE 1948–9

The Arab plan had been for the Egyptians to move on Tel Aviv, tying down Israeli forces while Transjordan, Iraq, Syria and Lebanon cut off and squeezed north-eastern Israel; a second stage might see attacks on Haifa and Tel Aviv. The plan was not followed through. The Egyptian advance seemed ominous but distinctly unhurried; no serious assault had been made on the Israeli positions covering Tel Aviv by the time of the first cease-fire (see p.261). It is also noteworthy that a smaller, but significant, Egyptian force was diverted inland to prevent Transjordan garrisoning Hebron. In the north-east the Syrians and Iraqis scarcely penetrated Israel. Instead of joining them, the Arab Legion concentrated, as it had always intended, on central Palestine, forcing the Iraqis to redeploy further south in Arab districts. Its commander, General Glubb, was later to claim that Transjordan had still hoped simply to occupy areas like Hebron, Ramallah and Nablus without serious fighting.[35] But the Legion got diverted into what proved the major struggle of this phase of the war, that for Jerusalem and its approaches. The UN had earmarked Jerusalem for a continued trusteeship, but attempts to arrange a truce there in early May had failed; the end of the Mandate saw Israeli offensives designed to relieve the besieged Jewish Quarter in, and take over the remainder of, the Old City. The Legion had initially been ordered to avoid Jerusalem, but Abdullah insisted that it intervene to protect the Holy Places; during 18–28 May 1948 it did so, reducing the Jewish Quarter and securing the Old City but not the Jewish areas to its west. It also occupied the village of Latrun, within the UN's proposed Arab state but astride the road to Jerusalem, and held it

34. Shlaim, *Collusion* p. 228; Cohen, *Palestine and the Great Powers* p. 334
35. On 12 Aug 1948: Shlaim, *Collusion* pp.271–2

against strong Israeli attacks. Further north the Iraqis, though not where they had originally meant to be, seemed nevertheless well placed to cut the Israeli coastal strip in two. However they proved singularly inactive, repulsing an Israeli attempt to dislodge them from Jenin, but making no forward moves.[36] Britain had soon started working for a cease-fire. Israel and Abdullah were agreeable. The Arab League at first refused, but by June exhaustion was widespread, and the UN mediator Count Bernadotte secured acceptance of a four-week truce to take effect on 11 June. At this stage the position on the ground was much as had been stipulated by the UN partition plan, save that Israel had not secured the Negev and that Jerusalem had, de facto, been split between Israel and Transjordan.

Thus far the Arabs had had the advantage, not in numbers (their regular armies were remarkably small, and they showed no wish to supplement them by mobilising the Palestinians) but in equipment. This advantage was soon to be reversed. The UN had embargoed arms deliveries to the area, and on 3 June 1948 Britain revoked all arms export licenses. This (and earlier Egyptian appropriation of supplies destined for the Arab Legion) left Transjordan and Iraq extremely short of ammunition. In 1947 the Haganah had had only some 10,000 rifles and nothing heavier than a machine-gun. By December 1947 the Zionists had established clandestine contacts with Czechoslovakia; with Yugoslav and French collaboration arms started to arrive in Palestine from 31 March 1948, just in time for the Haganah's first major offensives. This inaugurated a regular flow that, by the end of 1948, included tanks and aircraft. Czechoslovakia's chief motive was Zionist dollars.[37] But its actions were authorised by Stalin, whose reasons can only be guessed at. Probably in supporting first partition and then arms for Israel, he was seeking to undermine the British position in the Middle East and perhaps also to drive a wedge between Britain and the USA. He may, too, have been encouraged by left-wing Zionist emissaries to hope that Israel would develop into an anti-imperialist or even a fellow-travelling state. Vital claims that 'by the early 1950s' Israel figured in Soviet contingency planning 'as a potential "popular democracy" to be taken over by the left-wing elements in its

36. Shlaim, *Collusion* chaps 7, 8; Edgar O'Ballance, *The Arab-Israeli War 1948* (1956) chap. 5

37. It sold Syria $11 million worth of arms, but declined to make further sales for payment in inconvertible sterling: Arnold Krammer, *The Forgotten Friendship: Israel and the Soviet Bloc, 1947–53* (Urbana, Ill., 1974) pp.64–6

population who would then, in turn, provide the Soviet forces destined to thrust down into the Near East . . . with a welcome *point d'appui*'.[38]

On 27 June 1948 the UN mediator, Bernadotte, proposed abandoning partition and returning to a Jewish–Arab confederation. Israel naturally refused; so did the Arab League, since the plan seemed chiefly to benefit Abdullah. Bernadotte then sought to extend the truce. Arab military leaders were favourable, stressing their shortages of matériel; but to placate public opinion the League determined to renew hostilities, while standing on the defensive to conserve ammunition. In the ensuing fighting (8–18 July 1948) Israel drove the Arab inhabitants from Lydda and Ramle and took much of western Galilee. The Arab Legion held Latrun with difficulty; but its ammunition was exhausted, and the UN Security Council's insistence on a cease-fire came only just in time. Israel had now gained the initiative; the rest of the year was to see much debate as to whether to drive out the Arab Legion and annex all the land up to the Jordan, or to concentrate on removing the Egyptians from the Negev. The second course was chosen, largely because Israel did not wish to incorporate too many Arabs and preferred instead to concentrate on bringing over and absorbing a flood of Jewish immigrants.

In September 1948 Bernadotte made a second report,[39] this time recommending an independent Jewish state (now to include western Galilee but not the Negev) and a merger of Arab Palestine and Transjordan. Abdullah readily agreed, as did Marshall and Bevin. Truman thought otherwise; nor did the report commend itself either to Israel or to the Arab League, and it eventually became a dead letter.[40] By now the Arab states' common front was beginning to disintegrate; the League completely alienated Transjordan by creating, in Egyptian-occupied Gaza, a Palestinian government under the Mufti (which formally proclaimed an all-Palestine state on 1 October 1948).[41] When Israel launched a new

38. ibid, esp. chaps 3–5; O'Ballance, *Arab–Israeli War* pp.136–8; David Vital, *The Survival of Small States* (1971) pp.74–5. Vital also says that Stalin's foreign affairs advisers warned him not to alienate the Arabs by supporting the Jews; he replied that in ten years the conflict would probably have subsided, and, if it had not, one could always change course. Both claims derive from a 'Private source'

39. On 16 September; next day the IZL murdered him

40. Shlaim, *Collusion* pp.293–6

41. In December Abdullah countered by staging a Palestinian Congress in Jericho that prepared the ground for his annexation of the West Bank (formally implemented in 1950)

offensive against Egypt in October the other Arab states sat it out, though the Legion did intervene to stop Israel seizing Hebron. (Later that month Israel responded to an Arab Liberation Army attack by taking over the remainder of western Galilee.) Israel was now in receipt of armistice overtures from both Egypt and Jordan, and in the following months was effectively playing its military cards to maximise its political advantages. A further attack on 22 December bypassed the main Egyptian forces,[42] and left Israel well placed to cut their communications and so eventually force their surrender. On 4 January 1949 Egypt formally sought an armistice; talks opened in Rhodes (under UN mediation) and on 24 February an armistice was finally signed that left Egypt still in possession of Gaza. The withdrawal from the war of the leading Arab state opened the way for a general conclusion of hostilities.[43] However the Israeli Prime Minister, Ben-Gurion, had at one time played with the idea of capturing Gaza, then offering it to Abdullah as the sweetener that would justify his making peace. This might have proved the wiser course.

There had been tentative Transjordan–Israeli contacts since August 1948, and 30 November brought 'an absolute and sincere cease-fire' in Jerusalem. More general negotiations started, clandestinely, in late December, but now against the background of Israeli military superiority, which was utilised in Operation Uvda ('*Fait Accompli*'), the early March occupation of Eilat on the Red Sea (at the tip of the Negev). The small Arab Legion detachments there prudently withdrew, and a general cease-fire came into effect the next day. Converting this into an armistice proved difficult, as Israel insisted on further territorial cessions to improve its strategic position in central Palestine. But Abdullah made it clear that he was hoping for peace and friendly relations with Israel; on the night the deal was finally concluded, the Israeli delegates were sounded as to possible Israeli air assistance for a Transjordanian take-over of Syria (where there had just been a coup).[44]

42. In so doing Israeli forces entered Egypt proper. They withdrew after a British ultimatum, but shot down five planes that were monitoring the withdrawal. Nothing concrete followed; but the atmosphere was briefly very tense, with Abdullah invoking the Anglo-Transjordan defence treaty and British troops moving into Akaba

43. Lebanon had indicated to Israel that it could not be the first Arab state to conclude an armistice but would be the second. Its armistice was signed on 23 March, Transjordan's on 3 April, Syria's (after long negotiations) in July. Iraq avoided the embarrassment by turning its positions over to Transjordan and withdrawing

44. Israel was ready for benevolent neutrality but not assistance: Shlaim, *Collusion* pp.423–4

FAILURE TO CONVERT THE ARMISTICE INTO PEACE 1949–52

Other countries had not made such dramatic proposals, but a number expected the armistice to be followed by peace. However, as long as the armistice held, no country *needed* to make peace: Ben-Gurion said that, though he would 'get up in the middle of the night in order to sign a peace agreement', 'I am not in a hurry and I can wait ten years. We are under no pressure whatsoever'.[45] For Israel, the existing situation might be better than the concessions that would be needed to secure peace. For Arab leaders, concluding peace would mean risking trouble with their own public opinion and with each other – while as long as Israel was not recognised, one could always hope for a second round against it at some unspecified future time or even that the problem would somehow simply go away. The UN did gather most of the parties at a conference in Lausanne from April to September 1949. Formal proceedings were a complete failure.[46] But Israeli delegates held quiet discussions with their counterparts from all other participating countries and with representatives of the refugees. Jordan was, as usual, the most forthcoming.[47] Egypt at one stage seemed ready for a compromise settlement *if* Israel would give up the Negev (widely interpreted). Outside the conference, the new (and as it proved very temporary) ruler of Syria offered peace, diplomatic relations and the settlement of 300,000 refugees in exchange for an extension of Syria's borders to include half the Sea of Galilee.[48] Israel was not prepared to go this far, and also proved extremely resistant to US pressure to take back 200,000 refugees.[49]

After the conference's failure Israel sent messages to Abdullah and to King Farouk suggesting direct negotiations. Abdullah agreed, and between November 1949 and March 1950 twelve Israeli

45. ibid, p.465

46. Israel did agree to take back the refugees in the Gaza Strip if it could gain the strip itself, but backtracked on discovering how numerous they were. Egypt was never willing to surrender the strip: ibid, pp.470–1

47. For Israeli summaries of the Jordanian position, see ibid, pp.478–81, 499

48. ibid, pp.428, 484–8

49. When Truman threatened to reconsider his attitude to Israel if it did not soften its general stance at Lausanne, Ben-Gurion responded, 'We can be crushed, but we will not commit suicide'. The Israeli ambassador, when threatened with the cancellation of a $49 million loan if Israel would not take back 200,000 refugees, told his interlocutor (who thought he had White House backing) that he would never get away with it; within the hour the White House dissociated Truman from the move: ibid, pp.471–2

visits were paid to his palace. In December 1949 the common interest in partitioning Jerusalem (rather than allowing the UN to establish a special regime there) seemed to have produced a breakthrough. When the agreed 'Principles of a Territorial Settlement' came to be defined more closely, however, it transpired that the stretch of Mediterranean coast that Israel was offering Jordan would be of little use as a port, while the corridor to it (under Jordan's sovereignty) would be only some hundred metres (not two kilometres) wide. Discussions then stalled, but were revived in February 1950. They soon reached impasse, so Abdullah suggested, in place of a definite settlement, a five-year non-aggression pact. In late February this seemed to have been agreed, but now the Jordanians backed off. Details of contacts with Israel leaked, rumours abounded, and, amid a storm of protest, Syria, Egypt and Iraq threatened sanctions. Abul Huda resigned as Prime Minister; since the King could find no replacement, he had to promise to do nothing till after the elections. These duly enabled Abdullah to annex the West Bank – against only token opposition from the Arab League, which was now chiefly concerned to block any separate agreement with Israel. But the growing prominence of West Bankers within Jordan made it less and less likely that Abdullah could push through ratification of an Israeli deal even if he reached one. He continued to try, but things went steadily downhill, until by 1952 all that was being discussed was the full implementation of the armistice provisions about freedom of movement around Jerusalem. In July 1952 Abdullah was murdered, and even these discussions stopped. In retrospect Glubb was to comment that the negotiations with Israel had failed for two reasons:

> The first was the intense agitation raised by the other members of the Arab League, which frightened the [Jordanian] government, though not the King. The second reason was that the Israelis, though apparently desirous of peace, wanted it only on their own terms. They were not prepared to make adequate concessions. King Abdullah realized that, if he were to make peace, he would have to be able to show substantial advantages therefrom. With Israel unprepared to make concessions, there was little inducement to defy the other Arab countries.[50]

50. ibid, chaps 17–19 (esp. p.581), Appendix 4

ARAB FLIGHT DURING THE 1948 FIGHTING AND ISRAELI REACTIONS

The UN calculated that the settled population of the 'Jewish State' it recommended in 1947 would be 55 per cent Jewish, 45 per cent Arab.[51] In practice Jewish immigration would soon have shifted this balance; but in the longer run it might have been offset by the higher Arab birth-rate. Ben-Gurion was to declare, soon after the UN's decision for partition, that 'With such a [population] composition, there cannot even be complete certainty that the government will be held by a Jewish majority. . . . There can be no stable and strong Jewish state so long as it has a Jewish majority of only 60%'. The problem had already exercised the Peel Commission in the 1930s; this had recommended an 'exchange' of population (between its proposed Jewish and Arab states) that should 'in the last resort . . . be compulsory'. Zionist opinion had welcomed the idea. But, during the struggle to secure UN support for partition, it had dropped out of sight; and Ben-Gurion so far departed from his earlier attitudes as to tell UNSCOP, 'We do not claim that any Arab ought to be moved'.[52] Nor, in the early stages of the fighting that followed the November 1947 UN Resolution, did the Yishuv follow any policy of extruding Arabs. The Haganah's Plan D, drawn up in early March 1948, for the first time authorised the destruction of hostile Arab villages and those that could not be garrisoned; in April this began to be implemented, chiefly along strategic roads. But the people who (beyond their expectations) forced the surrender of the Arab sector of Haifa on 22 April 1948 were astounded at the Arab decision, reached during the cease-fire negotiations, to evacuate the city. Their responses varied: local Jewish civilian leaders tried both then and later to persuade the Arabs to reconsider, but the lower levels of the Haganah came increasingly to see such flight as convenient.[53]

This sequence was to be replicated on a wider scale. The initial Arab flight was largely spontaneous. It began with the gradual withdrawal, from December 1947, of the more wealthy (who had also often removed to safety during the disturbances of the 1936–9 Arab Revolt). Their flight helped demoralise other Arabs, especially where, in and after April 1948, communities under attack suddenly found themselves abandoned by their leaders. Apart from the

51. Shlaim, *Collusion across the Jordan* pp.117–18

52. *Parliamentary Papers*, 1936–7 xiv pp.633–6; Benny Morris, *The Birth of the Palestinian Refugee Problem, 1947–1949* (Cambridge, 1987) p.28

53. Morris, *Birth of the Palestinian Refugee Problem* pp.76 ff

evacuation of a few villages for strategic reasons, the Arab Higher Command (AHC) did not (as many Israelis subsequently maintained) deliberately instigate Arab flight. However their attitudes sometimes promoted it: the leaders who decided to evacuate Haifa did so because they believed that, while they could not resist the Haganah, extremists would murder them if they concluded a formal surrender; evacuation seemed their only escape from this dilemma. Nor did the AHC discourage it, though the process took over a week. Not until early May 1948 was anything done to check the exodus. A meeting in Amman then agreed that 'the Arabs should return to Haifa'; on 5 May King Abdullah praised those who had not fled Palestine, appealed for a general return, and (by way of reassurance) cited the Jewish Agency's condemnation of the Deir Yassin massacre.[54] But it was now too late. Over wide areas the Palestinians were completely demoralised by the privations of the collapse of order, the flight of many notables, the presence of refugees from other areas and (sometimes) the depredations of Arab irregular forces. So they frequently fled on (or shortly before) Jewish attack. Some Jews deplored this. At the other extreme the IZL massacre at Deir Yassin was intended to instil panic and precipitate Arab flight. This was exceptional. A more usual response was that of Israel Galili on 11 May: 'we must continue to implement the plan of military operations prepared a while ago, which did not take into account the collapse and flight of Arab settlements following the rout in Haifa . . . [but] this collapse facilitates our tasks'.[55] Military men tried to destroy Arab morale through noisy bombardments, threatening loudspeakers and psychological 'whispering campaigns', and often sought in this way to edge the Palestinians into flight. As time went on, they also became more ready to clear villages by force, but still only on a sporadic basis. An intelligence analysis during the June truce put the refugee total at about 391,000 (perhaps an overestimate): this was viewed chiefly as a direct response to Jewish offensives and the contagious influence of the flight they engendered, though both 'general fear' (resulting from a 'crisis of confidence in Arab strength') and local causes played a part; only 9 per cent was attributed (more or less equally) to evacuation by Arab or expulsion by Jewish commanders.[56]

54. ibid, esp. pp.83–4, 134
55. ibid, p.128
56. Morris, 'The Causes and Character of the Arab Exodus from Palestine: The Israel Defence Forces Intelligence Branch Analysis of June 1948', *Middle Eastern Studies* xxii (1986) esp. pp.6–7, 9–10, 14, 16

Fighting in the second half of the year occasioned a similar exodus. There was still no defined and comprehensive Israeli policy, partly because one party in the governing coalition (Mapam) was officially committed to coexistence with the Arabs. Although Ben-Gurion personally authorised the expulsion of the 60,000 inhabitants of Ramle and Lydda – where sniping had resumed after the Israel Defence Forces (IDF) thought the town had surrendered – he intervened to protect Christian Nazareth. In general, though, Israeli commanders were given to understand that Arab departure would be welcome, and allowed to handle the problem largely in their own way: General Allon in the south was far firmer for expulsion than his northern counterpart, Carmel. The success of Israeli arms took them into areas less lacerated by earlier fighting, whose inhabitants were (especially in the north) correspondingly readier to stay put rather than conveniently abandon their villages as the IDF approached. So, one historian concludes, 'the July and October offensives were characterised by far more expulsions and, indeed, brutality towards Arab civilians than the first half of the war'.[57]

By the end of the year, though there was still fighting with Egypt, Israeli thoughts were turning to the stabilisation of the new borders. In military terms, this could be best effected by the removal of their Arab residents, a policy pursued – albeit incompletely – over the next few years by a mixture of harassment and force. The process generated far fewer refugees than the earlier war, but in some areas it was more visible, since it came under the scrutiny of the UN Armistice Commissions. In the north-east it was to prove of considerable importance: Syria never accepted the extrusion of the inhabitants of the demilitarised zone below Lake Tiberias, and its periodic attempts to disrupt Israeli cultivation of the area by cross-border shelling were to keep tension dangerously high.

At first Arab flight had not been viewed as necessarily permanent. The Jaffa surrender agreement of 13 May 1948 envisaged the return of any bona fide former inhabitants provided that they constituted no threat to peace and security. In late May the radio station Kol Yisrael was still proclaiming that Israel would allow refugees back. But to other Jews, Arab flight seemed too good an opportunity to miss. Leaders from exposed areas threatened to leave if the Arabs were permitted to return. Activists (including Sharett and Sasson, who were in other contexts to feature as doves)

57. Morris, *Birth of the Palestinian Refugee Problem* chaps 6–7, p.293

lobbied for a 'transfer policy'. In June the army stressed the danger that returning Arabs would 'fortify themselves in their villages behind our front lines, and with the resumption of warfare [correctly anticipated after the first Truce] . . . constitute at least a fifth Column', watching which would tie down Israeli forces.[58] At Cabinet meetings in June, Ben-Gurion made it plain that he too was opposed to an Arab return, even after the war, and instead favoured resettlement by Jewish immigrants. Mapam felt differently, but the most it could do was to retain the issue as an open question. August 1948 saw a further hardening, with a meeting of senior non-Mapam figures unanimously deciding to do everything possible to prevent the refugees' return. Meanwhile pressures from Count Bernadotte and the USA were turned aside with the argument that the question could be considered only as part of a general peace settlement.[59]

FAILURE TO AGREE ON RESETTLEMENT 1949

The time for this finally came with the Lausanne Conference of mid-1949. By then the UN General Assembly had, in December 1948, voted that 'the refugees wishing to return to their homes and live at peace with their neighbours should be permitted to do so at the earliest practicable date'.[60] But on the ground Israel had created faits accomplis, bulldozing some Arab villages and settling others with the immigrants who were now flowing in (190,000 between May 1948 and April 1949): 'Generally', the Palestine Conciliation Commission was told, 'it can be said that any Arab house that survived . . . now shelters a Jewish family. There can be no return to the status quo ante'. Nevertheless Sharett thought it prudent to have prepared 'an absolutely secret plan for the event that the Cabinet feels itself compelled to agree to a return of part of the refugees to Israel'.[61] In April 1949 the USA did begin pressing for the return of 200,000–250,000, and Truman eventually

58. ibid, esp. pp.135, 138–40, 144
59. ibid, pp.141–3, 148
60. UN, *Official Records of the Third Session of the General Assembly, Part 1: 21 September – 12 December 1948, Resolutions,* Resolution 194 (III) para. 11. The Arab states voted against the Resolution because it spoke of achieving 'a final settlement of all questions outstanding between' 'the Governments and authorities' of the region (para. 6)
61. Morris, *Birth of the Palestinian Refugee Problem* esp. pp.195, 255, 259, 261–2 chap. 9

threatened to reconsider his 'attitude toward Israel' in default of 'tangible refugee concessions', but, publicly at least, Ben-Gurion was defiant.[62] At the Lausanne Conference itself, the Arab delegations gave the refugee question pride of place (largely because it would require Israel to make the first concessions), while the Western Powers hoped that agreement on it would lead to a general settlement. Israel's first response was to float the idea of taking over the Gaza Strip from Egypt in return for allowing the refugees there to go home; this would in fact have met the US 200,000 target. Britain and the United States were enthusiastic, but sought also to link Israeli acquisition of Gaza with territorial counter-concessions in the Negev that would preserve the physical contiguity of the Arab world (disrupted by Israeli seizure of Eilat). Egypt, however, formally rejected the whole idea in late June 1949. A second Israeli move was a plan, launched in June, for family reunions; but this never amounted to much.[63] Finally in July–August 1949 Israel indicated willingness to accept the return of 100,000 – or, more accurately, after various deductions had been made, of 70,000 – refugees. The offer prompted intense domestic opposition, and was presented as both final and available only as part of a general peace settlement. Unofficially some Arab delegates suggested that Israel take back just over half the refugees, in which case the Arab states would settle the remainder.[64] Officially they treated the 100,000 offer as derisory; Israel stuck to it, and the conference broke down. Now that the armistice agreements were in place, neither side needed peace badly enough to induce it to make unpalatable concessions.

THE PALESTINIAN REFUGEES

The chief victims were the refugees, probably numbering some 725,000 (though nobody knows precisely). This figure – about 58 per cent of the Mandate's Arabs – certainly justifies the later Palestinian name for the 1948 war, 'the Catastrophe'. It also far

62. See note 49, p.264
63. By 1956 only 35,000 had returned under it: Morris, *Birth of the Palestinian Refugee Problem* p.440
64. ibid, pp.266–82

exceeded the 226,000 displaced Jews in postwar Europe.[65] The comparison occasioned comment: 'It seemed to [Bernadotte] an anomaly that the Israeli Government should advance as an argument for the establishment of their state the plight of Jewish refugees and demand the immediate immigration of displaced persons [from Europe] at the same time that they refused to recognize the existence of the Arab refugees which they had created'.[66] By absolute standards, however, these refugees were far fewer than the 5 million Germans *expelled* from Poland, Czechoslovakia and Hungary with the prior sanction of the Potsdam conference,[67] let alone the 13 million people who fled between India and Pakistan in 1947 at independence.

What has given the Palestinian refugees their special position in international relations is that so little was done to settle them. This would have cost money, and posed problems of land reclamation, but not of language or culture. Apologists for Israel contrast its ability to accommodate (in its first decade) some 450,000 Jews extruded from the Muslim world,[68] with 'the Arab nation's' disinclination to do likewise. Only in Jordan were the Arab refugees accepted as citizens; even there not all were absorbed into the ordinary economy, with the remainder continuing to live in refugee camps. At the opposite extreme Egypt barred those in Gaza from travelling to it to seek work.[69] This was possible because the costs of their maintenance were assumed by the United Nations, which in 1950 established a Refugee Works Administration (UNRWA) charged with resettlement. The Arab states would not cooperate, since this would have implied acceptance of Israel's permanent

65. For a discussion of the numbers of Palestinian refugees, see ibid, pp.297–8; for the numbers of Mandate Arabs, Shlaim, *Collusion across the Jordan* p.117; for the Anglo-American Commission's estimate of Jewish refugee numbers in April 1946, Ovendale, *Origins of the Arab–Israeli Wars* p.123

66. A US report, quoted by Morris, *Birth of the Palestinian Refugee Problem* p.147

67. *Keesing's*, 7365, 7694, 8299, 8905. Also in people's minds at the time was Mustapha Kemal's 1922 expulsion of Greeks after Turkey's 'War of Independence' and their resettlement by the League of Nations. (Israeli apologists have further cited the expulsion of loyalists after the US War of Independence.)

68. Howard M. Sachar, *A History of Israel: From the Rise of Zionism to Our Time* (Oxford, 1977) pp.336, 396–402, 415

69. Sachar calculated (ibid, pp.334–5, 441–2) that 300,000 refugees went to Jordan, 180,000 to Gaza, 100,000 to Lebanon, 70,000 to Syria, while others (often the best educated) gradually dispersed throughout the rest of the Arab world. Lebanon had grounds for fearing that, if accepted as citizens, they would upset its delicate religious balance. Similar fears as to the possible political consequences inhibited acceptance of Palestinians in the late 1970s by thinly peopled oil-rich states, who often imported non-Arab labour instead. But other Arab anti-Palestinian discrimination is less easily explained

existence. Only relief remained: by 1982 this had cost $1.5 billion, mostly contributed by the USA (and Britain). It kept the refugees alive; indeed natural increase had taken their numbers to 1.3 million by 1967. But they remained an unassimilated diaspora with little reason to put their hatred of Israel behind them, in marked contrast with the Arab minority that remained there. Although their political organisations did not become important until the later 1960s, the early 1950s saw repeated individual attempts to infiltrate Israel, to take revenge, to steal, or simply to get back to former homes and property. In 1952 alone 394 such infiltrators were killed and 2,595 captured. Israel blamed its neighbours for permitting, or encouraging, this infiltration; when its citizens were killed,[70] it followed a policy of major reprisals to force them to control their borders. As we shall see, the international consequences were sometimes very serious.

70. From 1949 to Oct. 1954 134 Israelis were killed by infiltrators from Jordan, a further 24 in 1955: Sachar, *History of Israel* pp.444–5

CHAPTER ELEVEN

The Middle East in the 1950s

SECRET ISRAELI–EGYPTIAN CONTACTS (1952–6); US–BRITISH ATTEMPTS TO RESOLVE ARAB–ISRAELI TENSIONS

If relations between Israel and its neighbours remained both hostile and dangerous, a number of efforts were made in the early 1950s to bridge the gap. The two most important catalysts were the 1952 Egyptian revolution and the 1953 advent of the Eisenhower administration. Israel welcomed the new Egyptian regime, and established contacts with it (chiefly in Paris). Through these Israel offered compensation for the refugees and a right of passage across the Negev. In return it sought free use of the Straits of Tiran and the Suez Canal, the lifting of the economic boycott (instituted by the Arab League in 1950) and the ending of threats of war. Egypt's response was more nebulous: in 1953–4 it expressed interest in 'a peaceful solution' and wished to avoid border trouble, but said it could not afford publicly to deviate from the Arab consensus or relax the blockade (though it held out hopes of gradual progress and eventual passage of Israeli ships). Nasser told the US Ambassador in 1953 that 'although an eventual settlement with Israel is in his mind, his present contacts are for informational purposes only . . . in his opinion, any peace settlement is still a long way off'. What Egypt most sought, at this stage, was Israel's good offices with the USA and help in inducing Britain to evacuate the Canal Base.[1]

1. Shimon Shamir, 'The Collapse of Project Alpha' in Wm. Roger Louis and Roger Owen (eds) *Suez 1956: The Crisis and its Consequences* (Oxford, 1989) esp. pp.75–7; *FRUS*, 1952–4, ix p.1,251

In fact the prospect of evacuation alarmed Israel, once it became clear that it would not be combined with a treaty providing for general freedom of navigation. Israeli intelligence, probably acting autonomously, fire-bombed British and US property in Egypt in July 1954 to destroy British confidence in the Egyptian regime and so stall the evacuation process. This murky episode, known in Israel as 'the affair', soon came to light with the arrest of some of the agents involved.[2] Equally Egypt had, after temporary compliance with a 1952 UN Security Council Resolution, again tightened restrictions on the transport of goods for Israel through the Canal in neutral ships. So in September 1954 Israel sent the *Bat-Galim* to transit the Canal in the vain hope of prompting Great Power intervention; it was confiscated, and its crew imprisoned for three months. In December 1954 Nasser told Israel that these developments made its proposals untimely. But he still expressed interest in maintaining contact, and 1955 saw, for instance, a fruitless shuttle between Cairo and Jerusalem by a private US citizen, Elmore Jackson.

The Eisenhower administration determined 'that Israel will not, merely because of its Jewish population, receive preferential treatment over any Arab state', and resolved to seek 'a progressive reduction in [Arab–Israeli] tension . . . leading to conditions under which ultimate peace may be secured'.[3] As a first step it favoured a scheme for the shared usage of Jordan basin waters that would also permit substantial refugee resettlement on newly irrigated land. Trouble arose in September 1953 when Israel started works to divert water from within the demilitarised zone with Syria; the USA suspended aid till Israel agreed to stop them (pending a UN decision on their compatibility with the Syrian armistice), one of the very few cases of open US sanctions against Israel.[4] Meanwhile a US envoy, Johnston, was deployed to seek acceptance of a water plan (one of a succession drafted since 1944). By 1955 he seemed to have succeeded, but in October the Arab League, at Syria's instance, declined to ratify it.[5] The USA also eventually persuaded Nasser in January 1955 to receive a secret Israeli

2. Donald Neff, *Warriors at Suez* (New York, 1981) pp.56–62. 'The affair' contributed to Ben-Gurion's return to active politics in 1955; the question of whether or not it had been authorised by Defence Minister Lavon convulsed Israeli politics in the 1960s

3. NSC 155/1 – *FRUS*, 1952–4, ix p.402

4. Yaacov Bar-Siman-Tov, 'The Limits of Economic Sanctions: The American–Israeli Case of 1953', *Journal of Contemporary History* xxiii (1988)

5. *Keesing's*, 19975–7

emissary; but when he confirmed death sentences on participants in 'the affair', Israel called the visit off.

More ambitiously, in 1954–5 Britain and the USA sought (mostly in private) a far-reaching settlement, Project Alpha, on the basis of Israeli territorial concessions to Jordan; sovereign access across the Negev between Israel and Jordan; the return of a considerable number of refugees and compensation for the remainder; agreement on the Jordan waters and on Jerusalem; the lifting of the Arab boycott of Israel; and Western guarantees for the new frontiers.[6] Nasser was generally non-committal, but indicated that he would require most of the Negev, not simply a corridor across it; Israel would not contemplate territorial cessions on the scale envisaged. In January 1956 Eisenhower sent a personal emissary, Anderson, armed with economic and other carrots, to see whether there was any chance of a deal. His shuttles between Egypt and Israel were a failure; Eisenhower blamed both sides – but more especially Nasser.[7] But this did not entirely end peace efforts. In July 1956 the Egyptian Foreign Minister floated the idea of exploratory visits by the UN Secretary-General, Dag Hammarskjöld, followed by a conference; but when Hammarskjöld visited the region he found little ground for hope. Probably by then all the parties wanted to do was to *appear* to negotiate, Israel in the hope that this would bring it arms, Egypt in pursuit of economic aid.

DETERIORATING MIDDLE EAST RELATIONS 1954–6

While these initiatives were in progress, the Middle Eastern situation was steadily deteriorating. Several interconnected themes can be traced.

Initially the Egyptian–Israeli armistice lines had been comparatively calm, though the cycle of murders by Arab infiltrators and Israeli reprisal raids dates back to 1950. Matters worsened sharply from March 1954, with Egyptian army involvement becoming increasingly apparent. In May the Israeli Prime Minister, Sharett, appealed to Nasser (via Britain) to arrest the officers

6. Louis and Owen, *Suez 1956* pp.81–100. Dulles sketched the scheme in an August 1955 speech and Eden gave it greater publicity in November, but it was pursued almost entirely through quiet diplomacy

7. Louis and Owen, *Suez 1956* pp.80–1, 95; Neff, *Warriors at Suez* pp.197–8

involved and reimpose order in the Gaza Strip, as Israel could not hold back much longer. This had little effect. But in January 1955 Egypt did clamp-down on Gaza, though there is some question as to whether the resultant border calm was beginning to unravel in February.[8] Sharett authorised a retaliatory raid, but – in the hands of Ben-Gurion, who had just returned as Defence Minister – it killed thirty-seven Egyptians, four times as many as Sharett had expected. Nasser chose to treat it as a mortal affront, intensified his search for weapons, and started training Palestinian guerrilla units (*fedayeen*). Thereafter things got much worse, with *fedayeen* raids and Israeli retaliation killing seventy people on the Gaza border in August, and conflict over 'demilitarised' Al Auja accounting for ninety-three in October–November 1955. In 1956 Hammarskjöld visited the area three times in unsuccessful attempts to calm things down; although the summer did see a lull, this was only because both Ben-Gurion and Nasser were concentrating on other things.

Second, in October 1953 Ben-Gurion had retired temporarily from politics, but only after presenting the Cabinet with a plan to strengthen the IDF against a renewed Arab attack, which he forecast for 1956. The prospect prompted Sharett to seek a way out through negotiation, especially with Egypt, a course that led in December 1954 to an exchange of messages with Nasser and to Nasser's agreement next month to receive an Israeli emissary. As we have seen, this process was interrupted by the side-effects of 'the affair'. Ben-Gurion and his supporters had viewed it with apprehension; in February 1955 he returned to the Cabinet convinced that, if they conflicted, defence should take priority over negotiation. One consequence was the Gaza raid. The rest of the year saw tension, with Sharett and a Cabinet majority overruling several proposals from Ben-Gurion for more dramatic action. Strengthened by elections in July 1955, Ben-Gurion resumed the premiership in November. But he still allowed the Cabinet to veto a proposal to seize the Straits of Tiran, where Egypt had recently further tightened the blockade by barring passage to Israel of ships or aircraft of whatever nationality. By March 1956 Ben-Gurion had, as a result of the collapse of the Anderson mission, changed his mind and concluded that war with Egypt was inevitable.[9] In April

8. Michael B. Oren, 'Escalation to Suez: The Egypt–Israel Border War, 1949–56', *Journal of Contemporary History* xxiv (1989) esp. pp.356–7, 370–1; Louis and Owen, *Suez 1956* pp.390–1

9. Avi Shlaim, 'Conflicting Approaches to Israel's Relations with the Arabs: Ben Gurion and Sharett', *Middle East Journal* xxxvii (1983) esp. pp.195–6

his protégé Shimon Peres used this argument when seeking more weapons from France to counterbalance those that Nasser had secured from the USSR (see below); he also played on French fears that an Egyptian victory would establish Nasser as a new Pan-Arab *duce*, with ominous repercussions for the French position in Algeria. In June Ben-Gurion forced Sharett out of office, and authorised Dayan and Peres to offer to help France with commando raids on Egypt.[10]

Third, Nasser had been seeking arms for some time: he first approached the USA in November 1952 for a considerable increase on what had been promised to his predecessor. He was to be disappointed; the USA played it long, and even when Eisenhower promised $27 million worth two years later, British intercession prevented their delivery.[11] In early 1955 three developments made the need for arms appear more urgent. One was the Gaza raid. Another, some say, was the establishment of secret Franco-Israeli relations and the promise to Israel (in December 1954) of twelve obsolescent jet fighters.[12] Lastly there were the moves towards the Baghdad Pact that threatened to bring arms to Iraq, Egypt's chief rival for the leadership of the Arab world. Anyway Nasser now turned to the Soviet Union, to which end he secured the advocacy of China by representing himself as the spokesman of the 'new forces of Arab nationalism' as against the 'colonialists and reactionaries'.[13] By August 1955 he had landed a deal on an unprecedented scale for $320 million worth of modern weapons on easy terms (ostensibly from Czechoslovakia); his ally Syria also bought substantial (though lesser) quantities.[14] The deal did not precipitate an immediate breach with the West. The pursuit of Project Alpha continued. Nasser – who took non-alignment seriously – sought to balance his Soviet arms purchases by securing Western aid for his cherished economic mega-project, the Aswan High Dam; in December 1955 he seemed to have achieved it. Nevertheless his 'Czech' purchases bypassed the Western Tripartite Pact regulation of Middle Eastern arms and gave the Soviet Union an entrée into the region. They prompted Israel to redouble its search for weapons, though in 1955 France remained distinctly

10. ibid. pp.197–8; Neff, *Warriors at Suez* pp.234–6, 239–42

11. Mohamed H. Heikal, *Cutting the Lion's Tail: Suez through Egyptian Eyes* (1986) pp.33–4; Neff, *Warriors at Suez* pp.71–2

12. Neff, *Warriors at Suez*, pp.162–3; Sachar, *History of Israel* p.483

13. Heikal, *Sphinx and Commissar* p.58

14. Sachar, *History of Israel* p.474

cautious.[15] They also increased the attractiveness for Israel of a pre-emptive strike before Egypt had absorbed its new equipment.

The fourth and perhaps the most important thread was that of rivalry between Egypt, the largest and most 'developed' Arab country, and Iraq, the largest oil-rich state. This rivalry was not new, but with the Egyptian revolution it had acquired an ideological edge: Iraq was ruled by the Hashemite dynasty, feared the USSR and was committed to the West, while Egypt claimed to embody the modern and progressive, as opposed to the traditional, forces of the region. In 1954 there were negotiations between Nuri and Nasser, but to no purpose. In January 1955 Nasser summoned Saudi Arabia, Syria, Lebanon and Jordan to a conference, and bullied them into accepting that no signatory of the Arab Mutual Security Pact had the right to join another defence pact – which Nuri regarded both as interference with Iraq's internal affairs and as a breach of earlier Egyptian promises.[16] February brought the signature of a Turkish–Iraqi defence pact that broadened to include Britain in April, Pakistan and Iran in September–October 1955. Nasser countered in March 1955 with an alliance with Syria and Saudi Arabia, further consolidated in October by the establishment of Egyptian–Syrian and Egyptian–Saudi military commands.[17] In November 1955 the Baghdad Pact decided to seek Jordan's adhesion; in December the British Chief of Staff visited Amman to sell the idea to King Hussein (warning him, inter alia, that Nasser was considering converting Jordan into a Palestinian Republic under Amin al-Husayni).[18] Hussein initially complied, then backed off in response to massive Palestinian protest orchestrated by Egyptian radio propaganda and, Britain believed, by the combination of Egyptian agents and Saudi money. Britain took this as a serious rebuff. Another blow came when, on 1 March 1956, Hussein dismissed the British Commander of the Arab Legion, Glubb Pasha, albeit (it now seems) for personal rather than political reasons. This is commonly represented as the last straw for Eden, whose initial reaction was to blame Egypt and declare, 'Nasser's got to go, it's either me or Nasser'.

15. Twelve more Ouragons and twelve modern Mystère fighters were promised in October 1955, far fewer than their Egyptian counterparts: ibid, p.484

16. H.F. Eilts in Louis and Owen, *Suez 1956* pp.352–3; Heikal, *Cutting the Lion's Tail* chap. 5

17. Yemen (which regarded the long-standing British position in and around Aden as occupation of a part of its own territory) associated itself with both moves: *Keesing's*, 14105, 14485, 14518, 14886

18. Heikal, *Cutting the Lion's Tail* p.88

BRITAIN AND USA TURN AGAINST NASSER MARCH 1956

Probably Eden soon recovered himself; but March 1956 does appear to have seen a decisive change in British policy. Since the decision to evacuate the Canal Zone, this had aimed at conciliating Egypt. True there had been Whitehall explosions of anger (at the stream of Egyptian radio propaganda) and alarm, more especially at intelligence reports of communist penetration of the Egyptian government; but in November 1955 Eden's response had been to shut this out by lobbying the USA to *help* Egypt with the Aswan Dam: 'on our joint success in excluding the Russians from this contract may depend the future of Africa'. In March 1956 the British seem to have given up hope of working with Nasser; Eden sent Eisenhower 'a most secret note of Egyptian intentions[19] of whose authenticity we are entirely confident'. Eisenhower was, as we have seen, already receptive following the failure of the Anderson mission. At the end of the month he approved a range of measures, 'in the main [to] be coordinated with the United Kingdom', to isolate Egypt (while still leaving 'Nasser a bridge to good relations with the West if he so desires') and strengthen its Arab opponents. Further, 'Planning should be undertaken . . . with a view to possibly more drastic action in the event that the above . . . [moves] do not have the desired effect'. In the months that followed, Britain and the USA seem to have worked fairly closely together. Although the USA put a brake on the more extreme British suggestions for dealing with Saudi Arabia[20] and Egypt,[21] it

19. The note remains secret; but Macmillan next day recorded 'alarming views' of Nasser's plan to transform the Arab world into 'a sort of League of Arab Republics' and to attack Israel when the last British troops left the Canal Zone: Alistair Horne, *Macmillan* i (1988) p.388

20. Saudi–British relations were bedevilled by a border dispute over the Buraimi Oasis, occupied by Saudi tribesmen in 1952, resumed by British-led auxiliaries in October 1955. This dispute, and historic rivalry with the Hashemites, help explain the untypical Saudi readiness to fund and align with radical Arab causes. In April 1956 British intelligence is said to have suggested that the overthrow of the Saudi regime should follow that of the Syrian. Eisenhower's policy was rather to encourage King Saud to distance himself from Nasser and, if possible, to build him up as 'a prospective leader of the Arab world': Neff, *Warriors at Suez* pp.212–13, 215–16, 265, 316–17

21. Kermit Roosevelt of the CIA (who had had close relations with Nasser) successfully opposed the idea of a coup: Nasser was so popular that there was no way to depose him short of assassination. Americans appear also to have warned Egypt that the British were now desperate and determined to 'do a Mossadeq', and to have hinted at the possibility of assassination: ibid, pp.216, 265; Heikal, *Cutting the Lion's Tail* pp.104–5

provided secret aid for Jordan and joined Britain in planning a coup to topple the regime in Syria. The USA also agreed that negotiations on aid for the Aswan Dam should be stalled.[22] This was initially quite easy: part of the Western aid package was a World Bank loan, and Nasser disliked the economic monitoring that would have accompanied it. However shortly after the last British troops left the Canal Base, Nasser brought matters to a head by accepting all Western conditions and asking for a definite decision. So in July 1956 Dulles had to tell the Egyptian Ambassador that the offer had been withdrawn.

NASSER NATIONALISES THE SUEZ CANAL JULY 1956

Nasser responded a week later by announcing the nationalisation of the Canal, from whose profits Egypt would build the Aswan Dam. Supposedly he subsequently said that he had been planning to do so (at a propitious moment) for nearly two years (that is ever since the agreement on British evacuation of the Canal Base).[23] The move ought to have been anticipated; and it could probably have been deterred had Britain maintained the capacity for rapid intervention to counter it; for before reaching his decision, Nasser prudently reviewed British capabilities for immediate action and found them wanting.[24] The British Chiefs of Staff were to reach the same conclusion; instructed, when news of the nationalisation came through, to plan a rapid response, they reported next day that airborne landings would be unsafe and that to assemble a seaborne invasion force would take weeks.[25]

The Cabinet had little difficulty in agreeing to try to reverse the nationalisation, 'by the use of force if necessary'. Britain was ready to act alone, but preferred coordination with France and the USA. France presented no problem. Like Britain it felt instinctively that Nasser would have to be stopped; and it had an added concern – 'If

22. Neff, *Warriors at Suez* pp.210–13, 317; Louis and Owen, *Suez 1956* pp.191–2; Wilbur C. Eveland recounts much covert planning in *Ropes of Sand: America's Failure in the Middle East* (New York, 1980) chaps 14–20, but he was clearly sometimes left in the dark

23. Dwight D. Eisenhower, *Waging Peace* (1965) p.34

24. Heikal, *Cutting the Lion's Tail* pp.119, 121–2

25. David Carlton, *Britain and the Suez Crisis* (Oxford, 1988) p.35; Robert Rhodes James, *Anthony Eden* (1986) pp.457–8

Egypt's action remained without a response', declared Foreign Minister Pineau, 'it would be useless to pursue the struggle in Algeria'. During his visit to London in late July 1956, he sought to convince politicians there that it was better to 'act bilaterally [with France] rather than [for Britain, France and America to] do nothing trilaterally'. Pineau also offered the services of French troops.[26]

The United States was another matter. Eisenhower sympathised with the British predicament, and even noted that, 'thinking of our situation in Panama, we must not let Nasser get away with this action'. He was anxious to play it long, however, and concerned that, if the USA joined Britain in using force, it 'might well array the world from Dakar to the Philippine Islands against us'. This judgement was not universal – Senate Majority Leader Johnson, Governor Stassen and the Joint Chiefs of Staff all, at various times, wished to support Britain; but Eisenhower's view firmly set the administration's course, and was especially strongly seconded by Treasury Secretary Humphrey, who saw the British as 'simply trying to reverse the trend away from colonialism, and turn the clock back fifty years'.[27] US efforts were, therefore, devoted on the one hand to dissuading the British – largely through a series of moderate but impressive letters from Eisenhower to Eden – and, on the other, to spinning out diplomatic initiatives in the hope that they would produce a solution or at least allow the psychological pressure for British military action to evaporate. Dulles 'thought there is a chance – just a chance –' of dissuading 'them, perhaps a bit at a time, gradually deflecting their course of action'.[28] This approach fitted well, though of course unconsciously, with Nasser's initial calculation that Egypt would be most exposed immediately after nationalisation:

> up to, say, 10 August there would be a 90 per cent risk of an armed attack . . .; for the rest of August the risk would decline to about 80 per cent; in September . . . 60 per cent; in the first half of October . . . 40 per cent; in the second half . . . 20 per cent, and thereafter, thanks to the mobilization of world opinion which Nasser confidently looked forward to, the risk would virtually evaporate.[29]

26. Maurice Vaisse, 'France and the Suez Crisis' in Louis and Owen, *Suez 1956* pp.137, 139; Rhodes James, *Eden* p.470

27. Ambrose, *Eisenhower* pp.331–3; Neff, *Warriors at Suez* pp.293, 391

28. On 31 July: Louis and Owen, *Suez 1956* p.199

29. Heikal, *Cutting the Lion's Tail* p.119. So confident indeed was Nasser in late October that the crisis was evaporating that he ordered the resumption of other *fedayeen* attacks from Gaza: Oren, 'Escalation to Suez' p.364

ATTEMPTS AT A MULTILATERAL DIPLOMATIC SOLUTION

In fact the Anglo-French attack ('*Musketeer*') could not be mounted till 15 September 1956, so August was bound to be devoted to diplomacy. Initially the British were only looking for a pretext. On 30 July the Cabinet's Egypt Committee was ready to accept the US idea of an international conference, but only to produce a policy declaration to be embodied in a British Note (or 'virtual ultimatum'): 'If Colonel Nasser refused to accept it, military operations could then proceed'. But the exercise took on a life of its own, at least to the extent that British politicians came to see it as necessary to secure US acquiescence; thus Macmillan understood that 'if every peaceful means had first been used, and force then used, Dulles believed that the world would understand'.[30] Dulles laid himself open to such misinterpretation because he had to sound sympathetic enough to the British position to induce the UK to go along with his delaying tactics. It has also been argued that, at least in some moods, Eden (to say nothing of more dove-ish ministers) hoped for a successful outcome from negotiations. To the extent that he would have been prepared to forgo military action against Nasser if 'effective international control over the Suez Canal [were] . . . re-established', this seems true. That he was contemplating any further concessions is more problematic, but by 26 September he was complaining of Pineau's hardline: the French Premier, Mollet, 'as I believe, would like to get a settlement on reasonable terms if he could. I doubt whether Pineau wants a settlement at all'. In Cabinet on 3 October Eden seems to have envisaged negotiations at the UN 'for a satisfactory settlement' if the Egyptians were prepared for them, though this would be 'more difficult' than 'If they continued to be obdurate' – in which case 'world opinion might be readier to support a recourse to forceful measures'.[31]

Meanwhile Britain mingled diplomacy with pressure, intimidation and subversion. Pressure began with the freezing of Egyptian financial assets in Britain, France and (to a lesser extent) the USA. Intimidation stemmed from the Anglo-French military build-up, but it was supplemented by broadcasts beamed from southern France.[32] The Egyptians also believed that attempts were made to assassinate

30. Rhodes James, *Eden* pp.469–70; Horne, *Macmillan* i pp.408–9 (22 Aug. and 26 Sept.)
31. Carlton, *Britain and the Suez Crisis* pp.53, 138–9; Rhodes James, *Eden* pp.504–5
32. Louis and Owen, *Suez 1956* p.119

Nasser.[33] August was largely devoted to a conference in London of the signatories to the 1888 Constantinople Convention on the Canal plus its largest users. With Dulles's full support, this produced (by eighteen votes to four) a strong resolution to the effect that the Canal should be run by an international board and not be closed to any user for political reasons. It also decided to send a mission, headed by the Australian Prime Minister Robert Menzies, to put this to Nasser. Menzies was a declared supporter of the British position, and in Cairo in early September 1956 he was at pains to stress that the military preparations were not (as Nasser had recently declared) a bluff. But none of his colleagues (from the USA, Sweden, Iran and Ethiopia) seconded him in this, and he was further undercut by Eisenhower's remark in a press conference that 'We are committed to a peaceful settlement of this dispute, nothing else'.

Menzies's failure could have led directly to military action, but there were signs that British public opinion, and indeed some ministers, were beginning to turn against this. Nor were the Chiefs of Staff happy with the plans that they had drawn up. Also Eisenhower was both advising strongly against the use of force and floating another of Dulles's schemes, for a Suez Canal Users Association (SCUA) that Eden understood as 'the running of the canal by the users in virtue of their rights under the 1888 Convention', Eisenhower as 'a semi-permanent organization . . . to take over the greatest practical amount of the technical problems of the Canal, such as pilotage, the organization of the traffic patterns, and the collection of dues to cover actual expenses. This organization would be on the spot . . . and might work out a de facto coexistence [with Egypt] which would give the users the rights they want'.[34] France opposed further delay, but went along with the decision to give SCUA a try. This meant another London conference on 19 September 1956, against, it was hoped, the background of proven Egyptian incapacity to run the Canal. As the

33. Heikal claims that hit men were sent but gave up without making any attempt, that France scheduled a commando assault on the Egyptian Revolutionary Command Council building for the date originally set for *Musketeer* but cancelled it, and that Israel attempted to poison Nasser's coffee: *Cutting the Lion's Tail* pp.154, 215. Peter Wright says that a plan was developed to murder Nasser, but that Eden rescinded it once agreement was reached for joint military action with Israel; after this failed, a different attempt was to be made using disaffected Egyptian officers, but it came to nothing: *Spycatcher* (New York 1987) pp.160–1. MI6 says that no British plans were made to murder, as opposed to topple, Nasser: Keith Kyle, *Suez* (1991) pp.149–51

34. Carlton, *Britain and the Suez Crisis* pp.121, 124

Menzies mission was failing, France instructed the Canal Company's staff to leave on 15 September, and Britain sought to route more ships through the canal than the remaining pilots could handle; after Operation Pile-up had made the point, British and French warships would intervene in the name of SCUA to organise the chaos and see ships through. The only trouble was that Egypt had taken the precaution of recruiting new pilots and managed successfully to handle all the traffic.[35] Nor did SCUA prove much more than a mirage. Dulles found the way that Eden presented it to the House of Commons unduly belligerent, and promptly explained that 'the United States did not intend itself to shoot its way through' the Canal; it was thinking only of diverting its ships around the Cape of Good Hope.[36]

By 23 September the British had largely given up hope of SCUA and insisted, despite French reluctance and (for opposite reasons) US concern, on going to the United Nations – though whether in search of a settlement or as a final demonstration that no avenue remained but force was unclear. Eisenhower privately contemplated producing a US plan ('even though it falls somewhat short of the detailed requirements of Britain and France') and secretly encouraging Nasser 'to make an appropriate public offer'.[37] Officially the Security Council made little progress: a list of general principles (including unimpeded transit for all users, and agreement between Egypt and the users on the manner of fixing charges) proved acceptable to Egypt and was passed unanimously; but the USSR vetoed a Resolution endorsing SCUA and the declaration of the August London conference. Unofficially there were incessant discussions between Selwyn Lloyd, Pineau, the Egyptian Foreign Minister Fawzi, and a range of mediators. Nothing tangible was agreed; but Lloyd did later tell the Cabinet that, though there were difficulties, 'he would not exclude the possibility that we might be able to reach, by negotiation . . ., a settlement that would give us the substance of our demand for effective international supervision of the Canal' (the original demand had been for 'effective international control' and 'management'). Moreover the Cabinet did regard as an option seeking 'the sort of settlement of the Canal issue which might be reached by

35. Louis and Owen, *Suez 1956* pp.122–3; Neff, *Warriors at Suez* p.308

36. Rhodes James, *Eden* pp.513–15; Louis and Owen, *Suez 1956* pp.204–5. Later Dulles may have alienated Lloyd at a crucial moment by letting slip that he expected SCUA to hand 90% of the Canal dues to Egypt: Kyle, *Suez* p.290

37. Neff, *Warriors at Suez* pp.327, 329; Ambrose, *Eisenhower* p.351

negotiation – recognising that, by accepting such a settlement, they would abandon their second objective of reducing Colonel Nasser's influence throughout the Middle East'.[38]

FRANCO-ISRAELI-BRITISH COLLUSION

One of the difficulties that Lloyd mentioned was the attitude of the French government. France had always been more determined and impatient than Britain. It was also politically closer to Israel, and at the beginning of September it began putting out feelers as to possible collaboration. After the British had insisted on trying out SCUA and postponing *Musketeer,* the French Defence Minister broached the possibility of joint Franco-Israeli action. (The Israelis were later informed that, during the London SCUA conference, Pineau had told Eden that, if Britain backed off, France might act either alone or with Israel, to which Eden supposedly replied that he had no objection provided that Israel did not attack Jordan.) The French Cabinet then invited Israeli representatives to Paris to discuss joint action. At these talks (on 30 September 1956) Pineau sought Israeli agreement to attack Egypt in the hope that this would precipitate British intervention, though it was also decided to look into a purely Franco-Israeli undertaking. The Israelis were attracted, but certainly not committed. Ben-Gurion decided to continue planning on a contingency basis, but privately put the chance of France's finally deciding to go ahead at no more than 20 per cent.[39]

France now turned to managing Britain. On 3 October 1956 Eden was apparently able to tell his Cabinet that 'The Jews had come up with an offer' to attack Egypt; but what impact, if any, this had is not clear.[40] The story resumes on the 14th, when French visitors, General Challe and Labour Minister Gazier, presented

38. The UN negotiations are described in Heikal, *Cutting the Lion's Tail* chap. 15 and Selwyn Lloyd, *Suez 1956* chap. 10. For Cabinet discussion, see the extracts from its minutes (27 July, 18, 23, 24 Oct.) in Carlton, *Britain and the Suez Crisis* pp.133, 140–1, 143, 145–6

39. Moshe Dayan, *Story of My Life* (1976) chap. 13; Shimon Peres, *David's Sling* (1970) pp.185–97

40. One version has it that the Cabinet was unresponsive: David Carlton, *Anthony Eden* (1981) p.428; another that it was from this point that "'collusion' slipped into forward gear' in unminuted Cabinet meetings, and that Macmillan (at Eden's request) destroyed his diary entries after 4 October: Horne, *Macmillan* i pp.429–30

Eden with what Challe later described as 'the pretext or rather the scenario that he wanted':[41] Israel should be encouraged so to attack Egypt that Britain and France could claim there was a threat to the Canal and send in troops to separate the combatants. Selwyn Lloyd was summoned back from New York; after brief ministerial consultations, he and Eden flew immediately to Paris, where Pineau told them that Israel was getting desperate and was likely to act soon. Eden sought strongly to discourage operations against Jordan (which then seemed quite likely – see p.286): 'If they contemplated any military operations . . ., it would be far better from our point of view that they should attack Egypt'. If they did, he agreed that Britain would join France in intervening 'to safeguard the Canal and limit hostilities'. And they should go soon, for, Dulles had said, US forces could not be used without congressional authority; and 'if Israel were to act before the end of the American election campaign, it was most improbable that Congress could be re-summoned or, if re-summoned, would give this authority'.[42]

Israel, and more particularly Ben-Gurion, did not like being cast in 'the role of aggressor, while the British and French appeared as angels of peace to bring tranquillity to the area'. Although the French insisted that this was the only 'scenario' Britain would accept, Israel wanted a partnership and apparently insisted on meeting a leading British figure. Lloyd was accordingly sent off to Sèvres on 22 October, but did not allay either Ben-Gurion's sensitivities or his fear of being left open to Egyptian air-power in the interval before Anglo-French intervention. Ben-Gurion was, however, exposed to pressure both from France and from his own delegation. Next day he authorised sounding Pineau out on minor alterations to the scenario, which Pineau took to London. There Pineau secured Eden's agreement to a further meeting with the Israelis, and to various undertakings designed to calm Ben-Gurion's fears of Egyptian bombing. Two British civil servants were sent over on 24 October and finally concluded a deal providing for Israel to attack on the 29th.[43]

41. Carlton, *Britain and the Suez Crisis* p.56

42. Kyle, *Suez* pp.302–4; Lloyd, *Suez 1956* pp.173–5; Carlton, *Britain and the Suez Crisis* pp.141–2

43. To Ben-Gurion's delight and Eden's dismay they did so in writing: Bar-On in Louis and Owen, *Suez 1956* chap. 7; Dayan, *Story of My Life* chap. 14; Carlton, *Britain and the Suez Crisis* pp. 59–68

BRITISH REASONS FOR USING FORCE

There is probably no single explanation for the British decision to go ahead. The country was divided over the acceptability of using force, but the Conservative Party conference, held just before the crucial visit of Challe and Gazier, had been distinctly belligerent. There were also very real fears of collision with *Israel* over Jordan. The Israeli–Jordanian border was disturbed, partly because Jordan was now allowing Egyptian-trained *fedayeen* to operate from its territory and Israel was following its usual policy of retaliation. On 10 October Israel mounted a major reprisal against Qalqilia. During the fighting King Hussein invoked his treaty and appealed for British air support. He later asked Iraq to send troops. Israel regarded such a troop movement as ominous. Britain initially encouraged it to stop Hussein turning to Nasser for assistance, but on 15 October (after the Challe-Gazier visit) asked for a delay. Britain also brushed up its plans for operations against Israel: by 20 October fighters in Germany had been prepared, and Mediterranean forces were ready to act at shorter notice against Israel than against Egypt. In this context Eden's comment that an Israeli attack on Egypt 'would be far better from our point of view' than one on Jordan is quite understandable; once the 24 October deal was reached, British preparations against Israel were relaxed.[44]

Above all, though, the British decision was predicated on the view that, unless Nasser was checked, disaster would follow in the Middle East and consequently in Europe. As Eden put it to Eisenhower,

> In the 1930s Hitler established his position by a series of carefully planned movements. . . . His actions were tolerated and excused. . . . It was argued either that Hitler had committed no act of aggression against anyone, or that he was entitled to do what he liked in his own territory, or that it was impossible to prove that he had any ulterior designs, or that the Covenant of the League of Nations did not entitle us to use force and that it would be wiser to wait until he did commit an act of aggression.
>
> . . . Similarly the seizure of the Suez Canal is, we are convinced, the opening gambit in a planned campaign designed by Nasser to expel all Western influence and interests from Arab countries. He believes that if he can get away with this . . ., his prestige in Arabia will be so great

44. John Zametica, 'Suez: The Secret Plan', *The Spectator* 17 Jan. 1987 pp.11–13. Militarily Britain could have fought Egypt or Israel, but not both. The dual planning was operationally awkward; but measures to deter Israel also served inconspicuously to upgrade readiness for *Musketeer*. Kyle, *Suez* p.309

> that he will be able to mount revolutions of young officers in Saudi Arabia, Jordan, Syria and Iraq. (We know that he is already preparing a revolution in Iraq . . .)[45] These new Governments will in effect be Egyptian satellites if not Russian ones. They will have to place their united oil resources under the control of a United Arabia led by Egypt and under Russian influence. When that moment comes Nasser can deny oil to Western Europe and we shall all be at his mercy. . . . Even if the Arabs eventually fall apart again as they did after the early Caliphs, the damage will have been done meanwhile.
>
> In short we are convinced that if Nasser is allowed to defy the eighteen [London conference] nations it will be a matter of months before revolution breaks out in the oil-bearing countries. . . . In this belief we are fortified by the advice of friendly leaders in the Middle East.
>
> The Iraqis are the most insistent in their warnings. . . . Other warnings have been given by the Shah . . . [and the] Libyan Ambassador here, who was formerly Prime Minister. . . . King Saud . . . said that it would be bad if Nasser emerged triumphant, for he agreed that Nasser's ambition was to become the Napoleon of the Arabs and if he succeeded the regimes in Iraq and Saudi Arabia would be swept away.

Eisenhower shared this view of Nasser's intentions but questioned Eden's picture of the Arab world. Were Britain to attack Nasser, 'I think all Arabs would be forced to support him, even though some of the ruling monarchs might very much like to see him toppled'. Instead Eisenhower advocated 'slower and less dramatic processes than military force', like SCUA.

> There are economic pressures which, if continued, will cause distress in Egypt.
>
> There are Arab rivalries . . . which can be exploited if we do not make Nasser an Arab hero.
>
> There are alternatives to the present dependence upon the Canal. . . .
>
> Nasser thrives on drama. If we let some of the drama go out of the situation and concentrate on the task of deflating him through slower but sure processes such as I described, I believe the desired results can more probably be obtained.

The apparent weakness of Eisenhower's approach was that the second eventuality in which he expected 'the Arabs to rally firmly to Nasser's support' was 'a capitulation to Nasser and complete

45. On 24–5 Oct. the Cabinet was further told that Nasser 'was already plotting *coups* in many other Arab countries', that against Libya being 'far advanced': Carlton, *Britain and the Suez Crisis* pp.145, 147. Eveland claims that Nasser had earlier made 'several abortive attempts to overthrow the Sudanese government': *Ropes of Sand* p.194; and Egypt helped arm EOKA in Cyprus: Heikal, *Cutting the Lion's Tail* p.120

acceptance of his rule of the Canal traffic'.[46] A negotiated Canal settlement was, as we have seen, not inconceivable in October 1956; but it would have involved substantial British concessions and would not have been such 'as would diminish Colonel Nasser's influence throughout the Middle East'. Moreover at crucial points (during the Menzies mission, at the launching of SCUA, and again during the Security Council proceedings), the USA seemed always to weaken the British negotiating position by public statements rejecting any use of force. Ministers found this exasperating.[47]

Finally, as the autumn drew on, it was becoming more and more difficult to maintain the invasion force in being, since the mobilised reservists were getting restive, equipment needed maintenance and sea conditions were expected to worsen; but winding it down 'could not fail to weaken our bargaining position'. In the end Eden and Lloyd saw inaction, and the consequent extension of Nasser's influence, as the greater risk, and argued that, though 'from the point of view of opinion throughout the Arab States, Israel's intervention in our dispute with Egypt would be unfortunate . . . there seemed to be little prospect of any other early opportunity for bringing this issue to a head'. Some doubts were expressed, but the Cabinet eventually agreed.[48]

THE MILITARY OPERATIONS

Israel duly attacked Egypt in Sinai on 29 October 1956. Next day Britain and France summoned both belligerents to withdraw ten miles from the Canal and permit them temporarily to occupy it. They vetoed a UN Security Council Resolution requesting all countries to refrain from using force, then late on 31 October they began the destruction of the Egyptian air force.[49] Nasser accepted the loss of his planes and saved his pilots for another day. He also

46. Eden to Eisenhower (6 Sept.), Eisenhower's reply (8 Sept.): Carlton, *Britain and the Suez Crisis* pp.120–5

47. Thus Eden and Lloyd felt Eisenhower's 11 October declaration that 'here is a very great crisis that is behind us' could only relax the pressure on Egypt at the UN discussions. So Eden attacked it (indirectly) at the Conservative Party Conference (*Full Circle* pp.307–8) and the plaudits he received may have made him more receptive to the Challe/Gazier proposal next day

48. Minutes, 24 and 25 Oct: Carlton, *Britain and the Suez Crisis* pp. 143–8

49. This should, under the Sèvres agreements, have started twelve hours earlier. Eden delayed it to permit the evacuation of Americans, but Nasser did not (as Ben-Gurion had feared) take the opportunity to bomb Israeli cities

pulled most of his troops back to cover Cairo against Anglo-French attack. This transformed the Sinai fighting into a rout; by 5 November Israel had occupied the whole peninsula, including Sharm el-Sheikh, and taken over Gaza (which it proceeded forcefully to clear of *fedayeen*).

The Anglo-French *Operation Musketeer* was altogether more ponderous. The initial elimination of the Egyptian air force was to be followed by at least a week's bombing and radio propaganda, intended to shatter Egyptian will to resist and so permit a later unopposed occupation of the Canal Zone.[50] Despite French pressure for speed, Britain would deviate little from this schedule. The main invasion force left Malta only after the outbreak of hostilities, and so could not land at Port Said before 6 November. This period of waiting could easily have been compressed, given the foreknowledge of the date of Israeli action. As things fell out, it merely provided time for the orchestration of international pressure against the undertaking. Concern for civilian casualties, plus fears that the destruction of Egyptian oil facilities would lead to reprisals against British ones elsewhere in the Middle East, precluded any serious attempt to bomb Egypt into submission. But the idea that Egyptian resistance would simply collapse was not wholly fanciful: on 31 October Nasser came under domestic pressure to surrender; and the British believed that Egyptians could be found to serve in a viable 'friendly' government.[51] France, on the other hand, wanted action before it was too late, and pushed Britain to consider paratroop drops. It also secured Israeli agreement to seize El Quantara and cover a French drop until the arrival of the main invasion force; indeed Israel went further, offering French armour transit through Sinai to any part of the Canal Zone.[52]

Britain rejected this as inconsistent with the cover story that its intervention was designed to *separate* Israeli and Egyptian combatants, but it did agree to a drop on 5 November. Although this went well, it did not secure the surrender of Port Said; on 6 November the invasion force had to fight its way in, taking the city by afternoon and heading south. No great military difficulty was anticipated in occupying the whole of the Canal,[53] but London's

50. Louis and Owen, *Suez 1956* pp.118–19

51. ibid, pp.120–2; Heikal, *Cutting the Lion's Tail* p.180

52. Moshe Dayan, *Diary of the Sinai Campaign* (1966) pp.160–2

53. The invasion had been planned on the basis of its taking six days; its overall commander later claimed only two further days would have been needed: Eden, *Full Circle* pp.554, 558; Carlton, *Britain and the Suez Crisis* p.76, also pp.154, 156

will to continue in the face of international pressure collapsed. The French Cabinet reluctantly accepted London's decision and issued orders for a halt, while vainly hinting to its commanders that they could be disregarded.[54] So the invasion stopped a mere twenty-three miles down the Canal, and a cease-fire was proclaimed as from midnight.

THE BRITISH DECISION TO CEASE ACTION

The British decision to halt is puzzling. Cabinet minutes stress concern with the situation in the UN, and the need to draw closer to the USA in view of possible Soviet interference in the Middle East following Bulganin's threatening note of 5 November.[55] But Selwyn Lloyd doubts whether either factor was really important, and claims that the British UN representative, Dixon – though clearly unhappy with the whole episode – had just said the UN situation could be contained till the end of the week. More important, Lloyd felt, was the fact that Israeli–Egyptian fighting had already stopped.[56] This claim is plausible. Britain was, as we have seen, much wedded to its cover story that it had intervened to separate the combatants; on 4 November news that Israel had accepted a cease-fire led some ministers to favour deferring action lest Britain and France 'alone be responsible for the continuance of hostilities which it had been the professed intention of their intervention to stop'; only Israel's withdrawal of its cease-fire offer (at French instance) restored the consensus on proceeding. Israel secured its last object, Sharm el-Sheikh, early on 5 November, and then again accepted a cease-fire when pressed strongly by Eisenhower. So the British problem of prolonging the fighting returned; whereas, 'If we

54. Louis and Owen, *Suez 1956* p.337

55. The note asked, publicly, how Britain and France would like it if rockets were used against them. It was almost certainly a bluff, and Eden answered it as such: see *The Cold War*, chap. 7; Rhodes James, *Eden* p.573. But some ministers were worried by reports – apparently CIA disinformation – of the movement of Soviet arms and aircraft to Syria. 'Nigel West' indeed claims that 'A full scale war seemed imminent, and Dean [the Chairman of the Joint Intelligence Committee] was obliged to advise Eden that MUSKETEER should be terminated with immediate effect': *The Friends* p.155. Keith Kyle's magisterial study contains no mention of any such advice, and does not regard the USSR's stance as more than a contributory factor to a Cabinet decision reached basically for other reasons: *Suez* esp. pp.459, 460, 465, 615

56. Carlton, *Britain and the Suez Crisis* pp.153–8; Lloyd, *Suez 1956* pp.209–11

agreed to break off hostilities at once, we could maintain that we had achieved our primary objectives'.[57]

The other consideration was economic: Eden apparently told Mollet 'The pressure on sterling is becoming unbearable. The English can take a lot of things, but I do not think they would be willing to accept the failure of sterling which would have considerable consequences for the Commonwealth'. As part of the gradual reconstruction of its international financial position, Britain had restored the convertibility of transferable sterling, which increased the pound's exposure to runs on the exchanges. Foreign exchange reserves (at $2.2 billion on 31 October) were dangerously close to the psychologically crucial $2 billion level. They could have been bolstered by drawing on the IMF, as France did in October, but the Treasury regarded this as alarmist and possibly counter-productive. Although the Chancellor (Macmillan) had been warned in September that Britain might be 'unable to maintain the value of the currency' if it resorted to force against Egypt, nothing was done. The November fighting led to a run on the pound, possibly encouraged by the USA, and by the 6th this had convinced Macmillan that Britain would have to stop. He told the Cabinet that £100 million had been lost that month (though this figure seems to have been £32 million) and that telephone calls to Washington had shown that only a cease-fire by midnight would secure US support for an IMF drawing to salvage the pound.[58] Nor was the cease-fire alone enough to mend the situation. The Americans knew that Britain needed to be able to disclose support measures in early December, when its reserve figures were due to be released. So until Britain had set a date for withdrawing from Egypt, they withheld all support, while promising that it would be freely forthcoming as soon as this was done. A deal along these lines was finally struck on 3 December 1956, and the last troops left on the 22nd.[59]

The less open French economy had not been so vulnerable. But the British Cabinet had been told on 30 October that reserves 'were still falling at a dangerously rapid rate; and, in view of the extent to

57. Moshe Dayan, *Story of my Life* p.209; Carlton, *Britain and the Suez Crisis* pp.74–5, 150–4

58. Carlton, *Britain and the Suez Crisis.* p.77; Kyle, *Suez* pp.334–5, 464, 467; Lloyd, *Suez 1956* p.209; Horne, *Macmillan* i pp.440, 443; Macmillan, *Memoirs* iv p.164. November's losses eventually proved eventually to be just below the $300 million of which Macmillan had warned his colleagues on 25–6 October

59. Diane Kunz, 'The Economic Diplomacy of the Suez Crisis' in Louis and Owen, *Suez 1956*

which we might have to rely on American economic assistance, we could not afford to alienate the United States Government more than was absolutely necessary'. The assumption, though, had been that, while the USA might protest, it would acquiesce.

EISENHOWER'S TACTICS DURING THE CRISIS

For his part, Eisenhower, while aware of heavy Anglo-French radio traffic in late October, preferred not to ask embarrassing questions. Anyway he assumed that nothing would happen before the US elections, and intended to launch a new pre-emptive peace initiative the moment he won them. His biographer says he expected 'that the Israelis would attack Jordan, supplied by the French and with covert British sanction and that the British and French would then take advantage of the confusion to occupy the canal'.[60] Eisenhower later told a British friend he had 'realised that at some time we intended to strike at Nasser, but had thought that it would have been after the American elections'.[61] When the Anglo-French action broke, he was initially furious, but for the most part reacted more in sorrow than in anger: 'I've just never seen great powers make such a complete mess and botch of things'; and

> I think that Britain and France have made a terrible mistake. Because they had such a poor case, they have isolated themselves from the good opinion of the world and it will take them many years to recover. France was perfectly cold-blooded about the matter. She has a war on her hands in Algeria, and she was anxious to get someone else fighting the Arabs on her eastern flank so she was ready to do anything to get England and Israel in that affair. But I think the other two countries have hurt themselves immeasurably and this is something of a sad blow because, quite naturally, Britain not only has been, but must be, our best friend in the world.

Above all he deplored the 'opportunities that we have handed to the Russians. Every day the hostilities continue the Soviets have an additional chance to embarrass the Western world beyond measure.'[62]

60. Ambrose, *Eisenhower* pp.353, 356–7; Louis and Owen, *Suez 1956* p.208; Horne, *Macmillan* i pp. 434–5; Kyle, *Suez* pp.310, 345

61. Lloyd, *Suez 1956* p.218. Dulles, too, while privately conceding to Macmillan on 25 September, 'that he quite realised that we might have to act by force', appealed to him 'to hold things off until after November 6th': Horne, *Macmillan* i p.423

62. Neff, *Warriors at Suez* pp.376, 396

Eisenhower might have tried blocking the invasion with the US Sixth Fleet (which Admiral Burke regarded as capable of knocking off the 'British, the French and the Egyptians and the Israelis, the whole goddamn works'). But though the fleet shadowed the invasion force uncomfortably closely, it did not attempt any such provocative action. Instead the USA concentrated on economic pressure, of whose efficacy the administration was always confident, and on activity at the UN. Here a major concern was to prevent the Soviet Union

> from seizing a mantle of world leadership through a false but misleading exercise of concern for smaller nations. Since the Africans and Asians almost unanimously hate one of the three nations, Britain, France and Israel, the Soviets need only propose . . . immediate punishment of these three to have the whole of two continents on their side, unless a good many of the UN nations are already committed to something more moderate that we might immediately formulate.[63]

Accordingly the USA endorsed the move (under the 'Uniting for Peace' Resolution – see p.456) from the UN Security Council to the veto-proof General Assembly, where Anglo-French action was condemned on 2 November by sixty-five votes to five (with seven abstentions).

THE UNITED NATIONS EXPEDITIONARY FORCE

Since (unlike France) Britain was internally divided over Suez, and was hurt by the split in the Commonwealth (only Australia and New Zealand voted with Britain, while South Africa and – on a technicality – Canada abstained), UN condemnation had some effect. Also concern was voiced in the Cabinet about the possibility of the UN proceeding to oil sanctions.[64] But the UN's chief contribution was to provide a cover for British withdrawal. With an eye on the General Assembly debate, Eden had declared that, once Britain and France had separated the combatants, they would be glad to turn over to the UN 'the physical task of maintaining peace

63. On 1 November: Louis and Owen, *Suez 1956* p.210

64. Britain was vulnerable to these as the Canal had been blocked and the pipeline through Syria cut. But the USA had in any case at the onset of hostilities suspended joint contingency planning for Western Hemisphere supplies: Carlton, *Britain and the Suez Crisis* p.154; Lloyd, *Suez 1956* p.206; Louis and Owen, *Suez 1956* p.227

in that area'. Canada's Foreign Minister, Lester Pearson, independently suggested a UN force large enough to keep peace on the Egyptian–Israeli borders until a political settlement was worked out. Eden seized on this, and suggested that the Anglo-French invasion force form its nucleus. Pearson was initially attracted, but the USA was not.[65] The idea, as it had evolved by 4 November, entailed the absence of contingents from any of the Permanent Members of the UN Security Council, something Eisenhower valued as excluding any Soviet presence. The British Cabinet then regarded this exclusion of its forces as unacceptable and resolved to go on with the invasion – with a view to later handing over to a UN force charged with separating the belligerents, securing Israeli withdrawal, restoring traffic through the Canal (which Nasser had blocked after the Anglo-French attack), and promoting 'a settlement of the outstanding problems of the area'. Even after Eden had cut the invasion short on 6 November, he tried to persuade Eisenhower to make the UN force a general Western one – but in vain.[66] Eden also assumed that the Anglo-French presence in Port Said would be used as a lever to extract concessions from Nasser. Had Britain occupied the whole of the Canal, it might have had something to bargain with, but a mere twenty-three miles was useless; Nasser refused to permit the clearing of the remainder until the invaders had left. The immediate functions of the UN Expeditionary Force (UNEF) were, therefore, to facilitate their withdrawal and help clear the Canal. Secretary-General Hammarskjöld conducted delicate negotiations in November to secure UNEF's acceptance on Egyptian territory for these purposes, the chief problem being Nasser's feeling that a Canadian contingent would be too 'British'. Hammarskjöld also secured Egypt's renewal of its October offers on the management of the Canal within the framework of the 1888 Constantinople Convention and on tolls. The UNEF then successfully covered the Anglo-French withdrawal in late December, and General Wheeler of the World Bank had the Canal cleared by April.[67] These achievements were valuable, though a far cry from the controlling function that Eden (and others)[68] originally had in mind.

65. Louis and Owen, *Suez 1956* pp.308–10; Eden, *Full Circle* p.536; *Keesing's* 15185–6

66. Carlton, *Britain and the Suez Crisis* pp.150–2; Neff, *Warriors at Suez* p.411

67. Brian Urquhart, *Hammarskjöld* (1972) chap. 7

68. In early November Dulles had anticipated Nasser's collapse under Anglo-French attack and the creation of a three-man UN commission to devise a new Canal regime: Louis and Owen, *Suez 1956* p.312

ISRAEL'S FORCED WITHDRAWAL FROM SINAI 1957

UNEF's real importance was to come in connection with the Israeli withdrawal from Sinai. Israel left the vicinity of the Canal in December 1956 and in January yielded to UN pressure to evacuate Sinai. Its sticking points were the Gaza Strip and Sharm el-Sheikh. They gave rise in February to intense negotiations (principally between Israel, the USA, Hammarskjöld, Canada, France and Egypt). There was considerable pressure for a UN vote of sanctions to force withdrawal, which Eisenhower used (despite unhappiness in Congress) to put pressure on Israel. In particular he warned the US Jewish community that its $100 million per year private contributions to Israel might be blocked. Meanwhile Dulles was prepared to work out, with the Israeli Ambassador, ways of preserving freedom of navigation to Eilat and of preventing the resumption of *fedayeen* activities from Gaza. In both cases, if it had to leave, Israel hoped to be replaced for the foreseeable future by UNEF; it was brought, on 1 March 1957, to promise withdrawal on this basis.

Over Sharm el-Sheikh things went quite smoothly: Israel proclaimed the principle of free navigation and declared that it would regard interference as entitling it to exercise 'its inherent right of self-defence under . . . the United Nations Charter'; at Canada's suggestion, the USA, UK, France and ten other maritime powers undertook 'to exercise the right of free . . . passage and to join with others to secure [its] general recognition'.[69] Gaza presented more problems; Israel sought its 'take-over' by UNEF. The USA was reluctant to endorse this explicitly, but both Hammarskjöld and the West generally hoped to secure it de facto. Egypt appeared accommodating until Israel had actually left, then appointed a Governor. Given UNEF's dependence (in Hammarskjöld's concept) on Egyptian acquiescence, he could hardly be kept out – especially as UNEF had already had to use force to suppress pro-Egyptian demonstrations in the Gaza Strip. Egypt was, however, prepared to promise that there would be no more *fedayeen* raids; and the loose ends were tied up during a visit by Hammarskjöld to Cairo in late March 1957.

Nasser was obdurate in refusing passage through the Suez Canal for Israeli ships, but promised to 'close his eyes' over the Straits of Tiran. He also claimed to want 'peaceful conditions without a

69. Some states not only noted, but also expressly endorsed, Israel's claim that interference with such navigation would trigger action in self-defence: *Keesing's*, 15446–7; RIIA, *Documents 1957* pp.205, 210

settlement' with Israel, and accepted UNEF's right to patrol the borders of the Gaza Strip and fire on would-be infiltrators. But Nasser rejected Hammarskjöld's suggestion that UNEF be withdrawn only after a vote in the Security Council, and insisted that it could remain on Egyptian territory only with Egypt's consent. Ten years later this was to prove very important. In the mean time a workable settlement of Israeli–Egyptian frictions had been arrived at, apparently guaranteed by UNEF's presence in the former trouble spots of Gaza and Sharm el-Sheikh.[70]

THE EISENHOWER DOCTRINE 1957; JORDAN'S BREAK WITH RADICALISM

With these arrangements, and the reopening of the Canal, the Suez crisis had been resolved. There remained in Eisenhower's view, the problem of Nasserite and communist influence. At their meeting in late November 1956, the Muslim members of the Baghdad Pact had expressed concern about 'the rising tide of subversion in the Middle East', and had drawn a US declaration of support for the Pact and for their own 'territorial integrity' and 'political independence'.[71] In January Eisenhower went further, launching what would become known as the 'Eisenhower Doctrine'; this authorised military assistance programmes, provided an extra $200 million per year of economic aid, and declared that 'the United States is prepared to use armed forces to assist any nation or group of nations requesting assistance against armed aggression from any country controlled by international communism'.[72]

In so doing, Eisenhower suggested that the Middle East now lay at the centre of the East–West struggle.[73] The only entirely favourable response from a Middle Eastern state came from the Lebanon. But Eisenhower worked assiduously on King Saud, who

70. Ambrose, *Eisenhower* pp. 385–8; Sachar, *History of Israel* pp.508–13; Neff, *Warriors at Suez* pp. 431–5; Urquhart, *Hammarskjöld* chap. 8; Heikal, *Cutting the Lion's Tail* pp.203–8; Michael Oren, 'Ambivalent Adversaries: David Ben-Gurion . . . and Dag Hammarskjöld, 1956–7', *Journal of Contemporary History* xxvii (1992)

71. Heikal, *Cutting the Lion's Tail* chap. 18; RIIA, *Survey 1956–8* p.162

72. 'Experience', Eisenhower claimed, 'shows that indirect aggression rarely if ever succeeds where there is reasonable security against direct aggression; where the Government possesses local security forces; and where economic conditions are such as not to make Communism seem an attractive alternative. The programme I suggest deals with all three aspects . . . and thus with the problem of indirect aggression': *Keesing's*, 15305–7, 15417–19

73. See also *The Cold War* chap. 7

gradually detached himself from Cairo in the first half of 1957. This was immediately important in connection with Jordan, which seemed in 1956–7 to be moving into the revolutionary camp. In October 1956 it had entered the Egyptian–Syrian military pact; elections that month led to the formation of a fairly radical government. After Suez, this ended the 1946 treaty with Britain and replaced British subsidies with promises (not honoured) of Egyptian–Syrian–Saudi aid. However, King Hussein made informal approaches to the USA, and embarked on increasingly vocal denunciations of communism. Matters came to a head in April 1957 when army units surrounded the palace. Hussein managed to order them back to barracks, and followed up by dismissing the Premier. Bedouin troops rallied to him, radical officers fled the country, and by the end of the month Hussein had installed a government to his liking and imposed martial law. In this he had the backing, both financial and military, of King Saud, and the endorsement of the United States which immediately contributed $10 million. The Syrian brigade stationed in the north of the country might have made trouble, but Nasser supposedly secured its withdrawal to avoid giving the USA a pretext for direct intervention.[74]

THE STRUGGLE FOR SYRIA

Another crisis revolved around Syria. Syrian politics consisted of a succession of rival conspiracies and Syria was then the only Middle Eastern country in which 'communists' appeared to have a chance of gaining power. Both Turkey and Iraq were alarmed at the prospect; Iraq also hoped (as it generally has, almost irrespective of its regime) to absorb or dominate Syria. In 1956 Britain and Iraq had brought the USA to join in planning a coup. This was aborted, as action had been set for 29 October, the very day of the Israeli attack on Egypt. Preparations resumed in 1957, though now under US leadership, but proved a fiasco when some of the conspirators changed sides and told all. This probably contributed to the installation in August 1957 of a reputed communist as Chief of Staff and to a purge of pro-Iraqi officers. So, as Eisenhower puts it,

74. Uriel Dann, *King Hussein and the Challenge of Arab Radicalism: Jordan, 1955–67* (New York, 1989) chaps 3–5; David Holden and Richard Johns, *The House of Saud* (1981) pp.190–5; Tabitha Petran, *Syria* (1972) p.119

> Syria's neighbors, including her fellow Arab nations, had come to the conclusion that the present regime in Syria had to go: otherwise the takeover by the Communists would soon be complete . . .
> In these circumstances most Middle East countries seemed to believe that direct military action would be necessary . . .

Syria's neighbours accordingly agreed to mobilise to induce it to disperse its forces, after which Iraq would attack. The United States' part was to 'see that no outside countries – for example, Israel or the USSR – would interfere', and it staged demonstrative fleet and air movements. At this stage the Arab countries involved got cold feet, Iraq fearing that its oil pipelines across Syria would be cut, King Saud worrying about disaffection in his army, and so on. Turkey would have been prepared to go ahead on its own with the 50,000 troops concentrated for 'manoeuvres' on its Syrian border; but Eisenhower claims that, in the absence of any Arab support for intervention, the USA shifted in September to restraining Turkey. So, more openly, did the Soviet Union, which in turn, gave rise to US counter-threats; but much of this was for show, after the crisis had begun to subside.[75] Nasser's contribution to this phase was to airlift troops into Syria; he came to appear to the mutually suspicious Syrians as a possible saviour. In November 1957 a meeting of Syrian and Egyptian parliamentarians advocated a union of the two countries. They were strongly supported by the Syrian military. Nasser let himself be persuaded; in February 1958 the 'United Arab Republic' (UAR) was finally proclaimed in Damascus, amid enormous enthusiasm and with Nasser swearing at Saladin's tomb 'to follow Saladin's example to realize total Arab unity'.[76] The Yemen promptly, if superficially, associated itself with the new state. To counter it the Hashemite Kings of Iraq and Jordan formed a rival 'Arab Federation', though the USA failed to persuade Saudi Arabia to join too.[77]

Trouble next struck in Lebanon, whose President Chamoun had sought to amend the Constitution to gain himself a second term of office. Chamoun saw the resulting disturbances in (oversimplified) terms of a cleavage between conservatism and Nasserite Arabism,

75. Prados, *Presidents' Secret Wars* pp.128–30; Eisenhower, *Waging Peace* pp.196–203; Holden and Johns, *House of Saud* pp.195–7; Horne, *Macmillan* ii pp.41–4; *The Cold War* chap. 7

76. Petran, *Syria* p.128

77. Dynastic differences apart, the Kingdom had lost face after the revelation in March of Saud's attempt to block the formation of the UAR by bribery and (allegedly) murder; it now sought to lower its international profile

sounded out American willingness to intervene, and also appealed to the UN claiming UAR subversion. But by early July the crisis appeared to have passed, with Chamoun declaring his readiness to retire at the end of his constitutional term.

THE IRAQI REVOLUTION 1958; US TROOPS LAND IN THE LEBANON, BRITISH IN JORDAN

On 14 July 1958, however, some Iraqi units that had been ordered into Jordan (whether to stabilise it or, as the Egyptians claim, as a preliminary to an attack on Syria) staged a coup as they passed through their own capital. The king, the crown prince, and Nuri al-Said were killed, and a Republic proclaimed. Iraq had long been a pillar of pro-British and pro-Western configuration in the Middle East; its sudden revolution seemed to sweep all this away, leaving Nasserism triumphant. The obvious question was whether the West would take it lying down. Saud (whose family had admittedly now forced him to relinquish much of his power) secretly demanded 'that the Baghdad Pact powers intervene in Iraq, on pain of Saudi Arabia's having to "go along" with the United Arab Republic'. Turkey was very anxious to oblige, and countries that felt themselves more directly at risk sought stabilisation by US or British troops. The now neurotic Chamoun appealed to Eisenhower on the 14th, Hussein to Britain on the 16th.[78] Eisenhower activated contingency plans drafted the previous November; US troops landed on the crowded Beirut bathing beaches (supposedly much to the profit of local ice-cream vendors) on 15 July, in what was intended chiefly as a demonstration of strength; – by early August they totalled 14,000, including tanks and atomic-capable artillery.[79] The British paratroop drop of 2,200 on 17 July was a more modest and risky affair, large enough to secure Amman airport and if necessary to take on the mob, but not enough to handle Jordanian armour had the army mutinied.

Both forces in fact achieved their goals, but given the difficulties

78. Eisenhower, *Waging Peace* pp.265–72; Macmillan, *Memoirs* iv esp. pp.513, 516, 522; Horne, *Macmillan* ii pp.93–8. Sudan also enquired as to British aid should Egypt attack it

79. Eisenhower, *Waging Peace* p.286. Though chiefly demonstrative, US strength may also have helped its envoys discourage elements of the Lebanese army from resisting

of putting them in place,[80] neither the USA nor Britain would have had any spare capacity to invade Iraq. Nor, apparently, were they anxious to give the go-ahead for a Turkish invasion, or to risk in any way provoking an Iraqi attack on Jordan or Kuwait. Khrushchev, however, could not be sure of this, and sought to discourage intervention partly by staging army manoeuvres and partly by calling for a summit meeting. For a time drama and tension were high, but things settled down very quickly. A US envoy managed to negotiate a political settlement in the Lebanon; on 31 July the army commander, General Chehab, was elected to succeed President Chamoun when he retired in September. Meanwhile the new regime in Iraq had proved conciliatory. On 28 July 1958 a Baghdad Pact meeting in London decided that it should be recognised. At a special session of the UN General Assembly the Arab states all agreed on 21 August to propose a moderate resolution inviting Hammarskjöld to make practical arrangements to consolidate Jordan and the Lebanon. He accordingly made a negotiating tour of the Middle East; October–November 1958 saw US and British withdrawals.[81]

INSURGENCY IN OMAN

Less visible than the Fertile Crescent, but important by virtue of its oil potential (and position at the head of the Persian Gulf) was Muscat and Oman. Part of its mountainous interior had long enjoyed autonomy under the Imam of Oman. Trouble arose between a new Imam and his suzerain the Sultan of Muscat; in the aftermath of the 1955 reoccupation of the Buraimi Oasis (p.279n), the Sultan asserted his authority. The Imam's brother then sought support from Saudi Arabia and Egypt; arms were imported, an

80. The original plan had called for joint Anglo-American action in the Lebanon. When Eisenhower determined that it should be all-American (to leave British troops free for use elsewhere) the intervention force could be assembled in time only by overflying neutral Austria (which protested): *The Joint Chiefs of Staff and National Policy 1957–60* (National Archives, Washington, DC) esp. pp.426–7, 445, 454. British forces for Amman had to overfly Israel, which later made difficulties about their resupply (as did Saudi Arabia). It being impolitic to ship troops through Suez, the further battalion that reached Aqaba in early August had to come from Aden, which drew down reserves that might be needed to hold Kuwait: Macmillan, *Memoirs* iv pp.519–25. US Marines were sent to the Gulf as a possible reinforcement: Blechman and Kaplan, *Force without War* p.238

81. RIIA, *Survey 1956–8* pp.374–92; see also *The Cold War* chap. 7

Oman Liberation Army was established, and in 1957 the Sultan's forces were driven out. After some hesitation Britain responded to the Sultan's appeals, re-established his control and (over the next two years) largely quelled the insurgency. The United States, with its Saudi interests, was uneasy and in 1957 abstained when the issue came to the UN Security Council. But Britain had demonstrated a continued ability to act independently (at least on a small scale); its political pre-eminence in the Gulf was to survive for another decade.[82]

82. Macmillan, *Memoirs* iv pp.270–7; Horne, *Macmillan* ii p.43; *Keesing's*, 14782, 15709–12; Holden and Johns, *House of Saud* p.186

CHAPTER TWELVE

The 1967 Six Day War and its Aftermath; the Lebanese civil war

THE ARAB WORLD IN THE 1960s

From 1959 to 1961 the Arab world enjoyed something of a lull. The chief reason was Nasser's falling out with the independent, and increasingly communist-inclined, regime in Iraq.[1] This led to temporary reconciliation with the USA and to the mending of relations with Jordan and Saudi Arabia. Indeed after Kuwait had been challenged (on its independence in 1961) by Iraq, UAR troops served alongside Saudi and Jordanian ones in the Arab force assembled to deter Iraqi aggression. But almost immediately thereafter Syria, tired of the imposition of 'socialist' Egyptian controls and of being generally treated as a dependency, broke away from the UAR. Nasser tried, and failed, to reverse the coup that effected this. He took Syria's loss hard, blamed it on reactionary elements, withdrew his troops from Kuwait, and veered back to a more revolutionary course. As the semi-official Al-Ahram later put it, 'If Egypt as a state recognizes frontiers in her dealings with governments, Egypt as a revolution should never hesitate . . . but should carry her message across them'.[2] A further disturbing factor was the coup in Yemen in September 1962, in which young officers seized the palace and principal towns but failed to eliminate the new Imam. As his father had done in 1948, he fled to loyal tribes in the north and secured Saudi support. Egyptian troops started arriving in Yemen, and civil war broke out. By early

1. See *The Cold War* chap. 7

2. Malcolm Kerr, *The Arab Cold War: Gamal 'Abd al-Nasir and his Rivals, 1958–1970* (1971) pp.20–8; Steven R. David, *Third World Coups d'Etat and International Security* (Baltimore, Md, 1987) pp.139–40

November 1962 Egyptian planes were bombing Saudi border villages; in retaliation the Kingdom severed diplomatic relations (see pp.360–1).[3]

Accordingly the Arab world was, by January 1963, in a state of considerable confusion:

> Iraq refused to recognize Kuwait, and on this account had recalled its ambassadors from all other [Arab] League members. Egypt had never recognized the Syrian regime, and had broken off diplomatic relations with Jordan. After the Yemeni . . . revolution, diplomatic relations between Saudi Arabia and Egypt were broken off as well. Egypt, Iraq, Syria, and Lebanon recognized the Yemeni republicans; Saudi Arabia and Jordan . . . the royalists. Syrian–Lebanese relations had been spoiled as a by-product of the Syrian–Egyptian confrontation, and the frontier was closed.[4]

Such a situation reflected the curious half and half condition of Arab sentiment. Similarities in language and culture both facilitate and legitimise intervention by one state in the internal politics of another, generally through a mixture of propaganda and subversion. This leads to competition both between 'progressive' and 'traditional' regimes and between rival bearers of 'progressive' ideologies (few rifts have proved as deep as that between Syria and Iraq, both since 1963 ruled by the Ba'ath Arab Socialist Party). However the various states have generated their own political structures and loyalties, pursue their own national interests (Syrian–Iraqi rivalry can also be seen as natural competition for pre-eminence within the Fertile Crescent), and tend to operate on the basis that 'the enemy of my enemy is my friend'. A further destabilising factor in the 1960s was the frequency of coups (and their apprehension even in countries like Saudi Arabia and Jordan that managed to avoid them); subsequently there has been far greater stability, notably in Iraq under al-Bakr and Saddam Hussein since 1968 and in Syria under Asad since 1970.

Space will not permit a tracing of the kaleidoscopic shifts in Arab alignments, but some developments must be highlighted. Israel's announcement of the imminent completion of its Jordan waters diversion scheme (see p.274) prompted Nasser to call an Arab summit in January 1964. This summit, and its sequel in September 1964, abounded with anti-Israeli rhetoric. Admittedly most of their

3. *Keesing's*, 19297 ff. A minor consequence of the coup was that Yemen's currency ceased to be the silver thalers of the eighteenth-century Austrian ruler Maria Theresa

4. Kerr, *Arab Cold War* p.40

decisions (notably those for the pre-emptive diversion of the Jordan headwaters) were insubstantial. But the summits blessed and assisted the formation of a 'Palestinian entity', the Palestine Liberation Organisation (PLO) under Ahmad Shuqairi. This too did not amount to much, but the new prominence given to the Palestine cause may have encouraged competing states to play the Palestinian card.

SYRIAN–ISRAELI BORDER TENSIONS 1966–7; NASSER'S CLOSURE OF THE STRAITS OF TIRAN

Syria forced the pace. The new government that emerged from the February 1966 coup started to support a rival, and more activist, Palestinian organisation, Fatah, that had already started staging *fedayeen* raids against Israel. Clashes on the Syrian–Israeli border increased; Fatah also began passing through Jordanian territory to get at Israel, possibly with Syrian encouragement since Syria and Jordan had quarrelled violently that summer (ostensibly over the Palestinian issue). After three such raids Israeli tanks crossed the border in November 1966 and demolished the West Bank village of Samu. This triggered major Palestinian riots against King Hussein for not providing better protection. Egypt had just sealed a reconciliation with Syria with a mutual defence treaty; it felt inclined to punish Hussein for his support of Saudi Arabia, so it allowed its radio to join in the Palestinian denunciation of Hussein. Jordan responded with charges that Egypt would provide no real help against Israel and was hiding safely behind the screen of UNEF. By December 1966 Nasser took a personal hand in the abuse, and the row continued into 1967.

The Israeli–Syrian border went from bad to worse. In April 1967 an incident escalated into a substantial clash, with six Syrian fighters shot down; on 13 May Israel's premier, Levi Eshkol, warned that it 'may have to teach Syria a sharper lesson'. Meanwhile the USSR (to which Egypt had again drawn close in 1964 and which now also had good relations with Syria) started complaining about an Israeli military build-up and warning Egypt that Israel planned to attack Syria in mid-May. The Soviet Union's motives have never been clear; but since the Soviet ambassador declined an Israeli invitation to inspect the border on 12 May 1967 and the UN Secretary-General U Thant reported on the 14th that his observers had found nothing, there have always been suspicions that the USSR was chiefly anxious to keep the pot boiling.[5] Nasser ordered general mobilisation and the dispatch of troops to Sinai; by the time his Chief of Staff returned from a lightning visit to Syria convinced that it had been a false alarm, Nasser seems to have judged it too late to turn back.[6] He had in fact moved troops to the Israeli border once before, in 1960, with no ill effects;[7] if he did so again, he could claim the credit for having deterred an Israeli attack on his new Syrian ally. But this time Nasser went further, and on 16 May ordered UNEF to 'withdraw'.

There has since been controversy both as to Nasser's original intentions and over U Thant's actions. Nasser subsequently maintained that he ordered withdrawal only from the Sinai border with Israel and not from the Gaza Strip or Sharm el-Sheikh, but that – to frighten him into rescinding his order – U Thant insisted that withdrawal had to be all or nothing. Rather than climb down, Nasser demanded complete withdrawal, to include Sharm el-Sheikh, then found himself impelled to occupy the latter and close the Straits of Tiran. There are problems with this account, though also with U Thant's denial.[8] Even if Nasser did not intend at the outset to close the Straits, he did nothing to make this clear either to his subordinates or to U Thant. Nor did the UN do much to stop him. On 17 May UN forces were simply pushed aside at two points on the border, and the UN was understandably reluctant to expose them to further violence. In any case they were stationed on Egyptian territory only – Israel resolutely refused to allow them on its side of the border – and conditionally (it had always been accepted) on continued Egyptian acquiescence, which was now apparently withdrawn. Hammarskjöld had envisaged that any request for their withdrawal would be referred to the UNEF Advisory Committee and thence to the General Assembly, which might stall. However the Advisory Committee was divided (as were the Permanent Members of the Security Council); without solid support U Thant did not feel able to take the question to the General Assembly. He therefore agreed on 18 May 1967 to UNEF's withdrawal, but invited himself to Cairo for general talks.[9]

5. Heikal seems to adopt this explanation: *Sphinx and Commissar* p.175

6. George Gawrych, 'The Egyptian Military Defeat of 1967', *Journal of Contemporary History* xxvi (1991) p.278

7. Donald Neff, *Warriors for Jerusalem: The Six Days that Changed the Middle East* (New York, 1984) p.63

8. They are discussed by Robert Stephens, *Nasser* (paperback edn Harmondsworth, 1973) pp.474–7

9. Neff, *Warriors for Jerusalem* pp.65–72; Urquhart, *Hammarskjöld* pp.193, 226; Stephens, *Nasser* pp.471–2

While he was in the air, Nasser pre-empted by publicly broadcasting the closure of the Straits. Before Nasser did so, Sadat later claimed, he told his colleagues that closure would transform the chances of war from evens to 'a one-hundred-percent certainty', and received assurances that his armed forces were ready.[10] In the next few days he may in fact have hoped (as he had done after the nationalisation of the Suez Canal) that he would be able to get away with his fait accompli: for the superpowers sought to discourage recourse to force by either side, and, if they succeeded, Nasser would be left in control of the Straits. Nasser also believed the USSR had promised that it would not allow any country to interfere.[11] Although the USA condemned his actions, it also declared that it would be 'against whoever fired the first shot' and (in June) agreed to receive the Egyptian Vice-President for talks.[12] On 4 June 1967 Nasser gave Western visitors the impression that he was not expecting an Israeli attack; next day the air defence system was apparently shut down to make it easier for his commander-in-chief to fly out to inspect positions in Sinai.[13] Yet whatever Nasser's real calculations, his speeches were bellicose, and those of most other Arab leaders even more so. The Arab world erupted into a torrent of rhetoric looking to the destruction of Israel and – in the case of Shuqairi – the liquidation of its inhabitants.[14] This further damaged Arab standing with the West, but it led to the rallying to Nasser even of his Arab opponents – most importantly of King Hussein, who flew to Cairo on 30 May 1967 and placed his army under Egyptian control.

WESTERN REACTION

For Israel the blockade of the Straits of Tiran oil route was objectionable in itself. If accepted, it would lead to further pressures; indeed Nasser told his National Assembly that 'if we are

10. Neff, *Warriors for Jerusalem* pp.88–9; Stephens, *Nasser* p.477

11. His Defence Minister read too much into a conversation with Marshal Grechko, and the Egyptian ambassador's letter of correction was fatally delayed in transmission: Heikal, *Sphinx and Commissar* pp.179–80

12. Neff, *Warriors for Jerusalem* pp.137, 178–80. By June some US diplomats were advocating the negotiation of a compromise with Nasser. Knowledge of this was a factor in Israel's decision to strike

13. Neff, *Warriors for Jerusalem* pp.196, 202

14. ibid, pp.71, 88, 181; Sachar, *History of Israel* pp.633–4; Stephens, *Nasser* p.480

able to restore conditions to what they were before 1956, God will surely help and urge us to restore the situation to what it was in 1948'.[15] Most Israeli generals believed that it need not be accepted since they could win a war fairly easily; but the longer they waited, the better would be Egypt's preparations and the higher Israel's casualties. Accordingly the cautious premier, Eshkol, was to come under growing pressure to strike.

Immediate action was pre-empted by a request that Israel hold its hand for forty-eight hours to give the USA time to come up with other ways of opening the Straits; the Foreign Minister, Eban, was sent abroad to consult. France promptly distanced itself from the 1957 Declaration on free passage through the Straits (see p.296), and instead suggested referring the whole Arab–Israeli question to the Four Powers. Britain and the USA were more forthcoming, and set about arranging a naval demonstration to uphold the right of passage. But, like SCUA in 1956, this turned out to have no teeth. On examination, it proved that assembling a fleet powerful enough to be sure of being able to force the Straits would take considerable time. Also countries were slow in coming forward to participate; by June 1967 Britain was making it clear that it did not contemplate the forceful escorting of Israeli ships. The United States also developed cold feet, partly as a side-effect of Vietnam. So, though President Johnson was full of sympathy for Israel, he was concerned that a request for a blanket congressional declaration of support (like the Eisenhower Doctrine or his own Gulf of Tonkin Resolution) could 'become bogged down in acrimonious dispute'; without congressional backing he could not give Israel the categorical promises it was seeking. He thus preferred that Britain make the running, and eventually told Israel 'our leadership is unanimous that the United States should not move in isolation'.[16]

All this, however, took some time to emerge. France apart, Eban's visit was initially judged a success; on 28 May the Israeli Cabinet decided to wait for a further two weeks. But Eshkol's broadcast speech that evening appeared weak and bumbling; domestic Israeli pressure mounted for a Cabinet reconstruction; and on 1 June – in the aftermath of Hussein's flight to Cairo – a national coalition was formed with (by public demand) Moshe Dayan as Defence Minister. On that day, too, Eban withdrew his

15. Stephens, *Nasser* p.480 (29 May)

16. Neff, *Warriors for Jerusalem* pp.94, 165, 177, 187–8, 192 and passim; Harold Wilson, *The Labour Government, 1964–1970: A Personal Record* (1971) pp.398–9; Sachar, *History of Israel* p.631; Dayan, *Story of my Life* pp.273, 277

opposition to military action. Meanwhile the head of the secret service, Amit, had gone on a follow-up mission to clarify the USA's real intentions; he sent back reports that, while little could be expected from the international maritime force, 'there is a growing chance of American political backing if we act on our own'. On his return on 3 June Amit briefed a group of leading ministers, who concluded

> that the United States was not going to be able to involve itself unilaterally or multilaterally in any enforcement action within a period relevant to our plight. But we all felt that if Israel found means of breaking out of the . . . blockade, the United States would not now take a hostile position.[17]

Formal Cabinet decision on war followed next day. Israel's calculation – that, if it disregarded formal US advice not to fire the first shot, it would nevertheless enjoy tacit US support – was very much that made by Britain in 1956. But the threat from the closure of the Straits appeared more immediate than that to Britain from the nationalisation of the Canal, and Israel's response that of self-defence by a small and beleaguered state not an anachronistic attempt to preserve an Empire. It is also possible that Israel had received quiet encouragement: Eban records a hint from 'an American, known for his close contact with government thinking', while Walt Rostow did not protest at the suggestion that it might be more convenient for the USA if Israel simply acted without involving it.[18]

THE SIX DAY WAR 5–10 JUNE 1967

On the morning of 5 June Israel staged a spectacularly successful air strike, taking Egypt by surprise and destroying 90 per cent of its serviceable planes. Later that day, after some Jordanian and Syrian reprisals, Israel wiped out the bulk of their air forces. Having thus gained air supremacy, it proceeded to conquest on the ground. The

17. Neff, *Warriors for Jerusalem* pp.180–2, 190–2

18. ibid, pp.180–2, 191–2. There have indeed been claims, supposedly based on interviews with participants and Pentagon officials, that US aircraft flew to Israel on 4 June and then helped provide reconnaissance over Sinai: Stephen Green, *Taking Sides. America's Secret Relations with a Militant Israel* (New York, 1984) pp.204–11, *Living by the Sword: America and Israel in the Middle East 1968–87* (Brattleboro, Vt, 1988) p.235

Egyptian army was outclassed; within three days it had been shattered, and Gaza and Sinai occupied. Hussein had been told at the outset that if he kept out, Jordan would be left alone, but if not, not. He replied with bombing, shelling, and a move on to a UN-occupied hill overlooking Jerusalem. This response may simply have been emotional – he had wished to attack Israel in 1956. Hussein may also have been influenced by Egyptian lies about the outcome of the initial Israeli air raid, and by the calculation that if he broke his new alliance with Egypt he might lose his throne to an outpouring of Palestinian and Arab nationalism. His decision cost him the West Bank. That night, after debate as to whether the international community would stand for it, the Israeli Cabinet decided to take East Jerusalem. This surrendered on the 7th. Amid emotional scenes troops rushed to pray at the Wailing Wall, from which all Jews had been excluded since 1948; Dayan announced that 'We have returned to the holiest of our holy places, never to part from it again'. By the end of the day Israel had taken the whole of the West Bank, though with rather higher losses than those incurred in Sinai.

Meanwhile the Syrian front had been fairly quiet. Dayan seems to have opposed launching an attack until early on the 9th, then suddenly changed his mind. (Some have seen as a preliminary to this change the disabling Israeli attack of the 8th – in circumstances that can hardly be accidental – on the US electronic intelligence ship, *Liberty*.)[19] Again it took only two days to break Syrian resistance; hostilities ended on the 10th (under strong Soviet pressure)[20] with Israel ensconced on the strategic Golan Heights, from which artillery had in the past shelled its northern settlements and that now enabled it to look down on Damascus.

19. Neff, *Warriors for Jerusalem* chap. 18 and pp.264–6; Green, *Taking Sides* chap. 9. One CIA report suspected that the attack had been authorised by Dayan. The presumption was that he may have feared that, if the *Liberty* could monitor Israel's military communications, the USA would gain foreknowledge of an assault on Syria and simply forbid it (Rusk had already deplored any such assault early on the 8th). But Dayan was still refusing to sanction an attack long after the *Liberty* was strafed, and his change of mind on the morning of the 9th May may have been quite unconnected

20. See *The Cold War* chap. 11

UN RESOLUTION 242; SECRET ISRAELI–JORDANIAN TALKS ON THE WEST BANK; US RELUCTANCE TO IMPOSE A SETTLEMENT

Victory had been crushing. Israel hoped to use it to secure a definitive peace, trading some of its conquests in return. President Johnson sympathised with this approach. (He had opposed Eisenhower's action to force Israeli withdrawal in 1957; the solution it had produced now appeared to have fallen apart.) Kosygin thought otherwise, and tried unsuccessfully to get the UN to prescribe unconditional withdrawal. After his failure, an Arab summit in Khartoum resolved in August 1967 on a policy of 'No peace with Israel, no negotiations with Israel, no recognition of Israel and maintenance of the rights of Palestinian people in their nation'. Like many other summit pronouncements, this could not be taken at face value: there appears to have been some disposition to negotiate in the wings of the UN session in November. According to King Hussein, Nasser had turned down an Israeli offer of withdrawal from Sinai in exchange for peace, but had authorised Jordan to negotiate to recover the West Bank (for whose loss he probably felt he was to blame). In New York Hussein plunged into indirect negotiations in which the USA, Israel and Egypt joined. These paralleled the official UN proceedings, which ended with Security Council adoption of a British compromise Resolution 242 – calling for withdrawal 'from territories occupied in the recent conflict' and for acceptance of the right 'of every state in the area . . . to live in peace within secure and recognized boundaries'.[21] Hussein later said he had

> sought clarification of the withdrawal provision . . . and was told the United States was prepared to make a commitment that would be understood to require Israeli withdrawal from all the occupied territory of the West Bank, with 'minor border rectifications' conditional on mutual agreement. . . . An essential part of the understanding . . . was that Israel had acquiesced in the agreed interpretation of what Resolution 242 would require. The specific term used was that Israel was 'on board'. And furthermore, that six months would be the outside limit for its implementation.

However, on East Jerusalem (which Israel had already annexed) the

21. Neff, *Warriors for Jerusalem* pp.344–5. The ambiguity of the call for withdrawal from 'territories' rather than 'the territories' 'occupied in the recent conflict' is not found in translations into other official UN languages

USA apparently promised only 'to obtain for Jordan the best possible deal'.[22]

None of this was to be. Direct (though secret) talks started between Israel and Hussein in December; but (like their predecessors with Abdullah) they never quite succeeded. For though in September 1967 Eban had been asking only for the West Bank's demilitarisation, by December Israel insisted on the retention of strategic positions along the Jordan, whereas Hussein, though offering normal peaceful relations, demanded a full withdrawal in exchange. During 1968 hopes for a formal settlement dimmed. In 1969 Hussein suggested to Washington some kind of swap whereby he acquired Gaza in exchange for substantial concessions on the West Bank, and in retrospect Kissinger regrets that this was not followed up more seriously.[23] In 1970 Hussein resumed his secret talks with Israel. Progress was made on the basis of Dayan's idea of 'functional cooperation', whereby Israel retained control of West Bank security but left Jordan (which continued to pay most Palestinian civil servants) much influence over other matters. Secret meetings were fairly frequent (ten between Golda Meir and Hussein during her premiership), but agreements were reached only on technical and security cooperation.[24]

This, of course, was all *sub rosa*, and did not expose Hussein to the odium of publicly betraying the Arab cause. Nor were there any other serious negotiations. For though Gunnar Jarring, the UN Representative charged with securing the implementation of Resolution 242, shuttled around the Middle East, he met with very little cooperation. Nor did the USA devote much real effort to seeking a settlement: it was absorbed with Vietnam. As Kissinger saw things,

> we were being asked to pressure an ally [Israel] on behalf of countries which, with the exception of Jordan, had broken off relations with us [in 1967], pursued policies generally hostile to us, and were clients of Moscow. I therefore doubted the advisability of American pressure for a general settlement until we could see more clearly what concessions the Arabs would make and until those who would benefit from it would be America's friends, not Soviet clients.

22. Neff, *Warriors for Jerusalem* esp. pp.340–2, 349; Kissinger, *Memoirs* i p.345
23. Kissinger, *Memoirs* pp.362–3
24. Dan Raviv and Yossi Melman, 'Revealed: Hussein's Secret Peace Path', *Observer*, 10 May 1987 p.8; Kissinger, *Memoirs* ii p.220; Sachar, *History of Israel* pp.678, 680, 691; Steve Posner, *Israel Undercover: Secret Warfare and Hidden Diplomacy in the Middle East* (Syracuse, NY, 1987) Part 2

Nixon occasionally considered 'taking strong steps unilaterally [to impose a settlement and] to save Israel from her own destruction'; but he feared both the domestic political costs and the likelihood of failure. So he mostly left things alone – which meant allowing them to be run by the politically weak Secretary of State, Rogers, rather than by the White House.[25]

THE EGYPTIAN–ISRAELI WAR OF ATTRITION 1969–70

After his 1967 victory over Egypt, Dayan had originally wished to hold Israeli troops back out of harm's way at the strategic Sinai Mitla and Gidi passes. But against his better judgement he allowed them to take up positions along the Suez Canal. Here sniping grew readily into military exchanges. Then, in October 1967, Egypt sank an Israeli destroyer patrolling offshore, and in response Israeli artillery destroyed most of Egypt's oil-refining capacity. Despite UN efforts to damp them down, such episodes continued, and then from October 1968 escalated sharply. In April 1969 Egypt declared that, since Israel had not implemented UN Resolution 242, it regarded the cease-fire as at an end, and so launched the 'War of Attrition'. Nasser's reasoning was that, with its vastly greater population, Egypt could continue such border action longer and take more losses than Israel. He had miscalculated again: with complete command of the air, Israel embarked on 'deep penetration bombing' against which Egypt was defenceless; the Canal cities were ruined and evacuated, and the vital Nile irrigation pumps at Nag Hammadi hit. By January 1970 Nasser was desperate and flew to Moscow in search of an air defence system that really worked. As he explained,

> If we do not get what I am asking for, everybody will assume that the only solution is in the hands of the Americans . . . as far as I can see, you are not prepared to help us in the same way that America helps Israel. This means that there is only one course open to me: I shall go back to Egypt and I shall tell the people . . . the time has come for me to step down and hand over to a pro-American President. If I cannot save them, somebody else will have to do it.

25. Kissinger, *Memoirs* i pp.351, 372–3; Nixon, *Memoirs* pp.477, 479

The threat – Nasser privately said a real one – worked, and the USSR got involved. This worried Israel and restricted its bombers, but Egypt's casualties remained high. Accordingly in July 1970 Nasser determined to accept a US initiative for a cease-fire 'so that we can finish our [anti-aircraft] missile sites. We need . . . a cease-fire, and the only cease-fire the Israelis will accept is one proposed by the Americans'.[26] His judgment was borne out: Israel went along – reluctantly, as it rightly anticipated circumvention of the provisions against the advance of missile sites to the front line.[27] In August an uneasy calm descended over the Canal.

ENHANCED PALESTINIAN ACTIVITY; JORDAN'S 'BLACK SEPTEMBER' SUPPRESSION OF THE PLO 1970–1

In the Arab world as a whole, the 1967 War had given an enormous stimulus to Palestinian consciousness and organisation. Fatah blossomed, largely taking over the PLO in early 1968, and it was flanked by many smaller and more extreme – or less disciplined – groups. One Fatah leader (Abu Jihad) was to write that *fedayeen* operations increased 'from a monthly average of 12 in 1967 . . . [to] 279 in the first eight months of 1970': Dayan claimed that, between the war and August 1970, 141 Israelis were killed in actions launched from Jordan.[28] Israeli reprisals caused serious clashes with Jordanian and Syrian forces. Raids deep into Lebanon led Syria's forces to seek to control the PLO. This in turn prompted mediation from Cairo and agreements in 1969–70 that permitted continued PLO activity, but only at a safe distance from Lebanese civilians; the agreements also enjoined the PLO not to provoke Israel by firing across the border.[29]

Above all, the PLO came to constitute a major problem within Jordan. By 1970 King Hussein had had enough. The 1967 war had produced a second flood[30] of refugees (again encouraged, though

26. Mohamed Heikal, *The Road to Ramadan* (paperback edn, Fontana, 1976) pp.85, 93–4

27. ibid, p.94; Sachar, *History of Israel* i pp.694–5; Kissinger, *Memoirs* i pp.584–6, 592

28. Posner, *Israel Undercover* pp.182, 184

29. *Keesing's*, 23704, 23843

30. 178,000 crossed the Jordan to the East Bank, of whom only 14,000 were eventually allowed back. A further 102,000 left the Golan Heights for Syria and 38,000 fled Sinai – Neff, *Warriors for Jerusalem* pp.320–1

seldom directly compelled, by Israel). Their camps proved fertile soil for Palestinian organisations; as Abu Jihad put it, 'The Jordanian regime was [at first] too weak to oppose us'. Indeed after the March 1968 Israeli raid on Karameh, Hussein declared that 'we have come to the point where we are all *fedayeen*'. However clashes between private Palestinian armies and the Jordanian state were almost inevitable: there was fighting in November 1968, February and June 1970. Further trouble in August, leading Hussein to declare that he would not tolerate efforts to 'undermine the absolute sovereignty of Jordan', brought a second attempt on his life, and caused a crisis with Iraq. The last straw was the hijacking of three foreign airliners plus hostages to a remote Jordanian airfield under *fedayeen* control.[31] As soon as most of the hostages had been released, Hussein declared martial law and demanded the surrender of all *fedayeen* weapons. This united the Palestinian movements, and the PLO (which had previously sought to restrain the more extreme factions) called for his overthrow. By 17 September 1970 civil war had begun.

Nobody seems to have doubted that Hussein could win if other Arab states did not intervene. Iraq had threatened to do so in early September, but did not implement its threat.[32] Syria did send in tanks on 20 September, but the prospect of Israeli intervention (concerted with Jordan and the US[33]) and lack of support from its own air force led to withdrawal on the 23rd. By then Nasser had convened an Arab summit to calm things. However he was in bad health and the effort of hosting it killed him. The summit produced yet another cease-fire between Jordan and the Palestinians. But the situation deteriorated, and in mid-1971 Hussein determined to finish things off. Most of the remaining *fedayeen* were captured, and a few even fled for refuge to Israel.[34] By then Hussein had re-established security cooperation with Israel, and subsequently the border has been generally calm.

31. Posner, *Israel Undercover* pp.179, 182; *Keesing's*, 23064, 23896, 24059–60, 24203–9, 24225–30

32. It may have been restrained by quiet Soviet diplomacy and/or fear of an Israeli riposte

33. *The Cold War* chap. 11

34. *Keesing's*, 24769–70

CIVIL WAR IN THE LEBANON 1975–90

Syria never staged a similar showdown with the *fedayeen*, and indeed always continued to support some Palestinian factions. However Asad, who took over in November 1970, was careful not to permit cross-border raids. This did not prevent deep Syrian–Israeli hostility, Israeli strikes against Palestinian bases in Syria, and numerous air clashes between the two countries. But the chief locus of Palestinian activities shifted to Lebanon, whither many of the *fedayeen* extruded from Jordan had moved. This led to increasing Israeli raids, designed inter alia to push Lebanon into curbing the Palestinians as Jordan had done. Some Lebanese tried to do this; President Frangieh's declarations in 1973 that he would not tolerate an 'army of occupation' or a Palestinian 'State within a State' echoed Hussein's. However whereas Jordan had been largely built around its army, the Lebanese army was too weak to make such declarations good. This led, after clashes in 1973 between the army and the Palestinians, to the build-up of political and confessional militias. In 1975, when Palestinians got involved in a clash between (Muslim) fishermen and the army, Christians responded by campaigning against their continued armed presence. This soon spread to street battles in the capital (Beirut), attacks on a Palestinian refugee camp, and a PLO statement in May that

> The Phalangists [a Christian militia] today are risking the entire destiny of Lebanon . . . by aiming to explode the situation and ultimately to remove the Palestinian presence from the Lebanese theatre . . . the Palestinian revolution, having learned from its . . . experience in Jordan, will know how to defend itself. . . .[35]

This prophecy proved only too true. The Lebanon had a history of communal clashes, and had never really been the model consociational state that some observers depicted. Still it had managed (after 1949) to keep out of wars, to maintain neutrality in inter-Arab quarrels, and to prosper as a liberal and fairly stable entrepôt for the Arab world. In 1975–6 it collapsed into civil war. This was broadly between the Phalange – defending an internal status quo that endowed the Maronite Christians with more political power than their current numbers warranted, and seeking to curb the Palestinians and thus save the Lebanon from Israeli reprisals – and

35. *Keesing's*, 25932, 27287–8; M.C. Hudson, 'The Palestinian Factor in the Lebanese Civil War', *Middle East Journal*, xxxii (1978)

a '''National Movement'' comprising leftist-oriented sections of the Moslem community . . . backed by Palestinian guerrilla elements, which from mid-1976 played an increasingly prominent role in the fighting'.[36] In March 1976 the official Lebanese army split along confessional lines, and ceased to be an effective force. By then the Christians were losing. From April Syria started to intervene, partly to protect them, partly to curb the PLO in favour of its own organisation Al Saiqa, and largely to establish its overlordship over the Lebanon. In October this intervention was legitimised by the Riyadh agreement to constitute a primarily Syrian 'Arab Deterrent Force'. The fifty-sixth cease-fire (since April 1975) was then arranged, and in November Syria ended hostilities by occupying most major towns.

Israel was pleased by Syrian action against the PLO; and there was talk of 'tacit agreement . . . that has permitted the Syrians to [cut] their military forces on the Golan Heights and reassign the troops to Lebanon without fear of Israeli attack'.[37] But for strategic reasons Israel was not prepared to see Syria establish itself on the Lebanese–Israeli border, and so made it clear that Syrian forces should not cross the 'red line', generally taken to be the Litani river. That left a vacuum on the border, where *fedayeen* were already well established. So cross-border raids and reprisals continued; in March 1978, after an unusually successful raid had killed 35 people, Israel invaded (in operations that, on one calculation, left 1,000 civilians dead). The USA demanded withdrawal (threatening otherwise to cut off all military aid).[38] The UN established an 'Interim Force' (UNIFIL) to interpose on the border; UNIFIL still continues, but its achievements have been slender. Israel preferred to rely on the militia of a Christian Lebanese officer, Major Haddad; in 1979 he declared an eight-mile-wide border strip to be an 'independent free Lebanese state', since 'the major part of the Lebanon is still under the occupation of Syria, the PLO and some foreign organisation [the UN]'.[39]

Trouble continued in a minor key, with guerrilla activities prompting Israeli raids and, sometimes, air clashes with Syrian planes sent up to intercept them. Meanwhile Syrian forces increasingly fell out with the Christians: April to June 1981 saw

36. *Keesing's*, 27765, 28117
37. *Keesing's*, 28124
38. Zbigniew Brzezinski, *Power and Principle. Memoirs of the National Security Adviser 1977–1981* (paperback edn, 1985) p.107
39. *Keesing's*, 30093

them besiege the Christian town of Zahle. An Israeli plan was formulated, to occupy South Lebanon; expel the PLO from the only front-line country from which it could operate freely; install as President the Phalange commander Bashir Gemayel (with whom Israel had maintained relations since 1976); and conclude a peace treaty with the Lebanon that would also secure Syrian evacuation. The plan was put into effect in June 1982 (on the attempted murder of the Israeli ambassador in London). The Lebanon was rapidly overrun as far as Beirut, Syrian forces were pushed aside, and over 60 Syrian aircraft shot down. Prolonged bombardment then induced the PLO to agree to evacuate its headquarters – to Tunisia – and some 14,000 *fedayeen*, moves that were effected with the aid of a US-French-Italian peace-keeping force. Bashir Gemayel was also elected President, but was then murdered in September 1982 before he took up office. His murder prompted Israel to move into Muslim West Beirut and to let the Phalangists loose on the Palestinian refugee camps there, supposedly to root out PLO control. Two nights of slaughter followed, which did much to damage Israel's reputation abroad and to intensify domestic opposition to intervention in Lebanon. Bashir Gemayel's weaker brother Amin was elected President in his stead, but proved an inadequate substitute. He did, however, in May 1983 eventually conclude what came close to being a peace treaty with Israel. This looked to a parallel evacuation by both Syria and Israel, after which the Lebanon would recover health under the tutelage of the Western peace-keeping force (which had been rushed back after the massacres in the refugee camps). However Asad had no intention of leaving, denounced the way in which the agreement effectively preserved Major Haddad's position in the south, and made trouble for Israel by arming the Druze militia. Unprepared to face constant losses from sniping and bomb attacks, Israel withdrew by stages, even though Syria not only stayed put but eventually induced the Lebanese government to cancel the May 1983 agreement. Israel's withdrawal was completed in June 1985. The Western peace-keeping force had already been pulled out for similar reasons in early 1984.[40]

The vacuum was filled by rival militias, and a war of all against all ensued, perhaps the most tragic of Middle Eastern political

40. *Keesing's*, esp.27765–73, 28117–24, 28733 ff, 29646 ff, 30093, 31914 ff; Robert Fisk, *Pity the Nation: Lebanon at War* (Oxford, 1991 edn); Howard M. Sachar, *A History of Israel: Volume II – From the Aftermath of the Yom Kippur War* (New York, 1987) chaps 8, 9

catastrophes and second only in bloodshed to the Iraq–Iran war.[41] It was marked by a further horrific siege of the Palestinian camps in Beirut (1986–7), this time by the Shia Amal militia, and by the taking of a number of Americans and Europeans as hostages by groups strongly influenced by Iran. In February 1987 Amal blundered into a losing battle with other militias and appealed for Syrian assistance. The appeal was echoed by the Lebanese 'government'; Syrian troops moved in, declaring that they had come 'to take control of security in West Beirut for good'. They effected a moderate, but only moderate, improvement. In 1988 it proved impossible to elect a successor to President Gemayel, and the country further fragmented with rival Muslim and Christian 'governments'. The latter, headed by General Aoun, embarked in 1989 on a 'war of liberation' against Syria.

From this nadir, things started to recover when Arab League diplomacy managed (in October 1989) to assemble most of the surviving MPs (both Christian and Muslim) in Taif (Saudi Arabia). They agreed on the desirability of constitutional reform to equalise political power between Muslims and Christians, and planned for the recovery of central government authority over two years with Syrian assistance. In November 1989 they elected a new President, then (when he was assassinated) a second, Elias Hrawi. Aoun did *not* accept him, but in 1990 plunged the hitherto less disturbed Christian sector into heavy fighting. By October 1990 Hrawi felt strong enough to invite Syria to remove him, which it did with alacrity. Thereafter reconstruction proceeded with Syrian aid, and was marked in May 1991 by the conclusion of a comprehensive treaty of Syrian–Lebanese 'brotherhood, cooperation and coordination' and the disarming of (most) militias. But the process has not so far (1993) extended to the Israeli-backed South Lebanon Army; indeed clashes with both this and the Israeli forces themselves became more frequent as other conflicts lessened.[42]

41. Casualties are now put at 152,000 dead or 'disappeared' between 1975 and 1990: *Keesing's*, 38836

42. Economic revival began in 1991, and 1992 saw general elections (albeit largely boycotted in some Christian areas): *Keesing's*, 35344–6, 35672, 36986, 37163, 37754–5, 38067–8, 38124, 39165–6, 1992 R142

CHAPTER THIRTEEN

Arab–Israeli Relations since 1970

SADAT'S DEALINGS WITH THE SOVIET UNION AND THE USA

In the early 1970s, of course, nobody foresaw the catastrophe of the Lebanon. The prevailing Western view of the Middle East, after Egypt's ending of the War of Attrition and Jordan's curbing of the Palestinians, was complacent. It was, admittedly, tinged with disgust at Palestinian terrorism (notably the murder of eleven Israeli athletes at the 1972 Olympic Games) and with concern at the extent of Soviet penetration of the area. The general feeling, though, was that Israel was invincible and that its neighbours recognised this. Egyptian rhetoric to the contrary was dismissed, and some amusement occasioned by the way in which Nasser's successor, Sadat, kept postponing the 'Year of Decision'. In fact Sadat was determined to prevent the 1967 cease-fire lines becoming 'a *fait accompli,* political lines similar to the 1949 armistice lines'.[1] To stop this, he could either challenge them by force, which meant securing the necessary arms from the USSR, or enlist real US diplomatic pressure on Israel. From 1970 to 1973 he followed both tracks.

It was an uphill task. The USSR was quite well suited by the existing situation of 'no war and no peace'. It was contemptuous of Arab military capacity, and not anxious to encourage another war which, on past form, its clients would lose and then need to be resupplied. So its arms deliveries always fell short of Sadat's requests (and, in Sadat's view, of what the USA was allowing Israel). Sadat

1. D. Neff, *Warriors Against Israel* (Brattleboro, Vt, 1988) p.45

was constantly complaining. Both sides then got cross and started to needle each other. The last straw came when, despite Sadat's earlier pleas, the 1972 Brezhnev–Nixon summit produced only banalities on the Middle East. Sadat concluded that Brezhnev was not really interested, and drew further confirmation from the tone of his tardy reply to Egypt's remonstrance. At just this time Saudi Arabia conveyed to him a US message that the United States would place no pressure on Israel while Soviet advisers remained with the Egyptian army, and itself advised their dismissal.[2] Sadat was given to sudden decisions, and he ordered the advisers out. This jolted the USSR. Later Sadat reassured it by promising to renew its lease of naval base facilities. Also Saudi Arabia came forward with hard currency. After these inducements, Soviet weapons came through readily, more arriving in the first half of 1973 than in the previous two years. By April 1973 Sadat was in a position to decide on war in October.[3]

Meanwhile he had been making overtures to the USA. In December 1970 he sent Nixon the message, 'I want peace: move fast',[4] and next year proposed a partial Israeli withdrawal in Sinai and the reopening of the Canal. This seemed promising, since Dayan was making similar suggestions. But US Secretary of State Rogers could not bridge the gap between Egypt's insistence that the move should be merely the first stage of a general Israeli withdrawal and Israel's view of it as a self-contained act (with no further commitments beyond a prolonged truce). Such disappointments led Egypt to feel that it could make progress only by dealing with the White House, not the State Department. So 1972 saw 'back-channel' contacts and attempts to arrange a meeting with Kissinger. However Kissinger had other preoccupations, notably Vietnam; although Egypt suggested October 1972, his meeting with Sadat's security adviser, Hafiz Ismail, did not come off until February 1973. During his US visit, Ismail had wide-ranging discussions with which he initially seemed pleased; but Egypt continued to insist that an interim settlement would have to be conditional on Israeli acceptance of the principle of complete withdrawal. This the Israeli Premier, Golda Meir, derided when she visited Washington shortly afterwards – 'The trouble with Egypt is that they want the end

2. Neff, *Warriors Against Israel* p.88; Heikal, *Road to Ramadan* p.183; Robert Lacey, *The Kingdom* (New York, 1981) p.393

3. Neff, *Warriors Against Israel* pp.85–6, 88, 97–8, 109; Heikal, *Road to Ramadan* pp.168–71, 180; Lacey, *The Kingdom* pp.393, 398

4. Neff, *Warriors Against Israel* p.43

before they begin' – though she was prepared to see negotiations continue through Kissinger. She also secured the secret promise of further arms deliveries; when news of this leaked it did much to spoil the atmosphere in Cairo. Sadat now appears to have lost interest, though Kissinger and Ismail met once more (unsuccessfully).[5]

Quite possibly nothing could have been done; with hindsight, the White House should have addressed the problem more urgently. Kissinger was, in his own words, 'stalling' until after the Israeli elections in October 1973; Nixon privately suspected that he saw the political problems as too difficult, and so always wanted to delay. The Watergate crisis diverted Nixon's own attention elsewhere; the administration may have been reassured by King Hussein's judgement that it had two or three years to find a settlement before the Middle East exploded.[6] Whatever the reason, the USA remained confident that Egypt did not really have a military option. Nor was it impressed by Saudi Arabia's novel warnings that 'America's complete support of Zionism against the Arabs makes it extremely difficult for us to continue to supply US petroleum needs' – or by Brezhnev's demand, at the end of his US visit, that the superpowers agree on a Middle Eastern settlement along Arab lines, failing which 'we will have difficulty keeping the military situation from flaring up'.[7]

THE YOM KIPPUR WAR OCTOBER 1973

On 6 October (the Jewish holy day of Yom Kippur) Egypt crossed the Canal to seize the Israeli Bar-Lev Line fortifications, and Syria broke into the Golan Heights. They achieved almost total surprise. Israel was so over-confident that it saw any attack as self-evident folly, and Sadat had talked so often of fighting only to call it off that nobody any longer believed he meant it. There had also been a false alarm in May 1973. So analysts (reluctant again to cry 'Wolf') missed a surprising number of indications, and provided a definite

5. Heikal, *Road to Ramadan* pp.151–4, 202–3; Kissinger, *Memoirs* i p. 1,300, ii, pp. 221, 223, 226; Neff, *Warriors Against Israel* p.112

6. Kissinger, *Memoirs* ii p.296; Nixon, *Memoirs* pp.786–7; Neff, *Warriors Against Israel* p.105

7. Lacey, *The Kingdom* pp.398–402; Kissinger, *Memoirs* ii pp.296–9; Nixon, *Memoirs* pp.885–6

warning only in the early hours of the day itself. There might still have been time for a pre-emptive air attack, but Meir forbade it so as not to alienate Washington.[8] Although taken by surprise, Israel still won the actual fighting, but only after serious set-backs that occasioned moments of near-panic among some of its leaders.[9] The Arab armies had improved greatly.

Syria's armoured thrust was at first only just contained on the Golan Heights and kept from seizing the vital Jordan bridges. On 9 October its offensive ground to a halt, while Israel finally destroyed the Syrian missile screen and recovered control of the air. Two days later Israel largely regained its lost ground, then made as if to move on Damascus. It was, however, checked by the intervention (at considerable cost to themselves) of Iraqi and Jordanian units; the front finally stabilised, leaving Israel with only minor gains.

On the Canal, Egyptian missiles took heavy toll of Israeli aircraft and tanks charging in to relieve those parts of the Bar-Lev Line that still held out. Had Egypt simply stayed put and settled for a cease-fire,[10] it could have claimed a considerable victory. But from a mixture of over-confidence and a wish to relieve the pressure on a defeated Syria, Egypt advanced beyond the defensive range of its missiles, and suffered severely. Israel then staged a counterattack that (since Egypt did not perceive its thrust) largely succeeded in crossing the Canal and encircling the Egyptian Third Army. Eventually Sadat was brought to realise his danger and seek a cease-fire, to secure which the USSR invited Kissinger to Moscow. Kissinger was in no hurry; but terms were agreed on 21 October and formally voted by the UN to come into effect late on the 22nd. Israel had little choice but to accept, but it had not, by then, quite cut off the Third Army. During the next two days it broke the cease-fire and did so. The result was a major international crisis, with the Soviet Union making as if to relieve the Third Army itself and the USA signalling that it would not allow this.[11] Eventually things were resolved: Sadat was persuaded to ask for a UN peace-

8. Neff, *Warriors Against Israel* pp.137–9

9. It has been claimed that, after the first day's fighting, Dayan talked of catastrophe, though the Chief of Staff was less downcast – and even that there is 'some evidence' of the readying of Jericho missiles, presumably with nuclear warheads: Stephen Green, *Living by the Sword* pp.89–91; also Neff, *Warriors Against Israel* pp.167–8

10. Israel – but not Egypt – was apparently ready to accept a cease-fire in place on 12 October: Matti Golan, *The Secret Conversations of Henry Kissinger: Step by Step Diplomacy in the Middle East* (New York, 1976 edn) pp.65–7

11. See *The Cold War* chap. 11

keeping force instead; a final cease-fire was reached on the 25th; the USA insisted that Israel allow supplies through to the Third Army; and direct military disengagement talks opened between Egypt and Israel under UN auspices.

KISSINGER'S SHUTTLE DIPLOMACY

Sadat had achieved two things: the restoration of Arab pride by crossing the Canal and retaining a position on its eastern bank, and the redirection of international attention to the Middle East. In this latter, he had been helped by the oil exporting states' production cuts and price increases, and by an Arab embargo on oil deliveries to the USA and the Netherlands (see pp.351–2). The USA determined to sort things out, and in November 1973 Kissinger flew to the Middle East. He seemed remarkably successful: Sadat had decided to bet on the United States. Internal Egyptian considerations were involved,[12] as was his mounting dislike of the USSR. More important was his acceptance of US claims that, whatever the aid the USSR offered, 'territories you can only get from us'.[13] Soviet influence over Israel, never great, had been ended by the 1967 break – not repaired until 1991 – in their diplomatic relations. It had been shown that Israel could not be coerced as long as the USA backed it, but Eisenhower had forced an Israeli withdrawal in 1957, and perhaps Nixon (Eisenhower's Vice-President) would repeat the process. Also Sadat and Kissinger quickly established mutual confidence and respect.

Over the next few months Kissinger made five visits to the Middle East, and shuttled first between Egypt and Israel, then between Israel and Syria in highly visible negotiations. In January 1974 he secured an Israeli pull-back to a dozen miles from the Canal and the separation of Egyptian and Israeli forces by a narrow UN buffer zone, flanked by zones in which weapons would be restricted. In late May, with far more difficulty, he gained a similar

12. Sadat sought to improve Egypt's economy by opening it up, breaking with Nasser's socialism and hoping for Western investment. This policy of *infitah* did not prove very successful, brought considerable corruption, and explains much of the discontent of his final years

13. Privately Sadat thought that the USA held '60 percent of the cards, but it sounds better if I say "99 percent" ' in public: Daniel Yergin, *The Prize: The Epic Quest for Oil, Money and Power* (1991 edn) p.627; Heikal, *Road to Ramadan* p.174; Golan, *Secret Conversations of Kissinger* p.104

settlement for the Golan Heights, which returned the town of Quneitra to Syrian administration. It seemed to be, and probably was, a dazzling achievement which also made possible the clearance of the Canal, provided grounds for the lifting in March 1974 of the Arab oil embargo on the USA, and encouraged Saudi Arabia to expand production to ease the economic pressure on the West.

With hindsight a number of criticisms have been made. The most serious is that Kissinger never really attempted to follow his Egyptian and Syrian achievements with an agreement on the West Bank. In his *Memoirs* he says he wanted to do so while he could still deal with the friendly King Hussein rather than the PLO. But it proved impossible: the Israeli government had too small a majority to make concessions on so sensitive a subject, and had in any case promised not to conclude a West Bank agreement without first calling a general election. Furthermore, Egypt did not wish to lose the momentum of its own negotiating process by allowing the West Bank to take precedence over Sinai. Indeed, though Kissinger does not mention it, the Egyptian Foreign Minister threatened to 'veto' any agreement reached between Israel and Hussein (as opposed to the PLO). Nevertheless Hussein and President Ford issued a communiqué in August 1974 envisaging a Jordan–Israel disengagement. When Kissinger visited Israel in October, however, its Cabinet rejected all his ideas. Later that month an Arab summit in Rabat declared the PLO 'the sole legitimate representative of the Palestinian people in all liberated Palestinian territory'. Hussein appeared to accept the decision. Although it did not stop his secret talks with Israel, it led the Americans to give up on Jordan for the time being and concentrate again on Egypt.[14]

ISRAELI–EGYPTIAN DISENGAGEMENT AGREEMENTS 1974–5; US PROMOTION OF A MULTI-LATERAL CONFERENCE, 1977

Here Kissinger sought Israeli withdrawal from the Mitla and Giddi passes and the Abu Rudeis oilfields, and in March 1975 returned for another shuttle. This time he failed: Israel would not completely leave the passes, nor Egypt promise the ending of belligerency that

14. Kissinger, *Memoirs* ii pp.1138–41; Golan, *Secret Conversations of Kissinger* pp.217–27; Ismail Fahmy, *Negotiating for Peace in the Middle East* (1983) p.98; *Keesing's*, 26813

Israel sought in return. But mid-summer brought signs of movement; Sadat decided to go ahead with the reopening of the Suez Canal and the rebuilding of its war-shattered cities, and Israel facilitated this through minor unilateral withdrawals. Also the Israeli economy desperately needed US financial aid. September 1975 therefore brought the agreement that had fallen through in March, sweetened by the stationing of US civilians in no man's land to help both sides with electronic surveillance and by a whole raft of US promises to Israel. These extended from some $2 billion aid, and reassurances about Israeli oil supplies, to a pledge not to negotiate with the PLO till it accepted Israel's right to exist, and to an undertaking that any further negotiations with Egypt or Jordan should be not piecemeal but conducted within the framework of an overall peace settlement. For its part Egypt carefully did not promise an end to belligerency, but it did accept that the mandate for the UN force in Sinai should now be extended on an annual rather than a quarterly basis. The importance it accorded to the redevelopment of the Canal (which Israeli cargoes, though not ships, were now allowed to use) suggested that it did not wish the resumption of fighting. The 1975 disengagement agreement was therefore seen as qualitatively different from that of 1974, and drew Syrian protests accordingly.[15]

It also appeared to constitute the end of the road for Kissinger's piecemeal approach.[16] US Democrats reached the conclusion that further progress would demand an attempt at a more comprehensive solution. This the new Carter administration was anxious to promote early in 1977, so as to get it out of the way before pressuring Israel for concessions could become an electoral liability. Originally it hoped to secure, through prior diplomatic negotiations between the parties, agreements that could then be confirmed at a reconvention of the December 1973 Geneva Conference. When this proved difficult, it came to look to the conference as an end in itself, even without the conclusion of prior agreements. The State Department was anxious to co-operate with the USSR, which co-chaired the conference and might be able to influence Syria and the PLO. In October 1977 the USA and USSR issued a joint communiqué committing the conference to negotiate the

15. *Keesing's*, 27432

16. The USA had promised Egypt to make a 'serious effort' to secure further Israeli–Syrian negotiations; but the Israeli premier had been pessimistic about the scope for another interim agreement on the Golan, and (as far as we know) one was not attempted: *Keesing's*, 27429; Golan, *Secret Conversations of Kissinger* p.248

'withdrawal of Israeli armed forces from territories occupied in the 1967 conflict; the resolution of the Palestinian question, including insuring the legitimate rights of the Palestinian people'. The outrage of Israel and its friends was intense, and brought an undignified partial backtracking in a joint US–Israeli statement; it also led Carter to appeal personally to Sadat for a bold move to help him with his difficulties.[17]

SADAT'S VISIT TO JERUSALEM NOVEMBER 1977

By now Sadat tended to see himself as a man of destiny: he was already in direct contact with Israel. Israeli intelligence had discovered a Libyan plot to kill him; instead of passing the information on (as usual) via the USA, Begin's new right-wing government arranged for a direct meeting in Morocco in the hope that it might 'warm the atmosphere between us'. This was followed up first by offers (transmitted through Romania and the USA) of 'extensive satisfaction' in Sinai and some form of Arab autonomy on the West Bank, in exchange for peace and intelligence cooperation, then by a September meeting in Rabat between Foreign Secretary Dayan and the Egyptian Deputy Prime Minister. At this Egypt proposed that the two countries reach a settlement that could be surfaced at the Geneva Conference, on the basis of Israeli evacuation of Sinai and an arrangement linking the West Bank and Gaza to Jordan; Dayan had important reservations, but indicated flexibility.[18] Against this background, and perhaps encouraged by Carter's appeal, Sadat determined on a dramatic gesture to convince Israel of his good intentions. Its details varied,[19] but it always involved his visiting Israel personally and in effect taking control of the negotiating process. In the face of considerable reservations, both domestic and from other Arab leaders, he (in effect) invited himself to address the Knesset in Jerusalem, and on 20 November 1977 he did so – with a speech that offered Israel peace and acceptance, but demanded withdrawal from the territories taken in 1967. The emotional impact was enormous, but (as Begin's reply made clear) there remained a considerable gap between the two countries'

17. Jimmy Carter, *Keeping Faith: Memoirs of a President* (1982) p.295
18. Sachar, *History of Israel* ii pp.45–8
19. One option was an East Jerusalem summit meeting of the parties to the Arab–Israeli dispute plus the Permanent Members of the UN Security Council

positions. It was, however, determined to resolve this through direct negotiations (which Israel had always regarded as a prerequisite for peace).

They failed. When it came to the point, Israel was not only increasingly firm over the West Bank but also anxious to preserve its military position in Sinai (which, by providing defence in depth had, after all, enabled it to withstand surprise attack in 1973) and not prepared to abandon the settlements that boxed in the Gaza Strip. In July 1978 Sadat was warning that, if he did not do better by October, he would resign; later he ordered Israel's military negotiators to leave Cairo.

CARTER'S 'CAMP DAVID' MEDIATION OF THE EGYPTIAN–ISRAELI PEACE TREATY 1978–9

Carter responded to this impasse by inviting both Sadat and Begin to Camp David in September 1978. Negotiations were not easy, especially with Begin; both Carter and Sadat came close to breaking them off. But agreement was finally reached. Egypt should recover all Sinai over three years, and (if the Knesset agreed) the Israeli settlements should be evacuated. In return Israel was promised free use of the Canal and the Straits of Tiran, and the establishment of diplomatic relations after its initial partial withdrawal; the USA would construct replacements in the Negev for some of the military bases lost by withdrawal, while Egyptian forces in Sinai would be limited. Another, and much vaguer, 'Framework' provided for negotiations between Egypt, Israel and (if it was willing) Jordan to establish a 'self-governing authority' for the West Bank and Gaza for five years, during which time its final status should be settled by further negotiations. (Both sides reserved their position on East Jerusalem.)

A peace treaty was to be negotiated along these lines within three months. The process immediately ran into difficulties when Israel denied Carter's understanding that no new settlements would be established on the West Bank. By March 1979 deadlock had been reached, and Sadat was threatening to come to Washington to denounce Begin's intransigence before Congress. Carter's response was to embark on a personal shuttle between Cairo and Jerusalem; by offering various sweeteners, notably reassurance to Israel on oil supplies and further aid to both countries, he secured the signature in late March 1979 of the first (and – 1993 – so far the only) peace treaty between Israel and an Arab state.[20]

EGYPT'S POSITION IN THE ARAB WORLD

Opinion differs as to whether it has helped stabilise the Middle East. Though Israel had to use force to secure the abandonment of its settlements in Sinai, its withdrawal was completed according to plan in 1982. Nor has the Egyptian border given trouble since.[21] But Sadat's insistent pursuit of a settlement that not even Morocco or Jordan approved isolated Egypt within the Arab world. A group of 'rejectionist' states (plus the PLO) met in Tripoli to condemn his 1977 visit to Jerusalem and freeze diplomatic relations. A further, and much better attended, conference in Baghdad after Camp David threatened sanctions if he proceeded; accordingly when the 1979 treaty was signed, most Arab states broke off diplomatic relations with Egypt, and Saudi Arabia and Kuwait cancelled their subsidies. Some of this was for show: Saudi Arabia secretly promised the USA not to impose really damaging sanctions, and did not expel expatriate Egyptian workers whose remittances were of great importance.[22] But the linked phenomena of dislike of his Israeli policy and rising Muslim fundamentalism were among the factors that destroyed Sadat's domestic popularity and forced him to become increasingly repressive. In October 1981 he was murdered by a small group of fundamentalists. Vice-President Mubarak took over very smoothly, and continued Sadat's policies till he had secured the return of all Sinai. In general, though, he adopted a much lower diplomatic profile than did Sadat; his relations with Israel have been cool if correct; and his chief concern was to restore Egypt's standing in the Arab world. In this he was helped by Iraqi defeats in the Gulf War (see pp.373–4). Iraq had been strongly 'rejectionist', but now needed help from any country that would provide it (Syria, of course, would not); although Egyptian aid did not go beyond the technical and logistic, the Arab states would have been foolish to cold-shoulder their most significant power. Even so

20. Sachar, *History of Israel* ii chaps 3, 4; Carter, *Keeping Faith* pp.319–428

21. A dispute remained as to whether Egypt's original border included the beach of Taba (on which a large hotel had just been built). Arbitration was agreed on in 1986, and the territory returned to Egypt in 1989

22. Brzezinski, *Power and Principle* p.286; Sachar, *History of Israel* ii p.75

it was not until 1989 that Egypt was formally welcomed back into the Arab League.

THE WEST BANK AND THE GAZA STRIP

Part of the attraction to Israel of a settlement was that, with Egypt out of the way, none of its other opponents would be much of a threat. Some people claim that the peace treaty encouraged Israel's 1980 declaration of Jerusalem as its united and indivisible capital, 1981 annexation of the Golan Heights and 1982 invasion of Lebanon. This can only be speculation. What is clear is that the Lebanon invasion finally ended any prospect that the Camp David process would produce a solution of the Palestinian question. Sadat had always insisted that he was seeking not just the recovery of Sinai but a general settlement. No doubt this was partly to cover himself against Arab accusations of betrayal; both at Camp David and in the final treaty he accepted much more indefinite agreements on the West Bank than on Sinai, nor did he insist on a precise linkage between the two. But if Egyptian interests were his chief concern, he did not wholly abandon Palestinian ones; he may have hoped that Begin's successors would be more forthcoming. In the early 1980s Begin's government was distinctly unpopular; it was easy to see his 1977 election victory as no more than a one-off protest against a rash of scandals in the Labour Alignment that had dominated the country since its creation. In mid-1981 Begin's Likud was narrowly returned to office, thanks largely to the votes of the oriental immigrants and to its attractiveness to the religious parties that held the balance of power in Parliament. As King Hussein had found after 1967, it was not easy to negotiate over the West Bank even with Labour. Likud was emotionally committed to the retention of what it preferred to call Judea and Samaria, and had since 1977 deliberately stepped up Jewish settlement there to make it difficult to leave. In 1978–9 Begin had accepted, in principle, a measure of Arab self-government. But when the talks stipulated by the peace treaty began, Israel made it clear that this would not extend to security, land or water.[23] Egypt regarded this as quite inadequate, and the talks went nowhere. The USA regretted their

23. By 1983 one-third of the West Bank and Gaza Strip had been classified and appropriated as disused state land, and restrictions placed on drilling for water in the West Bank to preserve the underground flow to the artesian wells of the coastal plan: Sachar, *History of Israel* ii pp.95, 153

deadlock, but Carter seems to have felt that he had exposed himself quite enough and was reluctant again to intervene personally.[24] Periodic meetings, and indeed Egyptian–Israeli summits, continued down to 1982. Mubarak then responded to Israel's invasion of Lebanon by breaking off the Palestinian autonomy talks and (after the killings in the refugee camps) withdrawing his ambassador (until 1986). So the West Bank did not get even the limited formal autonomy Israel had proposed.

For many years, though, it was not particularly difficult to rule. Despite sporadic protests, strikes and incidents, administration continued through the existing Arab civil servants, and there was no need for major sustained counter-insurgency measures. The Gaza Strip had initially presented more problems; it took until 1971 for forceful measures to break the PLO's grip on the local population.[25] In both the West Bank and the Gaza Strip, material conditions were eased by economic incorporation into Israel and by the opening of employment opportunities (albeit on the lowest rung of the labour market) for commuters. Indeed apart from occasional clashes resulting from the presence on the West Bank of some 30,000 Israeli settlers,[26] the chief problems were moral. Israel was coming to look uncomfortably like South Africa, in that its people of state ruled over a non-European population living largely in homelands and doing the less well paid and less attractive jobs.

PALESTINIAN RESISTANCE (INTIFADA) SINCE 1987

In December 1987 there quite unexpectedly broke out, across both the West Bank and Gaza, a locally directed resistance movement,

24. Brzezinski, *Power and Principle* pp.437–8. Sachar claims that Carter promised Sadat (after Israel's 1980 proclamation of Jerusalem as its capital) that, if re-elected, he would call another Camp David summit to push negotiations forward: *History of Israel* ii p.91

25. Sachar, *History of Israel* i pp.683, 685

26. Until 1977 settlements on the West Bank (outside greater Jerusalem) had been chiefly military. But children of the Kfar Etzion settlements wiped out in 1948 lost little time in re-establishing them; 1968 saw squatting in Hebron (whose Jewish community had been murdered in 1929) by religious enthusiasts whom the government did not dare to deport; and by 1977 they had four other imitators. Still there were only 5,000 settlers in 1977. By 1983 Likud's financial incentives (and the attractions of cheap suburban homes) had taken this total to about 30,000 (plus another 67,000 in the ex-Jordanian part of greater Jerusalem). The pace then slowed considerably for both financial and political reasons, but picked up again in the early 1990s: Sachar, *History of Israel* ii pp.15–17, 95–100, 153–6, 241

intifada, of demonstrations, riots and stone-throwing (though not, for quite some time, shooting attacks on Israelis). It was handled extremely badly – the Israeli military had, interestingly enough, no real training in riot control – and the resultant Arab casualties, well reported by the international media, initially served to place Israel politically on the defensive.

Intifada also helped activate the diplomatic scene. It was at first hoped that talks on the West Bank could be resumed between Israel and a Jordanian delegation containing members acceptable to the PLO. The PLO backed away from this; so King Hussein disclaimed responsibility for the West Bank and cut off his payment of West Bank civil service salaries, leaving the PLO to replace them (with the help of subventions from the Arab Gulf). Later in 1988 the PLO, for the first time, proclaimed an independent state of Palestine (followed next year by a government in exile). The PLO was also brought by the USA to declare its acceptance of Israel's existence and the limitation of its aims to a state on the West Bank and Gaza (a step it had often edged towards but never previously been ready to take); it renounced terrorism outside Israel and the occupied territories. In return the USA opened public discussions with it, though these were discontinued after eighteen months. On the ground, however, conditions did not improve, By November 1992 the death toll stood at 1,605, and there was a drift towards extremes: on the one side trigger-happy vigilante Israeli settlers; on the other, the mounting appeal of the Islamic fundamentalist *Hamas*, which the occupation authorities had initially encouraged in order to undercut the PLO but which turned out to be a more active and implacable opponent.[27]

A REVIEW OF THE ARAB–ISRAELI DISPUTE

In 1990 the Arab–Israeli question would still have been in many ways recognisable to the protagonists of the 1930s. At its heart is the wish of the two groups to live safely in as much of Palestine as possible, and the belief of each that to do so requires a state of their own. In the 1930s the Zionists were already creating facts on the ground by land purchase and settlement. But both they and the 'Palestinians' had to devote themselves very largely to external lobbying, chiefly of the then Mandatory Power, Britain. The

27. *Keesing's*, 36120–1, 36131, 36436–8, 39211, 1992 R144

Palestinians had also staged a number of murderous anti-Jewish riots and, in the later 1930s, a widespread but episodic insurgency. This attracted some sympathy from the independent Arab states, and (with war looming) Britain decided that it was more important to conciliate the Arab world than the Zionists. One result was the move first of 'extremists' like IZL, then of the whole Yishuv, to self-reliance and independent action. Self-reliance is etched on the Israeli psyche: Israel often cites interwar Czechoslovakia as a state that in 1938 allowed the crucial decisions on its security to be taken for it by the Great Powers and that in March 1939 accordingly ceased to exist. This made it extremely difficult for the United States to 'deliver' Israel in any negotiations, Israeli dependence on US aid notwithstanding. But Israel was still the 'object' of international politics (as well as a significant actor) in the way that less controversial states (like New Zealand) were not. The Palestinians had never acquired statehood; and although the PLO was an actor in a small way, the Palestinian cause still relied chiefly on international lobbying.

Whether in action, lobbying or political realism, the Zionists/Israelis have generally outclassed the Palestinians. Despite some successes in cutting roads and isolating Jewish settlements in early 1948, Palestinian irregulars were neither united, disciplined nor determined enough to match the Yishuv on their own. Later that year, indeed, Israel proved able to hold off and then roll back attacks from all its Arab neighbours simultaneously (albeit partly because they too were not very united). Israel has maintained this superiority ever since, though through the quality rather than the quantity of its armed forces. But it needed to, in the sense that it was far less capable of absorbing defeat than were the much larger Egypt and Syria. The result was one of the world's major arms races, though the growth in technology did not lead to a corresponding growth in casualties.

To outside eyes, 'political realism' has been in fairly short supply on both sides. The Zionists were too slow to accept the Peel Commission proposals, and so found them withdrawn in response to pro-Arab lobbying and the 1939 White Paper substituted. They did accept the (fairly generous) 1947 UN partition proposals. Their opponents did not, and Israel used the resulting war to consolidate and extend its territory, while prudently refraining from taking over the entire West Bank. Afterwards it refused the comparatively small territorial concessions that might have enabled King Abdullah to make peace; this was to be repeated after 1967. Israel had been not unhappy with the Jordanian presence on the West Bank and had not sought war. Once the West Bank had been conquered, however, Israel could never quite bring itself to return it all, even to secure peace with King Hussein. The objections were initially strategic, but later grew to include the mystical devotion to the historic land of Israel that necessarily underlies Zionism.[28] Admittedly Israel did take the risk of abandoning Sinai to gain peace with Egypt; but even here the stiffness of its negotiation brought Sadat to the brink of despair, and it took remarkable US efforts to secure success. More controversially, Israel has been accused of counter-productive overkill in its policy of massive retaliation raids to punish *fedayeen* attacks. These certainly confirmed the Arab image of constant Israeli aggression; some have blamed the 1955 Gaza raid for shifting Nasser from an open-minded stance into that of a determined enemy. On the other hand the policy eventually led Egypt, Syria and Jordan to bar attacks from their territory; the Lebanon, unfortunately, was too weak to do so, and Israel's attempts to make it have proved disastrous.

The most glaring lack of realism has been on the Arab side. Even the 1939 White Paper, which would have led to a shut-off of Jewish immigration and an Arab-majority state, was rejected as inadequate. By 1948 there were suggestions that the Peel Commission borders might be acceptable, but not those of the UN vote. In the 1950s there was talk of reverting to the UN borders, as opposed to those resulting from the 1948–9 fighting. These, however, became desirable after the 1967 war, and the Arab states gradually edged towards what now seems a genuine readiness to accept Israel on the basis of Resolution 242. It has clearly been politically safer to allow the continuance of an unsatisfactory position than to reach a partial settlement with Israel: this deterred Abdullah and Hussein (though it did not prevent clandestine Jordanian–Israeli cooperation), and when Sadat made peace he was ostracised. Most unyielding, of course, was the PLO, as it had few vested interests to incline it to compromise.[29] Until 1988 it retained its commitment to Israel's liquidation, which made it easy for Israel to rule out talks.

28. 'Of course, the Land of Israel is everything to us', Begin is said to have explained. 'All of it. Otherwise why are we here rather than in the United States?'

29. In 1973 talks, it did suggest to the USA that its interest lay in Jordan, not Israel: Kissinger, *Memoirs* ii pp.626, 628. This did not endear it to the USA, which valued King Hussein; but there has always been a minority view in Israel that it should take over completely up to the Jordan, leaving a new Palestinian state to be built on the East Bank (which was part of the original 'Palestine' Mandate and whose population is now at least half 'Palestinian')

The Yishuv/Israel's final advantage over the Palestinians has lain in relationships with the outside world. It was been remarkably successful in securing at least the financial and political support of the Jews of the Diaspora, whereas Arab support for the Palestinians has been distinctly patchy. The Mufti of Jerusalem was always a divisive leader. In 1948 King Abdullah's prime concern was to shut him out and take over the West Bank, preferably through an arrangement with Israel. The other Arab League states were more concerned with thwarting Abdullah than with either helping the Palestinians or fighting Israel. Egypt did eventually allow the Mufti to establish a 'government', but only as a move in Arab politics. Until 1967 Egypt ruled in Gaza, Jordan on the West Bank, to the exclusion of any specific Palestinian identity. In 1964, admittedly, the Arab League created a Palestinian Liberation Organisation; after 1967 it proved a rival to Jordan as the prospective beneficiary of any liberation of the West Bank. The 1974 Rabat summit pronounced in its favour; since then the Arab states have sought to enhance the PLO's status at the UN and elsewhere. But there were limits to their commitment: Sadat eventually gave the recovery of Sinai priority over a settlement of Palestine, and he sought the latter through negotiations that would not involve the PLO. Meanwhile Syria attacked the PLO in the Lebanon in 1976 and helped the Christians reduce Palestinian refugee camps; these again suffered severely during Asad's 1982–9 breach with Arafat.

The Yishuv/Israel also enjoyed more success in its wider appeals. Initially things were not always easy: both the British and the US diplomatic and military establishments, until 1948, regarded the Arab world as more important, and would have preferred to incline towards it. So at several points over the years 1945–8 the decisive factor was the sympathy, partly personal and partly electoral, of President Truman. Presidents' personal sympathies vary more than Israel's political appeal within the USA. This has rested on a number of pillars: feelings of guilt for the Holocaust; dislike of British imperialism; admiration for Israel as a beleaguered outpost of Western liberal democracy; thankfulness for the way it has defended itself (and by extension Western interests) in a part of the world that at times seemed otherwise to look to the USSR, without demanding the involvement of US troops; the concentration of Jewish votes in electorally important states, and American Jews' above average political activism and monetary contributions. Not all these pillars remain constant; the political importance of the concentration of Jewish voters has been somewhat reduced by population shifts, but that of financial contributions has increased. Overall, however, the Israeli lobby remains strong, so strong that in Congress it is wise to link otherwise unpopular programmes, like foreign aid, to assistance for Israel. Official US–Israeli relationships became closer over time. To begin with, most financial aid for Israel came from private sources; and the USA was happy to see France serve as Israel's chief arms supplier. In the 1960s Democratic Presidents increased US sales (partly to reduce the opposition of Jewish liberals to the Vietnam War). Thus when de Gaulle stopped arms deliveries after the 1967 war and Israel's 1968 raid on Beirut airport, the USA took over the role of armourer, soon establishing an extremely close military and intelligence linkage. The 1973 war saw an enormous arms airlift; each stage in the subsequent disengagement process was sweetened by further US arms transfers. Of itself, Israel could not have paid for these, and increasingly the burden was assumed by US aid: after 1979 Israel became the world's largest recipient of official US assistance.[30] Such dependence is potentially dangerous; but Israel has managed to take the money without exposing itself, at least until very recently, to any really severe pressure.

The Arabs, of course, have also had their backers. Until 1955 they, too, looked to the West. Nasser then pledged his cotton crop for 'Czech' arms. Thereafter Egypt, and in due course Syria, were able to turn to Soviet aid to outfit their armies. Soviet support replaced the equipment lost in 1956 and 1967, and the USSR made it clear that it would not permit Syria's total defeat in 1967 or Egypt's in 1973. This also enhanced Israel's value in Western eyes, and Israel's standing with the West (de Gaulle apart) probably reached its peak in the aftermath of 1967.[31] Later the Arabs took another course. The 1973 war and OAPEC (Organisation of Arab Petroleum Exporting Countries) oil embargo, in combination, sensitised the West to Arab concerns; the new oil wealth drove home the truth (already seen by de Gaulle) that, in material terms, the Arab world was of more importance than Israel. Sadat also managed to enlist the USA in his drive to move Israel back from its 1967 conquests by negotiation. His readiness to negotiate served to undercut the Israelis' long-standing claim that peace could come quite easily were the Arabs only to talk to them. Finally, though Palestinian terrorism slowed the process, the spectacle of Israel's

30 Sachar, *History of Israel* ii pp.226–7

31. Black Africa, admittedly, broke off relations with Israel after 1967, but in power-political terms this was very marginal

prolonged 'colonial' rule over an Arab West Bank and Gaza gradually reversed its appeal to political liberals. The result was to swing support to the idea of a Palestinian state – but faster in Europe than in the more influential United States.

NEGOTIATIONS TO SECURE AN ARAB–ISRAELI PEACE 1989–93

By 1990, however, the United States had also begun to change. From the outset Bush gave the Middle East a high priority, declaring in 1989 during a visit by Mubarak that the USA and Egypt shared 'the goals of security for Israel, the end of occupation and the achievement of Palestinian political rights': 'These are the promises held out by a sustained commitment to a negotiated settlement'. The Israeli Premier, Shamir, countered by proposing negotiations for an interim settlement, but with a non-PLO delegation.[32] This refusal to talk to the PLO proved a major stumbling block; in early 1990 Labour broke up the Israeli government in an attempt to get it changed, but failed as Shamir proved able to form an alternative coalition. The USA was, however, soon given a new reason to persevere: to counter Iraq's seizure of Kuwait (see pp.376–7), it had to build an *Arab* alliance against Saddam Hussein. It was, in fact, remarkably successful: Syria had correctly read the decline in Soviet power and decided to mend its fences with the USA. This softened the stance of one of the traditional opponents of negotiations with Israel; the isolation and defeat of Iraq temporarily destroyed the influence of another.

The USA had undertaken to reconvene the Geneva Conference once the Gulf crisis was out of the way. It was as good as its word, and the conference met (under US-Soviet chairmanship) in Madrid in October 1991, though (as in 1973) only as a ceremonial prelude to subsequent bilateral talks. The scene had been set for it by Bush's insistence that Congress postpone approval of $10 billion worth of loan guarantees for which Israel had lobbied hard, and on which it was depending both for budgetary stability and to settle the flood of Soviet immigrants.[33] This was not heavy US pressure on Israel, but many people saw it as significant. There was a general

32. *Keesing's*, 36599

33. The USA was particularly concerned that it should not finance the use of ex-Soviet immigrants – 185,000 in 1990, 142,000 (less than half the total originally expected) in 1991 – to colonise the West Bank

expectation that a settlement could be achieved, but only if Israel was prepared to cede land for peace (in line with UN Resolution 242). For its part, Israel successfully excluded the PLO from attendance, but had to concede the presence of a group of West Bank Palestinians who were quite obviously in touch with the PLO. (At the conference, it even met with them separately.) Nothing tangible was agreed, save that further talks should be held – initially in Washington, a venue that Israel regarded as unwelcome since, significantly, it now feared that it would make it easier for the USA to stage-manage proceedings and press for Israeli concessions. At the first round of talks in December 1991, Israel therefore sought to play for time and focus on procedural points. In January 1992, however, it proposed an 'interim [Palestinian] self-government authority'. Two small right-wing parties pulled out of the government coalition in protest, thus precipitating elections. They were wrong: after he had lost them, Shamir incautiously admitted that he had meant to carry 'on autonomy talks for 10 years and meanwhile we would have reached half a million [Jewish] souls in Judea and Samaria. . . . I didn't believe there was a majority in favour of a Greater Israel, but it could have been attained over time'.

Much was expected of Rabin's new Labour-led government, which sought to implement, within a year, Palestinian 'self-rule as is written and spelled out in the Camp David accords'. It began by cancelling new 'political' – though *not* security-related – building for Israeli settlement on the West Bank. The Washington talks therefore resumed in a new atmosphere, and were to be accompanied by tantalising hints of progress in separate talks with Syria. However no tangible progress was made, and momentum was lost when Rabin responded (in December 1992) to the murder of a policeman by deporting 415 alleged *Hamas* militants. The Lebanon refused to admit them, and they were left uncomfortably stranded in no-man's land. Much as the PLO disliked *Hamas*, it could not ignore their presence as a very visible symbol of illegitimate Israeli rule. When Israel refused to let most of the deportees return, the PLO persuaded the other Arab delegations to walk out of the talks. In April 1993 the PLO was, with difficulty, induced to return; but little progress was made either then or in June, and there were complaints that the new Democratic US administration was now siding with Israel.[34] Both Israel and the PLO therefore seemed to be in trouble. Rabin's peace initiative had produced nothing; and he was mired in the familiar cycle of fighting

34. *Keesing's*, 37303–4, 38740–1, 39027–8, 39167, 39224–5, 39436, 39484–5, 39532, 1992 R139 and 145, 1993 R143

in southern Lebanon and repression of the Occupied Territories (whose population, for security reasons, he largely shut out of Israel proper, thus cutting off employment and imposing considerable hardship). Arafat's position was worse: his alignment with Iraq during the Kuwait war had dried up subsidies from the Gulf and plunged the PLO into financial crisis; his autocratic style of leadership was strongly criticised by the Palestinian delegation to the Washington talks; and the PLO was steadily losing support to *Hamas*, especially in Gaza.

Perhaps these factors helped make both Israel and the PLO more flexible. In any case it suddenly transpired in late August that, in secret talks under Norwegian mediation, they had reached a tentative agreement envisaging: direct negotiations on its implementation; a PLO takeover of Gaza and Jericho; elections; and a transitional period of Palestinian local self-government elsewhere in the West Bank, with the IDF assuming a markedly lower profile. The thorny questions of Israeli settlers and of Jerusalem were to be reserved for later discussion. This was consolidated by letters, in which Arafat accepted Israel's right 'to exist in peace and security' and appealed for an end to intifada, while the Israeli government recognised 'the PLO as the representative of the Palestinian people' (Rabin sombrely telling the Knesset that, despite considerable qualms, he had 'reached the conclusion there is no Palestinian partner besides the PLO . . . It was an enemy. It . . . still is an enemy, but negotiations you conduct with enemies').[35] The exchange was completed by the signature in Washington of a Declaration of Principles.

The agreement encountered massive opposition, in Israel, in the PLO Council, and in the Occupied Territories; but both the Council and the Knesset eventually blessed it, while public opinion on the ground appeared to move in its favour. Implementation, however, proved unexpectedly difficult: the December deadline for the start of Israeli troop withdrawal was missed; and in February 1994 a Jewish fanatic sought to derail the whole process by gunning down worshippers in a Hebron mosque. We cannot yet tell whether he has succeeded or whether the outcry will force Israel to make concessions it would otherwise have held back. But a consummated PLO deal with Israel would transform the Middle Eastern scene and legitimise other settlements. Of these, an Israel–Jordan peace treaty would be fairly easy, though the achievement of one with Syria appears to depend on Israel's first taking the difficult decision to evacuate the Golan entirely.

35. *The Independent*, 10 Sept. 1993 p.1; *Keesing's*, 39658–62

CHAPTER FOURTEEN

Oil

INTERNATIONAL OIL ARRANGEMENTS (TO 1950); ARAMCO'S 50/50 DEAL WITH SAUDI ARABIA

Middle Eastern oil production was surprisingly low in 1945 – only half that of Venezuela – but a geologist's report (for the US administration) saw that 'The centre of gravity of the world of oil production is shifting from the Gulf-Caribbean areas to the Middle East . . . and is likely to continue to shift'.[1] In the past the chief competition in the Middle East had been between British and US oil companies (both sometimes backed by their respective governments), though it had mostly ended in cartel agreements. During the Second World War tension arose again, as a result of US recognition of Saudi oil potential and the US Navy's determination to secure it as an oil reserve. One result was the extension to King Saud of aid that gradually brought the Kingdom to look more to Washington than London.[2] Another was an attempt to negotiate a general Anglo-American agreement to govern the management of Middle Eastern oil. Despite mutual suspicion, such an agreement was reached in 1944, but shelved when it met opposition in the US Senate; the same fate met a second agreement in 1947. So all that was achieved was British and French consent (necessary under a 1928 arrangement) for the restructuring of the US oil undertaking in Saudi Arabia, Aramco.

1. Anthony Sampson, *The Seven Sisters: The Great Oil Companies and the World they Made* (paperback edn, London 1981) p.112

2. British companies had shown little interest in prospecting for Saudi oil during the world glut of the 1930s, so the concession went to US ones. From 1943 the USA reinforced its position by providing more aid than Britain, and by its more careful cultivation of King Saud personally

Middle Eastern oil was ordinarily left to the major oil companies (the 'Seven Sisters')[3] to manage. Occasionally they had to turn to their respective governments for help, but usually they kept their distance. This in turn made it easier for Arab states to compartmentalise oil and keep it separate from the issue of US government support for Israel. Thus shortly after the USA had ensured the passage of the November 1947 UN Resolution partitioning Palestine and establishing a Jewish state, King Saud privately promised Aramco that it would not lose its concession.[4]

Between 1945 and 1950 Middle Eastern oil production doubled, but the host countries began pressing for a greater share in the proceeds.[5] The running in this connection had hitherto been made by the Latin American producers; Bolivia, Ecuador and, most importantly, Mexico had nationalised oil in the 1930s. The oil companies had responded by boycotting Mexican production, while both the USA and UK had imposed further sanctions. The general need for oil during the Second World War resolved the confrontation, but the oil majors' resultant preference for Venezuela, plus mistakes by the Mexican national oil company, set the Mexican industry back for a generation. Venezuela, therefore, did not seek nationalisation, but in the 1940s it insisted on taxing oil profits in such a way as to secure a guaranteed half share (or '50/50 split'). This precedent proved influential when, from 1948, Saudi Arabia started seeking more money. In December 1950 Aramco struck with the Kingdom a 50/50 deal that, though it did not stop continued haggling, proved broadly satisfactory. Aramco had been steered to this by a State Department that was concerned about general US interests in the country, and the deal was eased by a corresponding reduction in Aramco's US tax liablity.[6]

3. These were (in order of their 1972 oil production): Exxon; Shell (Dutch-British); BP (British Petroleum); Texaco; Gulf; Socal; Mobil

4. Cohen, *Palestine and the Great Powers* p.395

5. World energy needs had earlier been met chiefly from coal. Mining is labour-intensive. So, though coal exports had not generally been subject to special taxation – and so had set few precedents for it – they had benefited the producing countries. But once oil has been discovered, it costs very little to produce. So unless producing states impose substantial royalties, or obtain a share in the profits, they gain little from the depletion of their natural resources

6. Fiona Venn, *Oil Diplomacy in the Twentieth Century* (1986) pp.76–9, 120–1, 175–7; David Holden and Richard Johns, *The House of Saud* (1981) pp.152 ff

MOSSADEGH'S DISPUTE WITH THE ANGLO-IRANIAN OIL COMPANY 1950–3

Events in Iran went less smoothly. Here the situation was complicated by the long-standing British involvement in the country's internal affairs. Many Iranian politicians saw foreign involvement as an inevitable, and sometimes convenient, fact of life; but others resented it, and sought to rescue Iran from subordination to foreign influence. The first victim of this feeling was in fact the USSR, which had been promised (as an inducement to evacuate Iran in 1946) an oil concession in the north comparable to that possessed by the Anglo-Iranian Oil Company (AIOC) in the south. Under the influence of Dr Mossadegh, the majlis (Parliament) refused in 1947 to ratify it. Although Mossadegh may always have hoped to follow this up by ending the AIOC concession, the Iranian government was less ambitious. It did, however, seek revision, as the fixed payments provided for in 1933 were being eroded by inflation, and as British postwar 'austerity' dividend restraint also reduced Iran's take. In 1949 AIOC concluded a 'Supplemental Agreement' that would have increased the royalty rate by half. But the issue featured extensively in the 1949 elections, which returned a strong opposition 'National Front' bloc to the majlis. Successive governments sought further AIOC concessions as a sweetener before they made any serious attempt to get the Supplemental Agreement ratified. The AIOC was reluctant to reopen negotiations and mistakenly confident that this would not prove necessary. Alarm bells started ringing in Washington in the summer of 1950; the USA sought both to press Britain to be more generous and to warn it of the forthcoming 50/50 Aramco settlement with Saudi Arabia. AIOC at first thought it knew better, so it was not until February 1951 that it indicated willingness to negotiate on a 50/50 basis.[7] By then the majlis was moving towards nationalisation. March 1951 saw the murder of the apparently strong and moderate Prime Minister, General Razmara, the passage of the nationalisation legislation, and a strike of oilfield workers. In April 1951 the Shah accepted Mossadegh as Prime Minister, and in May the oilfields were formally taken over.

Britain considered using force, either to protect its nationals or, more ambitiously, to seize and operate the Abadan refinery (using

7. Venn, *Oil Diplomacy* pp.114–15; Dean Acheson, *Present at the Creation: My Years in the State Department* (1970) p.503

Kuwaiti oil if Iranian supplies were cut off). Militarily this would have been quite easy, especially as the Iranian commander had privately agreed to offer no more than token resistance; and there was considerable domestic pressure for such action. But it would have breached international law and lost Britain foreign sympathy; the USA strongly advised against it. During the summer of 1951 the Cabinet, though making military preparations, preferred negotiation and an appeal to the International Court of Justice. However the Iranian government brought matters to a head by ordering all British oil personnel to leave Abadan within a week. Attlee again ascertained Truman's attitude, and on 27 September took the issue to the Cabinet for a decision. He himself still opposed the use of force, but the Foreign Secretary (Herbert Morrison) had now changed his mind and wished to warn Mossadegh that 'the expulsion of the remaining staff from Abadan' would not be permitted:

> If . . . the Government's handling of the Persian dispute appeared feeble and ineffective, the repercussions throughout the Middle East and elsewhere would be very serious. Egypt might be emboldened to take drastic action to end the military treaty and possibly to bring the Suez Canal under Egyptian control, and British rights in many other parts of the world would be placed in jeopardy.

'It was, however, the general view of the Cabinet, that, in the light of the United States attitude . . ., force could not be used to hold the refinery . . . We could not afford to break with the United States on an issue of this kind.' The USA had made it clear that it would 'acquiesce in the use of force' only 'to protect British lives, or in the event of a Communist coup in Persia'; otherwise its chief concern seemed to be to avoid any British action that would give the USSR an excuse for similarly taking over 'the oil area in Northern Persia'. On this occasion, unlike 1956, US views prevailed, though the USA had to fall in with a face-saving British appeal to the Security Council in October – which in fact failed to garner sufficient votes even to trigger a Soviet veto.[8]

8. Cabinet Conclusions, esp. 16 July 1951 (PRO CAB 128/21 – no circulation record) and 27 September (CAB 128/20); memoranda by the Foreign Secretary, 20 July and 26 Sept. (CP (51) 212 and 257 – CAB 129/46 and 47); *FRUS*, 1952–1954 x esp. pp.207, 230–1; C.M. Wodehouse, *Something Ventured* (St. Albans, 1982) p.111. Britain was in fact prepared to accept, as did the eventual 1954 settlement, the principle of Iranian nationalisation *provided AIOC retained operational control*; but Morrison (once the architect of Labour's own nationalisations) easily got excited – Acheson recalls him as expounding 'what seemed oddly heterodox socialist doctrine – that Iran by setting the terrible precedent of taking over property without justification was making strong action necessary' (*Present at the Creation* p.510)

The alternative to force was boycott. In May 1951 the AIOC secured the backing of the other oil majors, who had every interest in discouraging nationalisation. Thus fortified, it refused to accept that oil offered for shipment was now the property of the National Iranian Oil Company; Mossadegh would not permit its export without such acceptance; so lifting from Abadan stopped in June. The AIOC closed the Abadan oil refinery in July. None of the large companies would touch Iranian oil; despite one or two picturesque episodes,[9] the boycott held. Oil was not in short supply, and the hole left by the disappearance of Iranian output was easily met by increased production elsewhere, notably Iraq and Kuwait.[10] So the AIOC could afford to wait, whereas the Iranian government (though less damaged than some had anticipated by the loss of its oil revenue) came under increasing pressure, fell behindhand in paying the army, and was eventually forced to raid pension funds.[11]

The United States was caught between Britain and Iran. Both Truman and Acheson had a certain sympathy for the Iranian position, and both accepted Mossadegh's claim that, unless he was enabled to succeed, Iran would go communist. On the other hand, Britain was their major ally. Truman was to express some of his frustration in a private letter:

> We tried . . . to get the block headed British to have their oil company make a fair deal with Iran. No, they could not do that. They knew all about how to handle it – we didn't according to them.
>
> We had Israel, Egypt, near east defense, Sudan, South Africa, Tunisia, the NATO treaties all on the fire. Britain and the Commonwealth Nations were and are absolutely essential if these things are [to be] successful. Then, on top of it all we have Korea and Indo-China. Iran was only one incident.[12]

In this situation the Americans tried repeatedly to mediate and get Anglo-Iranian negotiations going. They acquired additional purchase when, in mid-1952, the International Court ruled that it had

9. One tanker was forced into Aden, where a court pronounced its oil the property of AIOC. Twelve other ships loaded Iranian oil (mostly at a 50 per cent risk discount), and courts in Italy and Japan found against AIOC. But the Italian government stopped most of the oil being sold by refusing import licenses: *Keesing's*, 13170

10. Sampson, *The Seven Sisters* pp.135–6; Venn, *Oil Diplomacy* p.172; Acheson, *Present at the Creation* pp.509–10

11. Barry Rubin, *Paved with Good Intentions: The American Experience and Iran* (New York, 1980) pp.72, 80

12. Nov. 1952 – Farhad Diba, *Mohammed Mossadegh: A Political Biography* (1986) pp.131–2

no jurisdiction (since the 1933 oil agreement had not constituted a formal treaty). This led London to soften its stand; Churchill agreed in August 1952 to a joint Anglo-American offer whereby the International Court should rule on the amount of compensation that Iran should pay in respect of nationalisation, AIOC should take (at current prices) the oil then in storage, and there should be negotiations on marketing future production through AIOC. Mossadegh regarded this continued link with AIOC as unacceptable; he counterclaimed for prior payment of substantial back taxes and royalties, and negotiations collapsed.[13] In October he broke off relations with Britain, which he correctly suspected of plotting a coup against him.

Mossadegh worried about the difficulties of selling a compromise agreement to 'my fanatics', and he felt that the USA would eventually have to support him on his own terms. He nearly succeeded. By November Acheson was so afraid Iran was being driven communist that he persuaded Truman to authorise unilateral US action, if necessary. He then put to both the British and the US oil majors a plan whereby, provided Mossadegh agreed to arbitration on compensation, the USA would advance him $100 million. Both the compensation and the loan would be repaid from future Iranian oil production, to be marketed if necessary by US companies. Neither the British nor the US oil majors were enthusiastic, and their acquiescence took time to secure. So discussions with Mossadegh had only just started by the time that Eisenhower and Dulles took over in Washington in January 1953. At first they continued the negotiations; but when Mossadegh kept shifting his position, and ultimately (as the British now expected) turned down the proposed deal, they allowed Eden to persuade them in March to let it drop.[14]

Eden had always been 'unable to accept the American view that the only alternative to Mussadeq is communism', and in November 1952 he told Acheson that they would 'be better occupied looking for alternatives to Mussadeq rather than trying to buy him off'.[15] Initially the British simply hoped to persuade the Shah to choose another Prime Minister. Since they could not guarantee his throne if this turned Mossadegh against him, the Shah was reluctant to do

13. Carlton, *Eden* pp.315–16; Eden, *Full Circle* esp. pp.207–8; Acheson, *Present at the Creation* pp.680–1; Rubin, *Paved with Good Intentions* p.74

14. Eden, *Full Circle* pp.209–13; Carlton, *Eden* pp.316–17, 324–5; Acheson, *Present at the Creation* pp.681–5; Rubin, *Paved with Good Intentions* pp.68, 74–5, 77

15. Carlton, *Eden* pp.306, 316

so. In July 1952, however, he replaced Mossadegh (after a quarrel over domestic issues).[16] This led to mass demonstrations, and the Shah backed down.

Another approach was covert action. Morrison had authorised some initial moves, but his Conservative successors were more cautious. In October 1952, Eden decided the operation would have no chance without US backing, and this became all the more necessary as diplomatic relations were broken off that month, thus depriving Secret Intelligence Service agents in Iran of cover. So Britain turned to the CIA for assistance. Given Acheson's likely reaction, the CIA waited for the advent of the new Republican administration. This was quite as determined as Acheson to prevent Iran going communist, but was prepared to try another route. Joint planning with the British seems to have begun in February 1953; 'Operation Ajax' was approved in June; Eisenhower gave the final go-ahead in August, when Mossadegh opened trade talks with the USSR.[17] By then the National Front was breaking up, and Mossadegh was becoming both increasingly dictatorial and perilously dependent on communist support. Operation Ajax sought to mobilise against him the Shah, the army, and (with the aid of some bribery) the bazaar and a Teheran mob. It nearly went wrong, as the Shah was indecisive and as Mossadegh received prior warning of his impending dismissal. He hit back, and the Shah fled abroad to the accompaniment of anti-royalist communist riots. Mossadegh suppressed these, and so was accorded no communist support when the army and mob finally moved against him. The Shah was thus triumphantly restored, at a cost of (at most) $10 million–20 million, plus an emergency loan of $45 million to the new government,[18] a success that gave the Eisenhower administration an unduly favourable view of the potential of covert action.

16. Diba, *Mossadegh* pp.148, 153–5, 157, 180

17. Wodehouse, *Something Ventured* pp.111 ff; Edward Mortimer, 'When Britain Brought off a Coup', *The Times*, 27 May 1985 p.10; Ambrose, *Eisenhower* pp. 110–12; Rubin, *Paved with Good Intentions* pp.77–81; Prados, *President's Secret Wars* pp.92–8; Kermit Roosevelt, *Countercoup: The Struggle for the Control of Iran* (New York, 1979) *passim.* Eden became increasingly irresolute, but his 1953 illness left Churchill free to give the go-ahead; likewise the State Department tried to abort the operation in August when it seemed at first to have misfired, but the British held up the signal

18. Prados, *President's Secret Wars* p.97; *Keesing's*, 13169. The USSR was aware of the plots against Mossadegh, but apparently so distrusted him as a bourgeois nationalist that it took a detached view; not for some months did the true implications of his fall sink in: Vladislav M. Zubok, *Soviet Intelligence and the Cold War: The "Small" Committee of Information, 1952–53* (*Cold War International History Project*, Working Paper no. 4, 1992) pp.20–2

The road had been opened to a settlement of the oil question. Negotiations were difficult, but a settlement was reached, and approved by the majlis, in 1954. Nationalisation (with compensation) was allowed to stand. But the National Iranian Oil Company would sell for *sterling* to a consortium of which AIOC would have the largest share, while the risk would be spread by other companies buying into the remainder.[19] The consortium participants privately agreed a formula for determining the amount of oil they would lift in any given year. Iran's take thus improved to 50/50; but essential control remained with the companies, and Mossadegh's fall was a powerful encouragement to leave it there.

THE FOUNDATION OF OPEC 1960

This state of affairs continued until the late 1960s. But the Suez affair constituted a warning of the potential consequences of Middle Eastern instability: the Canal was blocked and the pipeline across Syria blown up. Middle Eastern oil cost less to produce than any other, and Eisenhower worried that the USA might become dangerously dependent on it; so in 1957–9 he introduced import quotas. The effect was to increase the competition, and thus lower the price, in other markets – notably Western Europe. So great was the competition that, in 1959–60, the oil majors cut their 'posted prices' in such a way as to reduce the host countries' revenue per barrel by 15 per cent. Iraq responded by calling a meeting in September 1960, attended by the chief Gulf producers plus Venezuela, that gave rise to an Organisation of Petroleum Exporting Countries (OPEC).[20]

OPEC's achievements in its first decade were not negligible; they were mostly defensive, however, and an attempt to support prices by limiting production proved unavailing. Such management remained the province of the oil majors; and they were chiefly pressed to pump more, particularly by states like Iran that badly wanted money for their ambitious development programmes.

19. The final outcome was a 40% share for AIOC (BP), 14% for the Dutch-British Shell, 6% for the Compagnie Française des Pétroles, and the remainder for the five US majors plus nine US independents: *Keesing's*, 13717–18; Sampson, *Seven Sisters* pp.144–7

20. Ambrose, *Eisenhower* pp.446–7; Venn, *Oil Diplomacy* pp.121, 125–6, 128–31; Sampson, *Seven Sisters* pp.174 ff; Daniel Yergin, *The Prize: The Epic Quest for Oil, Money, and Power* (1991) pp.511–23, 536–8

LIBYA'S REVOLUTION (1969) AND SUCCESSFUL CONFRONTATION WITH THE OIL COMPANIES (1970)

By the end of the 1960s, however, there were signs of a change. Libya started producing only in 1961, but by 1969 it was supplying one-quarter of Western Europe's needs. Its aged and conservative King Idris was then toppled in a coup; this would probably not have been difficult to reverse, but neither Britain nor the USA was prepared to try.[21] Some people claim that this refusal, and the imminence of British military withdrawal from the Gulf, made conservative rulers less likely to restrain their economic demands in order to secure Western protection. Be that as it may, the new Libyan ruler, Colonel Ghadaffi, was anxious to take control of his oil, and proved to be in a very strong position: with its tiny population Libya had no desperate need of money and could sit out a fall in revenue. Its oil was not easy to replace, both for reasons of quality and because, now that the Suez Canal had been closed by the 1967 Six Day War, it was the only oil within easy reach of Europe. It was worked not only by the oil majors but also by smaller independent companies. Since these often had no alternative supplies, they needed continuous Libyan production to meet their contracts; as they had prospered by price-cutting, they were resented by the majors at whose expense this had been done. When Libya's initial demands were resisted, Ghadaffi first concentrated on the independent Occidental, and in mid-1970 ordered it to cut its production sharply in the name of conservation. Occidental could afford a confrontation only if it could get oil from somewhere else, and so begged Exxon (which was also in dispute with Libya) for a cut-price supply. Exxon would offer oil only at commercial rates. Occidental therefore came to terms with Libya. It was soon followed by another concession largely worked by independents, though Shell refused to sign. Shell and BP (the former AIOC) then sought

21. Britain rejected a plea from Idris's entourage for immediate intervention. With Italy, it also blocked attempts in 1970–1 to mount a freelance mercenary raid designed to touch off a rising against the Ghadaffi regime. In the USA there was some consideration of covert action, but a general consensus that the USA should instead seek good relations with the new regime (which it in fact warned of one prospective coup): Patrick Seale and Maureen McConville, *The Hilton Assignment* (1973) pp.44, 180–1, and *passim*; Kissinger, *Memoirs* ii pp.859–60. In 1977 the USA dissuaded Sadat from invading Libya to topple Ghadaffi, but in 1985 it proposed to Egypt joint action against him and was turned down by Mubarak: *Daily Telegraph*, 23 April 1984 p.20; *International Herald Tribune*, 3 April 1986 p.1

both British government backing and a common front with the other oil majors, but to no avail. When the British Foreign Secretary consulted his West European counterparts he found no disposition to risk the interruption of oil supplies. Two of the oil majors proved reluctant to join a common front; nor did the US State Department encourage them. Instead the companies progressively settled with Libya.[22]

PROFITS AND PARTICIPATION AGREEMENTS 1971–3

This proved only the beginning. In December 1970 OPEC formulated new targets and called for negotiations. In response the majors and leading independents determined to negotiate a single deal with OPEC, and agreed to support any company that was picked off individually (especially by Libya). They secured US government blessing and diplomatic support, but the presidential envoy sent to the Gulf to prepare the ground gave way on the issue of the single deal; the episode did not encourage the companies to entrust governments with subsequent negotiations.[23] The producing countries then took a tough line and secured considerable price increases, but deals were struck in 1971 (with the Gulf producers and with Libya) that were intended to last for five years. Attention immediately switched to demands for 'participation'. Relatively harmonious negotiations yielded Saudi Arabia and the Gulf States a 25 per cent stake in oil operations on their territory, which was to rise to 51 per cent by 1983. Other countries were more precipitate. Libya nationalised all BP's operations (in retaliation for British acquiescence in Iran's occupation of the Tunbs Islands – see p. 366) and took a 50 per cent share in those of other companies. Iraq came close to a major confrontation in 1972, with the nationalisation of most of its oil-fields and threats (admittedly never implemented) by the Iraq Petroleum Company (IPC) to contest the legal ownership of Iraqi oil exports. Participation developed a momentum of its own; Iran was at first not interested, then changed tune abruptly in 1973 and demanded it.

Although the pattern varied from country to country, oil

22. Sampson, *Seven Sisters* chap. 10; Venn, *Oil Diplomacy* pp.136–8; Kissinger, *Memoirs* ii pp.859–62

23. Kissinger, *Memoirs* ii pp.863–74, 867; Sampson, *Seven Sisters* pp.231–2

producers demonstrated more solidarity than consumers. Thus OAPEC lent Iraq £54 million to cover loss of earnings during its dispute. But though France sought to block oil deals with (and World Bank loans to) its former colony Algeria when this took over French undertakings in 1971, it had since 1967 been helping Iraq to develop concessions taken from IPC;[24] on the latter's nationalisation, it readily agreed to continue to lift Iraqi oil. France was only on the fringes of the Seven Sisters oil establishment, and since 1967 had generally sought preferential relations with the Arab world through arms sales and the dropping of its earlier support for Israel. Italy too moved promptly to secure Iraqi oil in exchange for crucial expertise and equipment; it had long resented the dominance of the Seven Sisters and sought to bypass them both by importing cheap Soviet oil and by independent prospecting (often offering host countries better terms than did the oil majors). However the oil majors themselves now proved accommodating – more so than Kissinger wished – and were never prepared to resist for long; even IPC settled in February 1973.[25] Their chief concern was now no longer ownership but security of oil supply.

THE FIRST OIL SHOCK 1973

This reflected a fundamental change in the market. During the 1967 Six Day War Arab producers had sought to support Nasser by cutting off exports, more especially to Britain and the USA. US domestic production was increased, alternative supplies were forthcoming, and after Saudi Arabia had lost $30 million revenue in a month the boycott was dropped. The episode led to Western over-confidence; in 1969 the Nixon administration turned down an offer from the Shah of Iran (who was desperate for more revenue) of 365 million barrels of oil a year for stockpiling at $1 a barrel.[26] In fact US reserves were less than had been thought, and by 1971 all production capacity was being used. Imports rose from 19 per cent of petroleum requirements in the late 1960s to 36 per cent in 1973, as a result both of economic growth and of the relaxation of controls in response to consumer pressure for cheaper supplies.

24. *Keesing's*, 24647. This action was the more noteworthy since the Compagnie Française des Pétroles had a 24% stake in IPC

25. *Keesing's*, 25086–7, 25454–6, 25594–5, 25896–8; Kissinger, *Memoirs* ii pp.866–8

26. Kissinger, *Memoirs* ii p.857

The administration became mildly concerned, but not to the point of doing anything effective; indeed it let environmentalist pressure halt offshore drilling and the construction of a pipeline to the great new discoveries in Alaska.[27] International consultations were also held, but they too produced nothing concrete. Meanwhile a general economic boom raised consumption; in September 1973, for the first time in well over a decade, the spot market price for oil exceeded its official 'posted' price. Against this background, and further impelled by rapid inflation in the prices of the manufactures they bought from the West, the OPEC countries invited the oil companies to discuss 'substantial' price increases on 8 October 1973. The negotiations failed, OPEC demanding a price of $5 a barrel and the companies refusing to go beyond $3.75. OPEC then met in Kuwait and unilaterally determined on $5.12.[28]

By now oil prices had become entangled with the Arab–Israeli war of October 1973. We have seen that Saudi Arabia had threatened sanctions unless the United States modified its support for Israel (see p.322). Once the war had begun, Egypt lobbied for a cut-back in oil exports. After the Kuwait OPEC meeting, the Arab states went on to agree to cut production by 5 per cent a month until Israel withdrew from its 1967 conquests. The Saudi Foreign Minister proceeded to Washington to give a last warning of an embargo unless the resupply of Israel was stopped, but the day after the White House received him, it sought a $2.2 billion appropriation for deliveries to Israel.[29] So Saudi Arabia imposed both a 10 per cent production cut and an embargo on oil for the USA and the Netherlands; this reduced Aramco's planned November production by 29 per cent. Similar action was taken by other producers, though not by Iran or by Iraq (which seized the opportunity to unload oil stockpiled during its dispute with the IPC). The USA advocated a common consumer front in response; but it was disregarded since it was seen as shielded by its enormous domestic production (still the largest in the world) and was in any case blamed for having caused the trouble through its uncritically pro-Israeli policy. As far as they could, the oil majors reshuffled

27. Yergin, *The Prize* pp.567–74

28. Strictly speaking, the meeting was of OPEC's Gulf States committee: Sampson, *Seven Sisters* pp.188, 252–5, 261–5; Venn, *Oil Diplomacy* pp.139–41, 144, 176–7; Kissinger, *Memoirs* ii pp.869–70, 872

29. Kissinger claims (*Memoirs* ii p.873) that this was a largely technical request to ensure that the costs of resupplying Israel did not come out of Defense Department funds; people had worried about Arab reactions when the airlift started, but nobody thought the appropriation request would cause such resentment

supplies to circumvent the embargo, but they could do nothing about the cut-backs; nor, understandably, were they keen on supplying their independent competitors who had grown by picking up previously cheap surplus oil. So both the independents and some of the consuming countries scrambled for any extra oil that was going. Spot market prices shot up accordingly, and governments refused to limit them by withholding foreign currency. In December 1973 Iran staged an oil auction and secured bids of up to $17 a barrel, while Nigeria soon got even more. This enabled the Shah to argue that the $5.12 agreed at Kuwait was far too low. OPEC met again in Teheran; Iran now pushed for $14, but Saudi Arabia feared that too great an increase would precipitate a Western economic collapse with disastrous knock-on effects for the producers. Eventually they compromised on $11.65.[30]

THE POLITICAL EFFECTIVENESS OF THE OIL WEAPON

Over the next few months the cut-backs and embargoes related to the 1973 war were lifted, and they have not been repeated. They had certainly drawn international attention to the Arabs and their case against Israel; the United States now showed a degree of activity in promoting a settlement that had been strikingly absent after 1967. But though Kissinger was anxious to get the embargo lifted, the USA was not that heavily dependent on Arab oil. It was the Arabs' misfortune that the countries that were did not, or did not any longer, enjoy much influence over the Middle East. Thus Japan had before 1973 broadly followed the US pro-Israeli line. It was pressed to change by OAPEC, and, after some reflection and explanation to Kissinger, duly did so, thereby securing more favourable Arab treatment in future. The change was merely one of rhetoric, since Japan never sought to determine developments in the area.[31] European attitudes were a little more important, given the recent European ascendancy in the Middle East. Three Arab Foreign Ministers descended on the European Community summit in December 1973 to offer oil supplies – on condition that the

30. Sampson, *Seven Sisters* pp.264–6, 269–71, 273–7; Kissinger, *Memoirs* ii pp.872–85; Holden and Johns, *House of Saud* chaps 19, 20; Heikal, *Road to Ramadan* pp.267–71; *Keesing's*, 26224 ff., 26355

31. Kissinger, *Memoirs* ii pp.740–5; Venn, *Oil Diplomacy* p.148

Community pressed for a satisfactory Middle Eastern settlement. The Community obliged with a communiqué calling for the implementation of Resolution 242 'in all its parts, taking into account also the legitimate rights of the Palestinians'. Many West European states had doubts about US Middle Eastern policy that had led them to obstruct US resupply of Israel during the war. Kissinger suspected France of using these doubts to distance 'Europe' diplomatically from the USA. Little came of it. France certainly sought an official 'European–Arab dialogue', while Kissinger feared that this would encourage the formulation of extreme Arab positions and undercut his preferred step-by-step approach. Whether because of US hostility or of changes in many European governments, the dialogue was instituted so slowly as to have little effect: the first full meetings were held only in 1976, and then only at ambassadorial level.[32] In these contacts the European Community was pressed to endorse the Palestinian position. It did indeed issue a series of friendly declarations, notably that of its 1980 Venice Council that 'The Palestinian people' should, as part of a comprehensive settlement, be enabled 'to exercise fully their right of self-determination' and that the PLO would 'have to be associated with the negotiations'.[33] However, the Community did not follow through on its stated intention to inject itself into the peace process.

Direct political consequences of the 'oil weapon' are therefore hard to find, and the most that can be claimed is that it helped mould Western public opinion. After 1973 the availability of oil could no longer be taken for granted; the Arabs trusted that the combination of readiness to supply it, Saudi solicitude for Western economic needs and large purchases by the newly rich oil states would gradually reduce Western support for Israel. To some extent these hopes were justified: despite revulsion against acts of Palestinian terrorism, Western sympathies for Israel have indeed cooled. Oil may well have been a factor; but it can only have been one among many, since the decline in Israel's standing continued in the 1980s when oil was no longer in short supply. So it seems reasonable to look rather to the economic than to the political effects of the transformation in 1973 of the world of oil.

32. Kissinger, *Memoirs* ii pp.709 ff, 727, 898, 900; *Keesing's*, 26350–1, 26545–6, 27571, 28049

33. *Keesing's*, 28656, 29426, 30635

OPEC IN THE 1970s

Prices had nearly quadrupled, and the producing countries had taken over from the Seven Sisters the general control of production. There was some US talk of seizing oilfields if consumers were really held over a barrel; but nothing of the kind was ever attempted, and prices were left to more peaceful determination. For nearly a decade the negotiations and OPEC meetings that effected this held the international limelight (especially in 1976, when terrorists broke into one such meeting and seized the delegates). Saudi Arabia proved the most influential player. It had great capacity and could expand oil production to alleviate shortages; but, with its small population, it stood in no desperate need of money and could afford to cut production when oil was in over-supply. With these advantages, it embraced the mission of stabilising the market and leading OPEC, though it did not always prove successful. In September 1975 the other OPEC states insisted on a price increase; in May 1976 Saudi Arabia secured a price freeze. In December 1976 Saudi Arabia and the United Arab Emirates (UAE) refused to go along with a price increase implemented by the rest of OPEC, but in mid-1977 they accepted it on condition that there was no further rise. Iran, previously a hawk, then joined them in working for the continuance of this freeze throughout 1978.[34] Meanwhile, and partly in response to the 1973 increase, inflation had accelerated sharply in most developed countries and had started to erode OPEC's earlier gains.[35] So when demand for oil, which had been weak in 1977–8, started to recover, OPEC agreed in December 1978 to phase in a 10 per cent increase.

THE SECOND OIL SHOCK 1979–80

Iranian output had been much reduced by the unrest accompanying the 1978–9 collapse of the Shah (see pp.369–70), and

34. Holden and Johns, *House of Saud* chap. 23 and pp.484, 489; *Keesing's*, 27529, 28065, 28895–7, 29981 ff. Yergin ascribes Iran's switch partly to the Shah's recognition that he could not spend all the money it was earning, and partly to his need to conciliate President Carter (whose human rights policy was potentially destabilising): *The Prize* pp.645–6

35. One index of the relationship between oil prices and OPEC imports from industrial countries moved from 28 in 1972 to 100 in 1974, 92 in 1976 and 77 in the second half of 1978 : *Keesing's*, 29982

Saudi production was raised close to capacity to offset this loss. On 26 December 1978 Iranian exports stopped altogether, resuming only in late February 1979 and at levels deliberately reduced by the new regime. The combination of a tight supply situation, cold weather, and alarm on the part of Iran's previous customers led to another scramble. The spot price for Gulf crudes was $2.90 a barrel above the official OPEC price in January 1979, $9 in February and March. Late in January Abu Dhabi held an auction and secured strong Japanese bids; other countries followed suit or levied surcharges; a March OPEC meeting gave member-states *carte blanche* to set their own rates. By July 1979 prices varied from 42 per cent to 69 per cent above those of the previous December.

When the dust settled it transpired that the problem had been more one of disorientation of the market than of absolute shortage: in 1979 world oil production rose by 4.1 per cent, OPEC production by 3.3 per cent, and world consumption only by 1.2 per cent.[36] But the disorientation continued. One factor was the Iranian detention of US diplomats as hostages, which led in November 1979 to a US embargo on Iranian exports and an Iranian refusal in return to sell oil to any US company. Another was the tendency of surcharges by one OPEC country to set off leap-frogging increases elsewhere. Together this took the weighted average of official OPEC prices from $21 a barrel in October 1979 to almost $32 in May 1980, a level then formally adopted by OPEC.

Here consumer resistance began to be encountered, and in September 1980 OPEC started to talk of production cuts to defend price levels. In October the outbreak of war between Iraq and Iran raised the prospect of another price explosion, but this time it did not happen. Spot prices rose, but the volume of trading did not. The consumer countries' International Energy Agency (founded in 1974, but completely ineffective in the 1979 crisis) managed to persuade them to draw on their now considerable stockpiles. By early 1981 the crisis had passed; the hostages were released, sanctions on Iran eased, and both Iraq and Iran were anxious to push exports to pay for their war. Demand fell in the importing countries, partly through economic recession and partly because past price rises had at length brought energy savings and switches to other fuels. Yet Saudi Arabia continued to expand production – to a peak of 10.2 million barrels per day (bpd) in August 1981, or half OPEC's total output – to force OPEC to reunify its pricing. In

36. *Keesing's*, 29987, 29993, 30563

October it gained its point with the adoption of a $34 per barrel marker price, and cut production to its preferred level of 8.5 million bpd.[37]

FALLING OIL PRICES 1982–7

By 1981 trends were broadly adverse to OPEC. Since 1973 its success had multiplied its members' incomes and further hastened their take-over of operations on their territories.[38] It had also helped them conserve their reserves, since they could now get the same income from pumping less; even Saudi Arabia, which sometimes raised production to offset shortfalls elsewhere and so relieve pressure on the West, never approached the target of 20 million bpd that had been under discussion in 1972.[39] But if OPEC production was thus contained, higher prices stimulated development elsewhere, notably in the North Sea, much of which would have been uneconomic at pre-1973 price levels. By 1982 Mexico and the UK had overtaken all OPEC members except Saudi Arabia, and OPEC production had fallen to below a half of non-communist oil output (from two-thirds in the 1970s). OPEC was thus on the defensive, and 1982–3 brought a cut in the marker price and the introduction of production quotas for its members. By mid-1985 such measures no longer sufficed. The ending of a British coal strike cut demand for heavy fuel oil, and spot prices started falling. Most OPEC states introduced discounts. To preserve the system Saudi Arabia kept up its prices and lost sales sharply, its production falling to 2.3 million bpd. In July 1985 it formally abandoned the role of swing producer and began to compete for market share. In December OPEC started a price war, with Nigeria promising to 'match the North Sea producers barrel by barrel and cent by cent'. North Sea Brent crude, which had stood at $27.92 for most of 1985, accordingly fell to a trough of $9.63 in July 1986. In real terms this took oil prices back to levels obtaining before the great 1973 rise.[40] The UK, much of whose economy stood to gain from cheap oil, was unmoved. But Vice-President Bush (who had a Texas oil background) was not; in April 1987 he urged Saudi Arabia to take

37. *Keesing's*, 31237 ff; Yergin, *The Prize* esp. pp.685–90, 702–6, 711–14

38. This was not now resisted; indeed compensation for such takeovers constituted a convenient way of 'recycling' surplus oil revenues

39. Neff, *Warriors Against Israel* p.111

40. Yergin, *The Prize* p.792

action, hinting that otherwise the USA might itself firm up prices through a tariff. In May a small meeting of oil ministers in Saudi Arabia focused on $18 a barrel as a level that might prove acceptable to both producers and consumers. Wall Street (scarred by recent losses on oil-related loans) and Japan (whose balance of payments surplus was being embarrassingly swollen by cheap oil) found the idea of stability at this level attractive. In August OPEC reintroduced quotas; it later secured promises of production restraint from Mexico, Norway and the USSR; in December 1987 it agreed to aim at a price of $18.

IRAQ'S ANNEXATION OF KUWAIT 1990 AND THE CONSEQUENT GYRATIONS IN OIL PRICES

By and large this level was maintained, despite a crisis in the autumn of 1988.[41] In 1990 prices began to weaken. One reason was the tendency of some countries, notably Kuwait and the UAE, to exceed their quotas; there was a good deal of pressure on them to conform. This was led by Iraq, which had embarked on an extremely ambitious military build-up and physical reconstruction after the end of its war with Iran, and which was facing an annual deficit of $3.5 billion. It claimed that every dollar fall in the price of oil cost it $1 billion; in July Iraq accused Kuwait and the UAE of implementing an 'international scheme to glut the oil market', and moved troops towards the Kuwaiti border. Against this background, OPEC agreed to raise its reference price to $21. But the pressure on Kuwait continued, and in August 1990 Iraq suddenly seized and annexed it (see pp.375–6). Had this coup succeeded, Iraq would have controlled 20 per cent of OPEC production and would have had a formidable influence on oil pricing, especially as Saudi Arabia and the UAE would have been militarily at its mercy. Instead the UN blocked the export of both Iraqi and Kuwaiti oil. Some hawks wanted to take advantage of this shortfall; but, at the insistence of the (now thoroughly alarmed) Gulf States and of Venezuela, OPEC instead agreed to suspend all restraints, with the result that its overall production actually rose. Prices initially shot up, passing $40 in September 1990, then stabilised around $29. They were generally

41. *Keesing's*, 32705 ff, 34702 ff, 34721, 35099 ff, 36057 ff, 36573 ff; Yergin, *The Prize* pp.746–51, 756–62, 764

expected to return to $40 in the event of war, but the first bombing of Iraq seemed so successful that instead they collapsed to $20, and were prevented from rising by stockpile releases agreed through the International Energy Agency. The crisis was accordingly surmounted with far less disruption than had once seemed likely. By June 1991 the price was again down to $18, but Saudi Arabia set its face against production cuts to drive it back up to $21.[42] Over the next eighteen months, prices tended to weaken – despite disruption in the former Soviet Union and the UN's continued exclusion of most Iraqi oil from world markets – as OPEC found difficulty in holding members to their quotas. In November 1992 Saudi Arabia finally conceded token cuts in OPEC's production targets. Perhaps more serious was Ecuador's decision to leave OPEC, though it is too soon to say whether this will have any important sequels.[43]

42. *Keesing's*, 37299, 37631–2, 37641, 37758, 37930, 37943, 37988, 38315, 38459; Yergin, *The Prize* p.773

43. *Keesing's*, 39120, 39128, 1992 R157

CHAPTER FIFTEEN

Arabia and the Gulf

Before 1973 Arabia and the Gulf attracted little international attention: in 1968 Saudi Arabia received only half the *New York Times* coverage of Albania. In part this is because both the oil companies and most of their hosts preferred a low profile. Also the area lacked the high drama of the Arab–Israeli conflict, and this often led people to overlook its real importance. There had, in the 1960s, been two basic and interlocking problems: domestic stability; and the question of whose influence would become dominant if the British abandoned their position in Aden and the small Arab Gulf sheikhdoms.

SAUDI ARABIA 1953–75

Saudi Arabia's stability was most immediately threatened by disputes within its ruling family. King Saud, who had succeeded his father in 1953, had not proved a success: he had distanced himself from the rest of the royal family, had over-spent to the verge of bankruptcy, and had been humiliated by the revelation of his attempts to buy influence in (and supposedly assassinate the President of) Syria. In 1958 his family forced Saud to turn over day-to-day control to his brother, Feisal, who embarked on an austerity programme. Although this proved successful, its unpopularity helped Saud resume power in 1960; for some time control alternated between the two, in response partly to Saud's health, partly to external developments. In December 1963 their rivalry led to ominous troop mobilisations, but in 1964 the royal family and religious leaders finally forced Saud to abdicate and go into exile (where he gravitated towards Nasser). Feisal succeeded to the throne. His reign was not without troubles – a religious attack on the newly introduced television station, some republican plotting, and an intended coup in 1969. In 1975 he was finally murdered by a radical young prince, but overall he had restored the Kingdom to an even keel.[1]

CIVIL WAR IN (NORTH) YEMEN 1963–70

Time was when this had looked most unlikely. In the aftermath of the September 1962 coup in the Yemen (see p.303), the dissident Saudi prince Talal announced plans 'to establish a national democratic government'. Nasser was soon allowing his 'Arab National Liberation Front' radio propaganda time. British newspapers concluded that the Saudi monarchy was now 'at the top of the list of prospective candidates for liquidation'. Talal had hoped that developments in Yemen 'would precipitate the evolution of events in the Arabian peninsula' towards his objectives.[2] In fact the Yemeni civil war became a proxy struggle over the peninsula's destiny. Saudi Arabia promptly started ferrying arms and money to the royalists;[3] common fear of Nasser led to the restoration of cooperation with the UK (discontinued after the Buraimi Oasis dispute) and to British weapons supplies via Aden.[4] On the other side, Egypt had probably had a hand in the original coup;[5] its backing for the Republic was early and massive. By November 1962 Egyptian forces were bombing and shelling Saudi border villages. The situation was temporarily stabilised by US air and naval demonstrations,[6] but subsequent attempts to mediate, and procure external disengagement from Yemen, first by the USA, then in 1963–4 by the UN, proved ineffective.

In dispatching troops, Nasser probably anticipated the rapid

1. Lacy, *The Kingdom* chaps 34–40, pp.426–7
2. ibid, p.342; Holden and Johns, *House of Saud* pp.227,237; *Keesing's*, 19298; admittedly Talal made his peace with Feisal in 1963
3. Four Saudi aircraft soon defected to Egypt in protest, and were later joined by the head of the Jordanian air force: *Keesing's*, 19298, 19300
4. Holden and Johns, *House of Saud* p.229. For the Buraimi Oasis dispute see p.279n
5. Holden and Johns, *House of Saud*, p.224; David, *Third World Coups* p.144
6. *Keesing's*, 19301; in exchange Feisal had promised President Kennedy a programme of internal reforms, including the ending of slavery: Lacy, *The Kingdom* pp.344–5

consolidation of the revolution in Yemen and perhaps its further expansion. But though it ruled the bulk of the population, the Republic could not control the tribes of the mountainous interior. Nasser thus found himself saddled with the continuing commitment of from 20,000 to 70,000 troops to a lengthy counter-insurgency, in the course of which he apparently used poison gas. In 1964–5 he did seek a settlement in negotiations with Saudi Arabia, but neither country could control its local partisans. Relations then worsened again as Nasser disliked Saudi advocacy of an Islamic summit. In 1966 Britain's unexpected declaration that it intended to leave Aden in two years' time provided Nasser with an incentive to stay on – especially as the USSR was covering a good deal of the cost. But after his sudden 1967 defeat by Israel, he needed his soldiers back and had to look to Arabia and the Gulf for subsidies; a deal was therefore reached with Feisal at the Khartoum summit, and Egyptian troops had withdrawn by December 1967. This appeared to leave the way open for a Saudi-backed royalist victory. But the Republic reconstituted itself, shedding the leaders that the Egyptians had imposed on it; with the aid of airlifted Soviet weapons and of Syrian pilots, it managed to beat back royalist assaults on the capital San'aa. Thereafter moderates gradually came to the fore within the Republic, and in 1970 Saudi Arabia mediated a settlement between them and their ex-royalist counterparts.[7] The Kingdom did not thereafter entirely resist the temptation to stir up the tribes; but for the most part it cemented relations with generous aid, and was further helped by friction between the Republic and South Yemen that led in 1979 to fighting. During this fighting North Yemen leaned heavily on Saudi and US support, but it would not seem to have played, or sought, a role in the internal politics of any country other than South Yemen.

THE BRITISH EVACUATION OF ADEN (1967)

Macmillan had noted of the 1962 Yemen revolution that 'This means great danger to Aden . . . and if we were to be driven out of Aden or faced with serious revolutionary troubles . . . which might make the [British] base useless, our whole authority over the

7. Stephens, *Nasser* chaps 14, 15; Peter Mangold, *Superpower Intervention in the Middle East* (1978) p.86; Holden and Johns, *House of Saud* chaps 15, 16; *Keesing's*, esp. 22204, 24053

Gulf would disappear'. Britain had been slow to decolonise Aden, but by the early 1960s had determined to do so by merging it with the protected states of the interior: 'The real problem', Macmillan had noted in 1961, 'is how to use the influence and power of the [inland] Sultans to help us keep the Colony and its essential defence facilities'.[8] In 1963 Aden was accordingly brought into the South Arabian Federation in the face of opposition from many sectors of its urbanised population, opposition that was encouraged by the republican regime in the Yemen and by the UN's Special Committee on Colonialism. In 1964 it was agreed that the Federation should become independent in 1968.

The intention was that the British base should continue to function thereafter (as had that in Malaya). But in February 1966 the British government announced that it would be discontinued. This decision put British backing for the Federation in doubt, and seemed to open up the whole future of south-west Arabia. It is widely credited with encouraging Nasser to stay on in the Yemen despite his 1965 disengagement agreement. King Feisal took the gloomiest of views, urging Wilson strongly in 1967 to reverse the decision and undertake to defend the Federation against attacks or subversion.

> He spoke passionately about President Nasser's expansionist aims; in most of the affected Middle-East states including the Gulf sheikhdoms, he said, there were seditious groups ready to go into action when . . . Nasser gave the signal. Unless we held firm in Southern Arabia, the Gulf would be subverted within months.[9]

Egypt's defeat in the 1967 Six Day War halted any plans Nasser may have had in this direction. But the Egyptian forces in Yemen had been supporting two rival South Arabian resistance movements, the Front for the Liberation of South Yemen (FLOSY) and the National Liberation Front (NLF). FLOSY, headed by Aden intellectuals and trades unionists, attracted more international attention, and the backing of the UN Committee on Colonialism. However in August–September 1967 the NLF unexpectedly drove out the sheikhs and took control of all the Federation except Aden itself. Sharp street fighting followed in Aden between FLOSY and the NLF (as well as against the British). Eventually both the British and the Federation's army recognised the NLF; in November 1967

8. Macmillan, *Memoirs* vi pp.265, 268
9. Wilson, *The Labour Government 1964–1970* p.396

the former Federation became independent as the People's (later the People's Democratic) Republic of South Yemen.[10]

MARXIST SOUTH YEMEN AND ITS NEIGHBOURS; THE DHOFARI INSURGENCY IN OMAN; UNIFICATION OF THE TWO YEMENS (1990)

Its name indicated Marxist leanings. These were strengthened in 1969 by a coup, after which the new government declared for the consolidation of relations with the USSR and promised increased aid to the 'Liberation Front of the Arab Gulf'. Relations with the Soviet Union prospered, and Soviet forces came in the 1970s to use former British base facilities. During the 1977–8 Somali–Ethiopian war South Yemen played a key role in the airlifting to Ethiopia of vital supplies and Cuban troops; when, for internal political reasons, it seemed about to disengage, Cuban and Soviet forces helped stage a coup to prevent it. The relationship was cemented in 1979 by a twenty-year treaty of friendship, and Soviet personnel supposedly increased to 15,000.[11] Domestic rivalries continued, however, with the most pro-Soviet leader, Abdel Ismail, moving to exile in Moscow in 1980. In 1985 he returned, and in January 1986 heavy fighting broke out in which the more extreme party triumphed. This time the USSR stood on the sidelines, and the world was treated to the spectacle of Soviet civilians being evacuated by the royal yacht *Britannia*, which happened to be passing by.[12]

Within Arabia, South Yemen certainly seemed an alien presence. From the outset the Saudis provided small-scale aid to the regime's opponents, and this was stepped up after 1970 (partly to ease South Yemen's pressure on its neighbours).[13] South Yemen retaliated in kind. It also, from 1968, provided facilities for the Marxist 'Popular Front for the Liberation of the Occupied Arab Gulf' (PFLOAG), and helped funnel Soviet, Chinese (until 1972), Cuban and Libyan assistance to the insurgency in the west Oman province of Dhofar. In 1973 PFLOAG claimed to control one-sixth of Oman, and announced its intention of liberating the Gulf Emirates. But the tide had already begun to turn. Oman had acquired a new and

10. *Keesing's*, esp. 19435–7, 21264, 21289–94, 22411–18; Stephens, *Nasser* pp.422–4
11. *Keesing's*, 23451–2, 29289–90, 30199; David, *Third World Coups* pp.89–91
12. *Keesing's*, 34393 ff
13. *Keesing's*, 25654; Holden and Johns, *House of Saud* pp.272, 281–2, 303–4

more effective ruler in 1970 (see p.366); from 1972 his (British-commanded) forces were able to take the offensive aided by Iranian and (briefly) Jordanian troops. South Yemen increased its involvement, but in 1975 its 300–400 troops were finally driven out and the Dhofari insurgents mopped up. In 1976 there was a formal Oman–South Yemen cease-fire.[14]

South Yemen, then, failed to destabilise its eastern neighbour, and its existence helped relations between Saudi Arabia and Yemen. For though in theory the two Yemens sought unity, in practice they were usually hostile. Against this background North Yemen was happy to accept Saudi aid; in 1975 Saudi mediation induced it to turn for arms supplies to the USA and to freeze dealings with the USSR (though these resumed in 1979). Border fighting between the Yemens had been particularly serious in 1972. Then in 1978, after a period of détente, South Yemen's power struggle spilt over into the assassination of the North Yemen President. Clashes followed, culminating early in 1979 in a South Yemeni invasion that precipitated a Saudi defence alert and US fleet movements before it was ended by Arab League mediation.[15]

Thereafter talks about Yemeni reunification resumed, to Saudi Arabia's concern. They were interrupted by the 1986 fighting in South Yemen, as the defeated President and his partisans fled to the North, where they were maintained as a military force on the border. The new hostility was inconvenient – border clashes disrupted the search for oil – and official North–South contacts gradually picked up. In 1988 it was agreed to resume the unification process; December 1989 to January 1990 saw the publication of a draft Constitution (envisaging, in tune with the times, a multi-party state) and the opening of the border. In May 1990 the two Yemens formally united, despite some resistance by strongly Muslim tribes in the North that was supposedly stimulated by Saudi Arabia. Saudi Arabia had in fact some cause for concern, as the new state had a population not far short of its own and could potentially complicate its domination of the Arabian peninsula. Their relations promptly deteriorated, as Yemen sympathised with Iraq during the Gulf crisis and the Kingdom retaliated by expelling some 800,000 Yemeni guest-workers.[16]

14. *Keesing's,* 25180, 25654, 26579–80, 26988, 27716; Mangold, *Superpower Intervention in the Middle East* pp.93, 99; John Akehurst, *We Won a War. The Campaign in Oman 1965–1975* (Salisbury, 1982) *passim*

15. *Keesing's,* 25654–5, 27682, 30197 ff, 30743; David, *Third World Coups* pp.89–90

16. *Keesing's,* 30745–7, 34393–7, 36176–8, 37106, 37138, 37266, 37470, 38075–6

BRITISH WITHDRAWAL FROM THE GULF 1961–71

In Aden the British had left behind them a state that was neither stable nor friendly. Their withdrawal from the Gulf proved smoother. It began with the ending in June 1961 of the 1899 treaty whereby Britain protected and controlled Kuwait. Instead a new agreement bound the parties to consult and committed Britain to supply assistance on request. In Baghdad, General Kassem saw this as a continuation of the relationship under another name, and immediately declared Kuwait 'an integral part of Iraq' on the grounds that it had once formed part of the province of Basra. Kuwait invoked British (and Saudi) aid, and troops were rushed in. In July 1961 the Arab League admitted Kuwait to membership, and from September an Arab League force progressively replaced the British. In 1963 the situation was eased by the overthrow of Kassem's regime. The Soviet Union (which had been close to that regime) now lifted its veto on Kuwait's application for UN membership. After receiving assurances that Kuwait would in due course end its treaty with Britain – and promises of a loan – Iraq accepted Kuwaiti sovereignty.[17]

Kuwait was in fact in no hurry to give up its British treaty, but Britain decided otherwise. Prime Minister Wilson was extremely reluctant to withdraw from 'East of Suez', believing the Indian Ocean to represent the area that Britain was best placed to stabilise at least cost. He was, however, under enormous party pressure to reduce defence expenditure and abandon any imperial or post-imperial role (save in connection with Ian Smith's Rhodesia). As late as November 1967 Britain was still giving assurances that it had no intention of quitting the Gulf, but it was then forced to devalue the pound. In pursuit of expenditure cuts to make devaluation stick, Wilson changed sides; and the Cabinet decided to leave by the end of 1971, despite particularly strong US pressure to stay, and Defence and Foreign Office warnings that 'any withdrawal would produce insurrection'.[18]

After this inauspicious beginning, planning for the British withdrawal went surprisingly well. The rulers of the seven small Gulf

17. *Keesing's*, 18159, 18187 ff, 18221, 18355, 19326, 19426, 19668

18. The decision to withdraw affected both Singapore/Malaysia and the Gulf; the USA deplored both, but was particularly concerned about the Gulf: Richard Crossman, *The Diaries of a Cabinet Minister* ii (1976) pp.624, 634–5, 639, 647, 650; Michael Dockrill, *British Defence since 1945* (Oxford, 1988) pp.97–8; *Keesing's*, 21494–5; see also *The Cold War* chap.14

sheikhdoms (Abu Dhabi, Dubai, Sharjah, Fujairah, Umm al-Qaiwan, Ajman and Ras al-Khaimah) agreed in 1968 to form a union. Implementation admittedly proved difficult; but eventually Bahrain and Qatar became independent on their own in mid-1971, while the remaining seven states (Ras al-Khaimah joining rather belatedly) constituted the United Arab Emirates (UAE) in December 1971. With plentiful oil money, and the use of British and other expatriates, these countries managed to consolidate themselves and, in the case of the UAE, to overcome their complicated constitutional problems. Oman was not associated with these moves; as we have seen, it had a serious insurgency problem that its ruler (who had no intention of permitting any departure from traditional practices) seemed quite unfitted to handle. In 1970 his son Qaboos displaced him with British assistance,[19] then over the next five years quelled the insurgency by a mixture of reform and military action.

External territorial disputes also had to be sorted out. One was that with Saudi Arabia over the Buraimi Oasis (see p.279n); a first attempt in 1970 failed, but the UAE and the Kingdom finally came to terms in 1974.[20] More serious were the historic Iranian claims to Bahrain and to strategic islets in the Gulf. Secret Anglo–Iranian negotiations led Iran to give up Bahrain (after a face-saving UN mission) in 1970. The Shah believed that he would secure the islets in exchange. Sharjah was persuaded to an arrangement over Abu Musa, but Ras al Khaimah was less accommodating; so Iran seized the Tunbs in November 1971, just before the expiry of the British treaty of protection. Radical Arab states made much of British acquiescence, Libya using it as a pretext for nationalisation and Iraq breaking off relations with both Britain and Iran.[21] But there were, at the time, no further consequences.

Three states were in some condition to replace Britain as the leading power in the Gulf: Saudi Arabia (which had money and diplomatic skill, but little military strength), Iraq (which was then unacceptably radical), and Iran. The Shah had always been ambitious; he was anxious to step into Britain's shoes, and in 1970 discouraged the new British Conservative government from having second thoughts about withdrawal. In 1972 Iran's position was

19. Abu Dhabi had seen the displacement of similarly unreconstructed rulers by more developmentally minded relatives in 1965–6; the ruler of Qatar was deposed in 1972: David, *Third World Coups* p.144; *Keesing's*, 21573, 25177

20. Lacey, *The Kingdom* p.447; Holden and Johns, *House of Saud* pp.276–7, 376–7

21. Holden and Johns, *House of Saud* pp.275, 300–1; *Keesing's*, 25010

confirmed by a visit from President Nixon: the two countries agreed to cooperate in supporting Kurdish insurgents against Iraq; and Iran was to be free to buy whatever US weaponry it wished. As Kissinger puts it retrospectively,

> The vacuum left by British withdrawal, now menaced by Soviet intrusion and radical momentum, would be filled by a local power friendly to us. Iraq would be discouraged from adventures against the Emirates in the lower Gulf, and against Jordan and Saudi Arabia. A strong Iran could help damp India's temptations to conclude its conquest of Pakistan.[22]

Iranian forces were only actually used in Oman. But, though it can never be proved, Iranian strength may well have been one of the reasons why the Gulf was far more stable in the 1970s than had been feared.

IRAN FROM 1960 TO THE FALL OF THE SHAH 1979

Ironically it was the Shah's regime itself that collapsed. It had gone through a difficult period in the early 1960s, when religious opposition, pressure from the bazaar, and resurgent (if illegal) National Front activity had forced the cancellation of the rigged 1960 elections. Further disturbances in 1961 compelled the Shah to appoint an uncomfortably independent Prime Minister, but in 1962 the Shah felt strong enough to force him out. The Shah continued, however, with a land reform programme that encountered massive opposition from (inter alia) clergy and tribesmen, and secured its endorsement by referendum in January 1963. Traditionalist forces were further alienated by the extension of the franchise to women; the final straw came with the renewal of privileges exempting US military advisers from prosecution. Ayatollah Khomeini, who shared the not uncommon view that the Americans surreptitiously controlled everything in Iran, burst into protest. His arrest in June 1963 touched off massive riots that were severely suppressed. Martial law was proclaimed, and a number of religious leaders placed under arrest (Khomeini himself was exiled in 1964). Thus fortified, the Shah held elections and inaugurated 'a 20-year era of construction', otherwise known as the White Revolution.[23]

22. *Keesing's*, 24500; Kissinger, *Memoirs* i p.1264
23. *Keesing's*, 17669, 18117, 18882–4, 19293, 19564, 19700; Rubin, *Paved with Good Intentions* pp.105–11

Initially this seemed a great success; in 1967 the USA felt able to end development aid since Iran (like Taiwan two years earlier) had achieved economic take-off. The Shah's policies had much in common with those of Taiwan (see pp.190–1) in that land was distributed to the peasants and landlords were encouraged to invest their compensation in industry; but they worked less well. Neither Iranian agriculture nor industry moved to export-led growth, and the country continued to depend on oil. Agriculture, indeed, retrogressed, partly because irrigation systems were neglected. Population flocked to the towns, where wealth was indeed spread, but very unevenly. The regime was seduced by the attractions of massive and high technology projects, some of them white elephants, to the neglect of more basic infrastructure and amenities. All were paid for from oil revenues, and the Shah was constantly pressing the oil companies first to expand production, then in 1973 to raise prices. The 1973 oil bonanza removed all restraints, and in 1974 the Shah decided to double the current Five-Year Plan and make Iran one of the world's leading industrial nations by the 1980s. The result was much dislocation and disastrous inflation, followed from mid-1975 by painful economic retrenchment and the harassment of bazaar merchants in the ineffective pursuit of price stability.

If the oil money was not spent wisely, other policies were probably even more damaging. The Shah was convinced that Iran was surrounded by enemies and instability, and was determined to build commensurate military strength. He had always been fascinated by advanced weaponry, and after 1972 could buy what he pleased. Unfortunately he could not operate it, so by 1976 there were 24,000 Americans in Iran to do so. They became highly conspicuous targets for xenophobia. Worse still, the Pahlavi dynasty took to insulting Islam, which the Shah (though a nominal Muslim) probably regarded as a hostile and retrogressive force. In 1976 the Islamic calendar was replaced by one dating from the accession of Cyrus the Great, from whom the direct descent of the Persian crown was somewhat unhistorically claimed. In 1977 the Empress's arts festival in Shiraz abounded in avant-garde obscenities, and also staged a Shi'ite passion play in a purely secular context for Western tourists. However the Shah's crucial mistake seems to have been his decision to liberalise his rule. He had, since 1963, tolerated no real criticism, and had operated a formidable secret police, SAVAK.[24]

24. Its activities were much exaggerated by foreign opponents and may well have been no worse than those of many of its counterparts. But, despite amnesties, the Shah admitted to holding 3,000 political prisoners in mid-1977, and moderate

Liberalisation is often represented as a response to President Carter's human rights policy, but the then British ambassador, Sir Anthony Parsons, maintains that it antedated Carter. The Shah knew that he had cancer, and was seeking to prepare the ground for his son's succession to the throne.

> He had tried in turn direct rule, a multi-party system, and a single party: none had succeeded. Why not therefore slacken the reins and see what happened? . . . If it worked, well and good. If it did not, then it would not be difficult to pull in the reins again.[25]

In fact liberalisation made possible the voicing of hitherto suppressed discontents, and their gradual merger into a renewal of the front (of political progressives, bazaar merchants and religious leaders) that had pressed the Shah hard in the early 1960s and that had extorted the 1906 constitution from his predecessors. In January 1978, nettled by the circulation of taped sermons and messages from the exiled Khomeini, the regime launched a newspaper attack on his morals. This touched off rioting in the religious city of Qum; the resultant loss of life inaugurated a growing cycle of riots, more deaths, more riots during the commemoration of the dead forty days later, more deaths. Some perceptive observers now realised that the Shah was in deep trouble, notably the Israelis who set about evacuating Iran's Jewish community. Most foreigners, however, and the Shah himself (who was dangerously isolated from real knowledge of developments on the ground), assumed that the army could, if necessary, always master the situation: not until the autumn did it become clear that the army was neither trained nor equipped for riot control. In August 1978 the fasting month of Ramadan brought nightly violence against symbols of the regime and of Westernisation. October saw protest closings of the Teheran bazaar, and the outbreak of strikes in the oilfields that gradually became insurrectionary. Meanwhile the government sought to put together a broad-based political coalition. If it failed, the Shah told Parsons,

> he would be faced with the choice of surrender – his own departure – or a complete clamp-down which would be bloody and would ultimately solve nothing. He had decided against a military government. . . .

estimates are that his regime had, by early 1978, killed some 5,000 people: *Keesing's*, 28940; Rubin, *Paved with Good Intentions* pp.176–81

25. Sir Anthony Parsons, *The Pride and the Fall: Iran 1974–1979* (1984) pp.48–9, 54, 69; Rubin, *Paved with Good Intentions* p.174

> The only answer was to find a neutral and prestigious figure . . . untainted by association with the regime over the last fifteen years[26]

In fact the Shah was more volatile than this quotation suggests. He was under considerable domestic pressure to try a crack-down, and often seemed anxious to pass the decision on to his US or British patrons. But Washington was quite as irresolute, Brzezinski hoping for action and Vance opposing it (as also did Parsons in Teheran). Riots in November 1978 did bring a military government and martial law, but no real attempt to suppress the strikes. Some demonstrations were broken up with significant casualties;[27] but on the holy days of Ashura (10 and 11 December) the authorities stood aside and vast crowds demonstrated support for Khomeini. The search for an alternative resumed; it was eventually announced that the former National Front figure, Shapour Bakhtiar, would form a government and that the Shah would go abroad for medical treatment. After further wavering, the Shah left on 16 January 1979. Had he gone in November, the more moderate religious leaders believed, it might have been possible to save the monarchy (albeit in a more constitutional form), but by January the momentum for an Islamic Republic was too great. It was, however, at this point that the USA intervened, dispatching a General Huyser to Teheran with the impossible mission of holding the armed forces together behind Bakhtiar's government, but preparing them for a coup if it failed. Huyser's impact was probably negligible. The armed forces and SAVAK gradually fell apart, with insurgents – stiffened probably by PLO and other trained militants – progressively taking over provincial centres. Khomeini was kept out for a few more days, but landed in Teheran on 1 February 1979 (to a welcome, supposedly, by 3 million people) and proceeded to appoint his own Premier, Mehdi Bazargan. Clashes continued, but on 11 February the army abandoned Bakhtiar, who resigned and fled.

THE US HOSTAGES CRISIS 1979–81

The United States reacted very mildly. Many officials took comfort from Khomeini's anti-communism, refused to credit evidence as to

26. Parsons, *The Pride and the Fall* p.85
27. Rubin puts deaths during the 1978 to January 1979 revolution at about 5,000: *Paved with Good Intentions* p.177

his other political views, and assumed that he would retire into the background leaving moderates like Bazargan to run things. Most of 1979 was spent trying to establish a relationship with these moderates. But the Shah was eventually admitted to the USA for medical treatment, and in November 1979 Bazargan and Brzezinski had a public meeting in Algeria. During a rally to protest against both developments, students occupied the US embassy in Teheran and held its staff hostage; Khomeini endorsed their action, and the Bazargan government resigned. As far as the USA was concerned, 1980 was dominated by attempts to secure the hostages' release, through UN (and even PLO and Libyan) mediation, through economic sanctions, and in April by an attempt at surprise military rescue that had to be abandoned when three helicopters broke down. Thereafter the USA could do little more than threaten massive reprisals if the hostages were put on trial. In September, possibly influenced by deteriorating relations with Iraq, Iran sought talks, in which it showed itself chiefly concerned to secure as much as possible of the money exported by the Pahlavi dynasty. The negotiations were difficult, and failure to secure the hostages' release by November 1980 may have cost Carter the presidential election. But, aided by Algerian mediation, their release was agreed before Reagan's inauguration in January 1981.

IRAN'S SHI'ITE PROPAGANDA

The Shah's fall was naturally unsettling. The United States' failure to maintain so long-standing and helpful a partner cannot but have worried Arab rulers who had also looked to the USA; and since much of the population on the south shore of the Gulf was Shi'ite (the religion of Iran), there was a distinct prospect that the revolution might spread. The new Iranian Deputy Prime Minister declared in February 1979, 'The success of the Islamic revolution in Iran has shown Arab neighbours that Islam provides the ideological basis for change within Moslem countries and can also replace Arab nationalism as a rallying point for Arab people'.[28] Such claims had some substance. It was perhaps in the Lebanon that Shi'ites were most responsive.[29] There were also Shi'ite disturbances in the

28. *Keesing's*, 30418

29. In the mid-1980s Iran was able to build up a radical Shia militia, Hesbollah, to challenge the more conservative Amal; it was generally believed to support and influence both terrorist and hostage-taking groups

Eastern Province of Saudi Arabia in November 1979, minor trouble in Kuwait in 1980, and an apparently Iranian-inspired attempted coup in Bahrain in 1981. Then in 1987 clashes with Iranian pilgrims to Mecca caused hundreds of casualties and a propaganda war with Iran, and this had further repercussions in 1989. November 1979 also saw the quite distinct seizure of the Grand Mosque in Mecca by armed Wahhabi fundamentalists proclaiming a Mahdi and denouncing Saudi corruption. Their action threw the country into an uproar, and it took a fortnight to overpower them (supposedly with French technical assistance).[30] Although all this occasioned considerable alarm, and caused some prudential reforms, none of the Gulf regimes appear to have been seriously endangered.

IRAN–IRAQ RELATIONS IN THE 1970s

So the most serious international consequence of the Iranian revolution was the opportunity that it provided for Iraq. Border friction was of long standing. An 1847 treaty had allotted the whole of the Shatt al-Arab waterway to the Ottoman Empire (which controlled what is now Iraq). Following the development of Iranian oil this was modified, notably by a 1937 treaty that extended Iranian rights in the immediate vicinity of its river ports but preserved Iraqi control elsewhere. In 1969 Iran denounced the 1937 treaty and sent ships down the river with a military escort. Iraq dared not challenge this, but expelled large numbers of Iranian nationals as a reprisal; Iran in turn started aiding Kurdish rebels in the north of Iraq. Matters worsened in 1970, when Iran backed an unsuccessful coup in Baghdad.[31] In 1971 Iraq broke off diplomatic relations, and in 1972 concluded a treaty aligning itself with the USSR. The Shah now feared that the USSR would 'try to squeeze Iran between Afghanistan [whose king had recently been toppled] and its Iraqi client', and saw Iraq as a threat not only to the Gulf but also to the whole Fertile Crescent. He therefore sought to tie it down by mobilising troops on its border and by supporting its Kurds.[32] Kurdish rebellion broke out again in 1974 with considerable Iranian assistance, but when Iraqi forces were clearly winning, the Shah was

30. *Keesing's*, 30702, 31353–4, 31563, 35676–7, 36835, 36906; Lacy, *The Kingdom* chap. 51

31. *Keesing's*, 23544, 23827–9, 31005; David, *Third World Coups* p.142

32. Kissinger, *Memoirs* ii p.675 (Nov. 1973 meeting with the Shah)

not prepared to risk open intervention and war. In 1975 he ditched the Kurds and concluded an agreement with Iraq, providing for minor redefinition of the land border and the adoption, for the Shatt al-Arab, of the normal international practice whereby the border runs down the middle of the deepest channel.[33]

Relations improved, and in 1978 Iraq was ready to oblige the Shah by expelling (and offering to murder) Khomeini. However in 1979 Iran fell into internal confusion and separatist ethnic risings: the chance seemed too good to miss. Moreover the Iranian revolution had evoked demonstrations among Iraq's depressed Shi'ite majority. So in October 1979 Iraq started demanding the revocation of the 1975 treaty, Iranian evacuation of the Tunbs islets, and autonomy for Iran's Arab, Kurdish and Baluchi minorities. This set off a downwards spiral, leading in April 1980 to Khomeini's call for the overthrow of the Iraqi President, Saddam Hussein, as 'an enemy of Islam'.

THE IRAN–IRAQ WAR 1980–8

In September 1980 Iraq formally denounced the 1975 treaty and invaded Iran, with, the then President of Iran believes,[34] encouragement from Brzezinski. Saddam apparently hoped to occupy most of the oil-rich, and largely Arab, province of Khuzestan within a fortnight, and to install a client government in Teheran. In fact the offensive soon bogged down, partly because of excessive Iraqi caution and partly because the inhabitants did not rise in Iraq's support. By late 1981 the initiative had passed to Iran, which lifted the siege of Abadan in September, recaptured Khorramshahr in April 1982, and crossed the border in July. It was now Iran's turn to talk of the punishment of Saddam Hussein and the establishment of an Islamic Republic in Iraq,[35] a prospect that worried not only the Arab Gulf states (with their Shia populations) but also many other countries. However Iraq's Shi'ites did not welcome their Iranian coreligionists, and its southern marshes proved difficult to

33. *Keesing's*, 26531–2, 27053, 27285; Parsons, *The Pride and the Fall* p.20; Kissinger, *Memoirs* i p.1265

34. John Bulloch and Harvey Morris, *Saddam's War* (1991) pp.75–6. (For Saddam's 1978 offer, not accepted, to arrange a 'suitable accident' for Khomeini, *The Independent*, 2 Jan. 1992 p.19)

35. *Keesing's*, esp. 30106, 31005 ff, 31851

penetrate. A long stationary war set in, with Iran spending its troops freely and Iraq countering with chemical weapons.

Considering the scale of the war, the world proved remarkably unconcerned. Mediation was attempted, but to no purpose. No effort was made to *compel* a halt to the fighting. The superpowers, for the most part, sat on the side-lines. Despite its 1972 treaty, Iraq had for some time been distancing itself from the USSR. In 1980 the USSR cut off supplies to Iraq and apparently hinted at assistance for Iran (much as it had recently switched its support from Somalia to Ethiopia); but Iran turned the feeler down, preferring complete independence.[36] The USA was initially concerned chiefly with its hostages; even after their release it continued officially to embargo arms (though, in the 'Irangate' affair, it was tempted by Israel to supply small quantities in 1985–6, to strengthen the Iranian 'moderates' and secure the release of US hostages held by Iran's clients in the Lebanon). Israel supplied Iran on a number of occasions despite Iran's vocal hostility, largely because it perceived Iraq as the greater threat.[37] The Arab world – apart from Syria and Libya – supported and subsidised Iraq, Egypt's usefulness in this connection facilitating its post-Sadat reacceptance into the Arab fold.

In 1986 Iran established itself in strength across the Shatt al-Arab, and in 1987 came close to taking Basra. Against this background Iraq attracted increased international sympathy and support, notably from France and the USSR. This put it in a position to attack Iranian cities and oil facilities by air and missile. Iran retaliated by attacking ships bound for Iraq or its Arab suppliers. In 1987 Kuwait chartered Soviet tankers, and transferred some of its own to the US flag to secure American protection. Iran's response (the indiscriminate sowing of mines, and repeated hit-and-run attacks on shipping by speedboats) drew into the Gulf Soviet and West European minesweepers and a major US fleet. By 1988 this latter was responding to Iranian attacks by destroying oil facilities; in July a US cruiser shot down in error an Iranian airliner. This growing US involvement helped convince Iran it could derive no benefit from continuing the Gulf war. The other decisive factor was Iraq's recovery of the military initiative, driving Iranian forces

36. Iranian–Soviet détente did not really come until late 1988: *Keesing's*, 31012, 36632

37. *Keesing's*, 35182 ff, 35212–13. Wilfrid Knapp sees in this the operation of a de facto balance of power system between the major Middle Eastern states (Iran, Iraq, Syria, Israel and Egypt) that had obtained for over twenty years

from its territory and staging raids over the border. So Iran now accepted the UN's 1987 call for a cease-fire, though as Khomeini declared 'taking this decision was more deadly than taking poison'. In August 1988 the UN supervised a cease-fire, but little came of subsequent peace talks under its auspices. The war had taken some 200,000 Iranian (distinctly fewer Iraqi) lives, and is estimated to have cost the two countries half of all the oil revenues they had so far earned.

IRAQ'S SEIZURE OF KUWAIT 1990

Saddam, however, saw it as a victory, and meant to profit by it. In 1988–9 he suppressed his Kurds, who had again taken up arms during the war with Iran. The process involved the use of chemical weapons and nerve gas, and also the destruction of half the Kurdish villages so as to create a cordon sanitaire around his borders. He also pressed ahead with ambitious programmes for the manufacture of long-range missiles, and chemical, biological and above all nuclear weapons.[38] It would have been wise to have waited till these were completed, but in 1990 Saddam showed himself increasingly irked by Western criticism (muted though this was by governments that still looked to Iraq to contain Iran and that did not wish to jeopardise their exports to it). He may also have been feeling the pressure of his enormous debts. Anyhow he decided to take the initiative. In May 1990 Saddam hosted an Arab League meeting to consider the dangers posed by massive migration from the USSR to Israel, represented Iraq's military strength as a necessary counterpoise, and alleged that Iraq was being subjected to 'war by economic means'. This was followed up in July by a battery of charges openly directed against Kuwait, and by the successful forcing up of the OPEC oil price (see p.357). Meanwhile he warned the US ambassador, April Glaspie, in a rather cryptic interview, not to intervene: 'Do not push us to consider war as the only solution to live proudly and to provide our people with a good living. We know that the United States has nuclear weapons but we are determined either to live as proud men or we will die'. 'Yours',

38. *Keesing's*, 35597 ff, 36167–71, 36567–70; Bulloch and Morris, *Saddam's War* pp.87–92

however, 'is a society that cannot accept 10,000 dead in one battle'.[39]

The pressure on Kuwait caused some alarm. Mubarak made a series of lightning visits, offering his services as a mediator, and (he said) securing Saddam's assurance that he had no intention of attacking Kuwait. Talks were eventually arranged between Kuwait and Iraq for 31 July. There Iraq demanded: the writing off of the loans it had spent on fighting Iran (protecting, it claimed, all Arab states); economic aid; compensation for Kuwait's alleged theft of oil from a field that straddled the border; and at least the lease of two disputed islands that would provide Iraq with a more secure outlet to the sea than that through the Shatt al-Arab.[40] Kuwait adopted a tough bargaining stance – though its Foreign Minister later claimed he had agreed to write off the debt and lease one of the islands – and the Iraqi delegation flew home. Next day Baghdad announced the collapse of the talks, then, on 2 August, invaded and occupied Kuwait. After vain attempts to coopt opposition Kuwaiti politicians, a highly incredible 'government' was installed; then on 8 August Kuwait was formally annexed.

Kuwait had thought that Iraq might push troops over the border, and April Glaspie had unwisely told Saddam that the USA had 'no opinion on Arab–Arab conflicts, like your border disagreement with Kuwait'.[41] Nobody had expected straightforward seizure, however: there was, indeed, no postwar precedent for the conquest of a state whose independence had been universally accepted. It was also the first major crisis of the post-Cold War era. US Secretary of State Baker happened to be in the USSR at the time; his friend Shevardnadze met him (albeit only after argument with elements of the Soviet government that did not wish to damage their special relationship with Iraq) and issued a statement of condemnation.[42] Given this common front, the UN Security Council had little difficulty in imposing a mandatory embargo on Iraqi trade and authorising naval operations to police it. The USA, Britain and France felt it safe to strip their forces in Europe so as to create a 'multinational defence force' to protect Saudi Arabia from what was represented as the 'imminent threat' of further invasion. That the

39. Bulloch and Morris, *Saddam's War* pp.1–3, 8–9, 11–12, 97–103

40. Iraq had moved on the islands in 1973, but withdrawn in the face of Arab disapproval and an Iranian ultimatum: ibid, p.125

41. ibid. pp.9–13, chap. 5; *Financial Times*, 18–19 Aug. 1990; *Keesing's*, 37631 ff, 38408

42. Shevardnadze, *The Future belongs to Freedom* pp.101 ff

Gulf states should welcome such deployment was unsurprising. Nor was Egyptian participation, especially given Mubarak's resentment at Saddam's breach of his personal promise not to invade. Less expected was Syria's contribution; this reflected not only long-standing dislike of Iraq, but also Asad's decision to use the crisis to mend Syrian relations with the USA now that the USSR could no longer continue its previous level of support. It enabled the Arab League to endorse the operation, though only by a narrow margin.

The UN had initially authorised only economic sanctions, but Iraq seemed remarkably unconcerned by the total blockage of its oil exports, and met shortages partly by trade with Jordan and Iran and partly by looting Kuwait. How long this could have continued was much disputed, but throughout the autumn of 1990 the multinational force built up an increasingly evident capacity to use force. Saddam gambled that it would not dare. On 15 August 1990 he suddenly accepted, in toto, Iran's position on the border, thus abandoning whatever gains he had achieved from the 1980–8 war, so as to enable him to concentrate his army in the south. Saddam seems to have relied on Western reluctance to take casualties in the process of overcoming it; he had some grounds for hoping, too, that Iraq's former friends, the USSR and France, would not indefinitely toe the US line. He grasped for the leadership of the Muslim and Arab world, playing on resentment at the Gulf states' selfish refusal to share their oil wealth, using the rhetoric of Nasser, and representing his move into Kuwait as an attempt to secure action on Israel's continued occupation of the West Bank. He was broadly supported by the PLO, Jordan (heavily Palestinian in population, and in any case closely tied economically to Iraq), and Libya; his rhetoric also went down well with some, but not all, of the Arab peoples further afield. In November 1990 the UN Security Council authorised the use of force; China, which could have vetoed this, chose only to abstain after the USA had resumed diplomatic contacts suspended after the Tiananmen Square killings. Frenzied negotiations continued until the mid-January UN deadline, with France, the USSR and the UN Secretary-General all trying (with little assistance from Iraq) to find a way out. Bush only secured congressional authority to go ahead by a five vote margin in the Senate.[43]

43. Bulloch and Morris, *Saddam's War passim*; *Keesing's*, 37870–1, 37934 ff

THE GULF WAR 1991

On 16 January 1991 the allies began a bombing offensive in which Iraq was technologically outclassed; as Iraqi fighters fled to neutral Iran, the allies enjoyed virtually uncontested control of the air. Saddam's chief response was to try to disrupt the Arab coalition against him by firing rockets at Israel so as to draw it into the fighting. Despite fears, the rockets did not carry chemical warheads; although they created great alarm they did relatively little damage. Nor did the other commonly foreseen catastrophes – a panic rise in the price of oil, and massive popular demonstrations in the Arab world – really come about. In mid-February 1991 Iraq offered to withdraw, but on manifestly unacceptable conditions. The USSR tried to build on this, securing the agreement of the Iraqi Foreign Minister but not obviously that of Saddam, to an improved peace plan in an attempt to forestall the imminent allied land attack. Faced with a possible unravelling of his coalition, Bush demanded much faster Iraqi withdrawal and, when his ultimatum was rejected, launched a ground offensive despite a private appeal by Gorbachev. It was spectacularly successful. In four days Kuwait was liberated – though only after the retreating Iraqis had set all its oil wells alight – and much of the Iraqi army encircled and destroyed. Bush then suspended operations, and Iraq concluded a very onerous cease-fire (authorising the UN, for instance, to search for and destroy its chemical and nuclear weapons facilities).[44]

AFTERMATH OF THE GULF WAR

With this victory the United States was clearly the preponderant power in the Middle East, and the margin of its pre-eminence further increased with the Soviet Union's collapse later that year. (Among those welcoming the abortive Soviet coup in August 1991 were Libya, the Sudan, and Iraq, which said it would lead to the restoration of 'international balance'.)[45] Whether the USA would prove able to use this pre-eminence to resolve the classic Middle Eastern problems was less clear. During the Gulf crisis it had been at pains to keep the issues of Kuwait and of the West Bank separate,

44. *Keesing's*, 37982 ff
45. *Keesing's*, 38370

but it subsequently rewarded its Arab allies by resuming the quest for a renewed Arab–Israeli peace conference (see pp.337–8). As we have seen, this did meet but to little immediate purpose. More rapid results were achieved in connection with the Western hostages in the Lebanon. For Syria had now improved its relations with the USA, and the (generally) prevailing Iranian faction of President Rafsanjani had been edging that way for some time. August 1991 brought the release of one hostage, who delivered a letter from his captors inviting the UN Secretary-General to take a hand. That autumn the Secretary-General's agent conducted complicated negotiations for a three-way trade of 'Western' hostages in Beirut against Lebanese militants seized and held by Israel and Israeli servicemen missing in action in Lebanon. By December 1991 all but two Western hostages had been released, but Israel still held many Lebanese, including the Shia leader Sheikh Obeid, while one missing Israeli was known to be still alive.[46]

Perhaps the greatest US failure lay in the handling of Iraq itself. It would have been militarily possible to occupy Baghdad. Bush refused to do so, for fear of exposing US troops to the sorts of attacks they had encountered when they were deployed in Beirut in 1983, and because many countries (notably the USSR) would have been concerned by any extension of the war beyond the simple liberation of Kuwait. But Bush had repeatedly declared the removal of Saddam to be the prerequisite for any real peace, and expected a military coup to effect it. So far (1993) no coup attempts have succeeded. When March 1991 brought widespread Shia revolt (with Iranian encouragement) in the south and Kurdish uprising in the north, it transpired that Saddam had conserved enough of his army to repress them, bloodily. The USA at first stood aside, fearful of precipitating worse confusion by destroying Iraq's unity as a state, and (with the USSR and China) resisted a French attempt to secure UN action. However the international outcry over the condition of the hundred of thousands who had fled to the Turkish mountains to escape the fighting became overwhelming: in April 1992 the USA reversed itself and accepted a British/European Community plan for the creation of an enclave to which the Kurds would feel it safe to return. US and European troops were deployed in northern Iraq from April to July 1992 to effect this, and after their withdrawal a presence continued in Turkey to deter the overt resumption of

46. The two remaining German hostages were released in June 1992: overall ninety-two foreigners had been taken hostage in the Lebanon since 1982: *Keesing's*, 38983, 1992 R142

hostilities. Iraq pulled out not only of the 'safe havens' but also of most non-oil-bearing Kurdish territory, and the Kurds have assumed its de facto administration. Despite lengthy negotiations, they have not yet (1993) reached a settlement with Saddam, who continues to harass and blockade them.[47]

Later in 1992 there was further news of the bombing and repression of the southern Shi'ites; in August the USA, Britain, France (and Russia) banned Iraqi flights in the area and inaugurated aerial observation. This led on, in December–January, to a game of chicken, with Saddam testing their resolve by intruding into the 'no-fly zone', mounting incursions across the Kuwaiti border, and calling for the overthrow of the Kuwaiti regime. With diminishing international support, President Bush responded with bombing and cruise missile strikes against Iraqi air defences and military plant that (he claimed) the UN had been prevented from demolishing. Saddam backed down, expressing the hope that relations would improve under President Clinton. However, Iraq still labours under UN sanctions. These have started to fray at the edges, and they appear to hurt the general population far more than Saddam's tight ruling circle; but the allies will not lift them until satisfied as to complete Iraqi compliance with the cease-fire terms.[48]

47. *Keesing's*, 38081, 38127, 38361, 39026, 39115, 1992 R138
48. *Keesing's*, 39026, 39068–9, 39247, 39291–2

PART IV

The Americas

CHAPTER SIXTEEN

The Inter-American Political System

CANADA

The two richest countries on the American continent (both absolutely and per capita) are the United States and Canada. From the Canadian perspective, much has been written on the difficulties of so 'Living with Uncle' as to preserve a distinctive cultural, political and national identity. But US–Canadian relations are so close, and undramatic, as scarcely to obtrude above the horizon in any general survey of postwar history. Perhaps the most notable clash was that between the Kennedy and Diefenbaker administrations. Diefenbaker was reluctant to acquire US nuclear weapons for the Canadian air force in Europe, or to let them be stationed on Canadian soil in peacetime in connection with the North American Air Defence Command (which some Canadians saw as operating in US interests but endangering Canada). It has been claimed that the White House manoeuvred, in 1963, to promote Diefenbaker's defeat and his replacement by the more congenial Liberal Pearson. But the only mention of Diefenbaker (or Canada) in (at least the Commonwealth edition of) Schlesinger's large biography of Kennedy is by way of recording that the President damaged his back at a tree-planting ceremony in Ottawa.[1]

1. H. Basil Robinson, *Diefenbaker's World: A Populist in Foreign Affairs* (Toronto, 1989) esp. chap. 29 and pp.308, 319; Schlesinger, *A Thousand Days* p.311 – though Sorenson devotes nearly a page to the issue and implies that Kennedy was better informed about Canada than his predecessors: *Kennedy* pp.575–6

THE LATIN AMERICAN WORLD

This chapter will accordingly focus on the United States' relationship with its southern (rather than its northern) neighbours, and on aspects of the international politics of Latin America. Like the Arab world, 'Latin America' extends over vast distances. It consists of markedly different states: thus Mexico is large, and has throughout our period seen an untroubled succession of strong Presidents chosen by the moderately authoritarian 'Party of Institutionalised Revolution' (PRI); Bolivia has a small population and is marked by frequent coups and risings; and so on. Although the identity and distinctiveness of the various states is not in question, activists pass between them and intervention by one country in another's internal affairs is not uncommon. There may also be something of a Latin American international style: war is not unknown, but it has (in the twentieth century) been rare;[2] armies exist primarily for the maintenance of *internal* security, which they may see as necessitating political take-overs and/or the violent repression of domestic insurgency or dissent. There has also, since 1945, been an apparent pendulum effect whereby a number of countries swing at much the same time from authoritarian rule to elected civilian government or back again. Another more slowly swinging pendulum relates to economic thought. Until the Great Slump of the 1930s, Latin American economies were mostly liberal, free-trade oriented and open to foreign capital investment. The Slump tended to discredit such policies; state-supported development, import-saving industrialisation, and the nationalisation and curbing of foreign companies became fashionable as an attempt to escape from what was perceived as an exploitative dependency on the developed capitalist world. This approach has, in its turn, been criticised as having contributed to the over-borrowing of the 1970s and resultant national bankruptcies of the 1980s; in the 1990s there has been something of a move back towards the privatisation of state industries and internal and external liberalism. The international relations of Latin America are inescapably bound up with the role played by that 'colossus of the north', the United States. In fact this role differs according to geographical area: US troops have, in the twentieth century, intervened periodically in Central America and the Caribbean, but never overtly in South America (whose states are

2. Since 1945, only the 1969 'Football War' between Honduras and El Salvador; the Organisation of American States stopped the fighting in a fortnight, though it took longer to bring El Salvador to withdraw: *Keesing's*, 23526–7

both further off and, mostly, much larger). Latin American governments do not (generally) dislike the USA, and usually see it as a natural leader within a hemispheric political system. Almost all stress the illegitimacy of such interventions, however, and of attempts to constrain the way in which they choose to deal with foreign (i.e. US) companies and nationals. Mexico, indeed, regards its 1918 Carranza Doctrine as a pioneer proclamation of many of the principles that were to be subsequently picked up by the non-aligned and Afro-Asian movements and to become the international norms of the postwar world.[3]

CREATING AN INTER-AMERICAN POLITICAL STRUCTURE 1940–8

Since 1823 it had been a fixed aim of US foreign policy (enshrined in the Monroe Doctrine) to ward off any external military involvement in the Americas. In 1904 President Theodore Roosevelt drew his 'Corollary' that, 'in flagrant cases of wrongdoing or impotence' on the part of local states, the USA should itself exercise an 'international police power'. Between 1898 and 1926 there were thirteen such interventions, including the taking over for long periods of the administration of Haiti, the Dominican Republic and Nicaragua. After the First World War this approach went into reverse, with US troops finally leaving the Dominican Republic in 1924, Haiti and Nicaragua in 1933–4. Franklin Roosevelt went further with his 1933 Good Neighbor Doctrine and acceptance at the Montevideo Pan-American Conference that 'No state has the right to intervene in the internal affairs of another';[4] for the rest of the 1930s he studiously cultivated Latin American sensitivities.

Come the Second World War, Roosevelt could draw on the goodwill he had thus accumulated. In the July 1940 Act of Havana, the Foreign Ministers of the American Republics resolved that 'any attempt on the part of a non-American state against the . . . territory, the sovereignty or the political independence of an American State shall be considered as an act of aggression against

3. R.E. Scott, 'National Development and Mexico's Foreign Policy', *International Journal* xxxvii (Toronto, 1981–2) pp.46–7

4. Harold Molineu, *U.S. Policy Toward Latin America* (Boulder, Colo., 1986) pp.23, 40–9

the States which sign this declaration'; they also authorised any states that wished to concert their defence preparations, and (by a smaller majority) sanctioned the pre-emptive occupation of any European colony in the hemisphere that seemed in danger of passing under Axis control.[5] This was complemented by US carrot-and-stick pressure on Latin American states to curb Axis activities and sympathisers. After Pearl Harbor the process was taken further at the January 1942 Rio Conference where almost all the Latin American states agreed to break off relations with the Axis Powers and coordinate their economic production to meet US defence needs. In return the USA promised to support Latin American industrialisation and held out the prospect of a conference to settle upon equitable economic principles.[6]

Pressure of business was one obstacle to the convention of such a conference, another being Argentina's refusal to break with the Axis. But in 1944 the question of hemispheric organisation became urgent as a result of the Dumbarton Oaks plans for a 'United Nations Organisation'. Latin American countries were anxious both to secure maximum representation on the new body and to make sure that it did not undercut the multinational regional system they had become accustomed to. In particular, they did not wish either to expose American affairs to a Soviet veto (the fear they most readily voiced in public) or to give the USA the opportunity of first exercising a UN veto and then acting unilaterally outside the UN. Their complaints led early in 1945 to a Mexico City conference at which, in the 'Act of Chapultepec', the USA accepted their position. Washington soon had second thoughts, however, the influential Leo Pasvolsky holding that to weaken UN authority over regional pacts 'would be tantamount to throwing all Europe into the hands of the Soviet Union'. At the UN's founding conference that spring in San Francisco, US Secretary of State Stettinius's initial inclination was to throw over Chapultepec. This raised a storm, with Mexico threatening to leave and several Latin American delegates being given an unusual opportunity to voice their discontents to Stettinius when he was trapped with them in a hotel lift for half an hour. They also made common cause with other smaller states

5. Department of State, *Peace and War: United States Foreign Policy 1931–41* (Washington, DC, 1943) p.563; *FRUS*, 1940 v pp.255–6. The Foreign Ministers had been meeting periodically since 1938

6. *FRUS*, 1942 v pp.40–1; Stephen Rabe, 'The Elusive Conference: United States Economic Relations with Latin America, 1945–1952', *Diplomatic History* ii (1978) pp.279–80

against various aspects of the Dumbarton Oaks agreements, and, in the end, broadly got their way. On regional organisation, the UN eventually accepted (for its Charter) a British compromise wording, referring to an 'inherent right of self-defence, either individual or collective' but not (as Latin America would have wished) specifically mentioning Chapultepec.

At Mexico City it had been agreed that American Foreign Ministers should meet annually and that there should be further conferences every four years. Chapultepec also picked up the Havana declaration to the effect that an attack on any American state should be treated as aggression against all. Truman promised, during the San Francisco Conference, to strengthen the American regional system with a permanent treaty.[7] Steps to achieve this were, however, delayed by a recurrence of the feud between the USA and Argentina.[8] It was not until August 1947 that a conference was convened and produced the Act of Rio whereby states undertook 'to assist in meeting' armed attacks within the hemisphere 'in exercise of the inherent right of individual or collective self-defence recognised by . . . the UN Charter'; a two-thirds majority could prescribe diplomatic or economic sanctions, though no state could be obliged to use armed force without its own consent. In the event of conflict between American states, the signatories would first call for suspension of hostilities and promote a peaceful resolution; only if this failed would they proceed to determine the aggressor.[9] The formalisation of hemispheric relations was completed next year by the conclusion at Bogotá of the 'Charter of the Organisation of American States' (OAS), providing for quinquennial conferences, annual (or emergency) meetings of Foreign Ministers, and interim direction by a Council composed of one member from each state,

7. *Keesing's*, 7413–17, 7565–6, 7725; J. Tillapough, 'Closed Hemisphere and Open World? The Dispute Over Regional Security at the U.N. Conference, 1945', *Diplomatic History* ii (1979) pp.28–40

8. Argentina had declared war on Germany at the eleventh hour in March 1945, and, in accordance with Latin American wishes, the USA sponsored it at San Francisco for UN membership. But the new US ambassador, Spruille Braden (who later became Assistant Secretary for Latin American Affairs) continued to denounce what he saw as the Fascist sympathies of the rising politician Colonel Perón, Perón to campaign – successfully – on the basis of opposition to such US interference. Braden was dismissed in June 1947 on the grounds that his ideological crusade was endangering hemispheric solidarity

9. *Keesing's*, 8881–3. The Rio Pact served as a model during the 1948–9 formulation of the North Atlantic Treaty, though the Cold War soon converted the latter into a supranational organisation (NATO) without parallel in the Western hemisphere

in practice their ambassadors in Washington.[10] The machinery thus established was soon in use: Costa Rica appealed to the OAS in December 1948 on the occasion of an invasion from Nicaraguan territory. In 1950 the OAS launched an investigation into charges and counter-charges between Cuba, Guatemala, the Dominican Republic and Haiti that found all but the last guilty of sponsoring mutual subversion, and threatened that any repetition would lead to 'the application of the procedures of the Rio Treaty'.[11]

ECONOMIC FRICTIONS AND THE SOURING OF RELATIONS WITH THE USA 1945–53

The creation of an American political system did not prove too difficult, but economics was more problematic. Wartime rhetoric had envisaged a conference to address the continent's economic problems, and the Act of Chapultepec had been accompanied by a pious if insubstantial 'Economic Charter of the Americas'. Latin Americans made it clear that, having helped the USA during the war, they now expected positive US support: the Mexican Foreign Minister had urged the USA to approach its neighbours' problems in 'a TVA [Tennessee Valley Authority] fashion'. Though the USA made conciliatory noises, it was in no hurry to convene an economic conference, partly from a feeling that, with the war over, 'the United States no longer deperately needs Latin America', but chiefly from a belief that a conference would prove a damaging fiasco that might (in Clayton's view) upset 'the broad commercial policy applecart'. The issue did, however, come up at the 1947 Rio Conference, where several states stressed that a sound hemispheric economy and security against aggression were two sides of the same coin. There were hopes that the USA would follow its Marshall Plan for Europe with one for the Americas. But Truman, though conciliatory, explained that US resources were limited, that Europe's needs were more important, and that, in the context of the undamaged Latin American economies, private initiatives should assume a much greater role than was appropriate for a programme designed to aid recovery by the war-torn European economies (a

10. The USA would have liked Canadian membership, but Canada did not join until 1980

11. *Keesing's*, 9235–6, 9293–4, 9727, 10815; the Rio Pact had been ratified and become operative in Dec. 1948

recovery that would, Marshall added next year, feed through into increased demand for Latin American products). The USA did nevertheless agree to the convention in 1948 of a special economic conference; in the event this never transpired.[12]

The underlying problem was, perhaps, Latin America's trade deficit with the USA: $2.7 billion over the years 1945–8. Postwar inflation meant that the $3.4 billion credits accumulated from wartime sales to the USA at controlled prices were largely exhausted; European purchases from Latin America were insufficient to bridge the gap. So (Acheson was briefed in 1950) reserves had reached danger point by 1948 and Latin America encountered serious dollar shortages in 1949. It looked, by way of solution, to a mixture of commodity price support and aid; it felt hurt that, by 1951, the Americas were the only continent without a US aid programme. The USA, by contrast, advocated 'enlightened private enterprise'; Acheson was briefed that 'The greatest single obstacle to economic development in Latin America is the slow rate of foreign private investment'. Here there was little meeting of minds, for the postwar period was rather one of nationalisation (though more especially of British-owned utilities in the south that the UK was happy to see taken over in settlement of its debts and deficits).

At Bogotá in 1948 US attempts to sell the remedies of free trade and investment provoked eight formal reservations over the principle of full compensation for expropriation of foreign capital. Thereafter some US officials sought to ease this discontent by accepting the 'Calvo Doctrine' that foreigners could not appeal to their home government for protection; but they were overborne by US business and by the business-oriented Secretary of State, Acheson. Admittedly the effects of these economic disagreements were not dramatic: their most important outcome was perhaps the role played by Latin American states in the coalition that pressured the USA into so many compromises, at the 1947–8 Havana negotiations to establish an 'International Trade Organisation' (see p.499), that Congress refused to ratify the result. But these differences may have led to a distinct cooling towards hemispheric co-operation. Acheson remarked privately that 'Hispano-Indian culture – or lack of it – had been piling up its problems for centuries'; in 1950 the State Department thought it wise to publish a *Foreign Affairs* article combating 'a Certain Impatience with Latin

12. *Keesing's*, 7565–6, 8881–3; Rabe, 'The Elusive Conference' esp. pp.279–85; Peter and Susan Calvert, *Latin America in the Twentieth Century* (Basingstoke, 1990) p.87

America'. Equally in 1951 the USA received only 'rhetorical' support at a special Foreign Ministers' meeting that had sought to persuade Latin Americans to mobilise their economies to meet the Korean War rearmament crisis. When the USA solicited Brazil to send troops to Korea, it was told that 'Brazil's present situation would be different and our cooperation . . . could probably be greater . . . had [Washington] elaborated a recovery plan for Latin America similar to the Marshall Plan for Europe'.[13]

The Truman administration did little to mend this state of 'sullenness', nor was it too concerned by the danger of communism, save, perhaps, in Guatemala. It resisted pressure from various Latin American governments for anti-communist pacts and policies, fearing that they would 'be directed against all political opposition, Communist or otherwise, by dictatorial governments – with the inevitable result of driving leftist elements into the arms of the Communist organization'.[14]

US CONCERN AND MILITARY AID 1953–9

The Eisenhower administration took the situation more seriously. John Foster Dulles claimed, in his confirmation hearings, that 'conditions in Latin America are somewhat comparable to conditions as they were in China in the mid-thirties when the Communist movement was getting started. . . . The time to deal with this rising menace in South America is now'. Actually the process had already started, after Allen Dulles had briefed the National Security Council in February 1953 that things were 'deteriorating not only in terms of cordiality of relationships with the United States but in the economic and political spheres of most of the Latin American states. The Kremlin was exploiting this situation'. As in the Middle East, there were 'trends in the direction of economic nationalism, regionalism, neutralism, and increasing Communist influence', with 'Communist infection' in Guatemala 'such as to mark an approaching crisis'.[15]

13. *FRUS*, 1950 ii esp. pp.593–4, 624; 'Y', 'On a Certain Impatience with Latin America', *Foreign Affairs* xxviii (1950) pp.565–79 (though the 'impatience' was more with Latin America's political than with its economic behaviour); Rabe, 'The Elusive Conference' pp.286–93, and *Eisenhower and Latin America: The Foreign Policy of Anticommunism* (Chapel Hill, NC, 1988) pp.16–19, 23
14. Rabe, *Eisenhower and Latin America* p.15; *FRUS*, 1950 ii p.624
15. Rabe, *Eisenhower and Latin America* pp.29–31

Accordingly 1953–4 saw demonstrative US attention to Latin American leaders and a reconciliation with Perón's (now bankrupt) Argentina; an increase of propaganda and support for anti-communist trade unions; and the stepping up of the military aid that had begun, in a small way, in 1951. The strategic case for such aid was not strong; and it encountered resistance in Washington, both for this reason and for fear that it might facilitate wars between recipient states and/or foster repressive regimes. Whenever military aid was questioned, however, the decisive consideration was always that it made friends with and maintained 'U.S. influence over Latin American military forces and through such forces on the political orientation of Latin American governments'. It was quite a cheap policy, accounting over the 1950s for no more than $400 million, and was, in its own political terms, fairly successful: Latin American armies, unlike those of the Middle East, have tended to be politically conservative and pro-United States.[16]

EISENHOWER'S VELVET-GLOVE TREATMENT OF BOLIVIA

In the early 1950s two countries in particular appeared to Washington to pose special problems – Bolivia and Guatemala. Eisenhower treated them very differently. In 1952 the National Revolutionary Movement had seized power in Bolivia, and workers successfully defended it in 1953 against an attempted right-wing counter-coup. The army was dismantled in favour of militias, land was distributed to the peasants, and the tin mines were nationalised. The new rulers sought US assistance, stressing that this would show the United States was not wedded to conservative dictators; the USA responded by rushing in food relief in 1953 and stockpiling high-priced Bolivian tin. This aid was forthcoming partly because things could have been worse – another right-wing coup attempt, it was calculated, would only strengthen the radicals, and 'we might virtually have a Communist state in the heart of South America' – but chiefly because the Bolivian President and Vice-President were perceived as being basically moderates (unlike the miners' leader). So Bolivia received $193 million of economic assistance between 1953 and 1961: 'I can only bet one dollar', Eisenhower once told a

16. ibid, pp.35–8, 88–9, 106–8, 146

golfing partner, 'for I have just lost two million dollars to the [pleas of the] Bolivian ambassador'. With this economic aid, though, went influence. The combination of high social welfare expenditure and falling revenues from tin led Bolivia through printing money to economic collapse. The USA responded not only by injecting money, both directly and through the IMF, but also by seeking to 'return Bolivia to a free market economy' that would service the external debts on which it had defaulted in 1931 and compensate the expropriated mine-owners. As for welfare spending, 'we had to tell the Bolivian government that they couldn't put their money into it and we weren't going to put ours'. Such policies provoked a general strike, but were forced through by President Siles. He and his successor Paz (both of whom had been central to the original 1952 revolution) gradually rebuilt the armed forces with US assistance; after 1960 Paz used them, together with peasant militias that had (after land reform) become conservative, to clamp down on the left and the miners. In 1964 Paz was displaced by a military coup.[17]

EISENHOWER'S PRE-EMPTIVE ACTION AGAINST GUATEMALA

With Bolivia Eisenhower used the velvet glove; not so with Guatemala. This had, after 1945, embarked on a social democratic programme that included the establishment of a right to strike and the break-up of large estates. These reforms alarmed the huge US-owned United Fruit Company and, perhaps as a result, the US State Department, which attributed them to Marxist ideology and reported on communist infiltration of the labour movement. Matters worsened with the 1952 land reform and 1953 nationalisation of United Fruit Company land with compensation set only at the value that had been previously declared for tax. Already in 1952 President Somoza of Nicaragua had interested the CIA, and indeed Truman, in staging a coup, but Acheson had scotched the idea.[18]

It has often been suggested that US policy was determined partly by concern for the United Fruit Company (with which many members of the Eisenhower administration had connections), and

17. ibid, pp.77–82; Calvert, *Latin America in the Twentieth Century* pp.76–8
18. Ranelagh, *The Agency* p.265

partly by a congenital inability to distinguish between moderate reform and communist revolution: as the Guatemalan Foreign Minister put it, the USA wanted

> to maintain the economic dependence of the American Republics and suppress the legitimate desires of the peoples, cataloguing as 'communism' every manifestation of nationalism or economic independence, any desire for social progress, . . . and any interest in progressive and liberal reforms.

Its dealing with Bolivia suggests that the Eisenhower administration was in fact more discriminating. Dulles insisted that United Fruit was not the real problem: 'if they gave a gold piece for every banana, the problem would remain just as it is today as far as the presence of Communist infiltration in Guatemala is concerned'. There were a few sceptics in Washington, but belief that the communists had real prospects in Guatemala went back some way: in 1950 Kennan had seen it as the only Latin American country where they might 'acquire the strength to come into power by majority opinion'. In fact neither Arbenz nor his government were communist; they followed the US line at the United Nations; and they claimed that their domestic reforms would undercut the appeal of communism. However, communists formed part of their parliamentary coalition; individual communists occupied important posts in the police, the labour movement and the Department for Agrarian Reform; Arbenz's refusal to break with them convinced Washington that he was at best their dupe. Eisenhower was appalled by the prospect of communism's taking over Guatemala and then spreading throughout Central America; 'My God', he told his Cabinet in March 1954, 'just think what it would mean to us if Mexico went Communist!'.[19] So he took what Dulles admitted was pre-emptive action: it was impossible, Dulles told the Brazilian ambassador in May, 'to produce evidence clearly tying the Guatemalan Government to Moscow; . . . the decision must be a political one and based on our deep conviction that such a tie must exist'.[20]

One US response was to seek to mobilise the rest of Latin America. Dulles wanted to extend 'the Monroe Doctrine to include the concept of outlawing foreign ideologies in the American

19. Rabe, *Eisenhower and Latin America* esp. pp.51, 56; *FRUS*, 1950 ii p.603; Ambrose, *Eisenhower* p.197

20. Even after the coup 'nothing conclusive' was found linking the Guatemalan communists to Moscow: Rabe, *Eisenhower and Latin America* p.57

Republics'. So in March 1954 he invited the Tenth Inter-American Conference (meeting at Caracas) to resolve

> That the domination or control of the political institutions of any American state by the international communist movement, extending to this Hemisphere the political system of an extra-continental power, would constitute a threat to the sovereignty and political independence of the American States, endangering the peace of America.

He got his resolution, but with some difficulty and the abstentions of Argentina and Mexico. Most states also specified that it did not justify either unilateral or collective intervention, or 'impair the inalienable right of each American state freely to choose its own form of government and economic system'. The US State Department concluded that, though most states opposed international communism, they were reluctant to transfer this opposition 'to the specific threat inherent in the Guatemalan system'. Indeed when (as we shall see) Guatemala subsequently imported Czech arms, the USA failed to secure the necessary two-thirds majority for action under the Pact of Rio to halt and inspect all further Guatemala-bound ships. So the USA proceeded on its own, both with a blockade (anticipating that imposed on Cuba during the 1962 missile crisis) and with the sponsorship of an émigré invasion. Guatemala appealed to the UN Security Council. Here Brazil and Colombia duly obliged the USA by moving that the hearing of the appeal be transferred to the OAS, but the USSR vetoed this. So intense pressure had to be exerted to prevent the casting of the seven affirmative votes needed for the Council actually to place the complaint on its agenda. Among the initial waverers were Britain and France, but Eisenhower had his UN ambassador threaten that if they 'felt that they must take an independent line backing the present government of Guatemala, we would feel free to take an independent line concerning such matters as Egypt and North Africa in which we hitherto tried to exercise the greatest forbearance so as not to embarrass Great Britain and France'. They duly fell into line, but reminded the USA of the episode when it refused to reciprocate over Suez in 1956.[21]

The United States' other policy towards Guatemala was covert action. CIA planning began shortly after the August 1953 displacement of Mossadegh from power in Iran (see p.346). With the enthusiastic support of Honduras and Nicaragua, it came to focus on an invasion by Colonel Armas and his 'contra'-type forces. This

21. ibid, esp. pp.50–3, 60; Eden, *Full Circle* pp.137–8, 566

was triggered when, in May 1954, Arbenz secured Czech arms with which to create a militia to balance his unreliable regular army. Armas's invasion was unimpressive, but it was magnified by skilful radio propaganda and backed by Nicaraguan and CIA bombing. The United States' hand was plain enough for the Guatemalan army to persuade Arbenz to resign to prevent further escalation. The US ambassador then negotiated his succession by Armas, and Eisenhower was able to thank the CIA: 'You've averted a Soviet beachhead in our hemisphere'. Armas did not take up a US offer to help build a non-communist labour movement, but in most ways he gave satisfaction: Nixon described him in 1955 as 'a good President who said, "Tell us what you want to do and that's what we will do" '. Judged by other criteria, Guatemala's subsequent social and political evolution was distinctly unfortunate; indeed about 100,000 people are said to have died in political violence over the next three decades.[22]

EISENHOWER'S GRADUAL CONVERSION TO ECONOMIC AID

To secure the Caracas anti-communist resolutions, Dulles had had to consent to the holding of the long-delayed economic conference. This duly met in Rio later in 1954, with the Brazilians encouraging the USA to come 'with an *Eisenhower Plan*'. Although his administration was divided, Eisenhower's policy was essentially that of his predecessor: Latin America (unlike South-East Asia) was not directly exposed to communist assault, and so should be developed by loans not grants, and above all through US business investment. At Rio the USA offered only an increase in Export-Import Bank lending; the conference amounted to little more than a resigned failure to agree. A sequel in 1957 also 'produced nothing better than a 10 per cent increase in the anthology of inter-American resolutions'.[23] However, in May 1958, what had been intended as an anodyne goodwill tour by Vice-President Nixon administered a major shock. Nixon was jeered and stoned by students in Montevideo and Lima, then nearly killed by a mob in Caracas, where the USA was blamed

22. Rabe, *Eisenhower and Latin America* chap. 3; Ambrose, *Eisenhower* pp.192–7; Cook, *The Declassified Eisenhower* pp.223–89; Molineu, *U.S. Policy Toward Latin America* pp.54–9; Ranelagh, *The Agency* p.265

23. Rabe, *Eisenhower and Latin America* pp.52, 72–3, 76–7, 95

both for past links with the recently ousted dictator and for its damaging economic policies.[24] This led to much heart-seaching in Washington. President Kubitschek of Brazil (among others) improved the occasion by deploring the riots but insisting that 'something must be done to restore composure to the continental unity'; 'the problem of underdevelopment will have to be solved if Latin American nations are to be able more effectively to resist subversion and serve the Western cause'. Specifically he suggested an 'Operation Pan America' to which the USA would pledge $40 billion over twenty years. Washington's horizons were more modest, but in 1958–9 it altered course to concede an Inter-American Development Bank with a capital of $1 billion (nearly half supplied by the USA).

A further stimulus was provided by the fall of the long-standing Cuban dictator Batista and the rapid leftwards move of the successor Castro regime (see p.404), which was by early 1960 concluding important trade deals with the USSR. There was, indeed, a general Soviet trade initiative, designed (the CIA felt) 'to erode and eventually eliminate United States influence in Latin America by promoting anti-American neutralism and ultranationalist movements and governments which will increase the vulnerability of America's "strategic backyard" '. Eisenhower's own 1960 tour of Latin America also convinced him that previous investment, public and private, 'had failed to benefit the masses'; he returned convinced that the USA would secure hemispheric support for its anti-Cuban policy only if it formulated 'a dramatic . . . democratic development program'. In July 1960 he announced a new $500 million 'Social Progress Trust Fund'; his administration now talked of making Latin American 'leaders, especially the traditional elite groups, fully aware of the critical need to do something to meet the rising expectations of their peoples in order to avoid violent changes brought on by over-long suppression of popular pressures'.[25]

KENNEDY'S ALLIANCE FOR PROGRESS 1961

Kennedy's incoming administration fully shared these attitudes and lost no time in proposing, in a blaze of publicity, a 'vast new

24. Kennan's 1950 tour had also provoked major anti-US demonstrations and required heavy police protection in Brazil

25. Rabe, *Eisenhower and Latin America* esp. pp.136–43

ten-year plan', the Alliance for Progress. This was endorsed in August 1961 at the Punta del Este Conference, which envisaged $20 billion aid over the next decade, to complement $80 billion of local Latin American investment and promote land reform, an equitable tax reform, cheap housing, health improvements and the eradication of illiteracy as well as economic growth. All this sounded good, except to Cuba, which described it as 'an attempt to buy the conscience of Latin America' and added (at Punta del Este) that it expected to do much better on the basis of aid from communist countries and its own non-exploitative development programme. Yet the Alliance's economic targets were less ambitious than they sounded: the Punta del Este Charter looked to 2.5 per cent annual per capita growth, and the influential Washington adviser Adolf Berle talked of a 50 per cent rise in the standard of living; but the Japanese premier, Ikeda, had recently promised to *double* living standards within the decade.[26]

In the event the USA met its commitments, providing $18 billion in aid over the decade (directly and through institutions like the World Bank) with a further $3 billion of commercial investment. But the net effect was less than it seemed: Latin American foreign borrowing was already high ($10 billion in 1960, nearly $13 billion in 1966), and debt servicing accounted for about 90 per cent of new aid. So much of the Alliance for Progress, especially in its earlier years, was, in effect, a refinancing operation, while new commercial investment was comfortably surpassed by repatriated profits. There was, too, considerable, if unquantifiable, flight of Latin American capital to safer havens abroad.[27] Latin America's economic performance therefore depended almost entirely on its own efforts. Naturally it varied greatly from country to country; but by 1963 Kennedy was saying, in language reminiscent of the Truman administration, that in Europe 'we helped to rebuild a shattered economy whose human and social foundation remained. Today we are trying to create a basic new foundation, capable of reshaping the centuries-old societies and economies of half a hemisphere'. This, in itself, need be no insuperable barrier, as the

26. *Keesing's*, 18035, 18378–9; S. Rabe, 'Controlling Revolutions: Latin America, the Alliance for Progress, and Cold War Anti-Communism' in Thomas Patterson (ed.), *Kennedy's Quest for Victory: American Foreign Policy, 1961–1963* (New York, 1989) pp.105–7; J. Levinson and Juan de Onis, *The Alliance that Lost its Way: A Critical Report on the Alliance for Progress* (Chicago, 1970) Appendices; see also pp.173–4, 176–7 for Japanese growth

27. Levinson and Onis, *The Alliance that Lost its Way* chap. 7; Schlesinger, *A Thousand Days* pp.674–6

Rim of Asia was beginning to show. Latin American experience was less fortunate: one notable, though not universal, feature was a propensity towards hyperinflation periodically reined back by harsh currency stabilisation programmes. Overall Latin American exports failed to keep pace with the growth in world trade; they did particularly badly in the burgeoning US market, falling from 27 per cent to 16 per cent of US merchandise imports between 1960 and 1968 (though this was partially offset by increased sales to Europe). General economic growth in the 1960s, at 1.5 per cent, fell well short of the Alliance's 2.5 per cent target and represented little improvement on the 1950s.[28] In short the Alliance did not constitute the demonstrative success that Kennedy had foreshadowed.

LATIN AMERICA, THE WEST, AND THE THIRD WORLD

It is not surprising that many Latin Americans continued to pursue their own ideas; for the most part this involved governments seeking economic development in ways too diverse to chronicle here, but it also saw them attracted by new approaches to the structuring of the global economy. Venezuela had taken the lead by making a major contribution to the foundation of OPEC in 1960.[29] Most states were not oil exporters, but all could see the attraction of attempts to support the prices of the primary commodities that were their chief exports. They were drawn (partly by Yugoslav diplomacy) into what became the Group of 77 (see pp.473–4); and the UN's Economic Commission for Latin America was to supply both the Secretary and much of the economic analysis underlying UNCTAD (United Nations Conference on Trade and Development – see pp.473–4). Intellectuals took these ideas further, developing (on the basis of Latin America's economic difficulties) a semi-Marxist *dependista* critique that saw the world's Northern capitalist core as restricting, or (with the aid of local elites) distorting, the development of the periphery.

All this led to a growing diversification of international attitudes. As before, many leaders identified with the Christian and capitalist West, and aspired only to develop and join it. But people were

28. Levinson and Onis, *The Alliance that Lost its Way* esp. pp.134–5, 164, 187 ff; Paterson, *Kennedy's Quest for Victory* pp.110, 112

29. Yergin, *The Prize* pp.510–18, 522–3; Ecuador joined OPEC in 1973

more ready than before to look beyond the United States. Thus the US policy of vetoing (as wasteful) purchases of supersonic fighters was swept aside by Peru's acquisition (after a nationalist military coup) of planes from France; over the next four years Latin American arms purchases from Europe were four times as high as from the USA; and in 1973 Nixon had to abandon the paternalist policy of controlling sales.[30] A few politicians (and many intellectuals) went further, preferring to see Latin America for some (or all) purposes as part of the Third World, but generally with caution: as Brazil's Foreign Minister put it in 1979, 'Our country is simultaneously part of the Western World and the Third World and we must know how to maintain a dialogue with both these spheres with equal proficiency'. So, as one scholar has written, the

> degree of alignment [with the Third World] varied greatly from country to country and regime to regime. Thus while Mexico . . . stood consistently in the forefront, Argentina changed its policy according to the character of the government in power . . . and in Brazil in the 1970s there was protracted conflict between the *terceiromundistas* and traditionalists.[31]

However tentative and qualified, such alignments constituted a major shift from the certainties of the 1940s and 1950s.

KENNEDY'S ATTEMPTS TO LINK AID TO DEMOCRATIC GOVERNMENT

Kennedy's 1961 vision had been not only economic but also political and social. 'Latin America', he declared, 'is seething with discontent and unrest'; accordingly 'political freedom must accompany material progress', and itself 'be accompanied by social change. For unless necessary social reforms . . . are freely made . . . unless the great mass of Americans share in increasing prosperity – then our alliance, our revolution, our dream, and our freedom will fail'.[32] This was, in a sense, a profoundly interventionist attempt to export to Latin America the liberal values

30. Anthony Sampson, *The Arms Bazaar* (paperback edn, 1978) pp.184–5. De Gaulle had sensed something of this potential detachment and undertaken a tour in 1964, denouncing 'hegemony' and stressing shared 'Latin' values

31. Andrew Hurrell, 'Latin America and the West' in R. O'Neill and R.J. Vincent (eds) *The West and the Third World: Essays in Honour of J.D.B. Miller* (Basingstoke, 1990) esp. p.162

32. Levinson and Onis, *The Alliance that Lost its Way* pp.338–9, 344

of his own domestic 'New Frontier'; it was for failures in these fields that the Alliance most quickly came to be condemned. Here we must concentrate on the insistence on democracy[33] (an insistence explicitly directed at the regimes of Cuba and the Dominican Republic). This came, in fact, at an unfortunate time, for whereas between 1956 and 1960 ten Latin American dictators had been ousted, in the 1960s the pendulum was swinging back: the Kennedy years alone saw six popularly elected presidents ousted by the military. Eisenhower's administration had reacted cautiously to the change, distancing itself from Cuba's Batista in 1958 and seeking to bring down Trujillo of the Dominican Republic in 1960. Although ready to give 'special encouragement' to democratic regimes, it defeated – with much anti-interventionist Latin American support – the 1959 Venezuelan proposal that the OAS recognise only 'regimes born of free election and respecting human rights'. By contrast, Kennedy was prepared to go some way down this road, breaking off 'diplomatic relations for varying periods with Argentina, Peru, Guatemala, Ecuador, the Dominican Republic and Honduras, when democratic regimes there were overthrown by military coups d'état. In each case economic aid was suspended as well'.[34] Thus when the Peruvian military took over in 1962, Kennedy invoked the Declaration of Punta del Este, briefly broke off relations, and managed to persuade the junta to hold elections in 1963. When a pre-emptive coup removed the possibility that Arbenz's leftist predecessor would win the 1963 Guatemalan elections, however, Washington was relieved and suspended aid only for three weeks. Although relations with Honduras were duly broken off after the October 1963 coup, the new leader correctly predicted that aid would be restored within six months. By then Kennedy had become resigned to such episodes, and approved a circular to US embassies that, while still regretting them, recognised the impossibility of 'keeping a man in office by the use of economic pressure or even military force, when his own people are not willing to fight to defend him'.[35]

33. For an assessment of social developments – largely undermined by the area's population growth – see ibid, Part 3

34. Rabe, *Eisenhower and Latin America* pp.104–6; *New York Times*, 19 March 1964 p.2. Kennedy's policy was also applied in Korea: relations and aid were broken off – briefly – after General Park's 1961 coup, and Park was later warned not to cancel the 1963 elections (see also pp.447–8)

35. Paterson, *Kennedy's Quest for Victory* pp.110–11, 113–15; Levinson and Onis, *The Alliance that Lost its Way* chap. 5; Molineu, *U.S. Policy Toward Latin America* pp.131–2

THE JOHNSON AND NIXON YEARS

Johnson's administration went further, the new Assistant Secretary for Inter-American Affairs telling diplomats (in what became known as the 'Mann Doctrine') that there should 'no longer be "good guys or bad guys" as far as United States policy was concerned'. Accurate classification of Latin American rulers as dictators or democrats was not easy, and he personally had difficulty in distinguishing politically between Lopez Mateos of Mexico, Paz Estenssoro of Bolivia and Stroessner of Paraguay. Accordingly he endorsed Mexico's 'Estrada' doctrine that the criterion for recognition should be effective control of the country by the new government. He laid down four principles only for US policy in Latin America: 'the fostering of economic growth in the area, the protection of $9 billion in United States investments there, non-intervention in the internal affairs of the hemisphere's republics, and opposition to Communism'.[36]

In the ensuing years, Latin American affairs were dominated partly by fall-out from the 1965 US intervention in the Dominican Republic (see pp.408–9), partly by widespread disappointment with the Alliance for Progress and mounting impatience with US trade policy. The Dominican intervention proved so divisive that it was thought best to postpone the scheduled inter-American conference for some months. When it finally met in Rio in November 1965, Colombia's motion censuring the USA attracted no votes. On the other side, Brazil (which had backed, indeed contributed to, the operation) proposed a permanent Inter-American Peace Force empowered to intervene when a country was threatened by internal communism. This appealed to the military in a number of other countries and also to the USA, but it attracted massive and predictable opposition, and was remitted for further study. Eventually it was withdrawn at the 1967 Buenos Aires Foreign Ministers' conference, which also defeated a more moderate Brazilian/ Argentinian proposal for a permanent OAS military advisory committee. Meanwhile a meeting of Chile, Colombia, Venezuela, Ecuador and Peru had called for non-intervention, more aid, Latin American economic integration, and 'greater respect by the United States for the rules of international trade'. What this meant became clearer at the April 1967 Punta del Este summit meeting. Ecuador

36. *New York Times*, 19 March 1964 pp.1–2 (leaked report, not claiming to be a *verbatim* quotation – cf. also Levinson and Onis, *The Alliance that Lost its Way* p.88)

was alone in actually attacking the USA, but Johnson's proposed aid increases (in fact more than Congress would wear) were found disappointing; a number of states pressed politely for tariff concessions, the elimination of export subsidies and the untying of US aid, on all of which Johnson had to stall.[37]

NIXON'S 'BENIGN NEGLECT' 1969–74

In 1969 unhappiness with the United States was still more evident in the disturbances prompted by a fact-finding tour on the part of Nixon's representative Governor Rockefeller; they led Venezuela and Chile to cancel his visit since 'far from achieving the fundamental objectives sought, . . . it has provoked events which could make difficult and even perturb the future relations between the United States and Latin America'. (He eventually produced a gloomy report noting that 'The United States has allowed the special relationship it has historically maintained with the other nations of the Western Hemisphere to deteriorate badly', and warning of the dangers of communist subversion.) In June 1969 twenty-one states met in Chile, whose President stressed the need 'to confirm a Latin American personality with its specific criteria and values in the sense of a continental nationalism', and called for 'a dialogue on an equal level, instead of a monologue however brilliant of one of the partners'. The Chilean Foreign Minister, Valdés, then proceeded to Washington to serve on Nixon the resultant 'Latin American Consensus of Viña del Mar'. The visit was a disaster: Valdés annoyed Nixon by stressing 'the impossibility of dealing with the United States within the framework of inter-American relations; the differences in power were too great', and by claiming that Latin America sent the USA $3.80 for every dollar it received in aid. Valdés allegedly collected the rebuke from Kissinger that Latin America 'is not important. Nothing important can come from the South. History has never been produced in the South. The axis of history' runs from Moscow via Bonn and Washington to Tokyo. Unsurprisingly the USA refused to embark on a continuous dialogue within the OAS on the basis of Viña del Mar. Although Nixon did show himself responsive to some of the specific

37. *Keesing's*, 22229 ff; Johnson, *Vantage Point* pp.350–1

demands,[38] he seems to have decided that Latin America was *generally* best left to its own devices in a low-profile policy of 'benign neglect'.[39]

EISENHOWER AND CUBA 1958–60

Under no US administration did such a hands-off approach extend to situations where there was a perceived danger of communism. In 1954 Eisenhower had perhaps been too prone to see reds under the bed in Guatemala. Surprisingly he was not quite ready enough to see them in Cuba. At the start of 1958 the authoritarian Batista regime had seemed reasonably in control. It was faced with urban terrorism (which it handled brutally) and a diaspora of small guerrilla groups in the mountains, mostly traditional bandits but including a few hundred men under Fidel Castro who had emerged (through skilful publicity and the division and discrediting of more orthodox politicians) as the leading opposition figure. Batista had enjoyed widespread sympathy after the assault on his palace in 1957, and as late as April 1958 the opposition's call for a general strike was a complete failure. But when Batista followed this up with a major assault on Castro's Sierra Maestra stronghold, first his army and then his regime disintegrated without any very serious fighting.[40] Washington had in fact begun to disengage from Batista in 1957 (*before* his rule appeared to be in any serious trouble), and in March 1958 it imposed an arms embargo that dealt him a serious psychological (though not logistical) blow. In November 1958 he was advised to leave, but the attempt to edge him out was badly handled, probably because it was accorded neither priority nor high-level political attention: in December 1958 Eisenhower was obviously not au fait with the Cuban situation.[41] US support was not thrown behind any particular successor, and in mid-1958 Vene-

38. His 1970 'Report on the "State of the World" ' untied AID ([US] Agency for International Development) funds, proposed to shift from bilateral to multilateral economic aid, offered support for tariff preferences for developing countries and for Latin American free trade areas, and accepted the Latin American desire to formulate policies by themselves before collectively discussing them with the USA: *Keesing's*, 23884–5

39. *Keesing's*, 23713 ff; Hersh, *The Price of Power* pp.262–3

40. Hugh Thomas puts the total casualties of the whole 1952–8 political crisis and civil war at between 1,500 and 2,000, plus some hundreds of subsequent executions for war-crimes: *Cuba or the Pursuit of Freedom* (1971) p.1,044

41. Ambrose, *Eisenhower: The President* p.505

zuelan intervention on behalf of Major Barquín was discouraged. By December direct pressure was finally placed on Batista to leave, as he did on 1 January 1959 – but still without any clear US planning for the succession, which fell into Castro's lap.[42]

From the outset Washington was concerned about some of Castro's associates; but it initially sought to treat his revolution as it had that in Bolivia, and it was not unhopeful of Fidel himself. In April 1959 Secretary of State Herter had a long talk with him, and reported to Eisenhower that he was an 'enigma' with good and bad points; Eisenhower's response was, '*File*. We will check in a year'.[43] Historians are still divided. The usual view is that Castro himself had, during his rebellion against Batista, no distinctive views on government beyond a general liberal nationalism. But between January 1959 and early 1961 he decided, probably by stages, that, in the face of internal opposition and external pressure, he could best conduct his revolution by taking over, and then working through, the Communist Party. From December 1961 onwards, however, Castro was to proclaim that he had always been at least loosely Marxist-Leninist, but had disguised these views in order to seize power. Partly, though not entirely, on the basis of such retrospective information, Tad Szulc argues that at the January 1959 take-over Castro paralleled the new official administration with a 'hidden government', the Office of Revolutionary Plans and Coordination.[44]

Be that as it may, by November 1959 Castro's domestic nationalisations, stridently anti-US tone at the United Nations and subversion elsewhere in Central America had led Herter to conclude that he would not 'voluntarily adopt policies and attitudes consistent with minimum United States security requirement'; this could have 'serious adverse effects on Free World support of our leadership, especially in the United Nations on such issues as the Chinese representation problem', and also damage US business interests in Latin America. So the USA should foster a 'coherent opposition' and seek to produce, by the end of 1960, either 'a reformed Castro regime or a successor to it'. In December Allen Dulles started calling for Castro's overthrow, and in March 1960, though Herter still had no 'hard evidence' of communist domi-

42. Ambassador Smith may have had some involvement in General Cantillo's attempt to establish a junta: Tad Szulc, *Fidel: A Critical Portrait* (New York, 1986) pp.457–8; the CIA bought the release from prison of Barquín, who then arrested Cantillo and turned power over to Castro: Thomas, *Cuba* p.1,028

43. Rabe, *Eisenhower and Latin America* pp.122–4

44. Thomas, *Cuba passim*; Szulc, *Fidel* esp. pp.472–80

nation, Eisenhower approved a programme for the creation of a government-in-exile and 'a paramilitary force outside of Cuba for future guerrilla action'. Building this took time. Meanwhile in July Eisenhower suspended imports of Cuban sugar, a major economic blow, and declared that the USA would never 'permit the establishment of a regime dominated by international communism in the Western Hemisphere'. Planning also went ahead, with the aid of the Mafia, to secure the assassination of Fidel Castro (and possibly of his more clearly pro-communist brother Raúl and of Che Guevara).[45]

KENNEDY AND CASTRO 1961–3

Little had come of all this by the time Kennedy succeeded Eisenhower in January 1961. In particular no government-in-exile had been constituted, though Eisenhower regarded the discovery of a credible leader as an indispensable preliminary to any invasion. But Cuban émigrés were receiving military training in Guatemala, and it was clear that their morale would suffer were they not used soon; also the Guatemalan government was anxious to see them leave. Kennedy thus inherited a bad situation, and soon made it worse. He decided to go ahead with the invasion (in April 1961); but he tinkered with the plan's details, moving the proposed landing site to the Bay of Pigs (an unsuitable choice). Worse still, the cover story for the preliminary CIA bombing of the Cuban air force fell apart,[46] and (for fear of repercussions in Berlin if the USA became openly involved) Kennedy refused to authorise the second strike that would have completed the job. The landing was accordingly shot up by the surviving Cuban planes, and the forces that came ashore were destroyed by the unexpectedly rapid deployment of the Cuban army; after heavy fighting, this took some 1,200 prisoners.[47]

Kennedys, however, do not give up easily, and their next step was

45. Rabe, *Eisenhower and Latin America* chaps 7, 9; Ranelagh, *The Agency* p.357; Szulc, *Fidel* p.672; Ambrose, *Eisenhower: The President* p.557; Powers, *The Man who Kept the Secrets* pp.186–92

46. Astute journalists soon concluded that the bombing could not have been the work of defecting Cuban pilots

47. Paterson, *Kennedy's Quest for Victory* chap. 5; Prados, *Presidents' Secret Wars* chaps 10–11; Thomas, *Cuba* chap. 106; Ambrose, *Eisenhower: The President* pp.608–10, 638–9

'Operation Mongoose', a mishmash of attempts to sabotage the Cuban economy (by, for instance, destroying the sugar crop), stir up rebellion, or simply assassinate Castro. 'Mongoose' may have convinced Khrushchev that he must do something to protect Castro's regime, and so helped bring on the Cuban missile crisis.[48] This ended with Kennedy promising not to *invade* Cuba provided 'Cuba itself commits no aggressive acts against any of the nations of the Western Hemisphere'.[49] But this did not prevent the resumption either of sabotage or of assassination plots, the nastiest idea being to take advantage of the December 1962 ransoming of the Bay of Pigs prisoners to present Castro with a poisoned diving suit. There have been suggestions that, by November 1963 (when he was murdered), President Kennedy was seeking a reconciliation; but equally another coup-cum-assassination attempt was then under way. President Johnson, however, did not share the Kennedys' vendetta with Cuba and ordered the discontinuance of operations against it.[50]

THE OAS AND CUBA IN THE 1960s

This left the Castro regime secure, but very much an isolated and alien body in Latin America. Eisenhower would have liked to secure OAS action against it. But, as Herter told him after a meeting in August 1960, the Latin Americans 'had two fears – the Cubans and us and were afraid we would take unilateral steps against Cuba' if the OAS in any way condemned it. These hesitations started to evaporate in 1961 as Castro moved towards a one-party communist state. Venezuela and Colombia broke off diplomatic relations; Colombia started pushing (with Central American and US support) for sanctions; and an OAS committee upheld Peru's complaint that Cuba was violating human rights and promoting subversion. On the other hand such major states as Argentina, Brazil and Mexico opposed anything punitive. The result, at the January 1962 Punta del Este Foreign Ministers conference, was a compromise to the effect that, by its actions, Cuba had 'voluntarily placed itself outside

48. See *The Cold War* pp.227–31

49. That Kennedy refused to give an unconditional assurance has only recently become known: *New York Times*, 7 Jan. 1992 p.A5

50. Paterson, *Kennedy's Quest for Victory* pp.152–4; Ranelagh, *The Agency* pp.383–90; Powers, *The Man who Kept the Secrets* chap. 9. After fuller briefing years later, Johnson declared that 'we were running a damned Murder Incorporated in the Caribbean'

the Inter-American system'; in addition arms sales were embargoed, but more general trade sanctions merely encouraged. Castro responded that the decision had shown the OAS to be 'nothing more nor less than the U.S. Ministry of Colonies', and by declaring the 'Latin-American revolution' to be 'inevitable'. By April 1962 fifteen states, though not Brazil, Chile, or Mexico, had broken off diplomatic relations; during the Cuban missile crisis the OAS offered unanimous support under the Rio Pact for US imposition of its 'quarantine' naval blockade. There was then something of a lull until the discovery in late 1963 of three tons of weapons shipped by Cuba to the Venezuelan guerrillas. Venezuela pressed for sanctions and in July 1964 the OAS voted not to maintain diplomatic relations, and to suspend all trade and sea communications, with Cuba. Mexico still stood out, on principle rather than for any love of Castro; but the air service to Mexico City was now the island's only official link with the Western hemisphere, and its trade had been oriented almost entirely to the communist world.[51]

Castro's dreams of industrial diversification were never realised, but the USSR paid quite well for his sugar and provided oil and other subsidies. What use he made of this is unclear. It certainly seemed, to begin with, that he had delivered social, if not economic, development, spreading health services and eliminating gross disparities in wealth, begging and prostitution in a way that contrasted favourably both with his predecessor's regime and with many of his neighbours. Recently there have been suggestions that, as in the USSR, privilege was more marked and social services were considerably worse than appeared on the surface.

THE USA AND THE DOMINICAN REPUBLIC 1960–5

Almost as important to Washington as isolating Cuba was stopping any other country from going the same way. The original US decision to distance itself from the Trujillo regime in the Dominican Republic long antedated Castro, but by February 1960 Herter was warning Eisenhower that Trujillo 'may soon create a situation like that in Cuba where the opposition is taken over by wild radicals'; by July 1960 Eisenhower had decided to 'link Trujillo

51. Rabe, *Eisenhower and Latin America* pp.158, 166; Schlesinger, *A Thousand Days* pp.670–3, 696; *Keesing's*, 18713–18, 20071, 20336

and Castro up and direct our actions against both of them'. He hoped that Trujillo's attempt to murder the President of Venezuela would induce the OAS to step in and enforce free elections, thus both forestalling a possible Castro-type revolution in the Dominican Republic and providing a useful precedent for subsequent action against Cuba, but the OAS would not go beyond the breaking off of diplomatic relations and certain trade sanctions. An alternative was to persuade, or bribe, Trujillo to leave, but he proved obdurate. A third possibility was assassination, which was much discussed in 1960 and which led to the supply of weapons to Dominican dissidents in January 1961.[52] Trujillo was in fact shot (though not with these guns) in May, and the nominal President Joaquin Balaguer took over. Kennedy's response was that 'The anti-communist liberals aren't strong enough. [So] We must use our influence to take Balaguer along the road to democracy', while also preventing an army take-over 'which could [by reaction] lead straight to Castro'. Accordingly OAS and US trade sanctions were kept in place until the brokered emergence in 1962 of a transitional government pledged to elections; the USA staged naval demonstrations to prevent a return to power of Trujillo's relatives. In December 1962 Juan Bosch won the elections and was initially accorded substantial US support. But he soon convinced the USA that he was too weak; in September 1963 it declined to prevent a coup against him, then in December resumed relations with the new regime against a promise of elections in 1965. Their imminence prompted another military coup attempt in April 1965, but it backfired and the military in its turn seemed likely to be overwhelmed by armed civilians.

Meanwhile the government had fled, and the United States concluded that real control was likely to pass to communists.[53] So it landed troops (23,000 by 9 May 1965): 'What can we do in Vietnam', Johnson is supposed to have said, 'if we can't clean up the Dominican Republic?' He later broadcast to the effect that 'The American nations cannot, must not, and will not permit the establishment of another Communist government in the Western Hemisphere'. Actually they were divided, though (as Johnson noted) US intervention seemed much more attractive to Latin American ambassadors in San Domingo than to their Foreign Ministers meeting in Washington. The OAS acted quickly to help arrange an

52. Rabe, *Eisenhower and Latin America* pp.155–61

53. Washington later named fifty-four communist and Castroist leaders, but its claims were categorically denied by the insurgents and by ex-President Bosch

initial cease-fire, but it was only after considerable debate that it accepted, on 6 May, a US proposal for the creation of an 'Inter-American Peace Force'; the vote of the Dominican Republic's pre-revolutionary delegate was needed to secure the necessary two-thirds majority. The Force consisted chiefly of US troops; but five other states contributed, notably Brazil, which sent a sometimes embarrassingly anti-communist general to assume formal command. Representatives of Brazil and El Salvador also joined the USA in mediating between the various Dominican forces, who were by the end of August brought to agree on a compromise government pledged to free elections. These were duly held next summer, with Balaguer defeating Bosch; US troops finally left in September; and competitive elections have in fact continued ever since.[54]

CIA INTERVENTION IN BRITISH GUIANA 1963

The Dominican Republic was not the only state to worry Kennedy, who had no intention of relying only on the Alliance for Progress to prevent communism since 'Vitamin tablets will not save a man set upon by hoodlums in an alley'. In British Guiana (Guyana) the Marxist Cheddi Jagan appeared likely to be the beneficiary of decolonisation. In 1963 a CIA-financed general strike induced the British to step in and change the electoral system to one of proportional representation that permitted Jagan's defeat by a coalition of his opponents.[55] Ironically the new leader, Forbes Burnham, subsequently developed into a Soviet-oriented Marxist, but his tenure was not disturbed.

54. J. Slater, 'The Dominican Republic' in Blechman and Kaplan, *Force without War* chap. 8; Schlesinger, *A Thousand Days* pp.660–4; Johnson, *Vantage Point* pp.187–204; *Keesing's*, 20813–18, 20855–6, 20985. In contrast to previous intra-American crises, the USA could not prevent lengthy discussion by the UN Security Council, but this led only to the appointment of a (helpful) special representative of the Secretary-General

55. Calvert, *Latin America in the Twentieth Century* pp.167–8; Ranelagh, *The Agency* p.390; Schlesinger, *A Thousand Days* pp.664–9 (a sanitised account, which, however, shows the British had warned Washington about Burnham)

THE USA AND THE COUP IN BRAZIL 1964

Far more important was the vast state of Brazil, which Schlesinger was to describe as (with Venezuela) the chief communist 'target of priority'. Its President, Goulart, was not basically anti-USA: during the Cuban missile crisis he advocated more forceful action than that taken, and at its conclusion had the ambassador in and drank 'To the Yankee victory!'. But both domestic conservatives and US observers were worried by his combination of inflation and economic nationalism, saw his leftist populism as opening the way to communist penetration, and feared that he was seeking to establish himself as dictator. The USA therefore reduced economic aid, but not military assistance, which was, according to Ambassador Gordon, 'a highly important factor influencing military to be pro-U.S.' Contact was also established with secret dissidents like the Chief of Staff Castelo Branco and ex-President Kubitschek. Their decision to stage a coup appears to have been taken independently, but in the knowledge that the USA would applaud it if successful. In fact Washington's worst nightmare was that an unsuccessful coup would precipitate Brazil to the left or lead to civil war; so, after a coup had been launched in March 1964, it decided to dispatch a naval force to supply oil and arms if needed. In fact they were not, since Goulart's administration collapsed while the force was still at sea: 'a great victory', Gordon wrote, 'for the free world' and one that eliminated the possibility of a 'total loss to the West of all South American Republics'.[56] Thereafter the military dug itself in, offering repressive government but for many years also rapid economic growth.

CASTRO AND CHE GUEVARA

On the other side, Castro had from the outset been interfering abroad,[57] and by 1962 he had come to call openly for general Latin American revolution. The Cuban revolution had been deceptively

56. Schlesinger, *A Thousand Days* p.664; Phyllis R. Parker, *Brazil and the Quiet Intervention, 1964* (Austin, Tex., 1979) p.82 and *passim*; Calvert, *Latin America in the Twentieth Century* pp.127 ff

57. Thomas, *Cuba* p.1,228 (the Dominican Republic, 1959); there were also attempts against Panama, Nicaragua and Guatemala, though Cuban government involvement is not clear

easy, and there were hopes that it could be generally replicated: 'Given suitable operating country, land hunger, and injustices', Che Guevara wrote in 1960,[58] 'a hard core of 30 to 50 men [Castro had started with about 20 in the Sierra Maestra] is enough to set off armed revolutions in any Latin American country'. Not so. There was, of course, much indigenous combustible material; in the mid-1960s this seems to have been supplemented by Cuban involvement in insurrections in Venezuela, Guatemala, Peru, Bolivia, and perhaps Colombia. None succeeded; Guevara's failure and death in an ambitious 1966–7 attempt to establish 'the continental command' in Bolivia became well chronicled when Castro published his diary.[59] Among the reasons for these failures were a lack of peasant support, greater strength on the part of most governments than had been anticipated, and the readiness of weaker ones (like Peru and Bolivia) to turn to the CIA for help.[60]

THE USA AND CHILE 1962–73; ALLENDE'S RISE AND FALL

A final dimension of US activity was the subsidisation of moderate political parties. This was especially important in Chile, where (as a National Security Council memorandum put it) 'We are not prepared to risk a Socialist or FRAP [Popular Action Front] victory [in the 1964 elections], for fear of nationalization of U.S. investments, the consequences of that action, and the probable Communist influence in a Socialist (or FRAP) government'. Accordingly the CIA spent some $4 million in 1962–4, and this may have helped the Christian Democrat Frei beat the Marxist socialist Allende in the 1964 presidential elections.[61] Frei could not constitutionally run

58. *Keesing's*, 23108. For a slightly different version see Guevara's very influential *Guerilla Warfare* (paperback edn; Harmondsworth, 1969) p.123

59. *Keesing's*, 23108 ff, 23235, 23855 (Bolivia – and Peru, for which cf. also 23101), 20071, 22119 (Venezuela), 24828 (Colombia); Richard Gott, *Rural Guerillas in Latin America* (paperback edn, 1973) esp. pp.52–6, 295–6; Ranelagh, *The Agency* p.424; V. Marchetti and J.D. Marks, *The CIA and the Cult of Intelligence* (1974) pp.123 ff

60. The CIA generally acted at the behest, and with the support, of local governments, but in 1962 it orchestrated anti-Cuban/communist demonstrations in Ecuador that proved the prelude to the army coup: Rositzke, *The CIA's Secret Operations* pp.190–2. The Bolivian Minister of the Interior during the Che Guevara affair later changed sides and claimed the CIA had blackmailed him into acting as an agent: Marchetti and Marks, *The CIA and the Cult of Intelligence* pp.130–2

61. Paterson, *Kennedy's Quest for Victory* p.116. From 1961 to 1973 the CIA was supposedly authorised to spend over $12 million on such covert support throughout the continent: Rositzke, *The CIA's Secret Operations* p.192

again in 1970, and as the non-Marxist vote was split, Allende just secured a plurality. The election was thus thrown into the hands of the Chilean Congress, but this was expected to choose Allende (as indeed it did). Hitherto the USA had stayed aloof, since the CIA had forecast a right-wing electoral victory. After the elections, plans were promptly drawn up to dissuade the Congress from choosing Allende, through either bribery or pressure on the part of the Chilean military; an attempt to organise the latter by kidnapping the army commander led to his murder, but not to any change in the army's constitutionalist stance. Allende therefore took over.

Three years later he was overthrown by a military coup, turning down the customary Latin American offer of a free passage to exile, and committing suicide or being killed in the subsequent fighting. This destruction of a democratically elected Marxist President (who had established warm relations with Cuba and made his country a mecca for Latin-American revolutionaries, but who might well have been prepared to leave office peacefully at the next elections)[62] became an international cause célèbre, and there are very varied assessments of the degree of US involvement. The USA did block Inter-American Development and World Bank loans (though not until after copper nationalisations with what the USA regarded as insufficient compensation) and US bank lending fell right off. It was replaced by loans from Western Europe, the USSR and China, however, so the Chilean economy was not really, as Nixon once said it should be, 'squeezed until it screamed' in any direct sense. More controversial is the question of foreign involvement in the numerous strikes. The CIA reported spending $8 million on propaganda and the general encouragement of opposition and potential putsch-ist groups. We are told that no such money went directly to the strikers. These had their own reasons for striking (inflation and a distaste for being nationalised); but they may also have been funded, in part, by Chilean business and by money sent from Brazil and other right-wing Latin American countries – the USA was not alone in wishing Allende's downfall. Finally there is the question of the spontaneity of the military coup. The USA had maintained military aid and been careful to cultivate the Chilean military; this must have known that a coup would be welcome. The USA, and very possibly Brazil and the Argentine too, had some prior knowledge of when the coup would come off. But there seems no

62. Which a re-formed anti-Marxist coalition would, on the showing of the 1972 congressional elections, have won comfortably

reason to doubt that the actual decision to mount it was taken by a Chilean junta, with the army deciding to move only at a very late stage.[63]

AUTHORITARIAN REGIMES IN SOUTH AMERICA IN THE 1970s AND EARLY 1980s

It had been widely expected that the coup would merely remove Allende and hold elections, but the US ambassador's forecast that 'If the Army should take over, I doubt very much that they will be prepared to give up power in a hurry' was to be amply borne out. For General Pinochet was determined to sort out the problems, political and economic, that he saw as having brought his country into its present state. Some of his methods did not bear examination: a 1991 report found that there had been 'a will to exterminate a category of people . . . [to whom the regime] attributed a high degree of dangerousness', and 3,129 political killings over the 1973–90 period have since been listed. Pinochet was only following, albeit far more ferociously, the course set by Brazil after 1964 and (more especially) 1968. Both were eclipsed by the so-called 'dirty war' between Argentina's post-1976 military regime and ex-Peronist guerrillas in which over 15,000 people are supposed to have been killed or 'disappeared'. For much of South America the 1970s saw a chicken-and-egg interrelationship between leftist urban terrorists and tough military rule (to which even Uruguay, the region's model democracy, succumbed).[64]

These regimes engendered growing concern in the USA, and from 1974–5 Congress restricted aid to countries 'engaged in a consistent pattern of gross violations of human rights'. The Ford administration opposed this, preferring 'quiet but forceful diplomacy'. Carter was more sympathetic; although he did not apply the policy to South Korea or China, he did so extensively (though not comprehensively) in strategically less exposed Latin America. Military aid was particularly affected, dropping from $234 million in 1976 to $54 million in 1979. This new approach was resented: in

63. Molineu, *U.S. Policy toward Latin America* pp.163 ff; Ranelagh, *The Agency* pp.513–20, 783–4; Powers, *The Man who Kept the Secrets* chap. 13; Hersh, *The Price of Power* chaps 21–2; Nathaniel Davis, *The Last Two Years of Salvador Allende* (1985) *passim*

64. Kissinger, *Memoirs* ii p.1,245; *Keesing's*, 38095; *The Independent*, 5 March 1994 p.8; Calvert, *Latin America in the Twentieth Century* pp.112–16 and chap. 5

1977 Argentina accused the USA of 'ignorance of Argentinian reality' and of setting itself up as an 'international court of justice', while the cutting off of economic aid was seen as 'intolerable meddling in the domestic affairs of Uruguay'. Argentina, Brazil, El Salvador and Guatemala refused further military aid on such terms. Nor did Brazil appreciate Carter's meeting human rights activists during his 1978 visit.[65] There was some loose talk of the authoritarian countries of the 'Southern Cone' going their own way: the USA charged Argentina with having played an 'important role' in the 1980 Bolivian coup;[66] Brazil, Paraguay and Uruguay were also quick to recognise the new regime, and the early 1980s saw something of a tussle in Bolivia between Brazil and the USA.[67] Both Argentina and Brazil also had nuclear programmes outside the Non-Proliferation Treaty; and there were contacts across the Atlantic with South Africa. But a May 1981 meeting of the Argentinian and Brazilian Presidents opposed the creation of any formal 'Southern Cone' bloc, and there were, in fact, serious frictions between its putative members. In particular shots were fired and sabres rattled in the Beagle Channel territorial dispute between Chile and Argentina. Accordingly Chile was critical of the 1982 Argentine seizure of the Falkland Islands, and is thought to have accorded some intelligence assistance to Britain's military response. Brazil, too, was quietly neutral.[68] Defeat in the Falklands, together with the economic disruption caused by British and other sanctions, contributed to the rapid collapse of military rule in Argentina itself and to the December 1983 restoration of elected government.

CARTER AND THE PANAMA CANAL 1977–8

Shortly after his election, Carter was told, in a joint letter from the Presidents of seven American countries, that the Panama Canal was 'the most urgent issue that the new Administration will face in the

65. Molineu, *U.S. Policy Toward Latin America* pp.135–41; *Keesing's*, 28343–4

66. *Keesing's*, 30586: President Videla declared that had Dr Siles taken over in Bolivia 'ideas contrary to our way of life and the permanence here of military government' would have threatened Argentina

67. David, *Third World Coups* pp.40–1; Calvert, *Latin America in the Twentieth Century* pp.125–6

68. *Keesing's*, 30951–3, 30981, 31449, 31534, 32781, 33517–18; for the Falklands War itself, see p.432

Western hemisphere'. To build the Canal, the USA had first sponsored the revolution that created the state of Panama, then in 1903 secured control of a ten-mile-wide Canal Zone as if 'it were the sovereign of the territory'. The Canal became an important communications link between the two sides of the USA, and must constitute the latter's chief interest in Central America. Negotiations over its by now anomalous status had opened in 1964 after the raising of the US flag outside a Canal Zone school had prompted rioting and shootings; but first Panama and then the USA had stalled for tactical or domestic reasons. Carter reactivated the negotiations, and in 1977 concluded treaties to transfer control in the year 2000 to Panama, which would then undertake to keep the Canal open and neutral. In 1978 the US Senate narrowly ratified these, though only after a great struggle and with reservations that made it clear that the USA would use force, even after 2000, if this proved necessary to keep the Canal open.[69]

CARTER AND THE NICARAGUAN REVOLUTION 1978–81

Carter's next major problem turned out to be Nicaragua, where the Somoza dynasty had become increasingly corrupt and repressive since the 1972 earthquake. In 1978 it was pilloried by an OAS human rights report, and other countries began to distance themselves. To begin with, Carter probably sought only its reform, but military aid was suspended in 1978 and economic aid in early 1979 (when many embassy staff were also withdrawn). Just as the cut-off of military supplies to Batista is supposed to have had a disproportionate symbolic effect in Cuba, so these moves heralded the fall of the Somozas, whose power came to rest on the National Guard alone in face of an opposition of growing breadth and cohesiveness. By mid-1979 it was clearly only a matter of time; in June the OAS called (with US consent) for an immediate change of regime. Vance would have liked to couple this with the dispatch of a multilateral force to Nicaragua to control events, but the USA could not secure agreement and would not act alone.[70] In July 1979

69. Johnson, *Vantage Point* pp.180–4; *Keesing's*, 28271, 28629 ff, 29044; Cyrus Vance, *Hard Choices* (New York, 1983) chap. 8; the Panamanian President later revealed that he had ordered his National Guard to attack the Canal if the Senate rejected the treaties: Carter, *Keeping Faith* p.178

70. Carter, *Keeping Faith* p.142

it managed to negotiate a transfer of power, with provision for the incorporation of the National Guard into a new army. The new government disbanded it instead, thus leaving the former Sandinista guerrillas in control of events.

Initially the USA sought to remain on good terms with the new regime, according it aid in 1980 in the belief that this would 'enhance the prospects for democracy' whereas its denial would 'almost guarantee that democracy will fail'. Congress would make no promises for 1981, however, and the 1980 Republican platform declared that 'we abhor the Marxist Sandinista takeover'.[71] As in the case of Cuba twenty years earlier, there is dispute as to how far Nicaragua was pushed into Marxism and hostility to the United States, and how far its revolution was already controlled by such elements. Whatever the truth, US conservatives saw the Nicaraguan revolution as inaugurating, in Brzezinski's words, a 'fourth central strategic front . . . in the world-wide US–Soviet contest', and some Sandinista pronouncements, at least, seemed to support their fears:

> The process of revolution in Central America is one . . . Guatemala will have its hour. Honduras its own. Costa Rica will live in a brilliant moment. The first note was heard in Nicaragua. [August 1980][72]

JAMAICA; US INTERVENTION IN GRENADA, 1983

The Nicaraguan revolution was accompanied by other worrying developments. The least important was Jamaica's shift, under Norman Manley, towards alignment with, and dependence on, Cuba; this was brought to an abrupt end by Manley's defeat in the 1980 elections. The new Premier, Edward Seaga, favoured capitalism and the United States; when Manley recovered office in 1989, he broadly continued Seaga's policies. Also comparatively minor was the March 1979 coup by the Marxist New Jewel Movement under Maurice Bishop in Grenada. The Reagan administration made much of the island's transformation into a Soviet-Cuban base. In 1983 it took advantage of Bishop's murder by more extreme colleagues to invade Grenada (and later hold elections); in the process it seized and published documents which,

71. ibid, pp.141–3, 178–9; *Keesing's*, 29805 ff.
72. Timothy Ashby, *The Bear in the Back Yard: Moscow's Caribbean Strategy* (Lexington, Mass., 1987) p.viii; Shultz, *Turmoil and Triumph* p.287

while they do not support all earlier claims, show that (from a mixture of revolutionary zeal and fear of US invasion) the Grenadan government did seek such a role and successfully pestered its allies for large quantities of arms.[73] Reagan's Grenadan intervention proved to be controversial in the Caribbean, as elsewhere; but the resolution it displayed seems to have encouraged other countries, notably Surinam, to distance themselves from Cuba.

EL SALVADOR 1979–92

More important, however, were events on the Central American isthmus. After the fall of the Somozas, El Salvador immediately appeared vulnerable; its army staged a pre-emptive coup in October 1979 to preclude a Nicaraguan-style débâcle by a controlled return to democracy. The USA encouraged the process, but cannot be said to have had much success. In 1980 insurgent groups coalesced into what was generally accepted as the communist-dominated Farabundo Martí Liberation Front (FMLF). Guerrilla warfare broke out, and right-wing death squads countered by fairly indiscriminate killing; in all 10,000 people are supposed to have been murdered in 1980. By 1981 the regime seemed on the point of collapse. The Reagan administration saw this as the product of aid for the insurgents from Nicaragua, Cuba, and Vietnam (which is alleged to have furnished plentiful supplies of US weapons that the FMLF could then plausibly claim to have captured from the El Salvador army). That the FMLF received such support is probable,[74] though its dimensions and duration are hotly debated. US Secretary of State Haig also assumed that El Salvador was intended to be only the first of a row of dominoes, whose fall would, in the end, threaten the stability of all Central America including Panama and Mexico.[75]

73. Ashby, *The Bear in the Back Yard* chap. 4

74. Nicaraguan officials told Molineu in 1984 that arms shipments 'may have' occurred before 1982, but insisted there had been none since then: *U.S. Policy toward Latin America* p.181; for allegations of more considerable involvement, see Ashby, *The Bear in the Back Yard* pp.123–37, and Alexander M. Haig, *Caveat* (1984) pp.123–4. Individual Nicaraguan officers were found to have stolen and transferred missiles to the FMLF in December 1991 (that is even *after* the end of the Sandinista government) and the FMLF still had arms caches in Nicaragua in 1993: *Keesing's*, 37956, 39503–4. Cf. also *New York Times*, 26 Jan. 1989 p.A10 for a Cuban defector's claim to have supplied weapons to guerrillas in El Salvador, Guatemala and Chile

75. *Caveat*, p.118; for a defector's endorsement of this claim, see Ashby, *The Bear in the Back Yard* p.137

The Reagan administration countered with a dual strategy of support for El Salvador and subversion of Nicaragua. Both tracks were seriously weakened by memories that the disastrous US involvement in Vietnam had begun with low-key support for an imperfect anti-communist regime, and by a determination (felt right across the political spectrum) not to commit US troops to the sustained suppression of insurgency in a tropical jungle. In supporting El Salvador, Reagan expanded, but did not significantly change, the work of his predecessor (Carter) who had in 1980 resumed military aid and supplied a few advisers. Financial aid was generous, as was military training outside El Salvador, but military advisers within the country were limited to about fifty-five in non-combat roles. Results were mixed: there was no military collapse, but the guerrillas were not defeated. El Salvador's manifest dependence on this aid gave the USA a political lever. It used this to deter coups and to push both elections and the moderate Christian Democrat Party, though not to force a real investigation of past death squad murders or a thorough reconstruction of the upper ranks of the army. The elections were indeed popular and turn-out high, despite rebel attempts to disrupt them; but the right-wing National Republican Alliance, which was seen as linked with the death squads, proved alarmingly successful. In 1988–9 it won first the parliamentary and then the presidential elections. The immediate result was an escalation of violence all round. However the settlement of the war in Nicaragua (see p.420) led both sides to agree to talk, with the aid of foreign, Church and from 1990 UN mediation. The talks proved difficult, but the FMLF no longer sought to disrupt the March 1991 elections. In September it offered a cease-fire and abandoned its call for the disbandment of the army; agreement was reached on the introduction under multi-party supervision of extensive reforms. Further details were tied up and a peace agreement signed in January 1992; implementation was slow, and the FMLF have retained arms caches, but a war that had cost some 75,000 lives may now be deemed to have ended.[76] 1994 indeed saw elections, in which the National Republican Alliance appears to have defeated the FMLF.

76. *Keesing's*, 35952 ff, 36393, 36460–1, 36520, 36846–7, 36890, 37270–1, 38093, 38415, 38716, 38759, 39361, 39503, 1993 R40. A UN inquiry later reported that most of the victims were civilians suspected of leftist leanings

NICARAGUA 1981–90

If policy on El Salvador did not change much as between Carter and Reagan, that towards Nicaragua did. Carter had hoped, by maintaining ties, 'to keep it from turning to Cuba and the Soviet Union'.[77] Reagan saw it as already having done so, and determined to apply against it what he took to be its own subversive tactics. In December 1981 he authorised the creation of an anti-Sandinista guerrilla force, soon to be known as the Contras. US involvement in the internal politics of the Contra movement was fairly open, as – generally – was US funding. But from 1984–5 Congress cut off all aid, and did not reinstate military aid until 1986. In the interim the CIA had to turn to other sources – private US money, contributions from friendly states ($32 million from Saudi Arabia, $10 million from Brunei), and (with Israel's assistance) a rake-off from secret arms sales to Iran. This was blown when a shift in Iranian politics led to the revelation of the arms sales in November 1986; the resulting 'Irangate' scandal did not enhance the administration's standing.[78] For this and other reasons no congressional funding for the Contras was sought in fiscal year 1987–8, and only 'non-lethal' grants were restored in 1988. The Contras never made much military progress, but they did damage Nicaragua's economy, both directly and by forcing it to maintain large armed forces. Their efforts were complemented by US trade sanctions (culminating in 1985 in a complete embargo), and by the CIA's 1984 mining of Nicaraguan harbours.[79] The upshot was shortages and massive inflation (5,884 per cent in 1988 and rising). This did not bring the Sandinistas down, but it probably reduced their readiness to export revolution and made them readier to compromise in other directions.

Of the many would-be mediators, the most important were the regional powers themselves. In 1983 Mexico (which emphatically did not see itself as a domino), Venezuela, Colombia and Panama met (on the resort island of Contadora), and called for an end to subversion, the removal of foreign military advisers, troop reductions, respect for human rights and a movement towards

77. *Keeping Faith* p.585

78. *Keesing's*, 35182 ff; Molineu, *U.S. Policy toward Latin America* chap. 8

79. The revelation of this mining prompted the first congressional cut-off of Contra funds. The USA was further embarrassed when Nicaragua took it before the International Court of Justice and the latter entertained the case; the USA announced that it would neither participate in the proceedings nor accept the verdict (which ultimately went against it)

democracy. In 1984 Nicaragua endorsed the approach, though not its further elaboration by the pro-US Central American quartet of Costa Rica, Honduras, Guatemala and El Salvador. The US remained wary, since the withdrawal of its military aid would be more easily verified than the ending of subversion. In 1987 President Arias of Costa Rica (previously a strong critic of Nicaragua) worked out – with the US administration and the Democratic Speaker of the House of Representatives – a development of Contadora. This was premised upon internal negotiations between the Nicaraguan (and El Salvador) governments and their insurgents, and provided for a measure of international verification. It was accepted in August 1987 by the Presidents of the five Central American states most directly involved; and though some of its prescriptions cannot have been meant too literally,[80] it did lead to measures of international accommodation in the area and to an uneasy 1988 cease-fire in Nicaragua. Then in February 1989, while the US administration was largely immobilised during the presidential transition, Ortega reached a settlement with the Presidents of Costa Rica, Honduras, Guatemala and El Salvador: he would bring forward elections (with international observers) to February 1990, permit press freedom and make other concessions; in return the Contras in Honduras (on Nicaragua's border) should be disbanded. The Bush administration was brought by congressional leaders to accept this in broad outline (though the now dispirited Contras were to be kept in being by non-military aid through to the 1990 elections). In July 1989 the Nicaraguan government and opposition agreed on ground rules for the elections, and in October the USA allocated $9 million for the opposition's expenses. The general expectation was that the Sandinistas would win and so finally gain full international acceptance. Bush conceded that relations with the USA could improve provided the elections had been fair. In the event the opposition coalition triumphed. The Sandinistas allowed its candidate, Violeta Chamorro, to take over as President, but remained both the largest single party and well dug in to the army and the public sector. Chamorro has since been very careful not to provoke them, even at the cost of seeing some former Contras again take up arms in protest.[81] With her victory, however,

80. Notably that all Central American states should create 'an authentic, democratic, pluralist and participatory process' with internationally-monitored 'free, pluralist and honest' elections; only Costa Rica would really meet this test

81. *Keesing's*, 32852–3, 35438 ff, 36421–3, 36460–1, 36520–1, 36653, 36680–3, 37269, 37272, 37326, 37450; *The Economist*, 28 Jan. 1989 p.61, 18 Feb. p.67, 4 March p.72, 1 April p.48; Molineu, *U.S. Policy toward Latin America* pp.192–3

Nicaragua (which had been a fashionable progressive cause) dropped out of the general international consciousness.[82]

WANING FEARS OF COMMUNISM

It is, of course, possible that the cycle might start again elsewhere: Peru has since 1980 had a Khmer Rouge-type guerrilla movement, the 'Shining Path', the struggle with which has cost over 22,000 lives and contributed towards the presidential coup of 1992;[83] but in view of the ending of the Cold War the geopolitical implications would be different. Meanwhile Cuba is again the only Marxist state in the Americas. With the USSR's collapse it fell on hard times: US calculations were that it received $3.25 billion of Soviet aid in 1990, $1.1 billion in 1991, and that it would get only $65 million from the Commonwealth of Independent States (CIS) in 1992; it has also had to scrabble around for trade to replace that with Comecon. The resultant shortages have cut production, forced draconian rationing, and apparently promoted discontent. Castro's response has been to change little in his rhetoric and nothing significant in the political system. The United States hopes, so far (1993) in vain, that enhanced propaganda broadcasts, a tighter trade embargo, and (possibly) sabotage raids from Florida will bring him down. Many Latin American states seek instead to encourage gradual economic and political reform: in 1981 and 1982 he was welcomed (inter alia) to the new Ibero-American summits and plied with ideologically unacceptable advice.[84]

82. Even the Bush administration, despite its delight at Chamorro's election, proved reluctant to go beyond $300 million in aid

83. *Keesing's*, 38846, 1992 R49

84. *Keesing's*, 38336, 38385, 38528, 38670, 38715, 38858, 1992 R36; it is, of course, impossible to say whether the raids are the work only of the Cuban opposition or whether they have CIA support

CHAPTER SEVENTEEN

The Americas since 1980

With the end of the Cold War, political attention in the Americas has shifted to such topics as drugs, debt, economic development and trade groupings – issues many countries had always regarded as more important than the supposed threat from communism.

DRUGS

The coca leaf has traditionally been grown and chewed in the Andes; there was some import of its derivative, cocaine, into Batista's Cuba. In the 1960s it began to be brought into Florida, first for Cuban émigrés, then for US users in general; demand grew rapidly in the 1970s, and later benefited from a switch away from other drugs. By 1979 it was worth negotiating a treaty permitting extradition from Colombia to the USA, since Colombian gangs were wresting the trade from Cuban ones; by 1984 Colombia's drugs exports were estimated to exceed its legitimate ones in value. In 1981 suppliers from the Medellín area formed a cartel and acquired an armed force to protect themselves. Colombia has since 1948 been a violent country with endemic local insurgencies. Although the drug barons' political preferences tended to be for the right, they apparently established a working relationship with both leftist guerrillas and Cuba: in 1981 a drug smuggler's ship was caught unloading Cuban arms for the guerrillas, and in 1984 the Colombian Defence Minister said 'Everyone knows that the planes leave Colombia with cocaine and that they return with weapons from Cuba'.

In 1984 Medellín responded to a massive government cocaine seizure by killing the crusading Justice Minister, which in turn led to the declaration of a state of siege. The cartel supposedly offered to inject $3 billion per year into the Colombian economy if it was left alone. But this was refused, and raids, kidnappings and murders continued, punctuated by negotiations and moderated by bribes. Further escalation came when a presidential candidate was murdered at a 1989 election rally. President Barco reacted with emergency decrees resuming extradition to the US (which the courts had invalidated on a technicality), seizing drug-related assets, and pulling in some 11,000 to 15,000 suspects. In return the 'Extraditables' declared war on the government. In 1990, however, the new President, Gaviria, changed tactics, offering traffickers softer treatment and a guarantee against extradition if they surrendered. In mid-1991 a settlement was reached: extradition was banned as part of a new Constitution, and the Medellín leaders surrendered on terms: the richest, Pablo Escobar, was to go to a prison of his own design and construction. A year later he simply walked out, and disturbances resumed. He was eventually shot in December 1993; but in the meantime much of his business had passed to the rival Cali cartel. In late 1993 the government was poised between accepting a plea bargain and seeking, with US military assistance, to suppress Cali.[1]

Colombia is perhaps the extreme case, but the drugs trade has affected many others. The 1980 coup in Bolivia, sometimes termed the 'cocaine coup', led to the abrupt ending of US anti-narcotics activities in the country. In 1983 Peru's President claimed that most of the 'Shining Path's' funds came from drug traffickers; in 1985 these supposedly offered (albeit in vain) to pay off the country's $14 billion foreign debt in return for an amnesty. Meanwhile Cuba would appear to have been involved in drug trading (though not manufacture), whether to facilitate the arming of guerrillas, to damage the United States, to raise money, or simply for personal profit. In 1989 it executed – or scapegoated – a general and punished other officials for helping Medellín smuggle cocaine into the USA. There has also been considerable concern about drug running through the Bahamas, with allegations made in US courts – though not sustained – against the Prime Minister.[2]

1. Scott B. MacDonald, *Mountain High, White Avelanche: Cocaine and Power in the Andes States and Panama* (Washington Papers 137, 1989) chap. 2; *Keesing's*, esp. 35756, 36844, 37772, 37851, 37957, 38283, 38332, 39001, 39186, 39774, 39812

2. MacDonald, *Mountain High, White Avelanche* chap. 3; *Keesing's*, 36731, 36844, 37000, 37068, 38226, 38857. Ex-President Noriega's trial saw many claims that he, Medellín and Havana were closely interlinked

Were the USA to curb its own demand, most of this would presumably cease. As it cannot, it has sought to destroy crops and disrupt drug traffic at source, in short to involve itself deeply in the internal affairs of other countries. We have seen that the attempt to extradite people from Colombia (whose judicial system was admittedly, in this context, suspect) encountered strong, if partly self-interested, nationalist opposition and has now been constitutionally barred. (Nor were US–Mexican relations improved when in 1992 the US Supreme Court sanctioned the kidnapping and trial of the supposed murderers of a Drug Enforcement Administration agent.)[3] In 1989 the US Attorney-General talked of military participation in Colombia's struggle with Medellín. It was made clear that this would not be welcome, but 100 US military advisers were accepted. In the Andes things sometimes went further: in 1986 170 US military personnel were deployed for four months in Bolivia with armed helicopters, a more direct effort than any in El Salvador; in 1987 US radio interception planes flew in support of Peruvian air strikes. Since 1989 such efforts have been integrated into a $2 billion Andean aid programme as part of the US 'National Drug Control Strategy'. But there have been complaints that the USA adopts an excessively military approach to crop destruction, without providing the peasant growers with adequate alternatives; and though regular presidential drug summits have been set up, they have not generated much substantive agreement.[4]

THE USA'S FEUD WITH NORIEGA IN PANAMA 1987–9

The deepest US involvement occasioned by drugs was in Panama. In the 1980s this was dominated by General Noriega. The CIA found him useful, but he seems also to have dealt impartially with all players in the Caribbean, anti-communist and communist, drug shippers and their opponents. In mid-1987 he was accused (not for the first time) by his domestic opponents of involvement in drug smuggling and murder; in June the US Senate called on him to step down until the charges had been independently investigated. He countered by securing an OAS Resolution against such 'unwarranted interference', but that autumn secretly tried to work out a settlement with the USA. It appeared that some arrangement

3. *Keesing's*, 38954
4. *Keesing's*, 34800–1, 35706, 36844, 36889, 37423–4, 37451, 377708, 38761–2

had been come to when he left the country in January 1988; if so, it broke down and he went back. In February the US Department of Justice (whose Drug Enforcement Agency had worked with and commended Noriega) indicted him for drug trafficking, apparently without notice to either the White House or the State Department. Noriega's hitherto tame President then tried to dismiss him, only to be thrown out himself; and in March the USA froze all Panamanian assets and barred the dispatch of dollars to Panamanian banks. Since Panama used the dollar as its currency, this hurt, but Noriega proved unexpectedly resilient. Negotiations were set in train to secure his departure abroad in return for an assurance that the USA would not seek his extradition. Most of the US administration opposed giving any such promise for fear of appearing (in an election year) soft on drugs; but Reagan insisted, believing the only alternative to be military intervention. In May 1988 a deal appeared to have been reached; but Noriega backed off at the last moment, explaining that junior officers feared for their futures if he left and had threatened a coup to stop him. Despite Noriega's general local unpopularity he hung on to power, riding out various coup attempts and fudging the 1989 presidential elections. Finally, in December 1989, the USA put in troops, defeated the Panamanian army in destructive fighting, and cornered Noriega in the papal embassy until (worn down by ghetto-blasters and demonstrations outside) he surrendered and was whisked off to Miami for eventual trial. Most Panamanians regarded the intervention as a liberation (though they have since cooled considerably towards the USA); but it was condemned by both the OAS and the UN General Assembly.[5]

THE DEBT SHOCK OF THE EARLY 1980s

Drugs are a relatively new issue, economic development an old one. Most of the South American military regimes of the 1960s and 1970s were committed to delivering it, and claimed that they were especially qualified to do so by reason of their insulation from trades union and electoral pressures. By far the most important case is Brazil, which has about half South America's population and has come to have more than half its GNP. The immediate sequel of the

5. MacDonald, *Mountain High, White Avelanche* chap. 5; Shultz, *Turmoil and Triumph* chap. 48; *Keesing's*, 35815–19, 36683–4, 37112–13, 37271, 38857

1964 coup was an attempt to curb runaway inflation and restore national solvency, accompanied by a severe recession. But from 1968 to 1974 Brazilian growth was some 10–11 per cent per year, declining after the 'oil shock' to a still impressive 4–7 per cent. Brazil's economy was still smaller than Canada's, but there was much talk of its soon realising the vast promise of its population and resources to become an industrialised Great Power. The World Bank has calculated that it doubled its per capita income in the eighteen years after 1961,[6] though this was marred by the growing inequality of its income distribution (always a marked feature of Latin American as compared with Pacific Rim states). Different countries naturally followed different trajectories, but most did well during this period.[7] Then 'After more than a decade of growth rates that exceeded the industrial . . . average, . . . Latin America's income suffered a historical reversal. From 1980 to 1985' average real per capita income in Argentina, Brazil, Chile, Mexico and Peru fell to levels 'prevailing in the 1970s, or, for Peru and Chile, to pre-1970 levels'.[8]

This phenomenon, commonly described as the 'debt shock', is not easy to explain since national circumstances differed so greatly: Mexico and Venezuela exported oil, most states imported it; Mexico, Argentina and Venezuela suffered from massive private capital flight abroad, Brazil and Chile did not; Chile was free trading and laissez-faire, Brazil protectionist and somewhat dirigiste. There were, of course, some common factors. Overall external debt leapt from about $75 billion in 1975 to $229 billion in 1980, facilitated by the 're-cycling' of OPEC oil money. Latin Americans had always worried about the repatriation of profits on private investment; now they had to service these new loans, which by 1978 accounted for a substantial proportion of new borrowing. This

6. Edwin Williamson, *The Penguin History of Latin America* (1992) p.429; *The Economist*, 13 July 1991 p.87. Pinochet's coup in Chile was also followed first by deep deflationary recession then by 8% per year growth from 1976 to 1981

7. A side-effect of such growth was the destruction of tropical rain-forest. Since the early 1970s foreign concern has mounted in the belief that forests represent a store of species invaluable for future medicine and biotechnology and that they are essential to the world's climatic balance. But traditional international law gives states the sovereign right to exploit their own resources; Brazil, in particular, has often resented outside interference. Such problems were addressed (in a UN framework) at the 1992 'Earth Summit' in Rio: *Keesing's*, 38947. This proved strongly reminiscent of the New International Economic Order wrangles of the 1970s; but it produced conventions on biodiversity and climate change, and created a 'Global Environment Facility' to help finance conservation in the South

8. James L. Dietz and J.L. Street, *Latin America's Economic Development* (Boulder, Colo., 1987) pp.273–5; Williamson, *Penguin History* p.367

borrowing was denominated in dollars (then a fairly weak currency), and much of it was conducted at floating, not fixed, interest rates. Accordingly the borrowers were badly hit by the post-1980 anti-inflationary strengthening of the dollar, and by the high interest rates with which the US Federal Reserve brought this about: 'Whereas . . . real rates of interest on external debt had been negative during much of the 1970s . . ., short-term real rates . . . rose abruptly to the 15 to 20 per cent range at the end of 1980, and remained very high for five years'.

Nor were most Latin American economies well placed to withstand such shocks. Since the 1930s they had concentrated on import substitution, but (unlike the Pacific Rim) they did not progress to high-volume manufactured exports. So, as at last became clear in the 1980s, their industries were mostly uncompetitive; this left them heavily dependent on exports of primary products (whose prices were low in the 1980s) and far less able than their (also heavily borrowed) Pacific Rim counterparts to profit from the import surge into the USA that accompanied the Reagan boom. Even so, the superficial drop in Latin American GDP (3.5 per cent in 1982, 4.7 per cent in 1983) did not appear devastating, and slow growth then resumed. Matters were, however, made much worse by high population growth, and by the fact that consumption bore the brunt of a probably long overdue fiscal restructuring (as when governments cut food subsidies, often on IMF advice).[9]

Fidel Castro was to term Latin American debt 'illegitimate' (as being the product of high interest rates and low primary produce prices) and to urge collective default, adding (in June 1985) that in such an event the capitalist system would collapse within three years. This, of course, was *not* what other Latin American leaders wished to see; there were incentives for them to cooperate. Mexico's 1982 declaration of inability to pay was worked out in cooperation with the US Treasury and international financial organisations, which put up emergency credit of $3.9 billion and induced private banks to add $5 billion to their existing loans. By contrast, as a Vice-President of the World Bank warned next year, unilateral action would 'without doubt eliminate a country for many years from receiving credit'.[10] Peru put this to the test in 1985, when – without discussion – President Garcia limited debt service

9. Dietz and Street, *Latin America's Economic Development* pp.274, 277–8; Philip Brock, M.B.Connolly and C. Gonzalez-Vega (eds) *Latin American Debt and Adjustment* (New York, 1989) p.33; Williamson, *Penguin History* pp.367, 370–1

10. *Keesing's*, 32071, 32619, 34156

payments to 10 per cent of its exports. This drew an immediate suspension of US aid, and escalated into a major row with the IMF, which was accused of being a US 'accomplice', of perpetuating colonialism, and of threatening democracy in the heavily indebted nations; it responded in 1986 by declaring Peru 'ineligible' for further use of the Fund's resources. Results were disastrous; the next President promptly secured a $2 billion bridging loan by promising to resume payments, then, on the basis of an internal austerity programme, mended Peru's relations with the IMF and restructured its debt.[11] Most states preferred to deal directly with the IMF and with their creditors; although there was considerable pressure (especially from non-governmental bodies) for a more collective approach, at the 1984 Cartagena Conference Brazil and Mexico pushed through a reaffirmation 'that each state is responsible for the negotiation of its own external debt'.[12] This has in practice continued to be the case, though there was much mutual consultation, both informal and (with the 1987 constitution of the 'Group of Three' and 'Group of Eight' indebted countries) formal.

DEBT RESCHEDULING AND RESOLUTION OF THE CRISIS 1984–92

By the end of 1984 all Latin American countries except Colombia and Paraguay had embarked on debt rescheduling negotiations. Not that these were easy: 1984, for instance, saw strikes and riots in São Paulo in protest against the cuts the IMF was seeking to impose on Brazil; the Chairman of the Central Bank tried in vain to persuade the IMF not to insist on the immediate ending of subsidies on imported wheat, and eventually resigned, denouncing such policies as 'socially perverse and economically inefficient'; the Brazilian Congress almost put a spanner in the works by initially refusing to reduce wage indexation; and, on the other side, it took months for the IMF to persuade creditor banks to advance Brazil a further $6.5 billion.[13] Initially it was hoped that such expedients would resolve the crisis, but by 1985 it was becoming increasingly

11. *Keesing's*, 33387, 34610, 37772–3, 38248, 38433, 1992 R48; there have, though, been calculated defaults as part of the negotiating process – Brazil imposed such a moratorium on debt payments for most of 1987 and again in 1989–91 (ibid, 35823–4, 36553, 37496, 38143)

12. *Keesing's*, 33214

13. *Keesing's*, 32665–7

clear that they would not. Although austerity improved Latin America's trade balance, its total debt continued to grow;[14] banks were reluctant voluntarily to inject new money, and Latin America became increasingly concerned at what it saw as a never-ending drain of resources to the North.

The first formal response to this situation was the 1985 Baker Plan, envisaging the provision of an extra $12 billion over three years by the World Bank and $20 billion by private ones. This in fact made little difference; by 1987–8 there was widespread demand for a more radical approach, underlined by Brazil's suspension of interest payments from February to December 1987. The uncertainty led major banks to make provisions against default (their ability to do so stilling fears of its engendering a spectacular collapse of the financial system) and also increasingly selling off their debt at a discount. In 1987 Bolivia established a precedent by buying back such discounted debt (using aid given for its cocaine eradication operations); it also allowed foreign groups to use such debt as a leveraged way of funding its forest conservation. Such schemes quickly caught on.[15]

In 1989 they became the centre-piece of the United States' new 'Brady' proposals, which envisaged IMF and World Bank lending to support them, conditional on the adoption of IMF-approved policies to 'encourage new investment flows, strengthen domestic savings and promote the return of flight capital'. The plan was much criticised, but Brazil and Mexico ensured a favourable response from the 'Group of Eight'. Mexico signed an agreement with the IMF in May 1989, and in July arranged with its bank creditors a general restructuring that appreciably reduced its debt burden.[16] Its example was widely followed, Argentina being the fifth state to conclude such a deal in April 1992 and Brazil following in July. With confidence thus (hopefully) restored, hot money has started flowing back to Latin America, new lending has resumed, and Chile's state credit has even returned to 'investment grade'.[17]

14. On one estimate, from $314 billion in 1982 to $368 billion in 1985; however, private citizens were thought to hold some $180 billion abroad, legally and illegally, which occasioned considerable resentment on the part of Latin America's creditors: Dietz and Street, *Latin America's Economic Development* pp.277, 286

15. *Keesing's*, 35419–20, 35763–4, 37017

16. In return for guarantees, they were required to choose between injecting new money and keeping their present debt, or accepting either low fixed interest or discounted bonds: *Keesing's*, 36812, 37243

17. *Keesing's*, 36541–2, 37078–9, 38860–1, 39002; *The Economist*, 5 Jan. 1991 p.72, 8 June p.505, 19 Oct. p.26, 22 Aug. 1992 pp.67–8

MEXICO'S MOVE SINCE 1982 TOWARDS ECONOMIC LIBERALISM; NORTH AMERICAN FREE TRADE AGREEMENT

The debt crisis had engendered the gloomiest of predictions: in 1985 the Colombian President described it as a time-bomb threatening the region's political and social stability. But if anything, the crisis hastened the swing from military to elected regimes that was so notable a feature of the 1980s. The crisis also called in question the wisdom of the import-saving orientation that had dominated development since the 1930s, and that was seen as having created corrupt and uncompetitive public sector corporations (many of which are now being sold to private and foreign investors). Nowhere was this more true than in Mexico, where both Presidents de la Madrid in 1982–3 and Salinas in 1989 began their administrations by targeting aspects of that symbol of the revolution, the nationalised oil company. Mexico's 1985 'letter of intent' to the IMF contained a commitment to trade liberalisation; privatisation of state enterprises began in 1986, and Mexico also joined GATT (General Agreement on Tariffs and Trade). Some of this was controversial: in 1988 the PRI presidential candidate Salinas had unprecedented difficulty in securing election, against competition from the son of the 1930s oil nationaliser President Cardenas; but this seems only to have spurred him to go faster. During 1987–91 there was a 20 per cent per year growth in US exports to Mexico.[18]

All this slotted in well with new directions in US foreign policy. Reagan, like Kennedy twenty years earlier, had sought to pre-empt communism through economic development – though his 1981–3 Caribbean Basin Initiative was geared towards encouraging private investment in, and access to the US market for, the manufactured products of the region. There is a sense in which this initiative, too, faded: its concessions were made permanent in 1990 only after they had been whittled down by US protectionist lobbying.[19] But it did lead first to the establishment in northern Mexico of factories using cheap local labour to work up products for re-export to the USA and then to a wider range of Mexican manufactured exports. In 1989 the USA concluded a (partial) free trade treaty with Canada; during Salinas's visit to the USA that year, he and Bush decided to try to remove trade barriers on a sector-by-sector basis. In June 1990

18. *Keesing's*, 32069–70, 33966, 34733, 34588, 36932, 37078; *The Economist*, 15 Aug. 1992 pp.55–6

19. *Keesing's*, 31565 ff, 32622, 37825; *The Economist*, 6–12 Aug. 1988 ('Caribbean Survey' pp.9 ff)

Bush followed with an 'Enterprise for the Americas' programme linking debt relief, investment and preferential access with the long-term goal of a hemispheric free trade zone. In November 1990 Bush declared the USA and Mexico to form a 'family', and he and Salinas decided to pursue a free trade treaty; Canada entered the negotiations in 1991, and in August 1992 a draft North America Free Trade Agreement (NAFTA) was initialled. It was to prove controversial: it only just scraped through the US Congress, and the Canadian Liberal Party was opposed (though, on gaining power in 1993, it confined itself to demands for 'renegotiations'). On 1 January 1994 Mexico was startled by a pre-planned Indian rising in the south that evoked the 1910 revolution and denounced NAFTA (on the day it came into effect) as 'the death certificate for the indigenous peoples of Mexico'. Militarily the rising was easily dealt with; but the Indian grievances behind it touched a chord, and foreshadowed a difficult run up to the August 1994 presidential election – which was to be further shadowed by the assassination in March of the PRI candidate. However, assuming Mexico remains on the course set by President Salinas, NAFTA could transform American relationships. For it was warmly welcomed by Caribbean and South American states; and President Clinton has held out the prospect of its extension to other free-market democracies.[20]

FREE TRADE AGREEMENTS IN LATIN AMERICA

NAFTA would not in any case stand alone: the creation of free trade groupings is again in fashion. In the past their record had been disappointing: the 'Central American Common Market' stalled with the 1969 Honduras–El Salvador war, the 'Andean Pact' with Chile's 1976 withdrawal in response to political ostracism, while little real effort was put into the 'Latin American Free Trade Area' (now 'ALADI') or the 'Latin American Economic System' (SELA). Since 1988, however, trade cooperation between the former rivals, Argentina and Brazil, has been more genuine; in 1991 they, Uruguay and Paraguay, decided to aim at a free market ('Mercosur') by 1994–5. The Presidents of the Andean Pact countries were still more ambitious, though Ecuador has reservations; there was a Chile–Mexico free trade agreement; the former British colonies of CARICOM (the Caribbean Common Market) are seeking a common market by 1994, and there are hopes of a revival

20. *Keesing's*, 36370, 36974, 37526, 37849, 38140, 38242, 39681–2, 39728–9, 39809–10; *The Economist*, 15 Aug. 1992 pp.55–6

of the Central American one. Some of this may again be rhetoric; but it is interesting to note that, whereas in the later 1960s Latin American integration had an anti-USA tinge – Mexico's President declared in 1967 that it must be 'an exclusively Latin American process' geared towards economic independence, not just a market to be exploited by US companies – in 1991 Mercosur and CARICOM were looking to take advantage of the US tariff concessions and aid to promote investment and free markets foreshadowed in the 'Enterprise for the Americas Initiative'.[21]

THE FALKLANDS

The Falkland (or, in Spanish, *Malvinas*) islands, some 300 miles off the Argentine coast, were claimed by both Spain and Britain in the eighteenth century. After 1811 neither exercised control, and they were effectively a no man's land occupied by temporary whalers. What was to become Argentina claimed them as the successor to Spain and sent a governor there in 1829, but he was expelled by a US warship. In 1832 the British took control, expelling the remaining Argentines, and in 1833 annexed and settled the islands.

Argentina never abandoned its claim, and began after 1945 to push it more seriously. From 1966 there were sporadic Anglo-Argentine negotiations at the UN. These resumed in 1980, and the Foreign Office seems to have been prepared to contemplate conceding sovereignty in exchange for either a lease-back of the islands or continued involvement in their administration. The Falklanders (1,813 in 1980) and the House of Commons were not, so little progress was made. In April 1982 an Argentine fleet suddenly seized the islands in the belief that Britain could not and would not respond, an action condemned by the UN Security Council. Attempts at mediation, notably by the USA and Peru, failed. In military operations between late April and mid-June 1982 Britain recovered possession at the cost of a thousand lives (mostly Argentine). Both countries were fighting at the limit of their reach, British victory being due to greater professionalism helped by covert US weapons supplies. Britain was also markedly more successful in mobilising its allies: the United States and the European Community imposed sanctions, whereas Argentina proved unable to invoke the Pact of Rio.

Argentina maintains its claim to the islands (which Britain had expensively to garrison), and regularly pursued it through UN

21. *Keesing's*, 22233–4, 37526, 38096, 38336, 1992 R57

General Assembly Resolutions. Britain lifted financial sanctions in 1983, Argentina reciprocated in 1984; trade was similarly resumed in 1985–6; but diplomatic relations were not restored until 1990. The then diplomatic thaw soon led to cooperation in the management of the profitable offshore fisheries, though not of offshore oil exploration or to the restoration of communication links between the Falklands and South America.

ANTARCTICA

There had been fears that Anglo–Argentine antagonisms would spill over into Antarctica. Here Australia, New Zealand, Norway, France, Britain, Argentina and Chile have territorial claims; the last three overlap, and 1947 witnessed some perturbation as fleets moved round asserting them. Neither the USA nor the USSR (the states most largely involved in Antarctic exploration) recognised any such claims. Potential conflict was avoided by a 1959 treaty demilitarising the continent, freezing all territorial claims, and providing for periodic meetings among the signatories 'on matters of common interest pertaining to Antarctica'. So Antarctica was left exclusively to research, with much cooperation between scientific expeditions from different nations (though Argentina and Chile continued to emphasise their territorial claims). The treaty was due to be renegotiated in 1991, and although Antarctica is at present valueless, it may not always be so. In 1981 the treaty signatories decided pre-emptively to draft a regime to control mining. This unleashed pressure for 'the international management and equitable sharing' of its benefits through the UN (no doubt along the lines of the deep sea regime proposed in the Convention on the Law of the Sea; see p.477), the exclusion of South Africa (a treaty signatory), and/or the designation of the continent as a World Park. The treaty signatories held off UN involvement, Australia arguing that 'any attempt to negotiate a new international agreement . . . would be likely to introduce uncertainty and instability into a region of hitherto unparalleled international cooperation'. In 1988, after lengthy negotiations, they agreed – to the UN's 'deep regret' – a regime that would permit seismic exploration but not full-scale mining. However, France and Australia (whose consent, as countries with territorial claims, was needed for it to come into effect) declined to ratify; they gradually won over other countries, isolating the USA and UK, and in 1991 a fifty-year ban on mining was concluded.

PART V

The International System

CHAPTER EIGHTEEN

The Nature of, and Leadership in, the International System

THE NATURE OF INTERNATIONAL RELATIONS

Most discussions of the nature of the international system cite the bleak vision of Thomas Hobbes. He saw it as a struggle of all against all: since there is no superior power strong enough to provide order, states 'for their own security enlarge their dominions upon all pretences of danger . . ., and endeavour . . . to subdue or weaken their neighbours by open force and secret arts . . .; and are remembered for it in after years with honour'. Accordingly kings

> are in continual jealousies, and in the state and posture of gladiators, having their weapons pointing and their eyes fixed on one another; that is, their forts, garrisons and guns upon the frontiers of their kingdoms, and continual spies upon their neighbours – which is a posture of war.
>
> (*Leviathan*, chaps. 17, 13 – punctuation modernised)

This picture well fits some of the modern world (the Korean peninsula, parts of the Middle East, perhaps also India and Pakistan) and certain postwar relationships (like that between East and West at the height of the Cold War); but it bears little resemblance to relations between Norway and Sweden or the USA and Canada. Most states' attitudes to each other lie somewhere along a continuum stretching from the model of the two Koreas to that of Norway and Sweden, and partake at least as much of cooperation as of conflict.

Cooperation and (generally) even conflict take place within a very loose framework of international law, deriving chiefly from treaties (including multilateral ones like the Kellogg-Briand pact,[1] the Nuclear Non-Proliferation Treaty and the UN Charter) and from common state practice (sometimes, as in the case of the law governing diplomatic relations and immunities, codified by treaty).[2] Enforcement, other than by self-help (as in the case of the British repossession of the Falkland Islands), is very limited, though provisions do exist for the blocking of World Bank loans to a country that has nationalised foreign property without compensation. The scope of international law is severely restricted both by the limited possibilities of enforcement and by the difficulties of creating new law without the consent of the states concerned. But, as the saying goes, most states adhere to the law most of the time – sometimes because they have internalised such adherence within their decision-making processes, usually because they have no reason for not adhering, and (to a more limited extent) because flouting international law carries with it costs in terms of a country's popularity and international standing.

It would be foolish to claim that the upshot is a degree of international governance comparable to that obtaining within a developed state. But most writers perceive an international system, composed chiefly of states that may squabble, but usually coexist and to an extent cooperate. Such cooperation is generally broad but quite shallow, most effective in non-political fields (like weather forecasting and the elimination of smallpox,[3] where the benefits are obvious and universal); but it goes far deeper in various subsystems (like Western Europe) where states share sufficient values and interests to constitute a community.

The international system consists primarily of states;[4] indeed one of the features of international law that commends it to newly independent (and generally weak) countries is its emphasis on the sovereignty and juridical equality of all independent countries. For descriptive purposes it is often adequate to refer to states as if they were individuals, saying (for instance) that India's relations with China worsened in the later 1950s. No states are completely

1. Of 1928, whereby almost all states promised 'not to have recourse to war as an instrument of national policy, and to settle all disputes between them by peaceful means'

2. The 1960 Vienna Convention on Diplomatic Relations

3. Between 1967 and 1979 a $112 million World Health Organisation programme eradicated smallpox, previously endemic in forty-three countries: *Keesing's*, 27548, 30252; for meteorological cooperation, see e.g. F. Kenneth Hare, 'Climate: The Neglected Factor', *International Journal* (Toronto) xxxvi (1981)

4. As is persuasively argued in J.D.B. Miller, *The World of States* (1981)

monolithic, however; even in Stalin's USSR different ministries had different interests in, and therefore policies toward, Eastern Europe, while in the USA presidential policies often founder on congressional, bureaucratic or public opposition. Even if states are the primary players, they are not self-contained homogenous bodies, and their interaction cannot simply be compared with that of billiard balls bumping into each other. Instead one government may appeal to another's public opinion, or even topple it by helping its domestic opponents stage a coup. Alternatively it may seek foreign help in its own political battles; thus to persuade Senator Abourezk to vote for the Panama Canal treaties, President Carter had to invoke the good offices of 'mutual Saudi friends'.[5]

Just as states are not monolithic, so too they are not the only international actors. They are joined, for instance, by national liberation/terrorist movements, like the Jewish Agency (which managed to turn itself into a state), the Palestine Liberation Organisation (which has not yet done so), and the Irish Republican Army (which is unlikely either to go away or to succeed in overthrowing the existing regimes in both Northern Ireland and the Irish Republic). There are also international organisations that do not aspire either to become states or to displace existing governments; some are quite old (like the International Red Cross or the International Postal Union), many (like the United Nations Educational Scientific and Cultural Organisation – UNESCO) of more recent growth.

THE ROLE OF MULTINATIONAL COMPANIES

There are great trading concerns operating in, and (less often) owned by, more than one country. These are in no way new; indeed some of their forerunners (like the British East India Company or the British South Africa Company) maintained armed forces and governed colonies or even empires. Today 'multinationals' may still have foreign policies: ITT lobbied for US intervention to stop the Marxist Salvador Allende from coming to power in Chile. But (Lonrho apart)[6] multinationals no longer deploy armed forces of their own, though some drug barons do.

5. Carter, *Keeping Faith*, p.177

6. During Mozambique's civil war collapse, Lonrho acquired a Gurkha-officered private force to safeguard its plantations: *The Independent*, 20 March 1993 p.13

Academics 'discovered' multinational companies in the later 1960s, and plunged into a debate as to their international importance that often generated more heat than light. It is clear that states can now, not only in theory but also in practice, nationalise foreign operations on their territory. This was not always so: Mossadegh's 1951 nationalisation of the Anglo-Iranian Oil Company was followed by his 1953 overthrow in a US-British managed coup. Nasser's 1956 nationalisation of the equally strategic Suez Canal, though it prompted an Anglo-French invasion, succeeded; subsequent nationalisations have not been so challenged, though they may incur lesser – economic – costs by alienating the international financial community. Nor is it any longer possible, as it was in the nineteenth century, for ordinary commercial companies (as opposed to drugs or foreign broadcasts) to force their way into a country whose government does not want them. Indeed some defenders of multinationals claim that the only choice these now have is that between investing new money in a country, not investing, or quitting and so losing their fixed assets.

Critics see this as too simple. States can undoubtedly insulate themselves from foreign investment and commerce: witness Albania and Burma. But, if they seek to attract foreign investment, they must make it worth coming, and this may have an impact on their internal arrangements; an obvious example is China which, in order to attract foreign companies, has since the early 1980s (particularly in the Special Economic Zones) modified much of what previously passed for socialism. Moreover, though conditions about investment, exports, ownership and the like are commonly imposed, if they are not, companies will behave in their own interests, which may diverge from those of the host country. It is indeed sometimes contended (especially in the Third World) that external companies constitute Trojan horses whose establishment within a state will tend to bring its economy, culture and society under foreign control. There are, however, counter-examples; despite some metropolitan pressure on them to combat apartheid, multinationals have had only a minor impact on the internal policies of South Africa. Even in Panama, a country that is peculiarly vulnerable since it uses the US dollar as its own currency, the USA failed to topple General Noriega by forbidding its banks to supply dollars (and had eventually to resort to direct military invasion).

MARKETS, CURRENCIES, AND INTERNATIONAL DEBTS

Linked, but not identical, with the influence of multinationals is that of markets. Again one must stress that states can opt out of foreign dealings – though the example of those that have is not particularly encouraging. But if states wish to sell abroad, they must do so either at market prices or at politically determined ones (much sugar is sold by special arrangements at above the 'world' price). Politically fixed prices generally involve an element of concession on the part of the purchaser; the possibility of their discontinuance carries with it that of the exercise of pressure. As for market prices, the producer/seller can sometimes manipulate them by controlling (alone or cooperatively) the production of a good with few substitutes and little (or lagged) elasticity of demand. More often sellers simply have to accept the ruling prices; where such exports are important to them, sellers are dependent, for better or worse, on the terms of trade. This is true of developed as well as of less developed economies; but fluctuations in the price of primary products tend to be the greatest, while less developed countries usually depend on a smaller range of exports than developed ones and so, again, are more affected by price fluctuations.

One internationally traded commodity is money. Here again states have options. A few – generally the richer ones – have internationally convertible currencies; most do not. Until the early 1970s, (as we shall see) the international currency system was controlled by reference to the US dollar and to gold. Coordinated attempts are still made from time to time to influence it, but the weight of money moving from one country to another is so great that control, as opposed to occasional influence, is no longer possible: a convertible currency cannot indefinitely buck the market. In open economies, currency and investment flows also have wider effects on interest rates and the money supply. Most countries are less directly exposed but if they wish to conduct international trade, they must have something to pay with – or, alternatively, borrow.

In the second half of the 1970s borrowing was rampant, but eventually most (not all) of the major borrowers proved unable to meet their interest payments. Simple default, however, would have cut them off from future loans for a long time to come. So most insolvent borrowers have placed themselves, to some extent, in the hands of the international community, seeking agreements on debt rescheduling and even new loans to pay off the interest on the old (see pp.427–9). In so doing the borrowers had some cards to play: it was not in the lenders' national interest to drive what were generally friendly states to alienation or despair; and many of the banks that had lent money were over-extended, hence for several years in no position to write off the capital of their loans lest this damage their own credit-worthiness. The result was a complicated minuet of concessions on both sides that revealed a degree of interdependence; but on the whole it is easier to be a creditor than a debtor.

Although most of the debt was commercial, the negotiations were moderated by international financial institutions, notably the International Monetary Fund (IMF). This brought pressure not only on creditors to lend and reschedule, but also on debtors to make the changes in (their often profligate) economic policies that would render future debt service possible. Agreements were therefore usually conditional on the IMF's certifying that such economic reforms had in fact been made, a process that enabled it to impose on the debtors – ostensibly sovereign states – internal measures (like the removal of subsidies, the trimming of uneconomic state enterprises, or devaluations) that were often highly unpopular, or at least against the interests of the local power holders.[7] This, too, was not new: British Treasury and League of Nations experts had played similar roles in the Eastern Europe of the 1920s;[8] while even before the 1980s many states had come under IMF surveillance and had to make some unwelcome changes in return for loans. But the 1980s scale of operations was far greater, and demonstrated to everybody that the great banks and the IMF could be significant international actors.

INTERNATIONAL POLITICS AS A TOURNAMENT ON MULTIPLE CHESS BOARDS

All this is a long way from, say, the Strategic Arms Limitation and Reduction Talks (SALT, START) of the 1970s and 1980s. The USSR was one of the two participants in SALT, and was generally regarded as a 'superpower'; but it was never a particularly important

7. In early 1993, twenty-seven Sub-Saharan African countries had such IMF/World Bank agreements: *The Independent*, 24 March 1993 p.12

8. Deflationary measures recommended by a British expert helped create the popular disaffection in Poland that led to Pilsudski's 1926 take-over

financial actor. One can extend such contrasts. The governments of small states like Jordan may exercise tight control internally and enjoy some influence over their neighbours, but their decisions probably affect fewer people than do those of a giant concern like International Business Machines (IBM), which sets global standards of computer operation and compatibility. Jordan and IBM operate in very different subject areas; and to some extent their relative importance lies in the eye of the beholder. Such considerations have led people to suggest, as a metaphor for the international system, a chess tournament on multiple boards. Some players, notably the United States, play on most (not all) boards; most play on many fewer (Saudi Arabia, for instance, chiefly on those of oil, finance, and the Middle East). There is, however, the important difference from a chess tournament that the play on one board can be affected by that on another.[9] Also, by common consent, some boards are more important than others, though there is much argument over the extent to which, in the modern world, military power can be converted into the currencies of influence or coercion.

Gathering these threads together – to give a picture of what Wilfrid Knapp calls the 'Warp and Weft of International Relations' – could be a difficult and lengthy task. So what follows will touch only on what I see as the system's most salient aspects.

'THE AMERICAN CENTURY'

International order rests chiefly on cooperation between states. But the part each state plays in this cooperation depends both on its resources – Burkina Faso's contributions are bound to be fairly limited – and on the role it seeks: for most of the postwar period Japan deliberately adopted a low international profile, whereas in the 1950s Nehru's India sought a position of moral leadership in world affairs. The USA has been well endowed with resources throughout the twentieth-century. Between the two world wars it was reluctant to use them; after 1941 this reluctance was perceived

9. By blocking the Suez Canal, the 1967 Arab–Israeli war helped damage the British balance of payments. Later that year Britain gave up trying to keep the pound at $2.80, thus diverting speculative pressure on to the price of gold. Devaluation also led it to decide to pull out of the Gulf, thus fully opening this up to the play of local power rivalries

as having been disastrous, and the USA has generally been ready to exert itself to mould international society to suit US interests and values (which are, of course, shared – to a greater or lesser extent – by many other countries). It has not always got its own way, nor, even when it did, was the end result necessarily what it would have wished. But there is a good deal of truth in the saying that the twentieth century, and more especially its second half, is the American century. Seldom has any country been so pre-eminent (economically, militarily, politically and culturally) as was the USA in the decades immediately after 1945. Its leadership extended both into geographically very disparate areas and over a wide range of topics, and was often institutionalised in both the security and the economic fields. The USA has clearly been a net provider, rather than consumer, of security, through a plethora of treaties both bilateral and multilateral – Dulles was often accused of 'pactomania'. In the most institutionalised such security system, NATO, the two main supreme commands are reserved for Americans.[10] In the economic field, the non-communist world was, in effect, on a dollar-exchange system for nearly three decades after the war. Although it is perhaps in the international monetary arena that the relative decline of US power has been most evident, the dollar remains the world's principal store of value: the price of commodities like oil and gold is fixed in terms of dollars even when none of the traders, producers or purchasers is American.

US leadership, therefore, must be seen as underwriting much of what is described in this book. However, it was neither unique nor exclusive: there was also the USSR. Indeed a whole host of lesser powers have provided a degree of leadership, to their neighbours, or to like-minded countries, or in functional fields such as the setting of oil prices (Saudi Arabia), or international banking (Switzerland) in which their position was particularly strong. Most of this is fairly intangible. But, as an organising principle of international society, it is quite as important as many more formal, and therefore visible, institutions; indeed it often underlies their operation.

10. Churchill begged emotionally in 1952 for an independent naval command. He was eventually consoled with a British Commander in Chief, Channel, who is officially on a par with SACEUR and SACLANT but at the same time subordinate to SACLANT for operations in the remainder of eastern Atlantic waters

SPHERES OF INFLUENCE AND GREY AREAS

Leadership, and the influence it affords, can be exercised in circumstances where coercion would not be possible. But it sometimes shades into coercion, or even rests on the possibility of coercion. Few East European states would have gone communist but for the post-1945 Soviet presence; both 1956 (Hungary) and 1968 (Czechoslovakia) saw overt military intervention to reverse political trends in nominally independent countries. Eastern Europe, in short, was a Soviet sphere of influence. This does not mean that its governments always did what the USSR wanted: Yugoslavia and Albania both broke away, and, as time went on, other communist governments gained in independence and assumed increasingly national characteristics. Nor does cooperation with the USSR necessarily imply coercion: East European governments shared many values and interests with their Soviet counterpart. However, in the postwar period, the relationship rested far more on force than did that between the USA and north-western Europe.

Of course other states besides the USSR seek or possess spheres of influence. After conquering the South in 1975, (North) Vietnam installed satellite regimes in Laos and (with more difficulty) Kampuchea, though in 1989 it pulled back from the latter. For much of the 1970s the Shah of Iran proclaimed his country's mission to stabilise the Gulf area and armed intensively to acquire the capability to do so. In 1979 the Shah fell from power, but his dream seemed to revive in a new form in 1982, when – after repelling Iraq's invasion – Ayatollah Khomeini called for the establishment of an 'Islamic' regime there and added that 'if Iran and Iraq unite . . . , the other, smaller nations of the region will join them as well'.[11]

The immediate catalyst for the Shah's ambitions had been British withdrawal from the Gulf in 1971, a withdrawal that brought to an end the last vestiges of a British sphere of influence that had in 1945 encompassed the Middle East from southern Iran to Greece and Libya. This rested on a mixture of military pre-eminence, defence treaties with independent (and treaties of protection with other) rulers, subsidies, the presence of pro-consular advisers, and a readiness to exert British influence in local politics, together with the anxiety of many local politicians to cooperate with such influence and harness it to their own benefit. Occasionally, as in the

11. Shaul Bakhash, *The Reign of the Ayatollahs* (1985) pp.232–4

displacement of Mossadegh, stronger measures were resorted to; a final instance was the help given in 1970 to the coup by the present Sultan of Oman, Quaboos, to depose his father (see pp.346, 366).

Britain's moment in the Middle East is over. But France still maintains a smaller scale, but not dissimilar, position in many of its African ex-colonies. Subsidies, and the services of French officials, are open to them; there are regular Franco-African summit conferences, and many of the African rulers are strongly Francophile. Embarrassingly so in the case of Jean Bokassa (ruler of the Central African Republic from 1966 to 1979), who bestowed diamonds on Giscard d'Estaing and his family,[12] and was so obsessed by Napoleon (his 'guide and inspiration') that he crowned himself Emperor in a ceremony costing some $26 million (largely borne by France). Bokassa murdered opponents in unpleasant ways; in 1979 he overdid things by beating a hundred schoolchildren to death. Either for this reason or because Bokassa had begun to cultivate Libya, France helped Dacko overthrow him; Dacko, however, proved to be a divisive President, and in 1981 France gave the Central African army the go-ahead to remove him. France maintains small numbers of troops in Africa – in 1964 they reversed a coup in Gabon – backed by a force d'intervention at home.[13] Such forces make possible occasional interventions to stabilise dangerous situations: the most important was probably the 1978 blocking of the Angolan-backed invasion of Shaba (Zaïre).[14] Less happy was French involvement in the 1970s in an endemic and unedifying civil war in Chad, from which it withdrew its troops in 1980; in 1983 they returned (after the failure in 1982 of an OAU peace-keeping force), and succeeded, at low cost, in holding Libya and its clients away from the African half of the country.

The location of certain spheres of influence is obvious. That of the United States' sphere is more controversial, partly because US influence extends so widely. De Gaulle regarded it as a 'hegemony', and was determined to extract France from it and reinstate its full sovereignty. Most people, though, would distinguish between the US position in north-western Europe and that in the Caribbean. Yet even if we do make such distinctions we are left with borderline cases. One such was Italy, where (at least until the 1970s) the USA

12. Giscard found the episode a liability in the 1981 French presidential elections: *Keesing's*, 30646

13. David, *Third World Coups* pp.144, 120–2; *Keesing's*, 28811, 29933–4, 31288 (Central African Republic/Empire), 20024 (Gabon)

14. See *The Cold War* chap. 11

has periodically deployed its considerable political leverage to keep the communists from office.[15]

Other borderline cases would include Greece and South Korea. By the 1950s the regimes of both owed their survival to extensive US support. It would have been surprising if US influence had not been considerable, and the disaffected often saw it as all-pervasive. But direct evidence of major US intervention in their internal affairs does not abound. There have been allegations that the USA was involved in the 1967 military coup in Greece; more probably it simply moved later to accept it on the basis of a shared anti-communism. The 'realism' of the Nixon administration would probably have led to this anyway; but the process seems to have been eased by campaign contributions on the part of Greek money and by personal friendships.[16]

In South Korea the United States was infuriated by the behaviour of President Syngman Rhee during the 1953 armistice negotiations, and considered the possibility of a coup if he remained obdurate (though only to reject it as unfeasible).[17] Thereafter relations were patched up, but Rhee's opposition to US attempts to build up Japan ensured that they would never be close. When electoral malpractice provoked riots in 1960 and the Korean armed forces declined to protect Rhee, the US ambassador was quick to call for the resumption of 'full democratic practices'; Rhee's resignation followed, and his departure for Hawaii was arranged. In 1961 a coup by General Park Chung Hee ushered in a period of military government. The coup was promptly denounced by the US commander of the UN forces (to whom Korean troops were theoretically subordinate) and by the US chargé d'affaires; but diplomatic relations and aid were soon restored, and the USA reverted to a policy of pressing the military to abide by their declared aim of restoring free electoral competition. In the spring of 1963 Park (who was by now President) proposed to scrap the original timetable for this, and received from Kennedy 'a friendly warning against the perpetuation of unconstitutional government'.

15. See *The Cold War* chap.13

16. Bell, *The Diplomacy of Detente* chap. 8; Hersh, *The Price of Power* pp.136–40 – given Hersh's antipathy to Nixon/Kissinger it is perhaps significant that his accusations are no worse. It certainly did not look good that Colonel Papadopoulos, one of the 1967 coup leaders, had received a CIA retainer since 1952; but such retainers were not uncommon in the 1950s: Ranelagh, *The Agency* p.758n; Victor Marchetti and John D. Marks, *The CIA and the Cult of Intelligence* pp.37–47

17. Ambrose, *Eisenhower* pp.101–3; MacDonald, *Korea: The War before Vietnam* pp.190–6

Park accordingly drew back, retired from the army, and that October was narrowly elected President as a civilian; he then dug himself in.[18] US wishes could therefore be overridden, and the United States' stake in Korea was so great that it felt it had to work even with distasteful regimes. Such considerations later inhibited President Carter from stopping military aid on human rights grounds, as he did to strategically less exposed friends like Brazil.[19] But South Korea could never feel quite certain, especially in view of the 1973 congressional cut-off of support for South Vietnam. So from 1972 (at the latest) until 1977 – when the matter came into the open as the 'Koreagate' scandal – Korea sought to purchase congressional goodwill through campaign contributions, gifts and entertainment. It is claimed that the operation was so managed as to reach only a few (and mostly uninfluential) Congressmen;[20] but the episode does serve to show that influence, even between a superpower and its dependant, can run more than one way.

In parts of Latin America and, from 1954 to 1975, Indo-China, US influence has been more obtrusive. Indo-China is discussed elsewhere. Here we need only note that the United States found itself helping in 1963 to depose President Diem of South Vietnam; between 1965 and 1972 it carried probably the major share of the fighting in Vietnam; a clandestine CIA-recruited army was also active in Laos; and by the early 1970s the regimes of South Vietnam, Laos and Cambodia were all dependent on US economic support.

US involvement in Indo-China was comparatively brief. The claim to a special position in the Americas dates back to the 1823 Monroe Doctrine, which depicted all attempts by European powers 'to extend their system to any portion of this hemisphere as dangerous to our peace and safety'. Its high point was the 1904 'Roosevelt Corollary' to the effect that, as the USA would not countenance intervention by (European) 'civilised nations', it might be forced, 'however reluctantly, in flagrant cases of . . . wrongdoing or impotence [on the part of local states], to the exercise of an international police power'. It is not admittedly to prevent European gunboat diplomacy that the USA has recently exercised a degree of

18. Robert T. Oliver, *Syngman Rhee and American Involvement in Korea, 1948–1960* (Seoul, 1978) esp. pp.468–9, 472, chap. 22; *Keesing's*, 18213, 19644

19. Brzezinski, *Power and Principle* p.128

20. Franck and Weisband, *Foreign Policy by Congress* pp.166–72. Spending about $750,000 a year was apparently envisaged; but the undertaking's full dimensions may not have emerged from the 1977 investigation

'international police power', but (generally) to exclude revolutionary communism or developments it sees as leading that way: President Johnson declared in 1965 that the USA 'will not permit the establishment of another communist government in the Western Hemisphere'; his chief Latin American policy-maker added that the possibility of a communist take-over anywhere in the hemisphere would warrant US intervention.[21] Like other hegemonic powers the USA has encountered difficulties since the Second World War, when existing rulers are attracted to ideas or alignments it regards as dangerous, or (more usually) when leaders with whom it is comfortable are displaced by opponents of a more hostile ideological cast. To control the situation, the USA has sometimes resorted to actions that clearly breach international law (like the 1965 occupation of the Dominican Republic, the 1984 clandestine mining of Nicaraguan ports and the 1989 invasion of Panama). Other states within or without the region may condemn these actions, but they are in no position to challenge them.

COLLECTIVE MANAGEMENT BY THE GREAT POWERS

It is of the nature of a sphere of influence that one Power has assumed a responsibility for the maintenance of a certain kind of order. Elsewhere, however, Great Powers have often acted collectively to provide order. In the nineteenth century the six Great Powers of the Concert of Europe, or a subset of them, intervened periodically to lay down the law in the Balkans (or, less often, outside Europe), sometimes enforcing their rulings by collective naval demonstrations.[22] After 1918 such Great Power behaviour was frowned on as part of the discredited old diplomacy. The practice nevertheless survived, to some extent in the Far East in the 1920s, but also from 1938 in Europe (where 'Munich' represented a Four Power revision of the peace treaties as they concerned Czechoslovakia, and was followed by the remodelling of Eastern Europe

21. Molineu, *U.S. Policy toward Latin America* pp.78–9

22. *One* of the causes of the First World War was their inability in 1912 any longer to control the local Balkan states and so prevent the outbreak of the Balkan Wars. These so expanded Serbia that Austria believed it a threat, and determined (with Germany's backing) to crush it without first agreeing action with the Great Power most nearly affected, Russia

agreed through the 1939 Nazi–Soviet Pact). During the Second World War the cast changed, but 'Big Three' summits at Teheran, Yalta and Potsdam took decisions both on border changes and on the establishment of the UN.

It was intended to continue this collaboration after the war, through regular meetings of the Four Power Council of Foreign Ministers. The Cold War largely blighted such hopes, and US–Soviet hostility proved too intense to permit much in the way of joint management of the international system. Admittedly the idea rather appealed to Brezhnev, who tried to draw Nixon into the joint handling of China and the imposition of an Arab–Israeli settlement – but to no avail. More headway was made in the field of nuclear weapons, where superpower pre-eminence was particularly marked: the SALT/INF (intermediate range nuclear force) talks were all bilateral, while the earlier Test Ban treaty was worked out on a Three Power basis. There has also been a very limited amount of crisis management à deux, as over Syria's involvement in the 1970 Jordanian–PLO fighting, and the 1967 Israeli–Syrian and 1973 Israeli–Egyptian cease-fires.[23] However, superpower participation was usually restricted to the coordination of more discreet pressure to promote negotiations, like those over Laos in 1961–2 or between South Africa and Cuba and Angola in 1988; even this was not common.

A variant is management by one or more Western powers. On a multilateral basis the most obvious example is the 1950 Tripartite Declaration, whereby Britain, the USA and France threatened action 'within or without the framework of the United Nations' to prevent violation of the borders established by the recent Arab–Israeli armistice agreements, and also undertook so to manage the supply of arms to the region as to prevent either side gaining preponderance. There is some dispute as to whether France complied with the provisions on arms sales. Egypt certainly managed to circumvent them through its 1955 arms deal with the USSR. In 1956 Eden hoped to plug this gap by inducing the USSR to accede to the Declaration, but to no effect.[24] The cover story for the Anglo-French Suez operation, that it was an intervention to halt Israeli–Egyptian fighting, drew on the same tradition of Great Power management of other countries' quarrels. This tradition shaded naturally into that of spheres of influence; it is not clear under

23. See *The Cold War* chap. 11

24. RIIA, *Survey of International Affairs: The Middle East 1945–1950* p.313; M. Heikal, *Nasser: The Cairo Documents* (1972) p.65 and *Sphinx and Commissar* p.66

which heading one would classify, for instance, France's intervention in Chad in 1983 and the laying down there of a 'red line' south of which Libyan military action would not be permitted. Similarly the 1950 US 'interposition' of its fleet between China and Taiwan, and perhaps also its subsequent handling of the Chinese offshore islands crises, can be seen either as the enforcement of calm in the West Pacific or as the extension and consolidation of its sphere of influence. However the 1964 and 1967 inter-positions between Turkey and Cyprus were squarely in the old tradition of Great Power regulation of Balkan rivalries. Unhappily subsequent US attempts to negotiate a settlement failed;[25] and the USA did not tangle with Turkey's 1974 invasion of the island.

25. Kissinger, *Memoirs* ii p.1,189; Cyrus Vance, *Hard Choices* (New York, 1983) p.144; Bell, *The Diplomacy of Detente* pp.142–3

CHAPTER NINETEEN

The United Nations

THE LEAGUE OF NATIONS AND THE UNITED NATIONS

After the First World War, liberals sought to replace Great Power management of the international system with a 'League of Nations'. The substitution was not completely successful, but the League enjoyed a very high international profile, higher, probably, than that of its successor the United Nations. Its values were sufficiently accepted for the leading interwar Power, Britain, to regard as improper Japan's detachment of Manchuria from China and Italy's conquest of Abyssinia, both of which would have seemed unremarkable in 1900. The League also appeared to be a major provider of 'collective security' with an obligation to assure the integrity of its member states (including Abyssinia and China). In practice, though not in intent,[1] this identified the League with the existing international regime: in the 1930s Germany, Japan and Italy accordingly signalled their rejection of this regime by leaving the League, the Soviet Union its apparent acceptance by joining. From this perspective, the League fell disastrously between two stools. It had so changed international values that Britain felt obliged to condemn Japanese and Italian action in Manchuria/ Abyssinia, and even to invoke economic sanctions against Italy; neither country was ever fully conciliated thereafter, and British diplomacy was nearly paralysed as a result. But Britain would not push 'collective security' to the point of forcing a war over actions

1. Its Covenant empowered the League to recommend treaty revision (Article 19)

that might violate League morality but did not directly affect British interests. Britain and the League could undoubtedly have defeated Italy (at a price); the League's engagement of its prestige, but failure actually to protect Abyssinia, destroyed it as a significant force in international affairs.

If the League's achievements in terms of security provision were in the end slender,[2] or even negative, we should not overlook the fact that in three respects it went beyond what the UN has subsequently attempted. The League itself took charge of some areas of great international sensitivity like Danzig. The UN, by contrast, refused in 1967 to accept responsibility for, and thus neutralise, Perim Island (which controls the Bab el Mandeb).[3] Second, the League sometimes attached political conditions to the loans it arranged in the 1920s for the economic rehabilitation of eastern Europe. The UN, as such, does not arrange loans; the IMF and World Bank (which do) are in practice largely independent of the UN, and even they have not sought to use their loans as direct instruments for the maintenance of the territorial status quo. Finally, the League was charged with overseeing states' compliance with their undertakings, in the East European peace treaties, to adhere to a defined code of rights for members of minority nationalities. Its efforts generated more heat than success; the UN has never attempted so to impinge on the sovereignty of its members.[4]

It has, however, mounted campaigns against three regimes that it found particularly obnoxious – Spain, Rhodesia and South Africa. At its outset it tried to reverse the outcome of the Spanish Civil War, voting (against US wishes) for the withdrawal of ambassadors on the unconvincing pretext that Franco's Spain was a 'potential danger to peace'. This was abandoned in 1950, and Spain worked its way back to acceptability and in 1955 UN membership (materially helped by the Cold War and a 1953 defence agreement with the USA). A similar embargo was placed, at British instance, on the breakaway Rhodesian regime in 1966 (see pp.68–9). It was not very successful, but the wish to end sanctions was a minor factor in the 1979 return to 'legality'. South African racial policies

2. Its only unequivocal success, the halting of a 1925 Greek attack on Bulgaria, was the kind of action not infrequently performed in the Balkans by the Great Powers before 1914

3. *Keesing's*, 22415

4. For a discussion of the League's role in the management of international relations – in the context of what preceded and followed it – see J. Dunbabin, 'The League of Nations' place in the International System', *History* lxxviii (1993)

attracted unfavourable UN attention as early as the 1940s. In 1962 the General Assembly condemned apartheid and urged a complete trade boycott – which the Security Council watered down to an advisory arms embargo in 1963 (made mandatory in 1987). This embargo influenced some states (Britain, South Africa's traditional supplier, had largely adopted it by late 1964), but the gap was for a long time more than filled by France, Israel, private arms dealers, and domestic production.[5] Since the 1960s many countries have imposed their own economic sanctions. These do not stem directly from the UN, but reviving international pressure in the mid-1980s would probably have led to UN measures except for the prospect of a veto by Britain and the USA.

THE UNITED NATIONS CHARTER AND THE DE-LEGITIMISATION OF THE USE OF FORCE

As the end of the First World War had seen an attempt to set the values of the new epoch through the League Covenant, so the end of the Second World War produced the United Nations Charter. This was only a mixed success: its Human Rights provisions, though further elaborated in a General Assembly Declaration of 1948, have remained essentially a dead letter, since any attempt to enforce compliance would be incompatible with national sovereignty. At most they are used as brickbats to throw at regimes that are widely disliked; no attempt was made to expel, say, Amin's and Obote's Uganda or Pol Pot's Kampuchea from the UN for their manifest non-compliance. Parts of the Charter have fared better, however, and it has – in conjunction with the League Covenant, the Kellogg–Briand Pact, and the International (war crimes) Tribunal at Nuremberg[6] – probably played an appreciable role in reducing recourse to open offensive war, something that had been entirely legitimate in the days of Cavour and Bismarck. In the run-up to Suez the Legal Adviser to the British Foreign Office called attention to 'the immense change that has taken place in the climate of world opinion on the use of force . . . Justification [notably the need to protect 'vital interests'] that would have been accepted

5. *Keesing's*, 19672–3, 20485; Anthony Sampson, *The Arms Bazaar* (paperback edn, 1978) pp.163–8. Although South Africa became an arms exporter, it was outgunned in 1988 in Angola by Soviet-supplied Cuban forces

6. This asserted the criminality of planning or waging an offensive war

without question fifty or even twenty-five years ago would by now be completely rejected'.[7] True, the British government did not take his advice, but the international reaction to its attack on Egypt proved him right. Admittedly war has survived as an instrument of policy in certain parts of the world, notably the Middle East and perhaps also the Indian subcontinent; and China has deliberately fought limited wars (against India in 1962 and Vietnam in 1979) for their demonstrative effect. Elsewhere, however, the incidence of open war has been remarkably low, and it has been avoided in a number of instances (like the Algerian–Moroccan border disputes) that might well have touched it off in the past. Unfortunately this decline in open war has led to a corresponding increase in 'covert action', in guerrilla activities by externally supported 'liberation movements', and in external intervention in civil wars. Even so, the effect has been to reduce the political advantages of large Powers: small ones have gained in security against external attack, even where they are themselves applying low-level force. Libya, for instance, could easily be conquered by either the USA or Egypt, but it has felt able to risk extensive support for 'terrorist' movements and for subversion in Africa, much of it directed against US and/or Egyptian interests.[8] At a lower level, Iceland could harass British trawlers in order to extend its fishing limits (see pp.476–7), secure in the knowledge that its gunboats would not be seized or sunk in return (as would once have been the case).

UN ENFORCEMENT ACTION – KOREA, AND THE 1950 'UNITING FOR PEACE' RESOLUTION

Although the UN Charter may thus have helped change international behaviour, the United Nations' founders did not (in the light of their recent experience) intend to take this for granted in the way that some of their predecessors had banked on the efficacy of the League Covenant. Roosevelt, indeed, regarded the UN as the vehicle through which the United States could be prevented from repeating its disastrous return to isolationism in the

7. Louis and Owen, *Suez 1956* p.114

8. The USA in fact dissuaded Egypt from intervention in 1977, while Egypt blocked joint action with the USA in 1985 (see p.348n). Admittedly the USA did then try to kill the Libyan leader in a 1986 bombing raid (*Keesing's*, 34456–7); but it never took its hostility to the point of a conventional invasion

1920s. He once said 'he saw the UN as the expansion of the United States; the United States had become the United Nations'.[9] So he had had expansive ideas of the UN's acquiring strategic territories like Dakar as bases and of its taking over the 'trusteeship' of French Indo-China. By 1945 such visions had been scaled down, but it was still hoped that the UN would succeed, where the League had failed, in providing collective security. Its Charter was therefore stronger in this regard than had been the League Covenant: the UN was intended to have its own military structure, and in 1945–6 there was much support for giving it exclusive control over nuclear production and weapons. The Cold War made this unrealistic; the chief result was to force the USSR to use its Security Council veto in ways that damaged its standing with Western public opinion.

UN coercive action came with the Korean War. This was fully in line with 'collective security' as it had been understood in the 1930s, when its advocates clearly envisaged the taking of military measures by one Great Power (Britain) through the League to repel actions (like the invasion of Abyssinia) of another (Italy). Truman saw things in this light. But doubts have grown up, probably because, instead of simply and rapidly repelling the North Korean invasion, the UN went on to try to unify the peninsula (in accordance with its 1948 Resolution) and found itself bogged down in a long war with China. Some people have therefore contended that the UN should not have let itself be conscripted into so firm an alignment with one side of the Cold War, and that the veto accorded to the Permanent Members of the Security Council[10] should be seen as a safeguard against such partisanship. The USA did not accept this view: in 1950 it secured a 'Uniting for Peace' Resolution that purported to empower the General Assembly to act by a two-thirds majority when the Security Council was paralysed by vetoes. It was only once used – during the Suez crisis – directly to condemn Permanent Members, and no UN sanctions were then deployed.

9. Also the Hot Springs conference to prepare the ground for a UN organisation concluded to the strains of 'The Star-Spangled Banner': J.W. Holmes, *Life with Uncle* (Toronto, 1981) pp.13–14

10. China, France, the UK, USA and USSR

THE UN'S ROLE IN THE DISPOSITION OF COLONIES AND MANDATES

The UN thus never played a primary role in the provision of security, and the 1940s and 1950s saw a mushrooming of alliances intended to fill this gap. However, the UN did involve itself in some colonial questions. Of Japan's colonies, Taiwan went to China (as promised by the 1943 Cairo summit), but the UN assumed responsibility for Korea. In practice decisions were made almost exclusively by the occupying Powers (the USA and USSR), but the UN's prescription (and in the South monitoring) of free elections in 1948 served to legitimise the Synghman Rhee regime (though not to secure unification). With respect to Italy's colonies, the UN exercised a more real influence: in 1949 the General Assembly rejected the Anglo-Italian agreement on Libya and called for its early independence as a unified state.[11] Earlier the UN had also intervened, chiefly at Australia's instance, to try to curb Dutch repression of the 'Indonesian Republic'. The Netherlands was to some extent responsive, complying with the UN call to break off its 'First Police Action' and accepting the mediation that produced the Renville Agreement. This did not, however, prevent further trouble and a 'Second Police Action', and the 1949 Dutch decision to leave owed more to other factors than to UN pressure (see pp.34–5). Nor did the UN interject itself into the not dissimilar fighting resulting from the French attempt to recover control throughout Indo-China.

The UN did, however, have a special role in connection with Mandates. In 1945 Britain had blocked French moves to repress Syrian nationalists. The issue was taken to the UN, which managed to secure the withdrawal of foreign troops from Syria and the Lebanon and their independence in early 1946. Palestine was more complicated. When Britain referred the issue to the UN in 1947, it initially anticipated stalemate, but the Soviet bloc's decision to back partition changed things. The General Assembly eventually drew up, and endorsed by a two-thirds majority, a specific partition scheme (see pp.253–5). This reflected not only support by the USSR and, still more, lobbying by the USA, but also, to some extent, a collective international decision on a difficult problem that accorded substantial legitimacy to the nascent state of Israel.

11. In 1950 the General Assembly also agreed (despite some local Muslim opposition) to the federation with Ethiopia of Italy's former colony Eritrea. In 1962 Ethiopia determined on full union; Eritrean insurrection broke out in 1966 and continued until successful in 1991

What the UN could not do was to enforce either its November 1947 partition scheme or, next year, the recommendations of its mediator, Count Bernadotte. So the final arbitrament was left to fighting, which the UN could influence by promoting cease-fires, but not control. Other Mandates proved less dramatic. But the fact that French Togoland had potential access to the UN encouraged its 1955 constitutional advance (with knock-on effects for other French African colonies) so as to avoid damaging comparisons with the Gold Coast; later British anticipation of difficulties at the UN accelerated Tanganyika's independence in 1961.[12] Also, though South Africa refused to place its League Mandate of South-West Africa under the UN, the latter managed in the 1950s to discourage South African annexation (which was not precluded by the terms of the League Mandate). The 1960s saw the start of a long campaign to end South African administration, which led South Africa to counter by itself embracing the idea of Namibian independence – on its own terms. Since these terms did not prove internationally acceptable, South African administration continued; agreement was, however, finally reached in 1988 for independence elections to be conducted under UN auspices, and Namibia duly gained independence in 1990.

THE UN'S CONTRIBUTION TO DECOLONISATION

Decolonisation was one of the areas in which the UN came to take a special interest as its ranks were swelled by an influx of new members that had themselves only recently become independent. In 1960 the General Assembly declared that 'All peoples have the right of self-determination', and that lack of 'preparedness should never serve as a pretext for delaying independence'. By then, of course, decolonisation was already very far advanced. Its timing cannot be closely linked with UN votes; but the climate of opinion in the UN probably helped persuade metropolitan countries to extend the process to the smaller colonies they had originally regarded as 'non-viable', and to strategic territories whose retention they had previously regarded as essential. It may also have encouraged some reluctant colonial politicians to take the plunge

12. Hargreaves, *Decolonization in Africa* p.154; Morgan, *Official History of Colonial Development* v pp.135–6

into independence.[13] In a few specific cases the UN became more directly involved. It successfully conducted votes to determine whether the British slice of Cameroun wished to leave Nigeria and rejoin Cameroun on its independence from France. However, the UN refused to ascertain the wishes of the people of 'West Irian' and assisted in their transfer to Indonesia; it blessed the incorporation into Malaysia of the British North Borneo territories (again exhibiting less interest in the inhabitants' wishes than had the earlier British Cobbold Commission); and its Committee on Decolonisation was determined to stop Britain from transferring power in Aden and its hinterland to the sheikhs of the South Arabian Federation.

UN JUDGEMENTS OF LEGITIMACY

Once independent, states naturally wish to join the UN as a symbol of their new sovereignty. The process is generally automatic, but in some controversial cases the readiness or otherwise of the UN – and of the appropriate regional organisation – to accord the new state membership is important in establishing its international legitimacy: thus Belize was acceptable,[14] but not Transkei.

This function of conferring legitimacy extends beyond the recognition of new countries, but in a rather inconclusive way. UN membership can crown and consolidate a settlement, as when East and West Germany joined the organisation in 1973; this represented a clear gain for the hitherto less accepted DDR. But nobody has ever doubted Switzerland's legitimacy despite its refusal to join the UN; nor did Israel's UN membership reconcile the Arabs to its existence. Also UN refusal to acknowledge the Kadar regime in Hungary after 1956, and the Mao Zedong regime in China from 1949, had eventually to be abandoned in the face of

13. In 1973 the General Assembly demanded independence for the Seychelles despite the wishes of its Prime Minister. But it was OAU financial support for his Opposition that he cited next year to explain his change of mind. Independence led to the former Opposition taking over in a Tanzanian-backed coup: *Keesing's*, 26500, 27852, 28485

14. Guatemalan territorial claims were the chief obstacle to Belize's independence. From 1975 to 1982 UN Resolutions encouraged attempts to resolve the problem; and growing support in the UN was a factor in strengthening Belize's position. In the end, though Guatemala deplored Belize's independence, it did not actively contest it; but Britain still had to continue its military protection of Belize: *Keesing's*, 27573 ff, 30348 ff, 31334 ff

facts; however, non-recognition of the Vietnamese-installed Cambodian regime did ultimately help bring it to the negotiating table.

UN PRESCRIPTIVE RESOLUTIONS

In making these judgements of legitimacy, the UN is the nearest thing we have to a world consensus: it is arguable that some of its Resolutions have acquired prescriptive power. In particular Security Council Resolution 242, though not so far implemented, has moulded a general belief that Israel should withdraw from its 1967 conquests, but that when it does it should be accepted and allowed to live without threats, as it was not before 1967. (Of course not all Resolutions have achieved this status – what was Resolution 241? There is, too, some competition in the selection of Resolutions on which to lay emphasis; thus the PLO naturally seeks to stress, and Israel to ignore, those bearing on refugees.)

Some people have taken this line of argument further. One of the sources of international law is the common practice of states. It is claimed that General Assembly Resolutions, when passed by massive majorities, can be taken as evidence of this 'common practice' and so of the state of international law. Condemnations of apartheid would presumably come into this category, but the 1975 General Assembly Resolution that (by seventy-two votes to thirty-five, with thirty-two abstentions) condemned Zionism as 'a form of racialism and racial discrimination' might not. In any case conventional treaties, like the Vienna Convention on diplomatic relations or the Nuclear Non-Proliferation Treaty, provide a far safer legal basis. The UN is accordingly more appropriately regarded as a political and deliberative than as a legislative body.

UN SECRETARY-GENERAL HAMMARSKJÖLD 1953–61

It is, I think, arguable that the most important decisions the UN has made were those of its early years.[15] But its prestige probably reached its peak under Secretary-General Dag Hammarskjöld

15. There were then more dependent territories on whose disposition the UN might be consulted. Now that the world consists almost entirely of sovereign states, the UN has less scope in this respect

(1953–61). He responded admirably to the Suez crisis, assembling the UN expeditionary force (UNEF) to cover the Anglo-French evacuation and persuading Nasser to accept it (see pp.295–7). UNEF stayed after the crisis was over; its presence on the border with Israel stopped the renewal of the cycle of *fedayeen* raids and Israeli reprisals, while its occupation of Sharm el-Sheikh preserved freedom of transit to Eilat. This appeared a most encouraging example of the 'preventive diplomacy' that Hammarskjöld regarded as the UN's hallmark; it provided a precedent for other 'peace-keeping' exercises. The two chief ones were ONUC for the Congo (of which more on pp.463–8) and UNFICYP for Cyprus. Cyprus had collapsed into communal violence in late 1963 (see p.242). This was curbed by Britain under the Zurich agreement. But British mediation failed to resolve the underlying political problems, and the Cyprus government preferred UN involvement to the Zurich framework; so in March 1964 there was established a UN force of 7,000. Over the next decade this protected enclaves into which the Turkish population increasingly withdrew, but did little to promote adherence to the original power-sharing Constitution. Although it might stop incidents arising, it was not intended to fight and could therefore be pushed aside. In any case its size made it irrelevant if Turkey decided to intervene. In 1967 the USA prevented such intervention; in 1974 it did not. So Turkey implemented partition amid communal killing and massive refugee flight. When the dust had settled UNFICYP was redeployed along the new border; the UN has attempted to mediate between the parties, but so far (1993) without effect.

After his 1956–7 Suez successes, and his election in September 1957 to a second term of office, Hammarskjöld assumed a higher political profile. He maintained that

> active preventive diplomacy . . . may be conducted by the United Nations . . . in many situations where no government or group of governments and no regional organization would be able to act in the same way. . . . [This] is explained by the fact that . . . [the UN] has begun to gain a certain independent position, and that this tendency had led to the acceptance of an independent political and diplomatic activity on the part of the Secretary-General as . . . [its] 'neutral' representative.[16]

These claims were quite widely accepted, and a common saying of the time was 'Leave it to Dag'.

16. A.W. Rovine, *The First Fifty Years: The Secretary General in World Politics* (Leyden, 1970) p.331

In retrospect one is more conscious of the limitations on UN activity. Hammarskjöld's attempt to visit Hungary in December 1956, and to send observers there, came to nothing. He did visit Laos in 1959 to try to encourage a neutralist government, but disengaged in 1960; Great Power mediation in the 1961–2 Laotian crises took place outside the UN framework. Khrushchev would have accepted a UN presence in West Berlin as part of his 'free city' scheme, but others saw it as a quite inadequate substitute for the occupation rights and military contingents of the Western 'Protecting Powers'; so the UN played no role in the 1958–62 Berlin crisis. Nor was it involved in the 1958 Chinese offshore islands crisis. But the UN did have a position in the Middle East. In May–June 1958 the government of the Lebanon complained that United Arab Republic support for its opponents constituted a threat to peace. The UN sent a small 'observer group' to check that arms were not being brought in. It reported that they were not, but (given the admitted limitations on its operation) this carried little conviction in Washington.[17] To Hammarskjöld's private concern, the USA responded to the Iraqi coup and to President Chamoun's panic by intervening in force, and proposed (as a necessary condition for its withdrawal) the dispatch of a UN peace-keeping force. The USSR vetoed this, and Hammarskjöld finally broke the deadlock by deciding on his own authority to expand the observer group. It was a testimony to Hammarskjöld's prestige, and to his distance from US policy in the Middle East, that when Khrushchev pressed for a summit meeting on the crisis, he proposed including Hammarskjöld or conducting it within the framework of the UN Security Council. This never came off; but Hammarskjöld presented a personal plan (originally intended for unveiling at the summit) to an emergency General Assembly meeting in August. The Arab states then developed it into a Resolution that they presented jointly and that substantially defused the crisis; afterwards Hammarskjöld toured the Middle East and helped tie up the ends.[18]

17. ibid, pp.300–1
18. ibid, pp.301–5; see also *The Cold War* chap. 7 and pp.300–1 in this volume

THE UN OPERATION IN THE CONGO 1960–4

High Noon came in 1960 with the collapse of the former Belgian Congo (Zaïre) immediately after the transfer of power.[19] Belgian troops intervened to protect expatriates and restore order; and Moise Tshombe, who valued continued Belgian assistance, took the opportunity to declare the independence of Katanga (the Congo's richest province, which contained most of its mines). Various central government ministers asked the USA for troops to replace the Belgians; but, to avoid providing any occasion for Soviet counter-involvement, the US ambassador instead encouraged an approach to the UN: 'This', he explained to Washington, 'should keep bears out of the Congo caviar. I assume most Americans have not yet developed a great taste for it either.' Prime Minister Lumumba duly appealed to the UN, and a UN force (ONUC) was assembled with commendable speed and 10,000 troops were deployed in the Congo in a fortnight. However they were refused admission to Katanga. Lumumba's chief concerns were the reinforcement of his own position and Katanga's reconquest. In July he flew to Washington to seek American arms to effect this, and he then demanded that ONUC be put at his disposal. Hammarskjöld instead tried to square the circle, insisting in early August that ONUC must enter Katanga and take over the great Kamina airfield, but that it should not 'in any way intervene or be used to influence the outcome of any internal conflict, constitutional or otherwise'. Tshombe was, therefore, left in control.[20]

Lumumba accordingly turned increasingly towards the USSR. This began, clandestinely, to fly in arms, and placed at Lumumba's disposal technicians plus a hundred lorries and fifteen aircraft to enable him to transport troops from his upcountry political base, Stanleyville. However his first attempt at military action led to a massacre of secessionist tribesmen in south Kasai. This result, along with his turn to the USSR and his generally erratic behaviour, lost Lumumba the sympathy of both President Kasavubu and the UN. When Kasavubu dismissed Lumumba from the premiership in September, ONUC (which had had some prior notice) closed down

19. The best account of the Congo crisis is Madeleine G. Kalb, *The Congo Cables. The Cold War in Africa – From Eisenhower to Kennedy* (New York, 1982), from which much in the subsequent paragraphs derives. See also pp.14–15, and *The Cold War* chap. 8

20. Kalb, *The Congo Cables* p.7 and *passim*; Rovine, *The First Fifty Years* pp.309 ff; *Keesing's*, 17758

Leopoldville radio and barred airfields to any but UN planes; a move that was ostensibly even-handed but in fact calculated to help Kasavubu. Hammarskjöld had not directly sanctioned this, but he certainly approved: he told the USA that 'what he was trying to do was get rid of Lumumba' without 'compromising' the UN ('gamesmanship – how to win without actually cheating'), and complained of Kasavubu's indolence (it was 'extremely difficult to break Hitlers when the alternatives were Hindenbergs [sic]').

The USSR was not deceived. At the General Assembly that autumn, Khrushchev denounced the 'one-sided' nature and pro-Western 'bias' of the UN machinery and proposed to remedy it by 'abolishing the post of Secretary-General' and replacing it by a 'troika'; one Western, one Soviet, and one from the non-aligned bloc. Hammarskjöld rode off this attack, gaining support even from radical Third World states that were unhappy with his Congo policy. But it had the effect of making him more cautious, as did the advice of his new political representative in Leopoldville (an Indian, who replaced an American). Accordingly the UN soon found itself protecting Lumumba from arrest after a Congolese army coup by Colonel Mobutu, despite the strong possibility that this would enable him soon to bounce back into office. In late November, however, after heavy US lobbying, the General Assembly in effect endorsed Kasavubu's dismissal of Lumumba by voting to seat his UN delegation, rather than the other which was pro-Lumumba. Lumumba then made a break for Stanleyville, where his supporters had established a rival government. The army recaptured him. But in January 1961 a brief mutiny on the part of his jailers indicated that Lumumba might be hard to hold; so Kasavubu and Mobutu had him transferred to Katanga, where he was murdered (perhaps by prior arrangement). The USSR denounced Hammarskjöld as an accomplice, and demanded his dismissal as Secretary-General and the immediate winding up of the UN's Congo operation. This did not go down well in New York. But Lumumba's murder prompted both the Security Council and the General Assembly to demand 'all appropriate measures', 'including the use of force', to 'prevent the occurrence of civil war'.[21] UN intervention had steadily increased; now it was in effect proposing to act as a colonial power.

The prospect prompted much negotiation among Congolese politicians, and led in August 1961 to the formation of an ostensibly

21. Kalb, *The Congo Cables* esp. pp.58, 67, 73–5, 80–2, 110–3, 184–7; *Keesing's*, 17784, 17938, 18421–2; Rovine, *The First Fifty Years* p.321

united central government under Cyrille Adoula. From this Tshombe stood aloof, denouncing the constitutional agreements that had been extracted from him when he was imprisoned after trying to walk out of one of the conferences. He also continued to buttress his position by recruiting European mercenaries, remarking privately that 'In these matters I trust only whites' (not mutiny-prone Congolese troops). Hammarskjöld encouraged the new Adoula government to demand the departure from Katanga of all non-Congolese soldiers. Then in late August–early September, the UN moved to arrest them, together with key figures in Tshombe's government. The attempt sparked serious fighting, culminating in the Katangan capture of 200 Irish UN soldiers. It is not clear whether Hammarskjöld had approved the operation, or whether it was the work of subordinates reading between the lines of his official instructions (as they had done at least twice before with his subsequent approval). When things went wrong, neither Britain nor the USA were inclined to rush arms to ONUC to redress the balance; both (though more especially Britain) feared that UN action might inadvertently 'hand the Katanga on a plate to the Gizengists' [Lumumba's successors]. Hammarskjöld seems to have shared their view that he would have to resume negotiations with Tshombe, who had withdrawn across the border into Northern Rhodesia. On the way he was killed in a plane crash; but the release of the prisoners and the return to the *status quo ante* were soon negotiated.

The net effect, however, was a swing of opinion against Tshombe. Immediately after Hammarskjöld's death, Kennedy decided to supply the UN with the planes and air cover he had earlier withheld; and in November, feeling in the Security Council was such that the USA decided that it would, with 'great reluctance', have to accept a resolution authorising the Acting Secretary-General (U Thant) to use force to arrest and deport Tshombe's mercenaries. So in December the UN had another go. This time it did rather better, but it was urged to stop by Madagascar, Congo (Brazzaville), the Central African Federation, Belgium, France and Britain. Macmillan, in particular, believed that his government (which had rashly promised the UN bombs for use against Katangan airfields) might well be toppled by a backlash among Conservative Members of Parliament. Macmillan managed to persuade Kennedy to avert this by insisting on a peaceful settlement. A meeting between Tshombe and Adoula at Kitona was duly arranged, and Tshombe promised to accept central government authority and participate in drawing up a Constitution.[22]

This appeared the prelude to a general restoration of unity: Adoula managed (with some UN help) to put an end to the rival Stanleyville government in January 1962, and later to force the Kingdom of South Kasai back into the fold.[23] But Tshombe stalled on the Kitona agreement. The USA, Britain and Belgium discussed this impasse at length, with Britain reluctant to accept UN military action and the USA compromising by inducing the UN to suggest economic sanctions instead. Acting Secretary-General U Thant incorporated these Western proposals into a 'Plan for National Reconciliation' that was in August 1962 served on Tshombe as an ultimatum. Again Tshombe's acceptance in principle led nowhere, and both Katanga and the UN built up their armaments. Kennedy occasionally considered pulling out and leaving the locals to it: 'every nation has a right to its own War of the Roses'. But he came to fear that, if the UN did not act, Adoula might either fall or turn to the Soviets, who were offering to provide, within two months of a UN withdrawal, enough military aid to subdue Katanga. This, the CIA concluded, would not pose an immediate threat to US interests, but could in the long run convert the Congo into 'a base from which revolution and instability' would flow into surrounding areas, notably Angola. Macmillan, by contrast, was afraid Adoula would prove a Kerensky figure soon to be displaced by Gizenga and the Russians; Tshombe should be preserved as an obstacle to this and a barrier to the spread of disorder to the Central African Federation, but should be made to join a loose Congo federation. However at their Nassau meeting in December 1962, Macmillan (then especially beholden to Kennedy for the promise of Polaris missiles to salvage Britain's independent deterrent) let himself be persuaded that force would have to be used to overcome Tshombe's resistance.

In December the UN had threatened Tshombe with an economic blockade, to be enforced by cutting his railway lines. Tshombe became increasingly suspicious and there were incidents between Katangese and UN forces. The former eventually overdid things, and the local UN commander persuaded U Thant to let him take the offensive in reply. This time UN troops were completely

22. Kalb, *The Congo Cables* esp. pp.193, 292–8, chap. 12; Rovine, *The First Fifty Years* pp.322–4, 351–2; Horne, *Macmillan* ii pp.402–4; *Keesing's*, 19341–4. UN forces were later accused of committing atrocities during the fighting

23. *Keesing's*, 19349–50

successful; in January 1963 Tshombe called off Katanga's secession, and soon went abroad.[24] In February U Thant (who had long been anxious to disengage[25]) reported that the UN's Congo mandate had been 'largely fulfilled', and recommended the withdrawal of ONUC by the end of the year. In fact its last troops did not leave till June 1964. More than half the country was then in revolt; and the subsequent restoration of central authority was due chiefly to Tshombe – who, somewhat improbably, became premier in July – with the assistance of Katangese gendarmes, anti-communist Cuban pilots (supplied by the CIA), South African mercenaries, and US-assisted Belgian paratroop drops that (besides rescuing European hostages) took over Stanleyville and Paulis.

It is not easy to cast the balance sheet of the UN operation. UN assistance often proved invaluable in preserving urban services. It must have prevented a number of disorders, though it clearly did not avert wide-scale flight, pillage and slaughter. It did not secure Congo's unity, but it did prevent the secession of Katanga. Whether this was a good thing can only be a matter for conjecture. Most African states were appalled by the prospect of Katangese independence: they were to set their faces firmly against *any* secessions, and a secessionist state backed by the Belgian *Union Minière* would have been still worse. As Macmillan wrote, 'An independent Katanga, and its friends, would have to face the hostility, both on the ground and in the UN, of most of the rest of Africa. This would provide the Russians with just the kind of opportunity they are looking for to enable them to line up the Africans against the West'[26]. In American eyes, the chief value of ONUC lay in its prevention of a Great Power clash; Kennedy 'used to say that, if we didn't have the UN operation, the only way to block Soviet domination in the Congo would be to go in with our own forces'.[27] At an overt level the UN certainly succeeded in preventing this. At a covert level it did not; the Central African Federation, Belgium, China, Egypt, Cuba, the USSR and the USA all dabbled in the Congo,[28] with the USA proving by far the most successful. Although Western policy on Katanga was ultimately determined by the

24. Kalb, *The Congo Cables* esp. pp.359–70; Horne, *Macmillan* ii pp.405–6; Rovine, *The First Fifty Years* pp.354–9; Schlesinger, *A Thousand Days* p.503; *Keesing's*, 19346–8. Macmillan had also been concerned that the Central African Federation (for which Britain was legally responsible) might intervene to protect Tshombe from the UN. Katanga again declared its total autonomy in 1993; *Keesing's*, 39766

25. Macmillan, *Memoirs* vi p.280

26. To Welensky, May 1961: *Memoirs* v p.440

27. Schlesinger, *A Thousand Days* p.501

28. See *The Cold War* chap. 8

imperative of not upsetting the anti-colonial majority in the UN or impelling the Central Congolese government to invoke Soviet aid, UN operations were less independent of the USA (and UK) than they appeared.

SOVIET FEUDS WITH THE UN; RE-ESTABLISHMENT OF IMPORTANCE OF THE SECURITY COUNCIL

Whatever one's final judgement, it is clear that the Congo strained the UN almost to breaking point. We have seen that the USSR broke with Hammarskjöld over the toppling of Lumumba. Khrushchev accordingly attended the 1960 session of the General Assembly to propose the replacement of the office of the Secretary-General by a 'troika' – representatives of the West, the East, and the non-aligned, each with a veto. It is a tribute to Hammarskjöld's standing with the Third World that the idea drew very little support. But his feud with the USSR continued – after Lumumba's murder, the USSR stopped recognising him as Secretary-General, a stronger move than it had made against his predecessor Trygve Lie.[29] This problem was resolved by Hammarskjöld's death. The USSR resumed pressing variants of its 'troika' proposals, but soon dropped them and allowed U Thant to take over as Acting (and from late 1962 full) Secretary-General.

What it would not do was pay its contributions to ONUC. These contributions were, on the model of earlier arrangements for UNEF, apportioned among UN members by the General Assembly, a practice upheld by an advisory opinion of the World Court. By late 1964 the UN was effectively bankrupt as a result of payments withheld from ONUC and UNEF. The USSR was the chief debtor; the USA decided to make an issue of it by invoking the clause that deprived a state two years in arrears of its General Assembly vote. The USSR refused to pay, claiming that the operations were unlawful, a position supported (inter alia) by France.[30] Few countries were prepared to go to extremes. So a showdown was

29. In retaliation for what it saw as Lie's abandonment of impartiality over Korea, the USSR vetoed his reappointment for a second term. The General Assembly then purported to extend his tenure, but the USSR would not recognise him after his term expired in Feb. 1951. This so reduced Lie's effectiveness that in Nov. 1952 he told the Assembly he would have to retire: Rovine, *The First Fifty Years* pp.265–8

30. *Keesing's*, 18901–2, 20153–4, 20641

avoided through an arrangement whereby the General Assembly did not formally vote during its 1964–5 session, operating instead by consensus. In August 1965 the USA backed off; but it warned that if other members could opt out of 'the principle of collective financial responsibility with respect to certain [UN] activities' of the UN, so too could the USA.[31] The USSR achieved further satisfaction from the adoption of 'guidelines' (for future peace-keeping operations) that stressed the 'primary responsibility' of the Security Council.[32] It is not certain that this had in fact been breached in the case of ONUC. But the intention was clearly to prevent future Secretary-Generals from behaving in as free-wheeling a fashion as had Hammarskjöld – and to end the practice (begun in 1950) of seeking to go to the General Assembly over the head of the Security Council, where the Permanent Members had vetoes. This intention has (so far) been realised, and the importance of the Security Council correspondingly enhanced – a development that was in due course to prove welcome also to the USA, whose control over the General Assembly had already passed to the new Afro-Asian majority.

UN ACTIVITY IN THE 1960s

Hammarskjöld had clearly overdone things, and the UN had to adopt a rather lower profile; but the 1960s nevertheless saw a good deal of activity. In 1963 the UN helped work out an agreement for Saudi and Egyptian disengagement from the Yemen civil war, though its subsequent attempt to monitor this failed abysmally. ONUC was ended in 1964, but UNFICYP was launched. The Committee on Decolonisation functioned as a gadfly; from 1963 onwards U Thant openly critised US policy in South Vietnam, though without either convincing US presidents or securing a role in the conflict.[33] Also, though the 1963 Test Ban Treaty was negotiated outside the UN, this provided a forum for the discussions that led

31. In the mid-1980s it exercised this right, partly for domestic budgetary reasons, but chiefly to punish the UN for its anti-American attitudes, to press less extravagant administration on it, and to seek (in vain) a change in the basis of UN voting; by late 1987 the USA had thus held back $320 million, whereas the USSR was at length moving to clear its debt: *Keesing's*, 35036–7, 35868–9

32. *Keesing's*, 20903–4

33. Rovine, *The First Fifty Years* pp.376–7, 400–9

to the 1968 Non-Proliferation Treaty.[34] By 1966, indeed, U Thant was thought to have done an excellent job in leading the UN out of the various crises he had inherited, and in December he was unanimously re-elected for a second term.

THE PATCHY RECORD OF UN PEACE-KEEPING IN AND AFTER 1967

Things then began to fall apart. Though opinion differs as to who was to blame for the 1987 withdrawal that proved the prelude to the Six Day War (see pp.306–7), the episode was an enormous blow to UN prestige; nor was this helped by UNFICYP's complete failure to keep the peace in Cyprus in 1974. It would clearly be rash to entrust one's security primarily to a UN presence. Although this diminished the UN's peace-keeping role, it did not end it. In 1973 Sadat had initially sought superpower contingents to enforce the cease-fire and extricate his troops from Israeli encirclement. The USA would not accept a Soviet presence; a nasty crisis was averted when Sadat changed his request to one for a UN force. This force proved completely satisfactory, as has (so far) that created for the Golan Heights under the 1974 Syrian–Israeli disengagement agreement. But a degree of Israeli scepticism was evident in the insistence on some US involvement in the 1975 Sinai disengagement arrangements. Since the Soviet veto would probably stop the UN covering the demilitarisation clauses of the 1979 Egypt–Israel peace treaty, the USA promised to arrange an alternative multilateral force.[35]

This readiness to do the UN's work for it was to be seen also in the Lebanon (see pp.317–18). In 1976 it was Syria who intervened to restore order, with Arab League blessing. In 1978 the UN created UNIFIL (United Nations Interim Force In Lebanon) to calm the southern border (where Israel would not allow a Syrian presence) and to deter another Israeli intervention. It has proved almost wholly irrelevant. After the 1982 Israeli invasion, the USA and other major Western countries provided a force to cover (successfully) the agreed PLO evacuation and then to control the situation after the killings in the refugee camps. Unlike a UN presence, this force was

34. See *The Cold War* chap. 6

35. To reassure Israel the USA supplied nearly half its men when it was constituted in 1982, but ten other countries contributed: *Keesing's*, 29948, 31906–7

acceptable to Israel; it was intended to act as a guide and guardian to a convalescent Lebanese state; and it was prepared to deploy heavy fire-power to defend itself. However it was not prepared to take casualties, and withdrew ignominiously in early 1984. From 1987 Syria has again attempted (with rather more success) to compel peace as the locally dominant power. Elsewhere a similar pattern underlay India's action in 1987 to impose a settlement on both the Sri Lankan government and its rebellious Tamil minority.[36]

The UN's role in the provision of security thus tended to decline after 1967. It reached a low point with the outbreak in 1980 of the Iraq–Iran war. This did not involve the superpowers, both of whom initially kept their distance from the combatants and later inclined towards Iraq. So the usual excuse for UN inaction – that intervention was precluded by the Cold War – did not directly apply, though US–Soviet relations were admittedly at a low ebb in the early 1980s. The UN confined itself to calls for a cease-fire and attempts at mediation, both quite ineffective. Although it did not halt hostilities, it later played a role in monitoring the 1988 cease-fire and in arranging subsequent (fruitless) Iraq–Iran negotiations.

POST-COLD WAR REVIVAL OF THE SECURITY COUNCIL; GROWING UN ACTIVITY IN THE SECURITY FIELD

Some claim that, in the détente of the late 1980s, the Security Council was coming to function more as had originally been intended, 'with the permanent members cooperating on a consistent basis in considering the problems before . . . [it], something that they have not done since the UN's inception'. [37] A major test was provided by Iraq's 1990 invasion and annexation of Kuwait. The UN quickly banned Iraqi trade; but though its oil exports were effectively blocked, Iraq kept its grip on Kuwait. The USA and Britain considered mounting a direct military response, at Kuwait's invitation, and invoking Kuwait's legal right of self-defence. However it seemed more prudent again to work through the UN; in

36. The Indian peace-keeping force came to number 40,000 (over twice the maximum size of ONUC), and resorted to hard fighting to suppress the Tamil Tigers. But its success was problematic, and Sri Lanka procured its withdrawal in 1990

37. Brian Urquhart, 'The United Nations and the Future', *International Affairs* lxv (1989) esp. p.229

November 1990 the Security Council was induced to authorise the use of force to liberate Kuwait if Iraq did not withdraw. Iraq stayed put, and was ejected with heavy losses. The outcome might be seen as a success for 'collective security'; but, as in Korea, the operation was under US command, drew primarily on US forces, and could therefore be seen as the victory of a mainly Western coalition (though this time with at least Soviet consent).[38] Cynics, indeed, have claimed that the UN risks becoming a mere vehicle for the legitimisation of pro-consular US interventions (which was, admittedly, the role Roosevelt probably hoped at the outset that it would play).

Kuwait was probably an exceptional case. But at the end of Secretary-General Perez de Cuellar's (1982–91) term of office, UN prestige stood high. Apart from the continuing questions of Iraq and Cyprus, it was involved in arranging a plebiscite for the West Sahara (see p.61n), in seeking a Yugoslav cease-fire (which was to lead in 1992 to yet another peace-keeping force), and in negotiating the release of hostages in the Lebanon. It had just secured a breakthrough in peace negotiations for El Salvador. In 1992 it undertook to help arrange and monitor elections in Angola; and it was to perform a crucial role in guiding Cambodia through to elections in 1993. The expectation was that, with the end of the Cold War and (possibly) a declining US readiness to act as a world policeman, the UN would take a more central role in the provision of international security, though not to the point where alliances like NATO become obsolete.[39]

This was perhaps over-optimistic. For the UN has ignored many major disaster areas – like Liberia (where such peace-keeping as there was stemmed from the intervention in 1990 of neighbouring states), the southern Sudan, Ethiopia (for all purposes but relief), and the ex-Soviet Caucasus and Central Asia. It took just enough cognisance of Somalia to get itself heartily disliked; but the distribution of famine relief proved largely ineffective until the United States intervened militarily (albeit with UN blessing) in December 1992. Then, when the USA formally turned over control to the UN in 1993, conditions deteriorated sharply: what had begun as a humanitarian operation developed into a vendetta with a local

38. The affair also high-lighted another facet of the UN's operation: the fact that once the Security Council has passed a Resolution, it cannot be rescinded without the consent of the Permanent Members (and more particularly of the USA)

39. NATO indeed decided in 1991 to create a Rapid Reaction Force for possible 'out of area' use. National interventions also continued, France sending more troops to Chad and (with Belgium) briefly taking control of Kinshasa to evacuate foreigners when the Zaïrean army mutinied: *Keesing's*, 38126, 38343

war-lord in which both UN and supportive US troops found themselves taking casualties and killing innocent civilians; the effect could be to discredit peace-keeping and destroy US readiness to participate. Other operations, too, could go wrong. For UN behaviour in the West Sahara has been much criticised. Its contribution to the 1992 Angolan elections was brought to nought when UNITA refused to accept the results and resumed fighting. Although the UN proved more successful than any other mediators in achieving a cease-fire in Croatia in January 1992, horrific fighting then spread to Bosnia; the UN mitigated its effects by escorting aid convoys and other humanitarian activity, but its forces had to stand aside and look on while people were being massacred. A tougher line was admittedly forced on the UN in early 1994 (chiefly by the USA and France), and (in March 1994) there were signs that, together with Russian and US mediation, this might lead to a definite improvement in conditions on the ground.

THIRD WORLD ATTEMPTS TO REFORM THE INTERNATIONAL ECONOMIC SYSTEM THROUGH THE UN: UNCTAD AND NIEO

Whatever the current position, the UN seemed, for many years, less important as a provider of security than as a vehicle for the politicisation of the international economic system. The 1950s saw pressure for a Special United Nations Fund for Economic Development, to counter which the West in 1959 conceded an offshoot of the World Bank, the International Development Association, to offer soft development loans. But the 1960s brought more positive organisation: the 1961 Belgrade 'non-aligned' summit led to a conference in Cairo in 1962 specifically on economic matters. This was attended by thirty-one countries, including seven from Latin America (whose anti-communism and lack of recent experience of formal colonialism had previously distanced it from the Afro-Asian movement); President Tito then travelled and lobbied assiduously in Latin America. As a result a United Nations Conference on Trade and Development (UNCTAD) met in Geneva in 1964. By way of preparation, seventy-five UN members had, the previous year, secured the passage, as a General Assembly Resolution, of a 'Joint Declaration of the Developing Countries'. They soon became the 'Group of 77', were joined by most subsequently independent countries, and continued to function as a loose unit, serviced by the

UNCTAD Secretariat. Together they constitute a clear majority of all countries, and can accordingly carry Resolutions in the General Assembly (or any other body operating on a one state one vote basis).[40]

The prospect of the Geneva UNCTAD conference produced a minor relaxation in IMF lending; a high US official warned of 'an economic Munich for the West'.[41] But the conference's chief outcome was the creation of a secretariat – located (by secret ballot) in Geneva rather than in the Third World it was meant to help – and the articulation of an economic philosophy by its Secretary-General, the Argentine Raúl Prebisch. This directed attention in three directions: the need to enhance and stabilise the prices of primary commodities, which, Prebisch held, were otherwise bound to fall *vis-à-vis* those of 'Northern' manufactured exports; the need to secure *tariff* preferences for 'Southern' industrial goods in 'Northern' markets; and an increase in aid, sometimes justified as reparation for past 'Northern' behaviour. Tariff preferences were accepted as legitimate by the developed countries' General Agreement on Tariffs and Trade (GATT) meeting, and were gradually introduced; UNCTAD's guesstimate was that in 1980 they increased 'Southern' exports by $4 billion.[42] There was some further relaxation in IMF lending rules. Otherwise UNCTAD's immediate impact was slight. But things seemed to change with the collapse of the Bretton Woods monetary order (see pp.494–5) and the post-1970 transformation of the international trade in oil. Already by September 1973 the Algiers non-aligned summit (which overlapped greatly with the Group of 77) was recommending 'the establishment of effective solidarity organizations' akin to OPEC 'to recover natural resources and ensure increasingly substantial export earnings'. Soon after came the deployment of the Arab 'oil weapon' and the enormous increase in oil prices. Thus encouraged, Algeria requested a special session of the UN General Assembly. In May 1974 this adopted a Declaration on the Establishment of a New International Economic Order (NIEO) and a Programme of Action designed to implement it.[43] Both drew heavily on Prebisch's economic philosophy.

40. Carol Geldart and Peter Lyon, 'The Group of 77: A Perspective View', *International Affairs* lvii (1981)

41. Nossiter, *Global Struggle for More* p.39

42. ibid, p.53. But the importance of tariffs had been reduced by the GATT 'Kennedy' and 'Tokyo' rounds of cuts, whereas that of quantitative restrictions (often directed against the cheap products of developing countries) has increased

43. Nossiter, *Global Struggle for More* chap. 3; *Keesing's*, 26548–9

The issue was at the forefront of the international diplomatic agenda for the next two years, and negotiations linked to it continued *diminuendo* until the 1981 Cancun North–South summit. Since they produced such meagre results it is not worth following them in detail. But they represented an ambitious bid for the United Nations, acting as a world legislature, to take control of the world economy, and replace the existing relationships (based partly on the market and partly, the South contended, on past Northern power) with a 'just and equitable relationship between the prices of . . . goods exported by the developing countries, and . . . [those of goods] imported by them with the aim of bringing about a sustained improvement in their unsatisfactory terms of trade'. In particular a massive 'Common Fund' would enhance and stabilise commodity prices. Aid should be raised to the 1971 UN target (for official assistance by developed countries) of 0.7 per cent of their GNP, the transfer of technology ought to be enhanced, and multinational corporations controlled. The international monetary system should be reformed to accord the Third World greater voting rights; the IMF's paper currency, Special Drawing Rights (SDRs), should become the chief international reserve unit; and when more international liquidity was needed, new SDRs should be issued and steered towards development assistance. Internally each state should have complete sovereignty, including the right to expropriate foreign enterprises without compensation, for

> Current events have brought into sharp focus the realization that the interests of the developed . . . and . . . of the developing countries can no longer be isolated from each other; that there is a close inter-relationship between the prosperity of the developed countries and the growth and development of the developing countries; and that the prosperity of the international community as a whole depends on . . . [that] of its constituent parts.[44]

This could be seen as a bid for a rapid transition to a social democratic one-state[45] one-vote world system. It failed because the 'North' (or 'West') – and in particular the USA, UK, and West Germany – was not prepared to move. In its initial 1974 enthusiasm the General Assembly had claimed that

44. *Keesing's*, esp. 24419, 26548–9, 27391–5; Nossiter, *Global Struggle for More* chap. 3

45. One of NIEO's presentational weaknesses was that it demanded new rights for poor *states*, not for poor people within those states. Many poor states were manifestly not run in the interests of their poorer citizens; the affluent (in some cases, ostentatious) life-style of a number of Third World leaders and elites attracted accusations of hypocrisy

> the developing world has become a powerful factor that makes its influence felt in all fields of international activity. These irreversible changes in the relationship of forces in the world necessitate the active, full and equal participation of the developing countries in the formulation and application of all decisions that concern the international community.

But though OPEC enjoyed remarkable success in the 1970s, the Saudi oil minister had made it clear in 1974 that the oil countries would not allow others to control oil prices as part of a general bargain. Oil, then, would look after itself, and other commodities would have to do so too. Some could: phosphate-exporting countries managed, though more inconspicuously, to raise their prices considerably. Most could not: copper and bauxite tried to form imitative cartels, but these did not work. Although General Assembly resolutions were easy to pass, they bound nobody. *Parturient montes, nascetur ridiculus mus* [mountains will heave in labour, but bring forth only a silly little mouse]. In 1976, for instance, UNCTAD unveiled a scheme for a $6 billion 'Common Fund' to finance commodity agreements; agreement on a much watered-down version was reached in 1980; by 1987 it had still not secured the ratifications necessary to bring it into existence.[46]

THE LAW OF THE SEA

To this general failure there long appeared to be one exception, the Law of the Sea. The traditional position, chiefly shaped by Dutch and then British naval predominance, was that, beyond a three-mile territorial limit, exploitation of the sea and of its underlying seabed was free for all. But in 1945 (with a view to oil exploitation) Truman proclaimed US sovereignty over its continental shelf out to 200 miles offshore. Other states, mostly Latin American, followed suit to control offshore fisheries. Attempts to make good these claims precipitated numerous arrests of fishing boats and other clashes. Perhaps the most dramatic incidents were the Anglo-Icelandic 'cod wars' of 1958–61, 1973, and 1975–6, when Iceland expanded its territorial limits to 12, 50 and finally 200 miles and sought to arrest and harass British boats fishing within these limits. Britain countered by offering naval protection (and in

46. Dell, 'The Common Fund', *International Affairs* lxiii (1986–7); *Keesing's*, 35549

1972–4 securing favourable International Court of Justice judgements). In each case, however, Britain had to desist as a result of cost, reluctance to ruin otherwise good relations with Iceland, and the fear of precipitating Icelandic withdrawal from NATO (which would have had serious strategic consequences).[47] By 1973 69 countries had claimed territorial seas of from 12 to 200 miles, and a general expansion was clearly inevitable. An adoption even of 12 mile limits could potentially inhibit naval traffic through, and air passage over, 116 straits, some of great strategic importance. Already by the late 1960s the USA and USSR had discovered a joint interest in keeping such sea-lanes open. All this led in 1973 to the opening of the Third UN Conference on the Law of the Sea.[48]

Conferences in 1958 and 1960 had achieved little. This time things went well, partly because the line-up usually reflected not conventional international differences but the possession or otherwise of a substantial coast. Negotiations eventually reached agreement on 200-mile 'exclusive economic zones', but with free transit not only through them but also through territorial straits. The only problem related to the distant ocean, whose resources the General Assembly had in 1970 declared to be 'the common heritage of mankind'. It arose in connection with the mining of the rare metals present there in the form of manganese nodules. Though this will probably not be viable for many years, North–South divisions reasserted themselves. A mining regime was devised as a prototype for the NIEO: extraction was to be controlled by an International Seabed Authority (guided by a one-country one-vote Assembly and a regionally balanced Council), to which private mining consortia would have to sell their know-how. The Authority would itself work half the deep ocean, and draw a small royalty from oil taken in the 200–350 mile zone; its profits would be distributed chiefly to landlocked countries and the Third World (including liberation movements) generally. Initially the USA had seemed ready to accept this, but the Reagan administration was not, and in 1982 joined Israel, Turkey and Venezuela in voting against the final Convention. That, for the time being, killed it. The Convention was widely signed, but by 1988 only 35 of the necessary 60 states had ratified it. Its shelving had no immediate consequences.[49]

47. *Keesing's*, esp. 16445, 18109, 26028, 26237, 26715, 27824

48. Nossiter, *Global Struggle for More* chap. 4

49. ibid; *Keesing's*, 24518, 31928, 35924. It may be, as the USA was to claim, that all but the mining provisions of the Convention had become incorporated into 'customary' international law; but this is debatable and therefore precarious

Little therefore came of the 1970s attempts to redraw the international economic order at the conference table. It continued to rest chiefly on the developed capitalist economies – the source of most of the world's trade and, to a yet greater extent, of its convertible currencies. The ground rules for their interaction had been set in the mid-1940s; and it is to this process that we must now turn.

CHAPTER TWENTY

Money and Trade in the Western World

US ATTEMPTS TO PROMOTE ECONOMIC LIBERALISM; THE CASE OF AIR TRANSPORT

A common view of the interwar period was that the collapse of its initial liberal international order owed much to the post-1929 Slump, to its worsening by 'beggar-my-neighbour' economic and monetary policies, to the disastrous effects on the political structures of Germany and Japan, and to their determination to extricate themselves by developing or conquering closed economic living-space in eastern Europe and East Asia respectively. The United States had already begun to act on this view in the later 1930s; the Tripartite Monetary Agreement of 1936 promoted limited exchange rate support between the USA, the UK and France (with some help from Belgium, Holland and Switzerland), and reciprocal trade agreements negotiated by Cordell Hull secured some lowering of tariffs and extension of the non-discriminatory 'most favoured nation' principle. In 1938 the van Zeeland report (commissioned by the British and French governments) proposed going considerably further.

The time was not then ripe. But during the Second World War the USA set itself to creating new international ground-rules and institutions, whose guiding principle, in economic matters, was to be non-discrimination. US delegates advocated this in high-flown language as a prerequisite for peace: 'No greater tragedy could befall', the 1944 Chicago conference on civil aviation was told, '. . . than to repeat in the air the grim and bloody history which tormented the world some centuries ago when the denial of equal opportunity and free intercourse made the sea a battleground instead of a highway'.[1] Other Western countries shared many of these goals, but they suspected that US zeal for liberalism covered a determination to open them up to devastating competition from US firms (that had emerged strengthened from the war and that would dominate any market they entered). Free trade has often been seen as the weapon of the strong: the United States' partners wanted to move towards it only gradually, and with safeguards until they had recovered.

In the bargaining that ensued the USA had formidable assets: the rest of the world needed it much more than vice versa. In 1947 the USA provided one-third of all exports, but took only one-tenth of imports.[2] It was, with Canada, the only source of substantial net economic aid. These advantages, together with the real merit of some of its proposals and/or ruthless lobbying, often secured success. Little was agreed that the US administration was not prepared to accept and did not feel it could steer through Congress. Still the USA clearly did not always get its own way. Thus of the five 'freedoms' of air transport proposed at Chicago, Britain would accept only two (the right of overflight and of landing for refuelling). Traffic rights had to be determined by subsequent bilateral bargaining, for which the 1946 Anglo-American Bermuda agreement provided a model. So scheduled air transport in fact developed into a cartel, with capacity shared between the chosen flag airlines of the countries involved, and prices (at least until the 1977 incursion of Freddie Laker on to the North Atlantic route) set by the air-lines' organisation, the International Air Transport Association (IATA).[3]

BRETTON WOODS AND THE INTERNATIONAL MONETARY FUND

In the more important international monetary field, both Britain and the USA began planning in 1941, each initially seeking to pre-empt the other. By 1943 US, British, Canadian and French plans had been published and lobbied for. The British proposals

1. Anthony Sampson, *Empires of the Sky: The Politics, Contests and Cartels of World Airlines* (1984) pp.66–7
2. W.M. Scammell, *The International Economy since 1945* (Basingstoke, 1983 edn) pp.21–2
3. Sampson, *Empires of the Sky* pp.67–9, 71–5, 92–3, and chap. 11

were the most ambitious, envisaging an 'International Clearing Union' that would create and manage the 'quantum of international currency' needed to sustain world trade and economies. International payments would be conducted through the credit and debit balances (denominated in this currency) that members maintained with the Union. Americans argued that most of the credit so created would be applied to the purchase of US goods, in return for which the USA would obtain only useless credits with the Clearing Union.[4] Instead the USA favoured a much more restricted 'Stabilisation Fund' consisting of resources contributed by members; the Fund would provide members with hard currency, but (beyond a certain point) only if they accepted the measures it recommended to cure their balance of payments deficits.

Subsequent bargaining was accompanied by a good deal of needle between the chief British and US economists, Lord Keynes and Harry Dexter White. But Keynes saw White's proposals as being, if not ideal, at least far better than an absence of US commitment. Concessions were made on both sides. The size of the Fund was to be well above the $5 billion envisaged by the US Treasury, though nowhere near Britain's original target of $30 billion; Britain resisted the US wish to internationalise the blocked sterling balances that had accumulated during the war, and that Britain wished to handle as an internal imperial problem.[5] On most points the USA got its way. Voting within the Fund was to be linked to each member's quota contribution in such a way as to give the USA a veto (though the British Commonwealth collectively secured nearly as large a quota). The Fund was to be located in Washington, where official US influence could be most readily deployed. The dollar – as the only major currency readily convertible into gold – was, effectively, to rank with gold for Fund purposes. Although some discrimination against 'scarce' currencies would be acceptable, most of the pressure for adjustment would fall on countries in deficit that would come to the Fund as suppliants seeking to borrow.

4. To some economists this has appeared a virtue, as it would have provided an incentive for *creditor* countries to import more and so adjust their balance of payments; at the time it simply seemed a device for enabling the rest of the world to help itself at the expense of Uncle Sam

5. Much of the Anglo-American difference stemmed from divergent attitudes to the continuation of a distinct British Empire/Commonwealth. Americans also felt that, in their existing form, the balances would seriously handicap the weak UK economy, while Keynes believed that it would be easier to repay debts to countries to which Britain had a tradition of exporting than debts denominated in dollars

Some of these details were not tied up until the inaugural meeting of what was now known as the International Monetary Fund (IMF) in 1946. Most had been agreed at the Bretton Woods Conference in 1944, at which quotas totalling $8.3 billion were apportioned between the participating countries. One important point was not really settled – the ease with which a state could devalue its currency. Minor adjustments apart, the USA wanted to forbid such devaluations without general IMF agreement, whereas the UK insisted on retaining the right to devalue unilaterally as a last resort. The Bretton Woods draft was ambiguous, and only future practice could decide.[6]

The Bretton Woods agreement was ratified, not without political difficulty in both the USA and UK, in 1945; the IMF was formally established that December with thirty-five member states. They did not include the USSR, though this had attended Bretton Woods and secured a quota only slightly below the British. Soviet participation was not inconsistent with certain interpretations of Bretton Woods; but its centrally planned economy could never have fitted into the liberal capitalist order that the Americans envisaged, and it was probably a minor convenience that the USSR did not join. The communist world accordingly developed in its own way. By the 1970s it was clearly being disadvantaged by the inconvertibility of its currencies; by the late 1980s the demonstration effect of the economic contrast with the West had become of great political importance.

THE 1945 US–CANADIAN LOAN TO BRITAIN; THE 1947 BRITISH CONVERTIBILITY CRISIS

It was initially envisaged that the Bretton Woods system would take five years to run itself in, but the USA decided to rush things, using the leverage afforded by British economic difficulties. Britain had expected the war against Japan to continue for eighteen months after victory in Europe, and had hoped to use the time to readjust its economy while still in receipt of Lend-Lease. Japan's surrender and the abrupt termination of Lend-Lease left the enormous UK trade deficit uncovered. Britain promptly sought US aid, and at first hoped for a gift of $5 billion. What it got, after long and fraught

6. Scammell, *International Economy* pp.15–18; A. Van Dormael, *Bretton Woods: Birth of a Monetary System* (1978)

negotiations, was a US loan of $3.75 billion (made up by Canada to $5 billion) with strings attached – including the ratification of Bretton Woods, participation in a conference that would seek multilateral trade, a vague promise to liquidate the sterling balances held in London, and the introduction of sterling convertibility (for current transactions) a year after the loan came into effect. Although most people in London regarded the loan as necessary, its terms aroused much resentment. Seventy-one Labour and twenty-three Conservative MPs voted against the loan; but they objected more to the provisos about multilateral trade (as incompatible with a planned economy) and to the possible threat to imperial preference and the sterling area than to the requirement to go convertible, on which attention has since concentrated.[7]

Congress approved the loan in July 1946. Sterling had therefore to become convertible in July 1947; since sterling then probably accounted for more than half of all international payments,[8] this would, if successful, have gone far towards realising Bretton Woods. By mid-1947 a wide range of countries had joined with the formal 'sterling area' in accepting payments, and undertaking to hold reserves, in sterling; in return they had gained the right to convert sterling into other currencies to cover current transactions. So it seemed that substantial convertibility had already been achieved between most of the British Commonwealth and Empire, countries closely associated therewith, much of Western Europe, and North America. The advent of formal convertibility in itself did little to extend this; no immediate problems were expected. Closer examination, however, should have revealed dangers. North America accounted for 43 per cent of British imports, but only 14 per cent of exports; sales to soft currency countries could do little to fill this gap; in any case Britain's trade performance fell back in 1947. In late 1946 British dollar holdings fell by $75 million a month, in the first half of 1947 by $315 million. The news that $400 million had had to be drawn from the US loan in the first three weeks of July set off a panic, with mounting sales of government stock and transfers (by foreign holders) into dollars. The first three weeks of convertibility cost $416 million, and the Cabinet decided that it would have to be suspended. The USA had reluctantly to accept suspension on 'an emergency and temporary basis', but froze the remaining $400 million of its loan. By December 1947 it had

7. Scammell, *International Economy* pp.25–8; Morgan, *Labour in Power* pp.145–50; (Sir) Alec Cairncross, *Years of Recovery: British Economic Policy 1945–51* (1985) chap. 5

8. Cairncross, *Years of Recovery* p.503

recognised that there could be no return to convertibility, and unfroze the $400 million.[9]

MARSHALL AID 1948–52

The episode had been mismanaged, but most European countries were in no condition to support convertibility. For the time being attention switched from the goals of Bretton Woods to attempts to keep West European economies afloat. US observers probably underestimated the degree of European economic recovery; but its pace could not have been sustained without some measures to bridge the 'dollar gap' and so secure the continued supply of goods that (in the circumstances of the time) could be obtained only from North America. As we have seen, Keynes had wanted an International Clearing Union to create and advance currency to this end. The USA would not underwrite it; nor would Congress allow more than limited loans. In 1947, however, fearing that without further assistance Western Europe would pass through economic collapse to communism, the US State Department advocated Marshall Aid, whereby $13 billion was to be appropriated for 1948–52, almost all as grants not loans; it is said to have financed nearly two-thirds of Europe's 1947–50 merchandise imports from the dollar area.

EUROPEAN PAYMENTS UNION 1950

American generosity was not unlimited: to restrict calls on its taxpayer, the USA insisted that the recipients so organise themselves that they came to the USA only for what they could not provide themselves. This necessarily entailed their according intra-European trade some priority over imports from the USA; it led to two Intra-European Payments Agreements. These were followed in 1950 by a European Payments Union (EPU), largely of US design but (save that the USA was not a member) strongly reminiscent of Keynes's Clearing Union. Trade deficits with one member state

9. ibid, chap. 6; Morgan, *Labour in Power* pp.341–7; Scammell, *International Economy* pp.29–30; Brian Tew, *International Monetary Cooperation 1945–56* (1956) p.133

were set off against surpluses with another, and countries then settled their net balances with the EPU, partly by drawing on their quota of EPU credits, partly in gold or dollars. This created a very wide area (Western Europe, its colonies, and the sterling area) within which questions of currency constituted no bar to multilateral trade – but one that was therefore separated from the 'hard currency' world of the dollar.[10]

THE REJECTION OF 'FLOATING' EXCHANGE RATES; WESTERN EUROPE MOVES TO CONVERTIBILITY (1958–61)

The abandonment of convertibility in 1947 had not cured sterling's problems. In 1949 these led to a 30 per cent devaluation against the dollar. Although 1950 was much better – with rearmament and the inflation accompanying the Korean War – matters again worsened, to the point where in 1952 the British government considered abandoning both the EPU and the principles of Bretton Woods in favour of a convertible but 'floating' pound (whose value would be set by trading on the exchanges). However, it eventually decided not to; for the next two decades the West put its faith in fixed exchange rates, with only Canada dissenting and often allowing its currency to float. The crisis of early 1952 rapidly subsided; thereafter the British and European economic environment became fairly benign. Although the USA continued to run a substantial visible trade surplus, this was counterbalanced by defence and economic aid, military expenditure abroad, and direct foreign investment. So dollars became less scarce, and it was possible to relax the discrimination against them. Also countries whose EPU or sterling area trade was in surplus pressed for either settlement in hard currency or full convertibility. There was a tendency to accommodate them, partly to keep them from leaving, partly because convertibility was regarded as desirable in principle, and partly because the UK saw it as essential to London's re-establishment as a world financial centre. So 1954–5 saw significant moves towards sterling convertibility, and the hardening of EPU payments until 75 per cent were effected in gold or dollars. Further moves

10. Cairncross, *Years of Recovery* pp.287–94; Brian Tew, *The Evolution of the International Monetary System 1945–77* (1977) pp.43–5

may have been delayed by the economic turbulence associated with Suez. But in 1958, to put an end to the embarrassing weakness of the French franc, De Gaulle decided to devalue sharply and then go for convertibility. This prompted the winding up of the EPU and a move by most West European currencies towards convertibility for non-residents, extended in 1961 to cover all commercial current account transactions.[11]

THE INTERNATIONAL MONETARY SYSTEM IN THE 1960s

The United States had thus secured most of the goals it had enunciated at Bretton Woods, but it remained to be seen whether the new international monetary system could be defended. Even in the control-laden environment of 1947 and 1949 normal commercial 'leads and lags'[12] could exert severe pressures on exchange rates. As time passed these were compounded by the growth of the volume of money that could flood across the exchanges in search either of safety or of the best rate of return. The advent of convertibility necessarily increased this volume, even though many countries still retained controls on capital transactions. In addition a net outflow of funds from the USA (see pp.485, 492) was steadily building up a pool of 'euro-dollars' not subject to national exchange controls. (British banks started using such dollars offshore in 1957, when the financing of foreign trade in sterling was cut back for balance of payments reasons. A further stimulus came from the USSR's decision to hold its dollars on deposit in London, for fear that they might be seized if they were placed in New York. The market was also advantaged by not being subject to US reserve requirements and interest controls.) From virtually nothing in 1957, 'euro-dollars' grew to some $9 billion in 1964, $57 billion in 1970 (as against total government holdings, in gold, dollars and 'Special Drawing Rights' combined, of $79 billion), and over $80 billion in 1972.[13]

11. Tew, *Evolution of the International Monetary System* pp.41–5, 107, 114–15; Scammell, *International Economy* p.20

12. Whereby if a currency seems likely to devalue, importers hasten to make payments at the existing parity, while exporters postpone receipts in hopes of a better rate

13. A. Shonfield (ed.) *International Economic Relations of the Western World 1959–1971* ii, Susan Strange, *International Monetary Relations* (1976) chap. 6

The international monetary system of the 1960s had three potential weak points – sterling, the price of gold, and the value of the dollar itself. All were addressed in 1961. A small revaluation of the deutschmark was followed by agreement that there should be no further changes, and arrangements were made for the mutual support of currencies under pressure. These were consolidated at the end of the year by the 'General Agreement to Borrow', whereby the ten leading Western countries undertook to lend the IMF up to $6 billion for this purpose.[14] At the same time most of these countries also joined in a 'Gold Pool' to help the US Treasury and the Bank of England stabilise the price of gold.

STERLING CRISES AND DEVALUATION 1964–7

Sterling was still the world's second currency, widely held both for purposes of trade and as part of other countries' foreign exchange reserves. Unfortunately the UK *appeared* to be in perennial balance of payments deficit,[15] the result partly of a high propensity to invest overseas, partly of substantial military expenditure abroad to underpin the international status quo.[16] Moreover Britain had recently come to realise that its economic growth in the 1950s had been well below the European average. This was widely blamed on a 'stop-go' policy that had choked off expansion whenever sterling came under pressure (most recently in 1961). So subsequent governments, both Conservative and Labour, decided to err on the side of expansion, even if this risked sucking in imports.

Although sterling was, therefore, often weak, most countries did not wish to see it battered by the markets. One reason was the fear, articulated by President Johnson in 1965, that this could lead to

14. The ten were (in order of size of commitment): the USA; the UK and West Germany; France and Italy; Japan; Canada and the Netherlands; Belgium; Sweden. This 'Group of Ten' came, somewhat to the irritation of medium powers like Brazil, to play a leading role within the IMF. Switzerland (which stayed outside the Fund to avoid compromising its neutrality) was an external associate

15. In late 1967 the OECD said that Britain had had current account deficits in six of the last eight years. In fact there were surpluses in five of the eight years, and a negligible overall deficit: Alec Cairncross and Barry Eichengreen, *Sterling in Decline: The Devaluations of 1931, 1949 and 1967* (Oxford, 1983) p.157. But markets are influenced by appearances, not retrospective calculations

16. Whereas in 1966 the USA believed that West Germany *gained* $1 billion per year from the USA and British forces stationed there: Johnson, *Vantage Point* pp.306–7

'British military disengagement East of Suez [as indeed it did in 1967] or on the Rhine'. Moreover if 'speculators' were allowed to knock down sterling, they would then turn on the next target. As the US Treasury Secretary remarked after sterling's eventual devaluation, the dollar was now 'in the front line'. Pressure might come either directly, or via the price of gold; when these fears were borne out in 1968, Johnson appealed for international help in avoiding financial disorders that could 'profoundly damage the political relations between Europe and America and set in motion forces like those which disintegrated the Western world in 1929 and 1933'.[17] It could not, of course, be proved that the collapse of the Bretton Woods system would have the same economic impact as the 1929–33 Slump, still less that it would lead to comparable political catastrophes. But many politicians and central bankers thought it possible, and did not want to run the risk.

There had been pressures on sterling (as on gold and the dollar) in 1961, but thereafter things went smoothly until 1964. The crisis broke in October, when the incoming Labour government was greeted with an alarmist prediction of an £800 million balance of payments deficit. It ruled out devaluation, not only for the general reasons given above, but also because Prime Minister Wilson feared that a repetition of 1949 would destroy Labour's financial credibility. Instead a temporary 15 per cent surcharge was placed on imports – which caused considerable upset since it breached Britain's European Free Trade Area (EFTA) obligations – and the Bank of England managed to secure $3 billion in foreign credits to bolster the pound. A further crisis in 1965 generated another support package from the USA, Canada, and eight European countries, though significantly not France. (In return the USA extracted a tacit undertaking that British troops would stay in the Far East and on the Rhine.) Worse followed in July 1966. Wilson still refused to devalue, and instead took measures to secure a £250 million balance of payments improvement. These entailed the abandonment of the new much-vaunted 'National Plan', and seemed politically wrenching. For a year they did curtail private consumption, but public investment continued to rise, and government expenditure abroad was not, in practice, reduced. Most other countries continued supportive, and President Johnson endorsed a British suggestion that 'the dollar and sterling should link arms'. But France, which was not enamoured of this axis, began to

17. ibid, pp.316, 319, 598; Strange, *International Monetary Relations* p.287

unsettle the market with hints that things could not continue; nor could they. In 1967 the combination of loose British fiscal policy, a damaging dock strike, and the closure of the Suez Canal by the Six Day War had adverse effects on oil prices and the British balance of payments. A run on the pound developed, and the reserves lost over £500 million in the third quarter of 1967. By October France was using sterling's weakness as a reason for vetoing Britain's application to join the EEC and urging the UK to imitate its own 1958 devaluations. Wilson might have been ready to soldier on if an attractive enough support package could have been arranged; the USA did indeed produce one contingent on further British defence efforts in Asia. But by now the existing parity was generally seen as unsustainable: in November 1967 Britain devalued by 14.3 per cent, the most France would allow without itself following suit and perhaps setting off the much-feared cycle of 1930s-style competitive devaluation.[18]

THE GOLD WAR OF THE 1960s

Although this did not end the pressure on sterling,[19] it did encourage speculators to move on to a new target, gold. In 1933–4 Roosevelt had sought to reflate the US economy by bidding up the price of gold and so depreciating the dollar. Gold thus went to $35 an ounce. Roosevelt meant this price to hold for a generation, and successfully defended it by standing ready to buy or sell, at that level, as much gold as the world offered or wanted. This became incorporated into the Bretton Woods system, since in practice the value of other currencies was defined in terms of the dollar, that of the dollar in terms of gold. At first the USA was well able to defend these arrangements, as it owned 70 per cent of the world's monetary gold in 1947, and 59 per cent in 1957.[20] However in

18. Cairncross and Eichengreen, *Sterling in Decline* chap. 5; Wilson, *The Labour Government* pp.250, 264–5; Strange, *International Monetary Relations* p.140; Alan Dobson, 'The Special Relationship and European Integration', *Diplomacy and Statecraft* ii (1991) pp.92–3

19. Borrowings to support it in 1968 amounted to nearly half the 1964–7 total. Moves were also made to guarantee and stabilise foreign countries' sterling holdings; these may have been meant also to lead on to the winding up of the sterling area, but they did not in fact do so: Cairncross and Eichengreen, *Sterling in Decline* pp.193, 211; Strange, *International Monetary Relations* pp.150 ff

20. But only 31 per cent in 1967: Strange, *International Monetary Relations* pp.42, 296

1960–1 a mixture of political alarms and US balance of payments deficits led to a rise in demand for gold and upwards pressure on the price; the USA accordingly reaffirmed its commitment to the $35 an ounce level, and in 1961 enlisted European help through the Gold Pool. In 1965, however, de Gaulle broke ranks, extending his critique of US 'hegemony' into the monetary field:

> The conditions that gave rise to the 'Gold Exchange Standard' have in effect been modified. The currencies of the West European countries have today been so far restored that the total gold reserves of the Six now equal those of the Americans, and would even surpass them if the Six were to decide to convert all their dollar holdings into gold. This means that the convention which attributes a transcending value to the dollar as an international currency no longer rests on its original basis, . . . America's possession of the greater part of the world's gold. Moreover, the fact that many countries on principle accept dollars on the same basis as gold . . . leads the United States to run [at no cost] into debt. . . . In effect, what they owe they pay . . . with dollars which it rests only with them to issue, instead of paying wholly in gold, the value of which is real. . . .
>
> [One result is a growing US tendency] to invest abroad. Hence there is for certain countries a kind of expropriation of various of their businesses.
>
> . . . We therefore consider it necessary that international exchanges should rest, as was the case before the world's great misfortunes [the First World War and its sequels], on an indisputable monetary basis bearing the mark of no particular country.
>
> What basis? Truthfully, . . . no other criterion or standard than gold can be seen. Gold, . . . which has no nationality, which is eternally and universally accepted as the unalterable fiduciary value *par excellence.*

De Gaulle's remarks attracted some German sympathy, albeit tempered by a preference for less risky incremental improvements to the existing system. The US Treasury was categorically opposed:

> President de Gaulle has recommended that the gold exchange standard based on the use of dollars freely convertible into gold at $35 an ounce, which has served the world well for 30 years, be abandoned. He has proposed instead we retreat to the full gold standard which collapsed in 1931 and which proved incapable of financing the huge increase of world trade that has marked the 20th century.[21]

France then announced its abandonment of the 'gold exchange standard' and its intention to convert its dollar reserves into gold (a process that had in fact started in 1962). Other countries also

21. *Keesing's*, 20667–9

moved into gold, but French transactions were on a significantly larger scale,[22] and came to be known as the 'Gold War' – yet another proof (to Anglo-Saxons) of the essentially disruptive nature of Gaullism. Furthermore France disengaged from the Gold Pool (and from support for sterling). Both its words and its actions encouraged private investors to pile into gold in hopes of a revaluation – something the USA was determined to avoid, not only because of its implications for the dollar, but also because the chief beneficiaries would be the USSR and South Africa (as the chief producers) and France (as the chief hoarder).

In 1965 the pressure was eased by Soviet gold sales (to finance grain imports), but they stopped in 1966; management of the Gold Pool then proved difficult even before sterling's 1967 devaluation. Thereafter much speculation switched to gold, the Pool losing $1.5 billion over the next month. American ability to hold the line was hampered by the high US deficit; unfavourable balance of payments figures in February 1968 set off another run on gold. The Pool lost $1.3 billion in the first fortnight of March 1968.[23] President Johnson pressed Britain to close the gold market and summoned an urgent meeting of the Gold Pool. This accepted US proposals for a two-tier system, with central banks still dealing between themselves in monetary gold at $35 an ounce, but not supplying the market (where prices would now be left free). The hope was that all new production would be funnelled into the market, causing prices to fall and burning the speculators' fingers. (South Africa had other ideas, and compromise as to the direction of its gold sales was not reached till late 1969.)

FRENCH DEVALUATION AND GERMAN REVALUATION 1969

In May 1968 de Gaulle's regime was shaken by riots and strikes; although it soon recovered, France's strong currency position did not. That summer the USA had the satisfaction of arranging a stand-by credit; de Gaulle's subsequent refusal to devalue prolonged

22. Official French gold holdings grew by $2.5 billion in 1962–7, German by $0.5 billion, other continental West European by $1.1 billion: Strange, *International Monetary Relations* p.296

23. Strange, *International Monetary Relations* pp.282–3, 289; Johnson, *Vantage Point* p.318

French weakness. The other side of this coin was a rush of funds into the mark, which Germany refused to revalue. France eventually devalued in August 1969 (Pompidou having replaced de Gaulle as President); pressure mounted, yet again, on the mark. This struggled on until the West German elections in September 1969, but the inflow of funds in election week was such that the German markets had to be closed. When they reopened after polling, a further $250 million came in in the first two hours; the mark had to be allowed to float until a new government was in place to decide on revaluation.[24] These currency realignments were perhaps most important for their impact on the working of the EEC.[25] But they did not augur well for the dollar, should it again weaken and come under market pressure.

THE WEAKENING DOLLAR; NIXON GOES OFF GOLD (1971); THE SMITHSONIAN AGREEMENT

The United States still enjoyed a comfortable surplus on ordinary trade in goods and services (averaging, on one calculation, $9 billion per year during 1960–7), but this was not enough to cover the combination of government spending abroad ($6.6 billion), private investment ($3.3 billion), pensions, remittances, and the like. The imbalance of about $2.5 billion was mildly disquieting,[26] and did prompt some remedial measures. Eisenhower had always doubted US ability to keep troops abroad for an indefinite period; one of his last acts was an attempt to reduce their foreign currency costs by $1 billion per year. Kennedy launched a 'See America First' campaign to narrow the 'tourist gap', and in 1968 Johnson urged people not to holiday outside the Americas. In 1963 and 1965 there were measures to discourage foreign lending, and 1968 brought a moratorium on capital transfers to continental Western Europe and South Africa (with lesser restrictions on those to Canada, Britain, Australia and Japan). But this did not amount to much. Johnson's chief interest was his 'Great Society' programmes, which entailed steadily rising federal welfare expenditures. He also sent troops to Indo-China and stepped up support of the South Vietnamese government. This brought unwelcome, though not overwhelming,

24. Strange, *International Monetary Relations* pp.324–30
25. See *The Cold War* chap. 13
26. Strange, *International Monetary Relations* p.83

foreign exchange costs.[27] At its peak, the war accounted for about 3 per cent of GNP, the Great Society programmes for rather more. Together the two overheated the US domestic economy, causing inflation and increased imports. Johnson was slow to react; when he did seek a tax surcharge in 1967, it took nearly a year to pass through Congress. Unsurprisingly the trade balance worsened. For the time being this was masked, since US banks reacted to restrictive monetary measures by borrowing euro-dollars. So in 1968 and 1969 the USA appeared to be in overall surplus. But when the economy cooled, a looser monetary policy first made such borrowings unnecessary, then in mid-1970 encouraged repayments. The currency outflow set off speculation against the dollar, both direct and through 'leads and lags'. The result was a deficit of about $11 billion in 1970, $30 billion in 1971.[28]

In theory Nixon might have resisted these pressures by increasing taxes and interest rates to cut domestic economic activity (and so imports) and to lure back hot money. Other countries (like the UK) had done this in similar circumstances, but the USA had never allowed external pressures to dictate its economic policy, a tradition that went back to Roosevelt in 1933. Johnson's Economic Council had rejected 'a more restrictive growth and economic policy. . . . No country could be expected to pay such a price simply to improve its balance of payments'. Nixon thought likewise: in 1970 he 'exploded', 'I hear all about the balance of payments and nobody worries about 8 percent unemployment'.[29] He had been disquieted by the poor Republican performance in the mid-term elections, which he ascribed to unemployment; to secure his own election in 1972 he needed to be seen to be tackling the USA's domestic problems. If he did not act, he feared that a protectionist Congress might. Matters were precipitated by the drain on US gold reserves, which sank below the psychologically crucial level of $10 billion when Britain and France converted dollars into gold to pay off their IMF debts. The USA was in danger of exhausting its automatic borrowing rights with the IMF, and so exposing itself to IMF surveillance. In August 1971 Britain asked that some of its

27. Overseas military expenditure and foreign aid were between $1.7 billion and $2 billion higher in 1968 than in 1964: ibid, p.83; Joanne Gowa, *Closing the Gold Window: Domestic Politics and the End of Bretton Woods* (1983) p.49

28. *Keesing's*, 19969, 22589–91; Tew, *International Monetary System 1945–77* pp.114, 162–5; Scammell, *International Economy* p.181

29. Andrew Shonfield (ed.) *International Economic Relations of the Western World 1959–1971*, i *Politics and Trade* (1976) p.57; Gowa, *Closing the Gold Window* p.135

dollar holdings be guaranteed against devaluation. A hasty crisis meeting produced a package of measures: the domestic economy was stimulated (subject to an anti-inflationary prices and incomes policy); a 10 per cent surcharge was slapped on most imports; and convertibility of dollars into gold was 'temporarily' suspended. The United States, Nixon proclaimed in an accompanying broadcast, would now look after itself:

> At the end of World War II the economies of the major industrial nations of Europe and Asia were shattered. To help them get onto their feet and to protect their freedom the United States has provided $143,000,000,000 in foreign aid. That was the right thing for us to do.
>
> Today, largely with our help, they have recovered. . . . Now . . . the time has come for them to bear their fair share of the burden of defending freedom around the world. The time has come for exchange rates to be set straight and for the major nations to compete as equals. There is no longer any need for the United States to compete with one hand tied behind her back.[30]

The aim was to secure a massive $13 billion turn-around in the US balance of payments, partly by extracting trade concessions from Japan and the EEC, partly by forcing other countries to revalue against the dollar. Their immediate reaction was to float (as the mark had already been forced to do in May); Japan tried to hold out, but after it had taken in $4 billion in a fortnight defending its existing dollar parity, it had to follow suit. Subsequent negotiations were not easy, partly because the combative style of US Treasury Secretary Connally put people's backs up, partly because their national interests in any case diverged. However in December 1971 (after much preliminary European discussion) a deal was worked out at a Franco-US summit and then unveiled, at a Group of Ten meeting, as the 'Smithsonian Agreement'. This re-established fixed exchange rates, with other currencies increasing their dollar values by between 7.5 per cent and 16.9 per cent.[31] There was a token increase in the price of gold, but no return of the dollar's convertibility into gold. Some people see this as crucial, in that it deprived the system of any external reference point or measure of value. In fact the European Exchange Rate Mechanism (ERM) operated quite successfully without one in the 1980s, so there is no a priori reason why the world should not have continued on the basis of fixed parities plus periodical changes of exchange rate.

30. Gowa, *Closing the Gold Window* p.149, chap. 6; *Keesing's*, 24997 ff

31. Strange, *International Monetary Relations* pp.339–44; Kissinger, *Memoirs* i pp.956–62

THE COLLAPSE OF FIXED EXCHANGE RATES – THE EUROPEAN 'SNAKE'

In practice flows of money in the 1970s proved too great; countries progressively let their currencies float (that is find their own value in the markets) as an easier alternative to allowing these flows to shape their domestic economic policies. Initially EEC members, plus Britain and the three other countries about to join, decided to keep the values of their currencies within a narrow band or 'snake'. But in March 1972 the British Chancellor of the Exchequer, Barber, was already saying 'the lesson of . . . the last few years is that it is neither necessary nor desirable to distort domestic economies . . . to maintain unrealistic exchange rates'; when sterling came under serious pressure in June he allowed it 'temporarily' to float.[32] By January 1973 the exchanges were again in turmoil, and the Swiss franc floated upwards. In February, after massive currency flows and hectic meetings, the lira and yen floated and the dollar was devalued by 10 per cent. All major exchanges closed during 2–18 March 1973, and reopened only in the wake of an EEC decision that the 'snake' (from which Britain and Italy had now withdrawn) should float freely against the dollar. By January 1974 the French franc was in trouble and left the snake; it rejoined in mid-1975, but left again in March 1976.[33]

SPECIAL DRAWING RIGHTS; THE ATTEMPT TO 'DEMONETISE' GOLD; OPERATION OF FLOATING EXCHANGE RATES

Floating had come about de facto, but it took time to adjust IMF rules to reflect this. Reforming the international monetary system had been something of an intellectual pastime since the 1960s. Europe, even while complaining of the inflationary flood of unwanted dollars, fretted as to whether there would be enough liquidity to finance the continued growth of international trade. De Gaulle's solution had been to double the price of gold. For the Anglo-Saxons, a more welcome alternative was an international fiduciary currency, 'paper gold', in the form of Special Drawing

32. He also imposed restrictions on overseas payments that effectively put an end to the sterling area; most currencies hitherto pegged to sterling cut the link

33. *Keesing's*, 25267, 25425–7, 25769–70, 25878–84, 26446, 27861

Rights (SDRs) on the IMF. In 1967–8 the Group of Ten was brought, despite French opposition, to devise a scheme for SDRs and seek the necessary amendments to the IMF's articles. These were achieved in 1969, but on the basis that not only the USA but also the EEC (if it voted together) could block the issue of SDRs; and the number initially issued represented a compromise.[34] After Nixon had suspended the dollar's convertibility into gold, Barber advocated a realignment of the international monetary system around the SDR; this led on to the creation of an IMF committee to devise a new system. By 1974 this had produced a 'Grand Design', but it had already been overtaken by events (notably the currency backwash of the oil price rise), and served chiefly to focus attention on three points – the definition of the SDR, the price of gold, and the question of floating exchange rates.

The Americans were now pressing for the 'demonetisation' of gold and its reduction to the status of just another commodity. Most Europeans thought otherwise, and the result was predictably a compromise. From 1974 the SDR's value was no longer defined in terms of gold but of an average of sixteen (later five) major currencies. In 1974–5 it was agreed that central banks should not be restricted to an 'official' gold price, though for two years they should hold off buying gold from the free market. The IMF would return one-sixth of its gold holdings to member states (as France wished), but would meet US desires by auctioning another one-sixth for the benefit of developing countries; it would stop using gold in its transactions.[35] The USA was also at odds with what France liked to term the 'Franco-Europeans' over fixed exchange rates. Originally it had strongly supported these, but by 1973 it was coming to have doubts. French pressure in 1973 and 1975 (that is, whenever the franc was strong) for their re-establishment proved unavailing, since the USA could not be forced to intervene in the markets to stabilise the dollar. In July 1975 President Giscard d'Estaing called for a summit conference on the question, remarking that 'what the world calls the crisis of capitalism is really a monetary crisis'. The meeting, in November 1975, led to annual gatherings of the leaders of the seven largest Western countries

34. *Keesing's*, 22691–7, 23492

35. The USA clearly hoped that these auctions (which began in 1976) would depress the price of gold, and sought to further the process by itself selling gold. Although some falls were achieved, the general trend was upwards, peaking in January 1980 at $875; the return to levels below $400 (which have been usual since 1984) owed more to the general re-establishment of financial and political confidence than to any specific attempts to manage the market

(accounting in 1975 for over 80 per cent of non-communist industrial production).[36] But it was itself chiefly significant as a venue for a US–French compromise on a range of outstanding monetary questions, which was then adopted by the IMF Board of Governors at its 1976 Jamaica meeting. Here, despite genuflection to the desirability of greater stability, the IMF's Articles were so amended as to give the USA a veto over any return to fixed exchange rates.[37]

Currencies therefore continue to float, though since 1979 those in the European Exchange Rate Mechanism have managed to stay linked together while floating against the dollar, the yen, and (save in 1990–2) the pound. Fluctuations are considerable: the dollar went from about $2.40 to the £ in 1980 to near parity in early 1985 and back to nearly $2 in early 1991, with similar swings against the mark. Such changes can play havoc with both the profitability of individual companies and the earnings of primary-producing countries (since most commodity prices are set in dollars). This cannot be helpful, but experience since 1973 has shown that floating exchange rates are no more than a minor obstacle to international trade. Indeed it is doubtful whether the Bretton Woods system could have accommodated the monetary dislocations that attended the 'oil shocks'. On the other hand, claims that floating exchange rates would make 1960s-type currency crises a thing of the past have also proved wrong. Countries cannot usually afford just to let their currencies slide; accordingly Britain had in 1976 to seek IMF help and accept IMF-imposed conditions as to its domestic economic policy, and similar conditions were imposed as part of Italy's 1976–7 rescue by the EC and IMF;[38] developing countries provide many more examples. Nor has concerted intervention to manage the markets been altogether abandoned: the hardening of the dollar in the mid-1980s provoked a good deal of concern. For some time this was confined to public declarations: within a month of the 'Group of Five's' January 1985 promise of coordinated market intervention, Reagan said that the USA would not 'artificially' depress the dollar and thus sent it higher. But he was eventually converted; after the Group's 'Plaza Accord' in September

36. Giscard had initially envisaged a meeting of the 'Group of Five' (countries with major internationally traded currencies). It was decided that Italy should also attend; Canada was not invited (perhaps because it would have supported the USA over 'floating'), but came to all subsequent meetings: *Keesing's*, 27501–3; see also *The Cold War* chap. 14

37. Tew, *International Monetary System 1945–77* chaps. 16–18, 20

38. *Keesing's*, 27298, 28181, 28494–5

1985, the dollar really was 'talked down', a process facilitated by the fact that it was already weakening and that intervention was therefore going with (not against) market trends.[39] (Equally the dollar was, in early 1991, successfully helped up out of a trough.)

POST-WAR TARIFF NEGOTIATIONS; THE 1947 GENERAL AGREEMENT ON TARIFFS AND TRADE; FAILURE TO SECURE AN INTERNATIONAL TRADE ORGANISATION (1948)

International money has on occasion provided high political drama. Trade and tariff negotiations have generally been lower key, but they have followed a broadly parallel course. The USA began with a vision of the system it would like; it met an early set-back in 1948, and had, therefore, to approach its goal more slowly than it had anticipated; by the end of the 1960s most of its desires had been met. Subsequently it became less sure that this was what it really wanted; and it negotiated with considerable force to protect what it now saw to be its own interests.

In 1943 a US committee viewed a great postwar expansion in international trade as 'essential to the attainment of full . . . employment in the United States and elsewhere, to the preservation of private enterprise, and to the success of an international security system to prevent future wars'.[40] Britain too believed the construction of a new multilateral order, monitored by a UN agency, to be the key to a lasting peace. But when discussions moved from high principle to practical measures, greater differences opened up over trade than had been the case with currency. In particular the USA wanted to end the tariff preferences obtaining within the British Commonwealth/Empire; Britain was prepared to contemplate this only if the United States agreed to cuts in its traditionally high tariffs (on a scale that US negotiators were clear that Congress would never accept). In 1945 the two countries could do no more than agree 'Proposals for Consideration by an International Conference' that fudged the issue.

In 1946 the UN established a committee to prepare for such a conference. Its 1947 Geneva meeting almost collapsed over the

39. *Keesing's*, 34135–6

40. R.N. Gardner, *Sterling–Dollar Diplomacy in Current Perspectives* (New York, 1980) pp.101–2

issue of 'Imperial Preference' (on which the US case had been weakened by its own recent concession of preferences to the newly decolonised Philippines). To save the conference, the USA had to accept a reduction in preferences considerably smaller than the tariff reductions it conceded in return. But the conference did conclude with a General Agreement on Tariffs and Trade (GATT). This was meant to be subsumed into the more ambitious Charter of an International Trade Organisation (ITO), which was finalised at a sixty-three–nation conference in Havana in 1948. During its drafting a coalition of non-industrialised countries, led by Australia, Brazil, Chile, and India, forced the USA to make major concessions – on states' rights to expropriate foreign-owned enterprises, to enter into new preferential regional groupings, and to impose quantitative trade restrictions to promote economic development. Nor did the USA get much joy over Imperial Preference, or secure anything more than a commitment to review discrimination against hard currency imports after 1952. It soon became clear that Congress would never ratify the Havana Charter, so the ITO proved still-born.

What remained was the GATT, which had been expanded in 1948 to incorporate commercial clauses from the Havana Charter, and which the USA continued to honour as an executive agreement. By 1951 GATT membership had risen to thirty-seven countries (accounting for 80 per cent of non-communist world trade). Rules were loose, but they did enshrine multilateral and non-discriminatory principles (except in agriculture); derogations, while common in practice, were viewed as exceptions to be lifted as soon as a country's economy was strong enough. A small secretariat remained in being; although without the supranational powers to compel compliance that the ITO would have enjoyed, GATT provides a forum to which complaint can be made, and has developed a network of precedent and case law. Above all it has provided the expertise for staging periodic negotiating 'rounds', where concessions made by one country in bilateral negotiations are generalised through the 'most favoured nation' principle, and where such concessions are traded to secure an overall package of tariff reductions.[41]

41. ibid, chaps 6, 8, 14, 17; Scammell, *International Economy* pp.41–9

GATT'S REVIVAL IN THE 1960s; THE 'KENNEDY' AND 'TOKYO' ROUNDS

The 1947 Geneva round had reduced US tariffs to their 1913 level. But Marshall Aid, by providing that Western Europe should buy from the USA only what it could not produce itself, tacitly sanctioned continued discrimination against US products. Some of these restrictions survived until 1961; against this background, the tariff reduction rounds of 1949, 1951, and 1956 were fairly minor. GATT was brought back to centre stage by the advent of an EEC committed to a common external tariff. The USA favoured European unification on geopolitical grounds, but did not want to lose the markets it had previously enjoyed in the less protectionist EEC member states, so it sponsored the 1960–2 Dillon round of negotiations. These led to little, since US negotiators were not authorised to match the tariff cuts the EEC offered, but it was agreed that there should be another round when Congress had voted sufficient powers. In seeking these, President Kennedy invoked high security interests:

> Our efforts to promote the strength and unity of the West are . . . directly related to the strength and unity of Atlantic trade policies. . . . If we can take this step, Marxist predictions of 'capitalist' empires warring over markets and stifling competition would be shattered for all time . . . and Communist efforts to split the West would be doomed to failure.[42]

Kennedy obtained authority to halve tariffs, and to abolish them altogether on products in which the EEC (enlarged, as was then expected, by UK membership) and the USA together accounted for 80 per cent of world trade. As this covered over half of US–European trade, it would have gone far to create an Atlantic free trade area in industrial goods. Since de Gaulle vetoed British membership of the EEC, this was not to be. In 1967, however, after five years of cliff-hanging negotiation, tariff cuts emerged that averaged 35 per cent on industrial products (agriculture was another story). Shortly afterwards the world was thrown into turmoil

42. Warning that things could also go wrong was provided by the celebrated 'chicken war' of 1962–3, when, in response to EEC levies that shut off its poultry exports to Germany, the USA threatened substantial tariff retaliation. After mediation by the GATT, this was compromised by allowing the USA to recoup its losses through a more limited range of tariffs (aimed chiefly at French and German products): Shonfield, *International Economic Relations* pp.51, 210–13

by the USA's 1971 closing of the 'gold window', imposition of emergency tariff surcharges, and determination to secure a $13 billion improvement in its balance of payments. The USA pressed for immediate trade concessions from the EEC and, more importantly, Japan. They did give some, but both preferred to negotiate in a more conventional manner, and the upshot was the launching in 1973 of the Tokyo round. This sought, ambitiously, to cover not only trade in industrial goods but also the pricklier questions of agriculture, non-tariff barriers, and special measures for developing countries. Some progress was made in all areas. But again industrial tariffs were the most easily addressed; it was agreed in 1979 to reduce them to an average level of 4.7 per cent, at which point their impact on trade can only be minor.[43]

JAPAN, GATT, AND NON-TARIFF BARRIERS

Initially GATT had been a largely Atlantic affair, but in 1952 Japan applied for membership. It enjoyed strong US support: the United States did not wish Japan to resume trade with China, and so sought alternative outlets that would anchor it firmly in the West. By 1955 the USA had overcome British resistance, and Japan formally joined GATT. In practice, though, most countries retained special controls on Japanese exports (then feared as the product of cheap labour), and only the USA can be said to have really opened its market. Its textile interests soon found the result uncomfortable, and in 1957 Japan was pressed 'voluntarily' to limit the flood. This did nothing to stop trans-shipment via Hong Kong, or (later) independent production and export by Hong Kong and Taiwan, so in 1961–2 the USA secured the negotiation of general agreements establishing national quotas and limiting the growth of cotton textile exports to 5 per cent per year. In 1973 this was replaced by a broader 'Multi-fibre Arrangement' covering all textile exports.

By now Japanese industry had moved on, and concern for the management of Japanese competition had spilt over into other areas; but the precedent of 'voluntary' trade restraints outside the GATT had been well established. Originally, as we have seen, most GATT members continued to discriminate against Japan. In the

43. ibid, pp.168 ff; *Keesing's*, 25130–1, 26393–5, 29783–4; *The Independent*, 13 Nov. 1990 p.29. In 1947 tariffs had averaged 40%

early 1960s they were persuaded to lift overt discrimination, but only on the basis that Japan would itself limit the growth of its exports. Limited this growth may have been, but it was also very fast. So 'By 1972 the whole of Western Europe was . . . negotiating self-restraint agreements with Japanese producers, covering electronic products, cars, steel, ball-bearings, chemical fibres, TV sets, . . . and even tankers'. The United States, now alarmed by its sudden yawning deficit with Japan, joined in too. Not, of course, that Japan was itself blameless. It had until 1964 been clearly mercantilist, not unreasonably given its balance of payments difficulties. As these improved, the USA pushed it to lift its overt controls on industrial imports, and such pressure intensified after 1968 (by which time Japan's trade surplus had become embarrassing). Accordingly between 1968 and 1971 most non-agricultural quotas were phased out, leaving the Japanese market (on paper) among the most open in the world.[44] Reality was very different; as we have seen (pp.180–2), a recurrent feature of US–Japanese relations since the early 1970s has been US pressure to 'open' the Japanese market, and its accommodation by successive Japanese packages, each billed as removing an important set of constraints whose existence had previously been denied. (There have been similar confrontations with West European countries and the EC, though Japan is less impressed with their political power and so less inclined to make concessions.)

GATT AND AGRICULTURE; THE URUGUAY ROUND

GATT has been mostly concerned with trade in industrial rather than agricultural products, and for good reason: a major element in the American New Deal had been its use of production limits and price supports to restore agricultural prosperity. The US Department of Agriculture insisted that these be allowed to continue; they were duly authorised by both the GATT and the Havana Charter, subject to some limitations that Congress promply overrode. This dereliction was noted annually by GATT, and in 1955 the USA covered itself by securing an open-ended waiver. But it gradually came to feel that this removal of agriculture from GATT's sphere had been a mistake, given its own strengths in that area. The USA pressed for its inclusion in the Kennedy round. Unfortunately the

44. Shonfield, *International Economic Relations* pp.253–80

nascent EEC was busy constructing a Common Agricultural Policy aimed at self-sufficiency, which became for France a sine qua non of membership. There was, therefore, no prospect of agricultural trade being treated in the same way as industrial. The EEC did offer to freeze agricultural support at existing levels; the USA hoped for more and unwisely turned this down, but finally had to settle for much less rather than risk the collapse of the whole Kennedy round. (It was, in any case, exposed to attempts by meat and dairy-produce exporting countries to use the negotiations to overturn its own almost total ban on these imports.)[45] Agriculture again featured in the Tokyo round, but once more only limited agreements were reached. Then in the 1980s it was placed on the agenda of what was to become the Uruguay round, with the United States being joined in 1986 by the 'Cairns Group' of fourteen major agricultural exporters.

By 1990 agriculture had become a crunch-point,[46] with the USA and the Cairns Group making the many other agreements reached during the round conditional on the EC's cutting farm support by 75 per cent and agricultural export subsidies by 90 per cent. The EC would offer no more than a 30 per cent cut in export subsidies, and received the general backing of Japan and South Korea. So talks broke down, amid US accusations of 'economic warfare' and Australian warnings of an imminent return to protectionism. In 1991 there was another failure. When talks were resumed in the autumn of 1992, they appeared to be going the same way; the USA responded by threatening punitive tariffs on $1 billion worth of EC produce. A trade war was averted by eleventh-hour EC concessions, which led to riotous anti-USA farmers' protests in France and much French denunciation of Britain's current tenure of the EC presidency as 'putting us in difficulty facing the Americans'. The EC–USA agreement appeared to presage a successful conclusion of the Uruguay round, especially as Japan also made conciliatory noises on rice imports. However French threats to veto the deal persisted, and the round did not achieve its cliff-hanging final agreement until December 1993.[47] Even then, though the scope of GATT (to be re-named the Multilateral Trade Organisation) was

45. ibid, pp.180, 345–7, 374–5, 382–6; Gardner, *Sterling–Dollar Diplomacy* p.149

46. Quite apart from the USA/Australia/Canada versus the EC/Japan dimension, the World Bank reckons that elimination of agricultural subsidies in industrialised countries would raise developing countries' exports by $50 billion per year: *The Independent*, 19 Dec. 1990 p.21

47. *Keesing's*, 35026, 37930, 39170, 39176–7, 39250, 39794, 1992 R154, 1993 R152

greatly expanded to include both agriculture and services, detailed negotiations as to the latter had to be held over to the future.

US OBJECTIVES OF THE 1940s AND THE OUTCOME – AN OVERVIEW

How far, then, did the United States achieve its wartime objectives in the economic sphere, and what has it made of the outcome? In both the monetary and the trade spheres progress was markedly slower than it had expected: the USA's overwhelming economic pre-eminence did not enable it to bulldoze through agreements that other countries could not afford to implement. But by the 1960s much of the desired multilateral system was in place. Growing prosperity, and the ending of the 'dollar gap', enabled Europe to implement the Bretton Woods monetary system, to lift quantitative restrictions on trade in manufactured products, and to negotiate deep tariff cuts. All this was accompanied, as both liberal economic theory and US politicians said it would be, by an almost continuous trade expansion (see p.506) that was clearly conducive to overall economic growth. But some European politicians, and many academics, saw the outcome as tailor-made for an American economic take-over: US-owned 'multinationals' were investing heavily abroad, both directly and by buying up foreign companies. They paid in dollars which, in a sense, it cost the USA nothing to issue, and whose general acceptability was believed to be underpinned by the Bretton Woods system. Moreover these US multinationals were seen as manipulative and super-efficient, and accordingly far better placed than local concerns to take advantage of the opening up of markets, whether by the Kennedy round or by the development of the EEC. Soon the world's third economic 'power' (after the USA and USSR) would be American corporations abroad.

In the 1970s things changed. In the monetary sphere the USA decided that the Bretton Woods system worked *against* its interests by preventing it from devaluing its currency. In 1971, rather than going on losing gold, or subordinating US domestic policy to external dictates, Nixon ditched it. There were still hopes that the managed international monetary system could be reconstituted around the SDR, but even before the 1973 OPEC oil price shock, this was by no means certain. The shock brought monetary disturbances that compelled currencies to 'float'; the USA decided that it was well suited by these new conditions, which the IMF duly sanctioned in 1976. The outcome was an unmanaged monetary regime. For though the IMF did issue a fiduciary currency in the form of SDRs, the major countries (whose weighted votes gave them control) made sure this was on a distinctly limited scale. Probably wisely, for the SDR was backed by nothing in particular, whereas, in the Western system, a national currency represents a claim on that country's economy. Trade, therefore, continued to be conducted in national currencies, chiefly in those of the three largest economies (the USA, Japan and Germany) and in sterling. Their relationship was determined primarily by the market pressures that had proved irresistible in the closing days of Bretton Woods. The most that can be said is that, after the 1985 Plaza Accord, coordinated intervention was again used with some (though far from complete) success to nudge the market in the desired direction.

Also left largely to the market was the initial shielding of weaker countries from the 1970s oil shocks. Although the IMF did provide cushioning 'oil facility' loans, and stood ready to lend more on increasingly stringent conditions, most borrowing was done from ordinary banks (partly to avoid having to submit to these conditions). At the time this seemed sensible. The OPEC states could not immediately spend the extra money brought in by the oil price rise; so they deposited it in Western banks, which lent it on to countries that would not otherwise have been able to pay for their oil. Sometimes this worked: South Korea borrowed very heavily, but continued with its economic miracle, met its interest payments, and started paying off its debt. But this was unusual; banks were too eager to earn money by lending and casually assumed that states would never default. Many Third World and East European countries borrowed from them precisely because they did not wish to make the painful economic adjustments that the IMF would have required. Most loans were denominated in dollars; the party ended when, after 1982, many states were squeezed by the combination of a hardening dollar and falling commodity prices.

The crisis was initially left to the banks, which handled it by 'rescheduling' the debt (that is by adding to the capital the interest payments that could not be made) in a series of one-off deals. Though its own lending remained small, the IMF was now drawn in, as the commercial banks generally made rescheduling conditional on IMF approval of the debtors' economic policies. But there was a general indisposition, strongly reinforced by the US, to adopt collective initiatives towards Third World debt. This began to change in 1985, when US Treasury Secretary Baker sought to cajole the commercial banks into advancing $20 billion of new money, and 1988 when the Toronto G7 summit decided on a special approach to the problems of the poorest countries. For the middle-income states that accounted for most of the outstanding debt, the summit reaffirmed the 'case-by-case' approach. It was not until 1989 that the 'Brady Plan' (advanced by the USA after strong Japanese lobbying) called for a 'great cooperative effort' to reduce Third World debt by about 20 per cent. The Brady Plan had a distinctly beneficial effect in Latin America (see p.429). Overall the picture was more mixed, with 1990 seeing the first surplus of lending over capital return since 1983, 1991 a decline in private lending, and 1992 a resumption of such lending and (more significantly) of direct investment. However this flowed to countries that (often as a result of changed policies) now seemed to have prospects for growth. Official, and especially World Bank, lending came to refocus towards the remainder; but, especially in Africa, the future of what was coming to be seen as a Fourth World – or, in the case of war-torn countries like the Sudan, Ethiopia and Somalia, Fifth World – appeared bleak.[48]

In the trade sphere, the international rules of the GATT held up better than had the Bretton Woods monetary system. They were admittedly bypassed by burgeoning 'voluntary' controls on exports, but the 1970s saw the successful conclusion of the Kennedy, the 1980s the launching of the Uruguay, round. Trade boomed, going from $30 billion per year after the Second World War to over $1,000 billion by 1980 and $3,500–4,300 billion by 1990, far outstripping inflation.[49] Clearly the system is suboptimal, but it works. How well it works depends on one's perspective: most trade is conducted between the industrialised Western countries that account for only a fraction of the world's population. An attempt was made in the 1970s to adjust the terms of trade by political action, and to create – in the NIEO – something of a global welfare state. But, with the partial exception of oil, it did not succeed.

48. *Keesing's*, 34139–40, 36214, 38254, 1992 R152, 1993 R150; *The Independent*, 19 Dec. 1990 p.21. According to the World Bank, debt stood at $829 billion in 1982; by 1987 it had risen to $1,268 billion, where it remained till 1989. In 1990 there was a further increase to $1,341 billion (with further small rises in 1991 and 1992); but debt has declined as a proportion of Third World exports

49. Gardner, *Sterling–Dollar Diplomacy* p.xvii; *The Independent*, 26 March 1991 p.23 (GATT estimate, the higher figure including some $800 billion of trade in services as opposed to merchandise)

Although most countries have, through the postwar period, secured an improvement in per capita income, in the 1980s most of Sub-Saharan Africa and much of Latin America fell back. How far this was due to the system, and how far to their own mismanagement, is a moot, and politically contentious, point. Certainly the system can be made to work, in the sense that at least some new countries can (in Lee Kuan Yew's words) 'plug into it' and use it to outdistance neighbours that, like Burma or Vietnam, for one reason or another choose to stand aloof. The economic contrast between Western Europe and an East Europe that had stood outside the system proved a powerful solvent of communism at the end of the 1980s.

So far, then, the American vision of the 1940s has been amply justified. There, however, have been some unexpected side-effects, notably the relative economic decline of the United States itself. Its position after the war (accounting for perhaps 43 per cent of *world* GNP in 1949) was no doubt exceptional. But whereas its 1970 output was 113 per cent that of the EEC and Japan combined, by 1987 the ratio had fallen to 67 per cent.[50] The 1960s expectations that its multinationals were bound to take over the rest of the world proved completely mistaken. For much of the 1970s the USA, with its low-priced domestic energy, was a good place in which to manufacture, so there was a welcome reversal of the flood of overseas investment that had been so much feared. In the 1980s, after a severe initial recession, the US economy expanded sharply under the stimulus of a huge budget deficit, while high interest rates drove up the price of the dollar. The result was a yawning balance of payments deficit, financed by foreign borrowing. For domestic political reasons, the deficit was not seriously addressed (at least before 1993). Although the weakening of the dollar in the second half of the 1980s did eventually make US industry more competitive, its initial effect was to make US assets seem cheap and so to attract massive inward investment. The result was the *apparent* transformation of the United States into the country with the world's largest foreign debt,[51] and a wave of foreign take-overs of US companies and property led by the British and Japanese. In the

50. UN, *National and Per Capita Incomes: Seventy Countries – 1949* and *National Income Statistics, Supplement 1938–50* (New York, 1950, 1951); John Zysman, 'US Power, Trade and Technology', *International Affairs* lxvii (1991) p.90

51. In 1990 the Bank of England put the balance of US overseas assets less liabilities at –$675 billion (Japan's being +$292 billion, Germany's +$254 billion, and Britain's +$174 billion); but this valued US assets only at historic cost, whereas they are probably now worth over $1,000 billion more: *The Independent*, 16 Nov. 1990 p.23; *Sunday Times*, 9 July 1988 p.D8

Japanese case this was the obverse of Japan's huge balance of payments surpluses, which induced Japanese companies and banks to spread their wings globally so that they now resemble the US multinationals of the 1960s. Many of these purchases in fact proved costly mistakes. But, as in the Europe of the 1960s, so in modern USA, they generated feelings of foreign domination, and were ascribed to imperfections in the international system, it being claimed that, while the USA maintains an open market, Japan and the EC do not. One response was a significant growth in direct protectionist sentiment. Another was a determination to prise open Japanese, European and other markets, in part through the Uruguay round demands that we have noted. Accordingly early 1994 saw the USA and Japan hovering on the brink of a trade war, with the USA (embittered by what it sees as the failure of past market-opening initiatives) demanding that Japan accord it 'objectively measurable' proportions of its domestic markets and Japan maintaining that this would imply 'managed trade' incompatible with GATT.

INCIPIENT REGIONALISM IN TRADE BLOCS?

It is, of course, US strategy to claim that failure to reach agreement would lead to trade war and split the West, especially if, with the end of the Cold War, the USA tired of the burden of providing international security and looked only towards its own domestic interests. A less melodramatic scenario might be the acceleration of an already perceptible trend towards economic regionalism, with roughly equal blocs centring on North America, Western Europe and Japan.[52] For the EC and EFTA are fast drawing together, with intra-European trade now out-weighing trade with the rest of the world. Similarly, despite Canadian attempts after 1957 to realign trade towards the UK and more general Canadian concern in the 1970s about foreign economic penetration, Canada and the US are each other's best customers; in 1989 a limited free trade area came into effect between them; Mexico soon managed to convert this into a North American Free Trade Agreement (with effect from

52. In 1987 the USA/Canada and Western Europe each accounted for about 25% of global GDP, Japan plus the Asian newly industrialising countries for 15.8%. Asian growth has subsequently been faster than American or European, but a Japan-centred bloc is more problematic than the other two: Zysman, 'US Power, Trade and Technology' pp.82–4

1994). Lastly there are some signs that trade is increasingly running along the rim of Asia rather than across the Pacific: in 1989 Japan's trade with Asia overtook that with the USA. The process seems natural, has developed within a relatively open world market, and may well continue to do so. But were the context to become one of trade rivalries and the emotions they generate, it could acquire a harder edge. With the ending of the Cold War, such questions are acquiring a distinctly higher political profile, though it remains to be seen whether, in the event of a real crisis,[53] they would be again pushed into the background (as they largely were by the 1990–1 Iraqi occupation of Kuwait) or further exacerbated along the lines of the US–EC tensions of the 1973 Yom Kippur War and oil embargo.

53. In March 1994 a Korean crisis was certainly possible. North Korea has built rockets and (probably) nuclear weapons. It has so far prevented serious IAEA inspection, and has threatened that, if pushed too far, it would attack the South. It also admits to grave economic difficulties; but it is not clear whether these make it more or less likely to reach a deal with the USA

Guide to Further Reading

While there are many things that we do not know, there is no quantitative shortage of secondary – or even primary – sources: one listing suggests that nearly half the published works on US foreign relations are on the period since 1945. Admittedly our sources have a serious bias towards the United States: not only has the USA been the most important single actor in international affairs since 1945, but also it has led the way in the release, publication, and (some would say) multiplication of historical documents. Scholars have tended to give it if anything disproportionate attention, partly for these reasons, partly (in some cases) from sheer insularity, and partly because, where space is short, it is easier to structure one's writing around an American, than around a multilateral, framework. There is also a question of national perspectives. Most scholars underplay the appreciable Canadian contribution to international diplomacy in the first two postwar decades; some Canadians err in the opposite direction; the result is a distinctive Canadian historiography. The same is true, to a lesser extent, in connection with Britain and France.

Postwar, like earlier, historiography has proceeded on the basis of a voluminous public record (of official documents and statements, parliamentary debates, press releases and comment, and the like). This is shaped and built on by memoirs, biographies, 'instant histories' (often by able and well-informed journalists), and comment and analysis by students of the contemporary scene. Even such recent events as the 1991 Gulf War have been so covered. But the blanket release of the confidential documents shaping and recording government deliberations and decisions takes much longer. Thus the UK operates a thirty-year rule (with derogations), which means that the frontier of classic document-based history now lies in the 1960s, with what one might term cultivated territory not extending quite so far. Much the same is true of the USA: study of the Truman and Eisenhower administrations is qualitatively different from that of their successors. But our knowledge of these is much expanded by a combination of: presidential libraries (each President is entitled to one, and, though security classification still applies, they make available documents that would in most other countries remain confidential); widespread declassification under the Freedom of Information Act; and massive leaks, plus investigations into the Central Intelligence Agency, in the 1970s.

The importance of archives is highlighted by the case of Israel. Like the UK this operates a thirty-year rule (and has also begun to publish *Documents on the Foreign Policy of Israel*); hence there is a lively historiography of the state's genesis and early years, with revisionist writers using primary sources to seek to challenge the received version at important points. There is nothing comparable for Israel's neighbours. Indeed most of our information about secret Arab–Israeli contacts comes from Israeli and/or British sources, while for Arab politics we depend chiefly on the public record and on memoirs by participants. Not that the Arabs are in any way unusual: the opening of postwar archives is rare outside Western Europe and North America. But the greater availability there of source material further enhances the natural tendency of historians, most of whom are American or West European, to look at the world largely from this perspective. Even in the case of the Vietnam War where many historians have sympathised with Hanoi, they have still based themselves primarily on US sources and concentrated chiefly on US decisions, since so much more is known of these than of their North Vietnamese counterparts. Nor is it unimportant in this context that far more historians can read English than Vietnamese.

For documents in the public domain, two convenient sources are J.A.S. Grenville, *The Major International Treaties 1914–1973: A History and Guide with Texts* (1974), and the series of *Documents on International Affairs* (nearly one volume for each year down to 1963) produced for the Royal Institute of International Affairs. The RIIA also published a companion series, *Survey of International Affairs* (whose last volume also covers 1963). An enormous amount of material is contained in *Keesing's Contemporary Archives* – since 1987 *Keesing's Record of World Events* – (until 1973, Keynsham, Bristol, thereafter London), a well-indexed press digest with (in recent years) annual updates of developments by country (especially useful for small countries) and international organisation. Also valuable are the (London) International Institute for Strategic Studies' (IISS) *Adelphi Papers* (short monographs on issues and developments of recent or current interest) and the similar *The Washington Papers* (Praeger, with the Center for Strategic and International Studies, Washington). *The World Today* (London) contains academic articles on recent events that emerge more rapidly than do their counterparts in heavyweight publications like *Foreign Affairs* (New York) and *International Affairs* (London); these in turn are less conventionally historical than *Diplomatic History* (Wilmington, Del.) or other scholarly journals.

Though both Britain and France have begun publishing their postwar documents, by far the most extensive published collection of primary sources is the Department of State's *Foreign Relations of the United States* (*FRUS*) (Washington, DC). Publication up to 1957 is nearly complete; a start has been made on later years, with the 1964–8 sub-series just beginning. Even *FRUS* cannot include everything, and the more recent sub-series are noticeably thinner than their predecessors. There is, too, a certain bias towards US State Department documents, which are not necessarily the most useful; the volume bearing on the Middle East in 1956 contains nothing on the US Treasury's crucial exercise of pressure on Britain via the IMF, and it has been noted that the editor ' "did not have access to the full range of documentation on US intelligence operations and the diplomacy of the Suez crisis". Those interested in the CIA-MI6 plot to overthrow the Syrian government . . . will have to look elsewhere . . . (e.g. to Anthony Gorst and W. Scott Lucas, "The other collusion: Operation Straggle and Anglo-American intervention in Syria, 1955–56", *Intelligence and National Security* 4:3, July 1989)'. Nevertheless *FRUS* constitutes an enormous quarry, useful for the history of many countries besides the USA. The trouble, for most people, is that *FRUS* is too large. This prompted a number of reviews by Geoffrey Warner, of which those most relevant to this volume are 'The United States and the Suez Crisis', *International Affairs* lxvii (1991) and 'The United States and Vietnam 1945–1965', two articles in ibid, xlviii (1972) surveying the leaked *United States–Vietnam Relations 1945–1967* based, as its common title *The Pentagon Papers* implies, on Defense Department documents, plus 'The United States and Vietnam: Two Episodes', ibid, lxv (1989) reviewing the *FRUS* coverage of the decision to extend aid to France in 1950 and the debate over American military intervention in April 1954. Supplementing *FRUS*, and often extending to a later date, are documents released under the Freedom of Information Act, which have been published on microfiche (initially by Carrolton Press Inc., Washington, DC, currently by its new owners Research Publications, Inc., Woodbridge, Conn., and Reading, England). Unlike *FRUS*, these documents are not edited into orderly volumes, but Carrolton and (from July–Sept. 1981) Research Publications have produced indexes in the form of *The Declassified Documents: Retrospective Collection* (3 vols, Washington, DC, 1976) and *Declassified Documents Quarterly Catalog* (Washington, DC, then Woodbridge, Conn., 1975–).

As for secondary sources, 'of the making of books there is no end'; new and valuable ones are continually emerging. Most of the works that I have used are referred to in my footnotes; but both that choice and the suggestions that follow here should be seen only as indicative rather than in any way comprehensive or exclusive.

Much of this volume has a regional orientation, or is directed towards specific themes such as decolonisation or the international economy. But many books will touch on more than one theme, or span several regions. For instance Barry M. Blechman and Stephen Kaplan (eds) *Force without War: U.S. Armed Forces as a Political Instrument* (Washington, DC, 1978) discusses, by way of case studies, the crises of 1958 in the Lebanon and 1970 in Jordan, that of Laos in 1962 and the 1971 Indo-Pakistani war, US handling of the Dominican Republic 1961–6, the 1958–61 Berlin crises, and US actions (or inaction) in connection with Yugoslavia in 1951 and Czechoslovakia in 1968. Robert Jervis and Jack Snyder (eds) *Dominoes and Bandwagons: Strategic Beliefs and Great Power Competition in the Eurasian Rimland* (New York, 1991) uses, to test and illustrate its theoretical argument, not only material from pre-1945 history but also a range of later episodes from 'the Eurasian Rimland' plus Angola and the Horn of Africa. Steven R. David reviews *Third World Coups d'État and International Security* (Baltimore, 1987). By the same token the secret services of the major powers are active in widely separated countries. We know most about those of the United States: John Ranelagh, *The Agency: The Rise and Decline of the CIA* (1966) is perhaps the best of many CIA histories, while John Prados, *Presidents' Secret Wars* (New York, 1986) is also very useful; more recent operations are described in Bob Woodward, *Veil: The Secret Wars of the CIA, 1981–1987* (New York, 1987) – though this was received with a good deal of scepticism – and Joseph E. Persico, *Casey: From the OSS to the CIA* (New York, 1990). Nor can top political leaders afford to specialise too narrowly. Accordingly volume 2 of Henry Kissinger's memoirs, *Years of Upheaval* (1982), discusses not only the US domestic political scene and US–Soviet détente in 1973–4, but also his dealings with Chile, Western Europe, Cyprus, Greece and Turkey, the Middle East, China and Indo-China (including a lengthy defence of his handling of Cambodia). In his equally vast *Turmoil and Triumph: My Years as Secretary of State* (New York, 1993), George P. Shultz covers US relations with not only the USSR, China and Western Europe, but also the Middle East, Central America, the Philippines and Southern Africa. Similarly Harold Macmillan's six rambling volumes of memoirs (*Winds of Change* – 1966, 1967, 1969, 1971, 1972, 1973) have much material on decolonisation, the Commonwealth and the Middle East, while Alistair Horne, *Macmillan* (2 vols, 1990, 1991) contains things Macmillan had not thought it yet proper to reveal (including some sharp insights into the UN's Congo operations in the years 1961–3). The three volumes of *Khrushchev Remembers* (Boston, Mass., 1971, 1974, 1990) are pure reminiscences, without the benefit of documentary support; but they contain important revelations on, for instance, the Korean War, the background to the 1954 Geneva Conference on Indo-China, and the 1962 Cuba missile crisis, as well as striking illustrations of his attitude towards both China and the Third World.

But if it is therefore important to look beyond works directed towards specific regions or themes, it will be natural for this bibliography to concentrate on them. Here one should stress that maps are almost indispensable, for 'where you stand' often, though not always, 'depends on where you sit'. A good atlas should suffice, since topography does not change rapidly. Economic and population statistics do, and are in any case less trustworthy. But those presented in, for instance, the annual World Bank *Atlas* are both interesting and useful, provided they are taken with a pinch of salt.

One of the most notable features of the post-1945 period is the decline of empires. D.K. Fieldhouse, *The Colonial Empires* (1966) gives an overview stretching from 'The First Expansion of Europe' to 'Decolonisation'. Decolonisation itself is more fully addressed in R.F. Holland, *European Decolonization 1918–81: An Introductory Survey* (Basingstoke, 1985), while M.E. Chamberlain's short *Decolonization: The Fall of European Empires* (Oxford, 1985) is useful for reference. Meanwhile Hedley Bull and Adam Watson (eds) *The Expansion of International Society* (1984) reflects on a much longer process of which postwar decolonisation formed only a part, albeit an important one. Each colonial empire differed; but the largest, the British, has (perhaps inevitably) attracted the most attention. John Darwin describes *Britain and Decolonisation: The Retreat from Empire in the Post-war World* (Basingstoke 1988), and returns to the subject in his assessment of *The End of the British Empire: The Historical Debate* (Oxford, 1991); Brian Lapping offers a more blow-by-blow account in *End of Empire* (1989). The second largest empire was the French. Syria, Indo-China, Tunisia and Morocco had all gone by the time de Gaulle returned to power in 1958, but he then disengaged rapidly from Sub-Saharan Africa and, with far more difficulty, from Algeria; the story is told in Alistair Horne, *A Savage War of Peace: Algeria 1954–62* (1987 edn) and Jean Lacouture, *De Gaulle: The Ruler 1945–1970* (1993 edn).

Another approach to decolonisation is by area. The British departure from India is discussed, from very different perspectives, by Ayesha Jalal, *The Sole Spokesman: Jinnah, the Muslim League, and the Demand for Pakistan* (Cambridge, 1985), Anita Inder Singh, *The Origins of the Partition of India 1936–1947* (Delhi, 1987) and R.J. Moore, *Escape from Empire: The Attlee Government and the India Problem* (Oxford, 1983); Philip Ziegler's *Mountbatten: The Official Biography* (1985) describes his time as the last Viceroy and as Governor-General, while the career of India's extremely influential first premier is surveyed in Sarvepalli Gopal, *Jawarharlal Nehru: A Biography* (abridged edn, Delhi, 1989). It will be convenient to consider both the Middle East and Indo-China below. But the confused period after the Japanese surrender, which was to prove crucially important in both Indo-China and Indonesia, is discussed in Louis Allen, *The End of the War in Asia* (1976), while Jan Pluvier gives us a general account of *South-East Asia from Colonialism to Independence* (Kuala Lumpur, 1974). J.D. Hargreaves covers *Decolonization in Africa* (1988); a gloomy view of the sequel is offered by D.K. Fieldhouse, *Black Africa 1945–80: Economic Decolonization and Arrested Development* (1986). Deeply involved in arranging one of the latest episodes of decolonisation, that of Namibia (with the concomitant South African withdrawal from Angola) was US Assistant Secretary of State for African Affairs, Chester A. Crocker, whose memoirs are *High Noon in Southern Africa: Making Peace in a Rough Neighbourhood* (1992); some of the broader context is spelt out and assessed in James Barber and John Barratt, *South Africa's Foreign Policy: The Search for Status and Security 1945–1988* (Cambridge, 1990).

Though much of the Middle East was formally independent in 1945, the area still lay within the British sphere of influence. Its subsequent history has been turbulent. Perhaps the best overview is M.E. Yapp, *The Near East since the First World War* (1991), while L. Carl Brown argues persuasively in *International Politics and the Middle East: Old Rules, Dangerous Game* (1984) that there is, and long has been, a distinctive Middle Eastern political culture, the product of the area's penetration by, and exploitation of, external power politics over the last two centuries. William Roger Louis gives us a large, if rather heavy, account of *The British Empire in the Middle East, 1945–1951: Arab Nationalism, the United States and Postwar Imperialism* (Oxford, 1984) and Peter L. Hahn describes British friction with, and ejection from, Egypt in *The United States, Great Britain and Egypt: Strategy and Diplomacy in the Early Cold War, 1945–56* (Chapel Hill, NC, 1991).

At least as measured by historiographical output, the most prominent sector of Middle Eastern politics has been the Arab–Israeli feud. Howard M. Sachar's *A History of Israel: From the Rise of Zionism to Our Time* (Oxford, 1977) and *Volume II – From the Aftermath of the Yom Kippur War* (New York, 1987) is useful and substantial, the second volume being less pro-Israeli than the first. Ritchie Ovendale's *The Origins of the Arab–Israeli Wars* (1992 edn) is at points strongly critical of US initiatives taken, as he believes (controversially in the case of Truman), for reasons of domestic politics. Michael J. Cohen provides a thoughtful account of *Palestine and the Great Powers 1945–48* (Princeton, NJ, 1982) and has edited a useful collection of primary sources in *The Rise of Israel: A Documentary Record* vol. 32 (New York, 1987). Edgar O'Ballance, *The Arab–Israeli War, 1948* (1956) gives us a short history of the fighting, the course and nature of which (though more important than most diplomacy) is often overlooked in accounts of 'international relations'; O'Ballance has written similar narratives both of later Arab–Israeli and of many other post-1945 wars. Arnold Krammer reminds us of the extent of early Soviet assistance to Israel in *The Forgotten Friendship: Israel and the Soviet Bloc 1947–53* (Urbana, Ill., 1974). Benny Morris uses archival material to challenge traditional views (both Israeli and Arab) of *The Birth of the Palestinian Refugee Problem, 1947–1949* (Cambridge, 1987). Avi Shlaim's *The Politics of Partition: King Abdullah, the Zionists and Palestine 1921–1951* (Oxford, 1990) contains extremely valuable discussion of the secret 1947–8 Zionist-Transjordan-British understanding on the partition of Palestine, of its shelving under the pressure of events, and of the abortive post-Armistice peace negotiations between Abdullah and Israel (for whose failure Shlaim chiefly blames Israel). Shlaim carries his revisionist interpretation further in 'Conflicting Approaches to Israel's Relations with the Arabs: Ben Gurion and Sharrett', *Middle East Journal* xxxvii (1983), arguing that alternatives were proposed to Ben Gurion's strategy of massive retaliation and underlining the effect of the 1955 Gaza raid in hardening Nasser's stance. More traditional is the picture given in Michael B. Oren, 'Escalation to Suez: The Egypt–Israel Border War, 1949–1956', *Journal of Contemporary History* xxiv (1989). In the aftermath of Nasser's nationalisation of the Suez Canal and in collusion with France and Britain, those border incidents burst in 1956 into open war. The antecedents of the crisis, and 'Suez' itself, are covered in William Roger Louis and Roger Owen (eds) *Suez 1956: The Crisis and its Consequences* (Oxford, 1989); among many other competitors, perhaps the leading account is Keith Kyle, *Suez* (1991). From the Egyptian side, Nasser's friend, the eminent journalist and politician Mohammed H. Heikal, gives us *Cutting the Lion's Tail: Suez through Egyptian Eyes* (1986) – to add to his earlier *Nasser: The Cairo Documents* (1972), *The Road to Ramadan* (1975 – on the 1973 Arab–Israeli war), and *Sphinx and Commissar: The Rise and Fall of Soviet Influence in the Arab World* (1978).

Arab–Israeli relations, and Great Power intervention, from 1955 to 1975, are covered, very readably, by the well-informed journalist Donald Neff in *Warriors at Suez: Eisenhower takes America into the Middle East* (New York, 1981), *Warriors for Jerusalem: The Six Days that Changed the Middle East* (New York, 1984) and *Warriors against Israel* (Brattleboro, Vt, 1988). There is also interesting material in Stephen Green, *Taking Sides: America's Secret Relations with a Militant Israel* (New York, 1984) and his (still more partisan) *Living by the Sword: America and the Middle East 1968–87* (Brattleboro, Vt, 1988). Kissinger's involvement during and after the 1973 war is recounted in his *Years of Upheaval* (1982), and by Matti Golan, *The Secret Conversations of Henry Kissinger: Step by Step Diplomacy in the Middle East* (New York, 1986 edn) – written from Israeli leaks and providing an interesting picture of Kissinger's negotiating technique. William B. Quandt looks at the 1979 Egypt–Israel peace treaty in *Camp David: Peacemaking and Politics* (1986); Shultz's *Turmoil and Triumph* (noted on p.514) contains much material on the diplomacy of the years 1982–8. But in the Middle East, even more than elsewhere, a great deal goes on unattributably and behind the scenes. This has generated a spate of works (including those, already noticed, by Green); Steve Posner, *Israel Undercover: Secret Warfare and Hidden Diplomacy in the Middle East* (Syracuse, NY, 1987) is particularly full on clandestine Israeli–Jordanian contacts; but the field is probably held by Yossi Melman and Dan Raviv, *The Imperfect Spies: The History of Israeli Intelligence* (1989) and Ian Black and Benny Morris, *Israel's Secret Wars: A History of Israel's Intelligence Services* (1991).

Though it takes the limelight, the Arab–Israeli dispute is only a part, and not always even the most important part, of the wider Middle Eastern picture. The most prominent postwar Arab leader was President Nasser of Egypt. Mohammed Heikal's works (noted on p.517) revolve largely around Nasser; and Robert Stephens offers us the useful *Nasser: A Critical Biography* (Harmondsworth, 1973). In *The Struggle for Syria: A Study of Post-War Arab Politics, 1945–1958* (1986 edn), Patrick Seale argues for Syria's centrality, albeit more as an object than an actor; with Maureen McConville he extends the story in his work on Syria's strong post-1970 President, *Asad of Syria: The Struggle for the Middle East* (1988). Malcolm Kerr guides us through the complicated politics of the 1960s in *The Arab Cold War: Gamal 'Abd al-Nasir and his Rivals, 1958–1970* (1971), while Edgar O'Ballance writes on *The War in the Yemen* (1971). The 1970s proved to be the oil decade; as such it naturally features in Daniel Yergin's general history of the industry, *The Prize: The Epic Quest for Oil, Money and Power* (1991 edn). With the 1973 'oil shock', awareness of Saudi Arabia burst on the world and led to two fairly similar explanatory histories, David Holden and Richard Johns, *The House of Saud* (1981) and Robert Lacey, *The Kingdom* (New York, 1981). The other great oil power was Iran, which was further highlighted by the 1979 revolution and its sequel. This occasioned Barry Rubin's *Paved with Good Intentions: The American Experience and Iran* (New York, 1980). Farhad Diba offers us a (probably over-sympathetic) *Mohammed Mossadegh: A Political Biography* (1986), written in the tradition that sees Mossadegh himself and his National Front (with its veneration of the 1906 Constitution) as a potentially viable middle way between the Shah's authoritarianism and Ayatollah Khomeini's theocracy. Kermit Roosevelt, *Countercoup: The Struggle for the Control of Iran* (New York, 1979) has interesting things to say on the ousting of the communists in 1946, but focuses chiefly on the coup he helped to organise to overthrow Mossadegh in 1953, the British share in which is described in C.M. Woodhouse, *Something Ventured* (St. Albans, 1981) chaps 8–9. Sir Anthony Parsons, British ambassador during the 1979 revolution, gives us one perspective on *The Pride and the Fall: Iran 1974–1979* (1984), Michael A. Ledeen (later to be involved in 'Irangate') and W. Lewis the diametrically opposed Debacle: *The American Failure in Iran* (New York, 1981). Either way, Iraq tried to take advantage of Iran's post-1979 confusion. Efraim Karsh (ed.) *The Iran–Iraq war: Impact and Implications* (1989) assesses the consequences. Efraim Karsh and Inari Rautsi also offer us *Saddam Hussein: A Political Biography* (of Iraq's leader) (1991 edn), while Lawrence Freedman and Efraim Karsh write on *The Gulf Conflict, 1990–1991: Diplomacy and War in the New World Order* (1993).

The Middle East is one region that has since 1945 had more than its share of international crises and fighting, East and South-East Asia another. A general introduction to its Cold War dimension is given by Nagai, Yonosuke and Iriye, Akira *The Origins of the Cold War in Asia* (1977) and Warren I. Cohen and Iriye, Akira (eds) *The Great Powers in East Asia 1953–1960* (1990). By the 1980s security alignments looked very different; an interesting portrayal is given in IISS's *East Asia, the West and International Security Parts 1–3.* (Adelphi Papers nos 216–18, 1987) and *Asia's International Role in the Post-Cold War Era* (Adelphi Papers nos 275–6, 1993). A pioneering overall view both of the region's security and of its economic development is given in Roger C. Thompson, *The Pacific Basin Since 1945* (1994). Jon Woronoff recounts the rise of *Asia's 'Miracle' Economies* (Armonk, NY, 1991 edn). He was also among the first to speculate on a *World Trade War* (New York, 1983). In lower key, the topic is addressed by, for instance, Bernard K. Gordon, *Politics and Protectionism in the Pacific* (IISS, Adelphi Paper no. 228, 1988), Jagdish Bhagwati, *The World Trading System at Risk* (Princeton, NJ, 1991), and C. Michael Aho, 'America and the Pacific Century: Trade Conflict or Cooperation?', *International Affairs* lxix (1993), as well as by some of the items listed below under Japan; but developments in this field stand in 1993 so much at a crossroads that we may expect these works, for no fault of their own, to date quite quickly.

The largest country in Asia (and the world) is China. Immanuel C.Y. Hsü provides a general history of *The Rise of Modern China* (including Taiwan) (New York, 1990 edn) in, and before, the twentieth century. Japan's invasion of China ended in 1945; but, with this gone, the pre-existent struggle between communists and the KMT resumed, leading unexpectedly to communist victory in 1949. Lloyd E. Eastman depicts *Seeds of Destruction: Nationalist China in War and Revolution 1937–1949* (Stanford, Calif., 1984), Steven I.

Levene examines a crucial theatre in *Anvil of Victory: The Communist Revolution in Manchuria, 1945–1948* (New York, 1987), and L.M. Chassin describes the (often neglected) military operations that led to *The Communist Conquest of China* (Cambridge, Mass., 1965). In *United States Relations with China* (Washington, DC, Aug. 1949), the State Department set out a documentary account of US dealings with China in order to justify its refusal to intervene to rescue its KMT ally. The reaction of the Truman and Eisenhower administrations to communist victory (which was far more complex and sophisticated than the public record would lead one to believe) is examined in John L. Gaddis, *The Long Peace: Inquiries into the History of the Cold War* (New York, 1987) chaps 4,6. Subsequent US–Chinese relations are described and assessed in Gordon H. Chang, *Friends and Enemies: The United States, China and the Soviet Union 1948–1972* (Stanford, Calif., 1990); see also Nancy Bernkopf Tucker's reflections on 'China and America: 1941–1991', *Foreign Affairs* lxx (1991), and (for Sino–Soviet relations) works listed in the bibliography of *The Cold War.* Meanwhile in the 1980s China departed drastically from its previous policies of socialist self-sufficiency, with results that bid fair to establish it as a major (perhaps eventually the major) economic power; this is described in Jude Howell, *China Opens its Doors: The Politics of Economic Transition* (Hemel Hempstead, 1993).

Fighting in the Chinese civil war was virtually over by 1950; the struggle by Ho Chi Minh and his successors for the liberation, control and unification of Vietnam lasted almost continuously (save for the second half of the 1950s) until 1975. Direct US participation in this war in the 1960s and 1970s proved traumatic, and has generated a mountain of literature. Other aspects are less well covered; developments in the area after the fall of Saigon are often ignored. The conflict's origins are explored in Stein Tønnesson, 'The Longest Wars: Indochina 1945–75', *Journal of Peace Research* xxii (1985) and Anthony Short, *The Origins of the Vietnam War* (1989). R.E.M. Irving, *The First Indochina War: French and American Policy 1945–54* (1975) covers events up to the temporary settlement at the 1954 Geneva Conference. US interest in Indo-China is also explored in Geoffrey Warner's 1972 and 1989 *International Affairs* articles (cited on p.512), and in Michael Schaller, 'Securing the Great Crescent: Occupied Japan and the Origins of Containment in Southeast Asia', *Journal of American History* lxix (1982) and J.W. Dower, 'The Superdomino in Asia: Japan in and out of the Pentagon Papers', *Pentagon Papers* (Senator Gravel edn, vol. 5,

Boston, Mass., 1971). For the end of the first Vietnam War, the partition of the country and the replacement of French by US influence in South Vietnam, see Lawrence S. Kaplan, Denise Artaud and Mark R. Rubin (eds) *Dien Bien Phu and the Crisis of Franco-American Relations, 1954–1955* (Wilmington, Del., 1990). The 'second' Vietnam War is covered in (among *many* other books): Stanley Karnow, *Vietnam: A History* (1984); William S. Turley, *The Second Indochina War: A Short Political and Military History, 1954–1975* (Boulder, Colo., 1986), which seeks to pay 'special attention to the view-points and strategies of the ultimately victorious parties, particularly the Vietnamese Communists'; and Jeffrey Race, *War Comes to Long An* (Berkeley, Calif., 1972), a study of a single province. International attention shifted away from Indo-China after the fall of Saigon in 1975, but events did not therefore stand still. Some account of subsequent developments is to be found in: Chang, Pao-Min, *Kampuchea between China and Vietnam* (Singapore, 1985); David P. Chandler, *A History of Cambodia* (Boulder, Colo., 1992); King C. Chen, *China's War with Vietnam, 1979* (Stanford, Calif., 1987); Charles McGregor, *The Sino-Vietnamese Relationship and the Soviet Union* (Adelphi Paper no. 232, 1988). Meanwhile David K. Wyatt, *Thailand: A Short History* (New Haven, Conn., 1984 edn) and J.L.S. Girling, *Thailand, Society and Politics* (Ithaca, NY, 1981) discuss a country often seen as a potential 'domino', but one that did not topple.

Events in Japan went more smoothly; so, though Japan is vastly more important than Vietnam, they have attracted much less attention from foreign scholars. An overview is given in Peter Duus (ed.) *The Cambridge History of Japan* vi *The Twentieth Century* (1988). Roger Buckley surveys both *Occupation Diplomacy: Britain, the United States and Japan 1945–1952* (Cambridge, 1982) and *US–Japan Alliance Diplomacy 1945–1990* (Cambridge, 1992). In *The Years of MacArthur: Triumph and Disaster, 1945–64* (1985), D. Clayton Jones gives us a biography of the very influential US general in charge of the occupation, while in *Empire and Aftermath: Yoshida Shigeru and the Japanese Experience, 1878–1954* (Cambridge, Mass., 1979) J.W. Dower writes the life of the possibly still more influential politician who recovered sovereignty for Japan and did much to mould its subsequent course. J.J. Stephan, *The Kuril Islands* (Oxford, 1974) explains Japan's surprisingly important, and still (1993) unresolved, territorial dispute with the USSR/Russia. Kent E. Calder writes on *Crisis and Compensation: Public Policy and Political Stability in Japan 1949–1986* (Princeton, NJ, 1988), Y. Satoh on *The Evolution of*

Japanese Security Policy (IISS Adelphi Paper no. 178, 1982), while Japan's more general stance is discussed in Kathleen Newland (ed.) *The International Relations of Japan* (Basingstoke, 1990). For many years Japan's primary concern lay with economic growth, discussed in Nakamura, Takafusa, *The Postwar Japanese Economy: Its Development and Structure* (Tokyo, 1981). With the emergence of Japan's huge trade surpluses and overseas investments, the subject has become controversial: is the Japanese economy as open as it seems on paper, or is it rigged in favour of local producers (to the detriment of both consumers and overseas competitors); and has Japanese efficiency been exaggerated, or is it in the process of establishing world economic dominance? Such questions are addressed, from different perspectives, in, for instance, Inoguchi, Takashie and Okamoto, Daniel I. (eds) *The Political Economy of Japan* ii (Stanford, Calif., 1988), Edward J. Lincoln, *Japan's Unequal Trade* (Washington, DC, 1990), Philip Oppenheim, *Trade Wars: Japan versus the West* (1992), Eric Helleiner, 'Japan and the Changing Global Financial Order', *International Journal* (Toronto) xlvii (1992) and Jon Woronof, *Japan As-Anything But-Number One* (Basingstoke, 1991). All this is of obvious relevance to future US–Japanese relations, for one view of which see Kent E. Calder, 'The United States–Japan Relationship: A Post-Cold War Future', *Pacific Review* v (1992). But the subject is, in 1993, particularly cloudy, since a split in the LDP (which had governed continuously since the 1950s) brought into office a broad coalition with a declaratory policy both of relaxing bureaucratic controls on the economy (to the benefit of consumers and – possible – foreign suppliers) and of adopting a higher profile in foreign affairs.

Japan's former colony and close neighbour, Korea, was the scene of the dramatic and important Korean War. Also South Korea has, since the 1960s, witnessed impressive economic growth. Again people have preferred to write about the first. A brief general introduction is given by David Rees, *A Short History of Korea* (Port Erin, Isle of Man, 1988). James Irving Matray writes on *The Reluctant Crusade: American Foreign Policy in Korea, 1941–50* (1985). On the other side we have Kathryn Weathersby's *Soviet Aims in Korea and the Origins of the Korean War, 1945–1950: New Evidence from Russian Archives* (*Cold War International History Project* [CWIHP] Working Paper no. 8, Washington, DC, 1993) and her 'New Findings on the Korean War', CWIHP *Bulletin* 3 (1993). The 1950–3 Korean War is also covered in: Peter Lowe, *The Origins of the Korean War* (1986), by Rosemary Foot, *The Wrong War: American Policy and the Dimensions of the Korean Conflict, 1950–1953* (Ithaca, NY, 1985), and by her review article, 'Making Known the Unknown War: Policy Analysis of the Korean Conflict in the Last Decade', *Diplomatic History* xv (1991). Recent evidence makes it clear that North Korea's invasion had been cleared with, and had received technical assistance from, Stalin; Chen, Jian *The Sino-Soviet Alliance and China's Entry into the Korean War* (*Cold War International History Project* Working Paper no. 1, Washington, DC, 1992) also demonstrates Mao's eagerness to intervene in the subsequent fighting. After the war South Korea recovered only slowly under its aged President Syngman Rhee, who is portrayed (over?-)sympathetically in Robert T. Oliver, *Syngman Rhee and American Involvement in Korea, 1948–1960* (Seoul, 1978). In the 1960s and 1970s it was transformed economically by President Park; by the 1980s it had clearly eclipsed North Korea (save, perhaps, in military power) and was beginning to embark on far-reaching political change. These themes are addressed by Donald S. Macdonald, *The Koreans: Contemporary Politics and Society* (Boulder, Colo., 1989), David I. Steinberg, *The Republic of Korea: Economic Transformation and Social Change* (Boulder, Colo., 1989) and Chong-Sik Lee, *Japan and Korea: The Political Dimension* (Stanford, Calif., 1985).

One of the side-effects of the Korean War was the extension of US protection to Taiwan. Thus given a second chance, Chiang Kai-Shek made good in a way he had not done on the mainland. The story is told in Ralph N. Clough, *Island China* (Cambridge, Mass., 1978), René Dumont with Charlotte Paquet, *Taiwan, le prix de la réussite* (Paris, 1987), and Joseph Bosco, Harvey J. Feldman *et al.*, *Constitutional Reform and the Future of the Republic of China* (Armonk, NY, 1991). South of Taiwan lie the Philippines: Benedict J. Kerkvliet describes *The Huk Rebellion* (Berkeley, Calif., 1977), John Bresnau (ed.) the deeper *Crisis in the Philippines: The Marcos Era and Beyond* (Princeton, NJ, 1986), and W. Scott Thompson – in *The Philippines in Crisis: Development and Security in the Aquino Era 1986–92* (New York, 1992) – the subsequent faltering recovery. As the Philippines' experience shows, both trouble and salvation are often largely generated internally; the same was true of Indonesia's vastly more traumatic experience in the 1960s, for which see H.W. Brands, 'The Limits of Manipulation: How the United States Didn't Topple Sukarno', *Journal of American History* lxxvi (1989) pp.785–808 and Harold Crouch, *The Army and Politics in Indonesia* (Ithaca, NY, 1978). But the non-communist countries of the area – the Philippines, Thailand, Malaysia, Singapore, Indonesia, and (later) Brunei – sought mutual diplomatic reassurance and support in the

Association of South-East Asian Nations (ASEAN). This took some time to make an impact; but in the 1980s it came to play an important role in first contesting the Vietnam-installed regime in Cambodia and then negotiating a general settlement there; in the early 1990s it developed into something of a diplomatic and economic magnet. In this connection, see Michael Leifer, *ASEAN and the Security of South-East Asia* (1989) and Alison Broinowski (ed.) *ASEAN in the 1990s* (Basingstoke, 1990) (though the latter's coverage really extends only to 1988).

In 1945 the American hemisphere seemed worlds removed from eastern Asia (or Europe), and most politicians, both US and Latin American, wished to keep it so. The best overview is probably given by Edwin Williamson, *The Penguin History of Latin America* (1992); but Peter and Susan Calvert, *Latin America in the Twentieth Century* (Basingstoke, 1990) and Harold Molineu, *U.S. Policy Toward Latin America* (Boulder, Colo., 1986) are also useful. Leslie Bethell and Ian Roxborough (eds) *Latin America between the Second World War and the Cold War, 1944–1948* (Cambridge, 1992) covers the crucial period of the establishing of the Organisation of American States and other aspects of the modern inter-American system. Stephen Rabe interprets US–Latin American relations in the two decades after 1945 in works well grounded in the US archival record: 'The Elusive Conference: United States Economic Relations with Latin America, 1945–1952', *Diplomatic History* ii (1978); *Eisenhower and Latin America: The Foreign Policy of Anticommunism* (Chapel Hill, NC, 1988); and 'Controlling Revolutions: Latin America, the Alliance for Progress, and Cold War Anti-Communism', in Thomas G. Paterson (ed.) *Kennedy's Quest for Victory: American Foreign Policy, 1961–1963* (New York, 1989). The end of the Eisenhower period saw the Cuban revolution, which was to become an obsession with Kennedy. Hugh Thomas provides us with an enormous history of *Cuba or the Pursuit of Freedom* (1971), Leslie Bethell (ed.) with *Cuba: A Short History* (Cambridge, 1993 edn). Tad Szulc offers us *Fidel: A Critical Portrait* (New York, 1986), Andres Oppenheimer the (perhaps premature) *Castro's Final Hour* (New York, 1992). The USA failed to reverse the Cuban revolution but did manage to stop it spreading, intervening frequently and eventually deploying troops in the Dominican Republic, as J. Slater recounts in Blechman and Kaplan, *Force Without War.* The USA was also cognisant of, and had decided if necessary to support, the vastly more important military take-over of Brazil, for which see Phyllis R. Parker, *Brazil and the Quiet Intervention, 1964* (Austin, Tex., 1979). The 1960s witnessed substantial guerrilla activity, especially in Venezuela and the countries of the northern Andes; this is described in Richard Gott, *Rural Guerillas in Latin America* (Harmondsworth, 1973 edn), while CIA involvement to help local governments counter it features in for example Harry Rositzke, *The CIA's Secret Operations* (New York, 1977). In 1970, however, the Marxist Salvador Allende won open elections in Chile, only to be deposed three years later in an extremely controversial coup that was to usher in a harsh military dictatorship: for this see Marc Falcoff, *Modern Chile, 1970–1989: A Critical History* (New Brunswick, NJ, 1989) and Paul E. Sigmund, *The United States and Democracy in Chile* (Baltimore, Md, 1993). In the 1970s the political pendulum in Latin America was swinging to the right. But the leftist 1979 revolution in Nicaragua (which was soon taken over by Marxists), together with the 1980 outbreak of civil war in El Salvador, aroused, in some quarters, fears of progressive collapse in Central America and the Caribbean, stimulated by Nicaragua, Cuba and the USSR; these are expressed in ex-Secretary of State Alexander M. Haig's alarmist memoirs, *Caveat: Realism, Reagan and Foreign Policy* (1984) and in Timothy Ashby, *The Bear in the Backyard: Moscow's Caribbean Strategy* (Lexington, Mass., 1987). Shultz's *Turmoil and Triumph* is calmer, but still supports the policy of harassing Nicaragua to induce it to desist that led to the 'Iran-contra' affair. He also has much to say on the 'Contadora' process that led in 1989 to a negotiated settlement with Nicaragua and, in 1990, to elections that were unexpectedly won by the anti- communist opposition (after which the world suddenly lost interest).

If stability, independence and international alignment constituted one cluster of Latin American issues, another cluster was economic. For nearly two decades after 1945, as Rabe shows, Latin American leaders were constantly pressing the USA for development assistance. The culmination of this process was Kennedy's 'Alliance for Progress'; it proved a great disappointment, as is shown in J. Levinson and Juan de Onis, *The Alliance That Lost Its Way: A Critical Report on the Alliance for Progress* (Chicago, Ill, 1970). Thereafter Latin American states either shifted their economic pressure to the forum of the United Nations (see p.527) or went it alone. In the 1970s the latter course involved massive borrowings that, by the early 1980s, could no longer be serviced. The resultant crash hit many countries hard, as is recorded in James L. Dietz and J.L. Street, *Latin America's Economic Development* (Boulder, Colo., 1987). However, as Philip Brock, M.B. Connolly and C. Gonzalez-Vega (eds) *Latin American Debt and Adjustment* (New

York, 1989) shows, it led not to the confrontation and debtors' cartel that Castro sought to promote so as to bring down capitalism, but to eventual settlements with the creditor banks on a country-by-country basis that did much to stimulate deregulation and economic liberalism. Nowhere was this more striking than in Mexico; it is reviewed by Riordan Roett (ed.) *Political and Economic Liberalisation in Mexico: At a Critical Juncture?* (Boulder, Colo., 1993). Another 1980s development was less elevating – the rise in the trade in drugs (most notably for the US market); this is described, and its contribution to the destabilisation of certain countries assessed, by Elaine Shannon, *Desperadoes: Latin Drug Lords, US Lawmen, and the War America Can't Win* (New York, 1988) and Scott B. MacDonald, *Mountain High, White Avelanche: Cocaine and Power in the Andes States and Panama* (Washington Papers 137, Washington, DC, 1989).

Moving now from a regional to a global focus, the hopes invested in the United Nations in 1945 have not, in general, been realised; but the UN has provided a forum for the conduct of international politics, and the nature and rules of this forum have had some influence on their outcome. Occasionally the UN has done more, legitimising (or stigmatising) certain policies and actors, taking initiatives on its own (especially, but not exclusively, in 'technical' areas), and – albeit rarely – exercising, or at least allowing a US-led coalition to exercise, coercive power. David Armstrong, *The Rise of the International Organisation: A Short History* (Basingstoke, 1982) provides a general context, while Adam Roberts and Benedict Kingsbury (eds) focus on *United Nations, Divided World: The UN's Roles in International Relations* (Oxford, 1993 edn). Amos Yoder writes on *The Evolution of the United Nations System* (New York, 1989). Peter R. Baehr and Leon Gordenker on *The United Nations in the 1990s* (1992). Before his premature death Evan Luard gave us *A History of the United Nations* i *The Years of Western Domination, 1945–1955* (1982) and ii *The Age of Decolonization, 1955–1965* (Basingstoke, 1989). Brian Urquhart (himself an eminent UN civil servant) has written a biography of its most activist Secretary, *Hammarskjöld* (1973). Henry Wiseman (ed.) *Peacekeeping: Appraisals and Proposals* (New York, 1983) covers the UN's innovative deployment of troops in a non-coercive role; but Madeleine G. Kalb's *The Congo Cables: The Cold War in Africa – From Eisenhower to Kennedy* (New York, 1982) shows that during the largest of these operations, that in the ex-Belgian Congo, United States' political influence probably outweighed that of UN personnel. In the 1960s and 1970s the UN, or at least its General Assembly, became responsive to a coalition of developing countries who used it to press (unsuccessfully) for a 'New International Economic Order'. This 'Group of 77' overlapped heavily with the older 'Nonaligned Movement', founded by India, Yugoslavia, Egypt and Indonesia to refocus world politics away from the East–West rivalry and towards the interests of the emerging countries. These two groups are described in Peter Willetts, *The Non-Aligned Movement: The Origins of a Third World Alliance* (1978) and William M. LeoGrande, 'Evolution of the Nonaligned Movement', *Problems of Communism* xxix (1980), and in Carol Geldart and Peter Lyon, 'The Group of 77: A Perspective View', *International Affairs* lvii (1981) and Marc Williams, *Third World Cooperation: The Group of 77 in UNCTAD* (1991). Bernard D. Nossiter gives us a useful appreciation, from the perspective of liberal economics, of *The Global Struggle for More: Third World Conflicts with Rich Nations* (New York, 1987).

However, the amount of economic activity that is controlled through the UN is distinctly limited. Joan E. Spero gives us an overview of *The Politics of International Economic Relations* (1992 edn); and Robert D. Putnam and Nicholas Bayne describe *Hanging Together: Cooperation and Conflict in the Seven-Power Summits* (of the OECD's G7) (1987), though these have since come to play a larger role in international consciousness. Another approach is by sectors. The well-connected journalist Anthony Sampson has written, extremely readably, on, inter alia, *Empires of the Sky: The Politics, Contests and Cartels of World Airlines* (1984), *The Money Lenders: Bankers in a Dangerous World* (1988 edn) and *The Arms Bazaar in the Nineties: From Krupp to Saddam* (1991). In this tradition is Daniel Yergin, *The Prize: The Epic Quest for Oil, Money and Power* (1991). Money, or the regime of international exchange rates, may also be regarded as an economic sector, often a very dramatic one. Brian Tew provides a general account of *The Evolution of the International Monetary System 1945–77* (1977), while John Williams describes *The Failure of World Monetary Reform 1971–74* (Sunbury on Thames, 1977). (Sir) Alec Cairncross and Barry Eichengreen tell of *Sterling in Decline: The Devaluations of 1931, 1949, and 1967* (Oxford, 1983), all of which had important knock-on effects, while Kathleen Burk and Alec Cairncross extend the story in *'Goodbye, Great Britain': The 1976 IMF Crisis* (New Haven, Conn., 1992). In *Closing the Gold Window: Domestic Politics and the End of Bretton Woods* (Ithaca, NY, 1983), Joanne Gowa demonstrates that, by contrast, Nixon's priorities when taking what proved to be important decisions ushering in the era of floating exchange rates, were purely domestic. Of that regime

Susan Strange has written briefly in *Casino Capitalism* (Oxford, 1986). The 1980s were the decade of the international debt crisis; this was mostly a matter of Latin American borrowings, and as such has been noticed above (pp.525–6); but African states, too, found themselves faced, if they wished new loans, with unwelcome IMF conditions as to their internal economic policies; the process is described, often with bitterness, in Kjell J. Havnevik (ed.) *The IMF and the World Bank in Africa* (Uppsala, 1987) and Bade Onimode (ed.) *The IMF, the World Bank and the African Debt* (2 vols, 1989).

At the present moment (September 1993) the European Community is by the ears over the Uruguay round of GATT and its implications for the Common Agricultural Policy. But this is unusual; international trade negotiations mostly generate less drama than currency crises – Andrew Shonfield (ed.) *International Economic Relations of the Western World 1959–1971* i *Politics and Trade* (1976) is therefore a fairly heavy book. Herman van der Wee gives us a general history of *Prosperity and Upheaval: The World Economy, 1945–80* (Harmondsworth, 1987), with a certain bias towards its quantitatively most significant economies, those of the OECD. Jon Woronoff describes what is clearly the principal postwar change, the rise of *Asia's 'Miracle' Economies* (1991 edn); other works noted above in the paragraphs on East Asia and Japan are also relevant here. Robert O. Keohane's *After Hegemony: Cooperation and Discord in the World Political Economy* (Princeton, NJ, 1984) Part III addresses the phenomenon of the United States' relative decline, as does, for instance, the more technologically oriented John Zysman, 'US Power, Trade and Technology', *International Affairs* lxvii (1991). In *Bound to Lead: The Changing Nature of American Power* (New York, 1991 edn), Joseph S. Nye contests the 'declinist' view (expressed in extreme form by Jacques Attali's prediction – in *Lignes d'Horizon* (Paris, 1990) – that the USA will fall behind both a European and a Japanese-led Asian bloc); instead Nye argues that the USA 'remains the largest and richest power' with (provided there is also the will to exercise it) 'the greatest capacity to shape the future'.

Index